W9-AQN-937

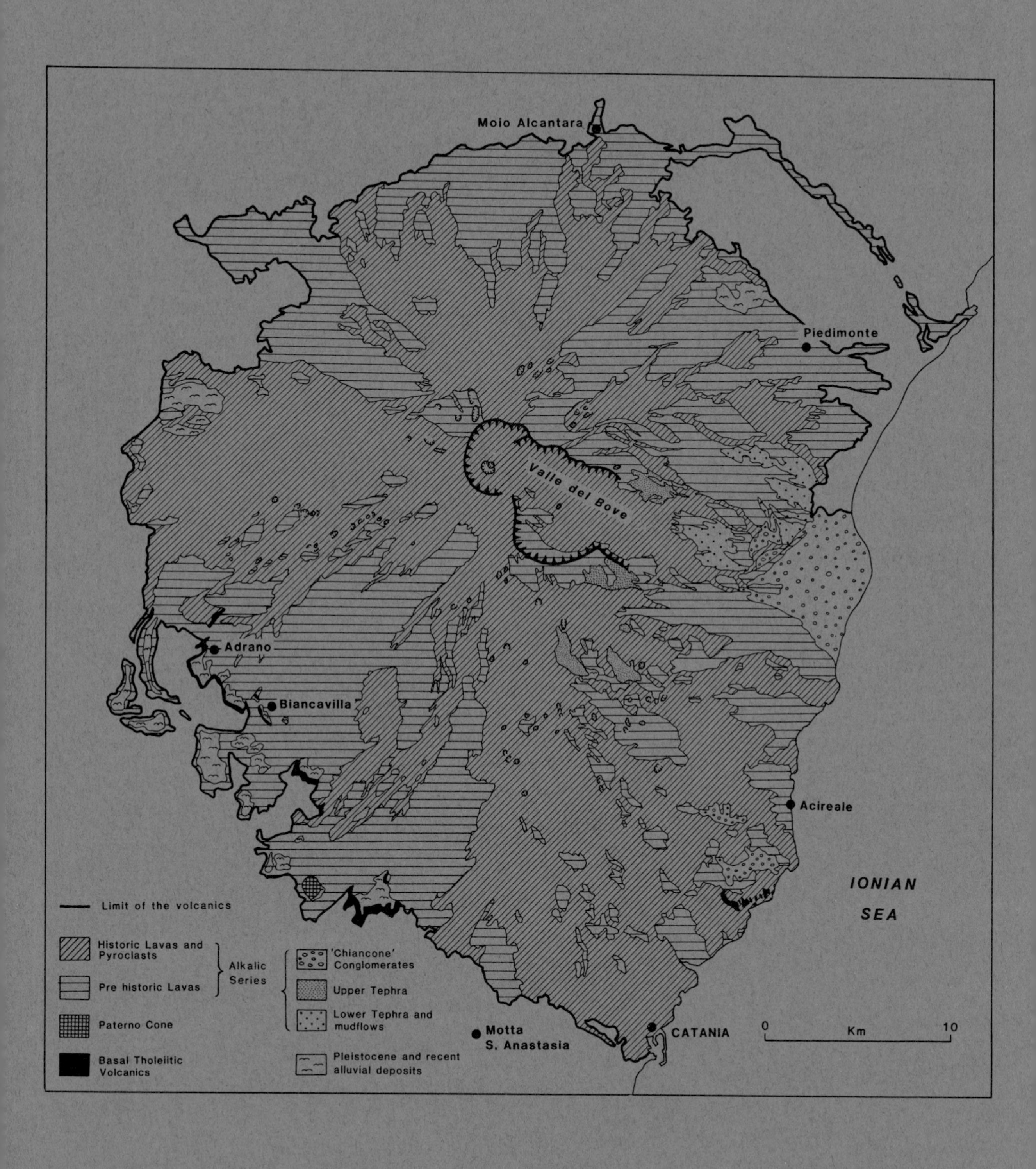
Moio Alcantara
Piedimonte
Valle del Bove
Adrano
Biancavilla
Acireale
IONIAN
SEA
Motta
S. Anastasia
CATANIA
0
Km
10
Limit of the volcanics
Historic Lavas and
Pyroclasts
Pre historic Lavas
Alkalic
Series
Paterno Cone
Basal Tholeiitic
Volcanics
'Chiancone'
Conglomerates
Upper Tephra
Lower Tephra and
mudflows
Pleistocene and recent
alluvial deposits

MOUNT ETNA
The anatomy of a volcano

To Chris Argent

MOUNT ETNA
The anatomy of a volcano

D.K. Chester
University of Liverpool

A.M. Duncan
Luton College of Higher Education

J.E. Guest
University College London

C.R.J. Kilburn
University College London

Stanford University Press
Stanford, California
1985

ST. PHILIP'S COLLEGE LIBRARY

QE
523
.E8
M685
1985

Stanford University Press
Stanford, California

© *1985 D.K. Chester, A.M. Duncan, J.E. Guest, C.R.J. Kilburn*

Originating Publisher: Chapman and Hall Ltd, London

First published in the U.S.A. by Stanford University Press, 1985

Printed in Great Britain

ISBN 0–8047–1308–1

LC 85–61960

Contents

083467

Note

% (v/v) is equivalent to vol. %
% (w/w) is equivalent to wt %

Preface

Since the Second World War interest in the active volcano Mount Etna, in Sicily, has been steadily increasing. This interest has not been restricted to Italy, and scientists from Belgium, France, Germany, the United States and the United Kingdom have played a part in volcanological studies. In 1972 much of this work was drawn together at a discussion meeting convened by the Royal Society of London and attended by representatives of most of the projects that were being conducted on Etna. The meeting served to draw together current knowledge of Etna, especially information derived during the 1971 flank eruption, and also to point out deficiencies in knowledge and methods of approach to investigating the volcano. In his opening statement to the meeting Professor A. Rittmann, one of the great leaders of Italian volcanology in general and a student of Etna in particular, stated, 'Much time and a great number of specialists are necessary to reveal the fascinating secrets of Europe's most important volcano. Such an extended and manifold research work can be carried out only in the frame of a well organised international collaboration.' (Rittmann, 1973, p. 16). Since that time considerable advances in the knowledge of Etna have been made, particularly as a result of work carried out by Italian, French and British geologists and geophysicists. Especially important amongst those advances were the construction of a new geological map at a scale of 1:50 000 by Italian and British workers, and as a result a better understanding of the historical development of the volcano; extensive geochemical studies by British, French and Italian geologists; the establishment of a seismic network by Italian geophysicists; studies of ground deformation by British and Italian groups; measurements of microgravity changes particularly by a British group; endeavours to improve analytical techniques for gases and sublimates by French and also Italian and British workers; pioneering work on rheology of lavas and growth of lava fields by British scientists; and greatly improved surveillance of activity, notably that occurring in the summit region.

It is a principal aim of this book to synthesize the results of these many different studies into a more complete understanding of the volcano. Inevitably the coverage is somewhat uneven; some fields of study have been researched more thoroughly than others. Isotope and trace element geochemical investigations and some geophysical studies are still very much at a preliminary stage. It must be remembered also that Etna is densely populated and has a growing agricultural and industrial economy; thus the presence of the volcano has a profound impact on this part of Sicily. Some consideration is therefore given to the level of risk and nature of the volcanic hazard, together with the kind of mitigating measures that could be adopted. It is hoped that the book will give some guidelines to gaps in present-day knowledge, and to the methods that need to be tested by future research; also that it will encourage new workers with new ideas to study this important and fascinating centre of volcanic activity.

Obviously a book such as this represents the collation of many people's work, sometimes derived from publications and hopefully suitably acknowledged, but also from numerous informal discussions which cannot be adequately recognized. Firstly the contribution of the late Professor A. Rittmann to Etna research should be recorded. He has had a lasting influence on many aspects of volcanology, and his efforts in stressing the need for an international and interdisciplinary approach to the study of Etna led to the production of the geological map of the volcano and the associated memoir. Over the last fifteen years Professor Renato Cristofolini and Dr Romolo Romano have made a major contribution to research on Etna and during this period they have played an important role in liaising with the various groups of different nationalities working on the volcano. The authors would in particular like to express their gratitude to Dr Romano and Professor Cristofolini for their guidance in the field, for readily making available their extensive knowledge of the volcano, and for always being willing to assist with the logistic problems of the various British research teams. Dr L. Villari and his colleagues at the International Institute of Volcanology, Catania, and scientists at the University of Catania have played the leading role in Etna research, and to them British scientists owe a debt of gratitude for their help and hospitality. French scientists have carried out much valuable research on Etna over the last fifteen years, and Professor H. Tazieff and Drs Jean-Claud Tanguy and Guy Kieffer deserve special mention for their contributions.

During the preparation of this volume we have received support from many colleagues and to these thanks are due. In particular Helen Anderson, Tom Huntingdon, Robert Preston, Stuart Scott, Søren-Aksel Sørensen and Maurice Wells have commented on specific parts of the manuscript. Over the years many people have supported the British contribution to Etna research; Professors E. A. Vincent and George Walker did much to encourage and foster the early work, and Chris Argent of the Royal Society worked hard to enhance the level of collaboration. The authors have benefited by working with many other people in the field on Etna and would like to acknowledge the following: Peter Baker, David Bell, Stuart Carter, Chris Durbin, Ronald Greeley, Ann Henderson-Sellers, Steve Habesch, Mike Hammill, Rosaly Lopes, Bill McGuire, John Murray, Harry Pinkerton, Ann Petrykowski, Andrew Pullen, Timothy Sanderson, Alastair Sharp, Steve Sparks, Geoff Wadge, Chris Wood and Jim Underwood. Over many years British workers have been hospitably accommodated at the Albergo Rifugio G Sapienza, and sincere thanks are owing to Signore and Signora A. Di Bella. Thanks must also to to Signore A. Nicoloso and Signore O. Nicoloso for their assistance in gaining access to the mountain and for overcoming many logistical problems. In the early days of the project Vinciento Barbagallo and Giovanni Carbonaro acted as expert guides on the volcano.

The majority of the figures were expertly designed and drafted by Alan Hodgkiss. Additional artwork was in the capable hands of Sandra Mather and Jennifer Wyatt. Most of the photographs were copied from colour transparencies by David Rooks and John Bell. Mike Ashton provided valuable technical assistance, and Valerie Peerless typed the drafts of many chapters. Thanks are also owed to our Heads of Department and academic colleagues for their encouragement.

The authors would like to acknowledge and thank the following for providing financial support for their research work on Mount Etna: the Leverhulme Trust (DKC and AMD), the Natural Environment Research Council (JEG), the Daniel Pidgeon Fund of the Geological Society of London (AMD), the Royal Society (DKC, AMD, JEG and CRJK) and the Central Research Fund of the University of London (JEG). AMD and CRJK received their introduction to Etna research as NERC-funded research students. The authors would also like to thank their own institutions, the University of Liverpool, University College London and Luton College of Higher Education, for providing funds at various times.

For general reference purposes the reader is directed to the location map and the geological sketch map of Etna which form the endpapers.

1 The forge of Vulcan

'A volcano is not
made on purpose to frighten
superstitious people into fits of piety,
nor to overwhelm devoted cities
with destruction.'

(James Hutton, 1788)

ST. PHILIP'S COLLEGE LIBRARY

Fig. 1.1 View of Mount Etna from the coastal town of Catania nearly 30 km away from the summit. The volcano has a maximum diameter of 45 km and covers some 1750 km^2. (Photograph: J. E. Guest.)

Mount Etna is the dominant feature in the landscape of eastern Sicily rising to a height of over 3300 m (Fig. 1.1). To a greater or lesser extent it is in an almost continuous state of activity and historical accounts of eruptions cover a period of more than 2500 years, providing a record of volcanism over a longer period than for most other volcanoes. Etna is relatively easy to reach, having an international airport near its foot, and, apart from a few areas which are remote and difficult of access, it has good road communications including drivable dirt tracks to the summit on both the northern and southern flanks. Amongst the basaltic volcanoes, therefore, it is virtually unrivalled as a place to study volcanic processes. As well as being an excellent laboratory in which to test out new techniques and ideas, Etna also has characteristics that are different from the more extensively monitored volcanoes such as Kilauea on Hawaii; thus new Etnean studies broaden volcanological experiences rather than just repeating those obtained elsewhere. In addition large parts of the volcano's flanks are heavily populated and cultivated, giving volcanological studies a critical social value.

1.1 The summit cone

At the hub of Mount Etna's volcanic activity lies the Summit Cone which forms an imposing feature at the top of the volcano (Fig. 1.2). It is constructed of interbedded lava and tephra (some of which are reworked by solifluction) and has a basal diameter of just under 2 km with a height of about 260 m. Its top is truncated by the 500 m-diameter Central Crater. Because the Summit Cone is built directly

Fig. 1.2 Oblique aerial view of the Summit Cone taken in 1943. At this time there was a single large lava-filled central crater at the top of the cone (cf. Fig. 1.3), and the North-east Crater (NE) was a relatively small vent surrounded by an apron of lavas. On the skyline is the rim of the lava-filled Piano Caldera.

Fig. 1.3 Oblique aerial view of the summit cone in 1972. The Central Crater is almost entirely filled with lava and tephra and has three fuming vents: the Chasm (C), the Bocca Nuova (BN) and a cone produced during the 1964 eruption. The North-east Crater (NE) has built up a more substantial cone than that seen in Fig 1.2 (in which the summit cone is seen from the opposite direction). In the background is the cloud-filled Valle del Leone. (Photograph: J. E. Guest.)

over the central conduit of the volcano it is the site of almost continuous activity in one form or another. There are several vents at least one of which at any time appears to be open to the main feeding system of the volcano (Fig. 1.3).

As a consequence, the summit region is constantly changing its form, and between consecutive visits separated by only a few months quite substantial changes may have taken place. The awesome nature of the Summit Cone area even at times of relative inactivity has made it a popular location for visitors since Greek and Roman times. Until relatively recently, nevertheless, the trek to the summit was not easy and the final climb involved the use of mules from the town of Nicolosi at about 800 m a.s.l.; but with the post-war expansion of Sicily's tourist industry, a cable-car system (La Funivia) has been built on the volcano's southern flank and a dirt track constructed from north to south over the summit of the mountain. The ascent therefore has become relatively easy and during the summer months many hundreds of tourists come every day to visit the upper reaches of the volcano.

Because of the constant turmoil of activity in the Summit Cone region no detailed description of its form can remain valid for long and neither can any visitor be entirely safe from hazard. These characteristics provide an exciting diversion for tourists from the coastal resorts, and the wide variety of types of activity cannot fail to arouse the curiosity of a visiting volcanologist.

Activity in the summit region is generally of the

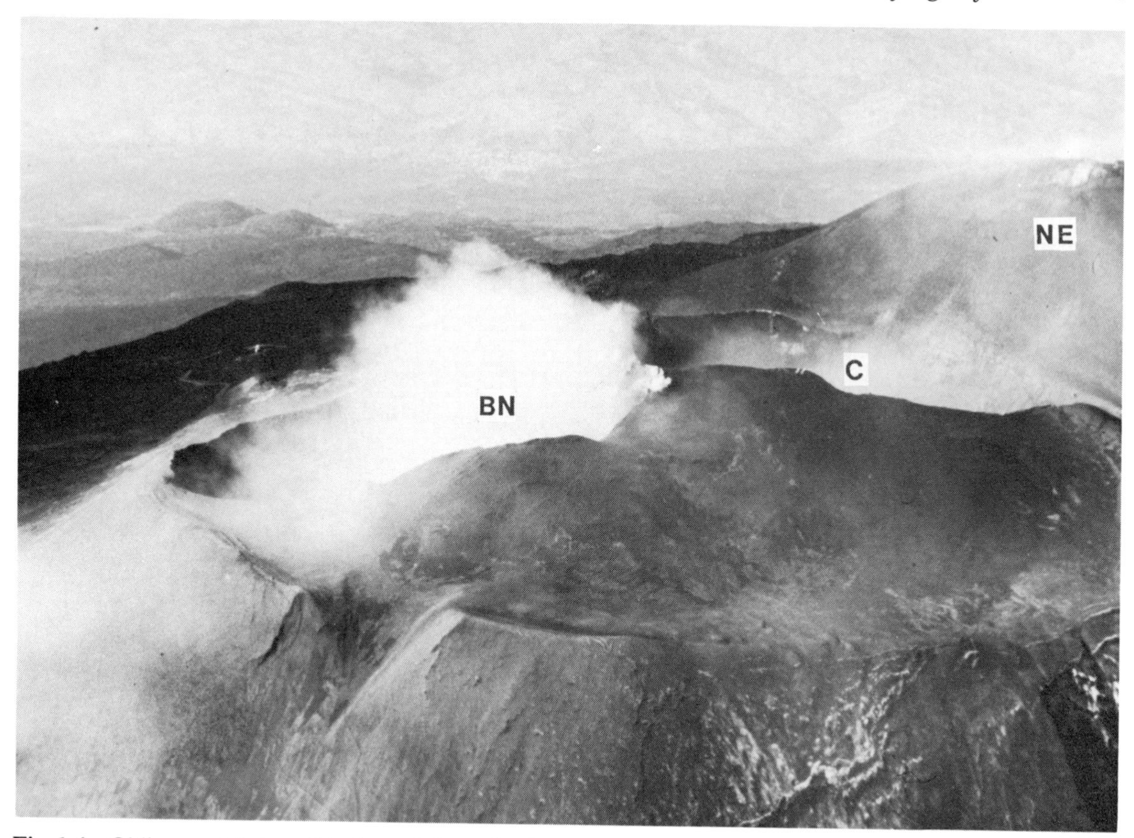

Fig. 1.4 Oblique aerial view of the Central Crater in 1983. Compared with the situation illustrated in Fig. 1.3 for 1972, the North-east Crater cone (NE) has built up to become the highest point on the mountain. The Chasm (C) is slightly enlarged but the Bocca Nuova (BN) is substantially enlarged so that it cuts the rim of the infilled Central Crater and has removed half of the 1964 cone. (Photograph: J. E. Guest.)

type known on Etna as *persistent* in which lava effusion takes place at a relatively low rate usually less than 1 $m^3 s^{-1}$. The actual effusion rate at any given time often approximates to the mean output of the volcano. In contrast *flank eruptions*, although sometimes occurring on the outer flanks of the Summit Cone, usually occur lower on the mountain and may have much higher effusion rates.

The type of activity occurring in the Central Crater is generally a reflection of the height of the magma column in the central conduit: with a low or falling column, collapse pits are formed or existing ones become enlarged and deepened. Throughout the 1970s to the present there were two such pits in the Central Crater: one called the Chasm (La Voragine) was established as early as the 1950s, while the other, known as the Bocca Nuova (New Mouth), began its life in 1968 (Figs 1.3 and 1.4). The magma columns in both these pits usually withdraw when there is effusive activity elsewhere. At such times the pits become progressively deeper by successive collapses in their floors accompanied by reverberating roars and the expulsion of brown, ash-laden clouds. Collapse has led at times to both the Bocca Nuova and the Chasm being close to 1000 m deep with near-vertical walls. To stand on the edge of a pit (Fig. 1.5) during a phase of deepening when the air is filled with a roaring sound, the ground is shaking, clouds of ash are billowing around the crater lip and the observer may be enveloped in choking sulphur dioxide fumes, is an experience not to be forgotten.

Of particular concern, especially when working

Fig 1.5 View of the Chasm from the flanks of the North-east Crater. The scale is given by a group of tourists standing on the edge of the pit. (Photograph: J. E. Guest.)

near the edge of the pits, is the possibility of wholesale ground collapse. The Bocca Nuova started life with a diameter of only 8 m but, as a result of several major collapses, had achieved by 1983, fifteen years after it was formed, a diameter of some 300 m. Fortunately such collapses have not yet resulted in loss of life, but they remain nevertheless a severe hazard to anyone visiting the Central Crater. This was brought home in a spectacular way during 1976 when another new pit, nearly 100 m in diameter, opened on the side of the North-east Crater only 80 m away from the vehicle park; a new parking area was immediately built at a safer distance.

Even when the major pits cease to collapse they are rarely quiet. Rapid gas expulsion in the pit floors produce loud bangs and the rattling sound of falling rock echoes around the walls. Because the pits are usually evolving copious clouds of white fume, it is not always easy to have sustained views into them and often the only clue that lava is present at the bottom comes from occasional red glows and the sound of strombolian explosions. When a pit is several hundred metres deep the only material ejected over the lip consists of fine fragments of glassy juvenile lava. However as a pit fills the larger strombolian explosions throw bombs and ash outside the crater for up to several hundred metres. On occasions the Chasm has filled to within a short distance of its upper edge and when activity ceased left it almost brimful of lava until the beginning of the next phase of collapse.

Although the summit crater has commonly been the site of persistent lava effusion, throughout the 1960s and 1970s most such persistent activity occurred from a vent that opened on the north-north-east flank of the Summit Cone in 1911. This vent, known as the North-east Crater (Fig. 1.6),

Fig 1.6 The North-east Crater seen from the Central Crater during a time of dormancy in 1978. Note the groups of tourists converging on the Bocca Nuova which is off the picture to the right. (Photograph: J. E. Guest.)

slowly built up in height from strombolian activity and lava effusion giving a series of cinder-cones one on top of the other, and by the late 1970s it was the highest point on the mountain (Figs 1.2 to 1.4). It appears that for most of its life this vent, like those in the Central Crater, has had an open conduit connected with the Central Crater system. Such vents close to the Central Crater but lying on the flank of the summit cone have often been termed 'sub-terminal vents' (Rittmann, 1973). This one lies on a fissure system running in a north-north-easterly direction through the Summit Cone where it is marked by a line of vents including the Chasm and the 1964 Crater which is the only Central Crater vent to have produced lava flows since 1960. On the south-south-east side of the Central Crater the fissure has formed a notch where the rim of the crater has collapsed (Fig. 1.7). A similar notch existed on the north-north-east side as a small graben in the early 1940s but has since been filled in by tephra and lava erupted from the Central Crater and North-east Crater.

Eruptions from the North-east Crater provide the visitor to the summit with a spectacular display which can be observed from the relative safety of the Central Crater. This is especially true after sunset (Fig. 1.8) when showers of red-hot bombs are thrown sometimes several hundred metres above the crater arcing down through the night to land on the side of the cinder-cone, while lava streams erupted from the foot of the cone form red glowing rivers down the mountain (Fig. 1.9). The duration of eruptions from the North-east Crater is variable ranging from those that last several years with a low effusion rate, to short eruptions of perhaps only a few hours that have relatively high

Fig 1.7 The Summit Cone showing the notch on the south-south-east side marking the main fissure zone through the summit. In the background behind the notch is the cone formed within the Central Crater during 1964. The dark lavas in this picture erupted from the 1964 cone and flowed through the notch to partly encircle a small cone built over the 1949 vent. Since this picture was taken in 1970 much of the area has been heavily mantled by ashes erupted from the South-east Crater, and much of the 1964 cone has been engulfed by enlargement of the Bocca Nuova. (Photograph: J. E. Guest.)

effusion rates. The longest continuous eruption from the North-east Crater occurred between January 1966 and April 1971. During that time lava effused at a steady rate of just under 1 $m^3 s^{-1}$ from vents scattered around the foot of the North-east Cone. Most of the lava was erupted from boccas (the mouths of vents) on the north-north-east side of the cone lying on the main fissure through the summit region. The position of the vents changed from day to day, many of the boccas being ephemeral and related to small lava tube systems developed in the vent area. The opening of a new bocca was often preceded by the surface creaking and groaning until it eventually split and lava was exuded. Although most of the gases escaped from the main crater of the cone accompanied by strombolian activity, gas was also released vigorously in the vent areas throwing up small splats of lava that fell around the vents, building hornitos and giving the whole vent area a macabre 'Tolkeinesque' atmosphere. It was continued effusion from these vents that built up the major part of a massive fan of lavas on the northern side of the volcano (Fig. 1.10). Such activity occurring on the shallow slopes of a volcano such as Hawaii, rather than the steep slopes of Etna, would have built up a low shield of lavas surmounted by a cinder-cone.

High effusion rate eruptions from the North-east Crater as for example occurred during 1977 do

Fig. 1.8 Time exposure at night in 1970 of a strombolian explosion from the North-east Crater showing the trajectories of bombs which rose to maximum heights of some 250 m. (Photograph: J. E. Guest.)

not always involve effusion from boccas at the foot of the cone. The pressure of lava within the cone can often push out and breach a sector of the cone allowing lava to pour out at a high rate from the main crater, drastically changing its shape (Fig. 1.11). Further modifications in morphology can occur during or after an eruption by collapses.

The beginning of activity at the North-east Crater is often preceded by several days of minor collapses producing billowing brown clouds and the occasional ejection of lithic fragments. Eventually, occasional juvenile bombs are thrown up and their numbers increase until the vent is clear and strombolian activity takes over. Although most eruptions are preceded by such minor 'throat-clearing' activity, it appears that the North-east Crater has been an open vent for much of its history. The evidence for this is the observation that North-east Crater eruptions are rarely preceded by seismic crises and that high-temperature fumaroles are present for much of the time between eruptions. These fumaroles have temperatures of several hundred degrees C as one British student found to his cost when, on his first visit to the North-east Crater, he had the misfortune to put his foot through the shallow crust over the fumarole; though withdrawing his foot rapidly, he found his socks and trousers to be already on fire. Nevertheless such fumarolic activity can be of benefit and an open fissure at the foot of the North-east Cone was a frequent haven for scientists working in that region during bad weather.

The North-east Crater is not the only sub-terminal vent to have opened up on the flanks of the Summit Cone. For example, in April 1971 three vents opened up immediately upslope from

Fig. 1.9 Small flow of lava erupted from a bocca at the foot of the North-east Crater. Surface velocities of the flow are about 10 cm s^{-1}. The surrounding congealed lava surfaces were formed by flows that were only a few days old when the photograph was taken in 1970. (Photograph: J. E. Guest.)

the Volcano Observatory sited near the foot of the summit cone. Lavas flooded down the southern flank burying the Observatory and much of the upper part of the cable-car system (Fig. 1.12). Inevitably any buildings erected in this zone face a high risk. Nevertheless the site of the Volcano Observatory had been occupied without mishap since 1811 when a three-roomed building known as the Casa Inglesi (Fig. 1.13) was erected by the British when they occupied Sicily during the Napoleonic wars. This small house was used as sleeping quarters for visitors to the mountain until 1879 when it was incorporated into an astronomical observatory. In the early part of this century the building was reconstructed as a volcano observatory (Fig. 1.14) which was eventually destroyed in 1971. Since then a new observatory, hopefully in a safer place, has been built on the northern flank (Fig. 1.15) affording fine views of the North-east Crater and the northern slopes of the volcano.

The opening of sub-terminal vents often precedes a flank eruption. In 1971, after the initial phase of activity from the Summit Cone region, fissures opened up progressively downslope, to 1800 m a.s.l. where another main phase of lava effusion took place. Similarly the South-east Crater, which opened up on the Summit Cone during 1978, gave rise to a series of eruptions which again migrated progressively downslope to give flank eruptions.

The summit region of Etna has left countless tourists with a feeling of awe and excitement, the lucky ones having witnessed sights of spectacular

Fig 1.10 Part of the fan of lavas erupted from the North-east Crater over the northern flank of the volcano. (Photograph: J. E. Guest.)

beauty, and numerous volcanologists have either worked there or made a pilgrimage to the top of Europe's most active volcano. However, visits to the summit were severely curtailed by an event that occurred on 12 September 1979. At about 17.47 (local time) a sudden and unexpected explosion occurred from the Bocca Nuova throwing out black jets of fragmental material. None of this was juvenile lava, but consisted of blocks of old rock and ash that had fallen in from the walls to block the vent ten days earlier. A build-up of gas, either from the magma below or derived from water in the collapse material, eventually caused the Bocca Nuova to throw out the obstructing material. The event was witnessed by a volcanological team working in the summit region (Guest *et al.*, 1980a). From 2 km south of the summit they saw the explosion (Fig. 1.16) which was followed by the rapid rise of a column of dense fume and ash fed convectively at the base and developing an expanding head rising to several kilometres above the crater within a few minutes. When the explosion occurred there were more than 150 tourists in the Central Crater region most of them to the north and north-west of the Bocca Nuova; many were near the edge of the Bocca Nuova while others were on the path leading from it to the vehicle park. For a few seconds the whole area was showered by dense blocks of lava some being 25 cm or more in diameter and having velocities of up to 50 ms^{-1}. Many tourists rushed for the Land Rovers in the vehicle park (Fig. 1.17) where a caravan was hit causing a gas cylinder to explode, burning a number of people before they could get into the Land Rovers. Others left the site on foot in fear and panic, running down the mountain in search of

Fig. 1.11 Oblique aerial view taken in 1983 of the North-east Crater with the fuming pits of the Central Crater seen behind. The conical symmetry of the cone has been destroyed by a breach on the north-west side caused by a high effusion rate eruption in early 1978 when lava in the conduit below the crater burst through the side of the cone carrying away part of it. (Photograph: J. E. Guest.)

safety. The first of the tourist Land Rovers to descend had a bomb hole in the roof, and its windscreen was shattered. There followed a horde of tourists many of whom were in a state of shock. Eventually all the tourists were cleared from the Central Crater; nine tourists had been killed and over twenty had received severe injuries.

Although the explosion was totally unexpected there had been evidence earlier in the day of impending activity. The volcanological team from the UK had set up a precise level in the morning some 400 m away from the Bocca Nuova. It was noticed that the rod was apparently vibrating up and down as seen through the level. This was caused by ground tremor, a common precursor to volcanic activity. However at this time the type of activity to occur was unknown and as most eruptions start relatively quietly on Etna giving observers time to retreat the team was not concerned. The tragic explosion that followed put a new complexion on attitudes towards the safety of visiting the Central Crater and since then restrictions have been placed on taking tourists to the summit region.

1.2 Flank activity

When eruptions occur on the flanks of Etna effusive activity in the Summit Cone region usually stops and it is not unusual for some collapse to occur instead. Flank eruptions are of much greater concern to the local inhabitants, since it is very likely that the lavas will flow through agricultural land and destroy buildings and even whole towns.

In consequence they may become more newsworthy and certainly throughout history have been better reported than activity at the summit which only rarely affects the local inhabitants, even those living high on the mountain. Thus the historical record of flank eruptions is considerably more complete than that for summit activity giving a rather biased view of the total eruptive behaviour of the mountain.

While some flank eruptions start as subterminal effusions only developing into true flank eruptions as fissures propagate downslope allowing magma to find exits at a lower altitude, many lateral effusions start well below the summit region even though open fissure systems associated with the vent area extend upwards towards the summit.

During historical times most flank eruptions have occurred from specific regions on the mountain. In common with many volcanoes, especially those of basaltic composition, Etna has rift zones, the most prominent of which runs down the north-east flank (Fig. 1.18) forming a ridge made up of coalescing tephra cones. As it approaches the summit the north-east rift swings around to become the north-north-east trending fissure zone cutting the summit of the mountain and then continues on the southern flank as a weak rift zone of scattered cinder-cones. Other prominent centres of activity include those marked by clusters of cinder-cones on the west and south-south-east flanks.

During the last four hundred years some 60% of flank eruptions occurring away from the summit region have formed cinder-cones as a result of continued strombolian activity over the vent. Where lava has issued quietly from fissures without strombolian activity, minor degassing of lava over the vent usually results in spatter being thrown up to form hornitos and spatter ramparts. Except in the most sluggish of eruptions the lava issues from the source vent as a silently flowing river of red lava (Fig. 1.19) at surface speeds that often exceed several metres per second. The top surface of the active lava, which has a convex transverse profile, only has a thin chilled skin which is continuously torn by the surface movement. In some cases the surface is also disrupted by bursting bubbles as exsolved gas escapes. Further downslope the surface skin thickens and is broken up into clinkers which abrade against one another making an eerie tinkling sound that is often a good guide to the proximity of the moving flow. At the flow-front itself and on the flanking leveés (Fig. 1.20) clinker and blocks of congealed lava roll down the slope with chinking and rumbling sounds.

The progress and effects of individual flank eruptions vary according to the eruption duration, the volume of lava emitted and their location on the mountain. The 1974 eruption on the west flank was a relatively small one with flows of less than 2 km long. It occurred entirely within the forest belt at about 1700 m a.s.l. and although causing loss of some trees, it did little damage, becoming a Sunday afternoon spectacular for the locals. On the other hand the eruption on the north flank in 1981 (Fig. 1.21) delivered some 20 million cubic metres of lava in less than three days with effusion rates that were at times in excess of $70 m^3 s^{-1}$. As a result, about 4 km^2 of agricultural land were destroyed, over 250 buildings were buried or knocked down and three major roads, together with two railways (Fig. 1.22), were cut. The speed with which events occurred gave little time for protective measures and fortunately the eruption stopped before a flow advancing towards Randazzo entered the town. Some houses and small plantations were stranded as islands (locally known as dagalas) in the middle of the flow field. In the days after the eruption it was a bizarre sight to see the people walking from their property across the still-hot, steaming flows.

The loss of land and buildings was also high during the 1983 eruption on the south flanks (Fig. 1.23). Damage was done to the tourist complex at the foot of the Etna cable-car system (Fig. 1.24) before the lava proceeded to cut at many points one of the arterial roads of the mountain. It was only the construction of embankments around the tourist complex in the late stages of the eruption that prevented the flow spreading over the whole of this area. The eruption lasted for 131 days and added to the volcano flanks some 100 million m^3 of lava.

By comparison another relatively recent eruption of similar volume to, but of longer duration

(a)

Fig. 1.12 Two views looking south from the rim of the Central Crater over the same area. (a) The upper view in 1970 shows the Torre del Filosofo (T), the top station of the cable car (F), the Volcano Observatory (O) and the Vulcarolo (V) a condenser over a fumarole area built to supply the Observatory with water. (b) The picture on p. 15, taken in 1972, illustrates the effects of the 1971 eruption. The Volcano Observatory and the cable-car station were both totally buried by lavas while the Vulcarolo was partly destroyed. Three vents formed during this eruption are seen: the Observatory Vent (OV), the Western Vent (W) and the Vulcarolo Vent (VV). On the skyline is the cone of Montagnola formed by an eruption in 1893 and to the left the edge of the cloud-filled Valle del Bove. (Photographs: J. E. Guest.)

than, the 1983 event occurred in 1950/51 on the eastern flank. However, most of the area occupied by the final flow field was uninhabited and despite the size of the eruption little damage was done.

One of the largest and most destructive eruptions in historical time was that of 1669. This famous eruption started near the town of Nicolosi (at about 800 m a.s.l.) and resulted in the growth of the gigantic twin-peaked cinder cone, known as Monti Rossi, still a prominent landmark today; the lava travelled more than 14 km down to the coast destroying in the process part of Catania the principal city of the region (Fig. 1.25). Based on historical records, eruptions similar to that of 1669 appear to occur from vents in this locality every few hundred years and any future such eruption on this now-highly populated area would be a volcanic disaster of a magnitude previously not experienced on Etna.

The flow fields from most historical flank eruptions, and indeed from persistent activity, have aa surface textures. Nevertheless pahoehoe flows have developed in historical time, the most notable from an eruption that started on the north flank in 1614 and lasted for ten years. The flow-field was fed by lava tubes and much of the surface is covered by unusually large tumuli caused by lava pressure in the tubes up-arching the surface material. Other pahoehoe flows were produced for example in 1651 on the west flank and during the 1792/93 eruption on the south flank. However, even on these extensive pahoehoe fields there are areas of aa especially on the steeper slopes.

The results of persistent activity and flank

(b)

eruptions have been to build up a mountain with progressively steeper angles of slope towards the summit. This shape has led a number of authors (e.g. Imbò, 1965) to classify Etna as a strato-volcano. However, strato-volcanoes (or composite volcanoes) owe their form to interbedded lava and tephra with the relative amount of tephra increasing towards the central conduit system. There is no evidence that this is the case on Etna and exposures several hundred metres in thickness in the rocks forming the upper and steeper part of the volcano show a predominance of lava flows.

The flanks of the volcano below about 1800 m rise generally at from less than 5° to 10°. Above 1800 m there is a sharp increase in slope at the base of a broad cone known as Mongibello, which, with a basal diameter of about 10 km, rises to the level of the foot of the summit cone. It is likely that this form resulted not from increasing amounts of pyroclastic activity from the summit but from the concentration in the summit region of persistent activity which produces short flows that only rarely extend below 1800 m. This continued activity has tended to build up the summit area faster than the flanks where there are less frequent eruptions. It seems likely that many volcanoes classified as being of the strato-volcano type may, like Etna, owe their form to this type of activity.

1.3 Other activity

The volcanic events outlined above describe the normal activity on Etna at the present time, and may well have been typical of eruptive phenomena

Fig. 1.13 The Casa Inglesi, a three-roomed building built in 1811 at the foot of the Summit Cone seen in the background. This building was used by visitors to the summit region. (Taken from Rodwell, 1878.)

Fig. 1.14 The Volcano Observatory at the foot of the Summit Cone and later destroyed by the eruption (Fig. 1.12) of 1971. (Photograph: J. E. Guest.)

throughout much of the history of the volcano. However there are other types of event that have occurred at infrequent intervals in historical time or only during the prehistoric history of the volcano.

One such phenomenon is caldera collapse. The Mongibello Cone has been truncated, or partly truncated, by at least four calderas, all apparently prehistoric (Fig. 1.26). They were subsequently filled or partly filled by lava to form the platform on which the present summit cone stands. It appears likely that these calderas were produced during a time span of about 15 000 years suggesting that caldera-forming events occur every few thousand years. There is no reason to consider that a caldera collapse of major proportions will not happen again in the future, although the earlier ones appear to have been associated with the existence of high-level magma reservoirs for which evidence is lacking at the present time. Nevertheless smaller collapses in the summit region, engulfing the whole of the Summit Cone, have been reported during historical times at intervals of a few hundred years and clearly could happen again.

Historical activity has also not been noted for explosions violent enough to have a wide-ranging effect. However, violent strombolian activity especially near the summit has on a number of occasions spread thin layers of ash for large distances downwind of the Central Crater. During 1979 an eruption deposited ash over much of the southern flank causing inhabitants to don raincoats and carry umbrellas as protection. The airport at Catania was also brought to a standstill for a short time by ash on the runway. However the

Fig. 1.15 The new Volcano Observatory built on the northern flank, construction of which was completed by 1983. In the background is the lower part of the North-east Crater. (Photograph: J. E. Guest.)

stratigraphic record shows that in prehistory violent explosive activity has occurred involving the production of pyroclastic flows and strong phreatomagmatic activity. Some of this violent explosive volcanism may well have been associated with caldera collapses. Pyroclastic flows are found associated with lava compositions that are more evolved than the normal hawaiitic lavas erupted during historical time, and violent phreatomagmatic activity was more prevalent some 26 000 years BP when the snowline on Etna was much lower than it is at present.

A rare form of activity is that of slope failure of one type or another. On the Summit Cone it is quite common for small mudflows to develop in the ashes as a result of snow melt in the spring. These are normally relatively slow movements but M. H. de Saussure (1879) gave a dramatic account of a mudflow/slide on the Summit Cone in 1879 when a local guide nearly lost his life as he sunk up to his middle in the mobile ashes. A much larger mudflow occurred in 1755 (Lyell, 1858) when a large flood of water was formed, possibly by melted snow.

Dramatic though these slope failures may have been to the onlookers, they were minor compared with the events that produced the Valle del Bove. This is a 5.5-km-diameter amphitheatre-shaped hollow in the eastern side of the volcano cutting deep into its flanks and being open on the seaward side. The evidence suggests that probably not long before the Greek occupation of the island major

Table 1.1

Before *c*.20 000 BC	Early man arrived in Sicily. Earliest remains in caves along N, W and SE coasts
c.4000 BC	Neolithic culture introduced from E Mediterranean
c.3000 BC	Metal working introduced. Increase in travel and trade
c.1500 BC	The Sicans (indigenous population in Etna region and E. Sicily) moved to W. part of island possibly as a result of violent eruption on Etna
c.1250 BC	Sicily invaded from mainland Italy by Sicals in the East and Ausoinans to the West. Bronze-age civilization forced inland
c.1000 BC	Phoenician trading began leading to colonization of W. side of island
734 BC	Greek colony of Naxos at foot of Etna was founded. Rapid Hellenization followed and within 135 years much of coastal and E. Sicily colonized to become one of the principal centres of culture and learning in Europe. The Greeks introduced vines, olives and figs
264 BC	Beginning of Roman conquest. The whole island was occupied by 210 BC. Island exploited and lost much of its prosperity established under the Greeks, but largely recovered under Imperial rule
AD 60	Christianity introduced to Sicily by St. Paul
Fifth Century	Vandals and Ostrogoths raided Sicily
535	Sicily incorporated into Byzantine Empire
827	Start of Islamic conquest of Sicily. The capital and cultural centre of the island transferred from Siracusa to Palermo by the Saracens
1061	Normans invaded taking Messina. Palermo finally taken ten years later. Greek- and Arab-based culture flourished under an initially tolerant, vigorous and efficient Norman rule
1194	Swabian rule of Sicily began
1268	Angevine rule of Sicily began at instigation of the Pope
1282	End of Angevine rule, Sicily becoming an independent kingdom under the House of Aragon
1377	Sicily collapsed into anarchy after death of Fredrich III
1409	The island lost its autonomy, to become a Spanish dependency ruled by a Viceroy
1720	Sicily ruled by Austria
1734	Bourbon rule began from Naples, the island becoming part of 'The Kingdom of the Two Sicilies'
1806	Britain leased the island as a base during the Napoleonic wars
1815	Revival of rule from Naples
1860	Garibaldi defeated Bourbons in Palermo and by the end of the year Sicily voted to become part of the new Kingdom of Italy
1943	Allied occupation of Sicily
1946	Restoration of Sicily as a Region of the New Republic of Italy, with its own regional government

Fig. 1.16 The explosion plume rising above the Central Crater following the Bocca Nuova explosion of 12 September 1979. The picture was taken from 2 km south of the Central Crater. (Photograph: J. E. Guest.)

landslides occurred on the seaward flank of the volcano depositing a huge fan of debris in the coastal region. Because of the inherent instability of the slopes of many volcanoes such huge landslide scars are not unusual and the recurrence of this phenomenon on Etna cannot be ruled out.

The loss of life directly by volcanic activity on Etna has been relatively small throughout history, amounting to the death of a few tens of people: but the same cannot be said for the effects of earth-

Fig 1.17 The vehicle park near the summit of Etna as seen the day after the explosion from the Bocca Nuova on 12 September 1979. Blocks lying on the surface were thrown out from the Bocca Nuova during this explosion. One of the larger bombs penetrated the roof of the Land Rover in the foreground. The rim of the Bocca Nuova is on the skyline immediately behind the hut. (Photograph: J. E. Guest.)

quakes. Though the volcano's frequent small earthquakes rarely involve fatalities (Fig. 1.27), there have been large earthquakes which have resulted in high death tolls. Notable earthquakes that have caused great devastation are those of 1169, when it is estimated some 15 000 people died and a tsunami engulfed part of Messina, and of 1693, when some fifty towns are thought to have been destroyed killing between 60 000 and 100 000 people. Thus, although the menace of the volcano itself is all too evident, the hidden destructive power of an earthquake must never be forgotten, and the need for earthquake engineering in all construction projects is of paramount importance.

1.4 From myth to science

Any synopsis of Etna's activity condenses in time events that are relatively localized and is thus liable to give an overdramatized view of life on the volcano. Even today with fast communications and media coverage, many of the people living close to Etna have never been to the summit where most of the activity takes place and most individuals may only see two or three eruptions – if that – during a lifetime. Thus, although throughout history the mountain has cast a shadow of fear over the whole

Fig. 1.18 The north flank of Etna with the town of Randazzo in the foreground. The ridge running from the base of the Summit Cone towards the left of the picture is the north-east rift. (Photograph: J. E. Guest.)

area, the majority of people live their lives on the mountain without personally encountering its relentless destructive power.

Attitudes to the volcano and its causes have depended on the density of population and the social and religious attitudes of the different cultures that have lived in Sicily (Table 1.1). For the Greeks, whose occupation of the Etnean region was restricted to the coast, volcanic activity only rarely touched their lives although clearly they were aware of activity at the summit and on the higher flanks.

Poetic descriptions of Etna's activity go back as far as Pinder (522 – 442 BC) who states 'whereout pure springs of unapproachable fire are vomited from the inmost depths: in the daytime the lava streams pour forth a lurid rush of smoke; but in the darkness a red rolling flame sweepeth rocks with uproar to the wide deep sea . . .'

They had little concern for rational explanations, attributing eruptions and earthquakes to the gods. Nevertheless these events were seen more as indications of the presence of the deities; and the Greek myths, rather than explaining natural phenomena, are generally more concerned with the activities of gods and men, especially the timeless preoccupations with war and seduction. In her fight against the Giants it is told that the warrior goddess Athene flattened the great Enceladus under a vast missile that became Sicily (Graves, 1955). Alternatively Virgil says that he was crushed under Etna and that each time he tires and turns over all Sicily quakes and growls and veils the sky with smoke. It is also told that the final monster to be slain was Typhoeus from whose shoulders sprang a hundred horrible dragons'

Fig. 1.19 Close-up view of a stream of lava flowing at about 5 m s^{-1} near to the vent in May 1978. The congealed ropes of lava in the foreground result from overflows. (Photographs: J. E. Guest.)

heads with eyes that spurted with flame. He was finally overwhelmed by Zeus's thunderbolts and buried under Etna (Guiraud, 1968).

Hephaestus (the Greek god of fire and volcanoes, later to be equated with the Roman Vulcan or Volcanus – from whom the word *vulcano* or *volcano* is derived) was to become the gaoler of Typhoeus under Etna. Having been born a cripple to Zeus and Hera, Hephaestus's mother threw him to Earth where he learned his fine arts as a worker in metal. In early life he made his name under the volcanoes of the eastern Mediterranean but eventually emigrated first to the active volcano now known as Vulcano and later developed Etna as his forge and home. Some stories tell of Hephaestus placing on the head of Typhoeus his heavy anvil on which he hammered bronze and iron, and of how the monster's attempts to escape caused earthquakes and eruptions (Guiraud, 1968). In his role as blacksmith of the gods Hephaestus turned out both weapons of war and fine items of beauty assisted by the Cyclops who toiled under Etna and whose hammer blows could be heard in the rumblings of the volcano.

But from these stories we learn little about Etna, although the activities of Hephaestus, and more particularly those of his amorous wife Aphrodite (Venus in later Roman mythology), have given delight to the present day. The dispassionate, generalized way in which the Greeks treated volcanic phenomena in their earlier myths is in marked contrast to mythology in other volcanic regions. The endearing stories from Hawaii of the wicked volcano goddess Pele and her beautiful and charming sister Hiiaka are equally concerned with describing the intricacies of human relationships,

Fig. 1.20 The rubbly edge of the 1983 flow crossing a road. The metre-sized blocks lying on the road to the left of the figure have rolled from the top of the flow. (Photograph: J. E. Guest.)

especially the forces of love and hate (Emerson, 1978); but they are clearly based on first-hand observations of dramatic volcanic happenings, and many of the stories can be related to the geology of Hawaii as it is today (Westervelt, 1963). These Hawaiian story-tellers were much closer to nature than their Greek counterparts on Etna (Macdonald, 1972).

The Greek myths were eventually adopted by the Romans. Thus the mythological tradition played an important part in people's lives for a long period. Nevertheless deistic thought about Etna did not satisfy the minds of all who saw the mountain in activity. Some speculated about the causes. The philosopher Empedocles (492–432 BC) realized the importance of observing natural phenomena: taking a particular interest in Etna, he spent several years living near the summit, making observations to test his ideas that the centre of the Earth was in a molten state and that volcanoes were formed when this liquid rock came to the surface. It is often said that he died either by falling or jumping into the summit crater but it is more likely he died in exile having been banished from Sicily and sent to Greece (Freeman, 1892). Unfortunately most of his work has been lost. Today he is remembered by the Torre del Filosofo (Tower of the Philosopher) a small eminence that once formed part of the rim of the Piano Caldera south of the present summit on which once stood a tower possibly constructed to celebrate a visit by the Emperor Hadrian.

The Roman philosopher, Lucretius, made known his views on Mount Etna in his poem '*The*

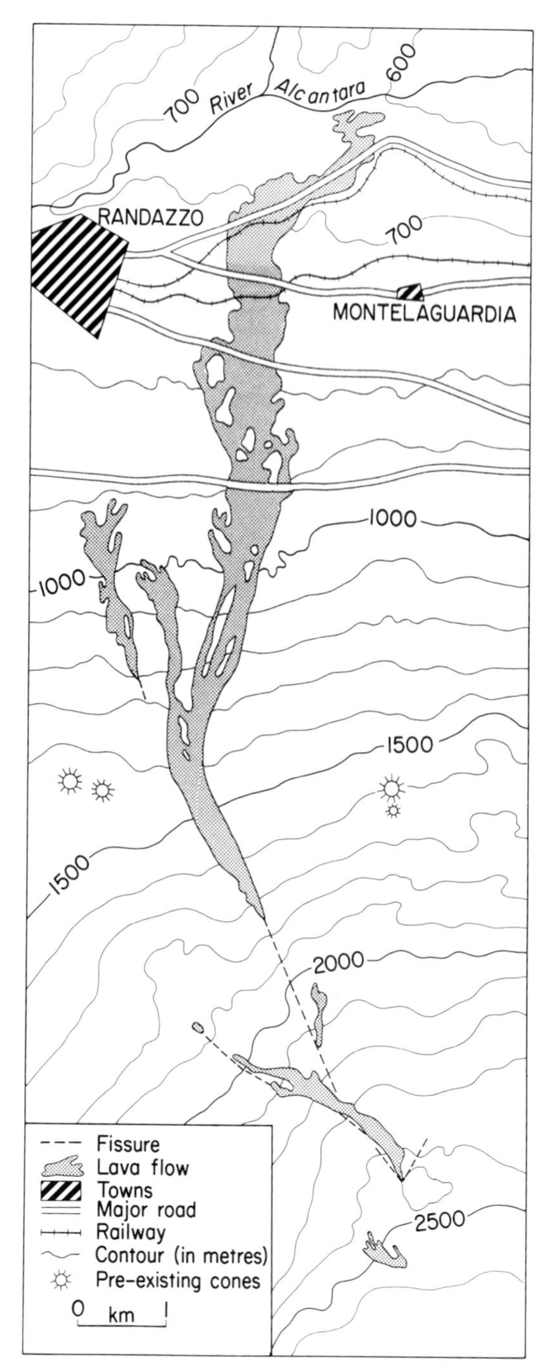

Fig. 1.21 Map of the lava produced by the 1981 eruption on the north flank of Etna. (From VEST, 1981.)

Nature of the Universe' published in about 55 BC. He followed Aristotle (384 – 322 BC) in believing that volcanic activity resulted from the movement of wind imprisoned within the Earth – a popular idea in Greek and Roman times. For Lucretius, Etna was hollow inside containing wind that when thoroughly heated and raging furiously melted the rocks around; fire was produced and the flames were swept up by the winds until they issued from the mountain-top throwing out rocks and black smoke. He also considered that water entering the subterranean caverns from the sea mingled with the air and was expelled in blasts of flame.

Strabo, who lived from about 63 BC to AD 30 studied several of the volcanoes in the Mediterranean. On Etna, he compared molten lava to a kind of black mud ejected from craters to flow down the mountain cooling and congealing as it descended. He considered volcanoes such as Etna to be safety valves for the entrapped subterranean winds, and that an eruption reduced the likelihood of a violent earthquake.

The temporal nature of Etna was also recognised and Ovid (43 BC to AD 17), writing in *Metamorphoses* on the teaching of Pythagoras, points out that Etna 'glowing with its sulphurous furnaces, will not always be fiery, nor was it always so.' He also likens Etna to a living animal 'possessed of many earth passages that breathe out flames, then as often as it moves, it can change the channels through which it breathes, putting an end to one set of holes and opening up another.' During Roman times many rejected the supernatural beliefs, and Lucilius Junior, the Procurator of Sicily under Nero, condemned the practice then prevalent of ascending to the edge of the summit crater to offer incense to the gods of the mountain. His explanation of the volcanic activity was similar to that of Lucretius, emphasizing the role of water filtering through cracks until it came into contact with the internal fires where it was converted into vapour and expelled with violence. The fires were nourished by winds which penetrated into the mountain.

And so the speculation ceased: volcanic eruptions were sometimes reported but seen more as portents of evil rather than phenomena to be studied, and the early explanatory ideas tended to be considered heretical. Superstition still prevailed

Fig. 1.22 Lava invading a railway track near Randazzo during the 1981 eruption. (Photograph: J. E. Guest.)

and, for example, it was believed by many that King Henry the Eighth's second wife Anne Boleyn was confined beneath Etna (Macdonald, 1972). It was not until the Renaissance that a free intellectual environment reigned once more allowing Etna to become a focus of academic pursuit.

Thus during the sixteenth, seventeenth and particularly the eighteenth centuries, philosophical thought turned away from invocation of supernatural forces, or deistic intervention. Natural phenomena were observed in meticulous detail with the principal aim of classifying objects and events, and so imposing a sense of order in the world.

The principal works on Mount Etna from the sixteenth century to the end of the eighteenth century are listed in Table 1.2. During this time the unusually large eruption in 1669 attracted considerable interest. Just over 100 years later Sir William Hamilton published *Campi Phlegraei*, generally regarded as the first modern work in volcanology (Macdonald, 1972, p. 31). Hamilton – perhaps better known for his second wife Emma, who became the mistress of Lord Nelson – was for over thirty years British Envoy Extraordinary to the Court of Naples. During this time he developed a considerable interest in Vesuvius whose eruptions he studied in great detail at first hand. He also travelled to the other Italian volcanoes including Mount Etna. These observations were published in *Campi Phlegraei* (Hamilton, 1776) which included a substantial chapter on Mount Etna (Fig. 1.28). On his visit to the summit he was accompanied by Canon Recupero who had devoted much time to the study of Etna and whose local knowledge greatly assisted Hamilton's des-

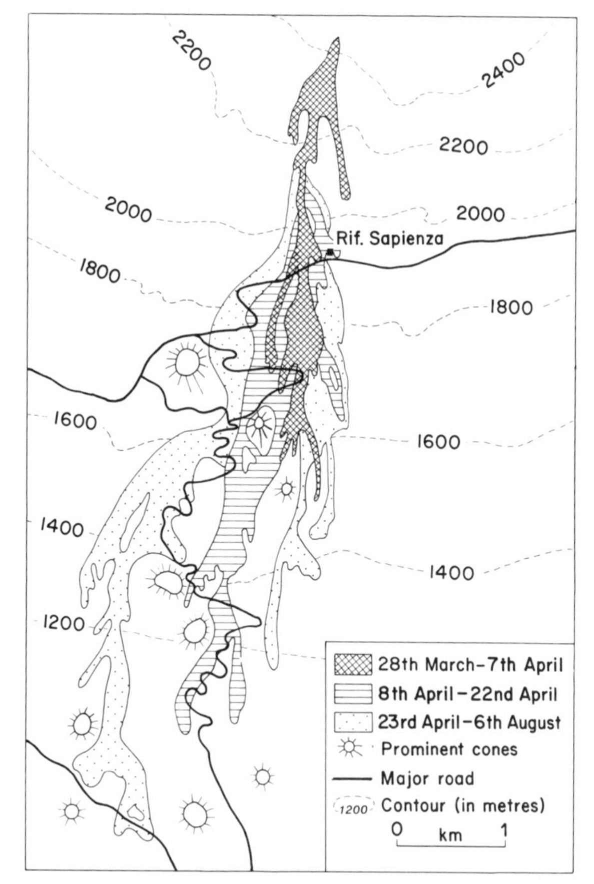

Fig. 1.23 Map of the lavas produced during the 1983 eruption on the south flank of Etna. (Compiled from data collected by A. Duncan, J. E. Guest, C. R. J. Kilburn and H. Pinkerton.)

criptions. Unfortunately Recupero's work was not published until 1815, nearly forty years after his death.

Because it was recognized as an active volcano Etna did not play more than a peripheral part in the famous dispute between the *Neptunists* and the *Plutonists* which was finally resolved in favour of the *Plutonists* in 1815 when Leopold vön Buch (1774 – 1852), a student of Abraham Werner, leader of the *Neptunist* camp, finally accepted the case for the volcanic origin of basalt. However vön Buch moved from one major controversy to another, developing the idea of 'Craters of Elevation' in which he argued that volcanic mountains owed their existence not to the slow accumulation of lavas from eruptive vents, but were formed by the up-warping of formerly horizontal beds of basalt as a result of pressures exerted by molten materials at depth (vön Buch 1818 – 19). According to Macdonald (1972) the reasoning employed by vön Buch was based on two critical field observations made in the Canaries: the occurrence of coarse-grained granitic rocks high in the crater of La Palma, which according to the conventional wisdom of the day implied elevation since granite was part of the lowest of 'primary' system; and his belief that the slopes of a volcano were too steep to have allowed lava flows to have solidified *in situ*.

The concept of 'Craters of Elevation' received immediate opposition. An early opponent was George Poulett-Scrope. In 1816, while still a student at Cambridge, he made a study of volcanic phenomena in the vicinity of Naples; later between 1818 and 1823 he extended his researches to include Etna, the Eolian Islands, dormant volcanoes around Rome and several other volcanic provinces in Europe. Following these excursions he published his now famous work *Considerations of volcanoes, the probable causes of their phenomena* (Scrope, 1825), in which he argued that volcanoes were not 'Craters of Elevation' but instead 'Craters of Eruption' formed by lava flows consolidating on steep slopes without any significant up-warping.

Scrope's work nevertheless did not end the argument for everyone, and in an account of Etna by Elie de Beaumont (1836) the ideas of vön Buch were strongly supported. De Beaumont was a meticulous field geologist and even Lyell, who was later to criticize him, graciously records that his monograph on Etna 'Is a most valuable memoir on the structure and origin of the mountain . . . in which he explains his views with uncommon perspicuity and talent' (Lyell, 1847, p. 399). Briefly de Beaumont's model for Etna envisaged the eruption of lavas on a sub-horizontal surface raised above sea level. These lavas issued from many fissures and the lava was erupted in thin sheets of uniform thickness with slope angles of around 3°, often interbedded with pyroclastic material. Eruptions were repeated for a long period of time until at least 1200 m thickness of material had been built up; whereupon the whole mass was

Table 1.2 Principal works of the pre-nineteenth century descriptive scientific tradition

Author	*Principal works*	*Main research findings*
Sixteenth century		
Fazzellus, T. (or Fazzello)	*De Rebus Siculis decades duae* (1558)	Describes the eruptive history of the mountain and indicates that at this time the volcano had a single crater
Filoteo, A.	*Aetnae Topographia* (1590)	Describes the volcano in the sixteenth century and the eruption of 1536 which he witnessed
Seventeenth century		
Borelli, G. A.	*Historia et Meteorologia* (1670)	
Winchilsea (Earl) (British ambassador to Constantinople)	*A true and exact relation of the late prodigious earthquake and eruption of Mount Etna or Montegibello as it came in a letter written to his Majesty from Naples. Together with a more particular narrative of the same, as it is collected out of several relations sent from Catania.* (1669, account sent to Charles II)	All these works and many more constitute the first detailed accounts of an eruption of Etna. In this eruption of 1669 attention is drawn to the following themes: (a) The type of activity and its exact timing; (b) The rate of advance of lava flow fronts; (c) The rate of cooling; (e) The effects of the volcano on the economy and settlements of the region; (f) The reaction of the inhabitants of the region and the civil authorities to this disaster. In addition to written accounts, this eruption stimulated the production of some of the first maps and engravings of the volcano; these being of varying quality
Anon.	'An answer to some inquiries concerning the eruptions of Mt. Aetna, 1669, communicated by some inquisitive merchants now residing in Sicily' *Phil. Trans. R. Soc., Lond.* **4:** 1028–34 (1669)	
Anon.	'A chronological account of several Incendiums or fires of Mt. Aetna' *Phil. Trans. R. Soc., Lond.* **4:** 67–69 (1669)	
Eighteenth century		
Massa, G. A.	*Della Sicilia grand'Isola del Mediterraneo in prospettiva e il Monte Etna o il Mongibello esposto in veduta da un religioso della Compagnia di Gesu* (1708)	Massa, D'Orville and Riedesel all ascended the mountain and provided detailed descriptions of its physical features
D'Orville, J. P. (Count)	*Sicula, quibus Siciliae veteris rudera illustrantur* (1764)	
Riedesel, J. H. (von)	*Reise durch Sicilien und Gross-Griechenland* (1767)	
Hamilton, Sir William	'Observations on Mount Vesuvius, Mount Etna, and other volcanoes' *Trans. R. Soc. Lond.* **57–61** (1768–72)	Hamilton ascended the mountain in 1769 and made many observations on volcanological phenomena. In particular Hamilton reviewed the eruption of 1669 and drew attention to a vineyard he had visited which had been carried over 500 m by a lava flow, yet had not sustained any damage
Hamilton, Sir William	'Account of a journey to Mount Etna in a letter . . . to Mathew Maty' *Phil. Trans. R. Soc. Lond.* **60:** 1–20 (1771)	

Table 1.2 (contd.)

Author	*Principal works*	*Main research findings*
Hamilton, Sir William	*Campi Phlegraei* (1776)	This work is devoted in the main to descriptions of Vesuvius and its surrounding areas. *Campi Phlegraei* contains many magnificent illustrations and one of these by the artist Antonio Fabris shows the volcano in the late eighteenth century, although certain features are clearly exaggerated
Brydone, P.	*A tour through Sicily and Malta* (1776)	Several chapters of this work are concerned with Etna and constitute the most complete account of the volcano which had appeared in English up to that time
Ferrara, F.	*Storia generale dell'Etna, che comprende la descrizione di questa montagna: la storia delle sue eruzioni e dei suoi fenomeni* (1773). Revised and reprinted in 1888.	The first reasonably complete history of Etna and its eruptions. The work begins with a general description of the mountain and continues with a history of eruptions from the earliest times. The third section discusses the volcanic products and the fourth certain geological and physical considerations
Recupero, G.	*Storia naturale e generale dell'Etna. Opera postuma con annotazioni del suo nipote Agatino Recupero* (Recupero died in 1778, but his results were not published until 1815)	Recupero accompanied Hamilton and Brydone on their visits to Etna and was employed by the government to report on the flood (possibly a mudflow), which devastated an area in front of the Valle del Bove in 1755. In the work published in 1815, Recupero gives a detailed discription of volcano, its eruptions and volcanic products

Based on information in Rodwell (1858), Vön Waltershausen (1880) and Hyde (1916). Bibliographical information from Johnston-Lavis (1918) and from the original sources.

suddenly uplifted to form the Etna construct. He further posited that uplift did not operate at one point but along a line now occupied by the amphitheatre-shaped depression on Etna's east flank known as the Valle del Bove (Fig. 1.29). From exposures on the walls of the Valle del Bove he observed that lavas were inclined at angles of up to 30° and yet maintained a uniform thickness, whereas historical lavas on slopes greater than 10–20° formed narrow strips, and their thicknesses varied with angle of slope. He also considered that the pattern of feeder dykes, their orientation and the nature of the faults observed in the region were all supportive of his model.

It was de Beaumont's paper which focussed the mind of Sir Charles Lyell on the question of how volcanoes came into existence. Lyell visited Etna in 1824, 1857 and 1858, and as well as using his observations on Etna extensively in *Principles of Geology* (Lyell, 1830 and later editions) to illustrate volcanic phenomena, he also wrote an important monograph for the Royal Society (Lyell, 1858) in which he not only condemns the idea of 'Craters of Elevation' but also gives a visionary account of the geology of the mountain that remains today an important document for any student of Etna.

Although Lyell had rejected the 'Craters-of-Elevation' hypothesis as early as 1830, during his visits to the volcano in 1857 and 1858 he assembled field data to argue against virtually all the evidence used by de Beaumont in support of his ideas. In his monograph Lyell first presents a mass of information on the morphology and flow characteristics of both historic and more ancient lava flows concluding that Etnean lavas can, and often do, consolidate on steep slopes and that subsequent elevation is

(a)

(b)

Fig. 1.24 (a) The upper photograph shows the Rifugio Sapienza which together with the base station of the cable car (just off the picture to the right) form the hub of a tourist complex at about 1900 m a.s.l. (b) The lower picture shows the same building during the 1983 eruption. The main flow forms the ridge on the skyline to the left but an overflow from the principal channel has swept around the Rifugio banking up against the back walls and entering the kitchen through the back door. (Photographs: J. E. Guest.)

Fig. 1.25 A contemporary engraving of lava invading the town of Catania during 1669. Note the clothes line by the flow to the right erected by the ingenious Catanesi.

Fig. 1.26 A drawing of the upper part of Etna as seen from the west during the mid-nineteenth century. The main cone with dark lavas on its surface has been truncated by calderas and later infilled by lava to form a platform on which stands the summit cone. The Casa Inglesi on the rim of the caldera is somewhat exaggerated. (From Rodwell, 1878.)

unnecessary to explain inclined flows of uniform thickness. However much of Lyell's argument relates to the Valle del Bove (Fig. 1.29) which had been considered by de Beaumont as the centre of uplift. The thick volcanic sequences exposed in the walls of the Valle del Bove allow the inner structure of the volcano to be studied in detail. It should be said that Lyell's observations must have benefited greatly from the field work being carried out in the Valle del Bove by members of the Gemmellaro family and Baron Sartorius vön Waltershausen. Using their observations, together with his own, Lyell argued that the distribution of dips of lavas and beds of pyroclastic material showed there was more than one centre that had played a part in the construction of Etna. The earlier centre to the east, known as Trifoglietto, had been partly buried by lavas from a centre near the present summit. He also noted that the frequency of feeder dykes increased in number towards the head of the Valle del Bove, implying that the centre of eruption was always near to the centre of the volcano and not distributed over a plain prior to uplift. Given these findings Lyell argued that the 'Craters-of-Elevation' hypothesis must be abandoned for 'although one cone of eruption may envelop another . . . , it is impossible for a cone of upheaval to mantle round and overwhelm another cone of upheaval so as to reduce the whole mass to one conical mountain' (Lyell, 1858, p. 761). Thus Lyell's argument brought to an end the controversy started by vön Buch forty years before; but as a by-product it directed attention on the origin of the Valle del Bove which is still being debated today.

Lyell's other important contribution to geology made from observations at Etna, related to the geological time-scale. He noted that at the base of the volcanic pile on the seaward side Etna's lavas were interbedded with sedimentary deposits containing shells that with one or two exceptions were

Fig. 1.27 Faults formed near the South-east Crater in the Summit Cone area during a local earthquake associated with eruptive activity. Displacements of up to 2 m are seen on the skyline which is the rim of a crater formed in 1819. People standing nearby watching the eruption were thrown to the ground. (Photograph: J. E. Guest.)

of the same species now living in the Mediterranean. One obvious conclusion to be drawn was that these sedimentary strata were not very old and that Etna had been built up extremely rapidly. However Lyell was impressed by the large numbers of adventive cones and vents on the present surface of Etna and the numerous individual flows recorded in the walls of the Valle del Bove. Assuming that eruptive behaviour had been similar to that in historical times, Lyell considered that the sedimentary strata containing 'modern' fossils must be very old indeed emphasizing the great age of the Earth.

Although the ideas of de Beaumont and Lyell based on their observations at Etna were expressed in detail, their visits to this volcano were of relatively short duration. The speed with which they were able to identify the structure and stratigraphy of the volcano was almost certainly helped by the work of others with long-standing programmes of research on Etna. The Gemmellaro brothers who lived and worked in the city of Catania made substantial contributions to knowledge of the volcano. In 1824 Dr Giuseppe Gemmellaro published a map showing 74 cinder-cones correctly located and the courses of the historic lava flows which had originated from these vents and from the area of the central crater. This map was re-published in London (G. Gemmellaro, 1828) and although being inaccurate in the location of certain towns and also variable in scale (Rodwell, 1878) was nevertheless a great improvement on the earlier maps contained in the works of both Ferrara and Recupero (see Table 1.2). Gaetano Gemmellaro mapped the Valle del Bove, and Mario made observations of the volcano for almost thirty years from 1803 to 1832 constituting the first example of regular monitoring of the volcanic activity. His

Fig. 1.28 View of Etna from the coast drawn by Peter Fabins to illustrate *Campi Phlegrae* (Sir William Hamilton, 1776).

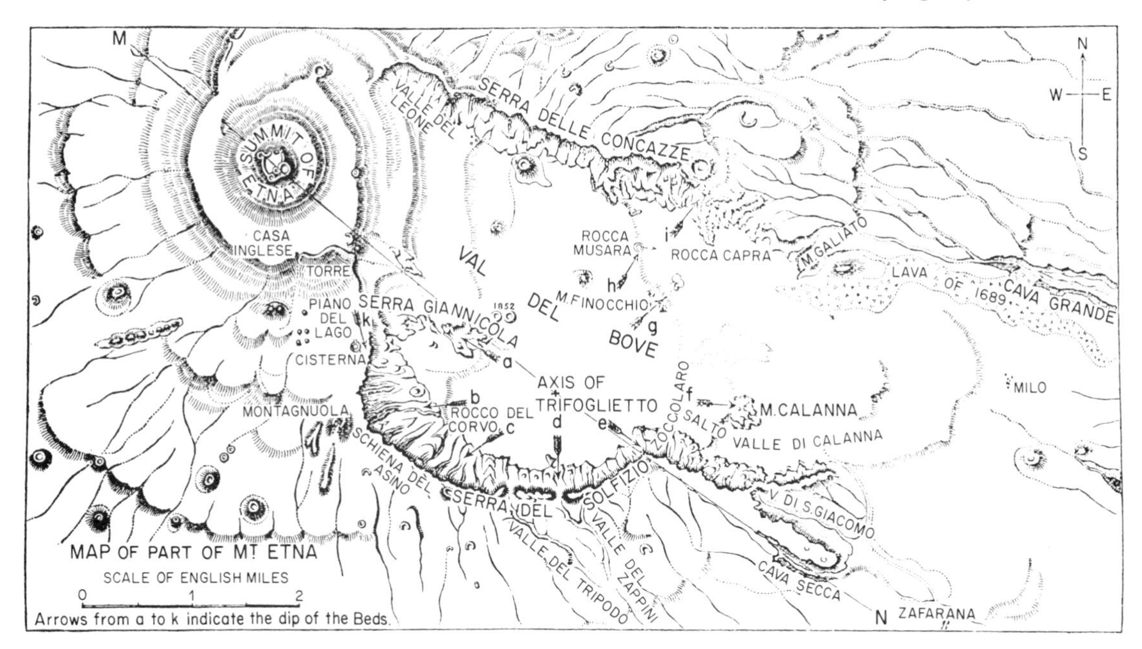

Fig. 1.29 Map by Baron Sartorius vön Waltershausen of the summit region and Valle del Bove. (From Lyell, 1847.)

researches were summarized and published by a fourth brother, Professor Carlo Gemmellaro (1860), who was an important figure in the development of the scientific ideas about Etna. Between 1819 and 1865 he produced detailed studies of most of the significant eruptions and wrote widely on a number of volcanological phenomena (Johnston-Lavis, 1918). In an important paper (C. Gemmellaro, 1860), he summarized the stratigraphy of Etna developed in part by discussions with Lyell who was a close friend; little advance was made on this work for very nearly 100 years.

Of particular significance in the history of Etnean studies is the name Baron Sartorius vön Waltershausen. Following in the footsteps of other German geologists such as vön Abich, who produced a detailed cross-section of Etna (vön Abich, 1836), and Hoffmann, who published a geological memoir of Sicily much of which is devoted to Etna (Hoffmann, 1839), the Baron started in 1836 a detailed study of Etna that was to continue for six years. His work involved a topographical and geological survey of Etna which was eventually presented in the form of an atlas that appeared in eight parts between 1848 and 1861 (vön Waltershausen, 1848–61). The death of the Baron in 1861 put an end to this project but his researches were continued by a colleague, von Lasaulx, and published as a two-volume work (vön Waltershausen, 1880) which supplemented the geological and topographical maps by providing an extremely comprehensive history of the volcano's eruptions from classical times onwards, together with an assessment of the effects of these eruptions on the people of the region. This work must stand as one of the most important landmarks in Etnean studies. In recognition of his work, the cinder-cones produced during the 1865 eruption were named Monti Sartorio.

The second part of the nineteenth century was less exciting in terms of development of ideas about Etna. Flank eruptions continued to be monitored. Professor Orazio Silvestri published accounts of all the eruptions which occurred between 1865 and the late 1880s (Silvestri, 1867, 1886) and also carried out some of the first chemical analyses of Etnean rocks (Silvestri, 1866). The mantle of Silvestri was then assumed by Professor Riccò of the University of Catania who not only compiled several fine narratives of flank activity (Riccò,

1892, 1909, 1910) but also produced excellent accounts of the more frequently occurring summit activity (Riccò, 1897). Riccò, being something of a polymath, also found time to produce reports on topics as diverse as gravity (1898), seismology (1894) and meteorology. The chronology was continued by Ponte (1911, 1923, 1953) who wrote at length on eruptions which took place between 1910 and 1951; by G. Imbò (1928, 1965) from Naples; and by Cucuzza Silvestri (1949, 1957) from the University of Catania.

The father of the modern surge in Etnean studies that went beyond just the reporting (important though that is) of volcanic activity was Professor Alfred Rittmann. Born in Switzerland in 1893, he carried out research in volcanology in a number of parts of the world, especially Mount Vesuvius. Having worked in several different universities around the world he eventually settled at the University of Catania in the 1950s. His interests on Etna were wide but perhaps his most important work was related to the petrogenesis of the lavas based on their chemistry. Little interest had been taken in the chemical composition of the Etnean rocks since the work of Washington *et al.* (1926) which contained the most-often-quoted chemical analyses for the lavas of Etna. Rittmann had a charismatic personality and penetrating mind and, although his views were often controversial, any discussion with him on volcanological matters was always stimulating. As well as encouraging his students to continue the work on Etna, Rittmann was a great source of encouragement to groups from other countries who were beginning research projects there. Much is owed to his enthusiasm that the new geological map of Etna produced by the joint labours of Italian and British scientists was started in 1972 and finally published in 1979, over one-hundred-and-thirty years after the map of Sartorious vön Waltershausen.

2 Etna and the Etna region

'The lava, where it
has been cultivated, is reduced
to fertile sand, in which vines
and fig-trees are planted – their
tender green foliage contrasting strangely
with the sinister soil that
makes them flourish.'

(J. A. Symonds, 1874)

To navigators of the Classical Age, Mount Etna was considered to be the highest point on earth (King, 1973a) and the names by which it has been known are indicative of the awe that successive cultures have felt when confronted by this distinctive volcanic environment. For Pindar writing in the fifth century BC it was the 'pillar of Heaven', while during the Arab or Saracen occupation of the island between the ninth and eleventh centuries AD it was known as *Gibel Uttamat* – the mountain of fire – and today its alternative names to Sicilians are *Mongibello* – mountain of mountains (from the Arabic and Italian words for mountain), and *Il Monte* – the mountain *par excellence* (Rodwell, 1878; Hyde, 1916). The etymon of the word Etna is not certain, most authorities suggesting that it derives from both Greek and Latin verbs to burn, but a minority view holds that it has its origin in the Phoenician *athana* – a furnace (Rodwell, 1878).

The linguistic origin of the name of the volcano correctly implies that Etna has always been a region that has attracted human settlement, in spite of the ever-present hazard posed by volcanic and seismic activity. Catania, the principal city of the region (Fig. 2.1), has been devastated on several occasions by these phenomena and, since the time of Christ, has been destroyed at least in part by earthquakes in 1169 and 1693 and by lava flows in 1371(?) and 1669. This apparent paradox between the hazardous nature of the environment and its attractiveness for human settlement may be explained by a combination of factors, both physical and human, which have made the region throughout most of its history one of the most densely settled, most agriculturally productive areas within the Mediterranean and one that has continually shown a quite different geography from the rest of Sicily and the Italian south.

2.1 The physical environment

2.1.1 Climate

The major influences on the climate of Etna are the height of the volcano and its location within the Mediterranean Basin. This means that, whilst at sea level the climate is similar to many other coastal locations in eastern Sicily, on the flanks it is modified both by the effects of altitude (the orographic effect) and by aspect, which combine to create a series of sectorially and altitudinally defined zones.

The climate of the Mediterranean region in general and of Sicily in particular is well known and documented (Admiralty, 1944; Meteorological Office, 1962; Houston, 1964; D. S. Walker, 1967; Pecora, 1968; Beckinsale and Beckinsale, 1975), its main features being relatively calm dry summers and windy moist winters. In summer, temperatures are fairly uniform in Sicily and a combination of the high angle of the sun at noon and long periods of daylight give mean temperatures of between 24–27°C over most of the island for the hottest months of July and August. The hottest places in the Sicilian summer are in the south-east and here temperatures often exceed 29°C, but many places are capable of reaching 35°C and figures of 40°C are not uncommon (King, 1973a). In winter temperatures are less uniform, being around 10°C on the coast but falling inland, mostly as a response to increasing height; so that Nicosia (800 m) has a January mean of 5°C and Floresta (1275 m – in the Nebrodi Mountains) one of only 2°C (Pecora, 1968); see Fig. 2.2. Because of the ameliorating effect of the sea and the combined influences of height and continentality, annual temperature ranges of 14 – 15°C are recorded on the coast and 20°C or greater in the centre of the island (King, 1973a).

The most notable characteristic of the rainfall of Sicily is its seasonality. In some summers no rainfall occurs and it is common for summer rainfall to amount to less than 5% of the annual total (Meteorological Office, 1962). These low rainfall totals, combined with high temperatures, mean that summer is a season when a constant battle has to be fought against drought. Any rainfall that does occur in summer is a function of localized convective activity, and short, but violent, storms are sometimes a feature of this season. The wet or winter season extends from October to April, and rain falls as a result of the passage of depressions from the west and north-west. Cold fronts tend to bring heavy rain in the form of showers, while light rain is a characteristic of less active warm fronts

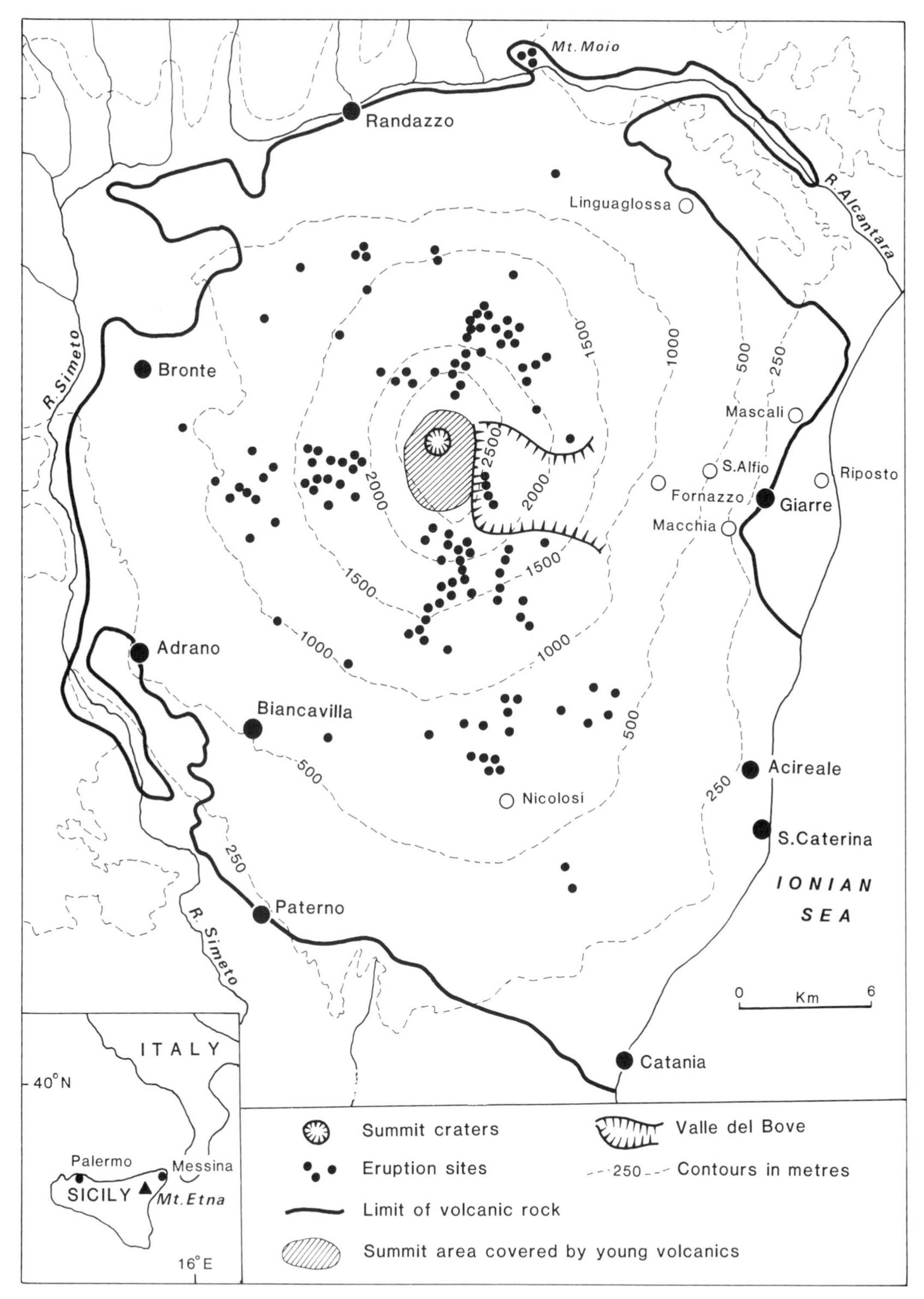

Fig. 2.1 The Mount Etna region. General location map. (After Chester and Duncan, 1982.)

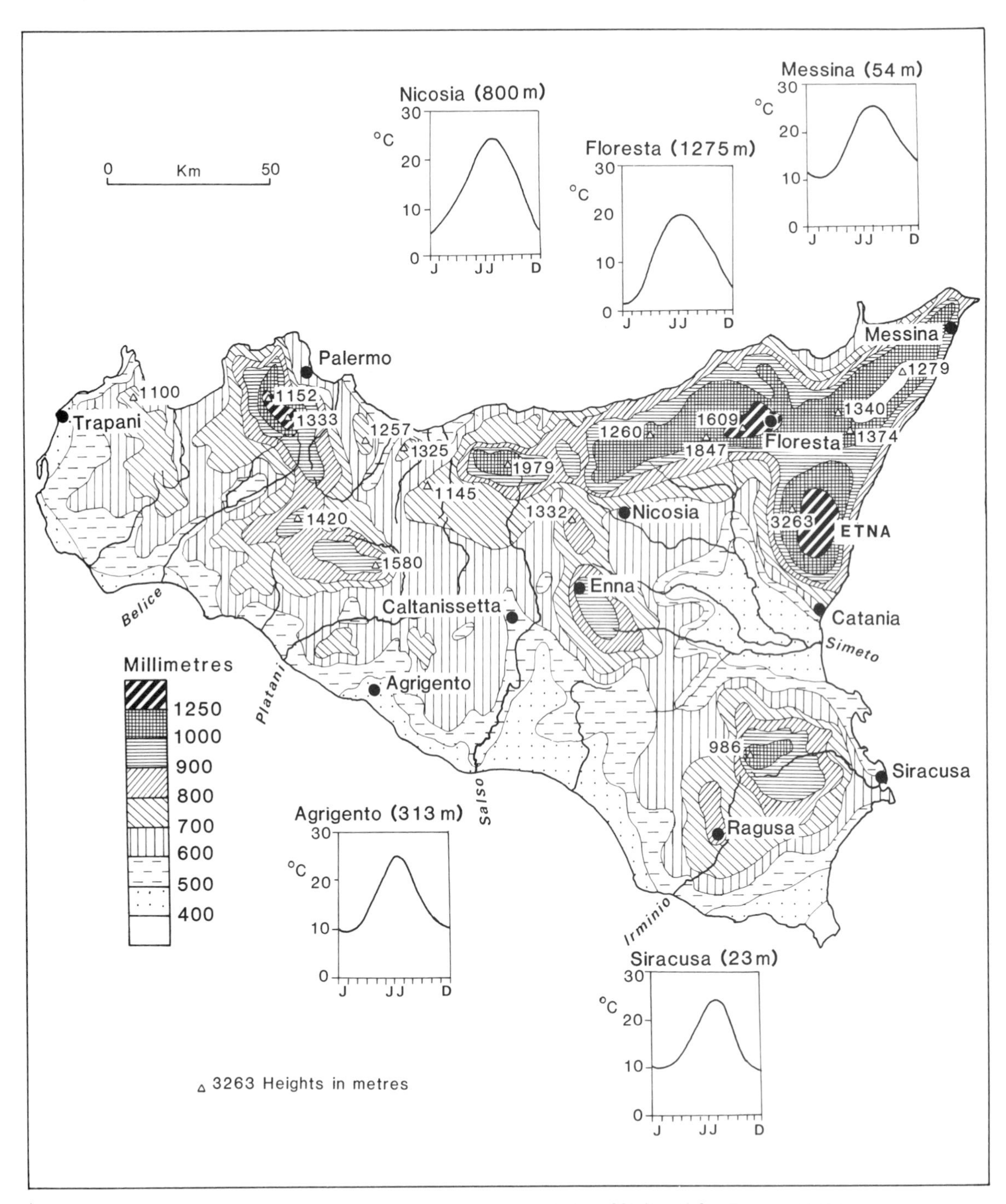

Fig. 2.2 The principal temperature and precipitation characteristics of Sicily. (After Pecora, 1968.)

(Durbin, 1981). Most of the island receives mean annual totals of 600 – 700 mm (King, 1973a), but great variations may occur from year to year and between different parts of the island. Because most rainfall is depressional, being derived from the north and north-west, there is a general decline in totals towards the south and south-east; however altitude is also important and these two factors combine to give annual means in excess of 1000 mm along the northern mountains and on the higher slopes of Etna. In both these areas much of this precipitation is in the form of snow. In contrast, along the southern coast of Sicily and on the Plain of Catania annual totals are below 400 mm (Pecora, 1968); see Fig. 2.2.

Regional winds are important elements in the climate of southern Europe, and four of these are of significance in Sicily: the *scirocco*; the *tramontana*; the *greco* and the *libeccio*. The scirocco is most common in spring and often brings premature high temperatures to Sicily. It originates in the Sahara, is always dusty and on the north African coast is dry and enervating, but when it reaches Sicily and southern Italy it usually possesses a higher humidity picked up during its passage over the sea. Sometimes, however, its descent from the northern mountains of Sicily may cause this wind to recover some of its Saharan characteristics and it can bring extremely high temperatures to the north coast (Admiralty, 1944). During one *scirocco* in 1885, temperatures in Palermo reached 49°C with a humidity of only 10%, while in the same city on another occasion a midnight temperature of 35°C was recorded. The *tramontana* and the *greco* both represent cold air from the European interior that penetrates into the Mediterranean by means of Alpine passes. Both winds are cold and dry and, although it is fairly rare for the *tramontana* to reach Sicily, the *greco* can bring cold wet spells, especially to the Straits of Messina and the north-east and east of the island. In contrast, the *libeccio* is associated with depressions and affects western Sicily in winter, bringing wet and blustery weather.

One notable feature of the climate of the Mediterranean Region, particularly in summer, is the occurrence of purely local winds. In summer under the prevailing anticyclonic conditions, local pressure differences play an important role in determining small-scale circulation systems and hence land and sea breezes and mountain wind systems are common.

Until comparatively recently the climate of Mount Etna had not been studied in detail, but over the last fifteen years a number of works have appeared that have partially remedied this situation (Affronti, 1967, 1969a, 1969b; Pecora, 1968; Durbin, 1981; Durbin and Henderson-Sellers, 1981). Problems still remain, however, the most significant of which is the poor spatial coverage of recording stations, whose frequency decreases with height, and in the higher parts information is only available from one station located at the astronomical observatory (Serra la Nave – Fig. 2.3). This station is by no means ideally sited (Durbin, 1981) and is over 1575 m from the actual summit. On an active volcano a further problem is continuity of records; the near-summit Volcanological Observatory, which periodically kept records, was unfortunately destroyed by lava in 1971. A new observatory on the north side of the mountain will possess continuous recording equipment.

On Etna the climate of eastern Sicily is greatly modified. The general effect of the volcano on temperature is to cause a decrease with altitude (Table 2.1) and, although estimates vary in detail (Affronti, 1967; Durbin, 1981), the mean lapse rate is around 6°C per 1000 m. Lapse rates do not seem to vary greatly with season, but mean annual and seasonal temperatures are both strongly aspect-dependent. For all seasons, temperatures recorded at stations on the east and south-east of the volcano are lower than those from stations at a similar height on the western flanks (Table 2.1). According to Durbin (1981) and Durbin and Henderson-Sellers (1981), enhanced cloud cover over the east and south-east of Etna, especially in and adjacent to the Valle del Bove, is responsible for this depression in temperature. Clouds develop for two reasons in this area: the proximity to the sea causes cooling sea breezes to develop, while the volcanic plume produces further enhancement. Since Etna is a continually active volcano displaying mildly strombolian activity (Duncan *et al.*, 1981) and because winds are from the west and

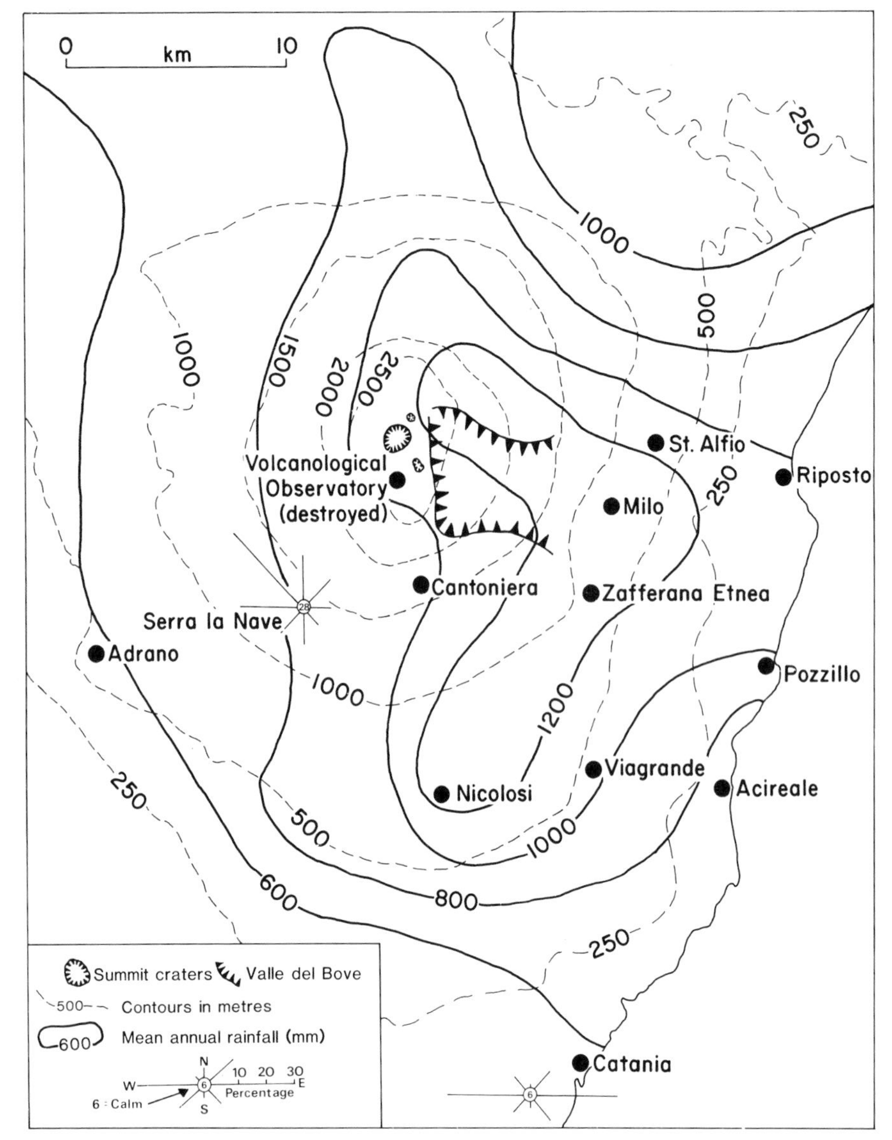

Fig. 2.3 Mount Etna. Mean annual precipitation and wind directions for selected stations. (From Durbin and Henderson-Sellers, 1981, with additions.)

north-west (Admiralty, 1944), the plume is an important climatological control on the lee side of the mountain. It should be noted that, although the effects of volcanic activity on world climate are still much debated, with an issue of the *Journal of Volcanology and Geothermal Research* (Vol. **11** (1), 1981) being devoted to this theme, it seems probable that mildly strombolian effusions have an effect that is strongly localized (Durbin and Henderson-Sellers, 1981; Walker, 1981b).

Throughout Sicily rainfall increases with altitude. This is particularly the case on Etna (Fig. 2.3) but as with temperature, so precipitation is also strongly influenced by aspect and again contrasts occur between the north-west and west sectors on the one hand and the south and south-east on the other. This asymmetry has been recognized for some time and many authors have noted

Table 2.1 Mount Etna: selected temperature statistics

Station	*Altitude (m)*	*Sector*	*Temperature (°C)*				
			January	*April*	*July*	*October*	*Mean annual*
Temperature variations with altitude							
Catania	65	South	10.4	14.8	25.8	19.9	17.7
Viagrande	405	South-east	8.5	13.8	22.5	18.1	16.6
Nicolosi	698	South	6.2	11.8	23.8	15.6	14.2
Cantoniera	1882	South	−0.8	3.6	13.2	8.8	6.4
Geophysical observatory (now destroyed)	2950	South	−5.7	−2.6	8.3	2.8	0.8
The effect of aspect on temperature							
St. Alfio	550	East	6.8	11.7	22.9	15.9	14.3
Zafferana	590	South-east	8.6	12.8	24.1	16.7	15.9
Adrano	589	South-west	10.7	13.6	25.4	17.9	17.2

the relative aridity of the north, north-west and west sectors of the volcano (Affronti, 1967; Durbin and Henderson-Sellers, 1981). Two reasons may be advanced to account for this pattern. In the first place air masses bringing rain in winter have increased instability due to their forced ascent over the northern mountains and because the lower northern slopes lie in the lee of these mountains a rain shadow occurs. As Durbin (1981) notes, however, it is reasonable to assume that rainfall again increases on the upper slopes of the northern side. A second reason for enhanced precipitation on the south, south-east and east flanks of Etna is probably again related to plume frequency and cloud cover, with these sectors being subject to clouds formed as a result of the persistant strombolian activity. An important feature of the precipitation regime is its variability. The mean annual rainfall variability of the Mediterranean lands may be over twice that of central Europe (Beckinsale and Beckinsale, 1975), due to the twin influences of periodic convective rainfall in summer and the varying frequency and character of cyclonic depressions in winter. In winter, rainfall on the higher slopes of Etna is strongly affected by the prevailing synoptic situation, which is accentuated by height, and at this time variability increases with altitude. Conversely in summer, variability decreases with increasing altitude and the lower slopes suffer large variations in rainfall as a result of occasional violent and short-lived thunderstorms.

A combination of enhanced precipitation and the lapse rate of temperature, means that on the higher slopes of Etna heavy snowfalls are common in winter. Mean monthly temperatures at the old Volcanological Observatory (2950 m), for instance, are below 0°C between November and May and at the present time snow and ice are preserved beneath lava and ash layers near to the summit. It is not known how long this snow and ice is preserved, but during the 'little ice age' (*c.*AD 1500 – 1920; Sugden and John, 1976) it is probable that a substantial snow and ice cover was maintained and, indeed, Lyell (1858) in the middle of the nineteenth century describes old ice layers at the summit covered by ash.

Data on winds, solar radiation, albedo and the role of Etna in their modification are neither detailed enough nor sufficiently well researched to allow definite statements to be made, but the limited information which is available suggests that these parameters are influenced both by the area and height of the mountain and by its volcanic activity. It has already been noted that the prevailing winds on Etna are from the west and north-west and it would appear that these preferred directions become more pronounced with altitude. This is probably due to the fact that because of its height Etna is unaffected by the shadowing effects of the mountains to the north, while near to the summit local winds are relatively unimportant. Because Etna is adjacent to the Ionian Sea, differential heating causes land and sea breezes, especially in summer, and this combined with gravity-sinking of cold air from high altitudes (the katabatic effect) produces differing microclimates at lower levels (Durbin, 1981). The influence of sea breezes on the development of clouds in and adjacent to the Valle del Bove has already been discussed, but the main effects of these winds are felt in the Simeto and Alcantara Valleys (Fig. 2.1), which form natural passages from the coast to the inland slopes of the volcano. In general onshore sea breezes build up during the day, while land breezes are features of summer evenings and nights. Sea breezes, together with topographic sheltering, are the principal determinants of the distinctive pattern of winds on the Plain of Catania. At Catania (65 m) July winds are predominantly onshore (easterlies) due to sea breezes, while in winter they are usually offshore (westerlies), as a consequence of topographic disturbance of the prevailing northwest winds of the island (Fig. 2.3). Gravity drainage winds are probably important in summer and in winter. In summer Durbin (1981) has noted that during the night katabatic winds reinforce the effect of land breezes, while in winter gravity sinking may bring low temperatures to sheltered areas low down on the volcano. At Paterno, for instance, power-driven fans are necessary to increase wind speeds and prevent cold air draining into hollows with disastrous effects on frost-sensitive crops.

Data on solar radiation for Sicily are even more fragmentary than those for other climatological variables, but from studies carried out elsewhere (Barry and Chorley, 1971) it might be supposed that solar radiation probably increases by a factor of about 10% (actually 5 – 15%) for every 1000 m increase in altitude. It is clear on Etna that the strombolian plume must have an effect on the receipt of radiation and that the gases and particulates involved may have varying effects on different wavelengths (Durbin and Henderson-Sellers, 1981). An experimental solar power plant has just been built near to Adrano (Fig. 2.1) and it might be expected that this aspect of Etnean climatology will receive more detailed monitoring from now on.

The development of convectional rainfall on the lower slopes of Etna is assisted by the fact that it is common for the reflectivity of surface materials to differ by large amounts. On Etna white snow may lie next to black lava and even the contrast between recent, unvegetated lava flows and those that are older and now cultivated may be of microclimatological significance in the initiation of localized convectional activity. This effect may be increased when large quantities of heat are emitted from newly erupted lava and Whitford-Stark and Wilson (1976) have noted that in these situations turbulence may reach the stage where small whirlwinds are developed and clouds are evaporated when passing over the hot flow.

2.1.2 Hydrology

Low summer rainfall and high evaporation rates mean that one of the main problems which has to be faced each year by Sicilians is a summer drought as severe as any in the Mediterranean region. This clearly restricts both the range and intensity of crops which may be grown without irrigation and means that at the height of summer very few rivers have a significant discharge. Lack of surface water is made more acute by the geology and physiography of the island. Many of the island's surface outcrops, for instance, are porous and/or permeable with the result that little moisture is retained at shallow depths to maintain river flow in summer. Not surprisingly permanent lakes are few in number (Admiralty, 1944; King, 1973a). The physiography of the island, with the main mountains lying close to the north coast are insufficiently high to maintain a permanent snow cover, and this also has a pronounced effect on the hydrology of Sicily. Watersheds in both the Peloritani and Nebrodi Mountains lie no more than 30 km from the north coast; and the north-flowing streams, suitably named *torrente* or *fiumare*, have short steep thalweg (longitudinal) profiles, are swollen by orographic rainfall in the winter season and by snow melt in spring, but are completely dry in summer. In contrast south-flowing rivers are much longer and tend to be less flashy (Pecora, 1968; King, 1973a). Partly as a result of a fairly small catchment area even the Salso, the longest river in Sicily, only maintains a significant summer discharge in exceptional years (Admiralty, 1944). The influence of man on river discharge cannot be overlooked. Throughout the Mediterranean region the long history of continuous human settlement has meant that since prehistoric times much of the natural vegetation has been removed and replaced by secondary *maquis* or *garrigue* scrub species (King, 1973a). Moreover in Sicily, as in the rest of Italy, traditional land-use practices have not protected the land from rapid erosion, and *frane* (landslips) are common in winter. The main effect of these anthropogenic land-use and the vegetation changes has been to reduce storage capacity and so increase runoff in winter and make summer discharges even smaller. It is also notable that as well as reducing the effectiveness of annual rainfall, land-use practices have also produced much alluviation within the river valleys of the island (Vita-Finzi, 1969, 1975; Delano-Smith, 1979).

The hydrology of Etna is quite different from that of the rest of Sicily. The volcanic lavas are highly permeable and act as aquifers, fed and recharged by winter rainfall and snow-melt at high altitudes in spring and early summer (Duncan *et al.*, 1981). More important is the fortunate circumstance that this large volcanic pile overlies largely impermeable and non-porous rocks, ranging from Cretaceous to Quaternary in age (Romano *et al.*, 1979), which means that Etna acts as a 'gigantic sponge' with plenty of water available for plant growth. Because the volcanic rocks are highly permeable there is little surface runoff, but at and near to the contact between the volcanics and the underlying sediments numerous springs occur. In a detailed study of the hydrogeology and water budget of Etna, Ogniben (1966) suggests that given a mean annual rainfall for the volcano as a whole of around 800 mm, which he admits is conservative because of the under-recording of snowfall, then only about 5% is lost through surface runoff and only 20% as a result of evaporation. Hence 75% is retained as groundwater. This figure of 75% represents an infiltration of some 600 mm of rainfall per annum, but this does not correspond to the volume of water which is yielded by springs and other extractions from the volcano. Most of the balance, of the order of 190 mm of rainfall equivalent, is lost to the sea. This is one reason why the areal yield of groundwater varies between the north and west and the south and east flanks of the volcano. As mentioned before, rainfall is enhanced on the south-east and east slopes (Durbin and Henderson-Sellers, 1981) and from this it might reasonably be expected that areal groundwater yields would mirror this pattern. In fact the opposite is the case, due in part to the outflow of freshwater seawards. A further reason is that the volcanic aquifer on the north and west flanks of Etna is partially recharged by water brought into the region in winter by the Simeto and Alcantara rivers.

The discharge characteristics of the principal rivers of the Etna region – the Simeto and the Alcantara – are quite different from those found in the rest of Sicily. Their hydrographs are generally less flashy and neither river is completely without water even at the height of the summer drought (Fig. 2.4). This is important, for it means that water is available for irrigation throughout the year. The main cause of this perennial flow is the addition of water to the two rivers from the spring line on the volcano, probably supplemented by at least some subterranean water movement. To the north of Etna, beyond the volcanics, both rivers are usually dry during the summer drought and, although in some years the Simeto does manage to maintain some flow because of the size of its catchment, both rivers are essentially very similar to those in other parts of Sicily.

2.1.3 Vegetation

Today over 90% of the area of Sicily is in productive agricultural use either for cultivation or for pastoral activities and little of the original post-Pleistocene vegetation remains (King, 1973a). The original vegetation cover of Etna, in particular the abundance of timber, was one of the main attractions of the region to man and, in contrast to most

Fig. 2.4 The river Alcantara, showing a significant discharge at the height of the annual drought. This is in spite of the fact that much water is removed for irrigation purposes. (Photograph: D. K. Chester.)

other areas of Sicily, the volcano still retains a significant yet greatly modified forest cover. Catania Province contains some 10 000 ha of forest and woodland and most of this is to be found on the middle slopes of Etna. Because relatively few detailed palynological studies have been carried out in southern Italy it is not possible to be precise in any discussion of the post-Pleistocene climax vegetation of Sicily (Delano-Smith, 1979) but, by means of the vegetation that remains together with inferences that may be drawn from the close association of vegetation on the one hand and geology, climate, relief and soils on the other, some idea of the original vegetation of the island can be pieced together (D. S. Walker, 1976).

According to D. S. Walker (1967), the vegetation of the southern Italian peninsula and islands is influenced at the broad scale by increasing aridity towards the south and east, and by altitude. At low altitudes land was colonized by the so-called ilex assocation. This is named after its dominant species, *Quercus ilex* (holm or evergreen oak) and the ilex association probably covered most of Sicily up to 1000 m or more. In less favourable environments a limit of only 300 m may have been reached, the limit at any place being determined by aspect, local geological conditions and the stage of colonization that had been reached (Delano-Smith, 1979). Within the ilex association, other tree types included *Quercus suber* (cork oak) on igneous rocks and western shores, *Pinus pinaster* (maritime pine) and *Pinus pinea* (stone pine) on sandy soils and *Pinus halepenis* (aleppo pine) on windy, dry sand-dunes (Rikli, 1943; Houston, 1964; Polunin, 1969). With increasing height the dominant evergreen oaks gradually gave way to deciduous species until eventually the vegetation reflected cooler, more temperate conditions. The main species of this zone included *Quercus pubescens* (white oak) and *Quercus cerris* (turkey oak), together with various types of ash, elm and walnut. Towards the upper limit of this zone *Castanea sativa* (sweet chestnut) became important, reaching 1400 m and even 1700 m in favourable localities. The semi-alpine zone lies above the limit of *Castanea sativa*, and various species of larch, beech, fir and pine colonized this arduous environment. The tree line probably occurred at between 1800 and 2000 m, which is roughly the same height as the highest peaks in the northern mountain range.

Although early man undoubtably had some destructive influence upon the vegetation of Sicily and in spite of the fact that the island was one of the granaries of the ancient world, it is generally accepted that most of the original vegetation survived until after the Classical Age (Frank, 1933; Delano-Smith, 1979). The system of agriculture that developed was closely adapted to the characteristics of the climate, and this involved the clearance of land to grow wheat, beans and other field crops in winter, while in summer tree crops (vines, olives, almonds, walnuts and pistacchio nuts) were introduced to exploit the water-retaining sub-soil. Unfortunately agricultural cropping, combined with the influence of grazing animals, caused a marked deterioration in soil fertility and massive soil erosion was initiated. When land was abandoned, lack of humus and the continuing grazing by animals meant that regeneration of the original vegetation was impossible and instead two new scrub associations developed: *maquis* and *garrigue*. Today these associations may be said to be far more characteristic of Sicily than the original vegetation that they have replaced. *Maquis* is a varied association of species that ranges from degraded patches of original vegetation with fairly widely spaced oaks and conifers, to a tangled mass of shrubby species that is almost impenetrable. The distinguishing feature of *maquis* is the predominance of evergreen shrubs and this association tends to thrive on siliceous soils and in moist locations. For these reasons it tends to form the secondary succession in the less arid parts of the island and it is generally confined to land below 400 m, though in places it may reach higher altitudes. Like *maquis*, areas of *garrigue* also tend to occupy land previously under the ilex association, but *garrigue* is adapted to withstand higher temperatures, stony soils and dryer winds (D. S. Walker, 1967) and for these reasons it is to be found in central and southern Sicily. Essentially *garrigue* is a much poorer, more sparse vegetation than *maquis* and is of little use even for rough grazing. It may represent a regression of *maquis* under further destructive human intervention, or else may be simply degraded forest. In places soils may be so eroded that parent materials exert a strong influence upon the vegetation assemblage, but in all areas the species are spiny and cactoid to survive the long summer drought. Plants include various species of cistus, heather, broom and juniper, together with a distinctive species of spiky grass (*Stipa sp.*). In areas covered by both *maquis* and *garrigue* two species introduced from Latin America are important. These are the prickly pear cactus (*Opuntia ficus-indica*) and agave (*Agave americana*) (King, 1973a).

Many authors have studied the vegetation of Etna and most conclude that in broad outline it accords closely to the patterns already discussed (Buscalioni, 1909; Milone, 1960; Speranza, 1960; Debazac, 1965; Pecora, 1968; Clapperton, 1972; Durbin, 1981). On Etna three altitudinal zones are recognized: the *regione piedmontese* (from sea level to 1000 m); the *regione boscara* or wooded area (from 1000 – 2000 m); and the *regione deserta* – which is to be found above the tree-line. The *regione deserta* is not well named, because above the tree-line alpine vegetation occurs. This includes a dwarf form of birch (*Betula aetnensis*) and varieties of juniper and other scrub associations. Colonization of these upper slopes is made difficult, not only as a result of low temperatures, but also because of the lack of surface water and the pollution caused by the volcanic plume (Garrec *et al.*, 1977; Hill, 1981). For these reasons vegetation is in the form of tussocks, with a large proportion of bare ground exposed. Near to the summit frequent ash falls and lava effusions also inhibit the growth of alpine species.

Commercial agriculture has virtually replaced all the original ilex association in the *regione pied-*

montese and factors controlling the nature and intensity of cultivation will be considered later in this chapter. It is a feature of this zone that where land has been abandoned or where historic lava flows have been re-colonized *maquis* is to be found, which suggests that on Etna, given sufficient time and no human interference, the climax vegetation could re-establish itself. Prickly pear cactus, introduced about 300 years ago, is particularly characteristic of the *maquis* of the Etna region and its distribution appears to be closely related to climate, although other factors including grazing and land management are also of importance. On the lower slopes of the more arid western and south-western flanks, for instance, it may colonize up to heights of 600 m, whereas on the southern and eastern flanks it had to compete with other species which are better adapted to higher rainfall and soil moisture conditions, and is rarely found above 250 m (Durbin, 1981).

The *regione boscara* is still covered by large areas of forest, although this is far less extensive than it was during the Classical Age. At the lower margin much forest has been lost to cultivation, while at and near to the tree-line many stands have been engulfed by lava flows. Timber has been exploited in this zone since the time of the Greek occupation and wood was exported to Greece, mainland Italy and to Malta during the Classical Age and later (Finlay, 1968; King, 1973a). In addition much wood was traditionally used for charcoal, the holm oak being particularly suitable for this activity (Polunin, 1969), and the net result of all this exploitation was that by the early years of this century the timber resources of Etna were severely depleted. During this century fairly large areas have been replanted, especially by the *Corpo Forestale* (forestry authority), and today the area in woodland is much greater than in the recent past. Planting has been carried out for a variety of reasons, including commercial forestry and land conservation and today this zone is characterised by stands of deciduous and evergreen oaks, chestnut and pine. In areas that have been cleared, but not replanted, the vegetation consists of brushwood and bracken, with an undergrowth of low bushes (Admiralty, 1944). Within the *regione boscara*, the altitudinal limit and the sectoral distribution of the different tree species is probably due to two variables. The first relates to the environmental conditions (mostly climatic) under which the various species can grow and thrive, and the second to past and present practises of felling and replanting. This information, so far as it is available from detailed maps produced by Speranza (1960) and Durbin (1981) is summarized in Table 2.2.

2.1.4 *Soils*

Except in the mountains and in areas underlain by calcareous and volcanic rocks, the greater part of Sicily was originally covered by Mediterranean brown soils. These are the zonal soils of the region, being developed under the distinctive Mediterranean climate, and were originally covered by the forests of the ilex association (Houston 1964). Under these conditions a fairly thick B-horizon was formed in which clay and humus were concentrated, having been washed down the soil profile during episodes of winter rainfall (D. S. Walker, 1967). Today few of these soils remain in their original state, because continuous occupation of the island and intensive cropping over 2000 years has caused most of the original vegetation to be removed, with the result that this association is eroded over wide areas. Indeed in mapping this association in the field Italian pedologists have had to make use of fairly tentative evidence, consisting of partial profiles and patches of undisturbed vegetation and their related soils (Mancini, 1966).

A distinction, however, may be drawn between the Mediterranean brown soils that are found on Pliocene and other clay outcrops and those which occur over other substrates (King, 1973b). In the case of the former, which are characteristic of large areas of interior Sicily, especially where the clays are *scagliose* or scaly, the soils are baked in summer, and in winter are waterlogged, viscous and impermeable. Under these conditions shallow ploughing in autumn and spring using the techniques characteristic of traditional peasant agriculture, has caused the upper layers of the profile to become unstable and subject to erosion. It is these areas in which landslips (*frane*) and other mass-movement phenomena are commonplace; and today little if any of the original soil profile remains. Problems in these areas are exacerbated by a long history of overgrazing and overcropping and today farmers are often forced to cultivate the actual bedrock (D. S. Walker, 1967; King, 1973a, 1973b). Italian pedologists have to classify these soils as a separate association of very low potential (Mancini and Ronchetti, 1968). The soils that are developed on other rock types are equally hard to work in summer, but in winter shallow ploughing may be practised without inducing much erosion (King, 1973b).

Mediterranean brown soils cover large areas of the Etna region (Fig. 2.5) up to a height of nearly 1000 m, this zone being approximately equivalent to the *regione piedmontese* (Comitato per La Carta dei Suoli, 1966). In the areas underlain by volcanic rocks, soils are little eroded and capable of supporting continuous cropping over a long period of time. Cultural factors (to be discussed later) combined with an abundant supply of ground water for irrigation, has meant that the characteristics of cultivation and the crops that are grown on the volcano are quite different from those that occur in other areas of Sicily, and a highly intensive system of land-use is supported with little obvious deterioration in soil quality. This is assisted by the ready supply of sodium, potassium and calcium which is naturally added to the soil from weathered lava (Rochefort, 1961; D. S. Walker, 1967). Beyond the limits of the volcanics the Mediterranean brown soils are of much lower potential. This is in part due to the more typically Sicilian agriculture that is practised, but the lack of easily

Table 2.2 Characteristics of the *regione boscara* on Mount Etna

Tree type	*Main species*	*Environmental controls*	*Human controls*	*Upper altitudinal limit (m)*[1]			
				North	*East*	*South*	*West*
Evergreen oak	*Quercus ilex*	Prefers dry stony slopes; concentrated on western flanks	Some may be original vegetation; now mostly managed	—	—	—	1400
Deciduous oak	*Quercus macrolepis*	Can be grown virtually everywhere on the volcano; west flanks too dry	As above; little grown on south and south-east flanks, due to competition with other land-uses	1200	1300	—	—
Chestnut	*Castanea sativa*	Similar requirements to deciduous oak, may be grown to higher altitudes	Popular for planting; nuts used for livestock	—	1700	1600	1600
Pine	*Pinus nigra* associated with *Fagus sp.* and *Betula aetnensis*	Can grow up to tree-line; upper northern slopes may be too dry	Dominant species on Etna; widely used for afforestation	1500	1800	2100	2000

[1] Absence of a height means that the species is not widely grown in this sector of the volcano. Compiled from Speranza (1960) and Durbin (1981) with additional data from Polunin (1969).

harnessed ground-water resources and the occurrence of readily eroded clay outcrops is also of significance. Particularly unproductive and infertile areas include outcrops of upper Cretaceous clay soils near to Bronte and Quaternary blue marly clays (*Argille marnose assurre*) that crop out between Paterno and Catania.

At heights above 1000 m, roughly corresponding to the *regione boscara*, brown volcanic soils are to be found. Given sufficient time, these soils will develop on both lava and pyroclastic materials and they have been protected from erosion by the deciduous forests that still cover much of this zone. Except on steep slopes, where they are thin, these soils have deep profiles, are well drained and rich in humus (Mancini 1966). Throughout this zone the prospects for afforestation are good and the soils allow root penetration to depth and rapid growth of wood, while at low levels they appear to respond well to cultivation. On Etna the conversion of ashes to productive soils is more rapid than is the case with lava. It is, however, also true that because of their loose texture these soils are subject to leaching if not correctly managed, and studies carried out on other volcanoes have shown that such soils are often deficient in phosphorus (Ugolini and Zasoski, 1979). Whether this is the case on Etna is not certain, but these ashy soils are often highly prized for the production of vines (Jashemski, 1979).

Summit and recent historic lavas on the flanks of the volcano give rise to volcanic regosols and lithosols (Fig. 2.5). These are soils that are still in the early stages of pedogenesis, the rate of conversion to mature and useful soils being governed by the speed of weathering processes which are strongly influenced both by altitudinal and climatic gradients and by aspect. Although in places deliberate intervention by man may bring these soils into productive use (Chapter 9), overall they can only support very low intensity rough grazing. Sandy regosols are a varied association that are to be found on the south bank of the Alcantara and adjacent to the coast (Fig. 2.5). Despite being immature these soils have a moderate potential and may be cultivated with vines and citrus fruits, providing slopes are not too steep and that sound land-management practices are followed.

The alluvial soils that occur on the Plain of Catania and near to the mouth of the River Alcantara, are the most fertile of the region. These are placed in the highest soil potential category by Mancini and Ronchetti (1968) and contain many of the materials which have been removed from the island by soil erosion. Until the time of Mussolini the inherent potential of the soils of the Plain of Catania was not realized, in spite of the fact that this area of 426 km^2 is the largest lowland in Sicily. This was because of frequent flooding by the Simeto, and the scourge of malaria; in 1931 the plain only supported a population of 700. Over the last fifty years massive investment in flood control, land drainage, public health and irrigation has transformed this region into one of the most productive in Sicily (Houston, 1964; King, 1971).

2.2 The human response

In describing the human geography of Etna volcano, it is easy to fall into the trap of being over enthusiastic in seeking links between elements of the physical environment and the use that is made of this region by its inhabitants. It is true that, notwithstanding the ever-present threat from the volcano, the combination of favourable climatological, hydrological and pedological circumstances gives this region far more potential, particularly for cultivation, than most others in Sicily. But while the physical environment has, and continues to exert, a very strong influence on patterns of settlement, on agricultural land use and on the distribution of population on the volcano, the distinctiveness of the region also reflects internal and external cultural and economic ties with the rest of Sicily, Mediterranean Europe and increasingly with other member states of the European Economic Community. The latter at the present time provide important markets for agricultural produce, sources of investment capital, jobs for migrant workers and a pool of tourists ready to spend money in the region and enjoy the pleasures of sun, sea, the historical heritage and the landscape. In addition since Italian unification in the nineteenth century, and especially since the

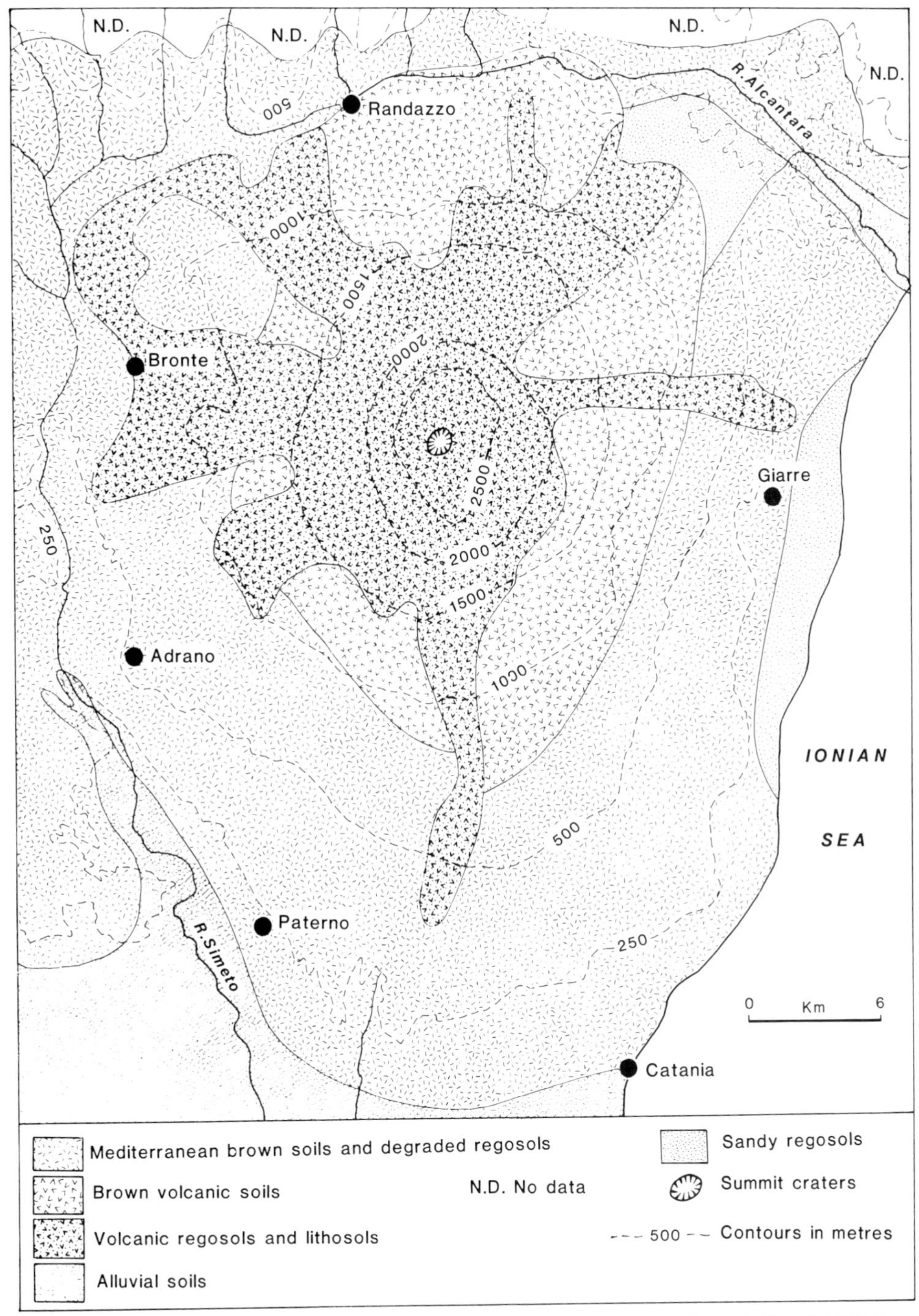

Fig. 2.5 Simplified soils map of the Etna region. (After Comitato per La Carta dei Suoli, 1966.)

end of the Second World War, the role of national government and the mainland economy have been crucial in stimulating economic growth and cultural and land-use changes. The case already quoted, of the latent high productivity of the soils of the Plain of Catania and their avoidance by the people of the region until appropriate technology and investment were available, is just one example which demonstrates that it is cultural and technological appraisals which in the end control the human use of the landscape, even though the natural potential has always been present.

2.2.1 Agricultural land use

The most striking feature of the agricultural land use of Sicily is the contrast between the relatively prosperous, intensively worked and often irrigated coastal margins and the poor, extensively worked lands of the interior (Milone, 1960). This contrast has been recognized by Italian geographers for some time leading to the island being described as 'an ugly picture in a frame of gold' (quoted by King, 1973a, p. 112) and from what has already been discussed it is clear that factors of the physical environment are important in accounting for this distribution (Fig. 2.6). In particular the higher rainfall of the north coast and on Etna, the fact that plains only account for some 7% of the total land area – these being concentrated near to the coast – and the greater soil and irrigation potential of the peripheral margins of the island, are all of significance. These variables, however, only provide a partial explanation of the distribution and character of land use in Sicily and must be placed in their historical, social and economic contexts.

By the Classical Age the distinctive dry-land agriculture so characteristic of the Mediterranean lands was well established in Sicily (King, 1973a) and, although most of the original forest cover remained intact (Frank, 1933) suggesting that the cultivated area was limited, the prosperity of the island led Strabo to comment 'as for the goodness of the land why should I speak of it when it is talked about by everyone' (quoted by Finley, 1968, p. 4). The main crops that were grown at this time were wheat, olives and vines; Sicily being one of the principal granaries of the ancient world and an exporter of wine to the Roman Empire (King, 1973a). Animals, a part of the rural economy since the Neolithic, were an essential element by the Classical Age and it seems highly probable that cattle, sheep and pigs were plentiful (Delano-Smith, 1979).

The distinction between core and periphery in Sicilian land use is mainly the result of techniques of farming, the social system and the economy that evolved under first Arab and later Norman, Spanish and Bourbon rule. These factors combined to produce systems of land use that remained fundamentally unchanged for centuries and which contributed to the poverty and backwardness of the interior lands. Although the Romans experimented with irrigation, it was only after the Arab conquest in the ninth century AD that these techniques became widespread. The diffusion of irrigation was mainly controlled by the availability of easily harnessed ground-water resources and even at this early stage the eastern slopes of Etna and the northern coastal fringes were important, with their prosperity being dependent upon newly introduced crops which included bitter oranges, lemons, sugar cane, probably cotton, mulberries, the date palm, melons and pistacchio nuts (Mack-Smith, 1968). By the early Middle Ages most of the crops that are to be found in Sicily today were being cultivated, the exceptions being the tomato, maize, tobacco and potatoes, which were all introduced from the New World from the sixteenth century (King, 1973a). The Arab and later expatriate rulers were largely to blame for the deterioration of soil potential in the interior. During the Arab conquest, for instance, land was cleared for settlement. Later, timber was exported to Africa or used for shipbuilding and by the close of the Middle Ages large areas of cleared land were given over to rough grazing with substantial quantities of hides, wool, meat and cheese finding export markets. Rough grazing is by no means the most appropriate land use for these interior lands preventing as it does full regeneration of the climax vegetation and so causing a long-term deterioration in soil fertility. By the sixteenth century declining cereal yields in existing cultivated areas, together

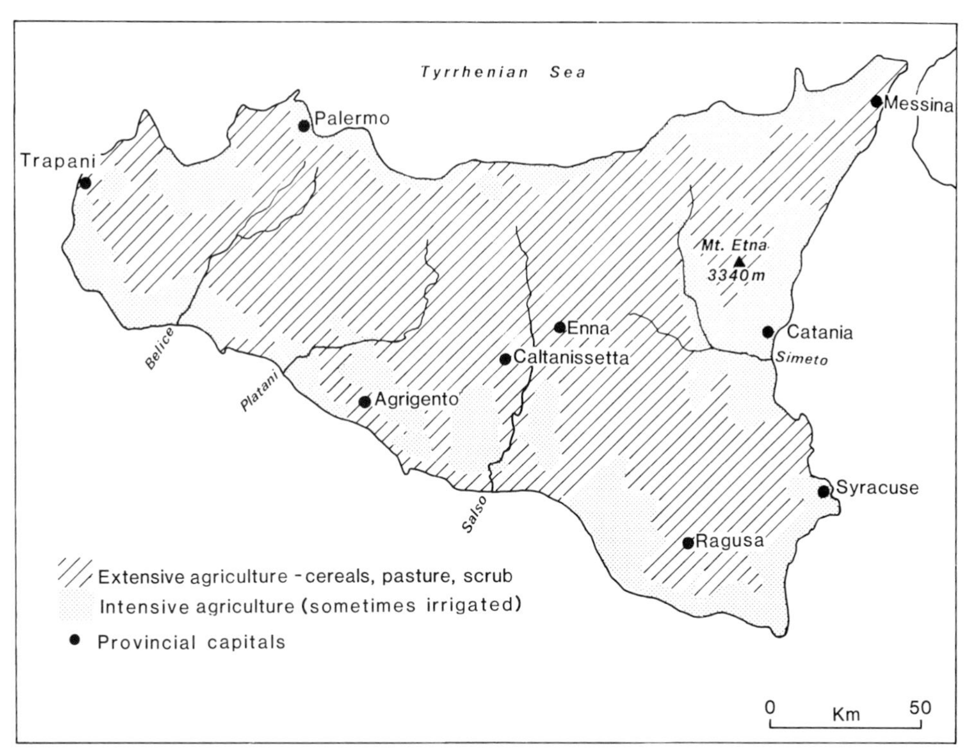

Fig. 2.6 The location of intensive and extensive agricultural areas in Sicily. (After King, 1971, courtesy of *The Geographical Magazine*.)

with population pressure, led to a progressive extension of the cultivated area with even greater deleterious effects on the soils. It is from this time that the strong contrast, between the coast lands and the slopes of Etna on the one hand and the interior on the other, became well marked (Mack-Smith, 1968).

The social structure of interior Sicily also differed from that found in the more outward-looking, more prosperous and more cosmopolitan coastal areas. This system has prevented and to some extent still prevents agricultural improvements being introduced in central and western Sicily and gives the landscape a timeless character (King, 1973a, 1973b). Although large estates or *latifundia* were established by the Romans, their diffusion over large areas of the island was largely the result of later rule, when they were used to reward politicians and other individuals who had given service. The *latifundia* were large only in terms of their ownership and usually subdivided and controlled by agents (*gabelloti*), who themselves rented out small holdings to peasant cultivators. The landowners or *baroni* were usually absentee and the *gabelloti* had tremendous power to bid up rents against the background of population pressure and land hunger. In this situation peasants were forced to engage in a virtual wheat monoculture to maximise their incomes, and over-cropping and the cultivation of steep slopes was widespread. To make matters worse these interior lands were strongholds of lawlessness with the *gabelloti* class being strongly identified with the mafia, crime and banditry being almost a way of life in parts of western Sicily. In contrast, the east of Sicily, including most but not all the Etna region, was relatively free of mafia activity (Rochefort, 1961; King, 1973a, 1975). Poverty and depression were most serious in the late nineteenth century and in 1876 a report by two Italian noblemen, Barons Franchetti and Sonnino, found that the *latifundia* areas of the island were almost a barren waste and that there was almost total illiteracy. They concluded that 'violence . . . is the only prosperous industry' (quoted by Mack-Smith, 1968, p. 465).

During this century the standard of living of the interior lands has improved under the stimulus of government intervention. Not all of this has been successful, and the campaign by Mussolini to increase wheat output in the 1930s and the incompetence and bureaucratic corruption of post-war policies of land reform has meant that the interior of Sicily is still one of the poorest regions in Europe and one of the least changed (King, 1971, 1973b).

Within Sicily, Etna is a prosperous agricultural region by virtue of the combination of environmental and cultural factors that have already been discussed. At a more detailed level of analysis it is clear that agricultural distributions on Etna are by no means uniform and often show a fine adjustment to small variations in the physical environment and to the actual and perceived economic potential of different height bands and sectors on the volcano. The agricultural land use of Etna is well documented in the literature (Milone, 1960; Speranza, 1960; Rochefort, 1961; Pecora, 1968; Clapperton, 1972; King, 1973a; Duncan, *et al.*, 1981; Durbin, 1981) and what follows is largely based on the research of these authors supplemented where necessary by direct field observation.

The most striking feature of the land use of Etna is the contrast between the north and west flanks on the one hand and the south and east on the other, with the former showing much less intensive cropping than the latter (Fig. 2.7). This may be partly accounted for by the asymmetry of the volcano and a much greater area of land below 2000 m is to be found on its south and east flanks. As already mentioned, cultivation on Etna is strongly controlled by altitudinal gradients and the observed positive relationship between the percentage of land used for intensive agriculture and the area in each sector below 2000 m is not unexpected (Table 2.3). Indeed this association would be even stronger if a significant proportion of the area of the south sector were not covered by historic lavas that are unsuitable for cultivation. An additional factor is the depression of rainfall totals in the north, northwest, and west sectors of the volcano, but against this must be set the lower solar radiation totals that are received on the south and east flanks due to the volcanic plume, and the fact that the ground water hydrology of Etna favours the north and north-west because of the loss of large quantities of water to the Ionian Sea. The difference between the potential of the physical environment for intensive agriculture and the observed pattern may be further explained by the relative isolation of the north and west of Etna from the main markets and export ports of the region. The prosperity of the volcano has always been based on the export of commercial crops to mainland Italy and to the rest of Europe (Formica, 1968). Even today after large-scale, post-war investment in roads and railways the towns of the north and west are still remote from Catania, the main market and port of the region. Indeed it is possible to recognize a gradient of declining land-use intensity on all the main roads leading from the city. The towns of Bronte and Randazzo and to a lesser extent Adrano (Fig. 2.7) still have a character more typical of central Sicily than of the Etna region and, even though Bronte is far more developed than it was a century ago when Rodwell (1878) compared it to ancient Pompeii, the effects of isolation and inertia

Table 2.3 The sectoral distribution of land below 2000 m and the percentage of land used for intensive agriculture

Sector	*Area of land below 2000 m (km²)*	*Percentage of land used for intensive agriculture*[1]
North	141	27
North-east	161	41
East	180	63
South-east	266	69
South	383	52
South-west	230	67
West	166	23
North-west	113	3

[1] Intensive agriculture includes land used for vineyards, orchards and plantations. Compiled from Duncan *et al.* (1981).

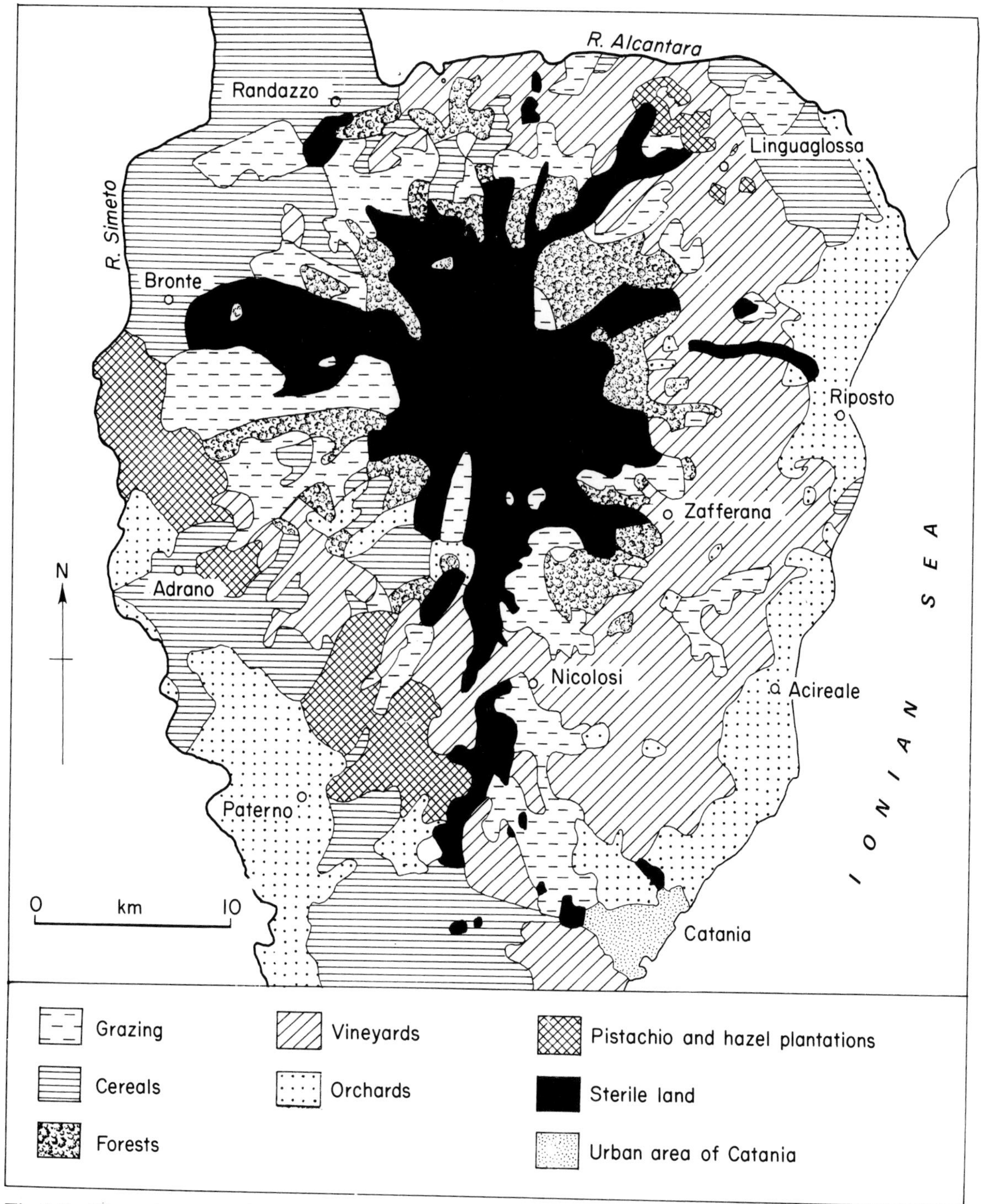

Fig. 2.7 The agricultural land use of the Etna region. (After Rochefort, 1961, and Duncan. *et al.*, 1981.)

mean that cultivation still has much in common with the interior of the island. Here cereals, especially rye and wheat with beans used for rotation, are cultivated both on the clay soils near to Bronte and up to 1100 m on the volcano. Pistacchio and hazel are commonly cultivated on partially weathered lavas up to a height of 800 m and these, together with a few vineyards, form a partial contrast to the interior.

Both vineyards and orchards have altitudinal limits and cultivated areas that are subject to change in response to social and economic factors. On Etna it is a matter of observation that the cultivated area is in a state of flux and abandoned terracing bears witness to the fact that once intensively worked areas are rapidly reverting to scrub vegetation. Over the last thirty years large amounts of capital have been applied to increasing yields through larger units and more modern techniques of irrigation and in this situation it is not surprising that the more marginal land, especially that found on steep slopes near to the margin of cultivation for the particular crop, has been abandoned (Fig. 2.8). A further factor is that traditional methods of intensive farming on Etna require heavy inputs of labour. Expanded job opportunities in the non-agricultural activities of the region, in northern Italy and in the EEC – particularly for young single men – has severely restricted the number of new entrants into farming. Again the effects have been felt most acutely on small farming units near to the margin of both profitability and climatic prudence. Durbin (1981), for instance, has shown that over the last twenty years the upper limits of both vine and olive cultivation have been lowered on all flanks of the volcano. The main area of recent expansion is the Plain of Catania and this has more than compensated for the loss of land on the flanks of the volcano, both through abandonment and because of the growth of Catania and other urban centres. Today the plain is important for traditional citrus crops and for vegetables. Although social and economic factors explain the present-day distribution of cultivation in part, the individual environmental tolerance of species are also of significance in accounting for this pattern. These data are summarized on Table 2.4.

Fig. 2.8 Abandoned agricultural terraces above the present-day altitudinal limit of cultivation. (Photograph: D. K. Chester.)

As elsewhere in Sicily pastoralism has declined, but it still remains an essential part of the land economy of Etna, especially at high altitudes, on slopes too steep for cultivation and on historic lava flows which have not yet weathered to soils able to support crops (Cumin, 1938). As King (1973a) has shown, this activity tends to involve large flocks of sheep (500 – 2000) whose ownership is split between members of the same family, individual members often combining grazing with part-time cultivation of small plots at lower levels on the volcano. High-level pastures are commonly under the ownership of large landowners and the church and are leased for the grazing season.

2.2.2 Population and settlement

The population of Sicily has grown from 2.4 million in 1860, to over 5 million in the late 1970s (Anon., 1979) and, unlike most countries in the EEC, a high proportion still depends on agriculture. The 1971 census of the provinces of Sicily showed that the percentage of the work force employed in agriculture varied from 20% to 40% (Rochefort, 1972), but at the same date it was estimated that nearer to 50% of the total population of the island still depended on income derived from this sector (King, 1971). Because agriculture still remains so important within the Sicilian economy, the distribution of population shows a close correlation with the intensity of cropping and nearly two-thirds of Sicilians live on or near to the fertile coastal lands, which are also the location of many of the large towns and cities. Etna is within this 'frame of gold' and as a result of its agricultural prosperity the Province of Catania contains nearly 20% of the total population of the island and has the highest density of any province in Sicily.

On Etna, population is concentrated within the *regione piedmontese*, especially in that part which coincides with the intensively farmed land found on the east, south-east and south flanks of the volcano. Near to the city of Catania some communes have densities of over 800 per km^2, while elsewhere in this zone figures of over 500 per km^2 are far from uncommon (D. S. Walker, 1967; Duncan *et al.*, 1981). Densities decline away from Catania both south across the plain and towards the extensively farmed lands of the north and west flanks and in these areas densities may be as low as 100 per km^2, although higher figures are more common. The very high densities of the south and east flanks are no longer supported by agriculture alone and it is a feature of the recent population geography of the region that an increasingly high proportion of the economically active population is employed in the factories and service industries of Catania. In some communes near to Catania only 20% or less may be classified as rural, but this increases rapidly in all directions away from the city (Pecora 1968) and is well over 50% in the more remote areas.

Emigration has traditionally acted as a safety valve by which population pressure in Sicily has been relieved and, out of the 2 million people who have left the island since unification, only one-third have returned (King, 1973a). Until 1925 emigration mostly involved out-of-work labourers and peasants, with the majority going to the United States; but since 1947 a new phase has developed in which young, often highly skilled, workers have left the island for the industrial cities of Northern Italy and other countries of Western Europe. In the view of King (1971, 1973a), post-war emigration has had a much more serious effect on the Sicilian economy than the earlier phase, which indeed could be argued to have been beneficial in reducing the pressure of cultivation on unsuitable land. Today it is mostly young men who leave the island, causing an imbalance in the population pyramids of many villages. The residual population tends to be aged and dependent upon remittances from abroad and these funds are often used to buy land as security, or for prestige, rather than for cultivation and development. For the same reasons migrants rarely sell either their land or their homes.

The influence of the post-1947 exodus on the abandonment of agricultural land has already been discussed and indeed, like all regions of Sicily, Etna has not been immune from its effects. In comparison with the interior of the island, the effect has been small and the Province of Catania has increased its proportionate share of the population of Sicily, through a combination of both natural increase and in-migration. This may be clearly seen in the population statistics which show that in 1861 the Province of Catania accounted for 15% of the population of Sicily, by 1901 this had risen to over 16% and is around 20% today (Anon., 1977). As it has been in the past, migration within the region continues to be important; and in a study carried out in the 1950s (Riccardi, 1958) it was demonstrated that between 1901 and 1951 very large increases in population of up to and in excess of 100% were recorded in two areas within the region. The first was the city of Catania and its suburbs – a reflection of its development as an industrial and commercial centre – and the second

Table 2.4 The location of vines and orchard crops on Etna in relation to the environmental requirements of individual species

Cultivated species	*Environmental requirements*	*Location on Etna*
Citrus fruits	(1) Requires irrigation (2) Intolerant of frost (3) Optimum temperature for photosynthesis 25°C (4) Minimum temperature for metabolic activity 12.5°C	Located from sea level to about 550 m. Upper limit defined by temperature decline with altitude and therefore may be cultivated to greater heights on the south-west flank (550 m) than on the east flank. Because of lower rainfall and higher potential evaporation on the south-west flank requires more irrigation than elsewhere on the volcano. Absent from the north and west flanks due to low temperatures. Ideal crop for intensive peasant cultivation as capable of producing high cash returns from a small area
Vines	(1) Minimum annual rainfall 500 mm (2) Not too drought-resistant (3) Needs a cool chilling period before the growing season	Located above citrus belt and may be grown on all flanks of the volcano, except the west and parts of the north due to aridity. Altitudinal limits: about 300–900 m
Olives	(1) Similar to vine but detailed differences (2) Low humidity required for proper fruiting (3) Will not tolerate frost for long (4) More drought-resistant than the vine (5) Long, hot, dry summers are essential	Similar altitudinal range to the vine, but more common on the dry west and south-west flanks

Compiled from Speranza (1960), D.S. Walker (1967), King (1973a) and Durbin (1981).

were those communes on the Plain of Catania where new irrigation projects were located. Although actual migration data are not presented by Riccardi (1958), it seems unlikely that these rates of increase can be explained by natural increase alone, and migration from both within the region and from the rest of Sicily appears to have been important. The communes of the *regione piedmontese* have shown a varied pattern of population change since 1901. Against a background of an overall increase in the population of Sicily of 26% in the first fifty years of this century, some communes recorded increases of over 50%, others had rates of increase less than the average for the island as a whole and a few actually declined. The only trend that may be detected is that some of the greatest declines in population are recorded in communes on the south-east flanks of Etna and this probably reflects the job opportunities that have been created in Catania and the impossibility of absorbing additional labour in agriculture, in an area where family plots are as small as two hectares or even less (D. S. Walker, 1967). Since the 1950s these trends in the population geography of the region have been maintained (Anon., 1977).

The most characteristic feature of the settlement pattern of Sicily is the relative absence of isolated farmsteads and the predominance of so-called *agro-towns* or peasant cities (Blok, 1969; King and Strachan, 1978). These towns contain the majority of the population of most communes and are most frequently found and best developed in the interior of the island. They represent a response to the *latifundia* system of landholding, allowing peasants, many of whom were traditionally landless, to cultivate their fragmented and insecure holdings by means of a daily journey to work. Today with the demise of the *latifundia* this settlement pattern persists because of social inertia (King and Strachan, 1978). Many *agro-towns* are sited on hilltops and this probably reflects a combination of factors including defence, scarce spring sites, the malarial nature of many lowlands and even protection from earthquakes (King, 1971). Generally these predominantly agricultural towns contain 3000–15 000 people, although some have as many as 20 000 and in extreme cases 40 000 inhabitants (Monheim, 1971). Today the percentage of the work force employed in agriculture is less than it was twenty years ago, but around 30% are still engaged in this sector and many more gain their livelihoods indirectly from agriculture by supplying related services. It has been suggested that this form of rural settlement is an obstacle to agricultural development (King, 1971; King and Strachan, 1978), primarily because many towns are sited on hilltops and as such are not close to major lines of communication. This both hinders the marketing of agricultural products and slows down the introduction of new attitudes and techniques. Additionally, journeys to work often involve a round trip of several kilometres, which not only alienate the farmer from his land, but also result in the land close to the town (the *corona*) being intensively cropped, while the remainder is not developed to its full potential.

The towns of the Etna region are *agro-towns* in terms of both their demographic and social characteristics; Fig. 2.9 shows their location on the volcano. Important differences exist between these towns and those found in the interior of the island. Because the density of population in the Etna region is so high, towns – particularly those on the south and east flanks – are closely spaced and almost appear to merge into one another. This means that daily commuting takes place over short distances and there is no evidence to suggest that agricultural intensity falls with increasing distance. Because export orientation has always been a feature of the agriculture of the Etna region, towns are located on roads leading to Catania; and the recent construction of new roads and by-passes has greatly improved access to Catania and the coast. Even on the sparsely settled north and west flanks, where overall agricultural intensity is lower, towns are still better served by communications than the majority of settlements in the interior, although longer daily commuting does bring about a small yet significant increase in the intensity of cropping in the immediate vicinity of these settlements.

2.2.3 *Industry, commerce and trade*

Until the mid-1950s the industrial base of Sicily was traditional in character and included the processing of agricultural products (including fish) for export, the manufacture of handicrafts and the winning of a variety of minerals especially sulphur from the so-called 'sulphur plateau' of central Sicily. In spite of the fact that the processing of food for export from the coastal margins of Sicily became more important, the other main industrial activities – handicrafts and mining – were in a much less healthy state in the 1950s than they were at the start of the century, or even at the time of the unification of Sicily with the mainland. At unification in 1860 it is estimated that 35% of the labour force was engaged in industry, the majority being artisans providing craft products for villages, towns and their surrounding areas (King, 1973a), but after unification these local handicrafts had to compete with manufactured household and personal goods from northern Italy and by the 1950s this sector had suffered serious decline. Decline, though noticeable throughout Sicily, was most marked in the eastern part of the island where better communications and closer proximity to the mainland ensured greater market penetration (Mack-Smith, 1968). In the 1950s the handicraft and manufacturing industries of Sicily were characterized by small concerns with the majority employing less than five workers, much precarious and seasonal employment and in many cases a lack of even rudimentary mechanization (Sylos-Labini, 1964; Stein, 1971).

Production of sulphur rose by 150% in the last thirty years of the nineteenth century and by 1900

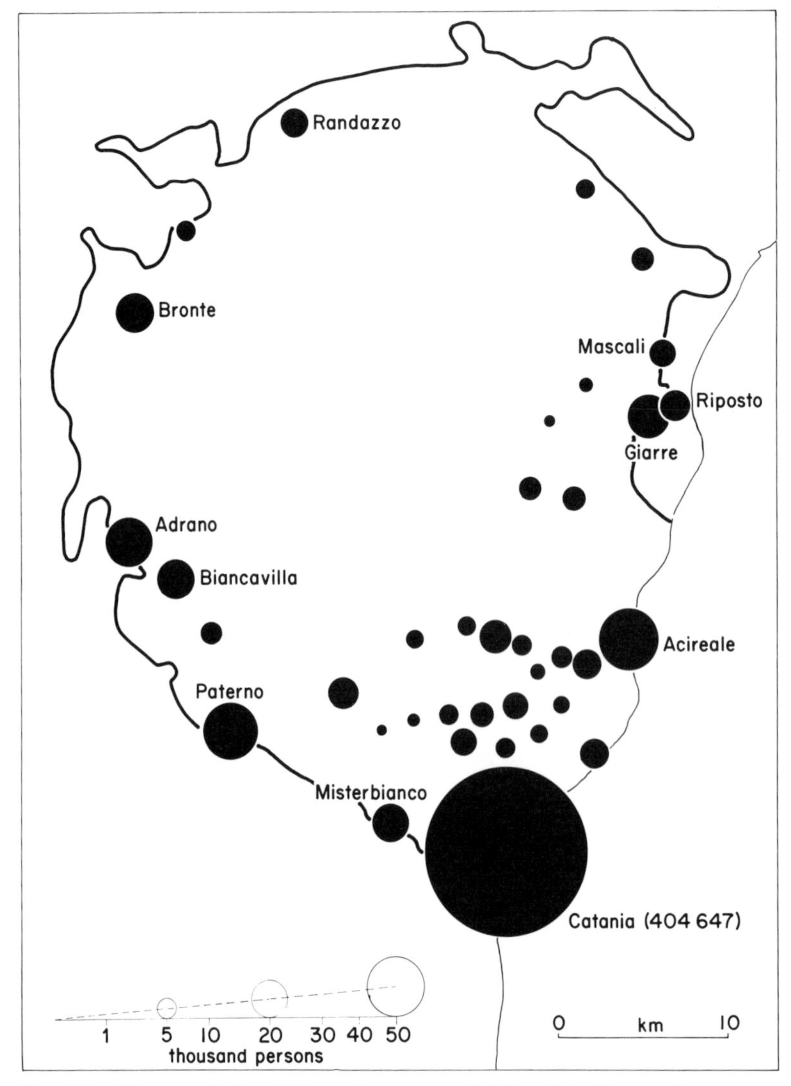

Fig. 2.9 The population of the main towns and cities of the Etna region.

50 000 workers were employed in this industry, but by 1955 this had fallen to 10 000 and was probably only around 3000 by the mid-1970s (King, 1973a). Competition from other suppliers was the principal cause of this decline, but the background of organized crime, an appalling safety record, poor labour relations and a lack of investment were also to blame.

In contrast to this general picture of stagnation, the Etna region in general and particularly the city of Catania did relatively well after unification and by the 1950s had become the major commercial and one of the main industrial centres of Sicily. The rich agricultural hinterland of the city was the major reason for this prosperity and gave a stimulus to the growth of industries processing the wealth of the land for export, so that by 1900 Catania had overtaken Palermo as Sicily's principal port. Social factors are equally important in explaining the growth of Catania as an industrial centre, and the relative lack of organized crime, the reasonably corruption-free politics of the city and the more cosmopolitan outlook of political and business leaders were all important in creating a climate in which industry and trade could prosper. Even the early post-unification decline in traditional handicraft manufacturing was turned to advantage by Catanesi businessmen, who became free to invest their resources in factories and other commercial ventures and, unlike the rest of Sicily where wealth was largely measured in land, these entrepreneurs placed a high value on investment and individual enterprise (Mack-Smith, 1968).

Developments since the 1950s have widened the commercial and industrial contrasts between the eastern coastal margins and the rest of Sicily. New industry has been brought to Sicily for two reasons: first as a response to the discovery and exploitation of new mineral resources, and secondly as a result of direct government intervention in the island's economy and infrastructure. In the fifties potash deposits were discovered in central Sicily, but although this brought some pockets of new prosperity to these interior lands and to the south coast town of Porto Empedocle where it is processed into fertiliser for export, this development has made little impact on the long-term economic problems of this region (King, 1973a). At the same time oil was discovered in south-east Sicily and, although the volume of these finds was small on a world or even a European scale, they provided a stimulus for the rapid capital-intensive industrialization of this corner of the island. The foci of this new industrial region are the cities of Siracusa and Augusta and by the late 1960s this area contained petrochemical industries (fertilisers, plastics, pharmaceutical products and industrial chemicals) and much refining capacity. Because of the island's strategic position in the Mediterranean, it is well placed for the import of crude oil from the Middle East and North Africa and there are large refineries at Gela on the south and at Augusta on the east coast. By 1969 Augusta had surpassed Catania as the island's major port and is today one of the top four in Italy in terms of tonnage handled (Beckinsale and Beckinsale, 1975). As well as the oil-based industries already mentioned, south-east Sicily also contains many new building and manufacturing enterprises which have been attracted to the region as a result of its new prosperity (Mountjoy, 1970; Stein, 1971; King, 1973a). The 'backwash' effects of this new investment have been felt throughout eastern Sicily, and Catania has benefited because of its existing role as the main commercial and service centre of the region. This is in spite of the fact that the only significant discovery of hydrocarbons was at Bronte in the relatively remote north-west sector of Etna. Here a small gas field was found on sedimentary rocks lying just beyond the limit of the volcanics and today its output is piped to Catania for use as a fuel.

Direct government involvement in the economy of Sicily has been of benefit to the industries of the Etna region. In 1946 the island was granted a measure of regional autonomy in matters affecting agriculture, forestry, mining, industry, commerce, public works and elementary education and, though the effectiveness of the assembly which meets in Palermo has been called into question (King, 1973a), there is little doubt that the agencies that have been set up to assist manufacturing have been important in widening the industrial base of Catania. In addition, and at a national level, investment funds have been available since the 1950s from the Italian special agency for southern development – the *Cassa per il Mezzogiorno*. Assistance from all these industrial agencies has been concentrated in so-called 'zones of expansion' and, apart from those which coincide with towns in the newly prosperous south-east (Gela, Ragusa and Siracusa – Augusta), the only others which have been to any degree successful are Catania and to a much more limited extent Palermo (Mountjoy, 1970; King, 1973a). Catania with its tradition of industry was quick to seize the opportunity of attracting new enterprises and expansion has occurred on a new industrial estate to the south of the city and more recently on the western margins of the urban area. In contrast to the successful industries of south-east Sicily, those of Catania are on a comparative basis far more labour-intensive and consist of small to medium-sized firms producing a variety of manufactured goods for the Sicilian market (Rogers, 1970). Today Catania with its well-established commercial and industrial sectors

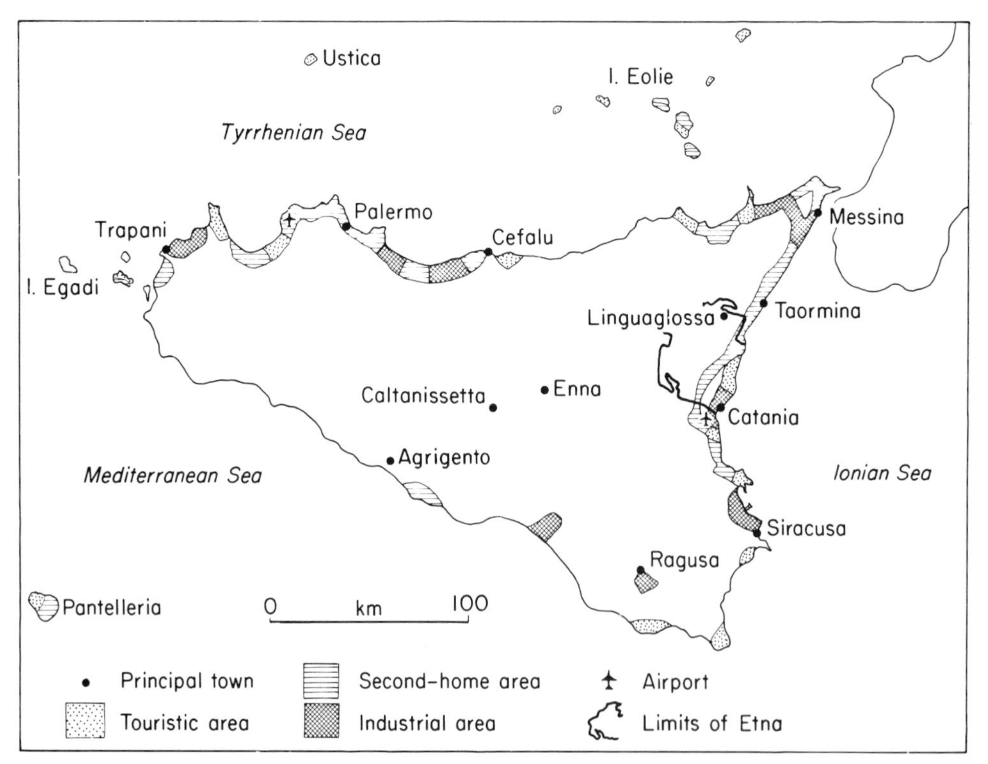

Fig. 2.10 The location of the main industrial, tourist and second-home areas in Sicily. (After Campagnoli, 1979, with additions and amendments.)

is a vital link in the chain of new prosperity that stretches from south-east Sicily to north of the Etna region and which, since the 1950s, has made this area the industrial heartland of the island.

Sicily has many advantages for tourism, since not only does it receive over ten hours of sunshine each day between April and September and possess many sites of historical, natural and cultural interest, but it is also centrally located in the Mediterranean, a region where annually over 85 million people spend their holidays. These advantages have meant that tourism is today a vital element in the economy of several coastal towns and cities (Fig. 2.10), bringing to the island much-needed foreign currency, providing a stimulus to local building and craft industries, and creating new employment in the tertiary sector. The Etna region has been at the forefront of the tourist boom for the last twenty-five years, because it is one of the few active volcanoes within easy reach of the northern European package tourist and is conveniently located near to the town of Taormina, one of the principal package-tour centres in Sicily (Fig. 2.10). Etna maintains a winter snow cover and this means that tourism is an all-year-round activity and, unlike other resort areas in Sicily, the region does not suffer to the same extent from the problem of seasonal unemployment which is common in the tourist sector. As well as the employment directly created by tourism, Catania airport has also been developed into one of the main arrival and departure points for people visiting the island and recent investment in a runway extension and a new terminal building provides better communications for the city and adds to its attractiveness to industries of all types.

Although Sicily as a whole and especially the Etna region has gained from tourism, it is also the case that the total benefits that have accrued to the island fall far short of their potential. During the 1960s the number of visitors to Sicily increased by an average of 18% per annum and, despite the fact

Fig. 2.11 A traditional Sicilian village. A major attraction for visitors to the region. (Photograph: D. K. Chester.)

that the number and quality of hotels improved and that communications were far better, by the middle of the 1970s this figure had fallen to only 0.3% per annum – a most worrying trend when viewed in the context of annual growth rates of 14% in Spain and 25% in Greece (Campagnoli, 1979). Campagnoli argues that the principal reason for this relative decline is the lack of an effective tourism policy, with insufficient funds being devoted to this sector even though it is more effective than most forms of development in creating new jobs. In the light of official indifference, the development which has taken place has been largely financed by outside capital, with most of the profits eventually finding their way to the already-prosperous regions of Northern Italy. In the main this development has included self-contained holiday complexes and luxury hotels on the coast, together with the mushroom growth of second homes in coastal and mountain areas (Fig. 2.10). Little attempt has been made to cater for either the mass tourist, with Cefalu and Taormina remaining the only two resorts of this type, or for the Sicilian holiday-maker who in spite of increased disposable income rarely spends his vacation away from home.

On Etna, fringe development on the eastern flanks of the volcano, particularly the growth of second homes near to the coast, is a problem because these housing schemes make little impact on the local economy since they are only occupied for a very short time each year. In addition, many of those located on the coast have private beaches and this has served to alienate land from the public domain, while elsewhere there has been a significant loss of land for agriculture and a lowering of overall scenic quality. Since the prosperity of the Etna region is based to a large extent on the agricultural and tourist sectors (Figs 1.24 and 2.11), this is a serious problem and recently the idea of zoning part of the volcano as a National Park has been put forward. This would involve strict planning control of all land above the 1000 m contour and would have the effect of preventing the worst excesses of free enterprise in the main tourist zone. Not surprisingly this proposal has been greeted with some hostility by certain sections of the business community and will do little to arrest the spread of second homes, which are generally to be found on the lower slopes of the volcano below the 1000 m contour.

2.3 Concluding remarks

The purpose of the present chapter is to demonstrate how, through the interplay of both environmental endowment and human ingenuity, Etna has developed into both a distinctive region of Sicily and one of the most prosperous in the Italian south. From what has been written it is easy to conclude that, notwithstanding the ever-present hazard from volcanic eruptions and earthquakes, over the long term the region gains more from the volcano than it loses through short-term though often catastrophic events. Although losses from eruptions are inevitable on a volcano like Etna, it is increasingly becoming apparent that carefully constructed planning policies – based on a thorough understanding of the processes involved in volcanic activity – can minimize losses in hazardous environments through well-designed land-use and disaster-contingency plans. Thus, even though the following five chapters are primarily concerned with reporting the results of pure research carried out on Etna during the last decade, the information contained within them has a direct bearing on the development of predictive models of volcanic activity (Chapter 8) and upon the formulation of policies, whereby the risks of losses resulting from eruptions may be minimized. The latter theme is dealt with in detail in Chapter 9.

3 Geological setting and volcanic history

'. . . for Etna is
the fairy godmother of the
neighbourhood, in her right hand
are riches, and in her
left terror and death.'

(Spencer C. Musson, 1911)

Mount Etna is one of many active or recently active centres of volcanism in southern Italy and before going on to consider the geology of this volcano in detail it is necessary to place the volcano in a regional context. Throughout the late Tertiary and Quaternary there has been a remarkably diverse history of volcanism in the central Mediterranean region (Fig. 3.1). In mainland Italy, potassic and silicic volcanism has occurred along the western coast from Tuscany in the north to Vesuvius in the south from the Pliocene to the present, though most of this volcanism is less than 1 m.y.old. The Tyrrhenian Sea is floored in part by basalt and is usually interpreted as a marginal basin which has formed during the last 7 million years (Barberi *et al.*, 1978). The Eolian Islands in the southern Tyrrhenian Sea, an arcuate archipelago of volcanic islands of Quaternary age composed of calc-alkaline and shoshonitic products, have been considered to represent an island arc in a senile stage of development (Keller, 1980). In Sardinia, which forms the western margin of the Tyrrhenian Sea, there were several episodes of calc-alkaline volcanism from the Oligocene to the lower Miocene

Fig. 3.1 Location of major centres of late Tertiary and Quaternary volcanism in Italy.

and this was followed in the upper Miocene by basaltic magmatism which continued into the Quaternary. The island of Pantelleria, in the Sicilian Channel, is built predominantly of trachytes and peralkaline rhyolites, while also in the Sicilian Channel, the island of Linosa is composed of volcanics of the alkali olivine basalt series. Activity still occurs in the Sicilian Channel as was shown by a submarine eruption in 1831. In Sicily between the upper Miocene and the lower Pleistocene there was eruption, under shallow marine and subaerial conditions, of tholeiitic and alkalic basalts on the northern margin of the Iblean carbonate platform. Since the middle Pleistocene, however, volcanism in Sicily has been concentrated in the region now occupied by Etna building up one of the largest continental volcanoes in the world. This wide range of types and styles of volcanism reflects the complex tectonics of the region and will be considered further in the next section.

3.1 Volcanism and tectonics in the central Mediterranean

The tectonic development of the Mediterranean throughout the Mesozoic is closely linked with the growth and closure of the Tethys ocean. There have been several accounts (Dewey *et al.*, 1973; Biju-Duval *et al.*, 1977) which have attempted to explain the evolution of the area in terms of plate tectonics. The lack of agreement between the various proposed models reflects both the gaps in the current information and the complexity of the problem. Another difficulty lies in the large-scale allochthony of basement and cover nappes and the destruction of much evidence through subduction and subsequent continent–continent collision (Bernoulli and Lemoine, 1980). In the Mediterranean area, tectonism since the Cretaceous has been largely controlled by continental collision but, as stressed by McKenzie (1977), the deformation of continental crust cannot be explained in terms of simplistic plate tectonic models as complex patterns may result due to the interaction between present motions and pre-existing structures.

In the pre-drift configuration of continental masses in the Trias the presence of a wedge-shaped split between Africa and Eurasia which opened up to the east (Bernoulli and Lemoine, 1980) has been interpreted as a late Palaeozoic palaeo-Tethys (Dewey *et al.*, 1973; Biju-Duval *et al.*, 1977). There is controversy, however, regarding the nature and status of a palaeo-Tethys ocean and, on the basis of the lack of Triassic ophiolites and the continuous passage of Permian facies across the position of the supposed palaeo-Tethys suture, Argyriadis *et al.* (1980) argue that the Eurasian and Arabian–African continents were linked from Gibraltar to Iran and did not break up until the opening of the Mesozoic Tethys. This rifting was initiated in the Trias with the early development of the Tethyan ocean (Bernoulli and Lemoine, 1980); the presence of calc-alkaline volcanics of middle Triassic age in the southern Alps, however, may indicate the occurrence of some subduction events at this time (Lucchini *et al.*, 1982). Throughout the Jurassic there was continued opening of the Tethyan ocean. Biju-Duval *et al.* (1977) consider that the palaeogeography of this time can be best explained in terms of three intermediate plates: Iberia, Apulia and Anatolia. Biju-Duval *et al.* restrict Tethys to the oceanic area that lay to the east of Apulia and give the name Mesogea to the oceanic area that opened up between Apulia and Africa during the Mesozoic. Towards the end of the Jurassic, consumption of the Tethyan ocean begins and, according to the model of Biju-Duval *et al.*, Apulia collided with Europe. Though the models proposed by the various authors are quite divergent in their tectonic reconstructions and configuration of plate boundaries and subduction zones, there is broad agreement that there was closure of the oceanic areas during the Cretaceous leading to continental collision and fragmentation in the Tertiary. This elimination of Tethys is related to the opening of the north and south Atlantic in late Cretaceous and Tertiary times. The consumption of oceanic lithosphere in the late Cretaceous and early Tertiary led to the opening of marginal basins, now represented by the Balearic and Ligurian Seas which are, in part at least, underlain by oceanic-type crust (Channell *et al.*, 1979). There seems to be a large measure of agreement between the various models (Biju-Duval *et al.*, 1977; Channell *et al.*, 1979; Scandone, 1979; Giese *et al.*, 1980) that there was consumption of oceanic lithosphere north-westwards beneath Sardinia throughout much of the Tertiary. The Eocene to Miocene calc-alkaline volcanism of western Sardinia is attributed to this subduction episode (Beccaluva *et al.*, 1977; Macciotta *et al.*, 1978).

An understanding of the formation of the Tyrrhenian Sea, a triangular area bounded by Corsica and Sardinia in the west, mainland Italy to the east and Sicily to the south, is of great importance in a tectonic reconstruction of the central Mediterranean since the Miocene. The Tyrrhenian basin is an area of high heat flow underlain by thin oceanic-type crust and has been interpreted as a marginal basin (Di Girolamo, 1978; Boccalatti *et al.*, 1984). Basalt recovered from the Deep Sea Drilling Project core (Site 373A, Leg 42A) from the Tyrrhenian Sea floor has the geochemical characteristics of a transitional-ocean floor basalt similar to basalts from marginal basins such as the Marianas Trough, but rather different from basalts of marginal basins associated with subduction (Hamelin *et al.*, 1979).

The opening of the Tyrrhenian Sea dates back at least 7 million years (Barberi *et al.*, 1978) and spreading was complete by the end of the lower Pliocene (Di Girolamo, 1978). Blocks of continental crust isolated during this rifting episode occur as non-volcanic sea mounts from which metamorphic rocks have been sampled (Heezen *et al.*, 1971). Since the lower Pliocene the Tyrrhenian Sea has been subjected to tensional faulting with eruption of tholeiitic to transitional basalts of 'within-plate' character from the Vavilov and Magnaghi sea mounts. More recent volcanics (around 100 000 BP) of alkalic affinity, alkali basalts and hawaiites, have been recovered in a piston core (Keller, 1981). The Pleistocene alkaline volcano, Ustica, which is an island in the south-west part of the Tyrrhenian Sea is associated with distensive faulting and is also related to this phase of activity (Romano and Sturiale, 1971). The most recent magmatic episode in the Tyrrhenian Sea was the development of the Eolian Island Arc. The Eolian Islands are a group of seven volcanic islands – Stromboli, Panarea, Salina, Lipari, Vulcano, Filicudi and Alicudi – and associated sea mounts which describe a broadly arcuate archipelago. The volcanics of the Eolian Islands are Quaternary in age and have been broadly assigned to two phases (Villari, 1980; Beccaluva *et al.*, 1981); the first phase being pre-*Tyrrhenian* Pleistocene stage with eruption of calc-alkaline basalts and andesites, and a second post-*Tyrrhenian* phase involving potassic products culminating in the shoshonitic activity of Stromboli and Vulcano at the present. Current activity is confined to Stromboli, which is almost continually active erupting shoshonitic basalts, and Vulcano which last erupted in 1888–90 and whose latest products include leucite tephrites and alkali rhyolites. The last activity of Lipari was in the sixth century AD with eruption of an obsidian lava flow in the north of the island (Pichler, 1980). An inclined seismic zone, dipping steeply to the north-west, exists beneath the Eolian Islands (Caputo *et al.*, 1970) and on the basis of this and the calc-alkalic affinity of the volcanics Barberi *et al.* (1974) suggest an island arc model with subduction of oceanic lithosphere north-westwards beneath Calabria and the Eolian Islands from the Ionian Sea. To explain the lack of oceanic-type crust at present in the Ionian Sea, Barberi *et al.* consider that consumption of oceanic lithosphere is now virtually complete. However, there is still uncertainty regarding the nature of the crust in the Ionian Sea; and Finetti (1981) suggests it is composed of very thin continental or even oceanic crust. Keller (1980) also considers that the Eolian Islands represent an island arc and supports the proposal of Barberi *et al.* that subduction is now almost complete and suggests that the shoshonitic affinity of the recent activity indicates that the arc is in a senile stage.

There are, nevertheless, some major complications to an island arc model for the Eolian Islands. The Palinuro and Marsili sea mounts are composed of calc-alkaline volcanics of similar age to the Eolian Islands but do not lie on the same arcuate pattern (Colantoni *et al.*, 1981). Palinuro is emplaced on a major east – west transcurrent fault and Marsili is situated within the centre of a basin which has undergone marginal distension. The presence of these two sea mounts with similar age and petrology to the Eolian Islands, but with a rather different structural setting, complicates the straightforward island arc interpretation. Another difficulty with the island arc model is the suggestion by Barberi *et al.* (1974) that the Tyrrhenian Sea represents the back arc basin to the Eolian Arc. However, as is pointed out by Di Girolamo (1978) and Scandone (1979) the spreading of the Tyrrhenian basin from about 7 to 5 m.y.old took place before the formation of the Eolian Arc which is less than 1 m.y.old. Indeed, Scandone (1979) interprets the Tyrrhenian Sea as a Neogene–Quaternary extensional basin initiated by rifting of a belt of deformed continental crust. Pichler (1980) questions the island arc model for the Eolian Islands considering that the evolution of the arc to a senile stage in less than 1 million years would require an unrealisticly high rate of sinking for the subducted lithospheric slab. In addition, if the Eolian Islands represent the volcanism relating to the consumption of the last segment of oceanic crust between Europe and Africa, the question must be asked where are all the calc-alkaline volcanics that resulted from the preceding subduction. In a study of the relationships between volcanism and tectonism in Sicily, Cristofolini *et al.* (1977a) find little evidence to support an island arc structural pattern to account for the different volcanic associations throughout the Quaternary in this region. From an investigation of earthquake data in the Tyrrhenian Sea between 1962 and 1979, Gasparini *et al.* (1982) have developed a detailed picture of the inclined seismic zone underlying the Eolian Islands and interpret it in terms of a strongly deformed remnant of a previously continuous Benioff Zone which extended from the north Apennines to Gibraltar. This Benioff Zone was sliced and partly consumed in the asthenosphere by the rifting event in the opening of the Tyrrhenian Basin and, with the anticlockwise rotation of Italy, distortion of this slab may have initiated magmatism. However, data from the International Seismological Centre and the USGS seismic files, plotted along a NW – SE cross-section, plot in a thin zone suggesting little curvature and no strong deformation of this Benioff Zone (H. Anderson, personal communication, 1984). From this general discussion it is clear that the relationship between the Tyrrhenian Basin, the Eolian Islands and conventional plate tectonic processes is as yet uncertain.

The eastern border of the Tyrrhenian Sea is characterized by volcanism on mainland Italy and adjacent islands from the late Tertiary to the present. This volcanism has taken place on the western side of the Apennines with the exception of Monte Vulture which is situated 120 km east of Naples. The Cainozoic volcanism of Italy belongs to three provinces: the Tuscan, Roman and Campanian areas of magmatism.

The magmatism of the Tuscan Province took place between Corsica in the west and the Apennines in the east. There is evidence of eastward migration of this activity with time, K/Ar ages from the Island of Elba range back to 7.0 m.y.old whereas the youngest K/Ar date for volcanics from Monte Amiata in the east is 180 000 BP (Alvarez, 1972; Bigazzi *et al.*, 1981). Geothermal activity continues at present in the Tuscan Province, at Amiata and Lardarello. The rock types of the Tuscan Province are predominantly rhyolites, quartz latites and small granite and quartz monzonite intrusions. The lavas contain xenocrysts of cordierite and quartz and have high $\delta^{18}O$ values, 11.2–16.4, and $^{87}Sr/^{86}Sr$ ratios, 0.713–0.720, suggesting an anatectic origin involving alumina-rich sedimentary rocks (Taylor and Turi, 1976). Some of the more recent complexes of the Tuscan Province such as Monte Amiata and Monte Cimini are considered to have been derived from mixing between crustal and anatectic magmas and potassic mantle-generated magmas of the Roman Province (Taylor and Turi, 1976; Bigazzi *et al.*, 1981). There have been several models proposed to account for the magmatism of the Tuscan Province. Alvarez (1972) suggested melting of sediments in a subduction zone. There is, however, little evidence to support such a model and Tuscan-type magmas do not occur in areas of known subduction (Taylor and Turi, 1976). The Tuscan region was subjected to considerable uplift during the magmatic episode and Marinelli (1975) attributes the volcanism to anatexis during high heat flow and crustal upwarping in what he terms the 'Etruscan Swell'. Civetta *et al.* (1978) associate the magmatism of the Tuscan Province with the opening of the Tyrrhenian Basin and the anticlockwise rotation of the Apennines, the pressure relief and mobilization of volatiles within the mantle, brought about by the rifting episode, causing the magmatism. This anticlockwise rotation would account for the eastward migration of the activity. Another important factor is that two crust – mantle boundaries have been located in the Elba – western Tuscany area, the first at 15 – 25 km depth and the second at 45 – 50 km (Giese *et al.*, 1980), and this thickened continental crust could provide a significant contribution of radioactive heat.

The potassic volcanism of the Roman and Campanian Provinces can be best considered together. The Roman Province includes the Monte Vulsini, Vico, Monte Sabatini and Colli Albani areas of volcanism. In the Campanian Province, Roccamonfina, Campi Flegrei, Vesuvius and Ischia, with Monte Vulture as a geographic anomaly, are the main centres. The rock types comprise classic potassic varieties, the high-K series, such as phonolites, leucite phonolites and leucite trachytes often associated with a low-K series containing latites and trachytes. The volcanism is marked by two main types of activity, firstly the growth of large stratovolcanoes and secondly the emplacement of large volumes of ignimbrite from central vents or fissures and generally associated with caldera collapse (Barberi *et al.*, 1978). The magmatism is associated with distensive tectonism and the volcanoes are related to normal faults and the development of grabens (Locardi *et al.*, 1977). Varekamp (1981) considers that the faults extend to considerable depth and tap magma sources in the lower crust or even the upper mantle. The volcanism ranges in age from about 2 m.y.old to the present.

There has been much discussion in the literature regarding the genesis of the potassic magmas of the Campanian and Roman Provinces and recent isotopic studies have provided useful data. Turi and Taylor (1976) demonstrate that there is an increase, from Ischia in the south to Vulsini in the north, in the $\delta^{18}O$ values, 5.8–11.7, and $^{87}Sr/^{86}Sr$ values, 0.706–0.714. This variation is explained by Turi and Taylor (1976) in terms of a two-component mixing model with progressive contamination, by a crustal component, of a mantle-derived unsaturated magma to the north. Hawkesworth and Vollmer (1979), however, from a study of $^{143}Nd/^{144}Nd$ and $^{87}Sr/^{86}Sr$ isotope data suggest two zones in the Campanian and Roman Provinces: a zone between Vulsini and Rome where there is evidence of crust–mantle-derived hybrid melts and one south of Rome where mantle-derived magmas have been largely unaffected by crustal contamination. Carter *et al.* (1978) consider that the Roccamonfina volcanics (Roccamonfina lies at the northern end of the Campanian Province) were derived from a mantle source enriched in light rare-earth elements. In a detailed study of oxygen and strontium isotopes of the Vulsinian district, Holm and Munksgaard (1982) show that even the more basic lavas with relatively primitive geochemical characteristics show a range of $\delta^{18}O$ and $^{87}Sr/^{86}Sr$ values suggesting a variation in the isotopic characteristics of the mantle source region. Holm and Munksgaard consider that this variation is due to the mantle having been subjected to metasomatism. They suggest that hydrous fluids enriched in large-ion lithophile elements, $\delta^{18}O$ and $^{87}Sr/^{86}Sr$ were derived from the dehydration of subducted continental crust into the overlying mantle wedge during the continent – continent collision of the Corsica – Sardinia block and the Adriatic plate. The work of Carter *et al.* (1978), Hawkesworth and Vollmer (1979), Cortini and Hermes (1981) and Holm and Munksgaard (1982) all indicate that metasomatic enrichment of the mantle source area has been an important process in accounting for the geochemical characteristics of the Campanian and Roman volcanic provinces.

Sicily forms the southern margin of the Tyrrhenian Sea. In the Straits of Sicily between Sicily and Africa there are several sites of Quaternary volcanism and the islands of Pantelleria and Linosa are both Pleistocene volcanoes. In historic times there have been observations of submarine volcanism in the Straits of Sicily. The most notable of these events was the eruption in 1831 which built up a small island called (by the British) Graham Island after the naval captain who landed and claimed it in the name of Queen Victoria (Bonney, 1899). The island was called Giulia by the French and Italians, and Ferdinandeo by the Germans; but fortunately the island was washed away before its sovereignty became a matter of embarrassment. The Straits of Sicily are characterized by tensional faults trending north-west–south-east with a north-east–south-west conjugate system and this has generated a horst and graben pattern in the area (Beccaluva *et al.*, 1981). Linosa (Di Paola, 1973) and the now-submarine volcanoes of Graham Island and Banco senza Nome (Beccaluva *et al.*, 1981) are characterized by alkaline magmatism and are situated on continental crust 25 – 30 km thick. Pantelleria, however, in the axial region of the Straits is situated in a graben and is built up of trachytes and peralkaline rhyolites (Villari, 1970; Mahood and Hildreth, 1983). Lava from the Banco senza Nome with a K/Ar date of around 10 m.y.old (Beccaluva *et al.*, 1981) represents the oldest recorded evidence of volcanism in the Straits and indicates the first sign of upper Miocene tensional tectonism in this area after the collision of the African and European blocks. This upper Miocene distensive tectonism may relate to the upper Miocene extensional phase identified in the Calabrian arc by Ghisetti and Vezzani (1981).

On Sicily there are two sites of Cainozoic volcanism: the Iblean Mountains and Mount Etna. Between the upper Miocene and the lower Pleistocene, in the Iblean Mountains there was eruption, under shallow-marine and sub-aerial conditions on a carbonate platform, of both low-K tholeiitic and alkali basalts (Romano and Villari, 1973; Cristofolini *et al.*, 1981). This volcanism is linked with tensional movements and located at the intersection of major faults. Etna rises from sea level to over 3 km and covers an area of around 1750 km^2 (Duncan *et al.*, 1981). The earliest activity of Etna took place in the middle Pleistocene with eruption of tholeiitic basalts (Cristofolini, 1973; Chester and Duncan, 1982), but the main bulk of the volcano is built up of mildly alkaline products of trachybasaltic affinity.

It is apparent from the preceding discussion that there is as yet no synthesis on the relations between magmatism and the tectonic evolution in the central Mediterranean area. In the tectonic reconstructions, proposed subduction episodes involving consumption of oceanic lithosphere seem to be associated with calc-alkaline magmatism. Some of the early tectonic reconstructions (Ninkovich and Hays, 1972; Barberi *et al.*, 1974), based on simplistic plate tectonic relationships, do not accord well with the chronological, seismic and geophysical data. Recent models are more cautious in their interpretation but invoke such processes as mantle metasomatism which are poorly understood. It is likely that the complex interaction between the Eurasian and African plates during the Mesozoic and Cainozoic with continental collision, the development of marginal basins and subduction of continental crust has left the mantle in a disturbed state as is evidenced by mantle diapirism. It is suggested that much of the magmatism in this area is related to localized mantle diapirism in a distensive tectonic environment.

3.2 Geological setting of Mount Etna

Situated at the junction of the Eurasian and African plates, Sicily presents a complex geological picture. This complexity is largely due to successive episodes of overthrusting and gravity-sliding from the north. The geology of Sicily is presented here in only a very introductory form; for further information see Caire (1970), Pieri (1975) and Wezel (1975). A simplified geological map showing the main structural units and the major faults is provided in Fig. 3.2; and a reconstruction of the probable original relationships of these units, based on the work of Pieri (1975), is shown in Fig. 3.3.

The oldest unit is the *calabride complex* which forms the Peloritani Mountains in north-east Sicily and is delimited to the south by the Monte Kumeta – Alcantara Line (Ghisetti and Vezzani, 1981). This crystalline sequence is made up of allochthonous units of Alpine provenance emplaced on to Apenninic thrust sheets (Ghisetti and Vezzani, 1981) and is composed of granites, gneisses, schists

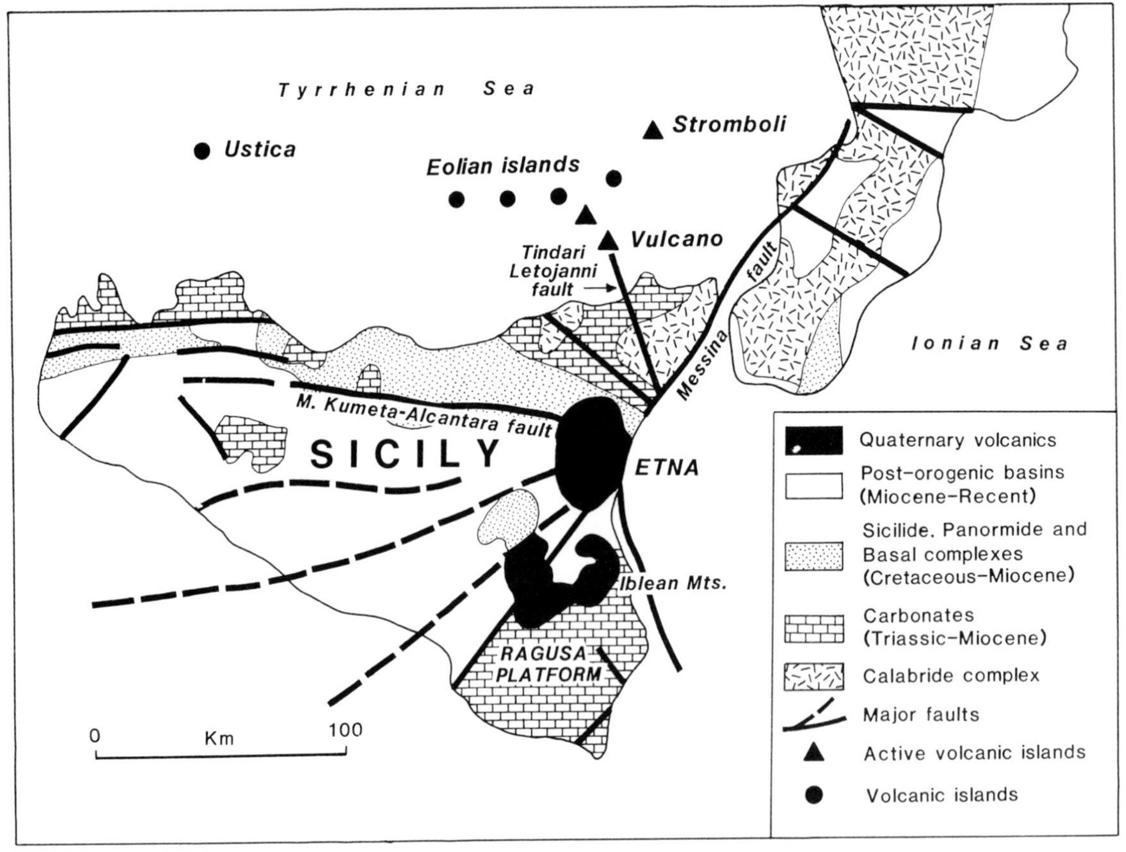

Fig. 3.2 Geological sketch map of Sicily showing location of Mount Etna in relation to the main fault trends. Adapted from Grindley (1973).

and phyllites. The granite intrusions and the metamorphism are Variscan in age and the phyllites have yielded Devonian fossils. In the Permo-Trias the Verrucano sandstones and conglomerates were deposited on this crystalline basement followed by a thin sequence of Mesozoic limestones and shales. In the middle Eocene there was a phase of folding and southward overthrusting followed by deposition of upper Eocene conglomerates. In the Miocene there was the main phase of Alpine movements with southward thrusting (Grindley, 1973).

The *sicilide complex* is composed of late Jurassic and younger flysch sediments which are allochthonous and have been thrust over the *panormide complex*. The sediments of the sicilide complex are interpreted by Ogniben (1960, 1970) as being deposited in a eugeosynclinal environment, whereas the predominantly carbonate succession of the panormide complex is considered to represent miogeanticlinal sedimentation. The Numidian Flysch and related sediments of the *basal complex* are attributed to a miogeosynclinal origin being deposited closest to the African foreland. The *Hyblean Foreland* of Ogniben (1960, 1970) is formed of mainly upper Triassic to Oligocene carbonates and, unaffected by the earth movements of the Alpine Orogeny, is a continuation of the Saharan Platform.

As described above in the sequence of events shown by the calabride complex, the main Alpine earth movements were in the Eocene and middle Miocene. In the Pliocene and lower Pleistocene uplift occurred in northern Sicily and there was

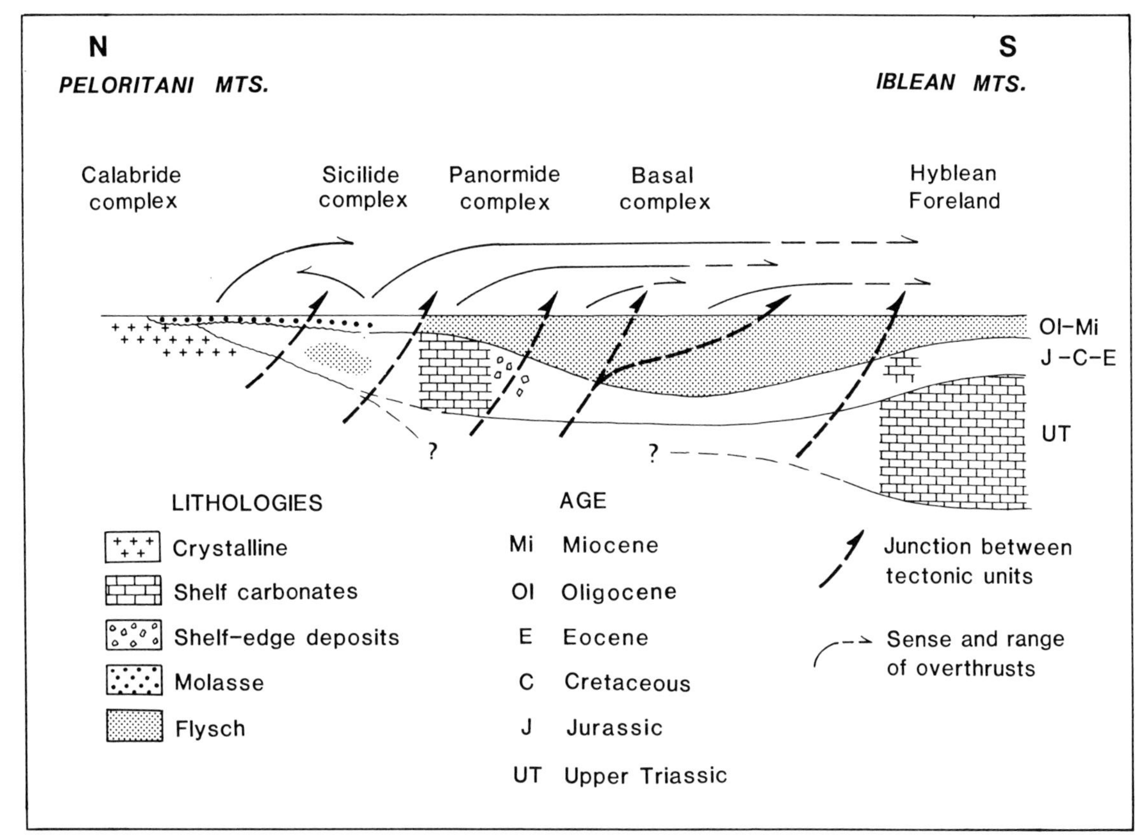

Fig. 3.3 North – south sketch section through Sicily showing pre-deformation relationships between different lithologies and the sense of tectonic movements. Adapted from Pieri (1975).

re-sedimentation of olistoliths and olistostromes in the rapidly subsiding post-orogenic basins of central Sicily (Grindley, 1973). Upper Pliocene to Pleistocene times were characterized by tensional tectonics with the major faults of Sicily and Calabria being reactivated with normal displacements (Ghisetti and Vezzani, 1981).

The crust is of normal thickness, about 35 km, in southern Sicily and thickens progressively northwards to around 40 km beneath the Peloritani Mountains and then rapidly becomes thinner in the Tyrrhenian Sea area. After a detailed seismic investigation, Sharp *et al.* (1980) identifed the Moho at a depth of 27 km beneath Etna. A reconstruction of the possible crustal structure beneath Etna is given in Fig. 3.4 based on the work of Ghisetti and Vezzani (1982).

Etna is in an area of active uplift, about 1 mm yr^{-1} (Grindley, 1973), at the intersection of three fault trends: a major trend of NNE – SSW step faults, a second trend that is ENE – WSW in orientation and a minor ESE–WNW trend (Rittmann, 1973). Evidence of the strong uplift in the Etna region is provided by the occurrence of lower Pleistocene marine clays at an altitude of 400 m on the south-east slopes and at 700 m on the north-east slopes of the volcano (Cristofolini, 1979). In a detailed structural analysis of the region (Ghisetti and Vezzani 1982), Etna is shown to be located where the Monte Kumeta – Alcantara line intersects with its major conjugate fault systems, the Messina – Giardini and Tindari–Letojanni faults (Fig. 3.2). Cristofolini *et al.* (1977a) argue that these tensional fractures could play an important role in transporting magma, generated under different physico-chemical conditions, to the surface in this very

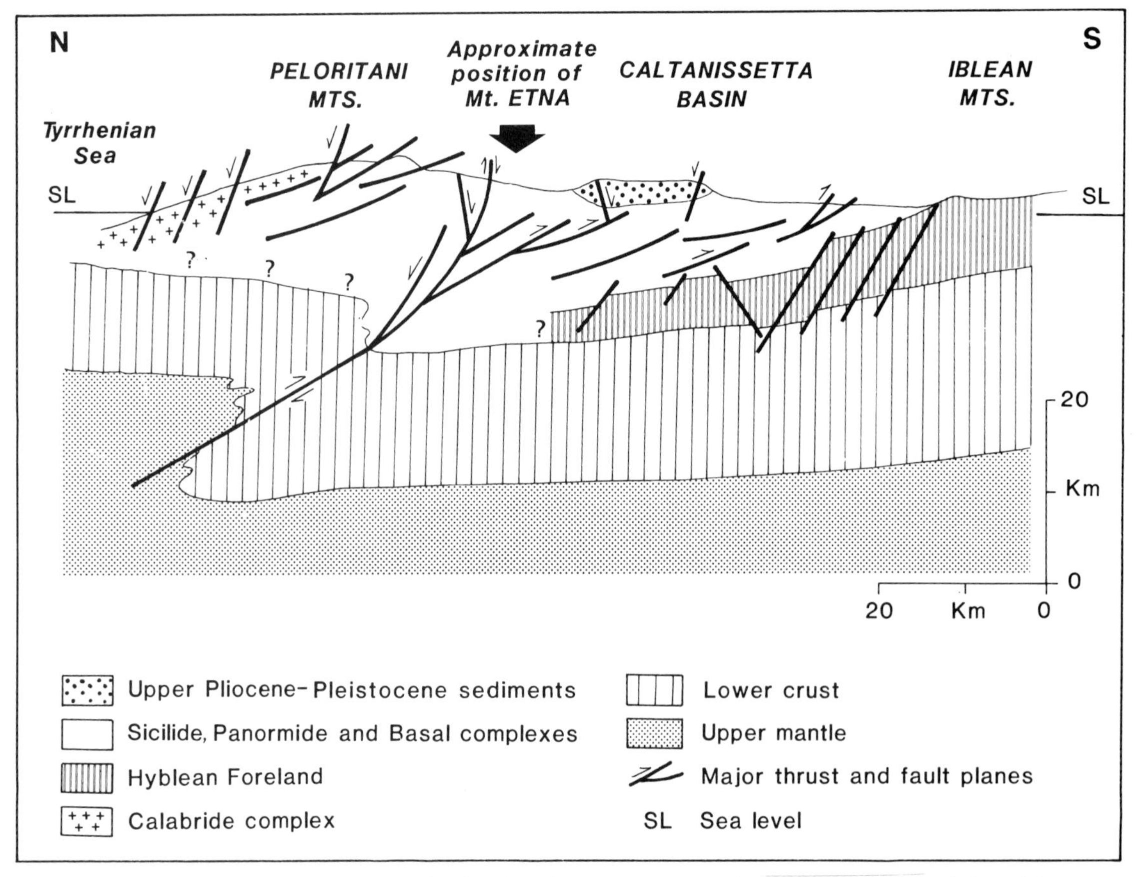

Fig. 3.4 North – south section through Sicily showing the crustal structure beneath Mount Etna. Adapted from Ghisetti and Vezzani (1982).

active structural system. In an analysis of structural lineaments on the slopes of Etna, Frazzetta and Villari (1981) suggest that the deformation pattern of the volcanic edifice is compatible with a deviating stress field dominated by an east – west sinistral shear.

Distinctive fault scarps (Fig. 3.5), locally known as *timpa*, occur on the eastern flanks of Etna orientated NNW – SSE and ENE – WSW (Cristofolini, 1979). The major fault scarps have a downthrow towards the sea; such fault scarps are not developed elsewhere on the volcano where the mountain is buttressed by the surrounding mountain ring (Guest *et al.*, 1984). A similar pattern of faults is developed on the seaward side of Kilauea volcano in Hawaii and this is interpreted by Duffield *et al.* (1982) in terms of gravity-sliding on the unsupported side of the volcanic pile. Although on Etna the pattern of faults is in part controlled by regional tectonic trends, Guest *et al.*, consider that much of the faulting is of shallow origin associated with gravity-sliding. The eruption fissures on the flanks of the volcano are not radial about the summit but are orientated along precise trends: the major trend is N 30° E which gives rise to the North-east rift system and two subsidiary trends along N 15° W and N 60° E (Lo Giudice *et al.*, 1982). The subordinate fissure trends are aligned parallel to the main structural lineaments with the major N 30° E fissure system developed perpendicular to the minimum principal stress direction. Lo Giudice *et al.* argue that inversions in the stress field, with alternations between compressive and distensive tectonics,

Fig. 3.5 Fault scarp by the coast on the eastern flank of Mount Etna. (Photograph: A. M. Duncan.)

could account for changes in the internal plumbing of Etna during its history.

There is much seismicity in this active structural system as the devastating Messina earthquake of 1908 bears horrifying witness, with over 100 000 deaths. There is, however, little evidence that earthquakes in regions adjacent to the volcano have had an influence on eruptive activity (Sharp *et al.*, 1981). Sharp *et al.* observe a correlation between local earthquakes and volcanic activity, with local earthquakes often preceding flank eruptions, and consider that this is due to a combination of magma pressure and lithospheric earthquakes fracturing the flanks of Etna and releasing lava from the partly charged plumbing system. Sharp *et al.* suggest that these observations lend support to the model that the volcanism of Etna is controlled by abyssal lithospheric fissures.

3.3 Nomenclature of the lavas of Mount Etna

With the wide variety of processes that can operate in the generation of magma and its subsequent modification during ascent, it is not surprising that there are a wide variety of volcanic rock types on a world-wide basis. Indeed, in terms of their detailed petrological character many rock types are unique to specific volcanic centres. In constructing a classification scheme for igneous rocks there are conflicting objectives: should the scheme recognize the wide variety of rock types with an equally wide variety of rock names, or should the rock types be grouped together into categories which have broad similarities? The International Union of Geological Sciences (IUGS) set up a commission chaired by Professor Streckeisen to develop a uniform nomenclature for igneous rocks. The IUGS recommendations regarding acid igneous rocks have been accepted to a large extent, however, there is still much debate regarding a classification for basic volcanic rocks. The problems of nomenclature of Etnean lavas are discussed in detail elsewhere (Cristofolini and Romano, 1982); in this account we use a classification scheme, described below, based largely on the recent literature on Etna.

On the basis of their petrography, isotope geochemistry and stratigraphic relationships the volcanic rocks of Etna can be assigned to three magma groups: the basal tholeiitic volcanics, the Paterno alkali olivine basalt and the alkalic series. The nomenclature adopted for the rocks within these three groups and their main characteristics are summarized in Table 3.1.

The basal tholeiitic volcanics represent a series of transitional to subalkaline basalts ranging from olivine-normative tholeiites through to quartz-normative tholeiites.

The Paterno alkali olivine basalt is limited in volume and outcrop occurrence and is nepheline-normative (<5%) and with a Thornton and Tuttle Differentiation Index (DI) of 33.5 falls into the alkali olivine basalt field as defined by Wilkinson (1974).

The lavas of the alkalic series comprise a mildly alkaline suite ranging from hawaiite to trachyte in composition. In the (Na_2O + K_2O) vs. SiO_2 plot of Cox *et al.* (1979) these lavas plot in the field of trachybasalts and, indeed, Duncan (1978) labelled this suite the Trachybasaltic series. Recent Italian literature, however, refers to this group as the alkalic series and this name is used here to maintain uniformity. The alkalic series, showing the greatest diversification in rock type of the lavas of Etna, poses the main problem in nomenclature.

Classically, the more basic members of alkali olivine basalt series have been identified in terms of their feldspar content (Muir and Tilley, 1961), hawaiite being characterized by andesine plagioclase feldspar and mugearite by oligoclase plagioclase feldspar. In fine-grained volcanic rocks the mineralogy is often difficult to determine and, also, there is usually a range of plagioclase compositions from phenocryst core to groundmass microlite within any one sample. More recently, classifications have been based on the CIPW norm using either the Thornton and Tuttle Differentiation Index or normative feldspar compositions. The CIPW norm, however, is sensitive to the FeO/Fe_2O_3 ratio which is susceptible to post-eruption processes. It is considered more satisfactory, therefore, to use major-element chemistry as a basis for classification of the lavas of the Etnean alkalic series. Silica content shows a continuous

Table 3.1 Nomenclature of Etna lavas

BASAL THOLEIITIC VOLCANICS		
General characteristics:	hy-normative, subalkaline, augite+pigeonite in modal mineralogy	
Rock types:		
Olivine tholeiite	(ol+hy normative)	
Quartz tholeiite	(qz+hy normative)	
PATERNO ALKALI OLIVINE BASALT		
General characteristics:	ne-normative, alkaline, Ca-augite in modal mineralogy	
Rock type:		
Alkali olivine basalt		
ALKALIC SERIES		
General characteristics:	ne-through to hy+qz-normative, alkaline, Ca-augite in modal mineralogy	
Rock types:		
Alkali olivine basalt	<47 % (w/w) $Si0_2$	Thornton–Tuttle DI <34
Hawaiite	47–52% (w/w) $Si0_2$	Thornton–Tuttle DI 34–46
Basic mugearite	52–55% (w/w) $Si0_2$	Thornton–Tuttle DI 46–56
Mugearite	55–58% (w/w) $Si0_2$	Thornton–Tuttle DI 56–65
Benmoreite	58–62% (w/w) $Si0_2$	Thornton–Tuttle DI 65–80

variation across the suite and is used as the criterion for distinguishing the different rock-types (Table 3.1). The hawaiites and mugearites defined by this scheme have modal plagioclase compositions more An-rich than would be anticipated by the petrographic criteria of Muir and Tilley (1961); this is due to the fact that Etnean magmas are richer in Al_2O_3 and CaO but poorer in Na_2O than most alkaline suites. The mugearitic lavas of Etna are subdivided into two groups – basic mugearites and mugearites – as there is a marked difference between the more basic mugearites which have a basaltic texture and the more evolved mugearites which have a trachytic texture (Duncan, 1978).

It is important to note the Continental terminology for Etnean lavas which is frequently used in Italian literature and which represents the main source of information on Mount Etna. Generally Italian scientists have used the classification system proposed by Streckeisen (1967) in which alkali andesite corresponds to hawaiite and latit-andesite to mugearite and benmoreite. The term, tephrite, is used to describe some of the more undersaturated basic lavas. Strictly speaking, however, tephrites should be olivine-free (Hatch, Wells and Wells, 1972) and, therefore, this term should not be used for basic lavas of Etna which generally contain olivine phenocrysts. Basanite would be the appropriate name for olivine-bearing undersaturated lavas with more than 5% normative nepheline.

3.4 Stratigraphy

The determination of the stratigraphy of an active basaltic volcano presents a complex task. Ribbon-like lava flows hamper any kind of lateral correlation and even pyroclastic deposits tend to be of limited aerial extent due either to prevailing wind conditions during eruption or as a result of subsequent fluvial erosion. Etna, in particular, with its high current rate of resurfacing by lava – Guest and Murray (1979) estimate a rate of 0.26 km^2 per year between 1000 m and 2000 m a.s.l. – provides only limited exposure of the more ancient products. There is a fairly extensive record of documented eruptions over the last 500 years and a rather more patchy record going back for almost a further 2000 years. However, for the remaining hundred thousand years or so of the volcano's history data are sparse. The Valle del Bove (Fig. 3.6), a major horseshoe-shaped incision into the eastern flank of the volcano, provides valuable exposure of some of the older volcanic centres and their structural relations. In addition, the interrelationships between lavas and the terrace sequence of the Simeto River have contributed to the stratigraphic framework. It is difficult to correlate the isolated patches of older volcanics which are surrounded by younger lavas and have no direct contact with the important exposures in the Valle del Bove; petrological and geochemical characteristics are rarely sufficient in themselves for correlation purposes.

A major factor in the development of the stratigraphy is the establishment of a chronological framework. With activity dating back to mid to early Pleistocene only the youngest ($< 70\,000$ BP) part of the history of Etna is suitable for ^{14}C dating and the lavas are generally too young and too low in potassium for K/Ar dating. Condomines and Tanguy (1976) used the $^{230}Th/^{238}U$ radioactive disequilibrium technique to provide radiometric dates for the Paterno alkali olivine basalt and an ancient hawaiite of the alkalic series. Further $^{230}Th/^{238}U$ disequilibrium dating has been carried out by Condomines *et al.* (1982) and these data are incorporated in the stratigraphic table (Table 3.2). A preliminary investigation into the use of thermoluminescent methods for dating lavas of Etna proved disappointing and it seems unlikely that at the present time a useful dating method can be established (Aitken *et al.*, 1968). Techniques making use of remnant magnetism have been investigated regarding dating of the historic sequence but as yet have provided little contribution. The association of lavas with fossiliferous sediments has been of value in the correlation of some of the older lavas.

On Etna a further complication is provided by the input of geologists from Belgium, Britain, France and Italy who have all worked on the stratigraphy of the volcano generating different schemes and nomenclature. The stratigraphic scheme

Table 3.2 A stratigraphic correlation of the volcanic rocks of Mount Etna

	Units	*Centres*	*Descriptions*	*Events*	*River Simeto terrace sequence*	*age* (see footnotes (1)–(10))
Alkalic Series	Recent Mongibello	Present Centre	Includes historic eruptions, mainly hawaiites	Minor collapse events in summit area	Terrace 1	
		Piano		Caldera collapse		
				Formation of the Valle del Bove		5000 BP [1]
	Ancient Mongibello	Leone	Hawaiites, basic mugearites	Caldera collapse		
		Ellittico	Hawaiites, basic mugearites, mugearites, benmoreites	Caldera collapse		?6000–5000 BP [2]
		Belvedere	Hawaiites, basic mugearites		?Terrace 2	
		Vavalaci	Hawaiites, basic mugearites, mugearites, benmoreites	Caldera collapse		?14 500 BP [3]
					Terrace 3	18 000 BP [4]
	Trifoglietto	Trifoglietto II	Basic mugearites, mugearites	Major phreatomagmatic activity		26 000 BP [5] ?65 800 BP [6]

	Pre-Trifoglietto	Calanna and other ancient centres of as yet problematic status, e.g. Tardaria Trifoglietto I	Poorly exposed, mainly hawaiites	Major caldera collapse Little known about early alkalic series activity	Terrace 4	?106 000 BP (7) ?143 000 BP (8)
Basal Tholeiitic Volcanics			Tholeiitic basalt	Intrusive neck at Motta S. Anastasia	Terrace 6	
	Alkali olivine basalt	Paterno Cone	Alkali olivine basalt	Eroded cone		210 000 BP (9)
			Sub-aerial tholeiitic basalts	Adrano	Terrace 7	300 000 BP (10)
			Submarine tholeiitic basalts and intrusives	Acicastello/Acitrezza		

(1) 5000±130 BP, radiocarbon date of final stages of the formation of the Valle del Bove (Kieffer, 1970a).
(2) 6000–5000 BP based on range of radiocarbon dates from the Upper Tephra which may relate to the formation of the Ellittico caldera or a later event (Guest *et al.*, 1984).
(3) 14 500 BP, $^{230}Th/^{238}U$ disequilibrium date for trachyte lava in west wall of Valle del Bove (Condomines *et al.*, 1982), possibly from the Vavalaci centre.
(4) 18 000±400 BP, radiocarbon date from palaeosol overlying Terrace 3 of the Simeto (Kieffer, 1979).
(5) Based on 26 380±340 BP radiocarbon date from the Lower Tephra (Guest *et al.*, 1984).
(6) 65 800 BP $^{230}Th/^{238}U$ disequilibrium date (Condomines *et al.*, 1982), from base of Trifoglietto II succession(?).
(7) 106 000 BP $^{230}Th/^{238}U$ disequilibrium date of lava capping Terrace 4 of the Simeto (Condomines *et al.*, 1982).
(8) 143 000 BP $^{230}Th/^{238}U$ disequilibrium date of ancient lava of the alkalic series exposed in Timpa S. Tecla (Condomines *et al.*, 1982).
(9) 210 000 BP $^{230}Th/^{238}U$ disequilibrium date of alkali olivine basalt from the eroded cone (Condomines and Tanguy, 1976).
(10) >300 000 BP is based on stratigraphic correlation (Chester and Duncan, 1982).

Condomines *et al.* (1982) consider that the error on age determination for their $^{230}Th/^{238}U$ dates is generally 10%, sometimes higher for greater ages.

Sample 709 of Condomines *et al.* is not included in this correlation as it is considered that this zeolite-bearing alkali basalt from the Cyclops Islands is likely to have been subjected to metasomation.

Fig. 3.6 The western wall of the Valle del Bove. (Photograph: T. J. O. Sanderson.)

adopted in this account is based on that of the Geological Map (Romano *et al.*, 1979), the Geological Memoir of Etna (Romano, 1982) and from recent literature; this is summarized in Table 3.2.

3.4.1 Basal tholeiitic volcanics

The earliest activity of Etna occurred in the Pleistocene with the eruption of tholeiitic basalts from fissures which transected the coastline of the time (Rittmann, 1973). In the west these lavas were erupted under subaerial conditions whereas in the east they were erupted in a submarine environment. In the south of the area now occupied by Etna the coastline at the time lay further to the west of its present position, somewhere between Paterno and Misterbianco.

The age of the basal tholeiitic volcanics is uncertain and the precise relationship between the activity in the east and west is difficult to establish. Nevertheless, as in both the east and west the tholeiitic basalts occur at the base of the volcanic sequence and as they have similar petrology it is generally accepted that they belong to the same phase of volcanism (Romano, 1982). The submarine volcanics of the east are intruded into marine clays, the *Argille marnose azzurre* (Wezel, 1967) of lower Pleistocene age and in places broke

(a)

(b)

Fig. 3.7 (a) Lavas of the basal tholeiitic volcanics resting on Terrace 7 of the River Simeto near Adrano. The lavas show well-developed columnar jointing. The River Simeto can be seen in the bottom left of the picture. (Photograph: A. M. Duncan.) (b) A quarry section near Paterno showing lavas of the basal tholeiitic volcanics overlying fluviatile sands and gravels, of the Terrace-7 deposits. (Photograph: A. M. Duncan.)

through to the sea-floor forming pillow lavas and hyaloclastites (Cristofolini, 1973). In the west the basal tholeiitic volcanics overlie the fluvial sediments of Terrace 7 (Fig. 3.7) the uppermost and oldest terrace of the Simeto River (Cristofolini, 1967; Kieffer, 1971; Chester and Duncan, 1979, 1982). The presence of clasts of tholeiitic basalt in some of the upper gravels of the fluvial sediments of Terrace 7 indicates that the basal tholeiitic volcanism was at least in part contemporaneous with the formation of Terrace 7 deposits. These terrace deposits rest on the Pleistocene sediments of the *Argille marnose azzurre* and the overlying sands and gravels of probable in-shore, estuarine origin (Chester and Duncan, 1982). Chester and Duncan propose the following sequence of events for the Lower Simeto area: before the onset of Etnean volcanism there was deposition of marine clays during the Portuensian (Sicilian) stage of the Pleistocene, this was followed by marine regression with the deposition of near-shore sediments throughout much of the lower Simeto area. Deeper water conditions, however, continued in the area to the north of Catania. It is uncertain exactly how much time elapsed after the deposition of the Pleistocene near-shore sediments before the fluvial sedimentation of Terrace 7.

On the basis of the association of the submarine basal tholeiitic volcanism in the east with the *Argille marnose azzurre*, Cristofolini (1972, 1973) suggests that this earliest volcanic activity is of late Sicilian age or younger. Chester and Duncan (1979, 1982) propose an age for the basal tholeiitic volcanics in the west based on their relationship with Terrace 7 of the Simeto. The alkali olivine basalt of the Paterno cone, which has an age between that of Terraces 6 and 7 of the Simeto, has been radiometrically dated by the $^{230}Th/^{238}U$ disequilibrium technique (Condomines and Tanguy, 1976) at about 210 000 BP. Terrace 7, therefore, has an age greater than about 210 000 BP, and Chester and Duncan (1982) suggest that this terrace may correlate with the continental Rianian stage of Ambrosetti *et al.* (1972), which is dated at between 200 000 and 368 000 BP, or be slightly older and relate to an earlier erosive phase. This is broadly in agreement with Rittmann (1973) who proposed an age of around 300 000 BP for the basal tholeiitic volcanics. It may be that the tholeiitic basalts in the Adrano area represent the final phases of the basal tholeiitic volcanism, indeed, Romano (1982) considers that the subaerial tholeiitic basalts are younger than the tholeiites in the east.

In the west the basal tholeiitic volcanics flowed into the Simeto valley as fluid lavas with pahoehoe morphology. This sequence of lavas is up to 40 m thick with several flow units exposed without intervening soil or detritus horizons and this indicates eruption over a limited time interval. Near to Adrano, pillow lavas wrapped in hyaloclastite occur at the base of the tholeiite lava sequence and these are interpreted as having formed when lava flowed into the river or a nearby lake (Kieffer, 1975). To the south of Paterno, an exposure in a quarry reveals the tholeiite lavas overlying a discontinuous palaeosol which is developed on top of the fluvial sands, gravels and clays of Terrace 7 (Chester and Duncan, 1979, 1982). This palaeosol, up to 0.5 m thick, is similar to the *rotlehm* type of Kubiena (1953) which is typically associated with a seasonally humid, semi-tropical climate. Further to the south-east, at Valcorrente, fragments of tholeiite pillow lava have been found by Professor R. Cristofolini and this may indicate that this area was close to the coastline of the time. Subsequent uplift in the south-eastern part of the Etna area has raised Terrace 7 and the overlying tholeiite lavas up to 350 m above the present level of the river forming a distinctive scarp feature between Adrano and Paterno.

To the east, the basal tholeiitic volcanics are exposed in the vicinity of Acitrezza and Acicastello (Fig. 3.8). Here they are emplaced as high-level intrusions in the Pleistocene marine clays, the *Argille marnose azzurre*; and pillow lavas and hyaloclastites have formed where the magma broke through to the sea-floor (Sturiale, 1968; Cristofolini, 1974). The extent of these volcanics is unclear as the area is largely covered by younger products of Etna. A more detailed account of this classic exposure of pillow lavas and hyaloclastites is given in Chapter 4.

The basaltic plug at Motta S. Anastasia (Fig.

Fig. 3.8 Pillow lavas of the basal tholeiitic volcanics at Acicastello. The seaward end of the cliffs is composed, largely of hyaloclastite which form beds dipping steeply inland. One of the Cyclopean Islands can be seen in the background. (Photograph: A. M. Duncan.)

3.9) just to the south of Etna, belongs to the basal tholeiitic volcanics and is interpreted as a high-level intrusion into the *Argille marnose azzurre* and overlying conglomerates (Cristofolini and Puglisi, 1974). The intrusion of the plug has tilted and lithified the conglomerates but there is no evidence to suggest that it fed any kind of volcanic activity. The relationship between these conglomerates and the Simeto terrace sequence is uncertain. The conglomerates are poorly sorted with clasts ranging up to 10 cm, including some basalt fragments, and in terms of altitude they most closely correlate with Terrace 6 of the sequence proposed by Chester and Duncan (1982). If this is so then it would indicate that the Motta S. Anastasia plug post-dates Terrace 6 in age and, therefore, the basal tholeiitic volcanism continued till after 210 000 BP.

3.4.2 *Paterno alkali olivine basalt*

The town of Paterno is built alongside on old, highly eroded volcanic cone which forms a distinctive mound some 70 m high on the very south-western periphery of the volcano. The mound is surmounted by a Norman keep which dominates the town and provides a fine view of Etna. As already discussed, the Paterno cone is considered younger than Terrace 7 but older than Terrace 6 of the Simeto sequence (Chester and Duncan, 1982) and radiometric dating by the $^{230}Th/^{238}U$ disequilibrium technique (Condomines and Tanguy, 1976) provides an age of 210 000 BP for an alkali olivine basalt from this cone. Erosion has revealed high-level dykes and plugs of distinctive olivine-phyric basalt within the welded spatter and ash layers of the cone. A vent agglomerate is exposed

Fig. 3.9 The Norman keep surmounting the basaltic plug of the basal tholeiitic volcanics at Motta S. Anastasia. (Photograph: A. M. Duncan.)

on the south-west part of the cone bounded by a sub-vertical sheet of basalt. The breccia is composed of angular blocks of basalt up to 1 m in size and smaller fragments of sandstone set in a matrix of very altered vesicular basalt. The alkali olivine basalt of Paterno is similar, petrographically and geochemically, to ancient alkali basalts that occur in the Piedimonte area of the north-east flank of Etna (Spadea, 1972; Cristofolini *et al.*, 1977b) and it may be that they belong to the same early phase of alkali olivine basalt volcanism. However, at present there are insufficient data to substantiate this relationship.

3.4.3 Alkalic series

Lack of exposure and difficulties of correlation create considerable uncertainty in the interpretation of the age and nature of the early stages of volcanism in the alkalic series. In the Simeto valley hawaiite lavas of the alkalic series occur in association with Terrace 4 (Chester and Duncan, 1982) and this indicates a considerable time-gap after the cessation of the basal tholeiitic volcanism and the eruption of the ancient alkali olivine basalts before the onset of the alkalic series activity. On the coast, to the north of Catania, hawaiite lava is exposed at the foot of the Acireale timpa (fault scarp) and this must be one of the oldest exposed lavas of the alkalic series and has been dated at about 95 000 BP by the $^{230}Th/^{238}U$ disequilibrium technique (Condomines and Tanguy, 1976). Bearing in mind the possibility that older volcanics of the alkalic series may be concealed beneath Etna, data currently available support a date of around 100 000–150 000 BP for the onset of this activity.

The activity of the alkalic series has constructed a series of volcanoes of central-vent type which overlap in space and possibly to some extent in time. The presence of these centres is best revealed

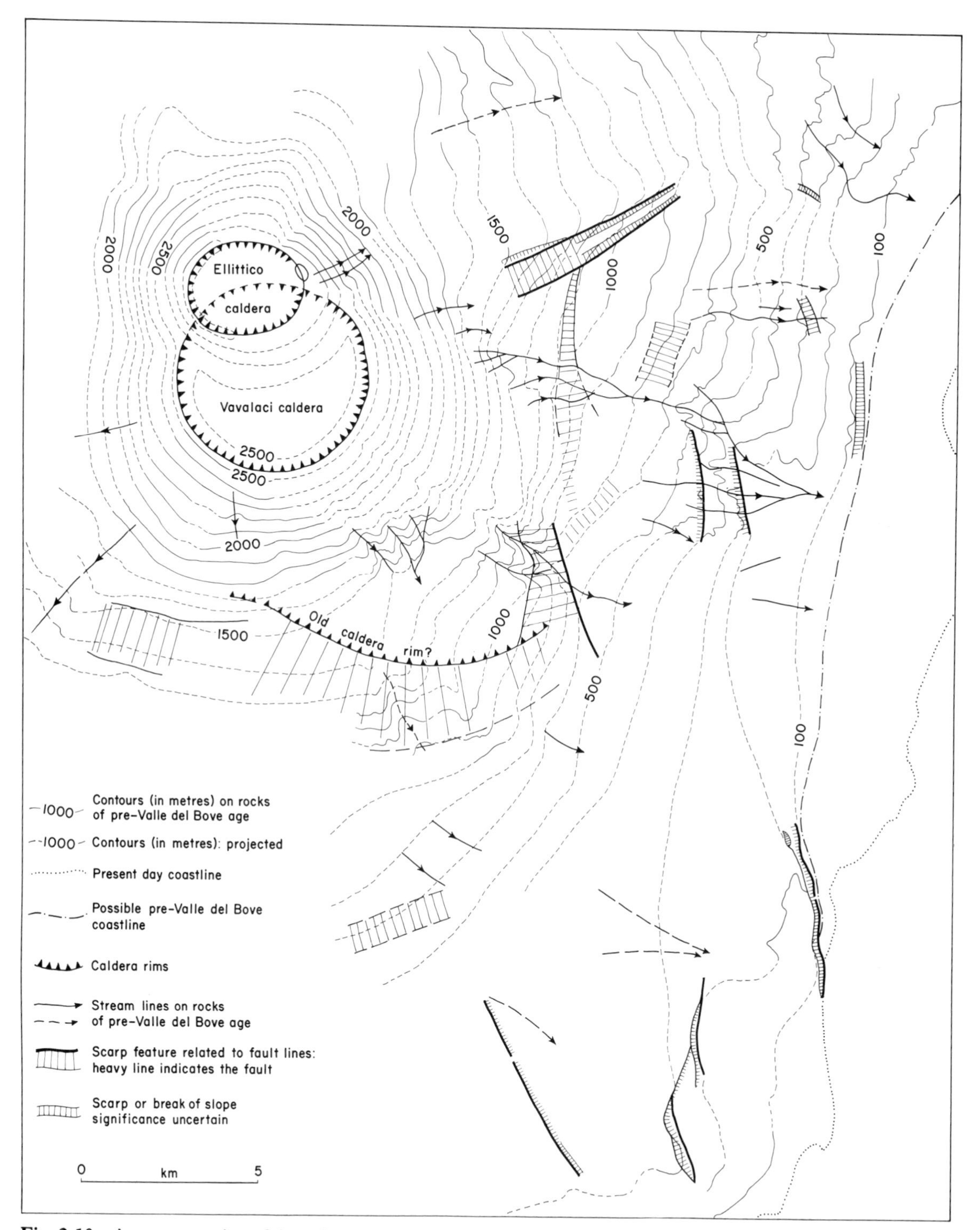

Fig. 3.10 A reconstruction of the palaeogeography of the summit and eastern flank of Etna immediately prior to the formation of the Valle del Bove. (From Guest *et al.*, 1984.)

by exposures in the walls of the Valle del Bove and, indeed, in the last century Sartorius vön Waltershausen and Lyell (1858) recognized the presence of an ancient volcano, Trifoglietto, which was located in the region now occupied by the Valle del Bove. The status and relationships of the Trifoglietto II centre are now well established and this centre is a convenient unit in the stratigraphy of the alkalic series (Table 3.2). Activity prior to this centre is not so well known and is referred to as pre-Trifoglietto (ancient eruptive centres) and is considered first.

The Calanna centre identified in the south-east corner of the Valle del Bove in the Valle del Calanna is the oldest exposed centre of the alkalic series (Klerkx, 1970; Romano and Sturiale, 1975; McGuire, 1982). The original Calanna cone has been strongly eroded and obscured by younger volcanics and all that is visible is a mass of vent agglomerate, intruded by dyke-like sheets of hawaiite, and scattered inliers of bedded ash and scoria (McGuire, 1982). The dykes are formed of porphyritic hawaiite, similar in chemistry to the historic lavas of Etna, but in addition to the normal suite of phenocrysts, kaersutite is also occasionally present (Klerkx, 1970; McGuire, 1982).

Recognition of ancient centres outside the Valle del Bove is based in the main on morphological criteria. As many of the centres have erupted lavas of similar composition, petrological criteria are often difficult to establish. A major aspect of the morphological interpretation is the recognition of annular kinks in the volcano profile as representing the rims of ancient infilled calderas, (see Fig. 3.10) (Guest, 1980). Such investigations have suggested the presence of an early volcanic centre situated to the south of the Valle del Bove. This has been recognized by a steep increase in slope rising to an arcuate crest and this is interpreted as the buried upper slopes of an old volcano truncated by a summit caldera which has been subsequently infilled (Kieffer, 1974a; Cristofolini *et al.*, 1982). This ancient volcano has been named the Tardaria centre (Romano and Sturiale, 1981) and though only a segment of the proposed caldera rim is preserved it does appear to centre on Calanna and it may be that this is part of the buried profile of the Calanna volcano. In the northern wall of the Valle del Bove, Klerkx (1970) identifies a further pre-Trifoglietto centre, Trifoglietto I. However, recent work (S. M. Habesch, personal communication, 1983) on the northern wall of the Valle del Bove casts doubt on the status of the Trifoglietto I.

The Trifoglietto II centre built up some 4 km to the south-east of the site now occupied by the summit of Etna. This centre probably built up within and subsequently overlapping the Tardaria caldera (see Fig. 3.14(a)). Although Klerkx (1968, 1970) refers to the major centre as Trifoglietto II, there may have been other centres of similar age now buried by younger volcanics. McGuire (1982) estimates that the Trifoglietto II cone reached a height between 2500 and 2600 m above present sea level. Most of the Trifoglietto II volcano has been removed by the formation of the Valle del Bove. The activity of Trifoglietto II began with an explosive phase building up a cone of predominantly scoria with thin interbedded lavas (Fig. 3.11). This pyroclastic sequence reaches a maximum exposed thickness of 300 m (McGuire, 1982). On the basis of granulometric and petrographic analysis, McGuire considers that this phase of activity was largely phreatomagmatic. The lavas are predominantly aphyric mugearites with minor amounts of plagioclase, augite, olivine and kaersutite phenocrysts. The initial explosive activity was followed by an effusive phase with pyroclastics forming a very subordinate proportion of the eruptive products. McGuire divides the effusive products into the upper, middle and lower lava groups. The lower lava group comprises mugearites, characterized by large augite and abundant plagioclase phenocrysts and reaches a thickness of 150 m. The middle lava group is the thickest – up to 400 m – and is mainly composed of basic mugearites whereas the upper lava group is thinner – around 125 m – and is made up of distinctive feldspar-phyric basic mugearites. Klerkx (1968) quotes a ^{14}C date of 25 000 BP for a sample of carbonized wood collected from within the effusive products of Trifoglietto II and this provides a minimum age for most of the activity of the centre. However, Condomines *et al.*, (1982) using the $^{230}Th/^{238}U$ disequilibrium technique obtain two

Fig. 3.11 Interbedded scoria and thin lava flows of the Trifoglietto II centre exposed in the southern wall of the Valle del Bove. (Photograph: A. M. Duncan.)

dates, 65 000 BP and 54 000 BP, from lava samples collected from the Trifoglietto II cone. These two lavas are separated by a vertical distance of about 100 m in the cliff face.

The age relations of patches of older volcanics surrounded by young lavas, exposed on the lower flanks of the volcano, are often extremely difficult to determine. On the southern and eastern sides of the volcano a series of prehistoric pyroclastic deposits occur and these have been divided by Romano *et al.* (1979) into the upper and lower tuffs. These deposits, however, are not consolidated and Guest *et al.* (1984) refer to them as the upper and lower tephra. The lower tephra consist of yellow-brown ashes with subordinate lapilli horizons and are up to 10 m thick. Granulometric and shape analysis indicate that these pyroclastics are predominantly phreatomagmatic in origin. The ash and particularly the lapilli horizons are rich in mafic crystals: clinopyroxene, olivine and kaersutite, indicative that the magma was basic in composition. The presence of kaersutite in these ashes suggests a relationship with Trifoglietto II materials in which kaersutite is relatively common. Fragments of carbonized wood from the lower tephra have provided a ^{14}C date of 26 380 ± 340 BP, dating carried out by the NERC Radiocarbon Laboratory and reported by Guest *et al.* (1984); this represents a close temporal link with the Trifoglietto II. These ashes are among the most voluminous pyroclastics of Etna and may correlate with an ash horizon dated at around 20 000 BP, attributed to Etna, located in submarine cores from the Ionian Sea (Keller *et al.*, 1978). The presence of amphibole in this ash horizon lends support to such a link.

Around Milo and downslope to the east there is an area of volcaniclastics, largely made up of mudflows, which Romano *et al.* (1979) termed the upper lahars and related to the upper tephra. The clasts in the mudflow units, however, are similar to material of the Trifoglietto II volcano and in one locality these mudflows are associated with ashes similar in their characteristics to the lower tephra. On account of this Guest *et al.* (1984) consider that these mudflows are of the same age as the lower tephra and have resulted from water-lubricated mass movement of material from the Trifoglietto volcano during a violent explosive phase. This explosive activity of Trifoglietto II around 26 000 BP correlates with the Italian Pontinian Pleistocene stage which is the approximate time equivalent to the northern European Würm glacial. During this cold phase it is likely that Etna supported considerable round-the-year snow cover, and Guest *et al.* argue that these climatic conditions might account for the phreatomagmatic eruptions and generation of lahars associated with Trifoglietto II.

The sequence of post-Trifoglietto activity can be most clearly established in the Valle del Bove. The southern wall of the Valle del Bove exposes lavas of the Vavalaci centre unconformably overlying the products of the Trifoglietto II volcano (Lo Giudice, 1970; McGuire, 1982). The lavas of the Vavalaci centre range from hawaiite to mugearite in composition and show a chemical trend distinct from that of the preceding Trifoglietto II volcano. A thin sequence of basic mugearite lavas which unconformably overlie the middle and upper lava groups of Trifoglietto on the southern rim of the Valle del Bove and form the capping to Monte Zoccolaro are assigned to a Zoccolaro centre by McGuire (1982). The relationship between the Zoccolaro lavas and the Vavalaci centre is uncertain. In the western wall of the Valle del Bove a sequence of flat-lying lavas, the Belvedere, occur overlying lavas of the Vavalaci centre (Lo Giudice *et al.*, 1974). The scoria, ashes and agglomerates that come between the Vavalaci and Belvedere lavas are called the Cuvigghiuni centre, by McGuire (1982). There is some controversy, however, as to whether the Cuvigghiuni qualifies as a separate centre (Romano, 1982; Guest *et al.*, 1984). Guest (1980) suggests that the activity of the Vavalaci centre was terminated by caldera collapse and that the well-defined break in slope at 2500 m a.s.l. on the southern part of the summit cone represents the rim of this ancient caldera and that the flat-lying Belvedere lavas infill this Vavalaci caldera.

The Valle del Leone and a covering of younger volcanics frustrates the correlation of the succession exposed in the southern and western walls of the Valle del Bove with the sequences exposed in the northern wall. Romano and Guest (1979) recognize a centre, which they name Ellittico, exposed in the northern wall and built up of thin lava flows, ranging from hawaiite to mugearite in composition. The activity of the Ellittico centre was terminated by the formation of a summit caldera about 3 km in diameter. This caldera is filled with thick (up to 20 m), flat-lying lavas ranging in composition from hawaiite to mugearite, but showing a rather strongly alkali-enriched trend, erupted from the Leone centre which built up on the eastern flank of the Ellittico volcano (see Fig. 4.40 of Chapter 4). The end of activity of the Leone centre was marked by the formation of a small collapse-pit or caldera, about 1 km in diameter, at the summit of the cone (Romano and Guest, 1979). It is of interest that in the case of both the Vavalaci–Belvedere and Ellittico–Leone sequences, mildly alkaline cone-building lavas are followed by caldera-collapse and infilling by a series of more strongly alkali-enriched lavas. McGuire notes this relationship and suggests that Vavalaci correlates with Ellittico and Belvedere with Leone. However, a detailed examination of the spatial relationships of the Ellittico and Vavalaci tentatively indicates that the Ellittico centre continued activity after the collapse of the Vavalaci caldera (Guest *et al.*, 1984) and it is suggested that there were two cycles of caldera collapse and lava infilling: Vavalaci–Belvedere followed by Ellittico–Leone.

Away from the Valle del Bove, on the lower

Fig. 3.12 Ignimbrite unit showing crude columnar jointing exposed in the walls of a ravine near Biancavilla on the south-western periphery of the volcano. Mount Etna is clearly visible in the background. (Photograph: J. E. Guest.)

flanks of Etna, it is generally difficult to relate prehistoric volcanics to the stratigraphy of the volcano. The hawaiite lavas that cap Terrace 3 of the Simeto River, stretching from S. Maria di Licodia in the south to the confluence with the River de Serravalle, are correlated by Romano *et al.* (1979) with pre-Trifoglietto activity. Kieffer (1979), however, reports a ^{14}C date of 18 000 ± 400 BP for a palaeosol developed on top of the Terrace 3 fluvial deposits but overlain by the capping of hawaiite lavas and this indicates that the lava has an age not much younger than 18 000 BP and is younger than the Trifoglietto II centre (Chester and Duncan, 1982). In the Adrano area, which forms the lower south-west flank of the volcano, there has been little resurfacing by historic lavas, and a substantial area of prehistoric volcanics are exposed (Duncan, 1978). Endogenous breccia domes of mugearite and benmoreite lava occur on the lower flanks of the volcano in this area near Biancavilla, S. Maria di Licodia and Poggio la Naca (Kieffer, 1974b; Duncan, 1978). Near Biancavilla these domes are overlain by ignimbrite and mudflow deposits (Fig. 3.12) of benmoreitic composition (Kieffer, 1974b; Duncan, 1976a). A carbonized tree trunk found in the ignimbrite deposit near Biancavilla has a ^{14}C age of between 15 000 and 15 500 BP (Romano, 1982). This would place the ignimbrites, mudflows and breccia domes in the Ancient Mongibello phase of activity (Table 3.2). The clasts in the ignimbrites and the lava from the domes have similar petrology, and the close temporal and spatial association would support that the eruptions of the domes and ignimbrites were closely related. Petrologically these mugearitic and benmoreitic volcanics are similar to the more evolved products of Vavalaci and Ellittico; indeed Cristofolini and Lo Giudice (1969) relate them to Vavalaci whereas Romano *et al.* (1979) include them with Ellittico. Kieffer (1973) suggests that the ignimbrites may be associated with the collapse of the Ellittico caldera, however with an age of around 15 000 BP it is more likely that they correlate with Vavalaci (see Table 3.2).

The upper tephra lie on the outer slopes of the Valle del Bove and are made up of two distinctive units. The lower unit consists of up to 2 m of fine-grained yellow ash with scattered lapilli and occasional accretionary lapilli. Grain size characteristics, the yellow colouration and the presence of accretionary lapilli suggest that these ashes originated from phreatomagmatic activity (Guest *et al.*, 1984). The occurrence of scattered carbonized wood fragments within the lower unit of the upper tephra indicates that the ash was hot enough to ignite vegetation and the fact that they are incorporated within the deposit might suggest surge activity, though as yet there is no direct evidence to support this. The ^{14}C dates of these carbonized wood fragments give ages ranging from 10 000 to 2400 BP (Romano *et al.*, 1979) and 6680 to 2710 BP (dating carried out by the NERC Radiocarbon Laboratory and reported in Guest *et al.*, 1984). The reasons for the range of dates from what appears to be the same ash horizon are unclear but values tend to cluster about 6000 BP and this would place the lower unit of the upper tephra within the ancient Mongibello phase of activity. One possible source of error in radiocarbon dating of active volcanoes is the localized influx into the atmosphere of magmatic CO_2 which contains little or no ^{14}C. Sulerzhitzky (1969) argues that the effect of volcanic activity giving a decrease of ^{14}C concentration in plants may be of significance in radiocarbon dating of objects less than 10 000 years in age by giving too old a date. Indeed, Carbonelle *et al.* (1982) note that in their measurements of June 1980 the CO_2 baseline in the ambient air on the slopes of the volcano was persistently more than the normal atmospheric background which suggests a contribution of CO_2 from volcanic sources. A black lapilli bed, 35 cm thick, forms the base of the upper unit of the upper tephra. This upper unit consists of dark lapilli and ash beds, the deposits are well sorted and show grain size characteristics typical of strombolian-style eruptions. The lapilli fragments consist of fresh, glassy scoria containing a suite of phenocryst minerals similar to those of historic lavas. These ashes may be rather younger than the lower unit and correlate with the recent Mongibello phase of activity (Table 3.2).

The excavation of the Valle del Bove must post-date the Leone centre as lavas from this centre are exposed in the walls of the depression. It is likely that the Valle del Bove formed as a result of gravity sliding towards the sea with the development of distinctive coalescing scallop features (Fig. 3.13 and Chapter 4). The Chiancone, a fan-shaped accumulation of sandy agglomerates developed on the coast in front of the Valle del Bove, is interpreted by Guest *et al.* (1984) as having been derived from landslide debris which has undergone substantial fluvial reworking. The Valle del Bove presents a valuable exposure of the interior structure of the volcano and largely on the basis of information provided by these exposures it has been possible, at least in part, to reconstruct the probable evolution of Etna (see Fig. 3.14). A geological map of the area is shown in Figure 3.15.

The activity of the last 3000 – 5000 years, since the formation of the Valle del Bove, belongs to the recent Mongibello phase and this is continuing at present. This period has been characterized by the eruption of rather basic lavas of hawaiite and basic mugearite composition. The eruptive activity during this time has been characterized by three types (Guest, 1973a): (a) nearly continuous emissions of lava at low effusion rates from the summit (the *terminal* activity of Rittmann (1973)) or near the summit (*sub-terminal* activity); (b) flank eruptions of limited duration with relatively high effusion rates; and (c) occasional short-lived eruptions at the summit.

One of the earliest recognizable features of the recent Mongibello phase of activity is the Piano caldera (Fig. 3.16). When Mount Etna is viewed from the west, the Cratere del Piano is clearly visible as a broad platform at 2540 m a.s.l. upon which the Summit Cone has developed (Fig. 3.17). This caldera was probably in existence at the time

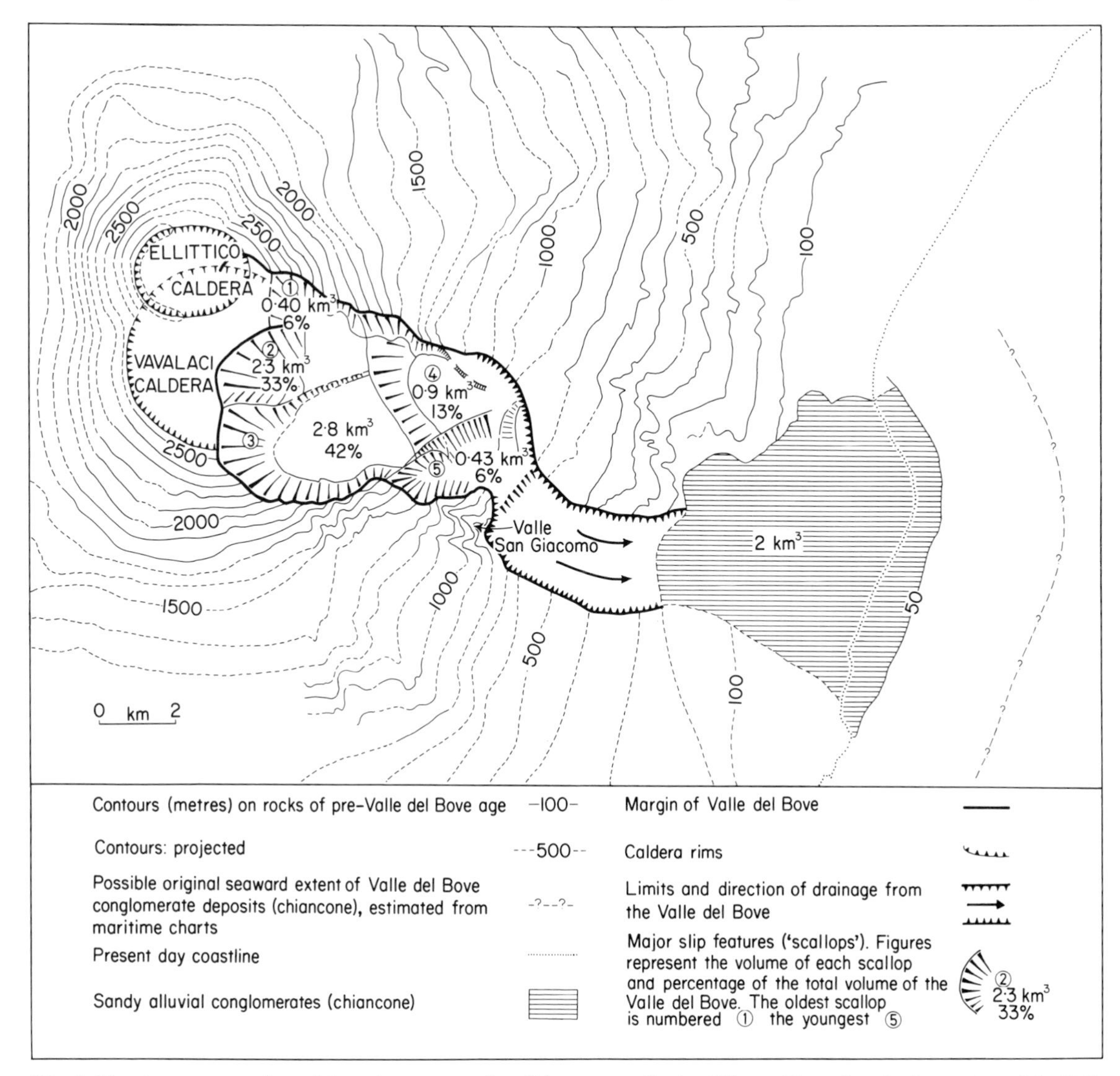

Fig. 3.13 A reconstruction of the palaeogeography of the eastern flank of Mount Etna after the formation of the Valle del Bove. (From Guest *et al.*, 1984.)

of Empedocles with further collapses occurring in 1444, 1537 and 1669 (Guest, 1973a). The last major collapse was probably the event described by Winchilsea (1669) in his eyewitness account of the 1669 eruption written to King Charles II. In these more recent events it is clear that documented observations provide a valuable source of information. There is a fairly complete documented record of flank eruptions going back 500 years and patchy accounts going back a further 2000 years (Fig. 3.18). This has enabled a reconstruction of the activity of the historic period to be carried out and is summarized in Table 3.3. This information provides a valuable and, by comparison with most other volcanoes, unique contribution to the interpretation of volcanic processes. Over the last fifteen years there has been a fairly complete study of eruptive activity and a record of changes in the topography of the summit area between 1973 and 1983 is shown in Fig. 3.19.

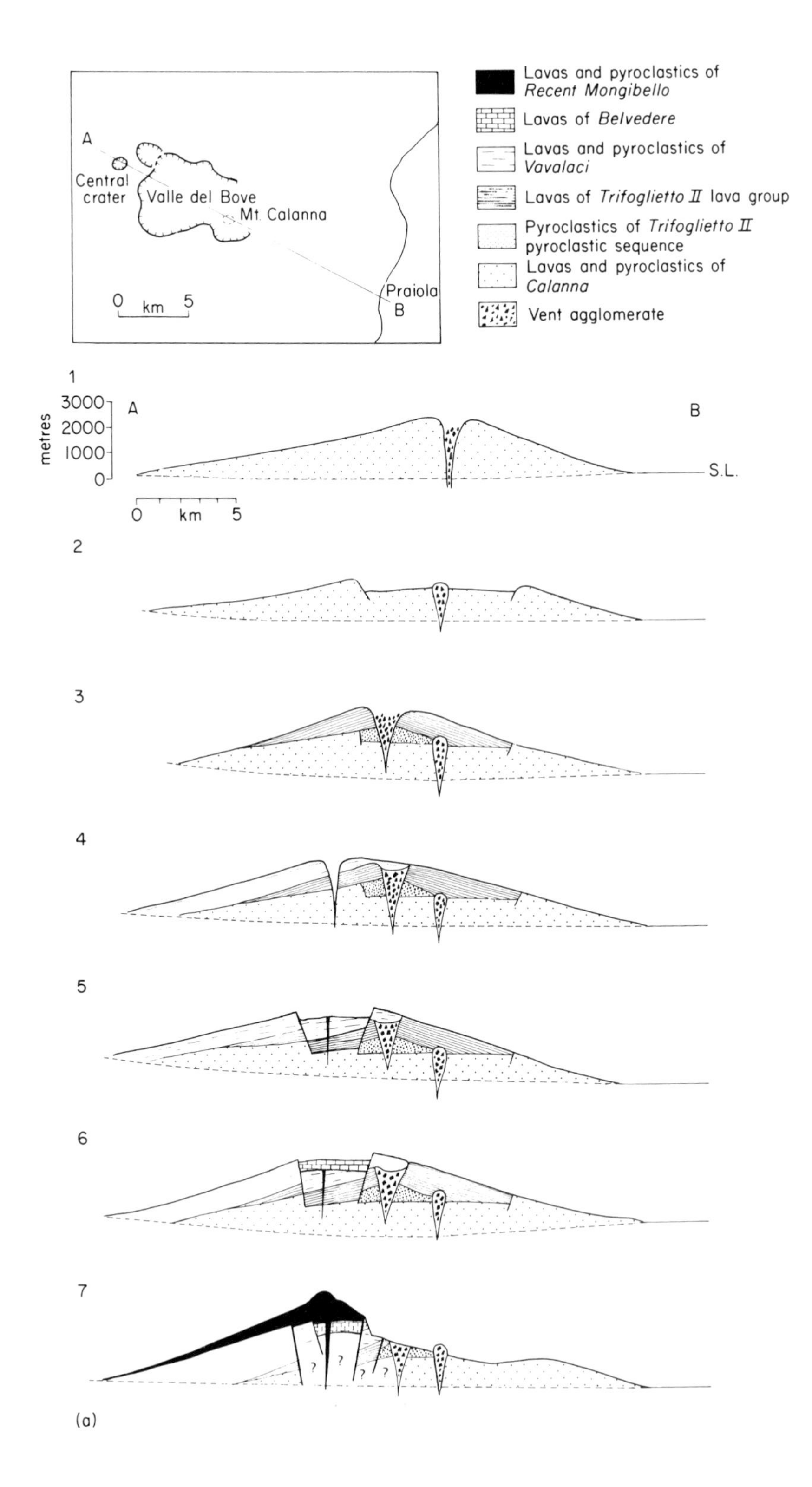

A
Central crater
Valle del Bove
Mt. Calanna
Praiola
B
0 km 5
Lavas and pyroclastics of *Recent Mongibello*
Lavas of *Belvedere*
Lavas and pyroclastics of *Vavalaci*
Lavas of *Trifoglietto II* lava group
Pyroclastics of *Trifoglietto II* pyroclastic sequence
Lavas and pyroclastics of *Calanna*
Vent agglomerate
1
3000
2000
1000
0
metres
A
B
S.L.
0 km 5
2
3
4
5
6
7

(a)

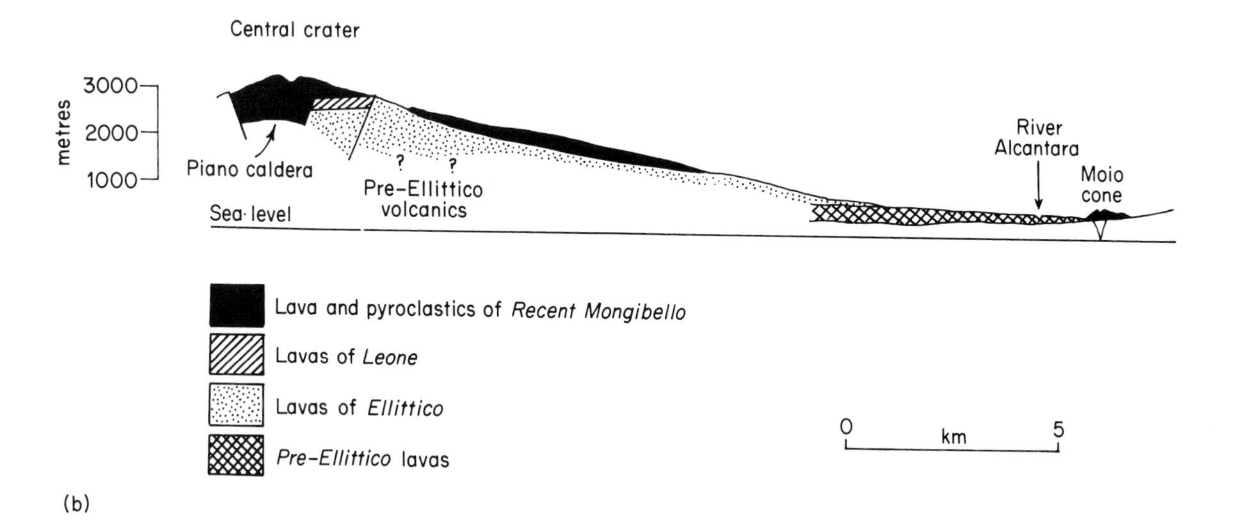

Fig. 3.14 (a) Diagram showing the construction of Mount Etna by means of a chronological sequence of simplified cross-sections along line A – B shown on insert map. There is no evidence that the basal tholeiitic volcanics were erupted along the line of this section and they are, therefore, not represented in this reconstruction. The Ellittico and Leone centres lie to the north of the line of section and are not included. Calanna is taken as the oldest centre of the alkalic series activity, though there may be older centres which are not exposed. Intrusive and flank activity are not represented. (1) Construction of the Calanna volcano. (2) Collapse of the Calanna volcano forming a caldera, this feature may have been considerably enlarged by gravity-sliding and fluvial erosion towards the sea. The vent agglomerate of Calanna is preserved as an upstanding knoll. (3) Build-up of the Trifoglietto II volcano within and partly overlapping the north-western margin of the Calanna caldera. (4) Construction of the Vavalaci centre just to the north-west of the Trifoglietto II volcano. (5) Activity of Vavalaci terminated by caldera collapse. (6) Infilling of the Vavalaci caldera by flat-lying Belvedere lavas. (7) Excavation of the Valle del Bove primarily by gravity-sliding and fluvial processes. Construction of the currently active Recent Mongibello cone to the north-west of the Vavalaci centre. (b) Diagrammatic cross-section from the Central Crater northwards to the Moio cone showing the relationships between the Ellittico, Leone and Recent Mongibello centres. (Adapted from Romano and Guest, 1979.) For information on the chronology of these events, see Table 3.2.

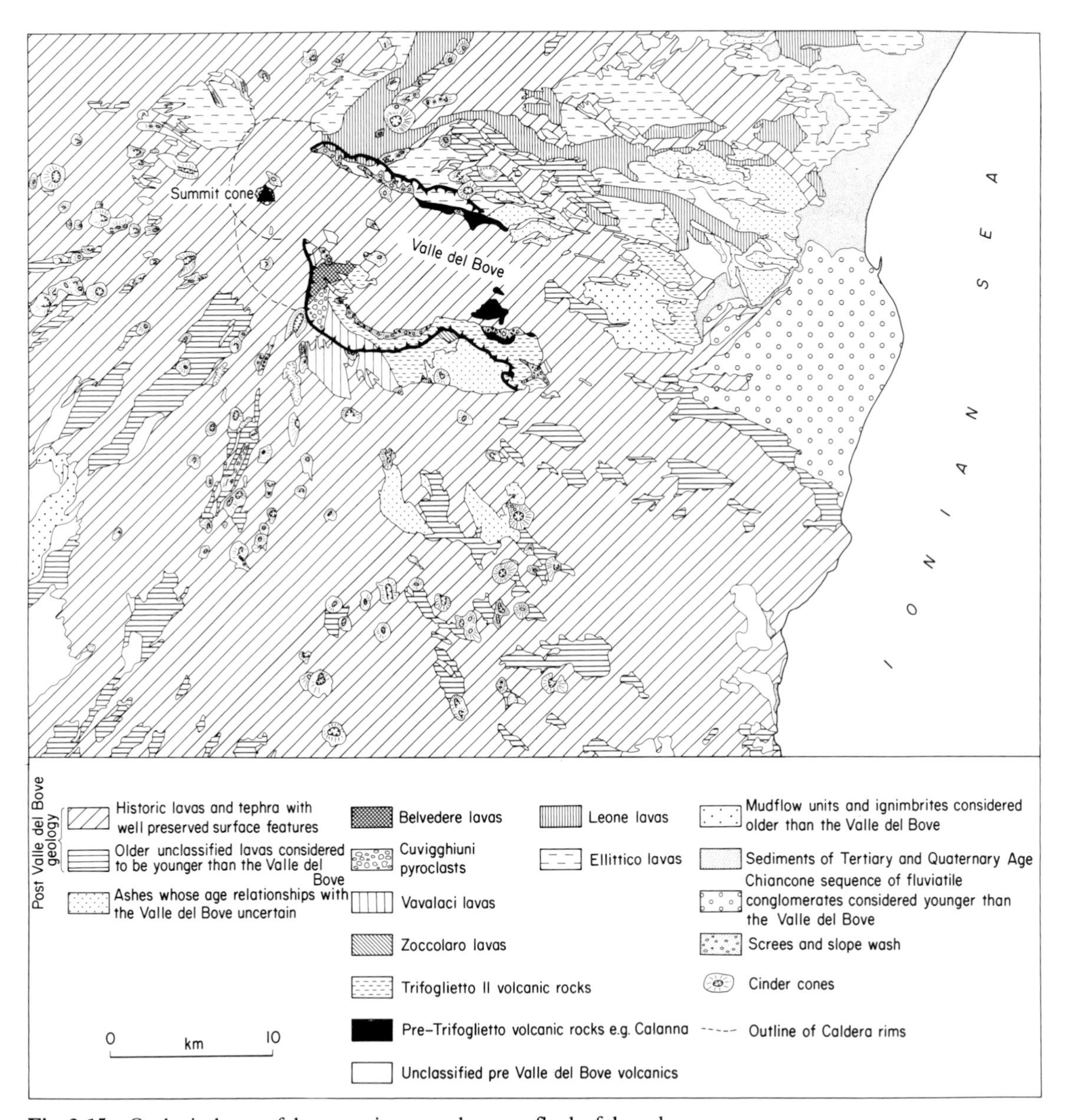

Fig. 3.15 Geological map of the summit area and eastern flank of the volcano.

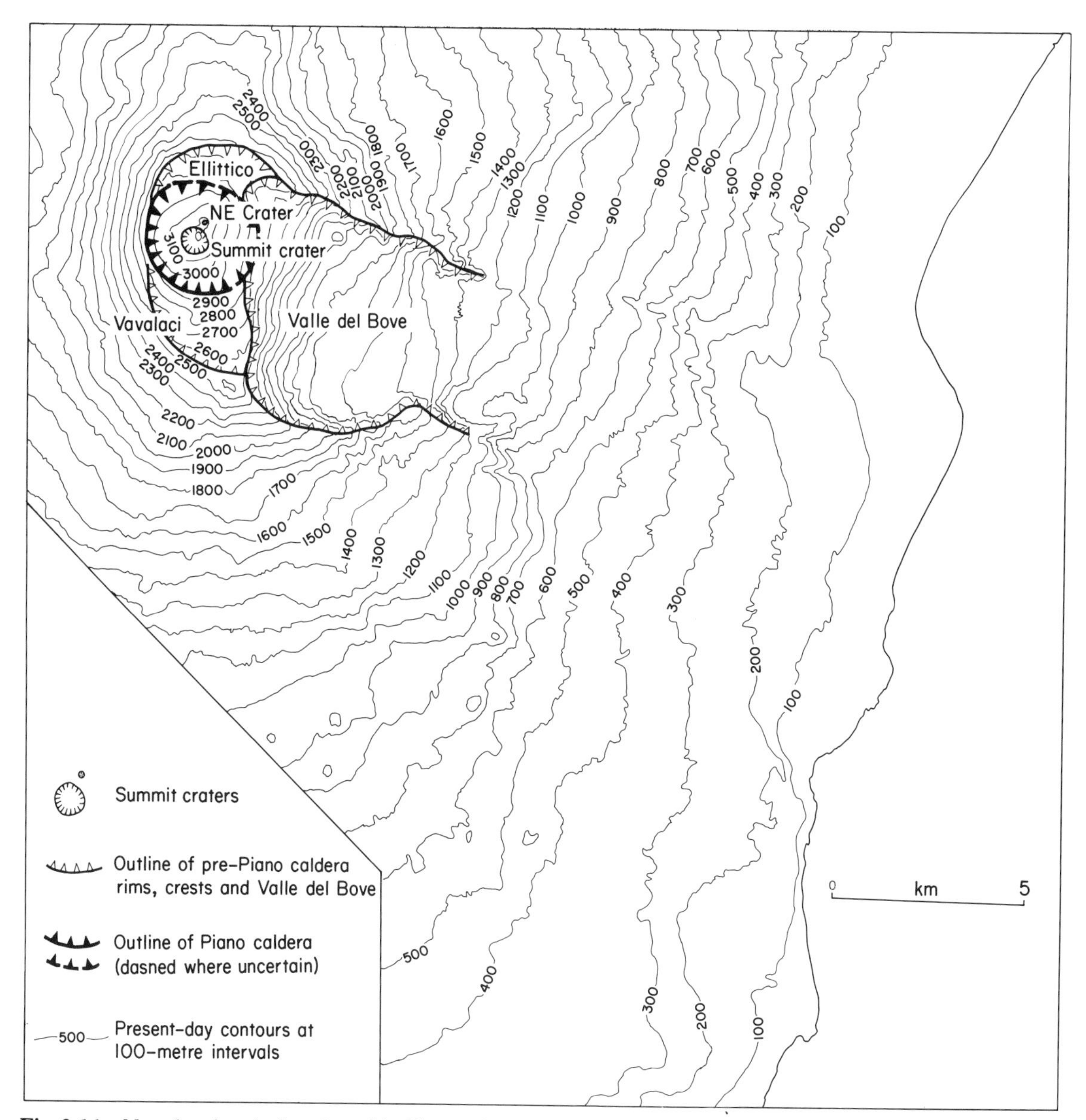

Fig. 3.16 Map showing the location of the Piano caldera. (After Guest *et al.*, 1984.)

Table 3.3 The documented record of the historic activity of Mount Etna collated from Tanguy (1981), Romano and Sturiale (1982), other sources and personal observations. Changes in the topography of the Summit Cone between 1973 and 1983 are shown in Fig. 3.19. (Dates in italics refer to eruptions which took place at or near the summit.)

Date	*Flank eruption*	*Persistent and other summit activity*
*c.*1500 BC	Date not known but reported as cataclysmic eruptions that drove the *Sican* tribe from E. Sicily to the western part of the island	
*c.*693 BC	Eruptions on the S. flank. Main vent probably Mt. Monpilieri 1 km S. of Nicolosi (650 m a.s.l.) other vents reported as at Campo Pio, 6 km NW of Catania. Lavas invaded Catania (town established in 729 BC). Eruption famous for the story of two brothers from Catania who saved their aged parents by carrying them on their backs away from the lava front; lava known as 'Fratelli Pii'	
479/475 BC	Vent area possibly on SSE flank	
425–424 BC	Vent area high on S. flank possibly Mt. Arso (950 m a.s.l.) 4 km N. of Nicolosi. Flows reached sea at Ognina just north of Catania, destroying part of town. Eruption lasted over 180 days	
396 BC	Cone of Mt. Gorna (Urna on older maps) built up at about 750 m a.s.l., 3.5 km N. of Trecastagni. Flows entered sea near Santa Maria la Scala just north of Acireale. The Moio cone at foot of Etna's N. flank and the lava in the Alcantara valley have been attributed to this eruption but are probably older. The lava prevented the Carthaginian General, Himileo, marching along the coast from Messina to Syracuse	
c.350 BC to *c.140* BC	No flank eruptions reported during interval of over 250 years. They may have occurred on N. and W. flanks, but were not reported	Activity reported at summit(?)
141 BC		Summit activity(?)
135 BC	(?)	
126 BC		Summit eruption and earthquake
122 BC	S. flank eruption from vent at 425 m a.s.l., 2 km S. of Trecastagni (Mt. Trigona). Large quantities of ash apparently broke roofs of houses in Catania. Romans granted inhabitants of city immunity from taxes for ten years	Possible caldera collapse

60 BC(?) *		Possible summit explosions
49 BC *	An eruption, possibly on W. flank, that occurred during the civil war between Caesar and Pompey	
44 BC *	Eruption mentioned by Livy as thought to portend the death of Caesar	
36–35 BC *	A violent eruption that occurred during civil war between Octavianus and Sextus Pompeius. E. flank or N.–NW	
0–32 BC *	(?)	Summit activity with possible lavas
AD *0–20* *		Persistent activity including strombolian explosions and lavas
AD *38–40*		Violent summit activity covering Catania and Taormina with ashes. Loud bangs heard for long distances. Caligula who was on a visit to Messina fled the town in fear
AD *c.80*		Two summit craters active
AD 252–53	Possibly formed Mt. Peloso 2 km NNE of Nicolosi. Lavas threatened Catania, but it is alleged stopped when the veil of the newly martyred St. Agatha was carried to the flow front. Eruption lasted nine days.	
812	An eruption in AD 812 was probably on the flanks. It occurred while Charlemagne was in Messina. The flow from Mt. Sona (1200 m a.s.l.) on S. flank has been attributed to this eruption but may be from eruption in 1169	Various reports of summit activity
1062–64	The SW flank eruption usually dated as 1595 may have occurred at this time according to Tanguy (based on palaeomagnetic measurements). Mt. Intraleo and adjacent cones formed between 1650 and 1350 m a.s.l.	
1157 1164	Possible eruptions	
1169 (February)		E. side of Summit Cone collapsed, accompanied by violent earthquake that was felt as far away as Reggio. Much of Catania destroyed with the death of (estimated) 15 000 people. A tsunami engulfed part of Messina
1194 1197 1222 1250	Possible eruptions	
1284–85	Large E. flank eruption in the Valle del Bove. At the time it was related to the death of Charles of Anjou	

* *Footnote*: Romano (1982) considers two eruptions of unknown date to have occurred in this period: one erupted from two cones on the site of Trecastagni and gave rise to a flow about 10 km long; the other formed Mt. Serra, N. of Viagrande

Table 3.3 contd.

Date	*Flank eruption*	*Persistent and other summit activity*
1329	On the evening of 28 June, accompanied by earthquakes, a new crater of Mt. Lepre (1825 m a.s.l.) opened in the Valle del Bove above the Rocca Musarra. Lava poured down the Valle del Bove. This vent ceased erupting on 15 July when a second crater opened 10 km to the south to form Mt. Ilice (800 m a.s.l.). Ashes carried as far as Malta. Date of end of eruption not known	
1333 1350/51	Details of eruptions not known	
1334	E. flank eruptions near Monterosso (500 m a.s.l.)	
1381	Started on 6 August from a long fissure (about 3 km) between 475 and 350 m a.s.l. between Mascalucia and Tremestieri. Lava flowed to sea just north of Catania. Destroyed olive groves	
1408	S. flank eruption at 950 m a.s.l. of Mt. Arso. Pedara and Trecastagni damaged. Eruption lasted nine days	Flank eruption preceded by explosions at summit. Ashes fell in Calabria
1444	S. flank eruption from two cones N. and NE of Mt. Arso (950 m a.s.l.). Eruption lasted twenty days	Violent earthquake accompanied collapse of Central Crater at end of eruption
1446	Eruption in Valle del Bove started 25 September. Probably formed Mt. Finocchio (1630 m a.s.l.)	
1447		Persistent activity constructed a summit cone. May have continued for some years. In 1533 Central Crater fumarolic
1536	23 March: flank eruption location of which is not clear; possibly lava from vent NW of Mt. Pomiciaro (flow threatened Randazzo), or from Mt. Nero degli Zuppini on S. flank, or both. 27 March: twelve boccas opened between Mt. Manfre and Mt. Vituri (1350–1600 m a.s.l.); fissure 1.5 km long on S. flank. One person reported killed by falling bombs. Eruption stopped 8 April	22 March: Strong effusion of lava from two boccas at summit Up to the end of April strong activity in Central Crater
1537	11–31(?) May: two main vents opened on S. flank to produce Mt. Nero la Bosco and Mt. Palombaro (1800–1500 m a.s.l.). Flow travelled 10 km in four days	Activity in Central Crater Violent summit activity accompanied by earthquakes. Many people prepared for their end by receiving Extreme Unction. Finally the Summit Cone fell in
1540		Two boccas reported in Central Crater
1566	1 November: eruption reported on NE flank at 140 m a.s.l. from short fissure. Flow threatened Linguaglossa. Based on palaeomagnetic evidence Tanguy considers this flow to be older. He suggests that this eruption may have formed Mt. Frumento delle Concazza. Eruption ended 5 December	

1579	9 November: occurred at same time as strong earthquake. Five eruptive boccas opened. Details unknown	
1595	Eruption may have occurred on SW flank but possibly confused with eruption in 1062 (see entry for 1062)	
1603		Persistent activity noted in July (?) SW side. Earthquakes
1607	Small N. flank eruption started 22 April. On 28 June SW flank eruption	Persistent activity noted in February on SE and W. side. Lava filled the lake in Piano del Lago
1607–10		Frequent persistent activity reported
1610	6 February: SW flank eruption 3 May: SW flank eruption forming a long lava flow that stopped close to Adrano. Eruption ended on 15 July. Adrano flow may have been from February eruption which is also mapped as 1607	
1614–24	Eruption started in early July at Mt. Deserti (about 2500 m a.s.l.) a small chain of cones on the NE rift. It lasted ten years. The enormous Due Pizzi hornitos were formed downslope from the vent area. Most of the flow field is pahoehoe, much is tube-fed and there are numerous tumuli, some of which are large	1619: contemporaneous activity in Central Crater
1633	Nicolosi was partly destroyed by a violent earthquake on 21 February	
1634–38	Following frequently felt earthquakes a vent opened on 18 (19?) December at 2000 m a.s.l. on S. outer wall of Valle del Bove. Earthquakes were felt on 22 December, and on 27 December a new bocca opened. Eruption continued intermittently until 1638	1 January and 15 February 1635: activity in Central Crater
1643	Small eruption on 20 February from two fissures on N. flank at 1370 and 1292 m a.s.l.	
1646–47	Large NE rift eruption that started on 20 November 1646 and formed Mt. Nero (1900 m a.s.l.). Flow almost reached the Alcantara river. Ended on 17 January 1647	
1651–53	17 January: earthquakes preceded an eruption on the W. flank from fissures at 2500–2100 m a.s.l. Initial flow travelled rapidly at rate of about 0.5 km h^{-1}. Flow field mainly pahoehoe and similar in form to that of 1614–24. Stopped close to Bronte. This eruption ended in 1653. Another 1651 lava has been mapped on the ENE flank. However, this flow is highly vegetated and based on palaeomagnetic evidence may be considerably older. A possible E. flank lava erupted at this time but not identified	

Table 3.3 contd.

Date	*Flank eruption*	*Persistent and other summit activity*
1654–56		Summit activity
1669	One of the most dramatic eruptions on Etna. Preceded by earthquakes starting on 25 February with increasing intensity causing great damage to Nicolosi. The eruption started on the 11 March (pm) by the opening of a 12 km-long fissure from Piano di S. Leo just north of Nicolosi to Mt. Frumento Supino 2 km from the summit (900–2800 m a.s.l.). Fissure 2 m wide and glowing lava seen in it. Successively lower explosive boccas opened accompanied by earthquakes in the late evening of 11 March and the main vent of Mt. Rossi opened and started emitting lavas on the night 11/12 March. Seven boccas opened venting lava that destroyed Belpasso. On 13 March lavas were close to Mascalucia, S. Pietro and Camporotondo 4 km from the main vent. One lava stream reached S. Giovanni di Galermo 6 km from vent on 15 March. Flow to west arrived near Valcorrente on 17/19 March. By 25 March the main flow had reached Misterbianco some 9 km from the main vent and arrived at the walls of Catania on 12 April having travelled some 12 km. Lava rose to the top of the wall and cascaded over; in one place a 40 m stretch was knocked down. Large portions of the town were destroyed. The lava finally reached the sea on 23 April. Lava stopped being erupted on 11 July and the eruptions ended on 15 July	There were violent earthquakes on 25 March accompanying the collapse of the Summit Cone
1669–82		Central Crater activity
1682		Eruption from near summit producing lava that poured into the Valle del Bove towards Rocca Musarra
1688		Another Summit Cone eruption with lava flowing into the Valle del Bove
1689	Flank eruption began on 14 March in the Valle del Bove at about 1300 m a.s.l. Lava flowed until it reached Macchia. Another vent at 1400 m a.s.l. may have opened on 19 March	
1693		On 9 January the Central Crater was emitting clouds of black ash accompanied by loud bangs and earthquakes. There was a violent earthquake on 11 January during which Catania was shaken badly, burying 18 000 of its inhabitants. Some fifty towns may have been destroyed killing 60 000–100 000 people. There may have been some collapse at the summit. Activity at the summit may have continued until November 1694. Ashes carried to Malta

1702	Three vents opened in the Valle del Bove on 8 March at about 2000 m a.s.l. Lava reached the Valle del Calanna in five days. Eruption ended 8 May	
1723–24		During early November 1723 earthquakes and bangs from Central Crater. 20/22 November: lava poured from W. side towards Bronte. Central Crater continued in activity until May 1724
1732–33		Summit activity reported from 9 December to January. Lava flow to SW
1735–36		Following earthquakes, summit activity started on 4 October. Lava was observed on 11 October flowing to E., NE and NW. Explosive activity continued until 15 July 1736
1744–45		Strong explosive activity forming a new terminal cone
1747–49		Activity in Central Crater reported with lava flowing E. into the Valle del Bove. Explosive activity continued until February or March 1749. Height of cone considerably increased
1752–55		Explosive activity (strombolian?)
1755	9 March an eruptive fissure opened in the Valle del Bove giving lavas flowing to E. On 10 March a vast quantity of water was liberated possibly as result of melting sub-surface ice. The flood descended at a rate of some 2 km in 1.5 min on the upper slopes of the volcano and carried large boulders. A deep channel was cut. On 11 March a new eruptive fissure opened below the first one. Eruption ended 15 March	On 2 March lavas flowed into the Valle del Bove to S. and E. until about 6 March. Explosive activity at summit continued until 9 March
1755–59		Continued intermittent activity at Central Crater. Earthquake and collapse in Central Crater on 1 November 1758. On 3/4 November lava flows. Three new cones built up in Central Crater. Several lava flows
1763	W. flank eruption between 6 February and 15 March. Preceded by earthquakes increasing in intensity. Two cones built up: Mt. Nuovo and Mt. Mezza Luna (1700 and 1600 m a.s.l.)	
1763	On 18/19 June vents opened at 2500 m a.s.l. on S. flank to form Montagnola and a thick compound flow forming a high ridge. Eruption ended 10 September	
1764–65	Extensive pahoehoe flow formed to NW from vents at $>$ 2600 m a.s.l. on NE rift. Eruption lasted about eighteen months	Possible summit activity resumed after period of quiescence

Table 3.3 contd.

Date	*Flank eruption*	*Persistent and other summit activity*
1766	Following earthquakes a vent opened on 28 April at 1900–2100 m a.s.l. on the S. flank building-up a small cone and producing a small lava flow that travelled rapidly. On the 29 April a new fissure opened at 1500 m a.s.l. The eruption ended on 6 November	
1767–80		Intermittent activity in Central Crater
1780	Near the end of April earthquakes felt widely on Sicily. On the 18 May a fissure opened from near the summit down to 1800 m on the S. flank. Lava boccas opened at about 2300 m and 1850 m on 18/19 May. Eruption stopped at end of May	
1781		Explosion in Central Crater during March and April. Lava flowed into Valle del Bove between 8 and 10 May. Summit vents then generally quiet until 1783
1783		A large Calabrian earthquake occurred on the night of 5 February. Copious fume was emitted from the Central Crater
1787		Summit activity began in June with lava flows from 16–22 July. Activity continued until 11 August
1792		Activity began in Central Crater and on W. side in early May having been heralded by earthquakes in April. Lava flows on W. and E. sides on 11 and 12 May. This activity continued until the flank eruption started
1792–93	On 25 May a long fissure opened on the W. wall of the Valle del Bove with a lava vent at about 1900 m. The 'Cisternazza' pit just above the Valle scarp collapsed. Lava poured onto floor of Valle. Another vent on the outer southern wall of the Valle del Bove opened on 1 June giving rise to an enormous field of pahoehoe that flowed westwards nearly to Zafferana. Activity was strong until April and eruption ended in May	
1793–1802		Intermittent activity in Central Crater. Some earthquakes. Lava flow in 1798
1802	On 15 November fissures opened on W. wall of Valle del Bove at about 1800 m a.s.l. Lava flowed onto Valle floor. Eruption ended on 17 November	
1803–09		Intermittent persistent activity with some lava flows and strombolian activity

1809	27 March: earthquakes felt in Castiglione and Linguaglossa, followed by opening of effusive boccas at NNE part of Summit Cone. The flow reached within 0.75 km of Mt. Santa Maria by 1 April. Between 28 and 29 March successively lower boccas opened down the NE rift to about 1400 a.s.l. Many of the craters purely ultravulcanian. Lava from the lowest bocca continued flowing to the NE until 9 April	Frequent explosions in March Minor collapse in Central Crater. Some strombolian activity until the end of year
1811–12	Following earthquakes a fissure opened on 27 October from the side of the Summit Cone across the floor of the Valle del Leone (about 3000–2000 m a.s.l.). Numerous effusive boccas opened but activity quickly diminished in the upper cones. By the middle of the next day activity was concentrated at the lower end of the fissure and Mt. Simone was built up. Lava was erupted until 24 April 1812 and the eruption stopped in May 1812	
1819	27 May (night): fissure opened with three boccas at about 2800 m a.s.l. on W. wall of the Valle del Bove. Thirteen hours later fissure extended and boccas opened lower down. Lava erupted and continued until 5 August	Activity in Central Crater and earthquakes on 27 May
1822–30		Activity in Central Crater intermittent from June 1822 to June 1830. Lavas may have erupted in 1830
1831		17 February: explosions started in Central Crater. Lava erupted on 4–15 March and again 2–3 April giving a flow on the N. flank. Minor collapse occurred on 30 September
1832	On 31 October or 1 November fissures on the W. and WNW flanks (between 2900 and 1700 m a.s.l.). Mt. Nunziata formed at bottom of W. flank fissure. Flow travelled to within 2 km of Bronte. The eruption ended on 22 November and earthquakes were felt for several days after	Fuming stopped in Central Crater during August and September. Some activity in late October and lava effusion on the S. flank of Summit Cone on 31 October
1833		Persistent activity with lava flowing to NNW reported in March
1838–39		8 July to 2 August: explosive activity in Central Crater. On 2 August slow effusion of lava began to SE until October when near the end of the month lava flowed to N. The eruption continued until February 1839
1842		Effusion in Central Crater on 18 November (probably ultravulcanian). On 26 November strombolian activity, and lava erupted on S. and E. sides on the night of 27/28 November. Eruption ended on 25 December. Small cone formed in the Central Crater

Table 3.3 contd.

Date	*Flank eruption*	*Persistent and other summit activity*
1843	Earthquakes were felt late on 17 November and shortly after, a fissure opened on the W. flank between 2400 and 1900 m a.s.l. Some fifteen boccas opened with lava flowing to W. The road between Adrano and Bronte was cut by lava on 23 November. Lava effusion stopped on 27 November and the eruption ended on 28 November. At least thirty-six people reported killed from phreatic explosion at lava front	Small collapses in Central Crater at end of eruption
1852–53	Late on 20 August a fissure opened in the Valle del Bove near the base of the Serra Giannicola venting lava. On 21 August there was explosive activity in the Central Crater and a strong earthquake. A new vent opened on 22 August to build up Mt. Centenari. The eruption ended on 27 May 1853 with summit activity	
1857		Some collapse in Central Crater on 6 September
1863		Strombolian activity in Central Crater starting 1 May. Intermittent until 25 July. Lavas erupted to S
1864		Persistent activity with lava effusion accompanied by strombolian activity in August and September
1865	Preceded by earthquakes, a fissure opened on 30 January on the NE flank with its highest point at about 2200 m a.s.l. On the following day the fissure extended down to about 1650 m a.s.l. and explosive activity between 1700 and 1650 m a.s.l. built up a chain of cones known as Mts Sartorius. Lava travelled 6 km in two days. Explosive activity ended on 10 June and the eruption ended on 28 June. An earthquake on 19 July killed 52 people in Macchia	
1868		Late November to early December explosive activity in Central Crater
1869		A short sub-terminal eruption that lasted 7–9 h on the morning of 26 September. Occurred on the E. flank of the summit cone with lava flowing into the Valle del Bove
1874	NE rift eruption from 29–31 August from vents at 2800–2030 m a.s.l. Two small lava flows	
1879	Flank eruption preceded by earthquakes felt as far away as Messina on 26 May. Later in the day two fissures opened, one on the NE rift and the other on the SSW flank at 2400–1690 m	Activity in Central Crater during March and May

	and about 2650 m a.s.l. respectively. The southern fissure erupted lava for about one day. The NE rift eruption gave rise to a long flow that cut the Randazzo-to-Linguaglossa road on 29 May. In early June the activity decreased and the eruption stopped on 6/7 June. Continuing earthquakes were reported from 1 June to August	
1879–82		Intermittent reports of summit activity until the next flank eruption
1883	Continuing seismic activity reported on 20–21 March culminating in the opening of a fissure from the Summit Cone to the S. flank (about 3000 m to 950 m a.s.l.) on 22 March (early afternoon). The main lava vents were between 1200 and 1000 m a.s.l., the principal vent being Mt. Leone at 1100 m a.s.l. The eruption ended on 24 March	
		Black fume noted above Central Crater on 25 March and activity continued intermittently until 1886
1886	Flank activity started in early morning of 18 May by opening of a fissure between 1500 and 1300 m a.s.l. on S flank. Mt. Gemmellaro was built up and lavas emitted. Most violent activity on 20 May. Eruption stopped on 7 June, having started to die down on 27 May.	On 18 May Central Crater inactive but several earthquakes noted. Some activity observed later in the day. Summit activity observed throughout eruption
1892	Early afternoon on the 9 July a fissure system opened, accompanied by quakes, between 2600 and 1800 m a.s.l. Eruptive boccas between 2000 and 1800 m a.s.l. over which built up the Mts Silvestri. Lavas had travelled about 6 km by the afternoon of 10 May. This long-duration eruption ended on 29 December	Activity noted in Central Crater in late June and early July. Earthquakes felt on 8 July around the mountain
1893–1908		Activity observed on various occasions including lavas starting in November 1899
1908	In the early morning of 29 April a fissure opened to the SE on E. flank at about 3000–2200 m a.s.l. Eruptive boccas developed between 2500–2200 m a.s.l. with lava flowing into the Valle del Bove. The eruption lasted less than 24 h	
1908–1909		Summit activity in April–June 1908 and April and September 1909
1910	In the early hours of 23 March there was strong seismic activity. A fissure opened on the S. flank between about 3000 and 1950 m a.s.l. and eruptive boccas opened below 2750 m a.s.l. Flows down the S. flank travelled 5 km in about the first ten hours of eruption. Explosive activity stopped on 13 April and eruption ended on 18 April	Activity in Central Crater observed in February

Table 3.3 contd.

Date	*Flank eruption*	*Persistent and other summit activity*
1910/11		Activity renewed in Central Crater on 27 December 1910 and continued into January and February 1911 with strombolian activity and short flows. Eruption of juvenile material ended on 6 February. On 27 May the NE Crater was formed to become the most effusive centre in the summit region to the present time
1911	Earthquakes of increasing intensity started on 9 September continuing into 10 September when fractures opened across the summit. In the early morning of the 10th, boccas started opening progressively down the NE rift from 2500 m to 1650 m a.s.l. The Linguaglossa-to-Randazzo road was cut by lavas in the late afternoon on the 12th. Explosive activity died down on the 17th and the eruption ended on 21/22 September	Summit activity noted at the time of fracture opening (probably collapse) Much summit activity at the end of eruption (probably collapse)
1912–18		Persistent activity reported again in August 1912 when lava appeared in the Central Crater. Lava was also observed in November 1913 and May 1914 when the NE Crater was active. In 1914 the Central Crater was active during May and the NE Crater in July. Further reports of Central Crater activity were made in December. The Central Crater and NE Crater were active from March to September in 1915 and the NE Crater alone in September–December. During 1916 NE Crater was active in March, June and July to September and again in November. There was a large strombolian eruption of the NE Crater on 24–25 June 1917 with Central Crater activity following; then in March–July 1918 the NE Crater produced its first flow which travelled to NE. During October–November that year a new cone was built up in the Central Crater
1918	Small NW flank eruption on 29–30(?) November from two fissures between 3100 and 1900 m a.s.l.	
1919–23		The Central Crater was active from March–September 1919, and again almost continuously from February to August 1920. In 1921 the NE Crater was active from the end of March to June while the Central Crater was active from early October to November. It was again active in mid-March 1922. The NE Crater was active from June to December 1922 with black ash (collapse) clouds in the Central Crater. During February to end-March 1923 Central Crater activity (strombolian), and in May to early-June NE Crater erupted lavas

1923	Earthquakes were felt later on 16 June through to the afternoon of the 17th when a fracture opened across the Summit Cone. Boccas opened successively down the NE rift at 2400 m, 2200 m and 1900–1800 m a.s.l. From the lower bocca lava travelled 7 km in 10 h. No cinder cones developed. An earthquake was felt in Puntalazzo on 27 June. By 29 June the lava front had stopped, and the eruption stopped on 18 July. Flow cut the Randazzo-to-Linguaglossa road	Activity in Central Crater at end of eruption (minor collapse?)
1924–28		The NE Crater reported with strombolian activity in July and December 1924 to February 1925. In 1926 it was observed fuming and in February 1928 part of the cone may have collapsed. Activity, possibly internal collapse in the NE Crater, took place in late-July to mid-August 1928
1928	On 2 November in the late-afternoon an eruptive fissure opened on the NE flank of the summit crater in the Valle del Leone giving a small short-lived flow. There was an earthquake shortly after the fissure opened. In the early hours of the next morning a 3.5 km-long fissure opened on the N. outer wall of the Valle del Bove with effusive fissures on the upper part between 2300 and 2050 m a.s.l. A line of small spatter cones was built up and lava was erupted until 4 November. On the night of the 4/5 November another effusive fissure opened on the Ripa di Naca fault scarp at 1200 m a.s.l. giving a large lava flow. Roads were cut and on 6 November lava cut the Circum–Etnean railway and entered Mascali which was destroyed by the 7th. The main-line railway was destroyed on the 11th. On 12 November effusive activity diminished and earthquakes were felt. The flow front stopped on 16 November and the eruption ended on 20 November. At least two people reported to have been killed in Mascali	NE Crater activity before flank eruption
1929–42		Various reports of fume and dark clouds, probably minor collapse. Between July 1931 and September 1933 explosive activity in the Central Crater built up a small cone. The NE Crater was active in September, October 1935; and intermittently between March 1936 and September 1938. Central Crater eruption between June 1939 and mid-1942 produced inter-crater lava flows and strombolian activity. An inter-crater cone was destroyed on 16 March 1940, the Volcano Observatory was damaged and ashes fell in Calabria. The NE Crater was active in June–August, and November 1940

Table 3.3 contd.

Date	*Flank eruption*	*Persistent and other summit activity*
1942	Accompanied by earthquakes a fissure opened on the SW flank between 3000 and 2240 m a.s.l. on the morning of 30 June. In the afternoon boccas opened on the fissure from 2780 m a.s.l. giving a small flow. Twelve explosive boccas and one effusive bocca. Eruption stopped on 5 July	Strong explosive activity at beginning and end of flank eruption
1942–47		Central Crater erupted 4–5 July 1942 with strombolian activity. The NE Crater was active with strombolian activity in February–March 1944, June–October 1945 and February–October 1946. A collapse pit opened in the Central Crater in late-October 1945. During 1947 the NE Crater opened on 5/6 February and was active intermittently until the 1947 flank eruption, often with vigorous strombolian activity. On 16 February the new collapse pit in the Central Crater was also in strombolian activity
1947	Late at night on 24 February a long fissure system opened between 3050 and 2200 m a.s.l. on the NE rift. Effusive fissures opened on the fissure system at 3050 m, 2350 m, 2275 m and 2225 m a.s.l. Spatter ramparts were built up at the boccas. The eruption ended on 10 March	Internal collapse in NE Crater after eruption
1949	There were stong earthquakes on 1 and 2 December before the eruption which started in the late afternoon of 2 December. Fractures opened across the summit and lavas flowed out at 3000 m a.s.l. on the S. side and 3100 m a.s.l. to the N. side. Late at night, accompanied by seismic activity, a new effusive fissure opened on the NW flank at 2400–2100 m a.s.l.. The eruption ended on the afternoon of 4 December	Strombolian activity at the NE Crater started just before the flank eruption finished
1950–51	Weak seismic activity in early-November 1950. On 25 November late at night a fissure opened in the Valle del Bove, between 2820 m to 2600 m a.s.l. Lava erupted for a short while, then stopped as the fissure extended downslope to 2250 m a.s.l. and a new flow started. Activity continued with occasional reduction in strength until 2 December 1951	NE Crater activity on occasion during and at end of flank eruption until end-May 1951
1955		A long period of eruption from the NE Crater started with seismic activity from early-January to mid-February. Strombolian activity started on 5 April. Lavas were erupted on 8 July and continued until the end of the year. The NE Crater cone was built up during this eruption. Activity also occurred in the Central Crater during September

1956

Mid-morning on 28 February continuous strombolian activity started in the Central Crater and by the 29th lava was flowing to the N. On 1 March lava flowed to the E. and a sub-terminal fissure opened on the E. flank of Summit Cone at 2750 m a.s.l. This phase of persistent activity stopped on 2 March. Earthquakes were felt on the SE flank of the volcano on 18–27 March. Activity renewed on the morning of 2 April filling the floor of the Central Crater with lava and giving flows to E., N. and NW. Flows stopped on 7 April

1957

Starting with collapse (?) and ultravulcanian activity on 5 February the NE Crater began strombolian activity on 8 February and continued with periods of quiescence and ultravulcanian explosions until 16 April when lava flowed to the E. and on the 17th to the NE and N. Diminishing activity continued to 3 May

1957–64

After a short period of quiescence, probably until August the NE Crater again became active mainly with strombolian explosions and continued in this state until late-1959. There followed a period of relative quiet although there were probably deep explosions in the Central Crater. Sporadic strombolian explosions at the NE Crater started again in April 1960 continuing until early-June. In July (17th) activity shifted to the Central Crater with strong strombolian activity spreading ash across E. Sicily to Calabria. Less violent activity continued until 5 August when again there was strong strombolian activity. Then during the latter part of August activity moved back to the NE Crater starting with ultravulcanian activity. Flows were erupted from the NE Crater on 30 December 1960 and several flows formed up until 23 April 1961. Sporadic activity in the Central Crater built up to strong strombolian activity on 12–13 May 1961 with flows to NW and E., but then activity returned to the NE Crater and continued with occasional periods of quiescence until late-January 1964. Numerous flows occurred and the NE Crater cone built up substantially

1964

Activity started in the Central Crater on 1 February with flow to N. and a fissure system opened on the E. flank of Summit Cone starting at about 3175 m down to 2900 m a.s.l. Spatter was thrown out from the upper part of fissure to give hornitos and a flow from the lowest bocca on fissure travelled into the Valle del Bove. This phase of activity terminated near the end of February. On 7 April strong strombolian explosions occurred in the Central Crater which over the next week built up a new

Table 3.3 contd.

Date	*Flank eruption*	*Persistent and other summit activity*
1964 (cont.)		cone in the Central Crater. Less violent activity continued (with some violent spasms) until early-July accompanied by lavas that ponded in the S. part of the Central Crater and overflowed especially to W. and breached a graben notch in the rim of Central Crater to SW. Eruption ended on night of 4/5 July with strong strombolian explosions and lava overflowing to SE in two streams
1966–71		The NE Crater reopened with ultravulcanian explosions on 10 January 1966. Strombolian activity started the next day. On the 13th lava began flowing. This activity continued almost without a break until April 1971. During this time a large fan of lavas was emplaced from the foot of the NE Crater cone on the N. flank of the volcano. One of the last phases of effusion during this period of NE Crater activity was the opening of a vent between the NE Crater and the Chasm and the eruption of lava to E. and W. Two other events occurred during this long period of persistent activity: a small sub-terminal eruption and the opening of the Bocca Nuova. The sub-terminal eruption began on 7 January 1968 when a fissure opened at 2550 m a.s.l. on the SE flank near Serra Giannicola Piccola. Lava flowed into the Valle del Bove. A further flow came from this fissure on 24–25 April. The Bocca Nuova opened as a small hole on the W. side of the Central Crater on 9/10 June 1968. It had a diameter of about 8 m and expelled gas at high temperature. During winter of 1970/71 it collapsed to form a pit of about 100 m in diameter and about 300 m deep
1971	The first phase of this flank eruption was technically sub-terminal, starting on 5 April (a.m.) with the opening of two fissures on the S. flank of the Summit Cone. These were the Vulcarolo vent (3050–3000 m a.s.l.) and the Observatory vent (2985–2975 m a.s.l.). Cones were built up over the vents by mild strombolian activity. Lavas flowed S. destroying the Volcano Observatory and the upper portion of the Funivia (cable car). An earthquake was felt in Macchia on 21 April. Another vent, the Western Vent, opened at 3500 m a.s.l. above the Observatory Vent on 22 April. Activity from these three vents stopped on 7 May. Three days before they stopped, a new vent opened in the afternoon at 2915 m a.s.l. near the foot of the Summit Cone on the SE side. This was named the Eastern Vent. It ceased erupting on 7/8 May when an ENE-trending	

fissure system opened along the back wall of the Valle del Bove with a series of small effusive boccas along its length. No cones were formed. These continued in activity until 15 and 16 May. Before they stopped on the 11th, late at night, yet another fissure opened on the same trend on the outer N. wall of the Valle del Bove at 1850–1800 m a.s.l. Apart from spatter there was no explosive activity. The flow from this vent extended through agricultural land, buried houses and narrowly missed Fornazzo

During the last phase of the eruption an explosive vent opened on the SE flank of the Summit Cone on 18 May with volcanic explosions. The main activity took place up to 26 May and then became spasmodic to the end of the flank eruption

The eruption ended on 12 June

1971–73

After the 1971 flank eruption the once-1000-m-deep chasm filled with lava to within 200 m of the lip by September. Strombolian explosions were observed. In late-March 1972 ultravulcanian explosions in the Chasm. Collapses deep in the Bocca Nuova occurred. In 1973 strombolian activity was taking place regularly from small vents in the Chasm and less regularly in the Bocca Nuova. In early-July only the Chasm was active. Heavy rockfalls in the Bocca Nuova were observed in late-July and early-August. On 3 August strombolian activity had again broken out in the Bocca Nuova. Continuing activity filled the Chasm to about 150 m below the lip and the Bocca Nuova to within about 50 m. The activity continued, to reach a peak on 6 November

1974

By the beginning of the flank eruption the Chasm was inactive with a collapse pit in the middle of the lava-filled floor about 75 m below the lip. The Bocca Nuova was several hundred metres deep with collapses occurring at intervals

Earthquakes were felt for ten days before the flank eruption started on the evening of 30 January. A vent opened at 1675 m a.s.l. and a cone rapidly built up. At first lavas were sluggish to W. but on the 8/9 February strong strombolian activity decreased to occasional explosions and a new, more vigorous lava came out from the S. foot of the cone. This phase of the eruption stopped on 17 February. On 11 March a new vent opened about 200 m to W. of the first, building-up another cone and giving rise to a thick, sluggish flow. The eruption ended on 29 March

Table 3.3 contd.

Date	*Flank eruption*	*Persistent and other summit activity*
1974–75		After flank eruption Chasm collapsed into funnel-shaped pit 300 m deep. Strombolian explosions observed during summer. Bocca Nuova about 150 m deep with roaring gas expulsion. The NE Crater began to clear its throat on 28 September with ultravulcanian explosions and on the night of 29/ 30 September strombolian explosions started. On 30 September the cone was breached and lava poured out. Activity continued until February 1975
1975–76		During the night of 23/24 February 1975 effusive activity occurred 1 km to N. of the NE Crater on NE rift at about 2600 m a.s.l. Hornitos developed at vent area and lava was emitted from numerous ephemeral vents. A low shield of lava was built up. During late-July and August activity became sporadic and during periods of quiescence untravulcanian explosions and collapse occurred at the NE Crater. NE rift activity stopped on 12 September. During this time violent gas expulsion and collapse occurred in the Chasm and Bocca Nuova in May. Both were >300 m deep. Explosive activity increased as well as collapse, especially at Bocca Nuova. The NE Crater started erupting on its W. side and continued until 28 November. The day after, new vents opened 1.5 km to NW near Punta Lucia. These were on NW-trending fissures along which hornitos were formed. Explosive activity centred on one vent and a small cinder cone was built up. Lavas poured down the NE rift. During January/February 1976 a pit was formed by collapse on the W. side of the NE Crater. Activity at the Punta Lucia vent continued with mild strombolian explosions; lava effusion was often from ephemeral boccas down the NE rift at about 2500 m. This activity ceased when a vent opened on the NE Crater cone giving strombolian explosions on 17 June. Activity continued for over a month, often violently, then quietened down to high-pressure gas emission for about three weeks. The eruption ended with a strombolian phase for a week stopping around 20 August 1976. At this time the Punta Lucia vent started erupting again until January 1977. During 1976 the Bocca Nuova and the Chasm showed varying degrees of explosivity and collapse. In June the Bocca Nuova had strombolian activity, small scoria fragments and Pele's hair landing on the crater lip
1977–78		In early-1977 the Chasm was >300 m deep with explosive phases. Explosions in Bocca Nuova. On 16 July there was a

		strong eruption from the NE Crater lasting six days. This was the first of numerous short, high-effusion-rate eruptions from the NE Crater lasting until 28 March 1978. The NE Crater cone built up considerably and was breached on the W. side
1978(1)	At about 20.00 on 29 April a bocca opened on the SE flank of the Summit Cone at about 3000 m a.s.l. with some strombolian activity. On 1 May a fracture system opened to SE and boccas opened at 2900 m a.s.l. where a hornito built up, but otherwise degassing continued from the upper vent. Lavas poured into the Valle del Bove. Another bocca on the W. wall of the Valle del Bove opened at about 2700 m a.s.l. On 2 May the last bocca opened further S. on the fissure system on the wall of the Valle del Bove at 2600 m a.s.l. producing a small flow which stopped after a short time. The eruption stopped on 7 May. Forceful emission of hot gas (glowing red at night) occurred in the upper crater until the next eruption	Bocca Nuova and Chasm quiet, but fuming At end of this phase of flank eruption the Chasm filled with ash and snow and no fume. Bocca Nuova had deep hole on SE side. Collapses and explosions occasionally
1978(2)	On the night of 23/24 August the upper crater of 1978(1) erupted to build a cone called the SE Crater cone. On the 24th lavas flowed E. into the Valle del Bove. Another bocca opened on the wall of the Valle del Bove at about 2725 m a.s.l. with a small flow down the S. side of the Serra Giannicola Piccola. The trend of this fissure was ENE. The eruption ended on 30 August	At the end of this phase of eruption the Chasm was funnel-shaped with a hole in middle – no fume; Bocca Nuova fuming but no activity
1978(3)	The SE Crater opened once again on 18 November with mainly ultravulcanian explosions. Strombolian explosions started on 23 November and lava erupted on the 25th. During that night a bocca opened at about 2600 m a.s.l. and on the 27th, others opened at 1800 m, 1700 m and 1650 m a.s.l. The eruption ended on 29 November	
1979		Lava entered the Chasm during June forming a small lake at about 130 m depth with strombolian explosions. Bocca Nuova fuming and very deep; no activity noted. The activity in the Chasm continued with increasing vigour through July
1979	Following an increase in evolution of high-pressure gas the SE Crater started small ultravulcanian and strombolian explosions on 16 July. Activity increased by the 17th with several active vents in the floor of the crater. Strong strombolian activity on night of 22 July. A series of felt earthquakes occurred on 29–30 July. Violent strombolian activity started in the	Collapse deep in Bocca Nuova in late-July

Table 3.3 contd.

Date	*Flank eruption*	*Persistent and other summit activity*
	SE Crater on 3 August. Ash fell on E. flank of volcano and later on Catania and Syracusa. Fissures opened to the SE of the SE Crater and lava poured into the Valle del Bove. Numerous earthquakes were felt. In the early morning of 4 August a fissure opened to the SE of Mt. Simone in the Valle del Bove (1800–1700 m a.s.l.) erupting lavas which reached Torrente Fontanelle by midday. Flow front, advancing at 100 mh^{-1} cut the Citelli–Fornazzo road at 14.30. Flow stopped in the evening 50 m from the N–S road through Fornazzo. On 5 August a fissure opened SE of the SE Crater cone with a flow into the Valle del Bove, and then another fissure opened below this on the wall of the Valle del Bove. Ash again fell on Catania and Syracusa. In the late afternoon a fissure with a NE-trend opened in the Valle del Leone near Mt. Simone and lava travelled down the Valle del Bove. During the morning of 6 August many earthquakes were felt and in the afternoon activity increased from the vent at Mt. Simone that had been active on 4 August. Late on 6 August a new fissure with a ENE-trend opened on the outer flank of the Valle del Bove above Rif. Citelli coinciding with the 1928 fissure. This vent stopped on 8 August and the eruption was over by 9 August	On 4 August magma level dropped in the Chasm
		Collapse started in both the Chasm and the Bocca Nuova on 2 September. A large chunk of the wall of the Bocca Nuova fell in and small collapses continued. On the afternoon of 12 September a strong explosion occurred at the Bocca Nuova throwing out lithic blocks that killed nine tourists and injured over twenty. Small internal collapses threw out fine ash for many days after
1980		Strombolian activity started in the Chasm on 14 April. Strong explosions occurred on 16 and 17 April when this activity ended having filled the Chasm to within 25 m of the lip. Explosions sporadically in Bocca Nuova. Collapse enlarged it to S. Strombolian explosions in the SE Crater started in late February and continued until late August. The NE Crater started ultravulcanian explosions and internal collapse on the morning of 1 September. Strombolian explosions started soon after. Ash fell on Fornazzo. Later in the day two lava flows formed to N. and NW. The eruption stopped in the early morning of 2 September. On 6 September there was another short eruption giving a small lava flow. On 26/27 September there was a third outbreak from the NE Crater of a few hours. Ash fell between Catania and Riposto.

1981		End-January, early February: ash emission from NE Crater. Strombolian explosions started on the 5 February. Lava flowed to W., NW and N. Activity stopped on 7 February
1981	This short-lived but major N. flank eruption was preceded by two days of numerous earhtquakes. The first fissure to open was on the NE rift at about 2625–2526 m a.s.l. Boccas on this fissure were observed to open at about 2550 m a.s.l. on 17 March (13.27). Fire fountains occurred along the fissure and two short flows formed to NW. During the next four hours more fissures opened progressively downslope first following the NE rift then at about 2450 m a.s.l. trending NNW and NW. Effusive boccas opened at about 2450 m, 2150 m and 1975 m a.s.l. producing flows; as each new bocca formed, the one above stopped. The fissure system was almost continuous with lava glowing in the cracks in many places where active boccas did not form. Ultravulcanian explosions occurred in places especially at the vent near the Grotta de Gelo (2150 m a.s.l.). At 18.55 a new fissure opened at about 1800 m a.s.l. downwards and a line of spatter cones developed accompanied by some ultravulcanian explosions. The flow from here travelled 5 km in the next four hours. This was the main flow of the eruption which destroyed large areas of agricultural land and numerous farm buildings. The flow cut the Circum–Etnean railway and a major road during the night. It then cut the mainline railway and the other major road link on the mountain's N. flank early in the morning. The fissure propagated downslope at 11.30 on 18 March to about 1400 m a.s.l. and produced a flow that headed N. towards Randazzo. By 16. 30 the front of the main flow had reached the edge of the Alcantara valley at 650 m a.s.l. Another fissure opened on 18 March at 1250–1125 m a.s.l. A line of spatter cones was formed (also large blocks from ultravulcanian explosions) the largest cone being near the lower end of the fissure. A flow travelled N. towards Randazzo but stopped 2 km from the town. The main flow reached the bed of the Alcantara at 11.00 on 19 March. By midday on the 20th the main flow had nearly halted and the lowest fissure above Randazzo was feeding a sluggish flow. Mild strombolian explosions took place from this lowest vent until the evening of the 23rd when the eruption stopped	During the flank eruption major collapses occurred in the Bocca Nuova causing brown billowing fragment-laden clouds to rise over the summit. This activity continued after the eruption had ended, and during the summer months collapse was punctuated by violent gas-release. Major collapses occurred at the Bocca Nuova's rim late in the year considerably enlarging its diameter
1982		On 27 May the lava-filled floor of the Chasm was punctured by an ultravulcanian explosion (and collapse) producing a small pit. The Bocca Nuova partly filled with lava to 150–200 m below the lip with explosive activity marked on the 8 August. Continuing strombolian activity to end of year

Table 3.3 contd.

Date	*Flank eruption*	*Persistent and other summit activity*
1983	A series of strong earthquakes were first felt during the night of 26–27 March. At midday on 27 March H_2S smelt at Mt. Silvestri. Seismic activity continued during the following night and at 08.45 on 28 March a fissure with NNE–SSW trend opened between 2450 m and 2250 m a.s.l. Weak explosive activity occurred along the length of the fissure. A lava flow was emitted which by evening had cut the Nicolosi–Sapienza road as well as destroying the ski-lift. From the top of the main fissure a N–S zone of fractures extended to near the Central Crater. On the morning of 1 April ash and old lava were thrown out of two craters at 2700 m a.s.l. By 3 April lava from main fissure had advanced 3.5 km from the vent area which consisted of at least four principal effusion points and some thirty hornitos. Between 3 April and 8 April the lowest points of the flow field moved only a short distance and flow field development was by breaching of the main channel to give small side flows. This type of activity intensified between 8 April and 12 April when one overflow from about 2100 m on the E. side of the channel surrounded the Rifugio Sapienza and touched the corner of the lowermost Funivia station at about 1900 m a.s.l. Another breakout on the W. side had reached 1650 m a.s.l. by 12 April, becoming the main flow. On 10 April the fissure hornitos stopped the explosive activity. From 12 April to 17 April the new western flow moved forwards at rates of 5–10 m h^{-1}. Flow front movement then slowed over the next few days the front stopping at about 1200 m. A new lava breakout occurred at about 1600 m producing a new flow to the west which stopped at about 1150 m in the first few days of May. On 4 May breakouts shifted to E. and on 6 May a lava front had reached 1450 m For the rest of the eruption individual flows were relatively short and during June a well-developed lava-tube system had developed feeding numerous ephemeral boccas especially below about 1900 m a.s.l. This resulted in a wide, thick fan of lavas between about 1700 m and 1900 m a.s.l. The eruption stopped after 131 days on the morning of the 6 August An attempt to divert the lava near the vent was made on 14 May and embankments built on the E. and W. sides of the flow at 1950 m and 1800 m a.s.l. respectively prevented lavas spreading at this level	Before and during the eruption collapses and explosions in the Central Crater area, especially in the Bocca Nuova, gave rise to billowing plumes of ejected ash After the eruption, collapses of the type seen during the eruption occurred.

Fig. 3.17 View towards the summit from an altitude of around 1800 m a.s.l. on the western flank of the volcano. The flat skyline overrun by recent-looking lavas is the Piano caldera rim. The grey area on the left represents the outer surface of the Ellittico cone. (Photograph: J. E. Guest.)

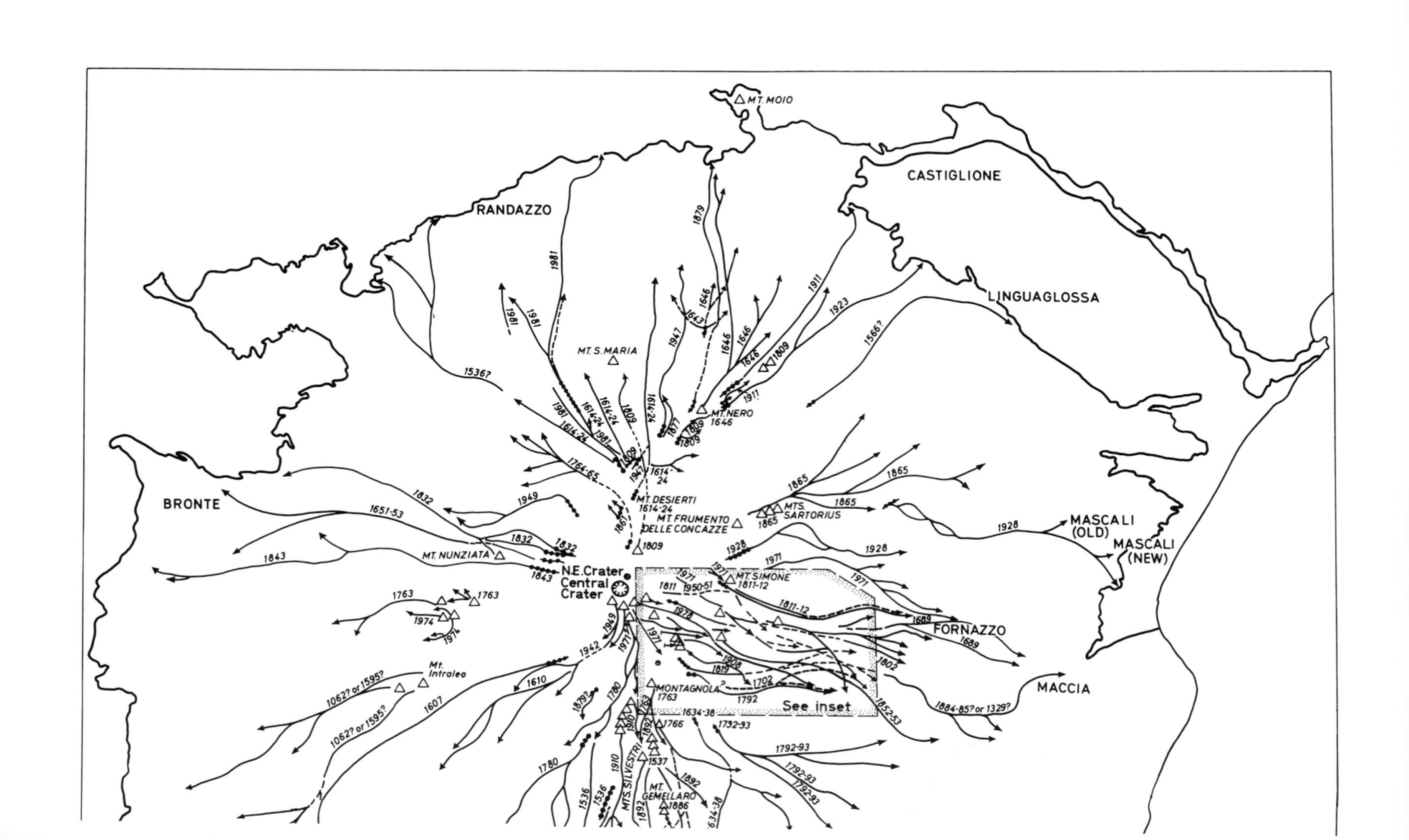
MT. MOIO
CASTIGLIONE
RANDAZZO
LINGUAGLOSSA
MT. S. MARIA
MT. NERO
BRONTE
MT. DESIERTI
MT. FRUMENTO DELLE CONCAZZE
MTS. SARTORIUS
MASCALI (OLD)
MASCALI (NEW)
MT. NUNZIATA
N.E. Crater
Central Crater
MT. SIMONE
FORNAZZO
Mt. Intraleo
MONTAGNOLA
MACCIA
See inset
MTS. SILVESTRI
MT. GEMELLARO

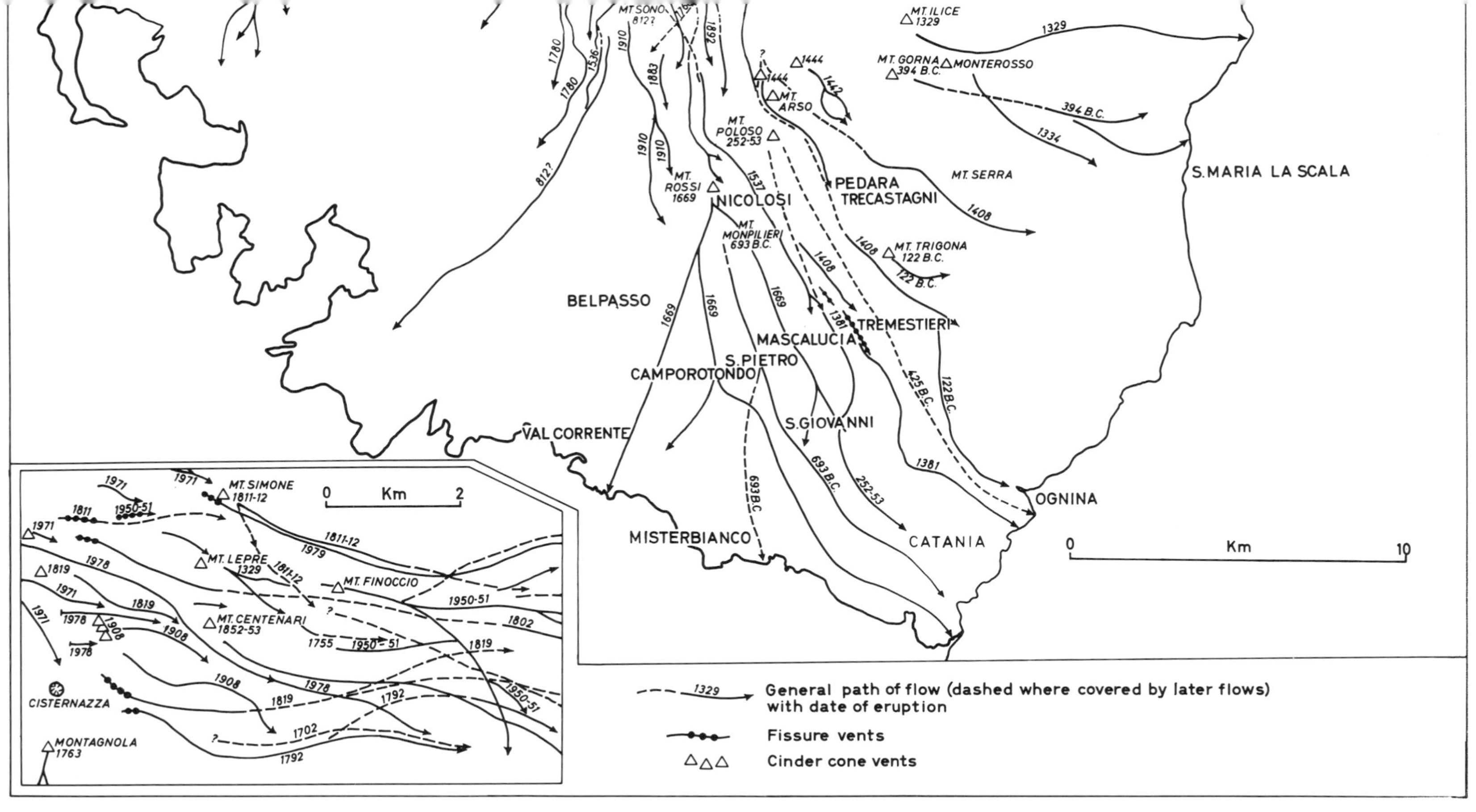

Fig. 3.18 Map showing the distribution of main historic lava flows, fissure vents and cinder cones.

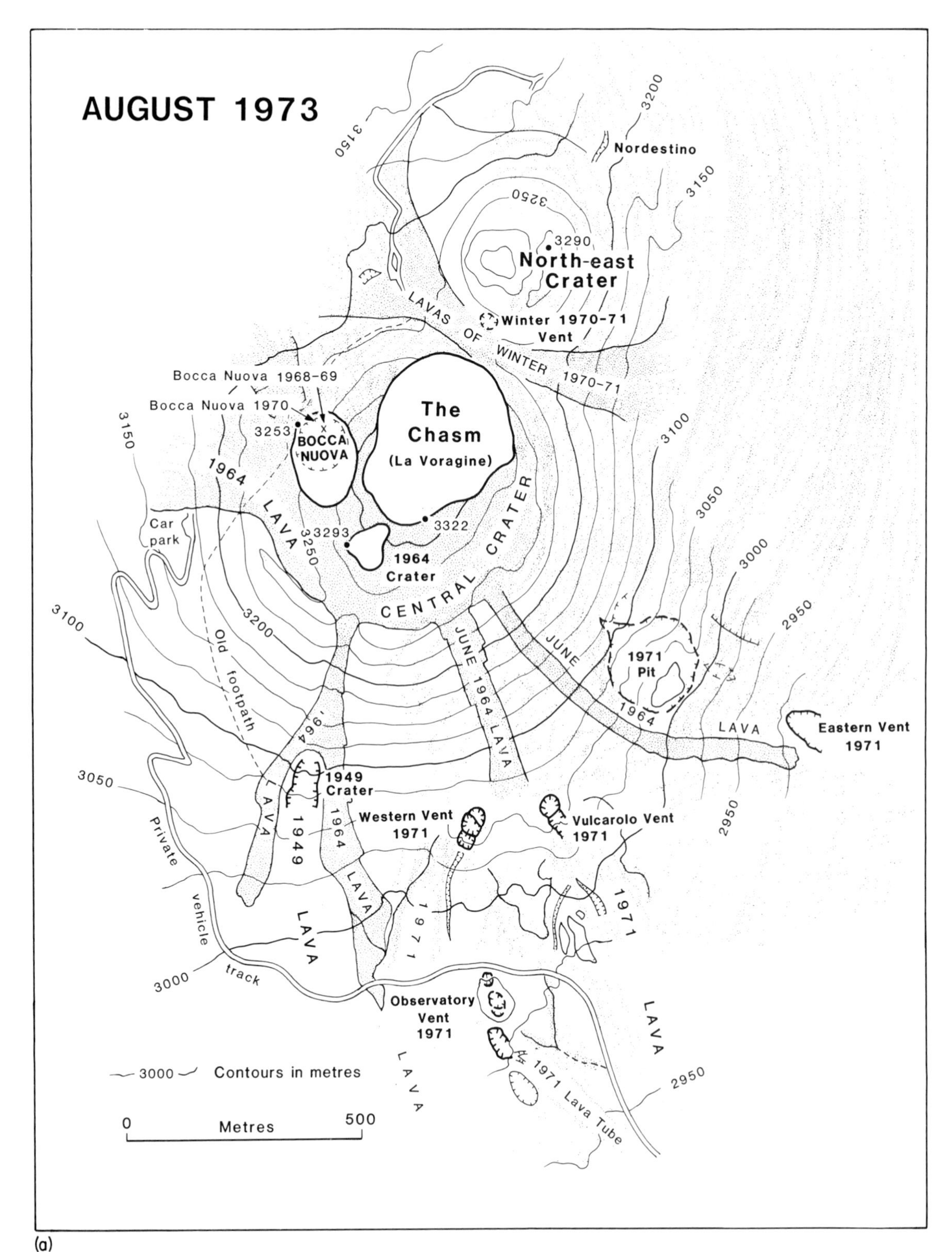

(a)

Fig. 3.19 Topographic maps of the summit area showing changes between 1973 and 1983. (Modified after Murray, 1975, 1980a, 1980b and 1982a). (a) August 1973. (b) September 1978, with insets for October 1976 and September 1977. (c) September 1981, with inset for September 1983.

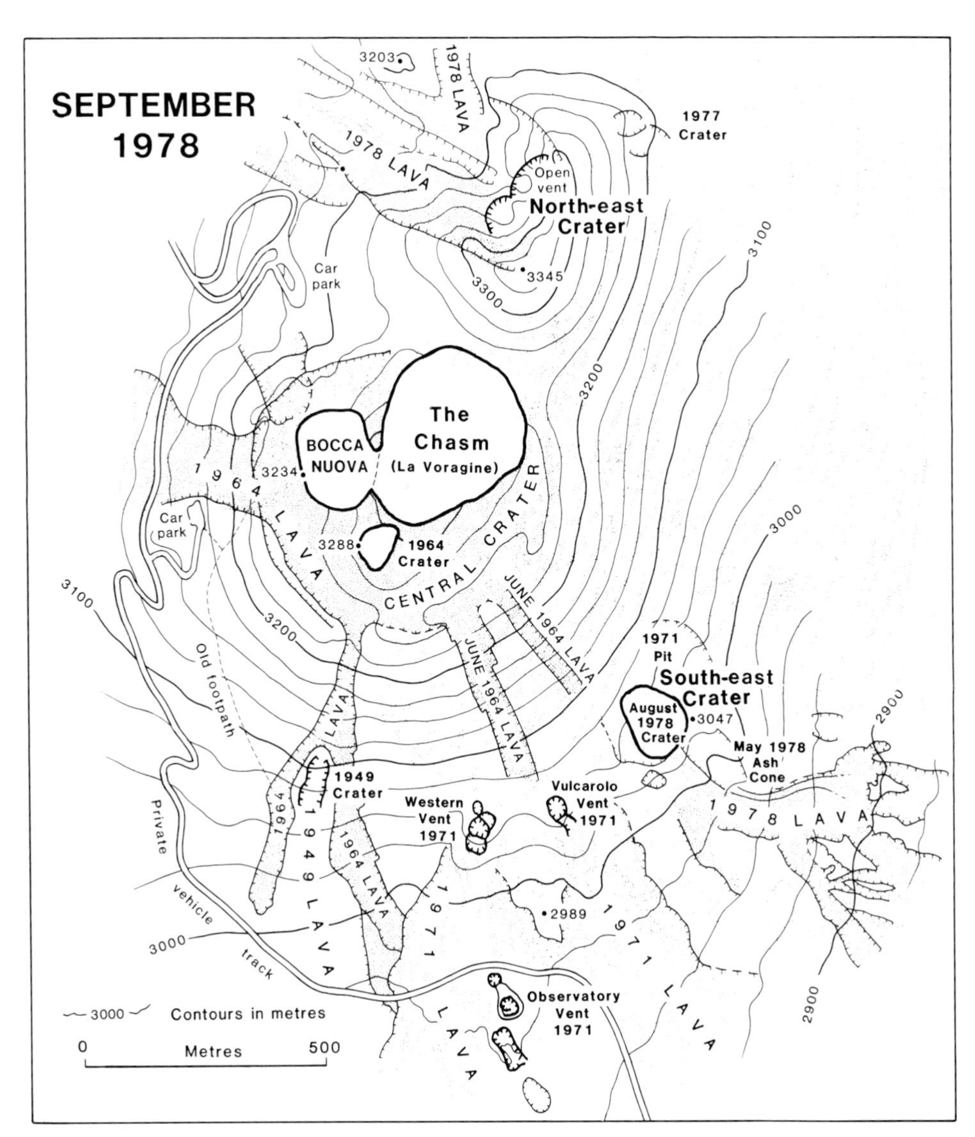
SEPTEMBER 1978
3203
1978 LAVA
1977 Crater
1978 LAVA
Open vent
North-east Crater
3345
3300
3100
Car park
The Chasm (La Voragine)
BOCCA NUOVA
3234
1964 LAVA
3200
Car park
3288
1964 Crater
CENTRAL CRATER
3000
3100
3200
JUNE 1964 LAVA
June 1964 LAVA
Old footpath
LAVA
1971 Pit
South-east Crater
August 1978 Crater
3047
2900
May 1978 Ash Cone
1949 Crater
Western Vent 1971
Vulcarolo Vent 1971
1978 LAVA
Private vehicle track
1964
1949 LAVA
1964 LAVA
1971
2989
1971 LAVA
3000
Observatory Vent 1971
LAVA
2900
3000 Contours in metres
0 Metres 500

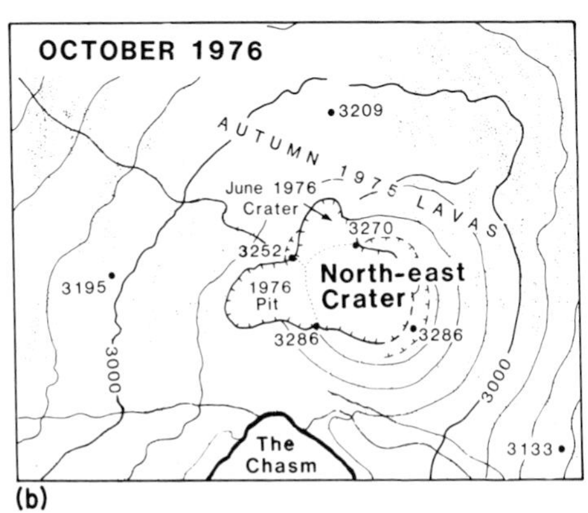
OCTOBER 1976
3209
AUTUMN 1975 LAVAS
June 1976 Crater
3270
3252
3195
1976 Pit
North-east Crater
3286
3286
3000
3000
The Chasm
3133

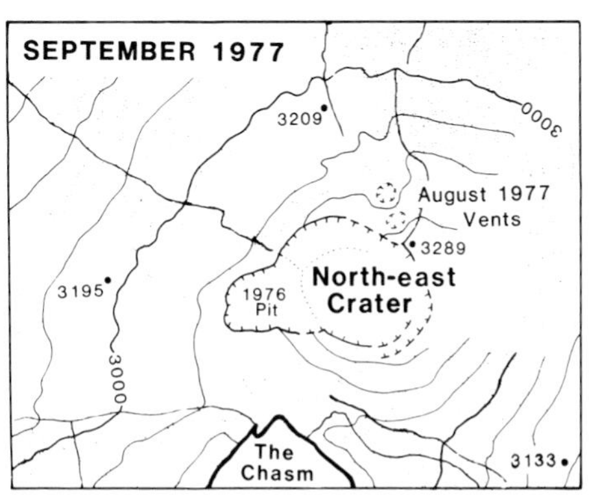
SEPTEMBER 1977
3209
3000
August 1977 Vents
3289
3195
1976 Pit
North-east Crater
3000
The Chasm
3133

(b)

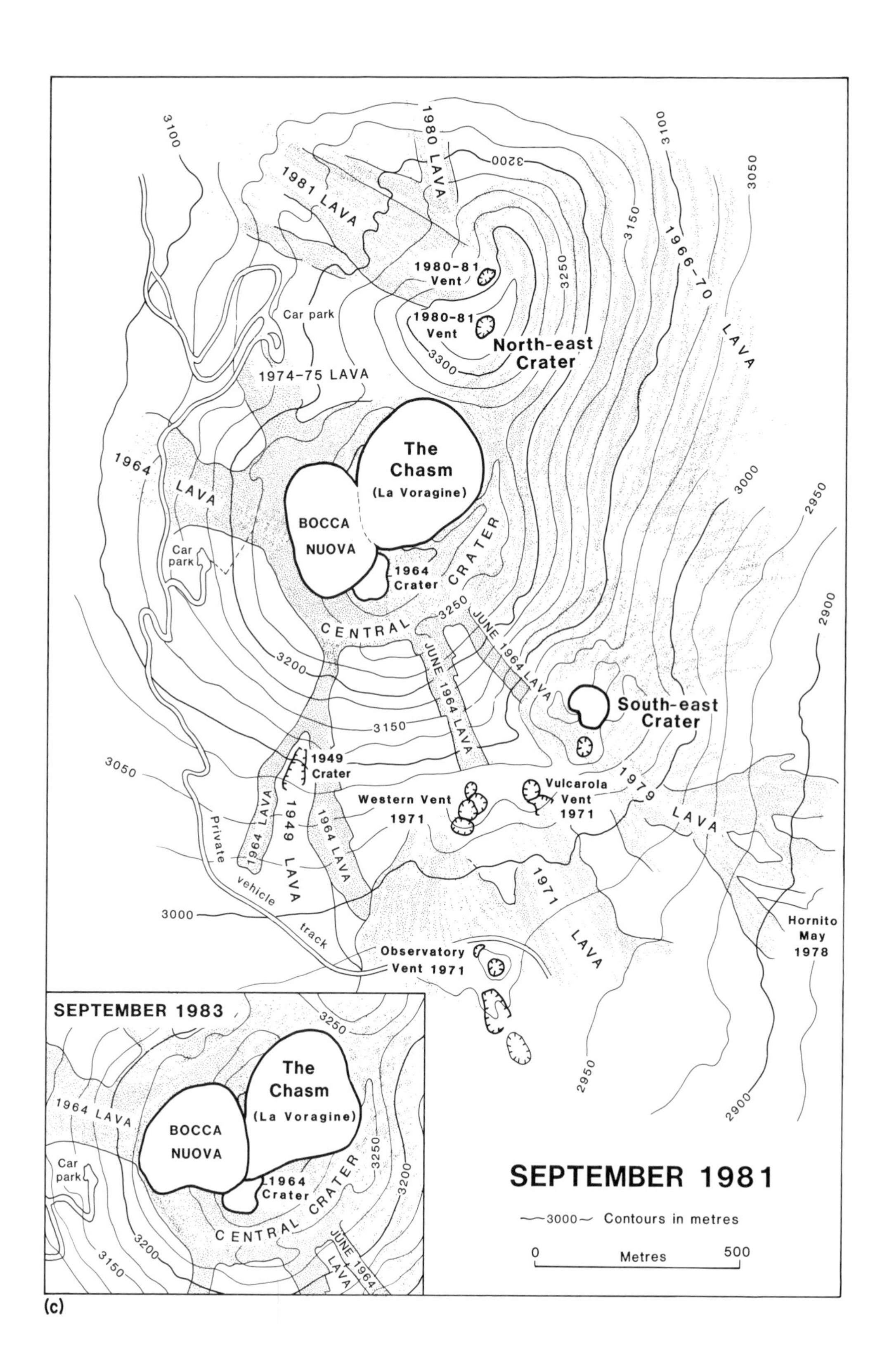
1980 LAVA
1981 LAVA
3200
3100
3050
3150
1966-70
LAVA
3250
1980-81 Vent
1980-81 Vent
North-east Crater
3300
Car park
1974-75 LAVA
The Chasm
(La Voragine)
BOCCA NUOVA
1964 LAVA
Car park
1964 Crater
CENTRAL CRATER
3000
2950
2900
JUNE 1964 LAVA
JUNE 1964 LAVA
South-east Crater
1949 Crater
Western Vent 1971
Vulcarola Vent 1971
1979 LAVA
1964 LAVA
1949 LAVA
1964 LAVA
Private vehicle track
1971 LAVA
Hornito May 1978
Observatory Vent 1971
SEPTEMBER 1983
The Chasm
(La Voragine)
BOCCA NUOVA
1964 LAVA
Car park
1964 Crater
CENTRAL CRATER
JUNE 1964 LAVA
SEPTEMBER 1981
3000 Contours in metres
0 Metres 500

(c)

4 Volcanic processes and products

'But close by Etna
thunders and its affrighting
showers fall. Sometimes it ejects up to
high heaven a cloud of utter black, bursting
forth in a tornado of pitchy smoke
with white hot lava, and
shoots tongues of flame
to lick the stars.'

(Virgil, 70–90 BC, *The Aeneid*)

Although Etna is best known for its outpourings of aa lava accompanied by strombolian explosions, a wide variety of volcanic phenomena have been exhibited by this volcano as indicated briefly in Chapter 1. Here each of the different types of activity is discussed, emphasis being placed on process rather than the overall importance of any one type of activity throughout the history of the volcano.

4.1 Explosive volcanism

4.1.1 Ultravulcanian activity

The term ultravulcanian is used, following Mercalli (1907), for those explosive events in which only solid fragments of older rocks are ejected. This definition is preferred here, although some authors (e.g. Wadge, 1977) have used 'vulcanian' to include explosions of non-juvenile material. The driving force of the explosion may be magmatic gases, vapourized groundwater, or both (Macdonald, 1972). On Etna the main products of such explosions are angular blocks typically up to 30 – 40 cm across and occasionally 1 – 3 metres across. The surfaces of the blocks are often chemically altered and they may be hot to the touch on emplacement. Such explosions are usually accompanied by non-juvenile fine ash.

Ultravulcanian explosions occur under a variety of conditions on Mount Etna. As on many volcanoes they are typical of the first few minutes or hours of an eruption. These are normally small explosions throwing material only a few metres to tens-of-metres away from the vent. Once the vent has been cleared, ejection of juvenile material becomes increasingly interspersed with the ultravulcanian explosions until strombolian activity dominates. However even when an eruption is well under way, ejection of lithic blocks may occur spasmodically between strombolian explosions and while one vent within the crater of a cinder cone may be ejecting juvenile material, an adjacent vent in the same crater may be producing ultravulcanian explosions. During the violent, strombolian activity at the South-east Crater during August 1979 numerous lithic blocks were thrown out by ultravulcanian explosions. Some of the blocks which were over 2 m in diameter came to rest some 300 – 400 m away from the vent although they may have rolled downslope for a considerable part of this distance.

As well as occurring in association with the production of cinder cones, ultravulcanian explosions can also occur during fissure eruptions. As Wadge (1977) has pointed out such explosions often occur at the upper end of the fissure while in the topographically lower parts of the fissure there are magmatic explosions and lava effusion. However these relations are not always followed as shown by the eruptive activity on the 8 km-long fissure system of the March 1981 eruption. Here, in addition to the more common cinder and spatter ramparts, several ultravulcanian craters surrounded by low block and ash cones were formed. These were not located on the upper part of the fissure system or restricted to the upper parts of individual fissures but instead were situated in topographic hollows along the fissure system. Some of the ejected blocks were in excess of 1 m in diameter and had been thrown 10 m from the vent. It seems likely that the explosions were caused by the magma in the dyke encountering groundwater or snow and ice accumulated in the hollows. Similar but larger block cones of low profile are found at about 2350 m a.s.l. on the north-east rift. Here the craters, probably associated with the 1809 eruption, are some tens of metres across. The surrounding blocky ejecta spread is only a few metres thick at the crater rim although the crater itself may be ten or more metres deep cutting through older rocks.

Dramatic ultravulcanian explosions occur occasionally from the summit pits, the Chasm and the Bocca Nuova. As described later in this chapter, the Chasm goes through cycles of filling with lava to near the rim and then collapsing to give a deep shaft. During April 1980 the lava level rose to within about 25 m of the edge of the Chasm accompanied by spectacular strombolian activity which littered the surrounding area with large bombs. By the summer of that year the floor of the Chasm consisted of the congealed surface of a lava lake with fumarolic activity around the edge. No further activity took place in the pit until the third week of May when seismicity increased suggesting the influx of new magma. During the afternoon of 27 May there was a magnitude-3.7 earthquake felt by local residents. Although there were no eyewitnesses it may be that this was contemporaneous with an explosion from the floor of the Chasm throwing lithic blocks as much as 300 m away. Some of the blocks near the crater rim were up to 1.5 m across and had produced small impact craters. From the distribution of the blocks it appeared that the explosion was not directed vertically but inclined in a north-west direction. Such explosions may be considered as 'throat-clearing' operations in advance of rising magma.

Under somewhat different circumstances the Bocca Nuova had a similar explosion on 12 September 1979, resulting in the tragic death of nine of the tourists standing near the crater edge as well as injuring many others some of whom were as far as 400 m away. The first signs of impending activity were given by seismic tremor although this did not identify either the type of forthcoming activity or its location. The explosion occurred at 17.47 local time when jets of black tephra were seen to shoot out from the Bocca Nuova followed by the crashing sound of falling bombs that could be heard as much as 2 km away. An eruption column of dense fume and ash continued to form above the explosion centre, being fed convectively at the base and developing an expanding head rising to several kilometres within a few minutes (Fig.1.16). During the eruption ejecta reached heights of several hundred metres giving impact velocities of 50 ms^{-1} or more. The ballistic range of the blocks was just over 400 m in a north-north-westerly direction but in other azimuths around the Bocca Nuova blocks fell much closer. This distribution suggests that the blast was directed. At distances of 400 m down-range the ground was strewn at intervals of several metres (Fig. 4.1) with blocks of 25 – 30 cm diameter each weighing 5 – 6 kg and having penetrated the ground to depths of 1 – 2 cm. Fragments of about 10 cm were more thickly scattered. It is estimated that something in the order of 200 000 kg of material was thrown out representing a volume of about 100 m^3 of solid rock. An eyewitness account of this explosion is given in Guest *et al.* (1980a).

The cause of this Bocca Nuova explosion has been much debated, Tazieff (1983) considering it to be the sudden release of pent-up magmatic gases in the central conduit following the flank eruption that had occurred the previous month. Kieffer (1982) and Murray (1980c) on the other hand argue that it was a purely phreatic event. In fact it is difficult to determine whether the sudden expulsion of lithic material was driven by magmatic gases or groundwater flashing to steam. Perhaps the most significant precursor to the explosion was the collapse of a shelf on the walls of the Bocca Nuova into the floor of the pit ten days before. This almost certainly caused a major blockage to the system. As Murray (1980c) notes, the Bocca Nuova gave off prolific amounts of white fume for some days prior to the explosion and some particularly heavy thunderstorms had occurred at the end of August and beginning of September. Murray suggests that these factors were the cause of the explosion, the waterlogged mass of collapse debris having been heated by magma from below until eventually some of the water flashed into steam, and ejected some of the debris plugging the vent. However it is also true that throughout its history the Bocca Nuova has emitted large amounts of fume, a high proportion of it being juvenile sulphur dioxide. Thus the possibility of magmatic gases playing at least a part in the explosion cannot be ruled out.

Despite the relatively small size of ultravulcanian explosions on Etna, they present, apart from ground collapse, by far the greatest hazard to life in the immediate vicinity of a vent. This is not because of the size of the explosion; even the September 1979 event was not a large one by comparison with some violent strombolian activity such as that which occurred during August 1979 from the South-east crater. It is the suddenness of the event that may catch spectators unawares. With normal strombolian activity even the most violent eruptions start with small strombolian events gradually building up in intensity and giving onlookers the opportunity to retreat. Some ultravulcanian events can follow this pattern, but

Fig. 4.1 Blocks ejected by the September 1979 Bocca Nuova explosion scattered over the vehicle park situated about 400 m away from the Bocca. (Photograph: J. E. Guest.)

more often they are unexpected, giving no opportunity for anyone in the vicinity of the vent to take precautionary measures.

4.1.2 Strombolian activity

Strombolian activity (Fig. 4.2), the most common form of explosive volcanism on Etna, consists of discrete explosions throwing lava fragments to heights of a few metres to many hundreds of metres. Maximum heights normally reached by bombs are 250–500 m, but occasional violent explosions may take place carrying material to 700 m or higher and some eruptions may have long phases of extremely violent strombolian activity. Other strombolian eruptions or phases within an eruption have very mild activity where small fragments are thrown up to a few metres above the vent.

The nature of the explosions depends on the physical conditions of the magma and to some extent the height of the top of the magma column in the vent. When the magma level is high in the crater of a cinder cone, fragmenting curtains of red hot lava are thrown above the lip of the crater. The larger shreds of lava, often several metres across, usually fall back into the vent or land just outside the crater, while smaller fragments are carried to greater heights and land further away. Smaller explosions even when the lava level is high usually produce bombs only a few centimetres to tens-of-centimetres across. Each explosion is accompanied by a loud bang and the accompanying shock wave can on occasion be painful to the ears. When the

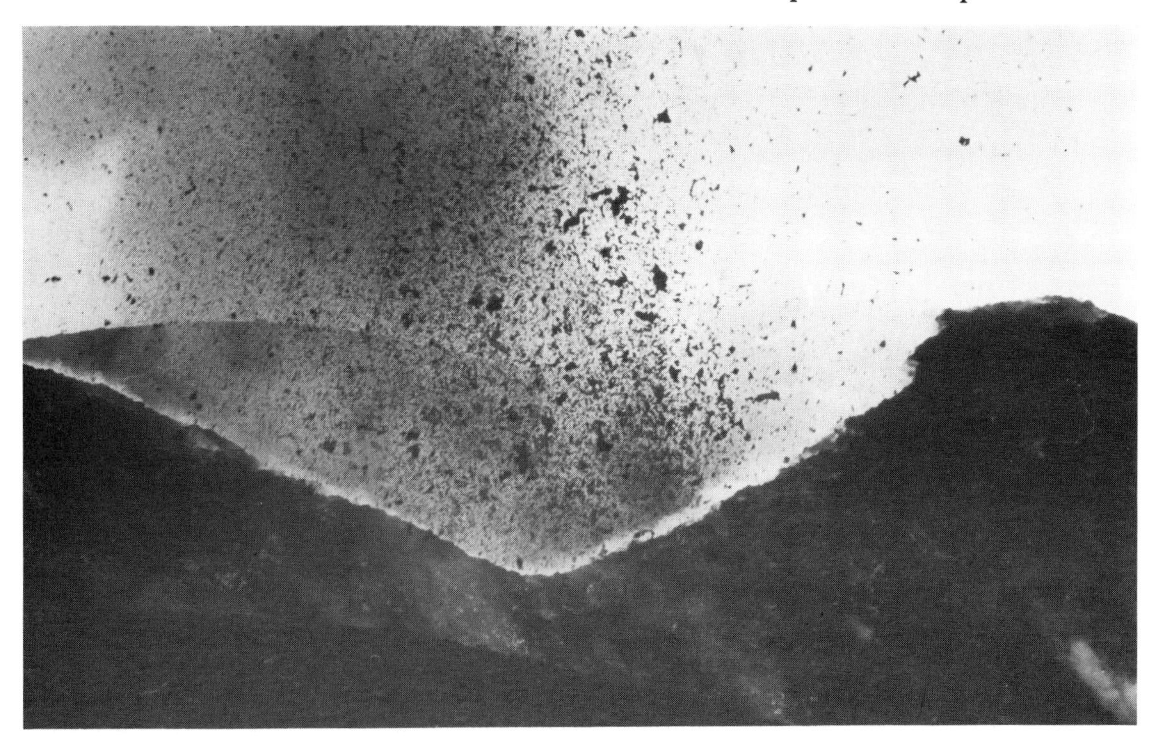

Fig. 4.2 Fragmenting clots of lava being thrown out of the crater of the first-phase 1974 eruption. (Photograph: J. E. Guest.)

level of magma is deeper in the conduit, explosions result in a shower of projectiles shooting out of the vent like pellets from the muzzle of a shotgun.

The essential dynamic characteristics of strombolian explosions have been attributed by Blackburn *et al.* (1976) to the effects of gas expansion and convection. When a bubble bursts through the magma surface, the melt fragments are initially expelled at a high velocity because of the decompression of the released gases. There follows a phase of rapid deceleration as the juvenile materials mix with the atmosphere, and most of the coarser pyroclasts fall out from the main jet along ballistic trajectories. The remaining cloud of gas and finer particles meanwhile continues to incorporate more of the surrounding air, generating a convective eruption column which may reach heights of several kilometres, one-to-two orders of magnitude greater than that of the gas jet column.

Typically explosions take place a few times per minute, larger explosions being interspersed by several mild ones. The North-east Crater in October 1969, for example, exploded at a rate of about 3 – 4 explosions per minute (Guest, 1973a). However, explosion frequencies can be much higher, following one another in quick succession at rates of 30–50 per minute; in some cases, although individual explosions can be recognized, the frequency is so high that it could virtually be classified as fire-fountaining of the Hawaiian type.

The products of explosion are extremely varied even within one eruptive phase and depend to a large extent on the rheology of the erupted lava. In a single explosion material from both the crusted-over surface of lava in the crater as well as less-congealed lava from below will be ejected together. Travel time in the air also affects the state of the final form of the bomb as this to some extent controls the amount of cooling before the bomb lands. Particularly close to the vent scoriaceous spatter is deposited, draping itself over the surface. Violent strombolian activity, as occurred during the August 1979 eruption from the South-east Crater, may throw metre-sized lumps of spatter up

Fig. 4.3 A typical spindle bomb ejected from the North-east Crater. The white scale in the background is 16 cm long. (Photograph: J. E. Guest.)

to 300 m away from the vent. Even at 500 m from the vent clots of lava with a maximum diameter of 0.5 m were emplaced.

The normal products of strombolian eruptions are scoriaceous fragments that have been sufficiently chilled so as not to deform on landing. These range in size from lapilli to bomb size. Occasional fusiform bombs occur ranging in length from a few centimetres to tens-of-centimetres (Fig. 4.3). A small number of dense bombs are thrown out consisting of lava which is poorly vesiculated. These are generally less than 10 cm across, the larger ones being egg-shaped, the smaller ones more like spindles. Their surfaces are finely crenulated and often have splits in the chilled carapace as a result of expansion of the interior by post-ejection vesiculation and a consequent increase in volume. Evidence that these bombs had thick congealed surfaces on landing is given by the observation that many of them possess only a single impact scar.

Although bombs are the most obvious products of strombolian explosions, much of the material produced is lapilli size scoria. Ash is usually less voluminous although with violent strombolian activity large volumes of fine material may be produced lifted in the convecting plume and carried down wind for considerable distances. For example, during the 1979 eruption from the South-east Crater fragments with diameters of 1 – 2 cm travelled as far as 3.5 km down wind and fine ash was deposited as far away as Catania airport 29 km away.

The actual vent can only be rarely observed during strombolian activity when mild explosions are occurring from vents inside the crater of the cinder cone. It is, however, sometimes possible to stand on the edge of the main crater and look down on the activity.

Although the Chasm and Bocca Nuova are normally filled with fume, permitting only glances of strombolian explosions, it is occasionally possible, if the nature of the evolving gases and the atmospheric conditions are favourable, to have an unimpeded view of the explosive activity in the floor of the pit, the Chasm in particular. When the pit is 150 m or more deep it is usually safe to view even fairly large strombolian explosions when ejecta is not thrown much above surface level.

Such conditions existed near the end of July 1979. At this time the pit was about 130 m deep below the lowest point on the rim. The pit floor was covered by a lake of lava that was crusted over with large blocks. Strombolian explosions took place from the surface of the lava lake at a rate of between one and six explosions per minute. Most of the material fell back into the Chasm and splendid views of the explosions could be obtained by peering over the edge of the pit. About 30 s before one of the larger explosions the whole surface of the lave lake slowly swelled into a giant blister causing gaping cracks to appear in the congealed crust and revealing incandescent lava below. Then the blister would burst with a resounding bang and eject material 150 m or more above the lava surface. Smaller explosions occurred around the edge of the lake each accompanied by loud hissing or sharp pistol-like reports. These smaller explosions only ejected material a few metres in the air.

As in the case just described where explosions of different magnitude were occurring from different parts of the magma column, so on cinder-cones there can be several vents of different character operating simultaneously. For example during the July 1970 activity from the North-east Crater, although there was a main vent giving rise to normal strombolian activity, there was a smaller adjacent crater which ejected mainly gas and sprays of small, heated lithic fragments with occasional incandescent juvenile bombs. Such essentially ultravulcanian explosions were accompanied by sharp reports.

Observations in the South-east Crater during mid-July 1979 showed a more complex situation. The activity had started on 16 July when Stuart Scott and Anne Petrykowski, who were examining fumaroles inside the crater, noticed that high-pressure gas was being evolved from a vent in the crater floor. The onset of minor ultravulcanian explosions caused them to beat a hasty retreat. Soon after, fresh magma was observed and the proportions of juvenile material increased steadily until the afternoon by which time strombolian activity had become established. The following day several vents had become active in the floor of the crater. On the northern wall there was a small cone of ash formed by explosions of ash mainly of a non-juvenile character. However, in the floor of the crater there was a cluster of three vents giving mild strombolian explosions. On 18 July the vent on the northern wall had largely died down and a new vent below this was giving much stronger strombolian activity. Next to it a small vent was blowing gas, which was burning with a blue Bunsen burner-like flame rising to 5 – 10 m above the crater floor, and giving occasional small explosions. Similar blue flames were observed in the main strombolian vent on the floor. These were almost continuous, increasing in height during a strombolian event so that the base of the explosion was surrounded by an expanding blue aureole. The cause of these blue flames has been much debated but the observation by Huntingdon (1972) that as much as 20% hydrogen occurred in high-temperature fumaroles emitting from hornitos over erupting lava has led him to the conclusion that these flames are the result of hydrogen burning in air.

Explosive activity is critically dependent on the vesicle content of a magma. Firstly, for a bubble to rupture a melt, its internal gas pressure must be greater than the total external pressure acting across its interface – typically a combination of the ambient hydrostatic pressure, surface tension effects, and the inertial and viscous resistance of the enclosing fluid. Secondly, for the wholesale disruption of the magma surface, the vesicles must be packed sufficiently closely together that they occupy a volume fraction of at least some 70 – 80% (Sparks, 1978). From gas-solubility considerations, such packing can be expected (at least, during the opening phases of an eruption) if the initial volatile content of the magma at depth exceeds about 0.06% (w/w), assuming all the gas to be H_2O, or 0.14% (w/w) if CO_2 is the assumed gas phase (Wilson and Head, 1981). And thirdly, the style of an explosion is further affected by the size distribution of the vesicles, which is determined by the relative rates of ascent of the exsolved bubbles and of the host melt (Wilson, 1980a).

In cases when the vesicles and melt are rising at comparable velocities, the opportunities for bubble coalescence are small and the size range of the vesicles remains comparatively narrow. Upon eruption, the gases stream forth as a jet, drawing with them blebs of magma that once formed the bridges between the vesicles. In the extreme, this behaviour produces the almost continuous, dramatic fire-fountains commonly observed on Hawaii. If, however, the melt ascends more slowly than the contained vesicles, coalescence assumes a greater significance, with larger bubbles rising more rapidly than, and amalgamating with, their smaller neighbours. In so doing, the bubbles become larger, are able to move yet faster and so increase the likelihood of further coalescence. Consequently, close to the surface of the magma, the vesicle population will consist of some very large bubbles, perhaps several metres across, mixed with others possibly one-or-two orders of magnitude smaller – as witnessed in the Chasm's lava pond in 1979. The style of activity will therefore be composed of comparatively frequent and small explosions, as the smaller vesicles escape, interrupted by the more violent bursting of the larger bubbles, the net result having the typical characteristics of strombolian behaviour.

In an attempt to quantify the conditions which favour either fire-fountaining or strombolian activity, Wilson and Head (1981) have numerically simulated the nucleation, growth and coalescence of vesicles rising through basaltic magmas. For the simulation, Wilson and Head (1981) assumed the rising magma to be Newtonian with a viscosity of 300 Pa s and a density of 2800 kg m^{-3}. Water vapour was considered to be the only gas phase present, at initial concentrations of either 1% or 2% (w/w). The effects of vesicle coalescence become pronounced only after the rate of magma ascent at depth has fallen below about 0.5–1.0 ms^{-1} (Wilson and Head, 1981). If the model is accepted as being reliable for at least order-of-magnitude estimates of magma velocity, then the predominance on Etna of strombolian activity over other styles of explosion suggests that the magma is rising through the volcano at rates of some 0.1 ms^{-1}. As will be discussed later, this result has fundamental implications for modelling the plumbing system within Etna.

4.1.3 Cinder cones

The vast majority of Etnean eruptions involve some strombolian activity. During the last 400 years this has been strong enough in more than 60% of flank eruptions to form a cinder cone (Guest, 1982). The cones range from a few metres to over 200 m in height and are either individual cones from which lava pours out at the base or are concentrated at the upper end of eruptive fissures, while at the lower end of the fissure lava flows out relatively quietly, sometimes building up hornitos and spatter ramparts. Generally speaking individual cones are not sites of repeated eruptions although in the summit region the North-east and South-east Craters are exceptions to this.

The general morphology of cinder cones is well known (e.g. Macdonald, 1972). They tend to have slopes close to the angle of rest and are often surmounted by multiple crater systems. In a study of cinder-cone morphology, Settle (1979) has determined that the modal basal diameter for Etnean cinder cones is about 400 m with a modal height of about 50 m. However these heights do not necessarily represent the original height of the cone as inward collapse of the crater rim, both during the eruption and as a post-eruption modification, enlarges the crater and reduces the cone's height. The initial rate of growth of the cone can be fast and for example the cone built up during the first phase of the 1974 eruption on Etna had reached a height of 100 m in less than one week from the beginning of the eruption (Fig. 4.4).

The size distribution of material ejected from a single strombolian explosion (McGetchin *et al.*, 1974) is difficult to determine as the tephra become

Fig. 4.4 A cinder cone forming during the first phase of the 1974 west flank eruption. Strombolian explosions are occurring from the crater (see Fig. 4.2) and the cone is about 100 m high. (Photograph: J. E. Guest.)

well sorted before emplacement. The larger bombs (greater than about 20 cm) tend to follow ballistic trajectories whereas the smaller material will be carried downwind with progressively finer particles being carried further. The extent of the tephra will depend on the height of the explosions and the wind velocity.

George Walker (1975) has made two studies of the scoria fall surrounding cinder cones of different sizes (Fig. 4.5). The larger one, Monti Rossi, a cone near the town of Nicolosi, is over 150 m high and was produced during the 1669 eruption. The second is the pair of cones formed during the 1974 eruption. The high maximum and median diameter values and the relatively low content of material finer than 1 mm is characteristic of the low degree of fragmentation which characterizes strombolian pyroclastics.

Figure 4.6 shows a cross-section of part of a cinder cone in a quarry face at Monterosso. In the formation of this cone the early phase of eruption produced a large amount of spatter which was emplaced in a hot enough state to weld together forming an agglutinate. On emplacement each individual spatter bomb had a cooled glassy selvage but the interior was mobile enough to allow the bomb to drape over the underlying surface. Cross-sections through the bombs show that the glassy rim is about 1 cm thick with small vesicles less than 1 mm in diameter. The middle of the bomb has larger vesicles up to 1 cm in diameter which are not strongly distorted. The upper part of the Monterosso cone has spatter close to the crater rim but for the most part consists of individually well sorted beds of different sizes of scoria. Although large bombs do occur in this sequence they are relatively

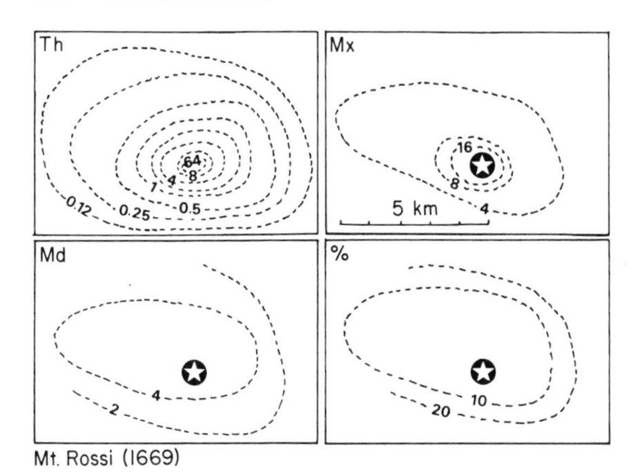

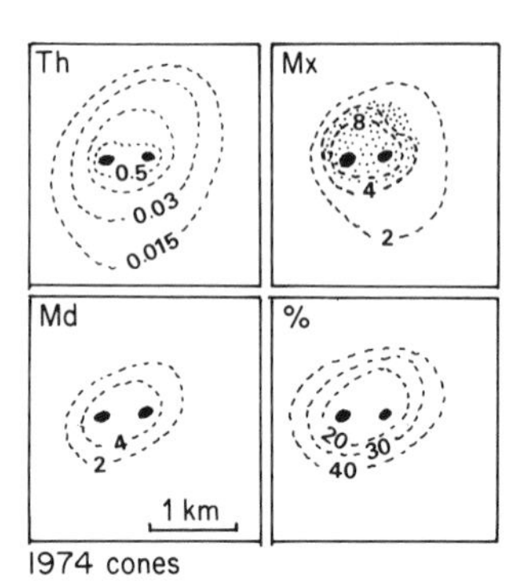

Fig. 4.5 Dispersal maps for the scoria fall deposits associated with the 1669 and 1974 cinder-cones on Etna. ('Th' is thickness in metres; 'Mx' is average maximum diameter of the three largest clasts in centimetres; 'Md' is median diameter in millimetres, '%' is weight percentage of material finer than one mm.) The figures on the 1974 Mx map relate to non-ballistic ejecta; the stippled area shows the approximate extent of ballistic (greater than 20 cm) ejecta. (After Walker, 1975.)

rare as most of the larger fragments emplaced on the flank of the cone during eruption tend to roll to the bottom of the cone. The steep angle-of-slope results from the fact that the surface of a cone at any one time is a talus slope, the emplaced tephra rolling downslope to maintain an angle of rest. Thus the larger bombs are generally only found at the tops and bottoms of cones. Although typically the material of cinder cones is black, close to the vent it can be various shades of red, orange and yellow as a result of fumarolic alteration during and after the eruption.

It is only with violent strombolian explosions that the finer grained tephra gets carried any distance from the vent. This occurred during the August 1979 eruption when tephra was carried some tens-of-kilometres from the vent to land in towns as far away as Catania. The local population protected themselves from the ash using umbrellas and raincoats. Such ash-falls tend to wash away quickly and cannot be analysed unless collection of samples is made during or immediately after the eruption.

Although most of the cones on Etna are monogenetic, polygenetic cones do develop in the summit region as mentioned earlier and the North-east Crater cone is the longest-lived of these. This vent which opened in 1911 (Guest, 1973a) has been the main site of persistent activity for much of this century. A summary of the historical development of this cone has been given by Guest (1973a, 1982). Activity here may be long-lived as with the continuous eruption between January 1966 and April 1971, or a series of short high-effusion-rate eruptions as for example occurred when there were a total of twenty-three individual eruptions each lasting just a few hours between mid-July 1977 and March 1978. The onset of eruptive activity at the North-east Crater is usually heralded some days or hours in advance by collapse in the crater giving dense yellow-brown clouds sometimes accompanied by the ejection of lithic fragments (Guest, 1982).

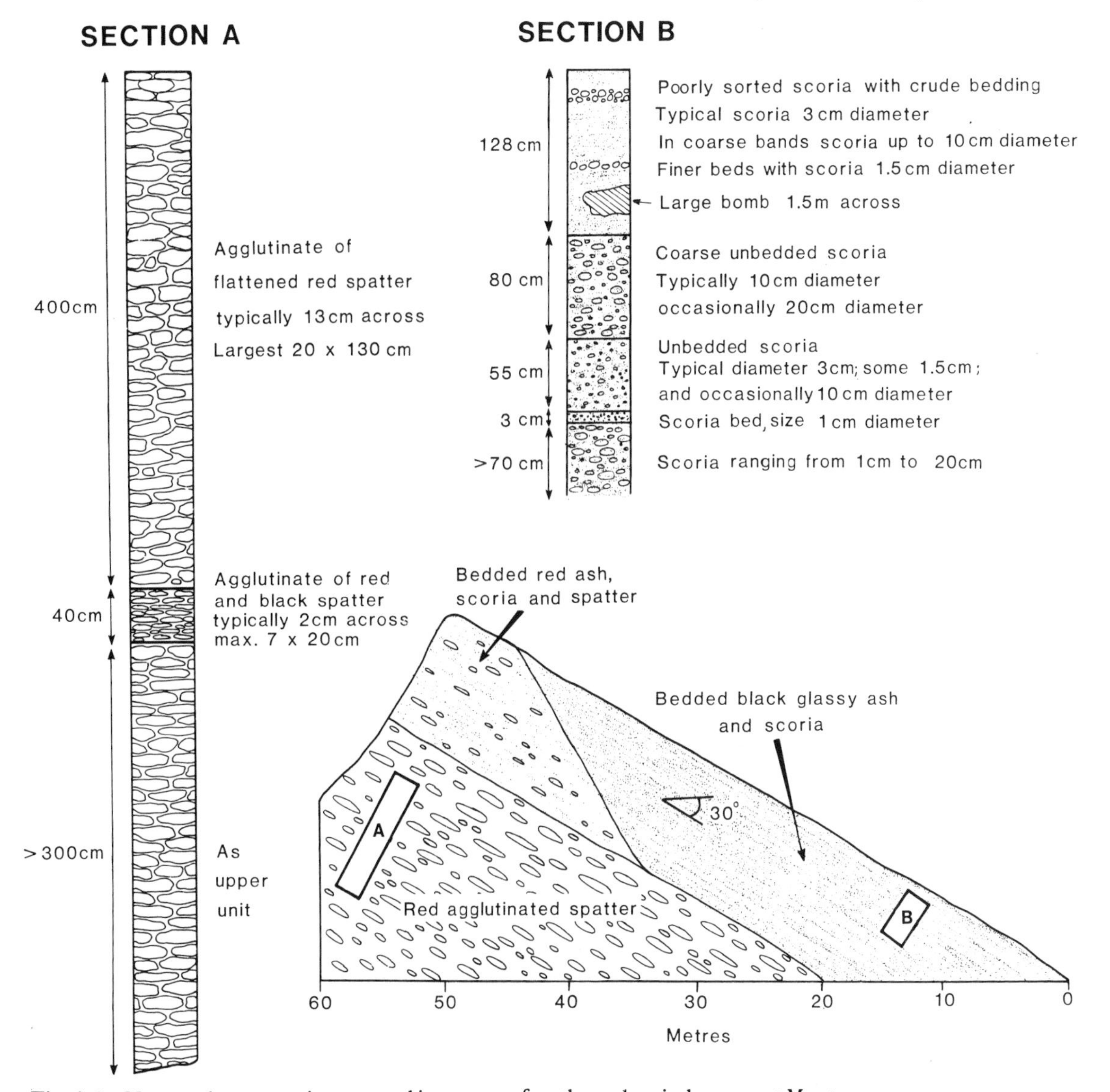

Fig. 4.6 Measured cross-section exposed in a quarry face through a cinder-cone at Monterosso.

Throughout the history of the North-east Crater cone its height has steadily increased. However, the base of the cone has also risen as a thick pile of lavas in excess of 120 m has accumulated at its foot. It may therefore be considered as a succession of cones built one on top of the other over the same general vent area, the original vent being at approximately 3100 m a.s.l., while the top of the cone was at about 3290 m a.s.l. in 1973 (Murray, 1975). By late 1978 the cone had reached a height of 3345 m a.s.l. (Murray, 1980a; also see Fig. 4.7). Because the North-east Crater consists of a series of cones built one on top of the other the internal structure is inevitably complex. This is enhanced by the fact that the site of the crater has moved from one eruption to another, extensive collapse of the rim has occurred between eruptions, the walls have been breached, and small shallow collapse pits have formed on the rim.

As in most cinder-cone fields many of the cones

(a)

(b)

(c)

(d)

(e)

(f)

(g)

(h)

(i)

(j)

on Etna have been breached on their downslope side giving them a crescentic shape. Hammill (1979) suggests that as many as 32% of all the cones on Etna have this form. Cones can develop a breached form in several ways. Continued lava effusion from the main crater of the cone may carry away newly formed tephra as it falls preventing build-up of the cones on the side where the lava is issuing, usually the downhill side. Although on many cones the lava effusion takes place from boccas around the foot of the cone, if the lava level in the main crater of the cone rises to a high level rapidly the pressure of magma may cause the cone to breach and segments of pre-existing cone material are then rafted downflow to be fragmented and incorporated in the flow or left as massive blocks on the flow surface. Once the breach has been made it will be maintained as long as the flow rate is fast enough to carry away the falling tephra. If effusion slows down or stops, continued strombolian activity will heal the breach and the cone may become roughly conical again. The most dramatic breaching event is when a whole segment of the pre-existing cone is bodily rafted away from the cone coming to rest at its foot. This again usually accompanies an increased rate of output of lava and is probably assisted by the cone becoming undermined as lava forces its way under the foot of the cone. Such an event occurred at the North-east Crater early in 1978 when it appears that a substantial part of the north-western side of the cone slid off to come to rest about 200 m away from its original position. The cone then had a horseshoe shape and lava was able to escape from the heart of the cone at a high rate (Murray, 1980b). Approximately a quarter of the cone was removed probably in much the same way as the dramatic descriptions of a similar event occurring on Paricutin in June 1943 (Foshag and Gonzalez, 1956).

Hammill has noted that on Etna pairs of cones associated with the same eruption often have an upper unbreached cone and a lower breached cone. An example of this is the pair of cones produced during the 1974 eruption on the west flank. This he attributes to higher volatile concentrations in the upper, early-formed cone causing the rapid build-up of the cone before lava effusion took place. The lower, later-formed cone was produced by volatile-depleted magma, and the effusion rate of the lava was higher than the rate of growth of the cone causing the breach to be maintained.

4.1.4 Phreatomagmatic activity

The conditions on Etna during historical times have not been suitable for phreatomagmatic eruptions in which the dominant product is juvenile material ejected by explosions that, at least in part, are generated by water entering the vent. None have been known to occur in historical times and it is unlikely that such an eruption will occur in the future unless a vent opens on the coast or under thick snow accumulated for example in the Valle del Bove; the latter situation would probably only result in a limited amount of phreatomagmatic activity before the relatively thin snow cover was melted and normal activity took over.

There is evidence nevertheless that large phreatomagmatic eruptions have occurred in the past apparently at times when the snowline would be expected to be low during glacial periods. The best exposed phreatomagmatic cone is that of Trifoglietto II which is considered to have formed during the Pontinian stage when the snowline in the Etnean region was lower than at present (Klerkx, 1970 and McGuire, 1982). The cone is exposed in the western wall of the Valle del Bove where it is seen to have an oval form in plan view. The original dimensions are unknown as only part of the cone is visible but it had a minimal basal diameter of 3 km × 3 km and a minimum height of 300 m (McGuire, 1982). By extrapolating the present surface upwards McGuire (1982) suggests that the original height of the Trifoglietto II cone lay between 2500 m and 2600 m a.s.l. However, this

Fig. 4.7 A sequence (a)–(j) of photographs of the North-east Crater to illustrate some of the changes that have occurred since 1969. All the pictures were taken from about the same place immediately west of the Bocca Nuova. For the eruption history of this vent during the time illustrated, see Table 3.3. (Photographs: J. E. Guest.)

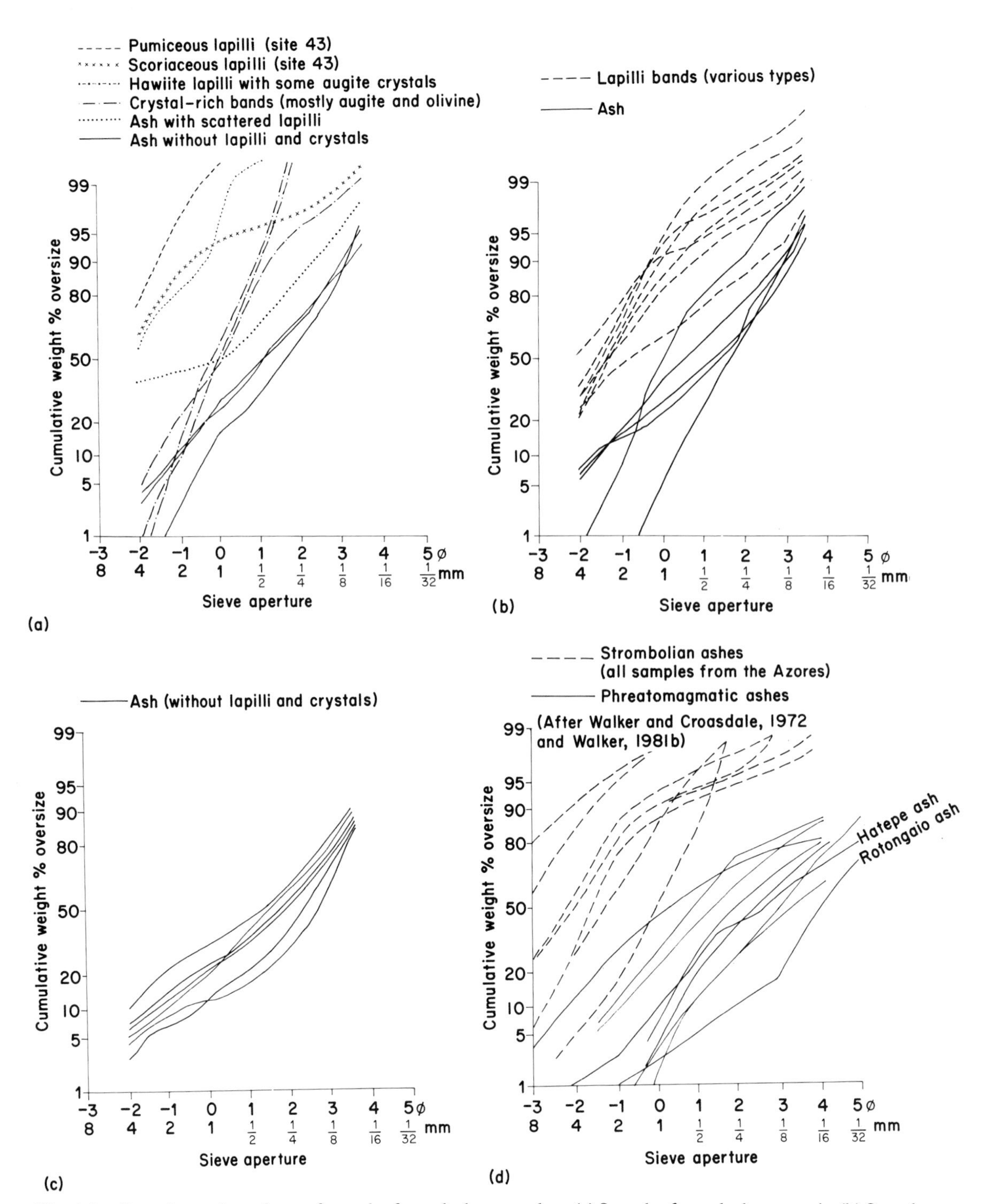

Fig. 4.8 Granulometric analyses of samples from the lower tephra. (a) Samples from the lowest unit. (b) Samples from middle unit. (c) Samples from the upper unit. (d) Comparison curves from other volcanoes. These analyses show that, while the units of scoriaceous lapilli plot in the region of strombolian deposits, the other units compare well with the phreatomagmatic ashes from elsewhere. (After Guest *et al.*, 1984.)

reconstruction is based on the summit crater being relatively small by comparison with the size of the cone and if a larger crater – as is typical for phreatomagmatic cones – had developed, the original height may have been several hundred metres less.

Most of the cone is made up of pyroclastic materials with some thin interbedded flows making up about 20% by volume of the cone (McGuire, 1982). The phreatomagmatic origin of the cone can be demonstrated by examination of the ash particles. Typical ash from the strombolian eruptions consists of curved glassy droplets which exhibit shapes that are largely controlled by surface-tensional effects on the particles when they were still molten; particles of this type have been termed achneliths by Walker and Croasdale (1972). However the materials of Trifoglietto II have a quite different form consisting of fragments that are bounded by angular fracture planes and phenocrysts broken out of their matrix. This highly fragmented type of ash with a high proportion of fines is typical of phreatomagmatic eruptions.

Guest *et al.* (1984) have examined the lower tephra, extensive ash deposits to the south-east of Trifoglietto II, and have correlated these deposits with that volcanic centre or a penecontemporary one of similar type nearby (see Chapter 3). The thickness of these ashes, which is in excess of 12 m at about 13 km from the vent, is suggestive of strong and sustained activity. Guest *et al.* (1984) divided the sequence into three main units based in part on lithology and to some extent on erosional unconformities. The basal unit is usually seen to be filling in valleys which are cut in either bedrock or hill wash material. It consists mainly of fine-grained yellow ash. Lapilli are scattered throughout the unit but in places there are discrete horizons or lenses up to 30 cm in thickness of dark lapilli and scoria. There are also thin beds rich in augite and olivine crystals broken from their matrix. However the bulk of the unit consists of fine-grained yellow ash showing the high degree of fragmentation (Fig. 4.8) leading to 65% of the material being less than 1 mm in diameter. Although the coarser bands are relatively well sorted and the crystal-rich bands clearly result from gravity-sorting in the eruption cloud, most of the material is poorly sorted perhaps as a result of rain flushing from the eruptive plume (Walker, 1981a). The highly fragmented nature of this material together with its yellow alteration strongly suggests that it is phreatomagmatic in origin. The lapilli bands, on the other hand, are more characteristic of strombolian activity, perhaps developing at times when water was prevented from entering the vent and 'normal' activity occurred for a short period of time.

This lowest unit has an erosional upper surface with channels sometimes as much as 10 m deep. The middle unit is draped over this surface and consists of lapilli and gritty ash horizons. The lapilli beds vary in thickness from 13 cm to 53 cm and individual fragments may be up to 3 cm with a mean size of between 0.5 cm and 0.75 cm. The material is mainly basaltic scoria but some horizons contain pale-gray lava and augite crystals, the latter being especially abundant near the base of the unit. The lapilli beds are well sorted with only about 9% of sub-millimetre size grains. Again this unit may be interpreted as alternating strombolian and phreatomagmatic explosions.

The upper unit is similar to the lowest unit and is considered to have formed in the same way. The ashes of the lower tephra unit are consistent in character with the type of activity apparently exhibited at the Trifoglietto II cone and their thickness and dispersal away from this vent (or a similar nearby one) indicates the strength of the eruptions.

In the closing phases of the development of the Trifoglietto II cone the production of lava suddenly dominated the eruptive style and the outer flanks of the cone are coated with several hundred metres of lavas with only about 5% interbedded pyroclastic material (McGuire, 1982). As is the case with many phreatomagmatic centres the source of water dried up or the cone had built up to such a size that water was prevented from entering the vent.

Although Trifoglietto II cone is the largest exposed cone produced by phreatomagmatic activity on Etna there are other ashes that may be interpreted as being of this origin. For example, the so-called upper tephra (Chapter 3) have a lower component of apparent phreatomagmatic origin material grading up into strombolian ashes and scoria beds (Guest *et al.*, 1984). These ashes were erupted around 5000 BP and may well be related to the collapse of the Ellittico Caldera.

4.1.5 *Ignimbrites and lahars*

Although local inhabitants of the basaltic volcano and volcanologists alike have been lulled into a sense of security by long periods of hundreds or even thousands of years when activity is of a relatively quiet nature, such volcanoes can sometimes provide unpleasant surprises. During the phreatomagmatic eruption of Kilauea, in 1790 a party of King Keoua's warriors and camp-followers were killed apparently by a surge consisting of a dilute mixture of ash particles in superheated steam that rushed out of the Halemaumau caldera (Swanson and Christiansen, 1973). Such surges probably accompanied phreatomagmatic activity on Etna described in the previous section but surge deposits have not so far been identified. However, evidence of rather more violent explosive activity has.

On the south-western flanks of the volcano where resurfacing by lavas has been relatively slow there are two deposits considered by Kieffer (1973) to be 'pumice flows' produced by Katmaian-type caldera-collapse in the summit region. The deposits have since been described by Duncan (1976a) who recognized both pyroclastic flow deposits – or ignimbrites – and units of similar composition that were emplaced as lahars. The two main areas of deposits of this type are at Biancavilla and Montalto. Carbon-14 dates suggest that these have ages of 15 000–15 500 BP (Romano, 1982) and 14 180 BP (Kieffer, 1979). The enclosed pumicious material has a benmoreitic composition similar to the more evolved lavas in the Vavalaci and Ellittico sequences around the Valle del Bove. Although Kieffer (1973) correlates the deposits with the collapse of the Ellittico caldera these dates would be more consistent with a Vavalaci age (see Chapter 3). Although ignimbrites have only been found in this one area on Etna it seems likely that similar deposits occur elsewhere but have since been covered by lavas.

The Biancavilla ignimbrite is particularly well exposed as it has been dissected by a canyon-like gorge. Duncan (1976a) recognised two units of distinctly different lithology (Fig. 4.9). The upper unit which has the maximum exposed thickness of 7 m has all the textural characteristics of an unwelded ignimbrite. It is poorly sorted with a homogeneous distribution of pumice fragments generally less than 10 cm across, set in a finer-grained matrix with no bedding. Most of the pumice is grey, although there is some red pumice and tachylyte. In some places the unit shows faint stratification and cross-bedding which may be a ground surge facies within the ignimbrite unit.

The lower unit which varies from 2 m to 8 m in thickness, although of similar composition to the upper units, has a different texture. There is normally no obvious stratification and the unit is poorly sorted but the fragments are distributed in a heterogeneous manner. In addition to the pumice there are abundant blocks of plagiophyric lava picked up from the underlying surface. These denser lithic fragments tend to be concentrated near the top of the unit. The heterogeneity of the unit has suggested to Duncan (1976a) that this unit is a mudflow or lahar rather than being an ignimbrite. This interpretation is supported by the observation that the denser fragments have been carried to the top of the flow. If this interpretation is correct then it would suggest that during this phase of eruption, material emplaced higher on the flanks of the volcano as a result of plinian eruptions or explosions associated with dome emplacement was remobilized into lahars which preceded the pyroclastic flows in this sector of the mountain.

The Montalto unit has a more extensive outcrop than that of Biancavilla. It is generally less than 5 m in thickness and shows a variation of lithology. However the characteristics are similar to those of the upper unit at Biancavilla, it being poorly sorted with fragments of black pumice and glass usually less than 20 cm in diameter set in a finer-grained matrix. Some of the glassy materials contain small sandstone inclusions. Lithic fragments picked up at the base of the flow consist of pale-grey plagiophyric benmoreite and fragments of plagiophyric lava. The variations in texture result largely from

Fig. 4.9 Pyroclastic flow deposits exposed in the wall of a canyon near Biancavilla. (Photograph: A. M. Duncan.)

differing amounts of lithic fragments within the unit. On stratigraphic grounds Duncan (1976a) considers this Montalto unit to be younger than that at Biancavilla and this conclusion is supported by the ^{14}C dates mentioned earlier.

It is not known how often small ignimbrite eruptions have occured on Etna. However they are more likely to occur with magma compositions that are more evolved than the normal hawaiitic lavas erupted during historical time and it is likely that they will only occur again should the volcano plumbing change to allow these more silicic lavas to be produced.

4.2 Effusive activity

4.2.1 Sub-aqueous volcanism

Among the earliest volcanism of Etna was the eruption of tholeiitic lavas into a shallow bay on the site now occupied by the mountain. The extent of that bay and the subaqueous volcanic deposits is unknown as these materials are now largely covered by younger flows, but good outcrops may be seen along the coast north of Catania (Fig. 4.10) especially near the picturesque fishing towns of Acitrezza and Acicastello and up to 2 km inland near Ficarazzi (Sturiale, 1968). At Acitrezza it appears that the magma intruded into wet 'Sicilian' sediments, the *Argille marmose azzurre*. The deposits are well exposed inland just at the back of the town, along the shore at Acitrezza and on the islands and sea stacks known collectively as the Isole Cyclopi. Viewed from the coast the Cyclopi form a spectacular seascape and legend has it that these rocks were those flicked by the giant Cyclops Polyphemus at the fleeing Odysseus. The well-known Castle Rock (Fig. 3.8) surmounted by a Norman keep consists of fine exposures of pillow lavas, hyaloclastites and hyaloclastite breccias;

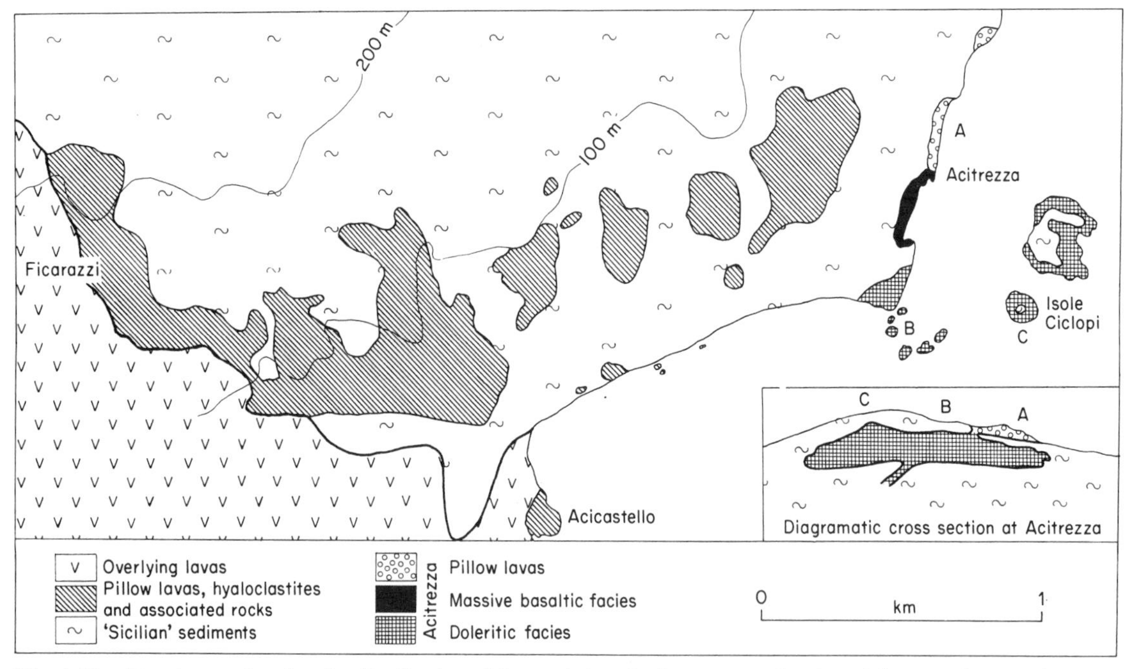

Fig. 4.10 Sketch map showing the distribution of the products of subaqueous volcanic activity near the coast between Acicastello and Acitrezza. (Compiled from Sturiale, 1968, and Wells and Cristofolini, 1977.)

photographs of this site have appeared in many textbooks of volcanology (e.g. Macdonald, 1972, p. 101).

Sartorius vön Waltershausen (1848 – 61, 1880) described these deposits and similar ones found more extensively in the Iblean volcanic field to the south of Etna. He considered that the pillows were volcanic bombs and the associated yellow fragmental deposits were tuffs. These latter he named palagonite after the town of Palagonia in the Iblean area where they are well exposed. Although several authors wrote on this subject in the last half of the nineteenth century and the beginning of the twentieth century it was Platania (1902–1903) who recognized their submarine origin suggesting that the pillows were the result of basaltic intrusions into a denze ooze. During the early part of this century the term *palagonite tuff* was widely used in the literature especially in Iceland where it became associated with sub-glacial fragmental deposits. Misuse of the term to include all deposits of glassy, basaltic ash in which the particles are mainly the altered isotropic mineraloid palagonite led Rittmann (1962) to suggest that those fragmental deposits resulting from submarine volcanism should be termed hyaloclastite from the Greek, meaning literally a rock made up of broken glass. This term has now been generally accepted for all fragmental rocks of this origin ranging from fine-grained sandy deposits to breccias.

Taking the Acitrezza and Isole Ciclopi area first, this has been studied in detail by Cristofolini (1974) and Wells and Cristofolini (1977). The main mass of basaltic material here is a shallow intrusion emplaced beneath a thin cover of marly claystones on the sea bed. The magma cooled sufficiently slowly to give well-defined columnar jointing (Fig. 4.11) and at one outcrop has prominent platy jointing. The capping white claystones now exposed on the tops of the two largest islands (see Fig. 6.6), have in places been pierced by the intrusion allowing the formation of pillow lavas on the sea floor.

Because of the special conditions of their emplacement, the Acitrezza rocks have an interesting crystallization history which is quite different from their subaerial counterparts. The intrusive nature

Fig. 4.11 Well-developed columnar jointing in an intrusive mass within the 'Sicilian' clays at Acitrezza. (Photograph: J. E. Guest.)

of the sill-like body is indicated by thermal metamorphism of the overlying sediments. Wells and Cristofolini (1977) have noted that the first event to be imprinted on the doleritic rocks of the sill was the development of planes of vesicles developed roughly parallel to the upper surface of the intrusive body. These pass uninterruptedly across zones of quenching which appear to have developed differentially along cracks as the de-vitrifying and crystallizing magma began to contract and solutions derived from the sea or wet sediments were able to penetrate the upper part of the mass. Continued hydrothermal activity resulted in the filling of the vesicles by zeolites. Deeper in the mass, vigorous growth of pyroxenes in the vicinity of joint planes (particularly horizontal platy joints) led to pyroxene-rich veins. The petrological and petrochemical aspects of this phenomenon will be discussed further in Chapter 6.

Most of the other outcrops of subaqueous volcanic deposits are of effusive character although in some places they are penetrated by strongly columnar and colonnade jointed auto-intrusive masses. The exposure at Castle Rock in Acicastello is one of the best examples of pillow lavas in the region. The outcrop consists of a jumbled interlocking mass of pillows draped over one another (Fig. 4.12). Patches of marly clay and hyaloclastite occur in places between individual pillows. The typical pillow size is about 70 × 20 cm. One large pillow-like mass in the upper part of the section has strong radial jointing and is more than 6 m across. Many of the pillows show radial jointing in addition to spherical fractures. Some have retained an outer glassy black selvage of about 4 mm thickness containing small vesicles of about 1 mm diameter

Fig. 4.12 Pillow lavas in the cliff face at Acicastello. Note the radiating joints and zeolite-filled vesicles. (Photograph: A. M. Duncan.)

or less. Inside the pillow vesicles occur in concentric zones with increasing vesicle size towards the centre of the pillow where they may be as much as 5 mm in diameter. The characteristics of the pillows are similar to those found elsewhere in the world and an understanding of their mode of formation comes particularly from observations of advancing flow fronts off the coast of Hawaii (Moore, 1975).

Hyaloclastite material occurs at the seaward end of Castle Rock where it is separated from the pillow lavas by a near vertical sharp boundary. Near to the pillows it consists of sandy yellow hyaloclastite shot through with stringers of lava bounded by glassy selvages. There are also sub-angular fragments typically 9 × 6 cm across, although sometimes as large as 40 × 20 cm, which have glassy selvages on some sides and appear to be broken pillows. The matrix has fragments of glass up to 1 cm, orange fragments, and chips and secondary zeolites. This unit grades into a unit containing up to 80% of pillows and fragments set in a pale yellow hyaloclastite matrix. The pillows normally have dimensions of about 90 × 40 cm and there are also pillow fragments of about 10 cm diameter. In this unit the secondary zeolitization is more prevalent in the pillows. The next unit away from the pillow mass has a crude semi-vertical bedding and about 40 – 50% of the material is made of angular fragments and scattered pillows of various sizes. The hyaloclastites exposed in this cliff section do not extend on to the marine platform which surrounds the base of the cliff.

The near-vertical disposition of these units in the Castle Rock has led to some debate about their origin. It is suggested by Di Re (1963) that this upstanding mass is a slab of pillow lavas and hyaloclastites that was originally emplaced in a sub-horizontal position but has been broken up and tilted by being rafted above an underlying flow. A similar explanation would be that it arrived in its present position by landsliding on the floor of the sea, a common phenomenon in subaqueous volcanic rocks (Moore and Fiske, 1969). Romano (1982) on the other hand suggests that the hyaloclastites were tilted by the mass of pillow lavas intruding from below.

The subaqueous deposits around Ficarazzi (Sturiale, 1968) are somewhat different in character and consist largely of breccias, chemically altered blocks and micro pillows. Sturiale considers that these represent material erupted close to the shoreline. It is also of interest to note that the 'Sicilian' clays in the general region of Acitrezza and Acicastello contain thin levels of vitreous lapilli and ash in their upper part.

Hyaloclastites are generally considered to be the result of spalling and decrepitation of lava flow fronts and pillows caused by the rapid chilling of lava surfaces. Where there are thick extensive hyaloclastite deposits they may have been formed by a more violent mechanism whereby auto-explosions generate cracks and the surrounding water is able to enter the cracks giving a high surface area in which water is in contact with hot lava. Further explosions lead to more cracking and the process continues while there is a supply of hot magma and cold water (Colgate and Sigurgeirsson, 1973).

Although the tholeiitic subaerial flows of comparable age to the Acitrezza – Acicastello complex are largely pahoehoe, there are, in the vicinity of Valcorrente and near the River Simeto at Adrano, outcrops of pillow-like character. These are interpreted as resulting from the flows entering lakes or lagoons in this region (Cristofolini, 1972).

4.2.2 Vent areas

The styles of activity and resultant landforms in the effusive vent areas depend on a number of factors including the effusion rate, the rates and amounts of de-gassing and the duration of the eruption. Vents usually open on fissures which range in length from a few metres to extensive systems of several kilometres. For the longer fissure systems effusive activity may be restricted to a short length, the rest of the system consisting of gaping cracks and normal faults; or, as in the case of the March 1981 eruption, effusion can occur for a substantial proportion of the length of the whole system (see Fig. 1.21).

With vigorous gas emission at the vent giving strombolian activity, or even on some occasions fire-fountaining, a cone of cinders or spatter and cinders builds up. If the rate of construction of the cone is high compared with the rate of lava emission, cone-building will dominate especially in the early phases of the eruption and lava effusion takes place from boccas at the foot of the cone. This may result from burrowing of the lava from the central column under the flanks of the cone, or where there is a pronounced fissure system that is longer than the diameter of the base of the cone, from vents along the fissure. If, on the other hand, the effusion rate is high the cone will remain breached on its lower side allowing lava to pour from the main conduit. Where activity takes place from several points along a fissure system the tendency is for (a) vents to open up progressively downslope and (b) for the upper vents to be more explosive than the lower ones. However, this is not always the case and during the 1910 eruption (Fig. 4.13) most of the lava poured out from the lowermost vent on the fissure system which was also the most explosive.

Where de-gassing at the vent is on a relatively small scale, spatter ramparts build up along the sides of the fissure system and quite commonly hornitos (Fig 4.14) of various sizes and shapes may be formed. These typically range up to about 6 m high and even when not expelling fragments of lava can be impressive features (Fig. 4.15) emitting gas at a high rate so as to produce a loud hiss or even roar. The largest such hornitos on Etna are found near the vent area for the 1614 – 24 eruption at about 2500 m on the north-east rift. These hornitos (Fig. 4.16) are about 100 m apart and are both some 30 m tall. Unfortunately these outstanding features known as the Due Pizzi are now slowly being buried by lavas from persistent activity at the

Fig. 4.13 The lowermost cone of the 1910 eruption. The lava issuing from it has a well-defined channel seen in the foreground. (Photograph: J. E. Guest.)

North-east Crater and from fissures on the rift. Although where vents are associated with cinder cones most of the de-gassing occurs in the crater of the cone, in some cases fields of hornitos can form in the vent area at the foot of the cone, a phenomenon commonly seen around the North-east Crater (Fig. 4.15). Normally, however, any activity at the base of the cone is confined to quiet effusion often from a bocca consisting of an open pool of lava up to about 10 m in diameter. In contrast, more sluggish flows may just break out through the side of the cone. Where lava is erupted from small vents on fissures without explosive activity it again forms a small (usually less than 4 – 5 m across) pool of lava around the vent area or over a length of fissure leaving, when the eruption is finished, a hole or series of holes where lava has drained back.

The duration of the eruption can also have a profound effect on the final form of the vent area. If the eruption is a short one or the effusive activity moves from one site to another, as in the case of the individual boccas opened up around the 1974 cone during its first phase of activity, then the vent areas are much as described so far. However, with sustained activity from the same vent over a period of one-to-two weeks a well-developed channel system may form. In time this may roof over to form a tube system (Fig. 4.17). This is particularly common where the eruption is occurring from a radial fissure when lava is flowing down the fissure near the vent. Complex tubes may develop within the fissure, sometimes at several different levels. This phenomenon, which has been noted in other volcanic districts (Greeley, 1971) can be seen in the

Fig. 4.14 A hornito, approximately 6 m high, expelling fragments of lava at a vent near the foot of the summit cone in May 1978. (Photograph: J. E Guest.)

1910 fissure, on the lowest fissure vent of the 1971 eruption near Citelli and in the 1983 eruptive fissure. The actual outlet of lava is thus moved further downslope from the vent itself. In the most extreme case distributory tube systems develop delivering lava to numerous ephemeral boccas. This phenomenon has occurred frequently as a result of persistent activity from the North-east Crater and on the north-east rift. It can be recognized because the boccas consist of open tube entrances (Fig. 4.18) and sometimes skylights in the tube can be seen further upstream. Another indication is the presence of tumuli aligned along the roof of the tube and the tumuli themselves are often sites of small emissions of lava. Ephemeral boccas also form at the toes of slowly moving or stationary flows, draining the flow upstream to leave an open channel (Pinkerton and Sparks, 1976).

The development of tubes in aa lavas deserves some discussion. Normally associated with pahoehoe lavas, they have rarely been described in the technical literature as occurring in aa flows (Macdonald, 1972, p. 83). However, on Etna (and probably on many other volcanoes consisting largely of aa lavas) tubes are especially common in the vent areas of aa flows. Indeed lava tubes have long been known by shepherds on Mount Etna as resting places, and sources of snow and ice for watering sheep in the hot summer months. Reference is made to them in classical and mediaeval literature (Brunelli and Scammacca, 1978) and one such was probably the home of the mythical Cyclops. Lyell (1847, p. 384) described these subterranean caverns as 'the most curious features on Etna'.

The lava tubes formed from the Observatory Vent during the 1971 eruption have been discussed in detail by Guest *et al.* (1980b). The Observatory Vent opened at an altitude of about 2980 m a.s.l. and consists of a cone 150 m in basal diameter and 40 m high. Lava was emitted continuously for thirty-two days from the base of the cone on the southern side to give a total length of flow of about 3.7 km. The thickness of lava at the site of the buried Volcano Observatory 300 m downslope is about 10 – 15 m.

During the later stages of eruption from this vent Huntingdon (1972) and Le Guern (1972) recognized that lava from the main vent at the foot of the cone was channelled in a tube and that the flow was being fed from a number of ephemeral boccas scattered up to several hundred metres further downslope of the cone. When the eruption had stopped and the lava cooled it was possible to explore the vent area both above and below ground. The lava vent at the southern foot of the Observatory Cone is a shallow, partly ash-filled amphitheatre about 30 m across surrounded by a rampart of blocks of lava. Extending downslope from here is a ridge about 170 m long and up to 5 m high consisting of buff-coloured chemically altered lava blocks about 2 – 3 m across that have been tilted up away from the centreline of the ridge,

Fig. 4.15 Small hornitos emitting gas at high pressure at the foot of the North-east Crater in 1970. Numerous ephemeral boccas were emitting lava in the surrounding area. (Photograph: J. E. Guest.)

giving it a castellated appearance in profile. Along the ridge axis is a depression as wide as 35 m across floored by a chaotic jumble of lava blocks similar to those along the margins of the ridge. The general structure is of a line of large collapsed tumuli over a tube. This tube probably formed in a fissure parallel to the Observatory Vent fissure but slightly offset from it. The chemical alteration of the lava blocks resulted from escaping gases from the lava below. At the lower end of the ridge of tumuli the tube is obscured by lavas, but 50 m to the east the conduit reappears as an east–west-trending shallow channel floored with lava slabs. Although there are no obvious tumuli, the southern side of the feature is bounded by upturned altered lava blocks. Here it appears to be a more typical collapsed lava tube.

After 50 m the collapsed tube turns sharply south as a more pronounced feature similar to the line of tumuli above, and terminates in a 'pit' some 30 m long, 20 m wide and 8 m deep (Fig. 4.19). The walls of the pit are veneered by fresh lava that appears to have draped the walls when it finally drained. This pit was probably at one stage a tumulus as it has uplifted blocks surrounding it but the roof presumably collapsed early in its history, leaving it as a large open skylight. Numerous overflows occurred from the pit as indicated by thin veneers of lava on the outer flanks and well-developed lava channels extending from the rim crest of the pit outwards. However not only was lava spilling over the edge of this pit, which might at this stage be treated as the main bocca for the eruption, but it was also escaping through exits in the wall of the pit into a system of lava tubes. These must have originated as channels radiating from the end of the main channel system but, because of the sustained activity, each later became roofed

Fig. 4.16 The two large hornitos known as Due Pizzi on the upper part of the 1614–24 lava flow field. The fissures in the foreground opened during the 1947 north-east rift eruption. (Photograph: J. E. Guest.)

over allowing lava to flow below ground. At this stage of the eruption, therefore, lava was being emitted from both the pit and through a series of lava tubes to feed the flow lower downslope. The exit points of the tubes in the walls of the pit consist of alcoves, the most pronounced of which is at the southern end of the pit. It is 8 m long by 3 m wide but like the other alcoves it is blocked by lava at the end and it is not possible to enter the tube system. Immediately above the alcove is a well-developed lava channel on the rim of the pit and a few metres downslope the floor of the channel has broken down giving access to the tube below. From this point the tube extends for about 15 m downflow but does not follow the line of the surface channel above. A branch tube extends back to the eastern wall of the pit but is filled with lava near the edge of the pit. This tube may have been joined by another, now-blocked tube, again associated with a surface channel. The lower end of the main tube is blocked by undrained lava but downslope from the tube are two boccas consisting of the open ends of lava tubes (Fig. 4.18). These were almost certainly fed from the main tube from the pit or another one (now inaccessible) close by. The 1971 eruption is one of many on Etna in which lava tubes became an important part of the near-vent flow field development of aa flows.

The preceding descriptions of vent areas pertain mainly to flow fields that in their final form were of the aa type. For pahoehoe flow fields on Etna the vent areas are relatively simple and are usually fissure type vents with little or no pyroclastic materials surrounding them. Spatter ramparts can form and on rare occasions, such as the growth of the Due Pizzi described earlier, hornitos may develop. The formation of lava tubes is normal, and in the extreme case virtually the whole of a pahoehoe flow field may consist of ephemeral boccas fed by lava tubes. This phenomenon will be discussed later in the chapter.

4.2.3 Aa lava fields

The aa lavas of Etna come in a variety of contrasting gross morphological forms. There are simple and compound flow fields, the latter predominating; long thin flows, which may or may not bifurcate downslope, and wide fan shaped flows; and thick short flows formed on the one hand by sluggish eruptive lava and on the other by numerous overflows from a single channel system. The development and final form of a flow field depends on a number of interrelated factors including the lava rheology, duration of eruption, rate of effusion, total volume of lava erupted and the underlying topography.

The rheology of lava, discussed in more detail in the next chapter, is itself controlled by interrelated factors, the principal ones being composition and temperature of the lava, its crystallinity and rates of crystal nucleation and growth, degree of polymerization, gas content and amount of vesiculation. For Etna's historical flows the bulk

Fig. 4.17 Main flow channel of the 1983 eruption near the vent where it is beginning to roof over to form a tube. (Photograph: C. R. J. Kilburn.)

chemical compositions of lava from individual eruptions are similar enough for this to be considered a negligible factor when comparing the flow field of one eruption with that of another. The other factors are, however, important variables. Initial eruption temperatures may vary from one event to another and temperatures measured at depths greater than 30 cm depth range from about 1060°C (with about 50% (v/v) crystalline phases) to over 1125°C with 35% (v/v) phenocryst phases or less (Archambault and Tanguy, 1976; Pinkerton and Sparks, 1978). There is a tendency for persistent activity to erupt lava at lower temperatures while flank eruptions and more violent summit activity tend to have higher initial eruption temperatures (Archambault and Tanguy, 1976). There is a strong temperature gradient within the top 20 – 30 cm of the flow, the thickness of this cooler 'crust' depending on the initial temperatures and distance away from the vent. Pinkerton and Sparks (1976) have measured temperature-drop with distance from the vent at depths of about 15 cm indicating the rate of cooling of the surface materials is slow and in their example about 4°C per 100 m; however, the rate of heat loss with distance from vent will depend on the velocity of the flow and mode of flow emplacement such as channel or tube flow. In general heat loss from the interior of the flow will be relatively slow because of the high insulating properties of the congealed crust. Nevertheless relatively small changes in temperature can result in orders of magnitude change in the viscosity and effective yield strength (Chapter 5). All the other factors controlling lava rheology will tend in time to increase the effective viscosity.

Lava rheology strongly controls the surface characteristics of flows. Some lavas on Etna are erupted with significantly higher effective viscosities than normal and have an overall surface texture

Fig. 4.18 A drained ephemeral bocca on the 1971 flow field from the Observatory Vent. In this case the bocca is the distal end of a small lava tube. (Photograph: J. E. Guest.)

comparable to the distal portions of flows that were erupted in a more fluid state. The lava is usually emitted sluggishly and is often accompanied by intense de-gassing in the crater of the associated cinder cone. This was exemplified during the first phase of the 1974 west flank eruption, in which the early main period of cinder cone building was accompanied by the effusion of a thick and short flow (Fig. 4.20), while during the later stages when strombolian activity was much reduced, lavas of more normal rheology were erupted (Guest *et al.*, 1974). The sluggishly erupted flow is 10 – 15 m thick and only a few hundred metres long. Its frontal talus slopes have settled at about 35° from the horizontal and were steeper during the eruption. The surfaces are covered by chemically altered red and yellow, rounded blocks of scoria and autobrecciated lava, typically about 20 cm in diameter but occasionally larger. The coarse rubbly nature of such flows is attributed to the relatively slow rate of advance of lava with a higher effective viscosity than normal, at least near the surface. Little drainage of a channel occurred and the flow eventually congealed with arcuate convex downslope pressure ridges or ogives (Fig. 4.20).

For 'normal' eruptions on Etna the lava has initial rheological conditions which allow it to congeal as pahoehoe so long as it sustains only a limited shear stress while it is cooling. Thus slop of lava over the edges of levées and the final material congealed in the middle of the lava channel in the near vent areas may have a pahoehoe form (see Fig. 1.19). However with distance from the vent the flowing lava develops a congealed skin

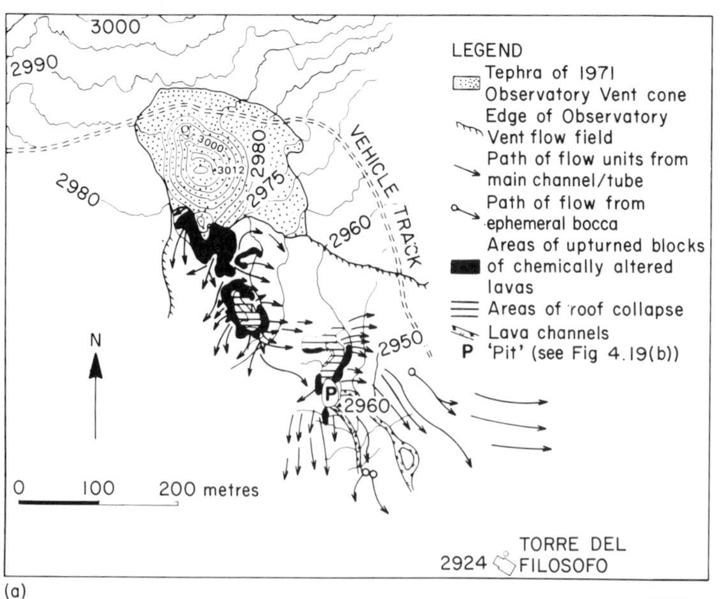

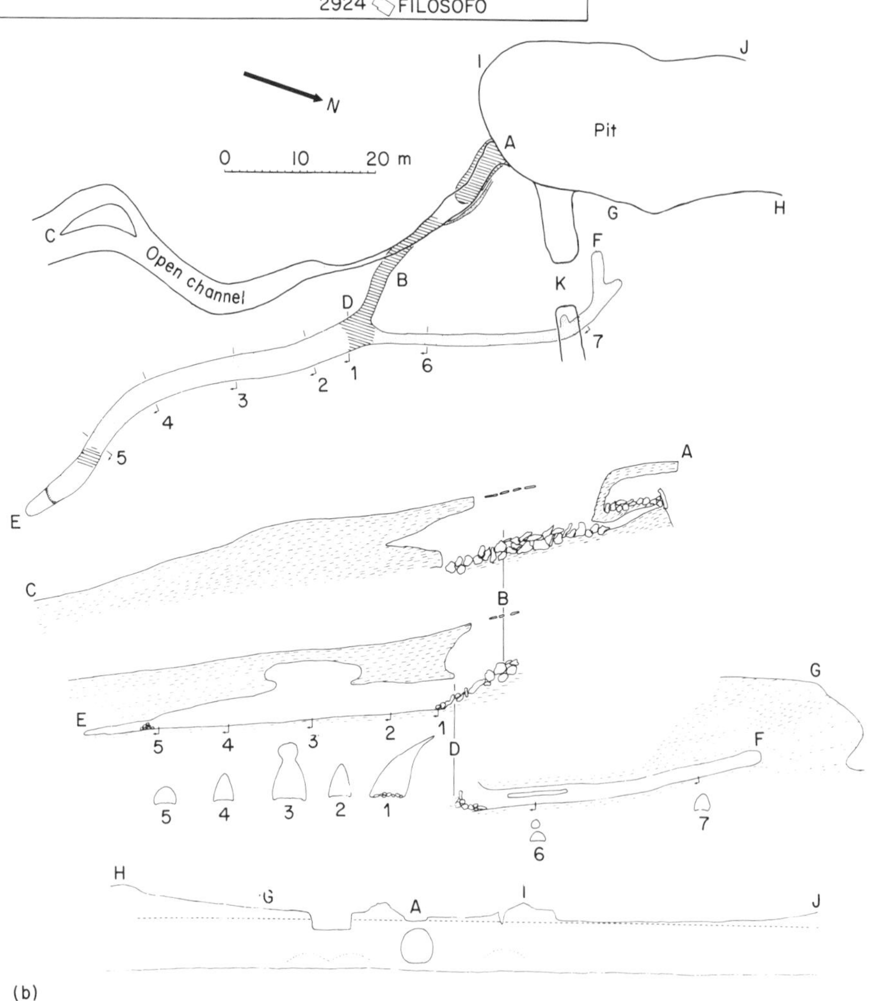

Fig. 4.19 (a) Map of 1971 Observatory Vent area. (b) Plans and cross-sections of the 'pit' area and associated channels and tubes near the 1971 Observatory Vent. The top figure is a plan of the pit and the channel and tube systems. Channels are indicated by thick lines. Where the tubes are floored by a lava they are dotted, while diagonal lines inidicate where there has been breakdown from the roof. The middle figures are cross-sections through the main channel system and the lower profile that of the inside of the pit. Letters and numbers indicate corresponding positions on the plan and profiles. (From Guest *et al.*, 1980b.)

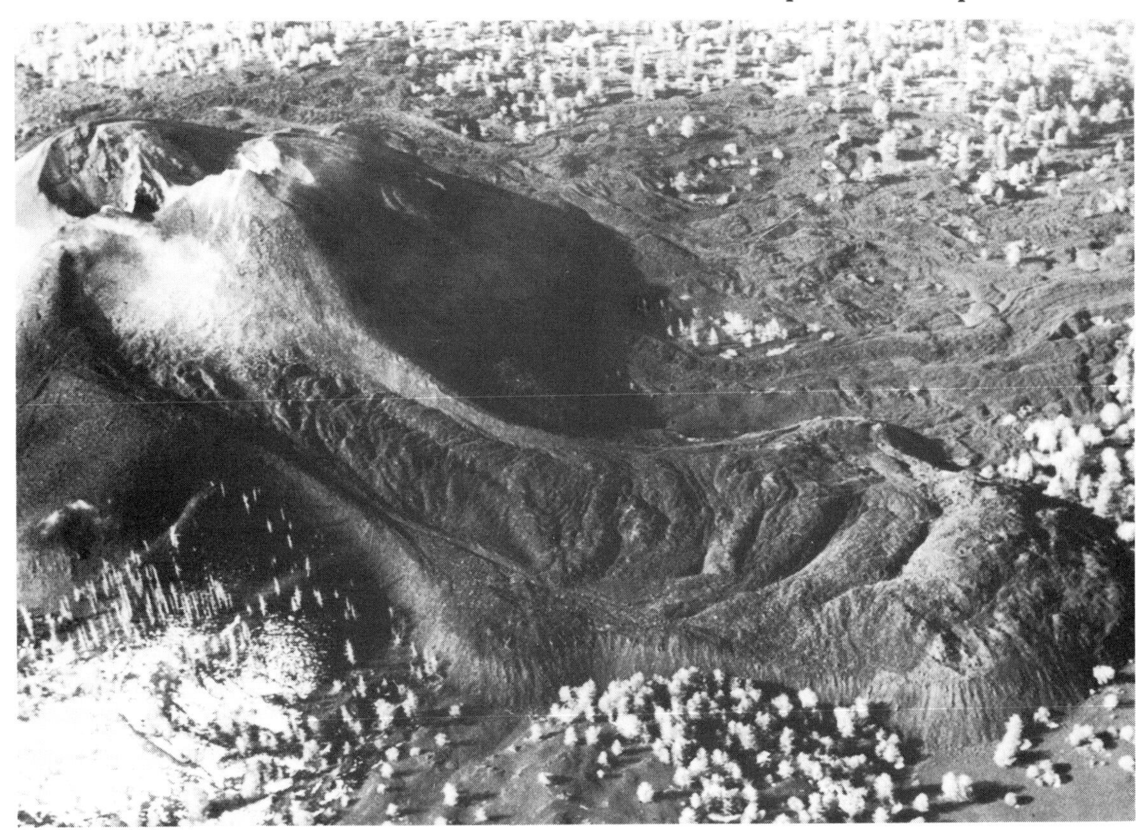

Fig. 4.20 Aerial view of the cone and lavas from the first phase of the west flank 1974 eruption. Note the thick, stubby flow with ogives in the foreground. (Photograph: R. Romano.)

which stretches, breaks up and gives the characteristic clinkery surface appearance of an aa flow. The spinose nature of the clinkers may not always be the result of stretching of the crust but may form by outgrowths on the clinker and the surface of the flowing lava giving cauliflower-shaped protrusions (Kilburn, 1984). The clinker developed close to the vent usually has a small diameter of typically about 5 cm (Fig. 4.21). However with distance from the vent the clinker becomes larger sometimes with typical diameters of 0.5 m (Fig. 4.22) presumably as a result of the broken crust being thicker; in the distal portions of the flow the blocks become rounded as a result of rolling and attrition against other blocks (Fig. 4.23). The clinkery and rubbly surface of aa flows is not only produced by this mechanism; chunks of friable autobrecciated lava can be squeezed up (Fig. 4.24) and sometimes break up during flow adds to the surface rubble.

Although the crust becomes thicker and cooler with distance from the vent the material inside the flow can retain a temperature close to that of the initial one. This is demonstrated by ephemeral boccas in the distal portions of a flow (in the case of the 1981 eruption some 8 km from the source area) where lava has squeezed out from beneath the scoriaceous rubbly surface to produce short flows of material that congealed as pahoehoe (Fig. 4.25), the surface form suggesting that the lava was in a similar rheological condition to that near the vent area.

Slabby surfaces (Fig. 4.26) may develop by break-up of pahoehoe surfaces in the near-vent area especially with low flow velocities allowing the surface to congeal as pahoehoe before it is stretched.

As pointed out by Sparks *et al.* (1976) levées may originate as a direct result of the rheological

Fig. 4.21 Clinker covered surface of an aa flow. (Photograph: C. R. J. Kilburn.)

characteristics of the lava. If lava is considered to have a yield strength, then stationary bodies having a characteristic width for a given slope must develop at the flow margins (Chapter 5). Consequently in the early stages of a flow there are two bordering zones of stationary incandescent lava (Fig. 4.27) which are termed *initial levées* by Sparks *et al.* (1976). With continued effusion other types of levée are built up over the initial one. Following the classification of Sparks *et al.* (1976), *accretionary levées* generally occur near the vent where the central portion of the channel consists of relatively smooth pahoehoe with thin margins of clinker. The clinker may remain incandescent and ductile during flow and may be reworked by the marginal shear forces. As the lava level rises with time, as commonly occurs, the marginal clinker builds up a bank on either side of the flow. The clinkers tend to weld together forming a solid levée, giving typical slopes as steep as 50 – 85°. Eventually the outward-sloping levées may converge over the top of the flow thus roofing it in.

Rubble levées occur in the parts of the flow where aa has fully developed as a surface characteristic. They are formed by avalanching on steep flow fronts and consist of a talus composed of unwelded aa debris. In addition unpublished observations (Pinkerton, Guest, Duncan and Kilburn) show that while these levées are active they tend to move forward whether they be at a flow front or on the flow sides. Lava pressure against the embankments causes them to bulge and fresh lava to squeeze through the embankment to be erupted as small toes. Sometimes the embankment may completely breach, perhaps as a result of the main flow being slowed further downslope, and a new flow develops fed through the breach.

Overflow levées occur when the lava in the channel rises and slops over the edge of the levée. Normally the increase in lava level is short-lived

Fig. 4.22 Typical surface texture of an aa flow in the more distal portions with larger blocks of clinker and rubbly material. (Photograph: C. R. J. Kilburn.)

and the overflows travel only a metre or so. However occasionally larger surges occur giving longer flows which rapidly break up to slabby pahoehoe and, if sustained long enough, become aa flows. Temporary increases in lava level may result from increase in effusion rate, back pressure as the advancing flow front slows down (Pinkerton and Sparks, 1978), or because the flow has become blocked downstream by a large chunk of levée that has broken off and been carried downflow.

Because each of these levée types results from a specific mechanism and because at any one point in a flow the conditions may change, many levées are hybrids of two or more types. In addition to this all of them may to a greater or lesser extent suffer from intrusion by lava in the channel thus giving a complex cross-sectional appearance.

The duration of an eruption can have a profound effect on the final flow field form. The median duration for Etnean flank eruptions is 22 days but eruptions may range from a few hours up to six months or a year. Exceptionally, eruptions may last for several years, especially persistent activity in the summit area. For example, the activity that started at the North-east Crater in January 1966 lasted more than five years. The longest known duration eruption is that of the 1614 – 24 flank effusion but this gave rise to an extensive pahoehoe flow field.

Those flow fields formed by eruptions of short duration (usually of less than 48 h) are often simple flows which over most of their areas consist of a fairly level field of surface clinker. Drainage tends to occur only on the steeper slopes where weak channels are formed. The main 1981 effusion on the north flank produced an example of such a flow field, which was emplaced in about 40 h and covered an area of about 4 km^2 (see Fig. 1.21).

With longer duration eruptions the flow field becomes compound, developing numerous overlapping units as a result of new flows starting near

Fig. 4.23 Surface blocks on an aa flow. Note the rounded corners resulting from attrition between the blocks on moving flow. (Photograph: C. R. J. Kilburn.)

the source, break-outs through levées and bifurcation of flows by topographical obstacles. In such flow fields many of the channels drain and may be occupied again by later flows. Depending on topography the main channel within the first kilometre or so of the vent may remain the principal feeding channel to the flow field throughout the eruption; but downslope once the main flow front has come to rest, the feeding channel may be breached higher upslope by the continuing flow of lava from above, and the new flow develops either parallel to the previous one or forms a new tongue depending on topography. This occurred several times during the 1983 eruption, so taking the active flow front progressively further downslope (see Fig. 1.23). With continued eruption the main channel near the vent may roof-over forming a lava tube retaining the temperature of the flowing lava and thus allowing it to travel further. Eventually, however, probably when the main flow field has reached its maximum length the flow may start spreading by repeated overflows and a complex tube system may develop extending progressively away from the vent. During the last phases of the 1983 eruption, a lava fan developed consisting of numerous effusive boccas up to 3 km from the vent, each bocca erupting small volumes of pahoehoe lava. Because the lava feeding each of the ephemeral boccas was thermally protected in the roofed-over conduits, the rheological properties of the lava appears to have been similar to those in the vent area despite being up to 3 km away; and because effusion was taking place from numerous ephemeral boccas effusion rate at each one was low giving slow moving flows which solidified as pahoehoe. A similar phenomenon was observed on Etna by Sparks and Pinkerton (1978) in 1975 when pahoehoe toes formed at individual boccas when effusion rates were less than 2×10^{-3} m^3 s^{-1}.

The changes in style for flow field development

Fig. 4.24 A lava pinnacle on the main 1981 Randazzo flow. While parts of the exterior of the pinnacle support collections of loose or partially welded fragments, its interior consists of a single massive unit, extruded from the flow interior. (Photograph: C. R. J. Kilburn.)

with time described above for the 1983 eruption relate to an eruption with moderate average effusion rates of about $10 m^3 s^{-1}$. The actual effusion rate near the end of the eruption, when the ephemeral bocca field developed, may have been lower although estimates of effusion rate are difficult when the feeding channels are encased in tubes. The changes took place over a period of 131 days. However, with higher or lower effusion rates, it may be predicted that similar changes may take place on different time scales.

The rate of effusion is controlled by the lava rheology, the shape of the conduit and the supply rate. Generally, all other things being equal, a fissure vent will have a higher effusion rate than a cylindrical conduit (Wilson and Head, 1981).

Effusion rates for Etnean eruptions vary considerably from one eruption to another and may fluctuate during a single eruption. The median effusion rate is $8 m^3 s^{-1}$ for flank eruptions. In general persistent activity has low effusion rates of $< 1 m^3 s^{-1}$ and long-duration, persistent eruptions probably have overall effusion rates comparable to the volcano's total output rate. Some short, persistent eruptions may have higher rates comparable to those of flank eruptions which range from a few cubic metres per second up to hundreds of cubic metres per second.

For most historical eruptions the effusion rate was not directly measured. Effusion rates may only be obtained from the total volume of erupted lava and the duration giving an average effusion rate (or the *eruption rate* of Wadge, 1976).

It is not easy to obtain precise quantities for either effusion rate or average effusion rate. Measuring actual effusion rates during an eruption is difficult because although the flow velocity and the channel width can be measured with precision, normally it is only possible to estimate the thickness of the flow from the levée height. This may be incorrect by as much as a factor of 2. Under some conditions it is possible to measure the flow thickness by inserting a probe to the base of the flow but for most eruptions the flow velocity is too high for this to be accomplished. In addition most estimates of effusion rate assume uniform velocity over the whole cross-sectional area and thus, even if the depth of flow is correctly estimated, an excessive effusion rate will be obtained. Estimates of *average* effusion rate suffer from lack of precision in obtaining the volume of the final flow (as discussed later in the chapter), again because thickness is difficult to estimate and because effusion rates may vary during the eruption. Also, although the starting date of an eruption is usually well defined, the date on which the eruption stopped is often not so clear, especially if minor explosive activity continued at the vent after lava effusion had ceased. While this may not be important for long-lived eruptions, it may be for those that lasted only a few days.

Fig. 4.25 A rootless bocca at the front of the 1981 flow in the valley of the River Alcantara. Lava extruded from this bocca has congealed with a surface close to that of pahoehoe and shows up in this photograph as being darker than the surrounding aa surfaces. (Photograph: J. E. Guest.)

The maximum effusion rates of Etnean eruptions appear to have some relation with the altitude of vent (Fig. 4.28); while low average effusion rates can occur from eruptions at any location, high-effusion-rate eruptions normally only occur at the lower altitudes, presumably as a result of higher 'hydrostatic' pressure. This phenomenon was first implied by the observations of Walker (1974a) that the longer lava flows occurred from low-altitude vents (see Fig. 8.5) and that the most positive control of lava flow length was effusion rate (Walker, 1973a). Clearly, many other factors control lava flow length including lava rheology, volume of erupted material, topography and whether the flow is tube-fed or channel-fed. However, Walker considers that these are all subordinate to effusion rate as a controlling factor in the final length of the flow. Further studies by Wadge (1978) and Lopes and Guest (1982) show that there is a good correlation between the flow length and average effusion rate for those flows longer than about 1 km (Fig. 4.29). Wadge (1978) relates the dependence of flow length on effusion rate to rate of cooling of the flow. Cooling increases the thickness of the crust and the flow front stops once the crust has reached a critical thickness. He assumes that the thickness of chilled crust increases as the square root of time (Shaw *et al.*, 1968) and thus that faster-moving flows will achieve a longer length before the critical crust thickness develops. The lack of correlation between effusion rate and flow length for the shorter flows may well be the result of many of them not having reached their maximum potential length for

Fig. 4.26 Slabby lava on the surface of a flow from the South-east Crater. (Photograph: C. R. J. Kilburn.)

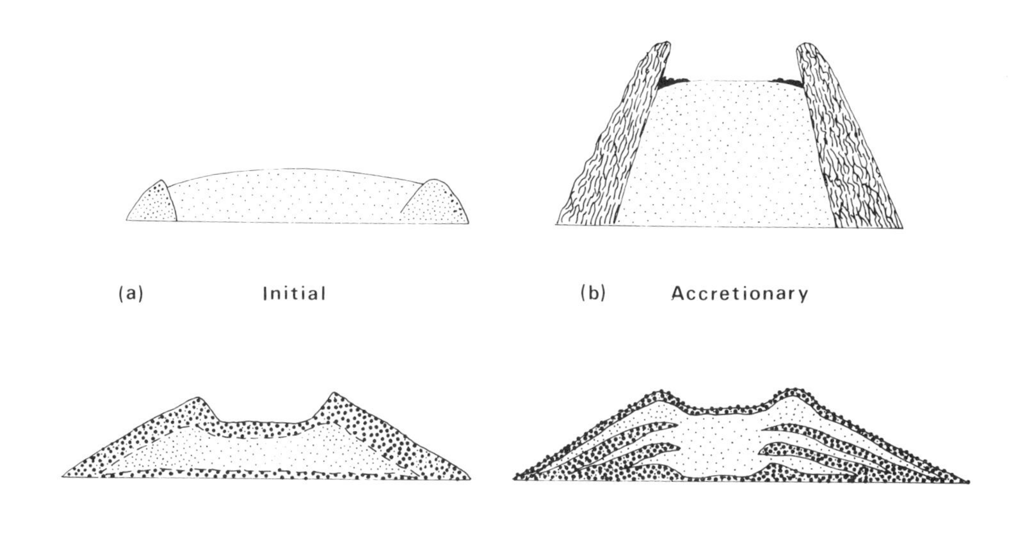

Fig. 4.27 Cross-sections through several different types of levée. (After Sparks *et al.*, 1976, courtesy of the Geological Society of America.)

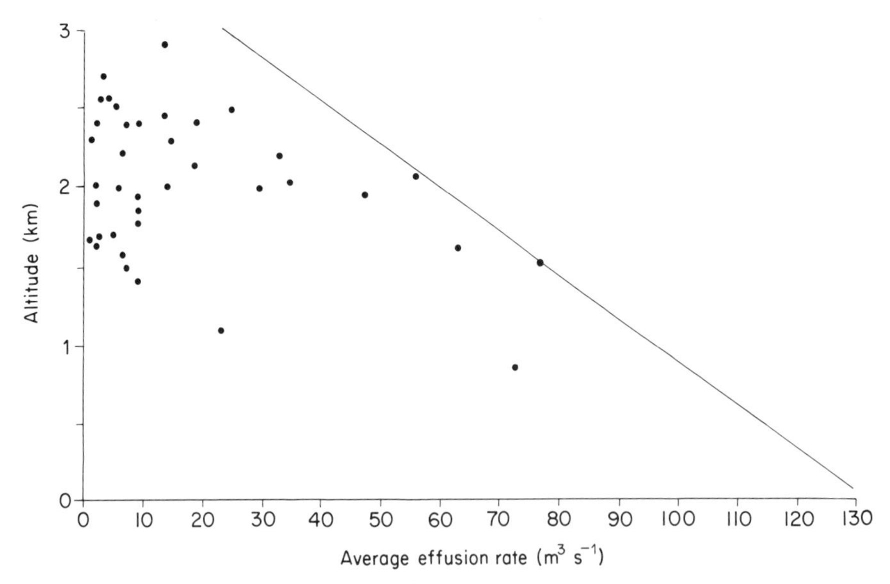

Fig. 4.28 Plot of average effusion rate against altitude of vent for historical Etnean eruptions. (From Lopes and Guest, 1982.)

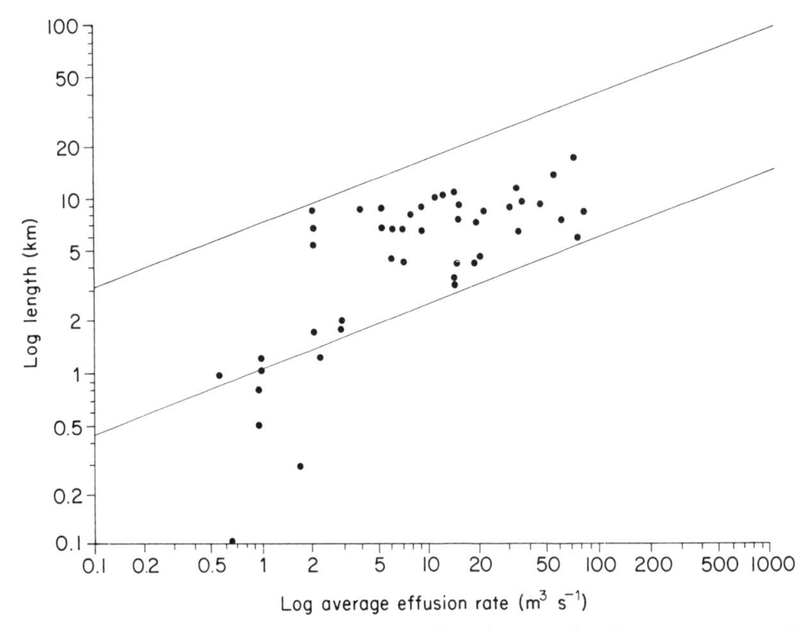

Fig. 4.29 Average effusion rate plotted against the length of flow for historical Etnean eruptions (From Lopes and Guest, 1982.)

a given effusion rate because the supply stopped before they had done so.

Although Walker (1973a) indicated that the association between flow length and effusion rate was a general phenomenon applying to all volcanoes, Malin (1980) has shown that the correlation is weak for Hawaiian eruptions and that for comparable effusion rates to those of Etna, Hawaiian lavas can be much longer. For the Hawaiian flows, Malin demonstrates a good correlation between their lengths and volumes suggesting that the principal controls on lava flow length in Hawaii are different from those on Etna, in part perhaps because many Hawaiian flows are fed by long, well-developed tubes. As shown in Fig. 4.30 even for Etnean flows there is a correlation between volume and flow length – a not entirely surprising result as in order to increase the length of a flow its volume must also increase. To examine this relationship further, Lopes and Guest (1982) grouped flows according to their volume and then examined length versus effusion rate for each volume group. Although the data are limited, for flows with volumes less than 5×10^6 m^3 there is a good correlation for flows longer than 1 km, length increasing with effusion rate (Fig. 4.31). For these flows there was no correlation between volume and length. Grouping flows with volumes between 5 and 50×10^6 m^3 also shows a correlation between length and effusion rate but only for flows less than about 11 km in length. Above this there appears to be no increase in length with increasing effusion rate, possibly because insufficient lava was available, or the flow front had reached shallower slopes lower on the mountain.

One exception to the correlation between volume and flow length is the flow produced during the 1763 eruption at Montagnola. This is a relatively high-volume flow with thicknesses in excess of 50 m but with a short length. The main part of this flow consists of a ridge with an axial lava tube system. The general form of the flow is that of a very large overflow levée and it is possible that this eruption progressed in a series of short effusions that overflowed the channel system building a high levée on either side. Each short effusion was of insufficient volume for any great distance to be covered.

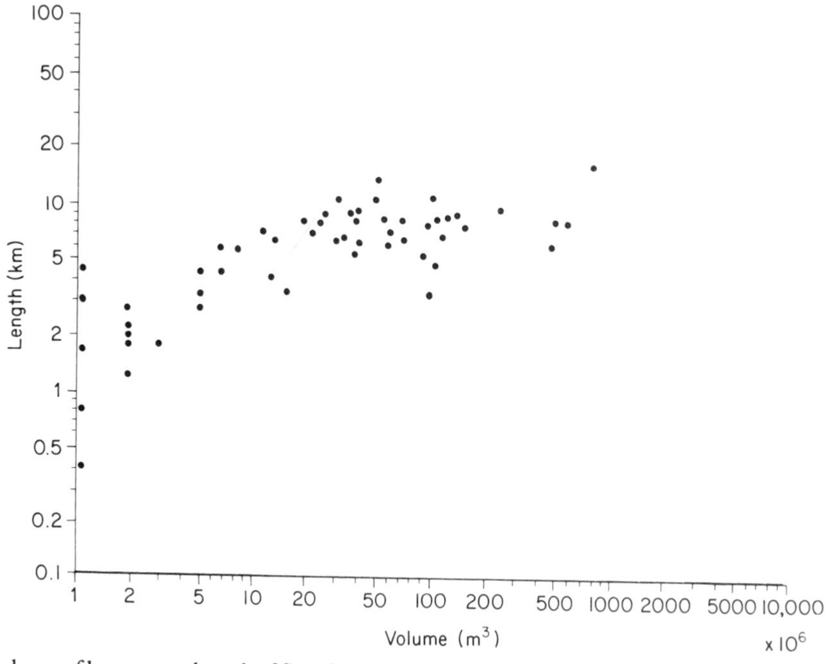

Fig. 4.30 Volume of lava versus length of flow for Etnean historical eruptions. (From Lopes and Guest, 1982.)

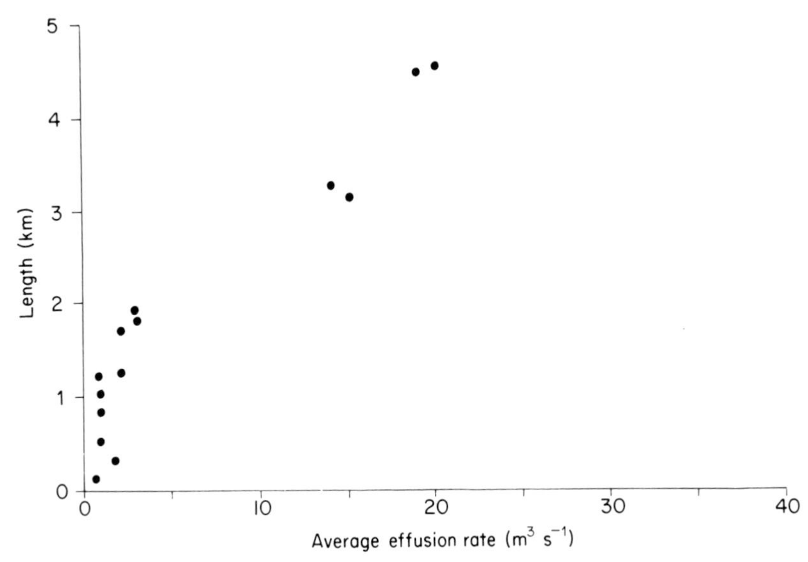

Fig. 4.31 Effusion rate versus length of flow for Etnean eruptions that produced less than 5×10^6 m^3 of lava (From Lopes and Guest, 1982.)

A comparable relation can be observed by considering volume and length for flows erupted at similar effusion rates. Lopes and Guest (1982) found that for average effusion rates below 8 m^3 s^{-1} (the median effusion rate for Etnean flank eruptions) flows do not advance further than about 8 or 9 km even if their volume is high. Continued eruption after maximum flow length has been achieved increases the total volume of the flow field by either thickening or widening of the flow field, or both.

Although for small flows the rate of advance of material at the flow front is comparable to the rate of effusion at the vent, with flows longer than a few hundred metres this may not be the case and the volumetric flow front advance rate may differ by factors of 2 or 3 from the effusion rate. These differences can result from a number of phenomena. With a flow in which channel drainage has not occurred, the thickness of the flow at any one point may be equal to or greater than the levée height. In this case lateral lava pressure causes the sides of the flow to advance like slow-moving lava fronts progressively widening the channel. If substantial parts of the side of the flow are spreading in this way then a proportion of the lava erupted at the vent does not reach the flow front. At times this may correspond to as much as two-thirds of the erupted material. Once the channel drains, the flanking levées become more stable and the flow does not increase in width by this mechanism. Channels drain when the rate of supply of lava in the channel is less than the rate at which it is flowing away. This may result from a drop in the effusion rate, blockage in the channel, overflows or breakouts higher upflow reducing the volume in the main channel or the lava flow front reaching a steeper slope causing it to move faster. All of these occurrences are also likely to affect the relationship between volumetric advance rate of the flow front and the effusion rate. In most cases the effusion rate will be higher than the rate of supply of material to the flow front, the main exception being when the eruption stops and for a short time the flow front continues to advance being fed by channel draining.

The median volume for a lava flow produced during an Etnean flank eruption is 30×10^6 m^3; most are less than 150×10^6 m^3, with only 10% of historical eruptions exceeding this value. The largest historical eruption on Etna was that of 1614 – 24 which erupted about 2 km^3 of lava. However this was mainly a pahoehoe eruption and was anomalous not only in its volume but in its

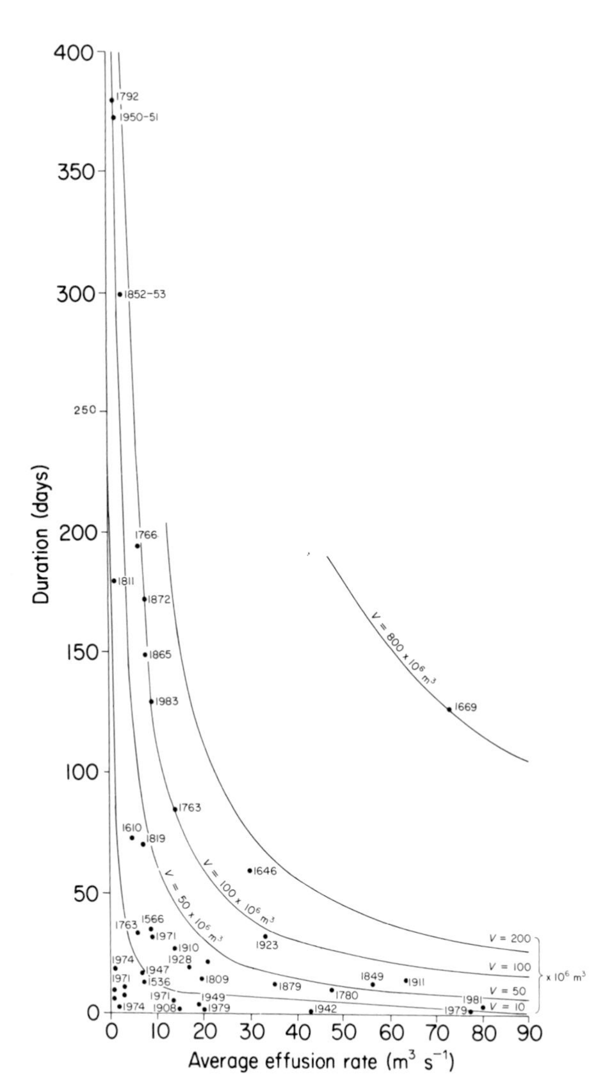

Fig. 4.32 Average effusion rate versus duration of eruption for historical Etnean flank eruptions. Volume (V) curves are plotted. (From Lopes and Guest, 1982.)

duration as is mentioned above. About 30% of eruptions have less than 10×10^6 m³ of lava. As shown in Fig. 4.32, there is no correlation of volume of material erupted with either duration of eruption or the effusion rate although small-volume flows of less than about 3×10^6 m³ have durations and average effusion rates that are much lower than the median value. Generally speaking those eruptions with high effusion rates (above 20 m³ s⁻¹) tend to be of short duration while those of long duration have low effusion rates (below 10 m³ s⁻¹). None of the volumes quoted here is corrected to their dense rock equivalent.

Topography controls flow field development in a number of ways not least of which is the direction of flow. G.P.L. Walker (1967) was the first to quantitatively assess the relations between angle of slope and thickness of flow (see Fig. 5.8) demonstrating that with increasing angles of slope the maximum thickness obtainable diminishes. On slopes steeper than 15°, flows rarely exceed 5 m in thickness whereas for flows to exceed 10 m, slopes less than 7° are required. The slope also affects the flow velocity and where a flow encounters an area of shallow slope it will slow down, spread and even stop if the applied shear stress is less than the effective bulk yield strength of the flow front.

Where flows follow steep-sided valleys they can become thick valley fills, the most dramatic example of which is the flow that followed the river Alcantara to the sea from an eruption at the Moio cone on the northern flank of the volcano. Tens of metres thick, this flow has been exposed by valley-downcutting to show the spectacular columnar jointing which has become a tourist attraction at Gole dell'Alcantara (Fig. 4.33).

Even small-scale topographic features can affect the flow. Where a flow advances over a pre-existing, deeply channelled flow, a wide flow front may be split up as it enters the several pre-existing channels. These lobes may reunite further down-slope or the flow may divide into a series of small tongues. Relatively small obstacles such as boulders of 2 m or 3 m diameter may temporarily slow down the rate of advance of the flow front causing thickening of the flow upstream. The advance of a lava may also be delayed when it enters a forested area, the trees acting as barriers to be either circumvented, burnt out, or knocked down. Where a flow front has almost stopped, obstacles of only 30 cm or so, or even wire-netting fences, may arrest it several metres before it would naturally have come to a halt.

4.2.4 *Pahoehoe flow fields*

Although patches of pahoehoe are found on many

Fig. 4.33 Well-developed columnar jointing in a thick flow filling a valley at Gole dell'Alcantara at the foot of Etna on the northern side. (Photograph: T.J.O. Sanderson.)

aa fields near the vent areas or at ephemeral boccas lower down the flow (Fig. 4.34), lavas made predominantly of pahoehoe material are less common on Etna. During historical times four major pahoehoe flow fields have been formed: those of 1614 – 24, 1651 – 53, 1764 – 65 and 1792 – 93. All these eruptions had durations that were longer than average, each lasting for more than a year. Hence, in spite of their relatively low effusion rates of a few cubic metres per second, they possess comparatively high volumes (Fig. 4.32). It is difficult to determine why these flow fields are predominantly pahoehoe. Sparks and Pinkerton (1978) have suggested that the low effusion rates may be largely responsible; however, many aa flows have comparable effusion rates. They also suggested that pahoehoe flows are more likely to develop where the initial lava is gas-poor so that on eruption the lava does not become undercooled by gas release. It is difficult to test this for Etnean lavas because although pahoehoe flows have little associated pyroclastic material in their vent areas the amount of de-gassing from the central conduit is unknown. For example, violent explosive activity in the summit area was reported during the 1614 – 24 eruption (Romano and Sturiale, 1982). Although high effusion temperatures may have been in part responsible for the pahoehoe flow fields the long duration may also have played a part. Each of these flow fields was fed by an extensive network of lava tubes and, as noted earlier, tube development is favoured by long-duration eruptions. Once a lengthy tube system is established then the flow is surfaced by relatively short individual flows erupted from ephemeral boccas scattered all over the flow field. Only where the flows travel over steeper slopes does aa develop. Thus it may be that duration of eruption is the critical factor in determining whether the final form of the flow field will be predominantly pahoehoe (Guest, 1982).

The lava tubes range from systems of surface

Fig. 4.34 A tongue of pahoehoe lava erupted from an ephemeral bocca in the middle of an aa flow. Such ephemeral boccas also give rise to ropy pahoehoe. (Photograph: J. E. Guest.)

tubes many of which are a metre or less in diameter (some are just large enough to stand up in), to main feeding tubes with diameters of several metres. They have all the characteristics of lava tubes on other basaltic volcanoes (Greeley, 1971; Wood, 1976), with glassy coatings to the walls, lava stalactites and stalagmites and benches of lava along the walls representing levels of flow at different times. In some tubes, notably the Grotta degli Inglese on the 1614 – 24 flow, large boulders of material fallen from the roof and walls of the tube litter the tube floor and are draped with lava, indicating that they became dislodged before flow stopped. Such boulders are sometimes observed to have jammed in the tube presumably reducing the flow rate. Tubes vary in profile from the pointed Gothic arch form to a semi-circular Norman arch profile. The original profile of the floor is difficult to assess because in most areas some lava has remained in the tube.

The surface of the pahoehoe flows are characterized by tumuli. In plan view these are sub-circular to boat-shaped and consist of slabs of upturned lava crust. These are commonly hollow inside and sometimes lead to tube systems below. They are considered to form by lava up-arching the roof of the tube as a result of increased flow rate in the tube or blockage of the tube further down. The steep slopes of Etna provide a good hydrostatic head in the lava tube to produce tumuli that are considerably larger than normal for basaltic volcanoes; the larger tumuli have basal diameters of about 1 km in the distal portions of the 1614 – 24 flow. These mega-tumuli are composed mostly of upturned slabs of the original pahoehoe surface, but on the downhill slopes they are often covered by streams of aa and pahoehoe lavas that have squeezed out from between the upturned slabs. The smaller tumuli may also be coated with numerous toes of mainly pahoehoe lava (Fig. 4.35).

The 1614 – 24 lava flow field (Fig. 4.36) is of particular interest in being made up in one area of a series of lava terraces giving the flow a step-like form descending from 2320 m to 1600 m a.s.l. Each terrace is relatively level although on a small scale the surface consists of typical pahoehoe with broad swales, short ropy flows, squeeze-ups, tumuli and driblet cones of entrail and toey lava. The steeper slopes of the terrace fronts have a high proportion of clinkery aa while the rest of the flow is largely made up of tumuli and mega-tumuli. These terraces appear to have developed as lava lakes that were trapped behind arcuate embankments built up in front of a slow-moving and growing flow front (Guest *et al.*, in press). The 1651 – 53 flow on the west flank has many characteristics in common with the 1614 – 24 flow field although terraces and mega-tumuli are not so well developed. Amongst the prehistoric flows there are many more examples of similar flow fields.

4.2.5 *Domes*

The term 'dome' is used here, following

Fig. 4.35 Typical view of a pahoehoe flow-field produced during the eruption of 1614–24. In the foreground is a small tumulus coated with small extrusions of toey lava. (Photograph: J. E. Guest.)

Macdonald (1972), for steep-sided lava masses accumulated over or near to a vent as a result of the extrusion of lava with a relatively high effective viscosity. They are comparatively rare features on Etna and are not known to have formed during historical time. The main examples of domes are found on the lower south-west flanks of the volcano and have been described by Kieffer (1974b) and Duncan (1976b). All the known domes have more-evolved compositions than the historical hawaiites, consisting of plagiophyric mugearites and benmoreites, or in the case of the dome at Poggio la Naca an aphyric trachytic textured mugearite. The lack of pyroclastic materials associated with the domes suggests that the magma was relatively de-gassed on eruption.

The chain of domes to the north of Biancavilla are the best-exposed examples in the region, as they have suffered relatively little burial by later lavas and because there are good sections provided both by extensive quarrying and by a gorge that dissects the whole length of the chain. The domes are aligned north – south and they were probably erupted along a fissure from several vents close enough to allow them to coalesce with one another.

The domes are composed mainly of autoclastic breccia consisting of sub-rounded blocks up to about 60 cm across but typically about 10 cm. These are set in a dusty matrix containing small centimetre-size fragments. Cutting through the breccia are sheets of massive lava (Fig. 4.37). In the middle of the domes these are sub-vertical but towards the margins they become dominantly sub-horizontal with thicknesses normally less than 2 m. The sheets are non-vesicular lava and have well-defined contacts with the breccia, although near the margins they often contain small xenolithic fragments of breccia.

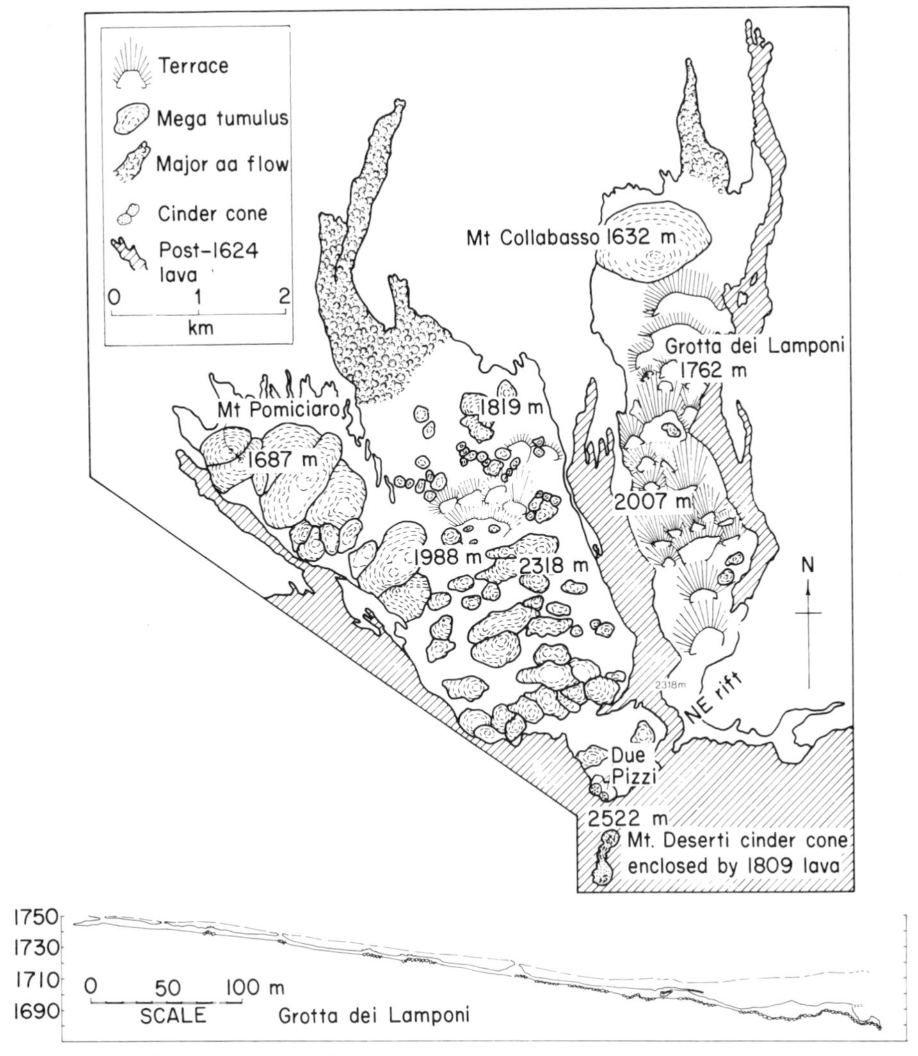

Fig. 4.36 Sketch map of the 1614–24 lava flows showing the distribution of mega tumuli and terraces. Also shown is a longitudinal profile of the Grotta dei Lamponi lava tube. (From Guest *et al.*, in press.)

Fractures within the crumble-breccia of the domes are coated with hematite while tridymite occurs within the powdery matrix (Kieffer, 1974b). These minerals are considered by Duncan (1976b) to be late-stage vapour-phase minerals.

The domes probably formed in much the same way as rubble breccia described earlier in the chapter. Lava was erupted slowly with a relatively high effective viscosity. It broke into blocks and continued expansion of the dome by the introduction of new material from below caused the blocks to become rounded by abrasion with one another, at the same time giving rise to the fine-grained matrix. Expansion of the breccia carapace allowed lava to invade the opening cracks so forming the massive sheets; some of these probably extended to the surface to produce small flow lobes covering the outer surface of the dome.

At the lower end of the chain of domes more fluid lava was emitted to form a flow some 2 km long extending down into Simeto Valley. This lava is heavily vegetated and weathered but close to the

Fig. 4.37 Cross-section through a dome exposed in a quarry at Biancavilla. The lower part of the section is autoclastic breccia while near the top is a sheet of massive lava. (Photograph: J. E Guest.)

dome it consists of toey pahoehoe. Kieffer (1974b) considers that this flow formed at a late stage in the development of the dome when lava of lower effective viscosity, possibly as a result of a higher P_{H_2O}, as suggested by Duncan (1976b), drained from the centre of the domes causing sagging of the upper surface. It was perhaps this drainage, together with lava withdrawal along the fissure, that allowed the axis of the dome to become a fluvial channel that was subsequently enlarged by snow-melt run-off.

4.2.6 Behaviour patterns and output

The long record of historical eruptions spanning a period of over two-and-a-half millennia provides one of the best data-sets of activity with time available for any volcano. However, lengthy though it is, the same cautious approach must be applied to this record as for any other which is based on human reporting. The problems involved with interpreting records of eruptive activity for volcanoes in general have been discussed by Simkin and his co-authors (1981) in their introduction to the Smithsonian Institution's *Volcanoes of the World*. Specific problems with the Etnean record are that: the quality of recording is variable; the record becomes less complete particularly before about AD 1500; reports may differ on important details such as the date or chronology of eruption; and, whereas the record is relatively complete for flank eruptions after AD 1500, reporting of persistent activity at the summit is probably only near complete for the last few decades. For most purposes the record is only meaningful for about the last 500 years, and then only for flank eruptions. One example of the uncertainty of the record before that time is given by the lack of any reported eruptions for nearly 250 years between BC 350 and 140 BC. Some have considered this a period when the volcano was quiescent (Rodwell, 1878) but there is no guarantee that eruptions were reported during this time perhaps because they occurred on then poorly inhabited northern or western flanks.

The majority of flank eruptions occur from well-defined regions that have a high density of cinder cones and fissure vents (see Fig. 8.11). Of the maverick eruptions that have occurred outside the zones of repeated eruptions there are those that produced the cinder cones on the perimeter of the volcano at Moio and near Linguaglossa, both at the foot of the mountain on the northern side, and near Bronte to the west. All these are prehistoric. During historical time the majority of eruptions have occurred in regions that already have more than one vent per km^2, exceptions being the eruption of 1669 which lies on the southern rift, the lower vent area for the 1928 eruption which was associated with a normal fault system, and 1981 which erupted along a fissure zone trending towards the north only occasionally utilized by erupting lavas on the northern flank. Even those vents that lie outside the high-frequency eruption areas are structurally controlled.

The highest concentration of vents lies on the north-east rift which turns north-north-east through the summit crater and then extends towards the south forming the southern rift. About half the flank eruptions on the volcano occur on either the north-eastern or southern rift system and occur on average every 35 years on each rift. The high-vent-density area near Citelli has eruptions at a similar frequency whereas the western vent area and that lower down on the south-eastern flank have eruptions once every few hundred years. Eruptions within the Valle del Bove are underestimated in Fig. 8.11 because they tend to be rapidly covered over by later eruptions. However eruptions in this region are generally associated with the southern rift or the Citelli vent area.

The above-quoted average frequencies of eruption are based only on the last 400 years of the historical record. Taking the mountain as a whole there have been since 1550 an average of one flank eruption every eight years. However eruptions are far from equally spaced in time. For example during the decade 1971 – 81 there were a total of seven eruptions that could be considered as flank events; whereas for eighty-six years after the large-volume 1669 eruption only two minor flank eruptions occurred. While such figures may have some relevance to the problem of general prediction, as it is flank eruptions that cause the most serious damage, they are only part of the eruptive history of the volcano; they do not take into account persistent summit activity and sub-terminal eruptions which until the last few decades have not been adequately reported. Thus a long gap in the historical record of flank eruptions may or may not have contained a fairly substantial number of unreported summit eruptions. Certainly the evidence over the last two decades suggests that between flank eruptions the summit region can be almost continuously active with the magmatic columns standing high in the central conduit.

The volumetric output of Etna is of particular importance. Charles Lyell (1830) with characteristic insight suggested that if the volumes of erupted lava from each dated historical eruption could be measured, then by knowing the total volume of the volcano it is possible to compute how long it would take to construct the whole edifice. This, of course, assumes that there were no long periods of quiescence, and would thus be a minimum age. Nearly 150 years later Wadge *et al.* (1975) attempted to do this and determined that the volcano *could* have been built in 65 000 years.

One striking feature of the output is that it has remained constant for relatively long periods. Since 1535 the output from flank eruptions can be divided into four phases, according to Wadge *et al.* (1975): (1) 1535 – 1610 when the output was low; (2) 1610 – 69 when there was a high output of 0.83 $m^3 s^{-1}$; (3) 1669–1759 when the output was again low; and (4) 1759 – 1974 when the output was 0.17 $m^3 s^{-1}$.

These conclusions have been criticized by Tanguy (1979) who considers that estimates of the volumes of historical lavas are not precise enough to draw such conclusions. It is of course difficult to

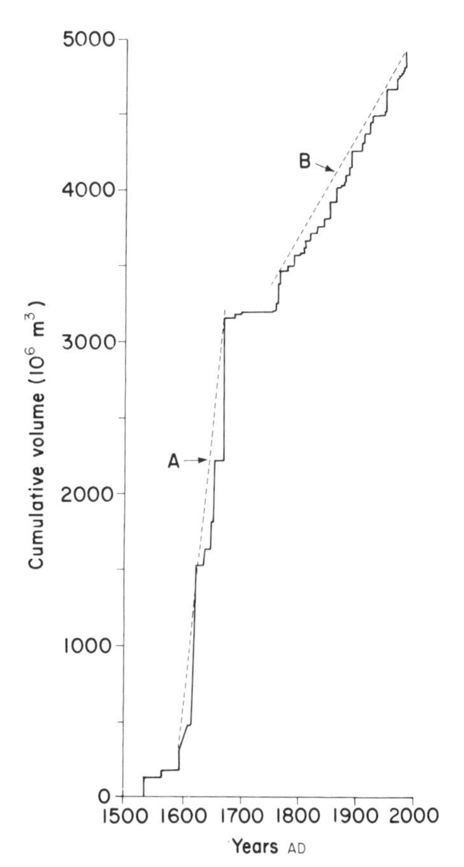

Fig. 4.38 Cumulative plot of lava output from Etna since 1500. Slope A corresponds to an output of 1.17 $m^3 s^{-1}$ and slope B to an output of 0.21 $m^3 s^{-1}$

obtain the precise volume for a lava flow unless the surface topography before and after the emplacement of the flow is known accurately. Measurements of the surface area of a flow are usually precise, although where a flow has been buried by a later flow it is necessary to estimate unless older maps are available. The average flow thickness on the other hand is much more difficult to obtain if surveys before and after the eruption are not available. Estimates of thickness are usually obtained by measuring the height of the sides and front of the flow and then estimating the total thickness taking into account the apparent form of the underlying terrain based on such observations as ground-slope immediately adjacent to the flow. However, there are considerable uncertainties, and estimates of average thickness could in some cases be wrong by as much as a factor of 2. The volumetric estimates made by Wadge *et al.* (1975) were made before the new geological map of 1979. Extensive field work involved in producing this map has led to new estimates of volume for historical flows and these have been re-plotted in the same form (Fig. 4.38) as in Wadge *et al.* (1975). These new estimates do not change the original conclusions and the same four periods of consistent output are again emphasized. The output rates are changed slightly and for the period 1610 – 69 the new figures give an output of 1.17 m^3 s^{-1}, while for the period 1759–1983 it was 0.21 m^3 s^{-1}.

These figures do not take into account persistent activity at the summit which is difficult to estimate for most of the historical record. However, observations of output during the last ten years have included summit activity and show that there is a ratio of 56:44 for summit-to-flank eruptive lava volumes. If we assume that this ratio is typical of the period from the present back to 1759 then we get a total output rate of just under 0.5 m^3 s^{-1}.

The output since 1971 is plotted from Wadge and Guest (1981) in Fig. 7.14 with the addition of the 1983 eruption. In this case the volumes of lava associated with persistent activity at the summit are included so that the total output may be determined directly. The data may be interpreted in terms of a steady state output, although the activity varied from continuous emission at the steady state to episodic eruptions (either because magma is stored for a short time in the volcano before release or the magma arrives in discrete batches resulting in a punctuated pattern of eruptions). Within the period 1974–81 the maximum capacity for volume erupted was about 25 $\times$ 10^6 m^3. However this pattern was punctuated by the two large flank eruptions of 1971 and 1983 which exceeded this capacity, although the repose time after 1971 still conformed to a steady state.

It would appear that a steady-state model is applicable to both the output for flank eruptions alone and the total output for a given period of time, a characteristic that must be consistent with any model of the internal plumbing and which could have value in forecasting future eruptions. However careful monitoring of output in the future should refine any conclusions drawn from our present knowledge of output. Clearly although the general output remains much the same for relatively long periods of time it would be difficult to recognize any sharp change in the output trend until after it occurred. Also, until we have refined methods of determining volumes of materials intruded into the volcanic pile but not erupted, we cannot determine the total volume of material rising from depth.

4.3 Collapse structures

Ground collapse in general is a relatively common phenomenon on Mount Etna, ranging in scale and frequency from rare wholesale caldera collapse and major slope failure on the volcano's flanks, to small-scale pit-formation or enlargement which occurs most often in the summit region although occasionally elsewhere. The features produced are comparable to those on many other volcanoes, especially those of basaltic type, although Etna does differ from volcanoes such as Kilauea in not having chains of pit craters along the rift zones.

4.3.1 Calderas

Not counting the Valle del Bove, which will be discussed separately, there are the remains of four major calderas in the summit region of the mountain. The timing of events that formed these

Fig. 4.39 The edge of the Piano Caldera now filled with lava as viewed from the summit. All the original rim is now buried but the morphology of the caldera is still retained. (Photograph: J. E. Guest.)

calderas has been discussed previously (Chapter 3) and based on our present knowledge of the ages of the volcanic centres they are associated with, it appears that the average frequency of major caldera collapse is about one every 4000 years or so. Because of subsequent flooding by lavas and dissection by later calderas, none of these major structures is now visible around the whole of their circumferences, but projection of the visible rims suggests that their original diameters ranged from about 4.75 km (Vavalaci Caldera) to 1.5 km (Leone Caldera). All the calderas are filled virtually to the brim with later lavas (Fig. 4.39), except that of Leone which is only partly filled (Fig. 4.40).

Because all the major calderas are prehistoric the mode of collapse is unknown. There is some evidence from the existence of phreatomagmatic pyroclastic deposits on the rim of the Ellitico Caldera that collapse was in part accompanied by explosive activity. However, whether collapse was wholesale or resulted from the coalescing of numerous pits, as suggested by Macdonald (1972, p. 298) for Hawaiian calderas, is not known.

As well as the four visible calderas, there are almost certainly others now buried or partly buried and thus difficult to recognize. Evidence for one such older caldera is given by the break-in-slope above Tardaria mentioned in Chapter 3.

Although the major calderas are all apparently prehistoric, there have been major historical collapses in the summit region that must be considered as larger-than-normal pit formation. Notable examples are the collapses of 1169, 1444, 1537 and 1669 (see Table 3.3). Each of these collapses, which resulted in the destruction or partial destruction of the Summit Cone, was accompanied by earthquakes and during the 1169 collapse an estimated 15 000 people were killed in Catania.

Fig. 4.40 View of the inner walls of the Leone Caldera. This caldera is partly filled by tephra forming the scree flow to the right of the picture and by lavas from the North-east Crater seen to the left. The flat-lying lavas exposed in the caldera wall in the middle of the picture are those filling the Ellittico Caldera. (Photograph: J. E. Guest.)

It is difficult to interpret caldera collapse in terms of the internal plumbing of the volcano. The evidence on Etna confirms the general view that they result from lack of support by the large-scale removal of magma from high-level storage areas. If this is so then the larger prehistoric calderas indicate magma storage areas at a few kilometres depth with horizontal extents of up to 4 – 5 km. The smaller historical collapses of the Summit Cone do not require large-scale high-level storage, but do suggest removal of a substantial column of magma within the central conduit. Certainly the larger calderas, apart from the Piano Caldera, are all associated with eruption centres that emitted lavas with chemical compositions indicative of high-level fractionation in a storage area before eruption. Little is known about the chemistry of lavas erupted from the centre that eventually collapsed as the Piano Caldera, because most of these lavas are now buried.

4.3.2 Pits

These are similar to calderas in that they presumably result from withdrawal of magma causing a lack of support at the surface. They differ from calderas in that they are smaller, can be caused by relatively small fluctuations in the level in a magma column below them, and their formation is far less dramatic – except to someone on or near the site at the time – as they are not accompanied by violent earthquakes. They range in size up to some 300 m.

The majority form in the summit region, either within the Central Crater, or as collapses over sub-terminal vents as occurred in 1966 over vents on the North-east Crater (see Fig. 4.7(f)). Occasionally they occur on the flanks as happened in 1792 when a pit, known as the Cisternazza, formed near the western edge of the Valle del Bove above an effusive fissure that opened on the inner wall of the Valle.

Although flank pits tend to be formed as the result of a single event, the pits formed within the Central Crater, being the main openings vertically above the central conduit, have long, complex histories of collapse and lava-filling. During the last decade there have been two pits within the Central Crater: the Chasm and the Bocca Nuova (see Fig. 1.3). The Chasm has a long history of repeated collapses and infilling by lava. The date of its opening is not recorded but following the 1956 eruption there was a large pit, some 100 m across, on the surface of lava filling the Central Crater in the region of the present Chasm. Between 1956 and 1974 explosive activity in this pit, together with at least two lava effusions, built a cone up to 65 m high around the pit. Collapse then occurred at the north-eastern side of the crater, forming a pit that by 1970 was in excess of 700 m deep according to the measurements of H. Tazieff and his team (Guest, 1973a). Immediately after the 1971 flank eruption, however, it filled with lava to within 150 m of the lip and strong activity during late-1973 filled it to within 75 m of the lip (Guest *et al.*, 1974). This was followed, at the end of the 1974 flank eruptions, by a new period of collapse. Since then, there have been repeated fillings and collapses within the Chasm tending to be associated respectively with times of quiescence and of activity at the North-east Crater (Guest, 1982). During periods of collapse, deep rumblings are frequently heard from the Chasm, apparently initiated by rock falls, and loud reverberating roars are thought to be the result of high-pressure gas release on the floor. Lava-filling episodes are often accompanied by strombolian activity described earlier in this chapter.

The other pit in the Central Crater, known as the Bocca Nuova (new mouth) or Bocca Ovest (western mouth), is of particular interest because its growth has been observed since it first opened on 12 June 1968 as a small gas-vent some 8 m in diameter (see Fig. 6.25). The early history of the Bocca Nuova has been described by Tazieff (1970), Guest (1973a), and Le Guern *et al.* (1982). According to the late V. Barbagallo, a senior guide on Etna for over forty years, the Bocca opened without any apparent warning between two groups of tourists being escorted by guides to the summit; the startled tourists scattered over the mountainside.

For over a year-and-a-half after it had opened, the Bocca Nuova retained much the same geometry and style of activity. The latter was quite regular consisting of alternating, strong gas-*blows* and the quiet expulsion of gas at low velocities. Blows occurred every minute or few minutes at rates of between 40 and 60 per hour. At night the Bocca Nuova was particularly impressive (Fig. 4.41). The walls of the shaft glowed red and the plume of gas formed an incadescent cone above the bocca.

Measured velocities (Tazieff, 1970) show that each blow consisted of a dozen-or-so distinct puffs with velocities ranging from about 50 ms^{-1} to 170 ms^{-1}. This puffing was accompanied by dull booms at the same frequency. If the shaft below the Bocca Nuova is considered to be similar to an organpipe, closed at the lower end, its length would be equal to a quarter of the wavelength. Correcting for the velocity of sound (Vs) in the measured gas-temperature of about 1000°C in the Bocca Nuova, we get 687 ms^{-1}. Using this figure and a period t of 1.8 s, the resonant length of the Bocca Nuova is given by

$$\frac{\lambda}{4} = \frac{v_s t}{4} = \frac{687 \times 1.8}{4} = 310 \text{ m}$$

This apparent length remained much the same throughout 1968 and 1969, although on 15 October 1969 the frequency was reduced to 1.5 s, possibly indicating that the length of the shaft became effectively shorter as a result either of collapse or of the magma rising to a higher level for a short period. Another variation in activity of the bocca was noted in October 1969, with occasional loud explosions throwing out small fragments of hot wall rock as well as equipment inserted into the Bocca. On one occasion a crucible was recovered

Fig. 4.41 The Bocca Nuova as it appeared in 1969 at night. The walls of the Bocca are glowing as is the gas ejected from it. In the background is the North-east Crater in strombolian activity. (Photograph: J. E. Guest.)

from about 200 m away. These violent expulsions of gas occurred at rates of about 1 every 3 h. The angle at which gas (Fig. 4.41) and rock fragments were expelled was 20° from the vertical towards the northwest. This implies that at least the upper part of the shaft dipped steeply into the mountainside.

On one occasion during October 1969 Haroun Tazieff was able to stand on the lip of the bocca to examine the shape of the interior of the shaft. He noted that the shaft widened just below the surface giving an overhanging rim. This important observation was made at the expense of his protective helmet which was ripped off by an unexpected explosion as he peered into the orifice. The shape of the bocca, together with the occurrence of more violent explosions and possible rising and lowering of magma in the shaft, suggested that with time the Bocca Nuova would enlarge itself at the surface. Also, the rocks surrounding the Bocca shaft had become deeply rotted by gases permeating through them to produce the fumarole field at the surface around the Bocca. Collapse occurred to a greater degree than expected at an unknown date during the winter of 1970 (possibly during February when a dark dust cloud was seen rising from the summit region). It is fortunate that the collapse occurred in winter, because during the summer months there would most certainly have been volcanologists and tourists alike observing the Bocca and standing in the region that collapsed. The collapse area was not symmetrical about the original Bocca Nuova but formed a pit nearly 100 m in diameter whose centre was about 20 m to the south-west. The walls were near vertical and the outer rim, especially on the southern side, was cut by open fissures concentric with the crater lip. The bocca became quiet

(a)

(b)

Fig. 4.42 Two views of the Bocca Nuova from near the same place showing progressive enlargement. The upper view (a) was taken in 1981, and the lower view (b) in 1982, when the pit had enlarged to near the edge of the Central Crater seen on the skyline in both pictures. (Photographs: J. E. Guest.)

Fig. 4.43 View from south of the Summit Cone showing ash-laden fume billowing from the Bocca Nuova in the Central Crater. (Photograph: J. E. Guest.)

evolving copius, white, choking fumes containing sulphur dioxide.

The cause of the Bocca Nuova collapse is not clear. However, the original bocca opening lay adjacent to a south-south-east-trending line of cones and the centre of the enlarged bocca lay close to the fissure over which the cones had formed. Based on increases in fumarole temperatures on the southern side of the central crater, Guest (1973b) argued that bocca collapse may have resulted from the original magma column 300 m below the surface bursting sideways into the fissure zone below the line of cones in a south-south-easterly direction, as a result of a fissure opening towards one of the sites of the future 1971 eruption.

Following its first major collapse in early 1970, the history of the Bocca Nuova has been dominated by progressive enlargement by collapse of the walls (Fig. 4.42) together with alternating uprise of lava in the floor and deepening by collapse. By August 1973 it had a mean diameter of just over 150 m (Murray, 1980c), the main enlargement being towards the south-south-east along the projected line of the underlying fissure mentioned earlier. In the early part of the year strombolian activity was occurring spasmodically at about 200 m depth, but, during the midsummer, activity was dominated by collapse producing a deep pit at the south-eastern end of the bocca. However by 8 August, strombolian activity had started again at the surface of a rising column of lava, which by the end of September had reduced the depth of the bocca to 15 m. During October fresh glassy bombs were thrown up to 50 m from the crater edge. Similar activity was occurring in the Chasm at the same time, suggesting that the two pits were joined at depth to the same magma system. This activity

Fig. 4.44 Aerial view of the Bocca Nuova in 1983 with the Chasm in the background. At this time the maximum diameter of the Bocca Nuova was about 300 m. To the upper right is the truncated 1964 cone. (Photograph: J. E. Guest.)

died down during the winter of 1973/74 until after the 1974 west flank eruption. Collapse began again in the Bocca Nuova with characteristic, brown, ash-laden clouds being evolved at frequent intervals. By the September of 1974 the Bocca was 150 m deep. Collapse continued through 1975, again mainly on the south-eastern side of the pit where it was over 250 m deep. However on the northern side a shelf remained at about 100 m below the lip, sloping towards the deeper part of the bocca. By late summer it had achieved a mean diameter of just under 180 m and was beginning to cut into the rim of the Chasm to the east.

During 1976 magmatic activity resumed with strombolian activity in the pit floor. Black ash fell out of the eruption cloud and occasionally fresh bombs were thrown up high enough to land outside the pit, while Pele's hair was collected downwind of the vent. By late summer the magmatic activity had decreased considerably but resumed again during the first half of 1977. In September of 1977 the Bocca Nuova was again collapsing deep in its interior, although the diameter at the crater rim remained much the same. This situation continued throughout 1978 by which time, according to Murray (1980c), the hole on the south-eastern side was over 700 m deep. Similar conditions prevailed during 1979 until the beginning of September when part of the bench on the northern side of the pit collapsed into the deep hole. As described earlier in the chapter, this was the prelude to the fatal explosion of 12 September, when material was ejected out of the pit in a general north-westerly direction suggesting that the original shaft inclination had been maintained throughout its history.

Following the September 1979 explosion the

Bocca Nuova remained relatively quiet with occasional collapses and gas-explosions deep within the pit. However during and after the 1981 flank eruption both surface and deep collapse became common phenomena often resulting in large plumes of particle-laden fume billowing high above the summit (Fig. 4.43). On some occasions collapse activity was extremely violent and the ash-laden cloud could be observed for many tens-of-kilometres downwind. In the intervals between collapse, reverberating gas discharge could be heard up to 10 km from the crater and caused ground vibrations that could be felt more than 300 m from the pit. Major collapses of the upper wall during the latter part of 1981 widened the pit to a mean diameter of nearly 300 m. Red glows observed deep in the pit heralded the start of strombolian activity in late-May 1982. This continued during the rest of the year depositing fine ash all around the lip of the Bocca Nuova. A collapse phase started again during the 1983 eruption, further enlarging the pit so that it intersected the edge of the central crater on the west side (Fig. 4.44).

Emplacement of magma in a conduit or dyke followed by magmatic withdrawal appears to be the most likely explanation of pit formation on basaltic volcanoes (Macdonald, 1972). In the case of Etnean pits occurring on the flanks, the evidence suggests that these result from a drop in magma level within a dyke as a result of dyke drainage from an eruption lower down the slope. Such pits are caused by single events related to one eruption and any later activity at the same site is fortuitous. In this respect the occasional flank pits are similar to those formed on the Hawaiian rift zones: the relative paucity of such features on Etna probably results from the magma rheology making it less mobile than would be the case for the Hawaiian tholeiitic magmas. On the other hand, pit-craters developed at the summit can have long active lives. They may be considered as representing surface openings above the central conduit complex, and their activity is dominated by a rising and lowering of the top of the magma column within them. When a lava column is high, lava lakes can develop on the floor of a pit, accompanied by strombolian activity, or strombolian activity can take place from individual boccas on the floor or walls of the pit. When the magma level is low, collapse occurs either as wholesale chunks from the walls or as the steady development of talus slopes. Even when the magma is low there are often gas vents at the bottom of the pits giving rise to steady evolution of gas or explosive releases, sometimes at rates of one nearly every second.

Although in broad terms these summit pits are relatively easy to understand, systematic study of them over the last two decades indicates that they are surface expressions of a central conduit plumbing system that is far from simple. During the period 1971 – 74 when the North-east Crater was quiescent, both the Bocca Nuova and the Chasm had simultaneous phases of lava-filling, both pits apparently operating in unison and related to the same magma plumbing system. However, during the period 1978 onwards, the two pits apparently operated independently and although when the North-east Crater was quiet the Chasm filled with lava there was no systematic lava-filling phase in the Bocca Nuova. This could suggest that the two pits had developed their own independent plumbing system and that the Bocca Nuova, no longer related at least at shallow depths to the Chasm – North-east Crater system, had instead become linked to the newly developed South-east Crater which was then active.

These observations alone raise yet another serious problem to our understanding of the summit plumbing system. It is not surprising that, owing to a drop in magma pressure in the central conduit system, collapse takes place in the pits when eruptions occur elsewhere on the mountain. However the antipathetic relation between the Chasm and North-east Crater is enigmatic to say the least. The North-east Crater lies only about 250 m away from the edge of the Chasm and yet when the North-east Crater erupts the Chasm collapses only to fill up again when the North-east Crater ceases to erupt. The extreme case was in the late 1960s when the bottom of the Chasm lay over 700 m below the eruptive vents at the North-east Crater. It is difficult to envisage why magma prefers to climb up to the summit of the North-east Crater rather than erupting into the already-existing hole of the Chasm. Moreover, to where does the material in the Chasm disappear during the repeated collapses? It is almost as if the Chasm acts as a piston of rock that rises and lowers, pumping magma during the lowering phase into the North-east Crater and then being pushed up again during the ensuing period of quiescence at the North-east Crater. One possible cause of the sinking of the Chasm magma column may be that the density of its upper level increases as a result of de-gassing and congealing, so allowing it to sink into less-dense underlying magma perhaps forcing material up the North-east Crater conduit. This subject requires further study.

4.3.3 The Valle del Bove

Carved into the eastern flank of the mountain, the Valle del Bove consists of a steep-walled hollow with a maximum depth of over 1000 m and a mean diameter of about 6 km. In plan view it has a keyhole shape narrowing towards a seaward opening (see Fig. 3.16). As described in Chapter 3 much of our knowledge of the history of the volcano comes from the study of strata exposed in its precipitous walls.

The origin of the Valle del Bove has been debated for over a century-and-a-half. Sir Charles Lyell (1858) summarized the views of the mid-nineteenth century scientists who had considered the problems suggesting that three possible origins should be considered:

(1) Engulfment by what is now accepted as normal caldera collapse.
(2) Excavation by violent explosion.
(3) Erosion by fluvial processes.

Following his first visit to Etna, he came to the conclusion, as did Sartorius vön Waltershausen, that the most likely cause of the depression was that of engulfment by a process we would now term caldera collapse. However in a later paper (Lyell, 1849) he had changed his mind suggesting that the Valle del Bove was entirely erosional as a result of marine activity prior to uplift of the region. He changed his mind yet again after a later visit to the mountain in 1857 when, having recognized the power of fluvial erosion and pointing out that torrents and rivers can rapidly erode volcanic mountains because of their steep inclination, he concluded that the Valle del Bove was largely the result of fluvial erosion and that the large fan of sedimentary material, known as the Chiancone, in front of the mouth of the Valle del Bove was the product of this erosion (Lyell, 1858).

Since the mid-nineteenth century each of the three possibilities – caldera collapse, violent explosive activity and erosion, or combinations of these – have been proposed in various forms by different workers. One of the first workers, after Sartorius vön Waltershausen, to take on the difficult task of mapping the geology exposed in the walls of the Valle del Bove was the Belgian student J. Klerkx who considered the Valle to be a collapse caldera over the 'Trifoglietto' centre of activity. Because of the evolved nature of some of the Trifoglietto lavas he considered that there was underlying it a high-level magma chamber, the emptying of which caused the Valle del Bove to collapse. Following caldera collapse, activity moved to the site of the present summit. The difficulty with this explanation lies in the sequence of events. The Valle del Bove was not formed immediately after cessation of activity in the Trifoglietto area. During the interval between these events, the Vavalaci caldera formed, the substantial cone of Ellittico to the north-west of Trifoglietto was built up and the summit of this cone collapsed to form the Ellittico caldera. The Valle del Bove cuts all these lava sequences and cannot be related in time to the Trifoglietto centres. Romano and Sturiale (1975) also considered the Valle del Bove to be the result of caldera collapse but suggested that it consisted of several coalescing calderas related to the various centres exposed in the walls of the Valle del Bove; but the same arguments against the ideas of Klerkx are applicable here. Thus present knowledge of the stratigraphy and history of Etna does not support the 'caldera formation by engulfment' hypothesis of the ancient Trifoglietto centre.

Both Kieffer (1970a) and Rittmann (1973) were impressed by the large aerial extent of ashes and lahars having an apparent spatial relation with the Valle del Bove (see Chapter 3). These ashes crop out around the seaward opening of the Valle del Bove and over the eastern side of the volcano. It was argued that the Valle owed its origin to violent explosive activity undermining the seaward flank of the volcano. A parallel was drawn between Valle del Bove formation and the activity that occurred at Bandai-San in Japan during 1883. Here, following a long period of dormancy, the outbreak of strong phreatic explosive activity on the side of the volcano caused the flank to be undermined and a major slope failure occurred resulting in huge mudflows and wide-scale destruction by surges from the phreatic explosions (Sekiya and Kikuchi, 1890). Following this model both Kieffer and Rittmann related the ashes on Etna to phreatic explosions that undermined the east flank and the Chiancone to mudflow and fluviatile deposits resulting from the collapse that gave rise to the Valle del Bove.

McGuire (1982) reiterated this explanation relating the events mainly to the Trifoglietto II volcanic cone. His model envisages the initial opening to have occurred in the later stages of the main production of the Trifoglietto cone followed by continuing slide collapses associated with occasional renewal of activity at Trifoglietto II while the main new cone was building up to the north-east. However, these Bandai-San type models are, like caldera collapse, difficult to reconcile with the now-known history of the volcano. The ash deposits are of two distinctly different ages (Romano *et al.*, 1979) and are of different petrological character. Studies by Guest *et al.* (1984) show that the older ashes have strong petrographic similarities and a comparable radiometric age to the materials of the Trifoglietto II volcano (see Chapter 3), and thus pre-date the Valle del Bove by some 20 000 years. The younger ashes which have a different composition from Trifoglietto materials, are dated at about 5000 BP and are more likely to be related to the Ellittico volcano (Guest *et al.*, 1984). It therefore seems unlikely that the Valle del Bove can be related to Trifoglietto II as suggested by McGuire and there is no evidence to directly relate it with any explosive activity.

Amongst the erosional hypotheses, in addition to the suggestion by Lyell that fluviatile activity was the main agent, it has been suggested that the Valle was carved by glacial activity (Vagliasindi, 1950), that fluvial erosion caused subsequent enlargement following the phreatic-induced landsliding (McGuire, 1982), and that it was formed entirely by a series of major landslips not directly related to explosive or caldera collapse (Guest *et al.*, 1984). It is extremely unlikely that glacial activity could have been the cause of the Valle del Bove, not only because of the lack of any distinctive glacial deposits but the hollow was carved during the Holocene age at a time when glaciers would have not developed on the cone. Although the Valle del Bove could have been formed at a time when the climate was wetter and increased run-off may have occurred, the shape of the Valle is not that normally produced by fluviatile erosion. As Guest *et al.* (1984) point out it consists of a series of coalescing scallops open towards the east. It is this morphology that strongly supports the view that the Valle del Bove resulted almost entirely from a series of major landslides. Following this explanation, the Chiancone conglomerates (Fig. 4.45) are considered to be the distal portions of the landslide deposits consisting of landslide debris and fluvially reworked material. Support for this conclusion is given by the observation that the volume excavated to form the Valle del Bove is roughly comparable to the estimated volume of the Chiancone materials. This series of landslide collapses probably occurred not much later than the formation of the upper ashes which partially fill valleys, the upper parts of which are truncated by the Valle del Bove thus removing the source regions for the water that carved the valleys. If there had been a long time gap between emplacement of the ashes and the carving of the Valle del Bove, continued stream erosion is likely to have removed these unconsolidated ash deposits.

In summary therefore the geomorphological and sedimentological evidence strongly support the view that the Valle del Bove consists of a series of coalescing landslide scars formed less than 5000 years ago. Although it is tempting on a volcano to associate all activity with eruptions there is no

Fig. 4.45 The Chiancone materials exposed in a marine cliff at Priaola. (Photograph: J. E. Guest.)

evidence that the Valle del Bove slides were triggered by eruptive activity. If they were triggered by phreatomagmatic explosions then the upper ashes are the most likely contenders for the deposits from these explosions; whether this is true or not the Valle del Bove cannot in any way be related to activity of the Trifoglietto volcanic centre.

Although large amphitheatre shaped hollows on the flanks of volcanoes were included by Williams (1941) as calderas in his famous monograph *Calderas and their origin*, he recognized that, although engulfment was a prime cause of calderas, some were produced by other processes such as fluvial erosion, landsliding and wholesale gravity-sliding of the side of the volcano. Caldera-like depressions produced by slope failure may nevertheless be more widespread than is recognized even by Williams. The nature and environment of a volcano makes it readily subject to slope failure in a number of ways; but as with failure in non-volcanic terrains this is rarely attributable to one cause (Varnes, 1978). Volcanic eruptive activity can induce landsliding as happened at Bandai-San, or at Mount St. Helens in 1980 when an earthquake dislodged a large portion of the side of the volcano that had been bulged up by an intrusion and in the process unroofed that intrusion causing violent explosive activity (Lipmann and Mullineaux, 1981). Another possible example of similar activity was that at Bezymianny (Gorshkov, 1959). Nevetheless eruptive activity did not apparently accompany the formation of the amphitheatre-shaped hollows of Oratava and Guimar on the island of Tenerife (Fuster *et al.*, 1968). Hollows formed by gravity-sliding also occur in Indonesia where lack of support at the volcano's flanks have led to the slow development of arcuate scars on the volcano's side (Williams, 1941, pp. 311 – 15).

Of particular importance to understanding the Valle del Bove are the studies of two other basaltic volcanoes: the Piton de la Fournaise on the island of Reunion and Kilauea on Hawaii. On Reunion the amphitheatre-shaped caldera of the Piton de la Fournaise has been attributed to the displacement of part of the volcanic shield in the form of huge landslide blocks sliding seaward on the unbuttressed flanks (Duffield *et al.*, 1982). This failure appears to have occurred in the angle between two intersecting rift zones. Duffield *et al.* compare this relationship with the well-documented landslide blocks on the seaward side of the Kilauean rift zones where parallel fault systems between the rifts and the coast are considered to mark the headwalls of active slump blocks. These relationships compare well with the Valle del Bove, the Valle lying between the angle of the north-eastern and southern rift zones. Also the presence of ancient fault scarps that pre-date the Valle del Bove suggests seaward sliding of the flanks in a similar form to that on Kilauea. Possible causes of major slope failure on a volcano's flanks are given in Table 4.1. Of these it is difficult to determine which played the major part in the Valle del Bove formation. It is likely that the water table was higher than at the present time; the Valle del Bove intersects the hypothesized Vavalaci caldera which could have held large accumulations of snow in winter and melt water in summer; the presence of seaward-dipping unconsolidated tephra layers associated with the Trifoglietto II volcano may have provided a suitable incompetent sliding layer; repeated dyke injections into the rift zones could have contributed to the instability of the seaward flanks; and the mass of the high Ellittico cone may have been too much for the seaward side of the volcano to support.

McGuire (1982), based on the explanation that the Valle del Bove was caused by phreatomagmatic explosions at a time when climatic conditions were

Table 4.1 Possible causes of slope failure on Etna

Cause		*Possible situation on Etna*
(1) Increased external shear stress	(a)	Overloading of slope by lavas, especially if erupted continually from the same source vent over a long period
	(b)	Excess weight at the top of the slope because of the build-up of a large cone, or a large area of summit lavas
	(c)	Lack of seaward support for the slope sometimes due to the presence of an active fault
	(d)	A rift zone, which is being dilated by dyke intrusions
	(e)	Earthquakes acting as a trigger and dislodging otherwise-stable slopes
	(f)	Faulting increasing angle of slope
	(g)	Dome activity increasing angle of slope
	(h)	Removal of support of phreatomagmatic explosions on the flanks
	(i)	Caldera collapse or sector graben
	(j)	Breaching of summit lake in large crater or caldera
(2) Low or reduced internal shear strength	(a)	Ash layer dipping down slope, overlain by lava. A similar situation would occur when old lava surfaces containing soils were overlain by new flows
	(b)	Shear strength of ashes covered by lavas reduced by waterlogging and mobilization by earthquake trigger mechanisms
	(c)	Increase in pore water pressure, aquifiers being trapped behind dykes

quite different from those occurring today, argues that the type of activity that produced the Valle del Bove is unlikely to occur again on Etna under the prevailing climatic conditions. If, however, we consider that it owed its origin to simple gravity-sliding, there is no reason why such activity should not occur again as a result of one or more of the causes listed in Table 4.1. Although this is most likely to take place on the unbuttressed seaward side, it should be noted that the north-east Crater has, since 1966, built up a substantial steep-sided fan of lavas high on the northern flanks. Evidence from precise levelling (Murray and Guest, 1982) shows progressive downward movement on these lavas which may in part be the result of slow sliding under gravity (Murray, 1982b; Guest *et al.*, 1984), and strong seismic activity or continued build-up of this fan could cause it eventually to fail forming a major landslide on the northern flanks. Thus, in any hazard assessment of the volcano, such a possibility should be considered.

5 The rheological behaviour of basaltic lavas

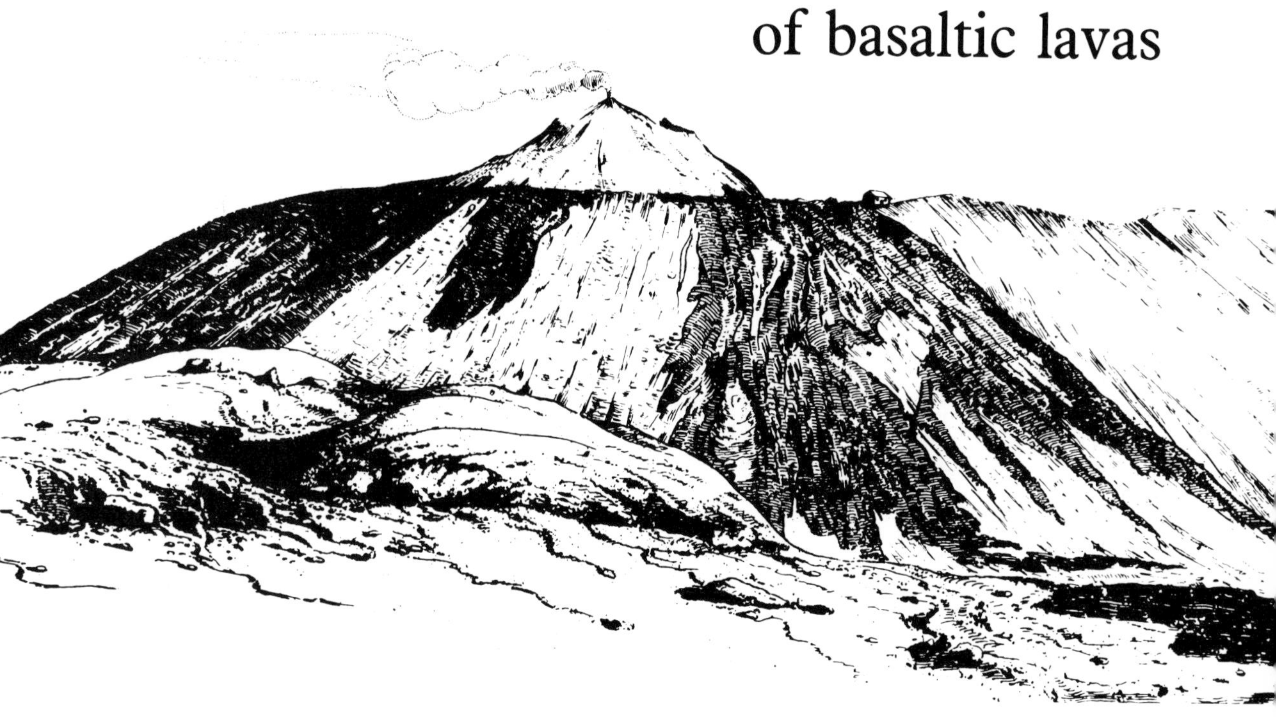

'This fiery and burning
deluge immediately spread
itself to above six miles in breadth,
seeming to be somewhat of the colour of
melted and burning glass; but, as
it cools, becomes hard and rocky,
and everywhere in its passage
leaves hills and pyramids
of that matter behind it.'

(The Earl of Winchilsea, 1669)

Used in the nineteenth century as a cornerstone for the 'Craters-of-Elevation' hypothesis (Chapter 1), the fact that the fronts of some of Etna's solidified lavas may be seen resting upon steep slopes, with dips of up to at least 35°, has since helped to initiate a fundamental advance in the understanding of lava flow evolution. Implicit in the earlier association between lava attitudes and 'Craters-of-Elevation' was the assumption that lavas, like large bodies of water, would continue to flow down an incline until being ponded behind an obstacle or within a depression, or until reaching a horizontal surface. In support of this contention, De Beaumont (1834) cited active Etnean lavas as examples of those which had been rarely observed to consolidate upon slopes with angles greater than 5° and which, in passing over steeper gradients, left behind only superficial veneers of solidified lava or coatings of scoriaceous debris. Hence the existence of old lavas lying on steep slopes was presented by De Beaumont as evidence that the underlying surface had been tilted to a higher angle after the emplacement of the flows.

De Beaumont's comments on the halting of a flow, however, are not applicable to the Etnean lava suite as a whole. Certainly the toes of many of the larger and low-level flank eruptions have come to rest upon the nearly horizontal slopes that mark the base of the mountain. Equally, it is common for a flow to become thicker on shallower slopes, the maximum:minimum thickness ratio being only exceptionally greater than 10:1. At the same time, though, many have consolidated upon appreciable inclines, such as the numerous flows coating the outside of the *Cratere Ellittico* which frequently never encounter dips of less than 10° before stopping; indeed, even De Beaumont (1834) himself recognized this to be sometimes the case, apparently in direct contradiction of his primary assertion.

It remains a matter of observation, therefore, that, when sufficiently solidified, a flow front will come to a halt whether on a shallow or steep incline – provided, of course, that the slope is not so steep as to induce the brecciation of the lava. The significance of this behaviour, demonstrating that crystallizing lavas are rheologically dissimilar from water, was first explicitly stated by Robson (1967), after analysing data collected on Etna by G. P. L. Walker (1967), and will be pursued in more detail in a later section of this chapter.

More generally, a knowledge of the rheological properties of a lava is essential for better understanding the morphological, dynamic and energetic development of a flow or flow-field, for each of these is determined by the variation, with time and position, of the sum of the force balances acting on every element of that lava. As a result, flow evolution reflects the complex interactions between the rate of eruption from the vent (controlled by the 'initial effusive force' driving the magma onto the surface), topographic irregularities (which affect the gravitational and any external frictional forces), and the rate and mode of lava solidification (which regulate the rheological and any self-imposed frictional forces, the latter possibly being generated, for example, along the inner margins of levées). Field observations (Kilburn (1984) has considered Etnean aa lavas in particular) indicate that, under steady conditions, the first of these components is usually of significance only within a few tens, or possibly hundreds, of metres from a vent. Beyond that, flowage for most of a lava's lifetime tends to be very nearly uniform (with the ground and lava surface gradients, away from the flow margins, being approximately equal), gravitational acceleration being the principal propelling agency, and lava effective viscosity – dependent on the rheological structure of the flow – and subsidiary frictional effects the retarding influences that ultimately bring a flow to a halt.

Analysing the rheological development of lava flows is thus a prerequisite for developing predictive models of flow growth, designing techniques for controlling lavas and reducing their threats to vulnerable communities, and for calculating the energy requirements of effusive processes. However, before concentrating specifically on the rheological characteristics of basalt lavas and on the role played by Etnean studies towards a better understanding of those properties, basic rheological concepts and definitions will first be introduced, followed by a discussion of the flow behaviour of comparatively simple suspensions containing solid particles and bubbles. Together, these considerations will provide a background against which the rheological investigations of crystallizing and vesiculating basaltic systems may be assessed.

5.1 Rheological concepts and definitions

Conceived from the Greek ρεοδ (a current) and λεγειω (to speak (of)), the term *rheology* was officially introduced in 1929 (Scott Blair, 1969) in recognition, as a science in its own right, of the study of the deformation (the change in shape or size) and flow (the rate of change of deformation) of materials under stress. Since then, an entire panoply of models, for the most part conceptual or semi-empirical, has been constructed to describe the rheological characteristics of widely differing materials, from foodstuffs and printing-ink to face creams and lava flows (see, for example, Reiner (1960) and Skelland (1967)). All of these, however, rely to some extent upon the classical notions of ideal viscous, elastic and plastic behaviour.

When subjected to a system of stresses, of any magnitude, that is both anisotropic (different in different directions) and inhomogeneous (different at different positions), an ideal *viscous fluid* will deform irreversibly as a consequence of flow, the degree of deformation changing continually with time. An ideal *elastic solid*, on the other hand, when exposed to a similar stress system, will suffer an instantaneous deformation, but will not experience flow. As summed up in Hooke's Law – '*ut tensio, sic vis*' (literally: 'how extended, thus the force') – the amount of deformation is directly proportional to the stress being applied. The deformation is also completely recoverable, with the body returning to its original size and shape after the stress has been withdrawn.

Bridging the gap between the purely viscous fluids and the elastic solids, and containing characteristics of both, is the family of *plastic* materials. If the applied stress does not exceed a critical value, a plastic body will behave as an elastic solid; but once this value has been overcome flowage will occur and the body will respond as a fluid. Since, for the most part, erupting magmas may be treated as solidifying fluids, it is with the viscous and plastic models that they can be most closely described.

The conventional classification scheme for flowing, incompressible media, whose properties do not change with time, is based upon the applied shear stress – shear rate (or deformation rate) relation displayed by a material when undergoing simple laminar shear at a specified temperature and pressure.

The conditions of simple shear are presented in Fig. 5.1. (A key to the notation used throughout the chapter is given in Table 5.1.) The shear stress τ is the force per unit area acting in the direction of flow on surfaces parallel with that direction, and the shear rate $\dot{\epsilon}$ is given by the velocity gradient across the moving layers (perpendicular to the flow direction). The resistance to motion within the fluid, an indicator of the amount of energy it loses as heat and which is thus not mechanically recoverable, is measured by its absolute viscosity η, mathematically described as the differential change in shear stress with shear rate ($d\tau/d\dot{\epsilon}$).

A plot of τ against $\dot{\epsilon}$ in laminar flow determines the rheological flow curve, or phenotype, of the

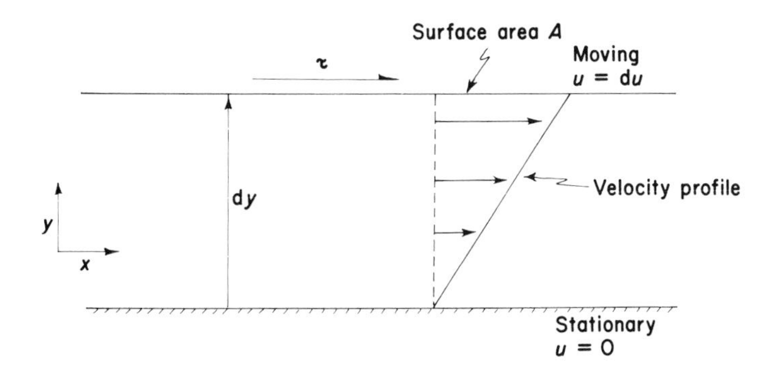

Fig. 5.1 The conditions of steady, simple, laminar shear flow between two parallel surfaces with an area A. A shear stress τ is applied parallel with the top surface, which subsequently advances with a velocity du. The lower surface, a perpendicular distance dy from the other, remains stationary. The shear rate $\dot{\epsilon}$ across the fluid is equal to du/dy.

Table 5.1 A list of the notations used in Chapter 5

English characters

Symbol	Meaning
A	area
A, A'	constants
B, B_{τ_y}	activation energy constant in, respectively, viscosity–temperature and yield strength – temperature relations
B	constant
C	crystal phase
C, C_m	actual and theoretical maximum, respectively, volumetric concentrations of particles in a suspension
C_c	critical volumetric concentration of particles, above which a suspension may develop non-Newtonian characteristics
c	velocity of sound
d, d_g, d_m	particle diameter and, respectively, geometric and arithmetic mean particle diameters
d_e	equivalent particle diameter, the diameter of a sphere with the same volume as that of the particle
d_h	characteristic length describing the geometry of the flow system of interest
g	acceleration due to gravity
H	flow thickness, perpendicular to flow surface
H_v	vertical flow thickness
h	depth within lava, perpendicular to flow surface
K	power-law coefficient (a 'consistency factor')
L	liquid phase
L	characteristic length of system
L_1, L_2	lengths of major and minor axes, respectively, of an ellipse or prolate ellipsoid
Lq	liquidus
M	constant
n	power-law exponent (a 'flow behaviour indicator')
N	constant
P	normal pressure
Re	Reynolds number; see Equation (5.17)
S	shape factor of a particle: the ratio of the surface area of a particle to the surface area of a sphere with the same volume
T	temperature (°C)
T	surface tension
ΔT	change in temperature; degree of undercooling below the liquidus
Ta	Taylor number; see Equation (5.15)
t	time
u	velocity
V, ΔV	volume and change in volume
v	velocity
w_b	basal width of lava levée
x	Cartesian coordinate direction
y	Cartesian coordinate direction

Greek characters

Symbol	Meaning
α	angle of slope
$\bar{\beta}$, β_g, β_m	average compressibility (of a lava) and the compressibilities of, respectively, gas bubbles and avesicular magma
Δ	gradient of line
ΔT	change in temperature; degree of undercooling below the liquidus
ΔV	change in volume
$\dot{\epsilon}$	shear rate
η, η_B	absolute viscosity (general) and absolute Bingham viscosity
$\eta_{B,H}$, $\eta_{B,L}$	absolute Bingham viscosities inferred for a non-Newtonian medium from observations made, respectively, at high and low rates of shear (Fig. 5.3)
η_e	effective viscosity
η_l	absolute viscosity of suspending liquid
η_r	relative absolute viscosity of a suspension (= absolute viscosity of suspension ÷ chosen reference viscosity)
η_{sp}	absolute viscosity of a suspension
$\eta_{sp,0}$, $\eta_{sp,\infty}$	absolute viscosity of a suspension at, respectively, limiting low and high rates of shear
θ	absolute temperature (K)
θ_0	reference absolute temperature
μ	Newtonian viscosity (absolute and apparent viscosities are identical)
μ_l	viscosity of a Newtonian suspending liquid
μ_0	reference Newtonian viscosity

Table 5.1 (contd.)

Greek characters

Symbol	Meaning
μ_r	relative Newtonian viscosity of a suspension (= viscosity of Newtonian suspension ÷ viscosity of Newtonian suspending liquid)
μ_{sp}	viscosity of a Newtonian suspension
μ'	apparent viscosity
μ'_l	apparent viscosity of suspending liquid
$\mu'_{l\infty}$	apparent viscosity of suspending liquid at limiting high rates of shear
μ'_{sp}	apparent viscosity of a suspension
$\mu'_{sp,0}$, $\mu'_{sp,\infty}$	apparent viscosity of a suspension at, respectively, limiting low and high rates of shear; in the first case, a non-Newtonian suspension may display essentially Newtonian behaviour, its apparent and absolute viscosities becoming virtually identical
ρ	density
ρ_l	density of lava or of suspending liquid medium
σ_g	geometric standard deviation of particle diameter
τ	shear stress
τ_b	basal shear stress
τ_T	'surface tension shear stress' acting around surface of a bubble (Equation 5.15)
τ_V	viscous shear stress acting on enclosing fluid in vicinity of a bubble (Equation 5.15)
τ_y	yield strength
$\tau_{y,H}$, $\tau_{y,L}$	yield strengths inferred for a non-Newtonian medium from observations made, respectively, at high and low rates of shear (Fig. 5.3)
τ_{y0}	reference yield strength
χ_g, χ_m	volume fraction of gas bubbles and magma in a lava

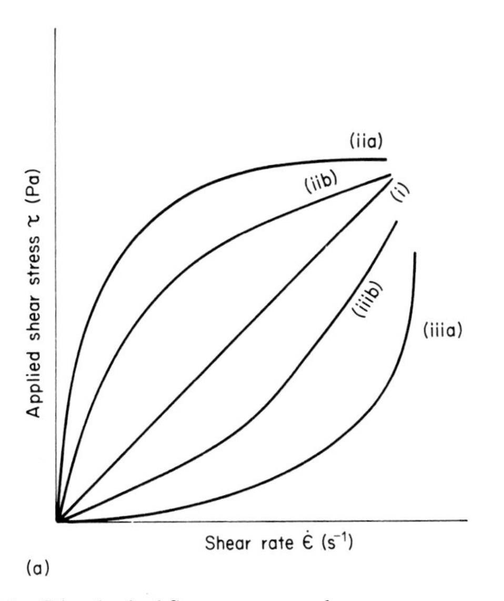

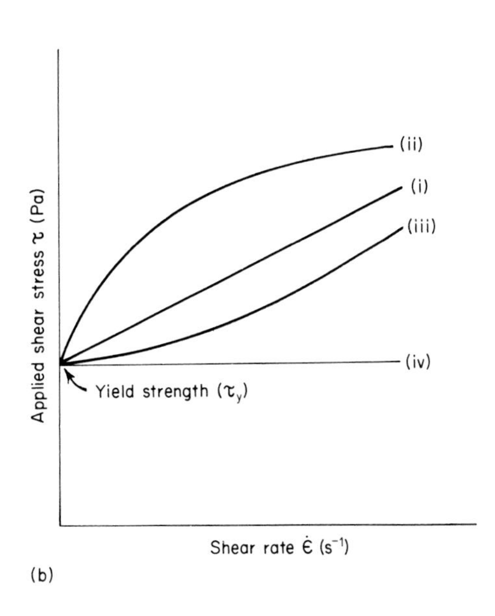

Fig. 5.2 Rheological flow curves or phenotypes.

(a) The principal flow curves of power-law fluids. (i) Newtonian fluid. (iia) Pseudoplastic fluid – ideal. (iib) Pseudoplastic fluid – real. (iiia) Dilatant fluid – ideal. (iiib) Dilatant fluid – real.

(b) The principal flow curves of plastic materials. (i) Bingham plastic. (ii) General plastic. (iii) Dilatant plastic. (iv) Ideal plastic (flows with zero viscosity when yield strength has been exceeded).

τ is applied shear stress; τ_y is effective yield strength; $\dot{\epsilon}$ is ambient shear rate.

material concerned. The principal types of flow curve for viscous fluids and plastic bodies are shown, respectively, in Figs 5.2(a) and 5.2(b). It is emphasized that these curves represent only idealized model materials, because, as encapsulated by Reiner's second axiom of rheology, 'real materials possess all rheological properties, although in varying degrees' (Reiner, 1960, p.11); it is merely the more prominent properties which a model phenotype displays.

Various workers have presented mathematical expressions to describe the shapes of these phenotypes (a useful summary is provided by Skelland (1967)). In view of the present level of understanding of lava rheology – still in its formative stages – there is little advantage in immediately delving into the more complicated of these expressions. It is accordingly sufficient to consider only the power-law characterization of viscous fluids (and later its extension to plastic materials), which is quite adequate for illustrating certain rheological principles and for permitting a preliminary analysis of the data available on the rheology of silicate magmas. Criticisms and discussions of the power-law model may be found in Reiner (1960), Scott Blair (1968) and Lenk (1978); further details of the alternative models are presented in most of the standard rheological texts, such as Reiner (1960), Bird *et al.* (1960) and Skelland (1967).

5.1.1 *Viscous fluids*

The power-law group of flow curves describing viscous fluids may be represented by the general expression:

$$\tau = K\dot{\epsilon}^{n} \tag{5.1}$$

where the power-law coefficient K denotes a 'consistency factor', and the power-law index n a 'flow behaviour indicator'.

The absolute viscosity is therefore given by:

$$\eta = \mathrm{d}\tau/\mathrm{d}\dot{\epsilon} = nK\dot{\epsilon}^{(n-1)} \tag{5.2}$$

The simplest of the power-law phenotypes is the linear Newtonian flow curve (Fig. 5.2(a), curve (i)), for which the rate of shearing is directly proportional to the applied shear stress, and the absolute viscosity remains constant. In this case, the power-law index is unity and so Equations (5.1) and (5.2) reduce to

$$\tau = \mu\dot{\epsilon} \tag{5.3}$$

and

$$\eta = K = \mu \tag{5.4}$$

where μ symbolizes the Newtonian viscosity.

The Newtonian model is of special interest, not only because of its historical significance as the first to formally define a quantitative measure of viscosity (Newton, 1687), but also because it is a good approximation to the behaviour of many common fluids (including water, but strictly only when its flow is laminar – a condition rarely satisfied by rivers, for example, whose motion is typically turbulent). Accordingly, most intuitive judgements on the consistency of a fluid are based, albeit subconsciously, upon the Newtonian model, whether or not it is truly applicable.

The psuedoplastic phenotype is characterized by a decrease in absolute viscosity as the shear rate increases (Fig. 5.2(a), curves (iia) and (iib)). This behaviour is generally attributed to structural rearrangements within the fluid (e.g. Mooney, 1958; Ram, 1967; Lenk, 1967, 1978). When at rest, non-spherical molecules or particles in the material are considered to be randomly orientated and probably entangled. Under increasing external shear stress, the particles become progressively disentangled and show some time-averaged alignment in the direction of shear, so reducing the fluid's overall resistance to motion. The linear portions of the flow curves therefore correspond to the conditions of total disorientation and ultimate alignment. An additional mechanism, suggested by Skelland (1967), invokes a greater shearing-apart of highly solvated particles to account for the decrease in absolute viscosity at faster rates of deformation.

In contrast to pseudoplastics, dilatant materials ($n > 1$) show an increase in viscosity as $\dot{\epsilon}$ becomes greater (Fig. 5.2(a), curves (iiia) and (iiib)). This response has been ascribed to an increase in the frictional interaction between neighbouring particles, even if initially aligned parallel to the direction of flow, owing to either inadequate 'lubrication' between the surfaces of adjacent flow laminae (Reynolds, 1885), or to the growth around the particles of secondary flow patterns, which are too localized to upset the general laminar motion of the fluid (Lenk, 1967, 1978).

Inspection of Equation (5.1) shows that the power-law model suggests that under certain conditions the absolute viscosities of a non-Newtonian viscous fluid may approach the extreme values of zero and infinity (for pseudoplastic materials ($0 < n < 1$), η tends to zero and infinity at very high and low shear rates respectively; for dilatant materials, the reverse η–$\dot{\epsilon}$ trend is apparent). In practice, however, the absolute viscosities of fluids which are satisfied by the power-law versions of the pseudoplastic and dilatant models, over the range of shear rates in which the greatest viscosity changes occur, appear to tend towards finite limiting maximum and minimum values (Van Wazer *et al.*, 1963; Ram, 1967; Lenk, 1978; see also Fig. 5.2(a), curves (iib) and (iiib)). The anomaly arises from the empirical nature of the power-law model and illustrates the danger of extrapolating a flow curve beyond the range of shear rates used for its construction. Several more realistic flow-curve equations for viscous materials have been listed by, among others, Reiner (1960), Bird *et al.* (1960), Skelland (1967) and Jinescu (1974).

5.1.2 *Plastic materials*

While the viscous fluids have the characteristic of being seen to flow under the smallest of shear stresses, plastic bodies appear able to do so only when the applied shear stresses exceed a critical value, identified as the yield strength τ_y of the material; when the external stresses are less than the yield value, the plastics instead appear to respond as if elastic solids. The fundamental phenotypes of plastic materials (Figure 5.2(b)) are thus distinguished from those of viscous fluids by not passing through the origin of the τ–$\dot{\epsilon}$ diagram, but in meeting the zero-shear-rate line (that is, the τ-axis), at a definite shear stress value corresponding to the yield strength. Hence, among the family of plastic materials, it is possible to distinguish (Figure 5.2(b)): (i) a Bingham plastic, representing a Newtonian material with a yield strength; (ii) a general plastic, representing a pseudoplastic fluid with a yield strength (including the special case of an ideal plastic which flows with zero viscosity); and (iii) a dilatant plastic, representing a dilatant fluid with a yield strength.

Hence, by analogy with Equation (5.1), and subject to its limitations as a conceptual model of real-fluid behaviour, the general τ–$\dot{\epsilon}$ relation for plastic materials may be expressed in the form:

$$\tau = \tau_y + K\dot{\epsilon}^n \qquad (5.5)$$

where $0 \leqslant n < 1$ for general plastics, $n > 1$ for dilatant plastics, and $n = 1$ for Bingham bodies. For shear rates greater than zero (that is, for $\tau - \tau_y > 0$) the absolute viscosity relation is the same as that for the power-law fluids (Equation (5.2)), η being replaced by the appropriate viscosity term; for applied shear stresses below the yield value, the absolute viscosity is effectively infinite, and Equation (5.5) is invalid. Thus, for example, the absolute viscosity relation for Bingham materials may be written:

$$\begin{aligned} \eta_B &= (\tau - \tau_y)/\dot{\epsilon} \quad \text{for } \tau > \tau_y \\ \eta_B &= \infty \quad \text{for } \tau \leqslant \tau_y \end{aligned} \qquad (5.6)$$

with η_B, the absolute Bingham viscosity, replacing the coefficient K of Equation (5.5).

In a manner similar to that used to explain pseudoplastic behaviour, the presence of a yield strength is usually explained in terms of a three-dimensional, rigidifying structure which permeates the material when in a condition of rest and, like a log-jam in a river, tends to stifle any tendency to flow. According to Reiner (1934) and Van Wazer *et al.* (1963), such a structure is more likely to be provided by the mechanical interaction within a second phase (for example, crystal or vesicle suspensions) in the host medium, rather than directly on a molecular level, since no single-phase liquids have yet been observed to possess a discrete yield value.

5.1.3 *The meaning of yield strength*

The yield strength or yield value of a material has

been formally defined by the British Society of Rheology (1966, p. 7) as that value of the load stress 'above which permanent deformations appear. It may depend on the precision with which the deformations can be detected. It may depend on the loading history, the temperature, and, in the case of an element, on the mean stress, the orientations and ratios of the principal stresses, etc.'

Such is the list of provisos that it is only with caution that independently determined yield values for the same material can be quantitatively compared, variations in quoted figures being as much indicators of different measuring conditions as of changes in a fluid's rheology. Discussing this problem, Reiner (1964) drew the analogy of the situation of two theology students praising the Almighty. Said one: 'For God, one thousand years are like a minute. And as He is the Creator of all, a thousand pounds are for Him nothing more than a penny.' Said the other: 'Wonderful! Next time I pray to God, I shall pray: "God, give me a penny." ' Replied the first: 'But what good will that do you? He will only say "wait a minute!" '

What the second student had forgotten was that his time-scale (of observation) was considerably shorter than that in Divine circles. Similarly, when applying very low shear stresses to a body, if the experiment is not conducted over a long-enough time-interval, or if the measuring apparatus has not a sufficiently high sensitivity, the amount of the permanent deformation which has occurred may be too small to be recorded.

Indeed it is open to question whether or not observed yield strengths are truly material properties (Reiner, 1964; Tozer, 1965; Houwink, 1971; Lenk, 1978). As Tozer (1965) has pointed out, there is no justification from solid-state physics that any solid should in fact possess a yield strength. Commenting upon the creep flow behaviour of ostensibly solid materials, he states (Tozer, 1965, p. 259, following Van Bueren, 1961) that 'the illusion of finite yield strength has arisen because there are creep processes contributing to the total creep rate that increase rapidly with stress and therefore suddenly become observable. It follows, without approximation, that because all solids have finite binding energy, processes exist that give rise to creep at vanishingly small shear stresses.'

Hence the detection of a yield strength delimiting the solid and fluid responses of a particular body may perhaps be more properly considered as an artefact of the conditions of observation, τ_y denoting the shear stress below which the absolute viscosity of the material becomes so large that the rate of deformation falls below the threshold of detectability. Accordingly, the plastic models discussed above emerge as special cases of the more general viscous class of materials, the distinction between their stress – shear rate relations (Equations (5.1) and (5.5)) being made for the purposes of practical description. As such, for meaningful comparisons to be made between the observed yield strengths of materials, it is necessary to ensure that the minimum threshold values of shear rate are of at least the same order of magnitude.

In addition, it is important to distinguish between the effective yield strength determined on the basis of the limiting shear rate (or absolute viscosity) and that quoted simply as a mathematical convenience to represent the flow curve of a material deforming at rates of shear much larger than the threshold value. As an illustration of the latter, consider a pseudoplastic material being investigated by two methods that utilize different rates of shear. Figure 5.3(a) shows the actual flow curve of a fluid superimposed upon the experimental data points as determined by the two methods. Treated in isolation (Figs 5.3(b) and 5.3(c)), both sets could be used to interpret the behaviour of the material, over the specified ranges of shear rate, in terms of a Bingham model, each characterized by a unique pair of extrapolated yield strength–absolute (Bingham) viscosity values ($\tau_{y,H}$,$\eta_{B,H}$, and $\tau_{y,L}$,$\eta_{B,L}$, corresponding to the appropriate pairs for the high- and low-shear-rate data sets shown in Fig. 5.3). Although the two Bingham viscosities provide measures of the average absolute viscosities of the fluid over the given rates of shearing, the associated yield strengths have no relevance to the stress below which deformation is undetectable: each is purely a device to allow the equation of the flow curve to be presented as a concise mathematical expression

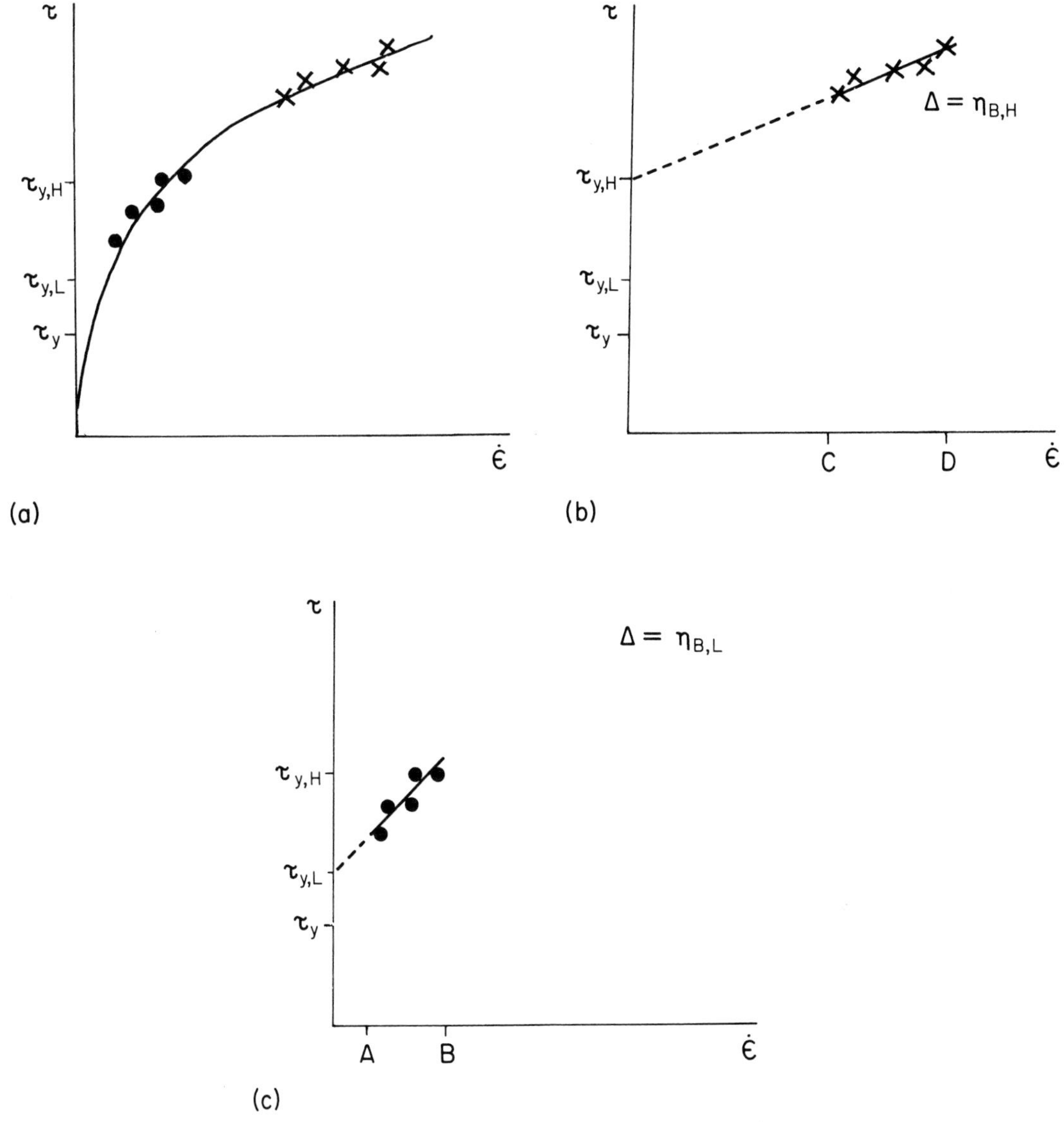

Fig. 5.3 The interpretation of a rheological flow curve (phenotype) using limited data.

(a) The true flow curve of the hypothetical fluid. Upon this have been superimposed the two data-sets obtained from rheometers operating over limited and different rates of shearing. The crosses denote the high-shear-rate data, the solid circles the low-shear-rate data.

(b) Interpretation of the high-shear-rate data. In isolation, the inferred part of the flow curve may be described by a Bingham plastic equation of the form: $\tau = \tau_{y,H} + \eta_{B,H}$ for $C \leqslant \dot{\epsilon} \leqslant D$

(c) Interpretation of the low-shear-rate data. As in case (b), the inferred part of the flow curve may be described by a Bingham equation, which, with the relevant parameters, becomes: $\tau = \tau_{y,L} + \eta_{B,L}\, \dot{\epsilon}$ for $A \leqslant \dot{\epsilon} \leqslant B$. Consequently, depending on the shear rate conditions of the measurements, the same material may be characterized by different rheological equations.

τ is applied shear stress; $\dot{\epsilon}$ is ambient shear rate; τ_y is effective fluid yield strength: the stress below which flowage cannot be detected; η_B is the inferred absolute Bingham viscosity of the material, over the shear-rate range of interest, = the gradient Δ of the flow curve; H are high-shear-rate conditions; L are low-shear-rate conditions.

which is valid only within the stipulated range of shear rates.

Even when considering only effective yield strengths the situation may be further complicated, especially in the case of suspensions of mixed particles, by the fact that the rheological properties which affect a particular process also depend upon the length-scale over which it operates. Viewing the suspension as a whole, its effective yield strength and absolute viscosity will be dictated by the properties of the liquid fraction combined with the influence of the whole population of contained particles. But when concentrating only upon the behaviour of one of the larger particles, the controlling rheological parameters will be those of the liquid fraction combined with the influence of the smaller size particles – those with mean diameters about an order of magnitude smaller than the particle of interest (Sparks *et al.*, 1977), the smallest particles being in turn influenced by the liquid phase alone. Thus, for example, if the falling sphere method is employed to determine the effective yield strength of a suspension (a sphere of known size and density being suspended in the fluid from one arm of an analytical balance, the imposed shear stress on the sample being varied, by placing differing weights on the opposite arm of the balance, until the sphere just begins to sink), the diameter of the sphere used must be at least ten times greater than the mean diameter of the largest suspended particles.

In summary, therefore, despite theoretical reservations, it remains a matter of observation that a wide range of materials do possess, for practical purposes, an effective yield strength, below which permanent deformation cannot be detected under the conditions of measurement. This value will depend on the duration of observation, the length-scale over which the process of interest operates, and the choice of measuring technique. Accordingly, to allow useful comparisons of yield strength to be made, quoted figures should be identified as either mathematical conveniences (in which case the range of shear rates of the experiment should also be presented) or as those defined on the basis of a minimum detectable shear rate, whose value should accompany the effective yield strength estimate.

5.1.4 *The meaning of viscosity*

Representing the amount of energy lost as heat from a fluid due to its motion and which is not mechanically recoverable (Van Wazer *et al.*, 1963), the viscosity of a material provides a measure of its resistance to flowage when undergoing simple laminar shear. However, because the concept of viscosity was originally based upon Newtonian behaviour, the subsequent recognition of non-Newtonian fluids has led to the proliferation of different types of viscosity, used to compare rheologically different materials under specific conditions of flow. Of particular importance are the absolute, apparent and effective viscosities. The additional effect of time-dependent changes will be discussed separately below.

5.1.5 *Absolute viscosity*

As previously mentioned, the absolute viscosity of a material may be defined as its absolute resistance to motion at any particular rate of shear, that is, $\eta = d\tau/d\dot{\epsilon}$. For both power-law viscous fluids and plastic materials whose yield strengths have been exceeded the absolute viscosity is given by Equation (5.2), which also describes the gradient of the appropriate rheological flow curve at the shear-rate of interest (Fig. 5.4).

5.1.6 *Apparent viscosity*

The apparent viscosity of a non-Newtonian material represents the viscosity which would be calculated for that material, at the chosen rate of shear, on the assumption that it possessed Newtonian characteristics (Fig. 5.4). It is mathematically defined as the ratio of the total applied shear stress to the corresponding shear rate, that is, $\tau/\dot{\epsilon}$. For power-law fluids, the apparent viscosity μ' is given by:

$$\mu' = K\dot{\epsilon}^{(n-1)} \tag{5.7}$$

while for plastic fluids it becomes:

$$\mu' = (\tau_y/\dot{\epsilon}) + K\dot{\epsilon}^{(n-1)} \tag{5.8}$$

For all non-Newtonian phenotypes, μ' varies with the value of $\dot{\epsilon}$ (in the Newtonian case, $\mu'\dot{\epsilon} = \mu$,

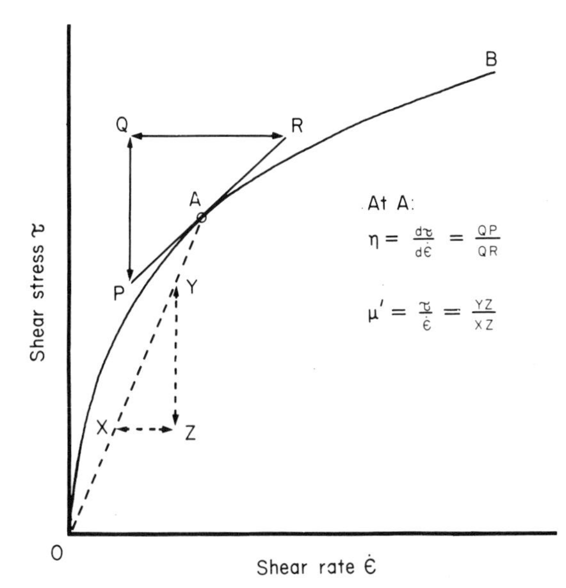

Fig. 5.4 The graphical interpretation of absolute and apparent viscosities.

The curve OAB describes the phenotype of a pseudoplastic fluid. Under the shear stress – shear rate conditions appropriate to position A on the flow curve, the absolute viscosity η is given by the gradient of the flow curve *at that point*, graphically equivalent to the ratio of the values covered by the lines QP and QR, or QP/QR. The apparent viscosity μ' at position A is given by the quotient of the ambient shear stress divided by the ambient shear rate, equal to the gradient of the dashed line OA, or YZ/XZ.

the constant Newtonian viscosity). Consequently, an apparent viscosity is a meaningless quantity unless accompanied by either the corresponding rate of deformation or the magnitude of the applied shear stress. Indeed, the principal attribute of an apparent viscosity is to provide a guide as to the material consistency which would be intuitively inferred without detailed rheological measurements.

5.1.7 *Effective viscosity*

The effective viscosity η_e of a non-Newtonian material is that quantity which may be substituted for the Newtonian viscosity in a mathematical expression for Newtonian flow under geometrically similar conditions, thereby allowing the use of similar sets of measurements and experimental techniques to investigate rheologically different substances. As a result, the precise relations between η_e and the apparent and absolute viscosities of a particular fluid will vary according to the geometrical conditions of flow (and therefore, unlike μ' and η in Fig. 5.4, η_e cannot be simply related to the shape of the appropriate rheological flow curve).

Consider, for example, the fully developed, steady flow of a fluid through a cylindrical conduit. In the case of a Newtonian medium, the mean flow velocity across a given section V may be related to the fluid viscosity by a form of the familiar Poiseuille equation:

$$V = \frac{D\tau_w}{8\mu} \qquad (5.9)$$

where D is the diameter of the conduit and τ_w is the wall shear stress, acting along the conduit perimeter.

For a Bingham plastic, the equivalent expression is (Skelland, 1967, p. 172):

$$V = \frac{D\tau_w}{8\eta_B}\left[1 - \frac{4}{3}\left(\frac{\tau_y}{\tau_w}\right) + \frac{1}{3}\left(\frac{\tau_y}{\tau_w}\right)^4\right] \qquad (5.10)$$

which, rewritten in the Newtonian form:

$$V = \frac{D\tau_w}{8\eta_e} \qquad (5.11)$$

gives the expression for the effective viscosity of a Bingham plastic flowing steadily through a circular conduit as:

$$\eta_e = \eta_B \Big/ \left[1 - \frac{4}{3}\left(\frac{\tau_y}{\tau_w}\right) + \frac{1}{3}\left(\frac{\tau_y}{\tau_w}\right)^4\right] \qquad (5.12)$$

For comparison, the apparent viscosity under these conditions is given by (Skelland, 1967, pp. 30 – 31, 74, 172 – 174):

$$\mu' = \frac{\tau_w}{\dot{\epsilon}_w} = \eta_B \Big/ \left[1 - \left(\frac{\tau_y}{\tau_w}\right)\right] \qquad (5.13)$$

where $\dot{\epsilon}_w$ is the shear rate of the fluid along the wall of the conduit.

Combining Equations (5.12) and (5.13) yields:

$$\eta_e = \mu' \left[1 - \left(\frac{\tau_y}{\tau_w}\right)\right] \Big/ \left[1 - \frac{4}{3}\left(\frac{\tau_y}{\tau_w}\right) + \frac{1}{3}\left(\frac{\tau_y}{\tau_w}\right)^4\right] \qquad (5.14)$$

Thus for Bingham materials, with finite yield strengths, η_e and μ' cannot be identical under the given conditions of flow. The advantage of using effective viscosity (η_e), therefore, is that, in contrast to the apparent viscosity (μ') which is generally useful only for qualitative analysis, it may be used in expressions derived for Newtonian fluids and the flow geometry of interest, so enabling quantitative comparisons to be made between the rheological and dynamical properties of Newtonian and non-Newtonian materials.

5.1.8 *Time-dependent fluids*

Implicit in the foregoing discussion of rheological models has been the assumption that the materials had time-independent properties, with any structural changes responsible for non-Newtonian behaviour having taken place instantaneously with an alteration of the shear stress field.

However, some steadily flowing materials do show a measurable change in their absolute viscosities with time, gradually approaching a limiting value which corresponds to that associated with their equilibrium structure at that shear rate. If the viscosity becomes smaller, the fluid is termed *thixotropic*; if, on the other hand, it increases, the fluid is described as *rheopectic*. The internal mechanisms promoting such behaviour are considered to be similar to, but much more sluggish than, those causing pseudoplasticity and dilatancy, respectively (Skelland, 1967). Indeed, thixotropic materials must inevitably be pseudoplastic (in the sense that their absolute viscosities decrease with an increase in shear rate and not, necessarily, that they follow a power-law relation), and rheopectic fluids invariably be dilatant; in neither case, however, can it be automatically assumed that the converse is true (Lenk, 1978).

Among time-dependent fluids, therefore, the period over which observations are made will influence the measured values of viscosity as well as, where applicable, the effective yield strength. The results will also vary with the amount of stirring to which a given volume of fluid is subjected by the viscometer. For further discussion of the details of time-dependent fluid behaviour, reference should be made to Van Wazer *et al.* (1963), Brodkey (1967), Skelland (1967), and Lenk (1978) and to the sources quoted therein.

5.1.9 *Viscoelastic fluids*

Although the family of models describing plastic behaviour combines elements of elastic and viscous behaviour, it only allows for one of the two responses to operate at any given moment. Thus when the applied shear stress is less than the yield strength, elastic behaviour is assumed, while at greater values the behaviour is considered to be viscous. Among real materials, however, the two responses may be expected to occur to a greater or lesser extent simultaneously. As a result, perhaps the best way to describe a real material is to regard it as *viscoelastic* (or *elasticoviscous*, depending on whether the viscous or elastic component is, respectively, the more prominent of the two).

The distinction is an important one. For example, over the range of shear stresses in which a plastic is supposed to behave as an ideal elastic, the stress corresponding to a given strain is independent of time, whereas for a viscoelastic material the stress will gradually dissipate. On the other hand, over the higher shear-stress range for which a plastic is considered to deform viscously, suffering a permanent deformation, a viscoelastic material will also flow, but will gradually recover a part of its deformation after the removal of the stress.

More details of viscoelastic behaviour are available in the references cited at the end of the preceding section.

5.1.10 *The concept of a generalized rheological flow curve*

In an effort to unify the common rheological phenotypes and to offer an improved conceptual understanding of the behaviour of real fluids, Lenk (1967, 1978) has introduced a generalized rheological flow curve (Fig. 5.5), derived intuitively from the structural changes (discussed at the beginning of the chapter) which may be assumed to occur in a fluid during laminar flow. In so doing, he is reiterating the views of Reiner (1960) that all fluids share the same basic rheological properties, but with some of the characteristics being more

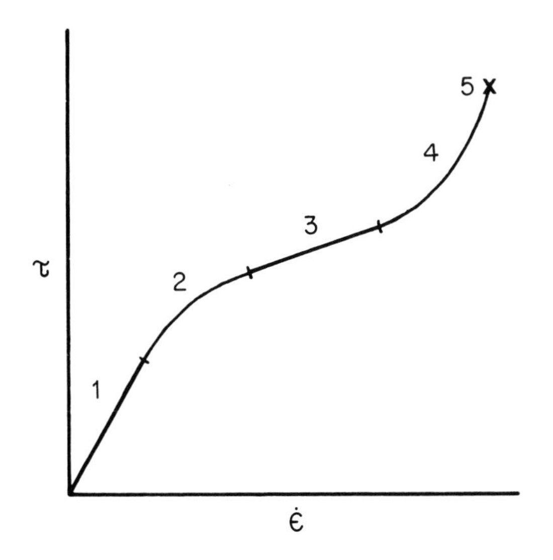

Fig. 5.5 A schematic representation of a generalized rheological flow curve.

The generalized flow curve embodies all the characteristics of the model phenotypes shown in Fig. 5.2 and provides a useful conceptual framework for linking those models together.

Five regions have been recognized according to the type of rheological behaviour which they show over the corresponding ranges of shear rate:

(1) Newtonian behaviour.
(2) Pseudoplastic behaviour.
(3) Bingham plastic (including ideal plastic) behaviour.
(4) Dilatant behaviour.
(5) Onset of turbulence or melt fracture.

The model phenotype chosen to describe the fluid will therefore depend on the range of shear rates covered during the time of observation, and also on the relative sizes of the depicted regions (here shown to cover comparable shear rate ranges solely for clarity). It is emphasized that the gradients of the curves are schematic as well.

(After Lenk, 1967, 1978.)

pronounced than the others.

Thus, provided that the shear rate at which turbulence or melt fracture becomes apparent (related to the intrinsic properties of the material and the geometry of flow) has not been exceeded, one or other of the Newtonian, pseudoplastic, plastic and dilatant phenotypes may be found to be useful approximations to the real characteristics of the fluid (Fig. 5.5), but only within, and not beyond, the range of shear rates covered by the observations. Hence, if only very low shear rates are being considered, for example, the observed portion of the flow curve may fall entirely within region 1 of Fig. 5.5, the fluid being then classified as Newtonian; at higher shear rates, on the other hand, only region 3 in Fig. 5.5. may be investigated, it being possible to describe that portion of the curve on its own in terms of either a pseudoplastic or Bingham plastic phenotype (the implied yield strengths and viscosities outside the measured region being simply mathematical devices for obtaining the equation of the flow curve over the observed range of shear rates, and having no material significance). Though not yet sufficiently far developed to be of quantitative value, Lenk's model does provide a useful conceptual framework for interpreting rheological data and gauging their limitations.

5.2 The rheological characteristics of suspensions

5.2.1 Introduction

The gross rheological properties of a material are determined by its physical composition. Hence in the case of a lava flow, crystal content, vesicularity, and degree of liquid polymerization will each contribute to its overall style of flow. But, such are the intricacies of their interactions, it is not yet possible to predict quantitatively how different combinations of these structural factors will affect magma rheology. Nevertheless, by comparing some of the relationships obtained for simpler suspensions of solid particles and bubbles, some insights may be gained into their probable modes of influence. A comprehensive review of published models will not be presented here, the purpose being merely to highlight certain essential features. Further discussions are available in Sadron (1953), Frisch and Simha (1956), Rutgers (1962), Goldsmith and Mason (1967), and Jeffrey and Acrivos

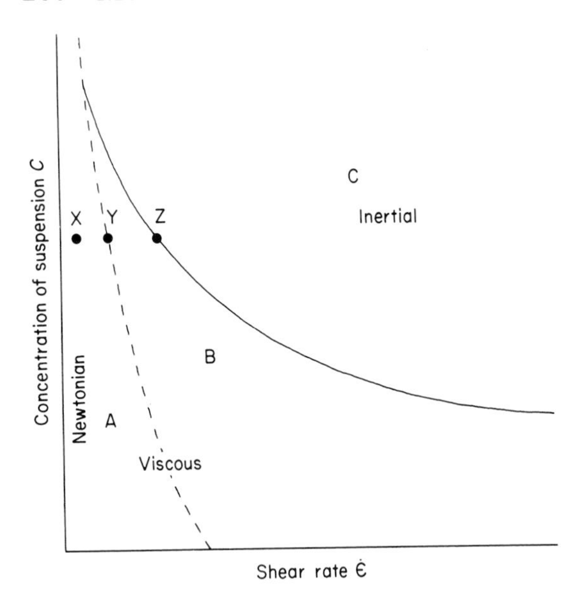

Fig. 5.6 A diagram showing schematically the tentatively inferred association between the total particle concentration (C) and ambient shear rate ($\dot{\epsilon}$) of a suspension and its observed rheological behaviour

Region A: Viscous-dominated – the shear rate is low enough at all concentrations for the suspension to display Newtonian behaviour (compare region 1 in Fig. 5.5).

Region B: Viscous-dominated – the fluid motion is controlled principally by the flow of the host medium through the gaps between the particles. The rheological response is expected to resemble that of the suspending phase alone, and may be Newtonian or non-Newtonian.

Region C: Inertia-dominated – the fluid motion is controlled principally by the inertial flow of the suspended particles. Non-Newtonian behaviour is anticipated, regardless of the nature of the suspending medium.

The junctions between the three regions will vary with the rheological properties of the suspending medium and with the relative density and size and shape distributions of the contained particles.

For a lava flow of constant crystallinity and vesicularity, for example, since the ambient shear-rate increases with depth, the points X, Y and Z illustrate the possibility of the deeper levels of the flow (at Z) showing non-Newtonian behaviour, while the upper layers (at X) display Newtonian characteristics.

(1976); the data concerning basaltic materials will be considered in a later section.

5.2.2 *The effect of rigid particles on the rheology of a fluid*

By interfering with the free motion of the host liquid, the particles in a suspension have a direct influence upon its rheological behaviour. The nature of this influence and whether or not it will encourage non-Newtonian behaviour appears to be governed by the relative significance of the inertial and viscous stresses operating within the fluid.

The inertial stresses are generated by changes in the momentum of the suspension owing to particle interaction – such as particle collisions or aggregation. At either very low total particle concentrations (C, by volume) or very small local rates of shearing, or both, the momentum transfer between particles becomes a subsidiary source of energy-loss compared with the viscous dissipation arising from the flow of the suspending fluid between adjacent solids (Frankel and Acrivos, 1967). Under these viscous-flow-dominated conditions, the type of the rheological response (that is, Newtonian, pseudoplastic and so forth) of the suspension can be expected to be similar to that of the suspending phase alone (Fig. 5.6, region B), all the types approximating to Newtonian behaviour at very low rates of shear (corresponding to region 1 in Fig. 5.5 and to region A in Fig. 5.6). As the particle concentration and shear-rate increase, on the other hand, so also does the degree of particle interaction and hence the significance of the inertial forces within the system (Ackerman and Shen, 1979). When the inertial flow dominates fluid motion, the suspension can be anticipated to show non-Newtonian behaviour (Fig. 5.6, region C), the exact nature of which will depend upon – in addition to C and local shear rate – the rheological properties of the host medium, and the relative density (the difference in the densities of the particles and of the surrounding fluid) and size and shape distributions of the particles (as these will affect the type of their interactions). In considering the influence of rigid second-phase particles on the rheology of a suspension, therefore, it is convenient to deal separately with the Newtonian and non-Newtonian regimes of flow.

5.2.3 Newtonian suspensions

Following the pioneering quantitative studies by Arrhenius (1887) and Einstein (1906, 1911) of the viscosities of very dilute ($C \leq 0.1$), low-shear-rate suspensions of spherical particles (Table 5.2), several theories have been advanced which extend these initial treatments both to higher-concentration systems and to those which contain particles of diverse morphologies. The majority have been based upon considerations of the kinematic, mechanical and hydrodynamic features of a mixture, restricted to specific ranges of particle dimensions and total concentrations, and to very low rates of shear.

A selection of the resulting viscosity – concentration relations is presented in Table 5.2. In each case, the relative viscosity μ_r (which is the ratio of the viscosity of the (Newtonian) suspension to the viscosity of the (Newtonian) suspending fluid) is represented as a high-order polynomial, sometimes exponential, function of C. This reflects the general property of concentrated suspensions with low particle inertia to display a dramatic variation in relative viscosity over comparatively narrow and critical ranges of particle concentration (Fig. 5.7). As a result, a suspension may attain a state of apparent solidity (with a viscosity sufficiently high that flowage cannot be detected over the time-scale of observation) before C has achieved its maximum theoretical value (dependent upon the geometries and size distributions of the particles). For example, Bagnold (1954, 1966) determined experimentally that mixtures of granular solids carried in a liquid medium have critical concentrations of about 62.5%(v/v). A similar feature has been noted among (non-Newtonian) crystallizing basalts, for which, over volcanologically reasonably applied shear stress conditions, the critical crystal content appears to lie in the approximate range of 50–55%(v/v) (Arzi, 1978; Marsh, 1981).

The form of the relations listed in Table 5.2

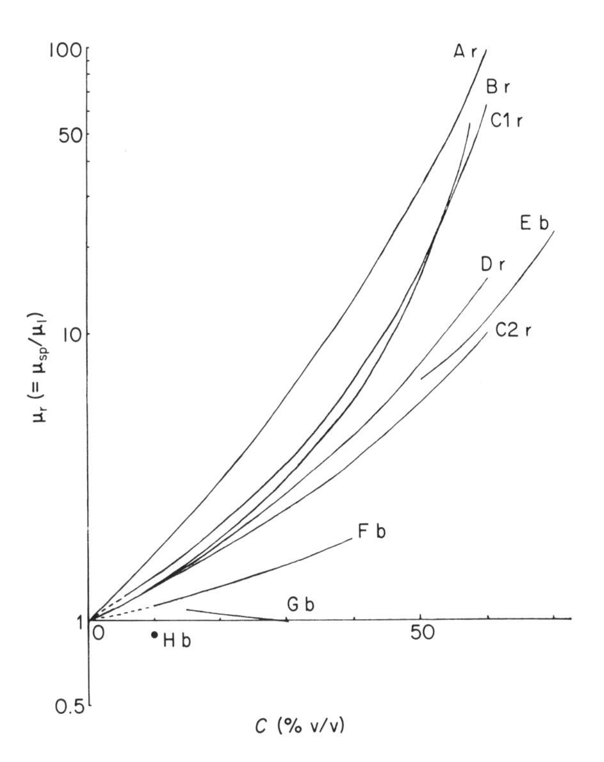

Fig. 5.7 A selection of theoretically and experimentally determined relations describing the variation with particle concentration (C) of the relative viscosities (μ_r) of assumed Newtonian suspensions of rigid particles (r) and bubbles (b).

Of particular note are the following:

(a) The trend among all the rigid particle systems to show a quickening of relative viscosity increase as the particle concentration increases:

(b) The inconsistent relative viscosity variations among bubble dispersions; and

(c) The position of the datum point for the bubble system H, which indicates a net reduction in bulk viscosity with respect to the host medium alone.

Both the suspensions and the suspending media are assumed to have behaved approximately as Newtonian media under the specified shear-rate conditions. The responses of the rigid particle and bubble suspensions may be compared within each category only qualitatively and for similar ranges of shear rate. The details of the relations shown are presented in Table 5.2.

Note that the relative viscosity values are referred to the (Newtonian) viscosities of the host fluids, and that they are plotted on a logarithmic scale.

Table 5.2 The change in the relative viscosities of suspensions with particle concentration: selected data. (Suspensions and suspending media are assumed to be Newtonian)

Curve letter (Fig. 5.7)	*Nature of suspension*	*Relative viscosity* μ_r $(= \mu_{sp}/\mu_l)$	*Shear rate* (s^{-1})	*Concentration C* (% *v/v*)	*Source*
Rigid particle suspensions (r)					
–	uniform spheres	$\exp(AC)$	'low'	'low'	Arrhenius (1887)
–	uniform spheres	$(1 + C/2)/(1 - 2C) \approx (1 + 2.5C)$	(?)'low'	<0.01	Einstein (1906, 1911)
A	uniform ellipsoids ($L_1/L_2 = 5$)		(?)	0–60	Bruggeman (1935) (also in Smit (1965))
D	uniform spheres	approximately $(1 - C)^{-3}$	(?)	0–60	Bruggeman (1935) (also in Smit (1965))
B	uniform spheres	$1 + 2.5C\,(1 \div 25C/f^3 \ldots)$ where $f \approx 11/9$	(?)	0–15	Thomas (1965)
		$1 + 2.5C + 10.05C^2 + 0.00273\exp(16.6C)$	(?)	25–60	Thomas (1965)
C1	uniform spheres	$(1 - 1.35C)^{-2.5}$	(?)	0–40+	Roscoe (1952)
C2	serial spheres	$(1 - C)^{-2.5}$	(?)	0–60+	Roscoe (1952)
Bubble suspensions (b)					
E	gas bubbles	$(1 - (AC)^{1/3})^{-1}$ $\{\mu_{sp} = \mu'_{sp,\infty}\}$	'very high'	50–70	Sibree (1934)
F	milk-fat emulsions ('spherical')	$\exp(C + C^{5/3} + C^{11/3})$ {inferred from original}	?moderate	0–40	Leviton and Leighton (1936)
G	gas bubbles	insufficient data	very high ((?)10^4–10^6)	15–30	Einarsson (1949)
H	gas bubbles	insufficient data	10	10	Shaw *et al.* (1968)
	gas bubbles	$1 - (5C/3)$	very low ((?) Ta $\geqslant$ 1)	'very low' ((?) < 0.01)	Mackenzie (1950)

Note: the behaviour of the rigid particle and bubble suspensions may only be compared (qualitatively) under similar shear-rate conditions.

depends not only upon the total solid concentration, but also upon the shape and size-distributions of the particles in suspension. Among dispersions of spheres of a given concentration, the relative viscosity appears to increase as the particles become smaller, provided that their diameters are less than about 1 μm. This association is generally attributed to an increase in the significance among smaller particles of flocculation or the growth around the solid phases of absorbed layers of stationary fluid (for example, Weltmann and Green, 1943; Rutgers, 1962; Chong *et al.*, 1971). At larger particle sizes, if the suspended spheres are uniform, the relative viscosity may appear to be independent of diameter (Rutgers, 1962; Chong *et al.*, 1971). Among bidispersed systems (that is, suspensions containing particles of two uniform size populations) of spheres with diameters greater than 1 μm, however, the more uniform is the overall size range (whether of the smaller or larger spheres) the greater generally is the relative viscosity of the fluid (Ward and Whitmore, 1950a; Eveson *et al.*, 1951; Roscoe, 1952; Eveson, 1959; Collins and Wayland, 1963; Chong *et al.*, 1971). De Bruijn (1951) has suggested that this variation may be due to 'colloid-chemical' effects acting on the surface of the particles, but it may also reflect changes in the intensity of the mechanical interaction of the particles, different amounts of energy-loss being associated with large – large, large – small, and small – small sphere collisions. More detailed explanations are presented by Chong *et al.* (1971), Jeffrey and Acrivos (1976) and Ackerman and Shen (1979), the last mentioned providing a simplified mathematical analysis of the behaviour.

5.2.4 *Non-Newtonian suspensions*

As the concentration and ambient shear rate of a suspension increase, so does the particle inertia of the system and hence the likelihood that it will display some non-Newtonian behaviour. Some of the experimentally determined critical solid-concentrations C_c above which non-Newtonian characteristics have become apparent for specific rates of deformation are listed in table 5.3. In addition to the shear rate conditions, C_c also varies with the nature, shape, relative density and size-frequency distribution of the suspended particles, as well as with the composition of the suspending medium, presumably because these factors influence the degree of physical and chemical interactions among the particles. Thus, for example, among suspensions of the same total solid concentration – while a system containing buoyant, uniform spheres, 1 μm or more across, may show Newtonian behaviour for a given shearing condition – non-Newtonian characteristics may develop among dispersions of:

(a) Smaller particles, owing to changes in the degree of flocculation and surface-chemical effects. This is likely to be the case only when the smaller particles are of submicron dimensions; when the particles among the suspensions are greater than 16 μm across, the bulk fluid viscosity may increase with particle size (Clarke, 1967), Newtonian behaviour being possibly retained because of the reduced relative significance of flocculation;
(b) More irregular particles, fluctuations in the amount of liquid trapped within the surface irregularities altering the effective solid concentration; and
(c) Heavier or more elongate particles, in which the degree of mechanical interaction between the particles – a process sensitive to the rate of shearing – may significantly affect the suspension viscosity.

As a general rule, however, for suspensions of spherical particles between 4 μm and 400 μm across, Rutgers (1962) considers that Newtonian behaviour cannot be expected with confidence when the solid concentration exceeds 25% (v/v), although this assumption has been maintained by Roscoe (1952) and Thomas (1965) for concentrations of up to 60% (v/v); see Table 5.2.

While some non-Newtonian dispersions display dilatant behaviour (Metzner and Whitlock, 1958; Alexandrovichi *et al.*, 1962; Clarke, 1967), the great majority possess the characteristics of pseudoplastics or general plastics. Accordingly, in trying to elucidate the dependency of the

Table 5.3 The effect of particle concentration on suspension rheology, indicating concentration ranges for Newtonian behaviour and the critical concentrations (C_c) above which non-Newtonian behaviour appears

Temperature (°C)	*Nature of particles*	*Size distribution (mean* diameter d_m *and length L;* μm)	*Suspending medium*	*Density contrast (particle – liquid; kg m* $^{-3}$)	*Shear rate* (s^{-1})	C_c (% v/v)	Rheological model	Source
30	irregular lead-zinc oxides	uniform 0.75 (d_m)	linseed oil	(?)0	up to 150	$\leqslant 5$	Bingham	Weltmann and Green (1943)
25	spheres, MMA	uniform (i) 38 (ii) 182	aqueous lead nitrate and glycerine solution	0	about 0.25–1	At least 20	no non-Newtonian behaviour detected	Eveson *et al.* (1951)
25	spheres, MMA	mixed 38 and 182	aqueous lead nitrate and glycerine solution	0	about 0.25–1	$\geqslant 5$	shear thinning	Eveson *et al.* (1951)
(?)	spheres silica	uniform (i) 0.025	standard oil and paraffin	(?)	<< 1–50	$\leqslant 6.1$	pseudoplastic /Bingham (and thixotropic)	Williams (1951)
		(ii) about 0.1	standard oil and paraffin	(?)	<< 1–50	6.1	Newtonian	
		(iii) 2–10	aqueous zinc iodide and glycerine solution	(?)	10–50	At least 50	Newtonian	

25	spheres, MMA	27.5–49.5 76–208 147–208 152–177	aqueous lead nitrate and glycerol	0	(?)	At least 30	no non-Newtonian behaviour detected	Ward and Whitmore (1950a)
		88–104	low-viscocity oil (about 0.005 Pa s)	300	(?)	$\leqslant 14$	Newtonian but thixotrophic (implying undetected psuedo-plasticity)	
		147–175	high-viscosity oil (about 0.089 Pa s)	300	(?)	$\leqslant 14$		
25	spheres, MMA rough	72–85 100–120 150–170 200–300 300 72–170	aqueous lead nitrate and glycerine solution	0	(?)	At least 15–20	no non-Newtonian behaviour detected	Ward and Whitmore (1950b)
20	spheres, glass	100–160	aqueous zinc iodide with glycerine solution	0	(?)	40–47	yield strength detected; implied dilatancy and rheopexy	Vand (1948)
30	fibres, cellulose	mixed (d_m = 30, L = 100–800)	aqueous glycerol	365	0.01–5	about 3–5	yield strength detected; (?)Bingham	Morrison and Harper (1965)

(MMA: methyl methacrylate polymer)

suspension viscosity (absolute or apparent) upon the particle concentration, a choice of reference viscosities is available for use: μ_l, the constant viscosity of the suspending medium, assuming it to be Newtonian; $\mu'_{sp,0}$, the approximately Newtonian viscosity of the whole suspension at very low rates of shear; and $\eta_{sp,\infty}$, the upper viscosity limit (ulitmate viscosity) at high rates of shear (it is emphasized that the values determined for $\mu'_{sp,0}$ and $\eta_{sp,\infty}$ will themselves be dependent upon the range of shear rates covered during the experiment). Hence, when comparing the values of relative viscosities (viscosity of suspension divided by the chosen reference viscosity) quoted from different sources, it is important to confirm which suspension viscosity (absolute or apparent) and which reference viscosity have been employed.

In cases when the absolute viscosity of a suspension at low shear rates becomes so large as to render flowage experimentally undetectable, or when only the flow characteristics over a restricted range of shear rates are required, the rheological behaviour of the fluid may be more conveniently described as that of a plastic material. Under these conditions, it is clearly desirable to establish how the particle content influences the bulk yield of strength of the fluid as well as its viscosity.

Because of their relative simplicity, most experimental investigations have been focused upon approximate Bingham systems, the results from some of which are shown in Table 5.4. Even assuming that it is justifiable to compare the *variations* in the yield strengths determined under the different experimental conditions (the quoted τ_y values not being comparable, as discussed in an earlier section), it is evident from the few data in Table 5.4 that there is as yet no simple, universal expression to link changes in τ_y (whether extrapolated from high- or low-shear-rate data) to variations in the physical composition of a suspension. This is possibly a consequence of different mechanisms controlling the rheological response of a suspension according to the concentration and size of the suspended particles. Nevertheless, viewing all the results in Table 5.4 together, some tentative inferences may be drawn that:

(1) Among suspensions with concentrations less than about 0.3, containing particles with mean diameters less than about 10μm, τ_y is likely to increase as C increases and as d_m decreases (the latter possibly being a result of the more equi-dimensional shape and of the greater relative influence of flocculation among particles with d_m of about 2 μm or less); of the two, particle concentration appears to be the more important factor;
(2) Among suspensions with particle concentrations between about 30% and 55% (v/v) mean diameters from 10 to 60 μm, τ_y increases as both C and d_m increase. This inference is based solely on the results of Gay *et al.* (1969), who assumed in the development of their model that a suspension will flow only when the distances between adjacent particles are of the same order as d_m, greater shear stresses being needed to separate the larger particles. Although the experimental results of these authors appear consistent with their model over the quoted ranges of particle size and concentration, the extrapolation of their equation to suspensions of larger particles leads to unrealistically high estimates of yield strength (Pinkerton, 1978); and
(3) Among crystalline solids, with mean crystal diameters between about 5 μm and 3.5 mm, τ_y again increases as d_m decreases, possibly reflecting a controlling influence of the rate either of slip propagation along grain boundaries or of micro-crack nucleation.

The data in Table 5.4 also suggest that the changes in suspension viscosity (whether absolute or apparent) with particle concentration follow a sympathetic general trend similar to that noted for Newtonian suspensions (Table 5.2 and Figure 5.7). There is also the implication from Thomas' equation in Table 5.4 that, for small particle diameter suspensions (with d_m between 0.1 and 20 μm), the apparent viscosity of a suspension increases with a decrease in mean particle diameter – again possibly a result of the greater significance of flocculation among the smaller, more equi-dimensional particles.

Table 5.4 Some of the experimentally determined relations, for assumed Bingham suspensions, between viscosity–yield strength and particle size and concentration

Nature of suspension	*Shear rate* (s^{-1})	*Concentration* C (% v/v)	*Size distribution (mean diameter* d_m; *μm)*	*Viscosity–yield strength – C,* d_m *relations*	*Comments*	*Source*
Uniform, irregular	10^{-3}–10^{-4}	0.02–0.2	0.1–20 0.1–2 2–20	$\mu'_{sp,\infty}/\mu_l = \exp(2.5 + (Ad_m^{-1/2}))C$ $\tau_y = BC^3/d_m^2$ $\tau_y \propto C^3/d_m$ (approximately)	Difference in τ_y relations possibly a result of (i) greater significance of flocculation among particles with $d_m \leqslant 1$ μm; and (ii) particles with $d_m \geqslant 2$ μm being more equidimensional than larger particles. Possible dilatancy when $C > 0.2$	Thomas (1961, 1963)
Uniform (?) spheres	(?)	0.06–0.09	0.025	$\tau_y \propto C^5$ or $\tau_y \propto C^6$	One particle size only, so τ_y–d_m relation not established	Williams (1951)
Uniform irregular lead-zinc oxides	max. 150	0.03–0.4	up to 4	$\eta_{sp,\infty}/\mu_l = [1 + (A/\mu_l)] \times \exp(BC)$ $\tau_y = M \exp(NC)$	A,B,M,N are dependent on particle size and shape, flocculation and adsorption features, and maximum rate of shear. A also depends on C: for $C < 0.05$, $A \rightarrow 0$	Weltmann and Green (1943)
Uniform spheres	max. 160	0.28–0.55	10–60	$\mu'_{sp,\infty}/\mu_l = \exp\{(2.5 + [C/(C_m - C)]^{0.48}(C/C_m)\}$ $\tau_y = 200\,[d_g/(C_m - C)\}\{C_m/(1 - C_m)\}^2\{S^{2/3}/\sigma^2_g\}$	C_m is maximum theoretical C; d_g is geometric mean particle diameter; σ_g is geometric standard deviation of particle diameter; S is a shape factor: surface area of particle divided by surface area of sphere with the same volume	Gay *et al.* (1969)
Mixed, irregular crystals in limestone and marble	detectable rate of slip propagation along grain boundaries or of microcrack nucleation	about 1.00	5–3500	$\tau_y \propto d^{-1/2}_m$	Solid media	Olsson (1974)

In the case of a crystallizing lava flow, the crystallinity – rheology relation will be yet more complex, continued crystal nucleation and growth changing the total particle concentration, the size- and shape-frequency distributions of the component crystals, and the chemical composition of the host magmatic liquid – by increasing its silica content and raising its effective viscosity.

Overall, however, it is to be qualitatively expected that the more crystalline a specific batch of lava becomes, the greater will be its resistance to motion. Only the exsolution of a discrete gas phase may potentially neutralize this trend, as discussed below.

5.2.5 *The effect of deformable gas bubbles upon the rheology of a fluid*

As with rigid particle systems, bubble dispersions, if they are observed at sufficiently low concentrations or at minimal rates of shearing, appear to behave as Newtonian media. Under these conditions, experimental and theoretical considerations suggest that the viscosity of the suspensions can be usually expected to be greater than that of the suspending phase alone, becoming high enough to be registered as a yield strength when a critical bubble concentration has been surpassed.

For a bubble to remain spherical, the surface tension stresses (τ_T) acting around its interface must be much larger than those (τ_V) generated by the viscous shearing in the host liquid (with viscosity μ_l). For fluids in simple laminar shear, the criterion may be written as (after Taylor (1932)):

$$\mathrm{Ta} = \tau_T/\tau_V$$

$$= \frac{4(T/d)}{\dot{\epsilon}\mu_l\,[19\mu_p + 16\mu_l]/[4(\mu_p + \mu_l)]} >> 1 \qquad (5.15)$$

which becomes, for gas bubbles in a lava:

$$\mathrm{Ta} = (T/d)/(\dot{\epsilon}\mu_l) \qquad >> 1$$

where T is the surface tension and d is the diameter of the bubbles in suspension, and $\dot{\epsilon}$ is the rate of shear. As the dimensionless ratio Ta (proportional to the more familiar Reynolds number divided by the Weber number) approaches and becomes smaller than unity (d being replaced by d_e, the equivalent diameter of a sphere with the same volume as the particle), the contained particles become more elongate and, if the effective viscosity ratio of the gas phase relative to the host fluid is greater than about 0.005 (Karam and Bellinger, 1968), they are eventually disrupted (Taylor, 1932; Goldsmith and Mason, 1967).

While assuming their elongate cross-sections (as seen in a section containing the direction of motion), the vesicles also tend to rotate so that their major axes are aligned parallel with the principal direction of flow (in the case of simple laminar shear). The bubbles thus offer a changing degree of resistance to motion and so may promote non-Newtonian behaviour within the suspension as a whole.

From limited theoretical and experimental data, it appears that the nature of the rheological changes brought about by the deformation of bubbles varies with their volume concentration and the imposed rates of shear. By analogy with the influence of porosity on elastic solids, Mackenzie (1950) has argued that as the vesicles first begin to lose their sphericity the viscosity of the suspension will fall below that of the enclosing medium (Mackenzie's relative viscosity relation is listed in Table 5.2).

Though explicitly derived for only very dilute ($C < 0.01$(?)), low shear rate (such that Ta $\geqslant 1$(?)) and, by implication, Newtonian dispersions, the mechanism considered by Mackenzie (1950) may in part be responsible for the behaviour observed by Shaw *et al.* (1968) of a 10% (v/v) suspension of bubbles within a pseudoplastic silicone liquid. Shaw *et al.* found that, after an initial region of high absolute viscosity ($\eta_{sp,0}$; detected as a yield strength), the relative viscosity of the suspension (η_{sp}/η_l) declined to about 0.75 (Shaw *et al.*, 1968; see Figs 5.4 and 5.11), until at higher shear rates (of the order of 10 s^{-1}), possibly coinciding with the emerging dominance of inter-bubble flow interference, η_{sp} began to converge towards the value of the corresponding absolute viscosity of the silicone base alone (η_l), with the apparent viscosity of the suspension (μ'_{sp}), though less than the silicone apparent viscosity (μ'_l) during the course of the experiment, seeming to gradually approach μ'_l at higher extrapolated values of $\dot{\epsilon}$.

These results, therefore, are not wholly incompatible with the observations made by Einarsson (1949) during his investigation of the 1947 – 48 lavas of the Icelandic volcano Mount Hekla. Under rather less rigorous experimental conditions and at considerably greater implied rates of shearing (10^4 – 10^6 s^{-1}) than those used by Shaw *et al.* (1968), Einarsson was unable to detect substantial variations in the apparent viscosities of glycerin – protein mixtures containing 0%, 15.2%, and 30.4% (v/v) of bubbles (curve G-b of Fig. 5.7).

Sibree (1934), however, also studying high-shear-rate suspension behaviour, found that, among froths with bubble concentrations between 50% and 70% (v/v), the apparent viscosities of the dispersions at assumed, but unspecified, upper limiting values of $\dot{\epsilon}$, such that the high shear rate absolute ($\eta_{sp,\infty}$) and apparent ($\mu'_{sp,\infty}$) suspension viscosities tended to the same value, were considerably greater than the corresponding viscosity (μ_l) of the suspending medium (assumed to be Newtonian). His expression for a relative viscosity (Table 5.3) is of the same form as that proposed by Hatschek (1911) for the flow of emulsions.

Assuming that no special mechanisms were in operation during any of the quoted experiments, it would appear that, in the first instance, the relative viscosity of a bubble dispersion is determined by a trade-off between bubble deformation and streamlining on the one hand, and vesicle interaction on the other. In the former case, provided that each bubble is sufficiently isolated from its neighbours and can deform freely to minimize the displacement of the streamlines within the host liquid, it is inferred from the work of Mackenzie (1950) that, since the gas within a bubble has a lower viscosity than the enclosing fluid, the net absolute viscosity of a gaseous suspension may be reduced below that of the suspending medium alone. This effect may possibly be enhanced by local vesicle coalescence, the larger daughter bubble being more readily deformable than either of the parents.

If, however, the bubble surface tension is sufficiently large to maintain bubble sphericity, the gaseous particles may be treated as effectively solid spheres of 'infinite' viscosity, and they will accordingly increase the relative absolute viscosity of the suspension. Moreover, at higher concentrations and at greater rates of shear, and assuming that bubble bursting is of minor importance under the conditions of flow, the effect of increased energy loss following more intensive vesicle interaction will also tend to increase the viscosity of the suspension. A similar effect may result from changes in the size distribution of the vesicles, the more numerous the smaller bubbles, which are relatively less easy to deform, the higher the viscosity – comparing similar concentration suspensions under the same conditions of shear. Furthermore, the closer the distance between adjacent bubbles, the more significant will be the action of any attractive chemical forces, also serving to upset the local flowage of the suspending fluid, and so raise the viscosity of the system.

5.3 The rheological properties of basaltic fluids

In order to use any of the models already discussed to describe the rheological behaviour of basaltic fluids, it is necessary to assume that a lava may be treated as an incompressible laminar fluid with insignificant time-dependent and viscoelastic rheological properties. The incompressibility and time-dependent assumptions will be justified (at least as a first approximation) towards the end of the chapter. The condition of negligible viscoelasticity is imposed by the paucity of the data required for a rigorous evaluation. It is noted, however, that under the conditions of steady laminar flow, the elastic characteristics of a viscoelastic material are only likely to have an appreciable influence in the regions where the channel or tube directing the flow changes in dimension or inclination, or at the entrances and exits of these pathways. Such behaviour may also become noticeable when considering very small-scale processes, such as the detailed motion of crystals and vesicles within a lava.

The general applicability of the assumption that the overall motion of a lava is likely to be laminar can be demonstrated by considering the nature of the forces acting upon the flow. In the case of an incompressible fluid moving unhindered across a surface, the principal forces to which it is subjected may be classified among the following categories:

(1) Body forces, arising from the action of external phenomena; for lava flows with free surfaces, the only body force is gravitational;
(2) 'Pressure' forces, due to the effect of external pumping and also, for fluids with free surfaces, to hydrostatic pressures;
(3) Effective viscous or rheological forces, produced as a result of the physical constitution of the fluid;
(4) Inertia forces, acting due to the change in momentum of the fluid; and
(5) Marginal retention forces, due to the processes acting around the periphery of the fluid – for example: the strength of a rigid crust and of an unconsolidated rubble coating.

Of these, it is the balance between the inertia and the effective viscosity forces which determines the essential style of motion. A measure of the relative influence of these forces is provided by the dimensionless Reynolds number (Re), defined as:

$$\mathrm{Re} = \frac{\text{inertia forces}}{\text{effective viscosity forces}} = \frac{\rho U d_h}{\eta_e} \qquad (5.17)$$

where ρ is the density of the fluid, U is its average velocity and η_e its effective viscosity, and d_h is a characteristic length of the fluid system (this varies with the geometry of the system; however, in the cases to be considered, d_h is taken to be the hydraulic radius of the flowing material, given by:

$$4 \times \frac{\text{cross-sectional area of flow}}{\text{wetted perimeter}}).$$

With the characteristic length so defined, experiments have shown that, among fluids in general, for values of Re smaller than about 2000, the rheological forces are sufficiently large with respect to the inertia of the system that flowage is laminar, a fluid *appearing* to move as a collection of infinitesimally thin layers sliding past one another. For Reynolds numbers greater than 2000, the individual fluid elements appear to move along quite irregular paths which on average represent the forward movement of the entire body; this is a characteristic of *turbulent* flow, in which the inertial energy is more efficiently disseminated than under laminar conditions.

In the particular case of Etna's basaltic lavas, the typical thickness of an individual stream lies between 5 m and 10 m, and rarely exceeds about 30 m. For lava channels with rectangular cross-sections, the corresponding maximum hydraulic radii are of the order of between 20 m and 40 m, and 120 m. Assuming a maximum velocity of 4 ms^{-1} and a bulk density of 2500 kg m^{-3}, the effective viscosity of the lava must be greater than about 100 – 500 Pas for the flow to be laminar. As discussed in more detail in the following sections, that this is invariably the case for subliquidus basalts is borne out by laboratory investigations (Shaw, 1972; Gauthier, 1973; Murase and McBirney, 1973; McBirney and Noyes, 1979) and by observations of active lavas in the field (Shaw *et al*, 1968; Pinkerton and Sparks, 1978; see also the reviews by Macdonald, 1972; and Williams and McBirney, 1979).

Under some circumstances, however, when considering local flow motion, the assumption of laminar behaviour may not be appropriate. If erupted at near-liquidus temperatures, for example, a lava may initially display some turbulence until crystallization has raised its effective viscosity to a sufficiently high value. Nevertheless, the above analysis suggests that, in general, the large-scale motion of Etnean lavas may be regarded as laminar.

5.3.1 *The rheological significance of the attitudes of Etnean lavas*

By virtue of their accessibility and frequent eruption, the lava flows of Mount Etna have proved instrumental in shaping ideas about the rheology of crystallizing basalts. Of special significance has been the fact that thick flows may come to rest upon appreciable inclines, a feature which led Robson (1967), using the data of G. P. L. Walker (1967), to present the first explicit statement that a congealing flow may be considered as a non-Newtonian material.

In Fig. 5.8 is reproduced the plot by G. P. L. Walker (1967) of the variation of thickness with angle of slope of a number of young Etnean lavas.

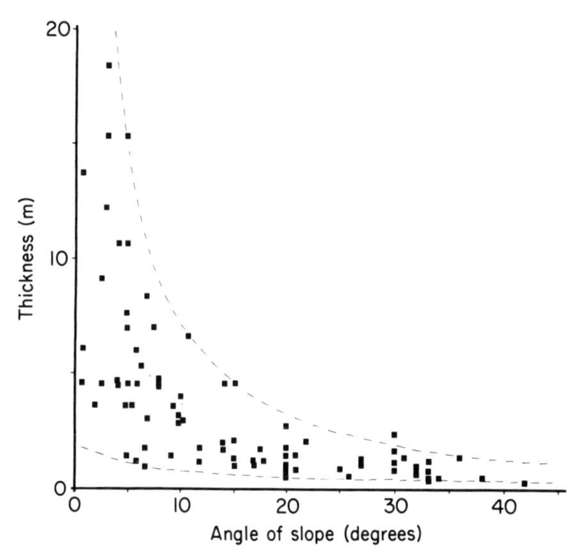

Fig. 5.8 The variation in thickness with angle of slope of young Etnean basaltic lava flows. The approximate limiting envelopes, shown by the dashed lines, suggest minimum and maximum effective bulk lava yield strengths of the order of, respectively, 10^3 Pa and 10^5 Pa. (After G.P.L. Walker, 1967, courtesy of *Nature*.)

Inspection of the shape of the upper envelope suggests that it may approximately be described by an equation of the form:

$$H \sin \alpha = \text{a constant} \qquad (5.18)$$

where H is the actual (that is, measured at right-angles from the ground surface) flow thickness and α is the angle of slope. In his analysis, Robson (1967) considered the vertical depth (H_v) of the flow, implying that $H_v \sin\alpha$, and not Equation (5.18), is a constant and is proportional to the imposed basal shear stress. This, however, is only valid for constant α, or approximately so for very shallow slopes, when $H_v \approx H$. Nevertheless, use of Equation (5.18) with Robson's line of reasoning leads to the same conclusion as in his original paper.

The more general term $h \sin\alpha$ is directly proportional to the shear stress imposed, parallel with the base of a uniformly thick flow, upon a lava at depth h, owing to the weight of the overlying material (Fig. 5.9). From Equation (5.18), it appears that as Etna's *thickest* lavas (relative to others on a similar gradient) slow to a standstill, the imposed *basal* shear stresses have an almost constant value. As a result, Robson (1967) inferred that these lavas may be considered as Bingham plastics (being the simplest rheological model material to embody both a yield strength and viscosity) which, as solidification progresses, acquire a maximum, limiting yield strength upon coming to rest, of the order of 2.5×10^5 Pa (Robson used a lava density of 2000 kg m^{-3}; applying an empirical correction factor to account for frictional effects (see caption to Fig. 5.9), this value may be revised to $6 - 10 \times 10^4$ Pa).

In addition, if it is assumed that the yield strength of a lava increases during the earlier stages of solidification and that the flow front may be considered to be at all times either rheologically homogeneous or to have yield strengths above its base which everywhere exceed the imposed shear stress, then a more molten flow may also come to a halt if it reaches a slope shallow enough to reduce the imposed basal shear stress below the prevailing yield value. On any given incline, therefore, lavas of various thicknesses may be expected to have come to rest, depending upon the flow depth and degree of solidity when that slope was first encountered, and upon the duration and rate of the effusion, which will determine whether or not any backflow thickening will occur sufficiently rapidly to overcome the increasing yield strength of the static and cooling flow front. It is thus possible to account for the scatter of points shown in Fig. 5.8. Furthermore, if the lower envelope in Fig. 5.8 is not the product of limited observational data, then it may also be inferred that, either upon or soon after eruption, Etnean lavas acquire yield strengths of the order of 10^3Pa. If so, one possible implication is that the plumbing system of Mount Etna is such that magmas are brought to the surface within a restricted range of rheological states which could, in turn, reflect that they have been subject to comparable melt-generation processes and crystallization histories during ascent.

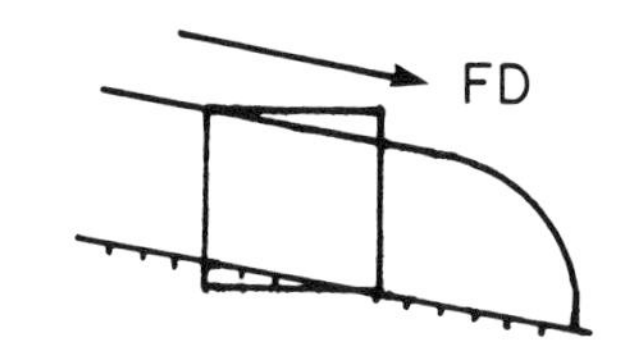

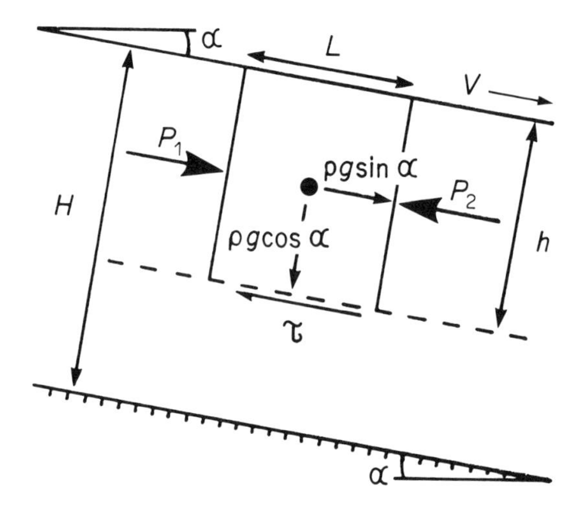

Fig. 5.9 Stresses acting on a lava moving down an incline in steady, uniform, simple laminar shear.

Consider the equilibrium distribution of forces acting upon an *element* of lava of unit width, uniform thickness h and length L. Assuming laminar motion, the force balance in the direction of flow is given by:

$$\tau L = (P_1 - P_2)\, h + \rho_l\, ghL \sin \alpha \tag{5.19}$$

Since for uniform flow the mean hydrostatic pressures P_1 and P_2 are equal, the relation reduces to:

$$\tau = \rho_l\, gh\sin \alpha \tag{5.20}$$

the imposed basal shear stress τ_b being obtained when $h = H$.

The shear stress is also equal to $\eta_e dv/dh$, where v is the local velocity. Inserting this relation into Equation (5.20), integrating over the whole thickness of the flow, and rearranging yields:

$$\eta_e = (\rho_l\, gH^2/BV) \sin \alpha \tag{5.21}$$

where V is the surface velocity of flow, and B is an empirical correction factor allowing for the influence of marginal friction. For an infinite sheet, $B = 3$; while for a narrow, semi-circular channel, $B = 4$.

Notice that if the effective yield strength is considered to be the shear stress below which the viscosity of the lava becomes so high for the rate of deformation to be undetectable, and if it is further assumed that at such minimal shear rates the lava shows approximately Newtonian behaviour with a limiting effective viscosity μ, then, for an homogeneous, nearly solidified lava of uniform thickness, on the point of coming to rest, the yield strength τ_y is:

$$\tau_y \simeq \tau_b \simeq \mu\, (V/H) \tag{5.22}$$

Substituting Equation (5.22) into Equation (5.21) and setting $\eta_e = \mu$ yields for a near-stationary flow:

$$\tau_y = (\rho_l\, gH/B) \sin \alpha \tag{5.23}$$

(FD is flow direction.)

5.3.2 Direct rheological measurements on basaltic fluids

Since the publication of Robson's conclusions in 1967, the non-Newtonian character of crystallizing basalts has been verified both in the laboratory and in the field (Fig. 5.10) by direct rheological measurements. That it had not been done so beforehand reflects the earlier concentration of interest upon the behaviour of supraliquidus melts, which appear to exhibit Newtonian characteristics. Partial summaries of these studies, as well as those on related materials, have been given by Birch and Dane (1942) and by Bottinga and Weill (1972).

For subliquidus basalts, data from Etna's alkaline lavas have been presented by Gauthier (1973), Sparks *et al.* (1976), Pinkerton (1978) and Pinkerton and Sparks (1978). Other studies on tholeiitic basalts have been conducted by Shaw *et al.* (1968; Makaopuhi Lava Basalt (MLB), Hawaii), Shaw (1969; MLB), Murase and McBirney (1973; Columbia River Basalt (CRB)) and McBirney and Noyes (1979; MLB and CRB). Scarfe (1973) has

Fig. 5.10 Harry Pinkerton using a shear-vane rotation viscometer to take rheological measurements from an active lava stream during the 1983 south flank eruption on Etna. (Photograph: J. E. Guest.)

also studied melts with a range of basaltic compositions.

Covering a combined order-of-magnitude range of shear rates from 0.001 s^{-1} to 10 s^{-1}, these studies have demonstrated that the rheological behaviour of subliquidus basalts may, in the first instance, be analysed in terms of the pseudoplastic or Bingham models. Some of the results are shown in Figs 5.11, 5.14 and 5.15, and Table 5.5. One of the most comprehensive sets of measurements is that of Shaw (1969), who investigated in the laboratory the behaviour of MLB samples subjected to different initial degrees of undercooling (ΔT is liquidus temperature minus the temperature to which the sample is rapidly dropped (and held at) for the experiment; see Fig. 5.11, curves labelled 'L'). Using a concentric-cylinder viscometer, each run was carried out when the system had apparently achieved crystal – liquid equilibrium (inferred from the good reproducibility of the results: Shaw, 1969, pp. 515 – 16). When considering only shear rates greater than about 2 s^{-1}, the rheological response of the sample can be approximated to the Bingham model (Fig. 5.11; dashed lines and their solid extensions to higher rates of shear); while at lower shear rates, evidence for pseudoplasticity becomes apparent.

The nature of this response clearly demonstrates the importance of the observation conditions upon the interpretation of the rheological data (as discussed in an earlier section). A further consequence of such non-Newtonian characteristics is that only those rheological measurements made under similar flow and shear rate conditions may be compared with confidence, even if all other factors, such as sample bulk composition and ambient temperature, and the attainment of crystal – liquid equilibrium, are carefully controlled. Especially in the field, therefore, where measurements are of necessity made in essentially uncontrolled conditions, comparative data analyses are likely to yield quite spurious results.

Table 5.5 The results of some direct rheological measurements upon subliquidus basaltic melts

Temperature (°C)	*Shear rate* (s^{-1})	*Rheological model*	*Rheological parameters*		*Laboratory (L) or field (F)*	*Crystal content* (% v/v)	*Vesicularity* (% v/v)	*Viscometer*[1]	*Source*
			τ_y (Pa)	η_B (Pa s)					
Makaopuhi Lava Basalt (MLB)									
1132 ±5	0.1–10	Bingham[2]	120[2]	650[2]	F	20–25	5	SV	Shaw *et al.* (1968)
1133 ±5	0.1–10	Bingham[2]	70[2]	750[2]	F	20–25	5	SV	Shaw *et al.* (1968)
1125	0.1–10	Bingham	2500	about 10^4 (Fig. 5.10)	L	(?)	0	RV	Shaw (1969)
1120	about 1	Bingham	about 8000	about 4500	L	(?)	0	RV	Shaw (1969)
1200 to 1120	0.005[3] minimum	Bingham	about 0–7000	(?) (Fig. 5.14(a))	L	(?)	0	(?)FS	Murase (1981)
Columbia River Basalt (CRB)									
1195	0.005–0.1	Bingham	about 10–60[5]	about 50–4000[5]	L	(?)	0	FS	McBirney and Noyes (1979)
1200 to 1120	0.005 minimum[3]	Bingham	about 0–7000[4]	(?) (Fig. 5.14(a))	L	(?)	0	(?)FS	Murase (1981)
Etnean Basalt (EB)									
1200 to 1150	0.01–10	Bingham	about 4.5–30 variable	about 90–180 variable	L	(?)	(?)0	RV	Gauthier (1973)
1086	0.001–0.1	Bingham	370 ±30	9400 ±1500	F	45	(?)	SP	Pinkerton and Sparks (1978)

(1) Types of viscometer: SV: shear-vane rotation viscometer; RV: rotation (concentric-cylinder) viscometer; FS: falling-sphere viscometer; SP: shear penetrometer.

(2) Data for viscometer speed increasing (different for decreasing speeds). These are considered to be closer to steady melt structure conditions: Shaw *et al.* (1968).

(3) Minimum shear rate inferred from McBirney and Noyes (1979, Fig. 2), who appear to have used the same data as Murase (1981).

(4) The quoted yield strength values are those which have also been published in Williams and McBirney (1979). The same data have been presented graphically by McBirney and Noyes (1979), but with the yield strength estimates, for corresponding shear rates, reduced by about one-third. McBirney (personal communication, 1984) has advised that the values as given here should, for the present, be accepted.

(5) Measurements taken after the sample had been held at 1195°C for 1 h (lower values) and 21 h (higher values). The yield strength values may be three times too small (see note (4) above).

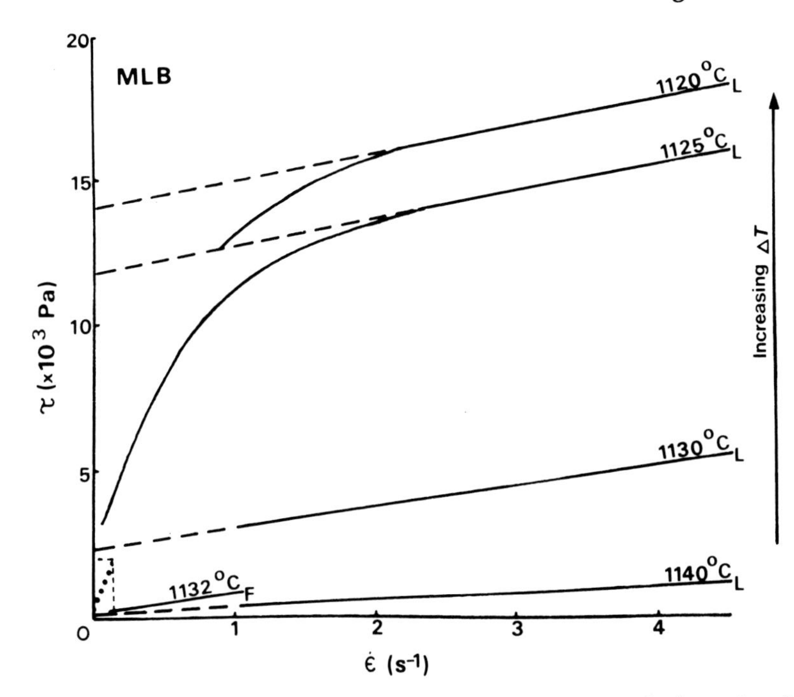

Fig. 5.11 Rheological flow curves of some subliquidus basalts. Curves determined from direct laboratory (L: Shaw, 1969) and field (F: Shaw *et al.*, 1968) rheological measurements on Makaopuhi lava lake basalt (MLB), showing the changes in its rheological characteristics with temperature. According to the range of shear rates under investigation, the phenotypes may be approximated to those of Bingham or pseudoplastic materials. A shear-vane rotation viscometer was used for the field study, a concentric-cylinder rotation viscometer being used in the laboratory. The dotted phenotype shows the Etna field data collected by Pinkerton and Sparks (1978). An enlarged version is presented in Figure 5.14. Further details are given in Table 5.5 and are discussed in the text. τ is applied shear stress; $\dot{\epsilon}$ is ambient shear rate; Δ is initial undercooling.

Consider, for example, two sets of measurements collected over the same applied rates of shearing from two chemically identical lava flows both of the same age and at the same temperature, but advancing with different velocities. Owing to the motion of the flows, vesiculation and continued crystallization, it cannot be expected that the two data sets will provide the same rheological flow curves. In the first place, even assuming plane parallel, steady laminar shear conditions, the difference in flow velocity will promote different mean crystal orientations and different local rates of agitation – the latter influencing the degree of disruption of already polymerized pockets of melt, the chances that a cluster of molecules will adopt the correct configuration to form a solid embryo, and the amount of crystal attrition, which may provide new sites for heterogeneous crystal nucleation. Secondly, the exsolution of volatiles such as H_2O (but not CO_2, which will have the opposite effect) may undercool the lava sufficiently to promote a surge in crystal nucleation and growth (Sparks and Pinkerton, 1978). It is worth noting that this effect appears chiefly to result from the rapid exsolution of volatiles throwing the melt into chemical disequilibrium; the physical loss of the volatile molecules themselves seems to be of lesser significance among basaltic materials, with Scarfe (1973) finding a negligible change in equilibrium viscosities when investigating tholeiitic (at 1150°C) and olivine (at 1250°C) basalts with water-contents from 0 – 4% (w/w). The subsequent growth of the gas bubbles may further accelerate crystallization by cooling the lava flow adiabatically (Sparks and Pinkerton, 1978), while other rheological changes may be induced in a lava by variations in the total quantity and the size-frequency distribution of the vesicles (a product of changes in the rates of bubble nucleation and growth, coalescence and escape), and the style, rate and degree of vesicle deformation, the latter processes being expected to have most influence at medium-to-low rates of shear (less than 10 s^{-1}?). Finally, even if it may be assumed that the sample material is undergoing effectively undisturbed, isothermal crystallization, the experimental studies of Murase and McBirney (1973; also mentioned in Williams and McBirney, (1979); and in McBirney and Noyes (1979)) and of Nabelek *et al.* (1978) indicate that it may take at least 24 h for a dry basaltic melt to approach crystal –liquid equilibrium (considering initial undercoolings of up to 54°C) to a first approximation applicable to a lava, since it is during the last stages of ascent, immediately before eruption, that the majority of a magma's volatile components come out of solution (Sigvaldason, 1974; Wilson and Head, 1981).

Accordingly, attempts to compare field and laboratory rheological data of the same composition material, or observations made on different composition materials, should be treated with caution. For example, Kilburn (1981), with a view to investigating the rheological nature of the pahoehoe – aa transition, suggested that a quantitative comparison could be made between the flow curves presented by Shaw *et al.* (1968: MLB) and by Pinkerton and Sparks (1978: Etnean basalt). Although the concepts presented in that paper are still considered to be valid, the quantitative treatments should not be accepted, owing to the different states of the sampled materials and of the conditions of observation. In addition, although the field ('F') and laboratory ('L') flow curves of Makaopuhi lava basalt shown in Fig. 5.11 appear superficially to be complementary, they should not, in the first instance, be combined to develop a quantitative relation between, for example, lava effective viscosity and temperature. This is not to say that they are incompatible data, only that models should be generated using one set of results alone, the other being examined to assess how closely it agrees with the first.

However, by themselves, Shaw's (1969) laboratory data are of particular interest, because the consistency of the observing conditions allows some conclusions to be drawn about the general rheological trends that may be expected within a cooling (or melting) basaltic magma. Specifically two features of the 'L' curves in Fig. 5.11 may be highlighted. The first is that as the lava temperature decreases (and crystallinity increases), the absolute viscosity of the lava *at any given shear rate* becomes larger. Thus, where insufficient subliquidus data are available, the limiting minimum absolute viscosity of a lava may be taken as its (Newtonian) value at the liquidus, so providing a constraint upon theoretical models. The second is that the transition from comparatively low to high absolute viscosity appears to occur at higher shear-rates as the lava temperature decreases. Hence, while a lava moving swiftly over a steep slope may show little appreciable change in its flow behaviour with cooling, the onset of its corresponding deceleration upon encountering a shallower gradient is likely to be more rapid. Small changes in temperature (about 10°C) and ground slope angle (less than 5°), therefore, may have a profound influence upon the rates of advance and spreading of a lava flow tongue.

These inferred trends are strictly applicable only to bubble-free portions of the melt: for example, problems concerning avesicular lavas or small-scale flowage around suspended crystals. Among Etnean lavas, however, final local vesicularities (that is, including bubbles which may have formed after the lava has stopped) may vary from virtually zero to 50 – 60% (v/v), the typical range of 10 – 30% (v/v) being comparable to values obtained from quenched samples of the surfaces of active flows. With surface tensions of about 0.3–0.4 N m^{-1} (Murase and McBirney, 1973), common vesicle diameters between 10^{-3}m and 10^{-2}m, *initial* host fluid (absolute) viscosities from 10^2 to 10^3 Pa s (using the empirical method of Shaw (1972) and considering only the liquid fraction of the lava), and a typical shear rate range during steady state flowage of 1 – 10 s^{-1}, the maximum Taylor number is seen, from Equation (5.16), to be unlikely to be much greater than unity. Indeed, apart from the case of a near-static (low $\dot{\epsilon}$) body of low-crystallinity lava, Ta is expected to be much smaller than unity, indicating that bubble deformation will be commonplace.

More significantly, the likelihood of pervasive bubble deformation raises the possibility that, considered in isolation, vesiculation will tend to reduce the absolute viscosity of a lava. The data on silicone fluids from Shaw *et al.* (1968; see also Fig. 5.12) suggests that, over the shear-rate range of about 1–10 s^{-1}, a 10% (v/v) concentration of deforming bubbles may lower the absolute viscosity of a suspension (relative to the avesicular state) by as much as 25%, the trend being enhanced or diminished at higher bubble concentrations, depending upon the nullifying influence of bubble interaction. Such a decrease, however, is likely to

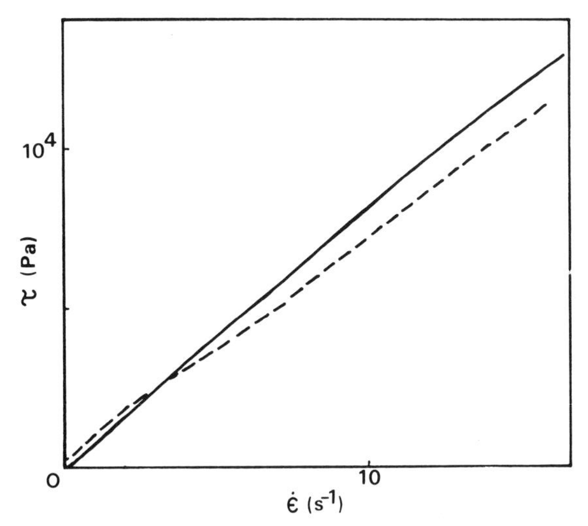

Fig. 5.12 One effect of moderate vesicle concentrations on fluid rheology at moderate rates of shear.
The solid curve describes the behaviour of an homogeneous silicone liquid. Though incipient pseudoplasticity is apparent at shear rates greater than 7–8 s^{-1}, the curve very closely approximates that of a Newtonian medium with a viscosity of 103 Pa s at 25°C ($\dot{\epsilon}$ up to at least 10 s^{-1}).
The broken curve describes the behaviour of the same silicone liquid containing a 10%(v/v) concentration of bubbles (diameters from about 0.1 mm to 3 mm; average about 0.5 mm).
Note that the introduction of the bubbles has given the fluid a yield strength, while at shear rates of 3–4 s^{-1} the absolute viscosity of the suspension becomes less than that of the host liquid – possibly the result of bubble distortion. At higher shear rates (10–15 s^{-1}), although the absolute viscosities of the two systems approach the same value, the apparent viscosity of the suspension remains less than that of the silicone liquid alone (by a small amount). (τ is applied shear stress; $\dot{\epsilon}$ is ambient shear rate. (Diagram and data from Shaw *et al.*, 1968.)

be adequately compensated for by the appearance in the melt of an additional 5 – 7% (v/v) crystals (estimated from the log η_e – C curves in Figure 5.13). In addition, as a lava advances, although its degree of crystallinity increases, its rate of residual vesiculation is not necessarily expected to equal the rate of either the loss of bubbles at the lava surface or their concentration in a narrow layer close to the crust, leading to an overall decrease with age in the vesicularity of the bulk of the active lava (this trend may be obscured by *post-emplacement* vesiculation). Hence, since also at high bubble concentrations and at low rates of shearing the presence of vesicles will increase a lava's absolute viscosity, it is inferred that, under the common conditions of emplacement, a subliquidus lava will always have a bulk absolute (or effective) viscosity greater than its liquidus equivalent.

Rather than assisting lava flowage, therefore, the contained vesicles may prove a significant factor in arresting the motion of an already-decelerating stream. Under sufficiently slow shear-rate conditions such that Ta becomes much larger than unity and the vesicles begin to behave as if rigid particles, a 20% (v/v) vesicle content within an only-30% (v/v) crystallized lava, for example, may raise its effective solid concentration above the critical value at which no motion will occur. Indeed, Shaw *et al.* (1968) have attributed to the presence of about 5% (v/v) vesicles the detection in the Makaopuhi Lava Basalt (up to 25% (v/v) crystallinity) of yield strengths of the order of 100 Pa (minimum detected shear-rates of about 0.25 s^{-1}), a drop of 1 – 2% (v/v) being associated with a yield strength decrease from 120 to 70 Pa.

Another complicating feature when comparing rheological data is the relative effect of local viscous heating. Hence the curves shown in Fig. 5.11 do not embrace temperatures less than 1120°C, nor shear rates greater than 4 s^{-1}, since at this minimum temperature Shaw (1969, Fig. 1) began to detect erratic flow behaviour, the sample basalt showing a sudden (almost discontinuous) decrease in viscosity in the shear stress – strain rate range of about 1.3 – 1.9 × 10^3 Pa and about 5 – 8 s^{-1} – a response which he attributed to localized melting. Under suitable circumstances, this can result in a self-perpetuating 'thermal-feedback' process, in which the melting reduces the local effective viscosity, so increasing the rate of shearing under the applied shear–stress conditions and thereby increasing the rate of viscous heat production still further (Shaw, 1969).

This mechanism has been postulated as having an important influence upon the partial melting of the mantle (Shaw, 1969) and on the rate of ascent and style of eruption of magmas (for example, Fujii and Uyeda, 1974; Hardee and Larson, 1977). The extent to which the effect is to be expected among lava flows is more difficult to assess quantitatively because the stress distributions assumed in the theoretical models (Gruntfest, 1963; Shaw, 1969) are not exactly duplicated in practice. Nelson (1981) and Kilburn (1984), considering acidic and basaltic lavas respectively, have suggested that local viscous heating may possibly encourage banding within flows and so influence their local rheological and dynamical behaviour.

5.3.3 *The influence of temperature on rheological properties: general considerations*

For an unconfined material, a temperature increase is generally associated with an increase in volume. Consequently, molecular and any second-phase structures within the host body become less restricted in their mobility, the former also becoming more highly energized and less highly organized (Lenk, 1978). As a result, the absolute viscosity and effective yield strength of most materials tend to decrease with an increase in temperature.

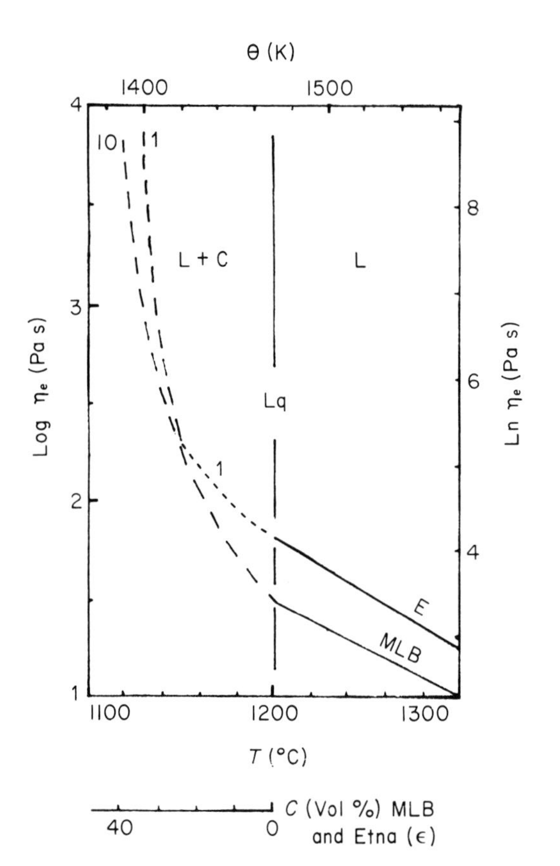

Fig. 5.13 The effective viscosities of dry, avesicular basaltic melts between 1120 and 1300 °C.

The solid lines indicate the supraliquidus conditions for which the magmas have Newtonian properties and follow an Arrhenius viscosity – temperature relation. The dashed lines for subliquidus conditions show marked increases in effective viscosity with falling temperature which cannot be accommodated by a single formula.

The large-dash curves and their solid extension are for Makaopuhi lava lake basalt (MLB: Shaw, 1969); the small-dash curve and its solid extension is for an Etnean basalt (E: Gauthier, 1973). The figures appended to each curve indicate the shear-rate conditions of the measurements. Note that, at a given temperature, lower effective viscosities are recorded at higher rates of shearing (only MLB data available).

The crystallinity scale (C; %(v/v)) is based upon the empirical $C-T$ relation used by Shaw (1969) for MLB. It is also consistent with the scattered crystallinity (typically phenocryst content) – temperature values quoted for Etnean lavas by Archambault and Tanguy (1976) and by Pinkerton and Sparks (1978).

The measurements were made in the laboratory with concentric-cylinder rotation viscometers. η_e is effective viscosity; θ is absolute temperature (K); T is temperature (°C); C is crystal concentration; L is liquid only; L+C is liquid with crystals; Lq is liquidus (nominal).

The temperature dependence of homogeneous Newtonian liquids may be expressed in terms of an Arrhenius-type equation of the form:

$$\mu = A \exp(B/\theta) \quad (5.24)$$

where A and B are constants, B being a measure of the energy required to activate viscous flow, and θ denoting the absolute temperature (Shaw *et al.*, 1968; Lenk, 1978).

This may be expressed in the alternative form:

$$\mu = \mu_0 \exp\{B[(\theta_0-\theta)/(\theta\,\theta_0)]\} \quad (5.25)$$

where μ_o is the viscosity of the fluid at an arbitrary reference temperature θ_0.

Among non-Newtonian media, the viscosity also varies with the shearing conditions with, at least for power-law materials (Lenk, 1978), the viscosity changes with temperature at constant shear stress and constant shear rates *not* being equal. Accordingly, when using Arrhenius-type temperature relations, two μ–θ functions have to be considered with different activation energy constants, one at constant shear stress, the other at constant shear rate (Lenk, 1978). Experimental data on polymer melts, however, have indicated that such Arrhenius relationships are generally restricted to narrow temperature ranges and do not hold well around the glass transition point (Miller, 1963, quoted by Lenk, 1978).

Since it has been argued that the yield value indirectly represents the maximum viscosity with which a material can be seen to flow, it follows that τ_y is in fact the measure of a rate process (viscous flow) and may therefore also show a temperature-dependence expressible in terms of an Arrhenius-type equation. Thus, by analogy with Equation (5.24):

$$\tau_y = A' \exp(B_{\tau_y}/\theta) \quad (5.26)$$

or, in modified form:

$$\tau_y = \tau_{y0} \exp\{B_{\tau_y} [(\theta_0-\theta)/(\theta\theta_0)]\} \quad (5.27)$$

where τ_{y0} is the material yield strength at an arbitrary reference temperature θ_0, A' is a constant and B_{τ_y} is the activation energy factor related to the initiation of viscous flow at the maximum observable viscosity.

5.3.4 *Temperature effects on the viscosity of basalts*

To illustrate the variation in effective lava viscosity with temperature, data from Shaw (1969; MLB) and Gauthier (1973; Etna) are presented in Fig. 5.13. The MLB plot is essentially identical to that of Shaw (1969, Fig. 2), no discrepancy being introduced by the use here of 'effective viscosity' instead of Shaw's 'apparent viscosity' because, under the steady (Couette) flow conditions employed with a rotation viscometer, the two viscosity terms are identical. At supraliquidus temperatures, the two flow curves obey Arrhenius-type relations, given by:

For MLB (Shaw, 1969):

$$\eta_e = 4.8 \times 10^{-6} [\exp(26\,500/\theta)] \quad (5.28a)$$

and, for Etnean basalt:

$$\eta_e = 3.1 \times 10^{-8} [\exp(31\,690/\theta)] \quad (5.28b)$$

At subliquidus values, Equations (5.28) are no longer applicable, the effective viscosities rising dramatically with only small decreases in temperature (and increases in crystallinity) at rates faster than those predicted by the extrapolation of the supraliquidus relations. The effective viscosity gradients also become steeper at lower rates of shearing.

Indeed, the subliquidus curves (for any given shear rate) cannot be simply described in terms of a single equation over the range of temperatures considered in Fig. 5.13. This reflects the complex rheological influence of particle interaction and changing liquid composition as crystallization proceeds, as well as the emerging importance of shear-rate at temperatures below about 1150°C (at least for MLB), presumably indicating its effect upon the degree of crystal alignment (notably of the feldspars) and interaction, and upon the stability of polymerizing liquid; that it appears to be of lesser significance between 1150°C and 1200°C possibly indicates that for crystal concentrations less than about 25% (v/v) (see scale in Fig. 5.13), basalt suspensions are too dilute for shear rates up to at least 10 s^{-1} to substantially alter the degree of crystal interaction. Nevertheless, Shaw (1969), in his discussion on the effect of viscous heat generation upon magmatic behaviour, has presented an approximate relation between the temperature of Hawaiian basalt and its viscosity at very low rates of shear, assuming for this condition essentially Newtonian flow behaviour (as in region 1 in Fig. 5.5). Taking the liquidus temperature and viscosity quoted by Shaw (1969) as reference values (the non-crystalline lava being treated as Newtonian), his low-shear-rate viscosity ($\mu'_{sp,0}$) – absolute temperature (θ) relation may be written as:

$$\mu'_{sp,0} = 31.62 \exp(33.97 - 0.23\theta) \quad (5.29)$$

The physical accuracy of this relation, however, remains to be verified.

5.3.5 *Temperature effects on the observed yield strength of basalts*

Effective yield strengths – namely those defining minimum detectable rates of shear under the conditions of the experiment, as opposed to the mathematically convenient extrapolations from higher shear rates – have been quoted for basaltic materials by Shaw (1969; MLB, laboratory), Pinkerton and Sparks (1978; Etna, field), and Murase (1981; MLB and CRB, laboratory), the last-mentioned compiling data which have appeared separately elsewhere (for instance, Murase and McBirney (1973); Williams and McBirney, (1979), and McBirney and Noyes (1979)). The corresponding limiting rates of shearing are approximately 0.05 s^{-1} (inferred from Shaw, 1969, Fig. 1), 0.001 s^{-1} (Pinkerton, 1978), and 0.005 s^{-1} (inferred from McBirney and Noyes, 1979, Fig. 2). The rheological measurements of Pinkerton and Sparks (1978) are shown in Fig. 5.14; Murase's data and the low-shear-rate measurements of Shaw (1969) are shown in Fig. 5.15(a).

As with the previous discussion of the flow curves in Fig. 5.11, while the data presented in Figure 5.15(a) may be quantitatively applicable only to avesicular material in crystal – liquid equilibrium and subject to the same flow conditions as in the experiments, the consistency of the observing conditions suggests that the trends apparent in the measurements may be used to assess qualitatively the behaviour of the more complicated natural lava in the field. Thus it is inferred that the low-shear-rate, high-viscosity zone of a lava's rheological phenotype extends rapidly to higher applied shear stresses during the early stages of cooling below the liquidus, its rate of increase apparently falling off later with further crystallization. In other words, the effective yield strength of the lava appears to increase rapidly following the onset of crystallization, tending towards a constant value before solidification is complete. If confirmed by further measurements made at lower temperatures, this behaviour would be consistent with the inference drawn earlier (discussing the study of Robson (1967)) that crystallizing lavas approach a limiting maximum yield strength.

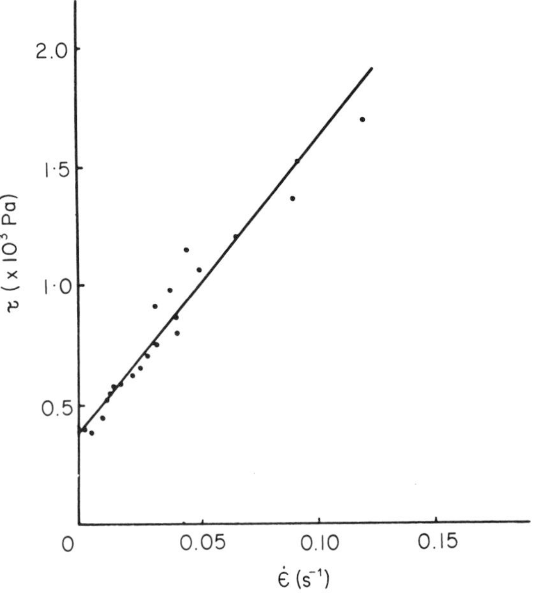

Fig. 5.14 Rheological data for an Etnean basalt. An enlarged view of the dotted phenotype in Fig. 5.11, showing the rheological data collected in the field by Pinkerton and Sparks (1978), during Etna's 1975 north-slope activity. In reducing the data, a Bingham model was assumed (Pinkerton, 1978). The measurements were made using a shear penetrometer, described by Pinkerton and Sparks (1978). Further details are given in Table 5.5. τ is applied shear stress; $\dot{\epsilon}$ is ambient shear rate.

Quantitatively, the high-temperature portion of the yield strength – temperature curves of Fig. 5.15(a) may be described by an Arrhenius equation

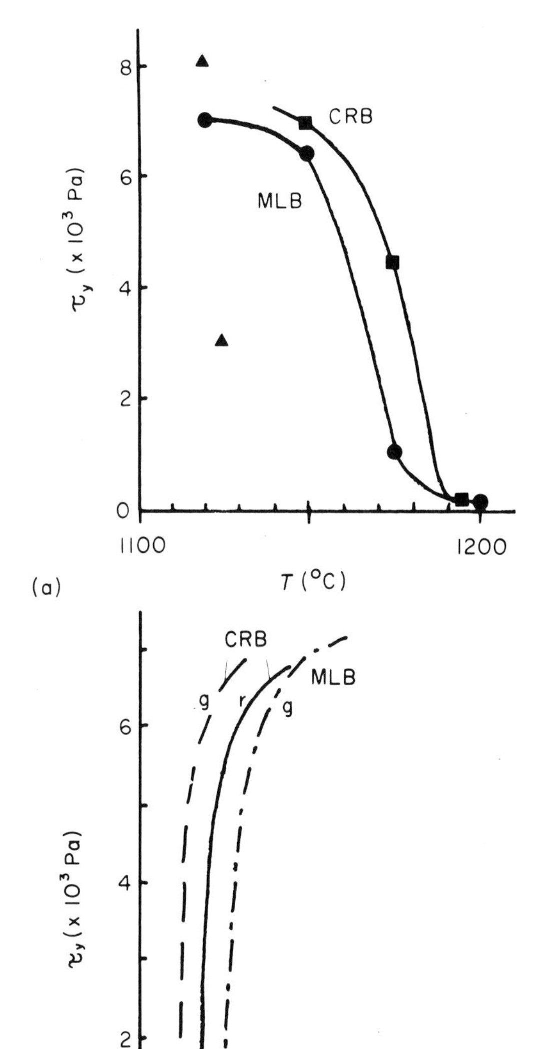

Fig. 5.15 The variation with temperature of the effective yield strengths of subliquidus basaltic melts.

(a) Curves showing the changes with temperature of the laboratory-determined effective yield strength of Makaopuhi lava lake basalt (MLB) and Columbia River basalt (CRB). All the samples were dry and avesicular. Note the rapid increase in τ_y immediately below the liquidus temperature (nominally 1200 °C) and the apparent trend towards a steady value at lower temperatures. The triangles show the τ_y values inferred from the laboratory data of Shaw (1969), assuming general plastic behaviour (see also Fig. 5.11). The conditions of the measurements are given in Table 5.5.

(b) The influence on the recorded yield strength of the starting condition of a sample. Among chemically similar materials, for a specified crystal content (C) during the measurements, higher yield strengths are recorded from those which started as glass rather than fine rock powder (compare CRB, 'g' and 'r' curves). (After Murase, 1981.) τ_y is effective yield strength; T is temperature (°C); C is crystal concentration; 'g' denotes glass as starting condition of sample; 'r' denotes fine rock powder as starting condition of sample. (After Murase, 1981).

of the form indicated by Equation (5.26), supporting the view that, for the relevant temperature range, what is being measured as τ_y is indeed an indicator of a rate process, such as a limiting rate of deformation. Thus, for Makaopuhi lava basalt between 1150 and 1200°C (the nominal liquidus temperature above which the fluid behaviour is Newtonian), the yield strength τ_y is given by:

$$\tau_y = 1.59 \times 10^{-40} [\exp(141\,113/\theta)] \qquad (5.30a)$$

while for Columbia River Basalt between 1150 and 1195°C:

$$\tau_y = 5.20 \times 10^{-97} [\exp(331\,562/\theta)] \qquad (5.30b)$$

where θ is the absolute temperature.

At temperatures below the quoted minima, the rate of increase in yield strength with falling temperature diminishes rapidly (as seen in Fig. 5.15(a), and the τ_y – temperature curves deviate significantly from the relations determined above. The change reflects a shift in the nature of the dominant mechanism resisting deformation. Two potential contributing factors are the packing of the solid phases and the composition of the residual liquid fraction. In the first case, during the early stages of crystallization, the increasing concentration of a disseminated solid phase should be accompanied by a rapid increase in effective yield strength, owing to more pronounced mechanical interaction between the crystals. However, upon reaching a critical crystal concentration, the lava may be considered (at least from a conceptual, if not physical, viewpoint) as – instead of a liquid containing solids – a skeletal framework through which the remaining liquid must pass. Accordingly, further crystallization will tend to fill in the gaps of the existing framework, a process which may result in a slower rate of increase in yield strength than during the earlier phase of skeleton building. At the same time, the appearance of the early mafic crystal phases will drive the residual liquid portion to increasingly siliceous, and more viscous, compositions. This effect is expected to be most in evidence during the early phases of crystallization because of the initially rapid nucleation and growth of olivines and pyroxenes close to the liquidus of basaltic melts. Thus, as solidification continues, the rate of increase in the residual liquid silica content will tend to diminish and, with it, the rate of increase in the effective yield strength of the fluid as a whole.

If all the measurements shown in Fig. 5.15(a) represent the characteristics of melts in crystal – liquid equilibrium, it is difficult to account for the discrepancy between the Makaopuhi lava basalt data of Shaw (1969) and of Murase (1981). Given that subliquidus lavas possess, at least in part, pseudoplastic characteristics then, because Shaw's (1969) yield values were determined from minimum shear rates an order-of-magnitude greater than those of Murase (1981), the former's estimates would have been expected to be consistently higher than the latter's – which is not the case for the quoted 1125°C values. Either, therefore, true crystal – liquid equilibrium was not attained in all of the experiments (an inference which strongly argues the need for more studies to test the deductions drawn above from the data in Figs 5.11 and 5.15(a)), or one or more additional mechanisms may have been influencing the rheological responses of the specimens.

One possibility could be the melting histories of the samples. From the data in Fig 5.14(b), it appears that the physical nature of the starting material has an influence on experimental results, initially glassy samples reaching relatively higher yield strengths at lower crystallinities than chemically equivalent samples starting as finely ground rock powder (compare the CRB, 'g' and 'r' curves in Fig. 5.14(b)). This trend may reflect that melt polymerization, before the appearance of a solid nucleus, is more extensive in initially glassy samples during the early stages of crystallization.

5.3.6 *Pressure effects on the rheological properties of basaltic flows*

In the case of materials at a specific temperature, it is common to intuitively anticipate that an increase in the externally applied pressure will lead to a reduction in volume and thereby an increase in absolute viscosity and effective yield strength (because of the reduced mobility of the fluid molecules and any contained particles). Thus, for example, Lenk (1978) indicates that, for polymeric materials, pressure increased viscosities become significant once the bulk compression of a system exceeds 10% (v/v).

The compressibility β of a medium (the reciprocal of its bulk modulus of elasticity) is defined as the fractional change in volume $\Delta V/V$ induced by a change in the applied pressure ΔP. For basaltic magmas in the melting range, β varies from about 10^{-11} Pa^{-1} when near the solidus to about 7×10^{-11} Pa^{-1} close to the liquidus (Murase and McBirney, 1973; Williams and McBirney, 1979, p. 30).

With the appearance of bubbles, however, the mean compressibility, β, of a magmatic fluid increases dramatically and may be estimated from (after Mallock, 1910):

$$\bar{\beta} = \chi_m \beta_m + \chi_g \beta_g \qquad (5.31)$$

where χ represents the volume fraction of the phase of interest, denoted by the suffices 'm' for melt and 'g' for gas.

Assuming that the vesicles contain water vapour, the compressibility of the gas phase at magma-melting temperatures is of the order of 10^{-5} Pa^{-1}, some 10^5 times greater than that of the melt. Consequently, for vesicularities (χ_g) larger than about 0.01% (v/v), the melt compressibility term of Equation (5.31) may be neglected. Equation (5.31) then reduces to:

$$\bar{\beta} \simeq \chi_g \beta_g \qquad (5.32)$$

indicating typical mean compressibilities of $1\text{–}30 \times 10^{-7}$ Pa^{-1} for solidifying basalts with vesicularities of between 1% and 30% (v/v).

Taking a critical compression value of 10% (v/v) (Lenk, 1978), therefore, rheological changes induced by bulk compression can be expected to be significant over pressure variations of about 2×10^9 Pa and 10^5 Pa for avesicular and vesicular basalts respectively. For a given section of flow, the hydrostatic pressure increase with depth h to which a lava is subjected may be estimated from $\rho_l gh$, where the mean lava density ρ_l is given the value of 2500 kg m^{-3}. Among avesicular lavas, therefore, significant rheological changes as a result of restructuring of the melt alone can be anticipated only near the base of a lava at least some 10^5 m thick – a plainly unrealistic situation. In passing, it is of interest to note that Kushiro *et al.* (1976; see also the review by Kushiro (1980)), investigating the rheological behaviour of a supra-liquidus and anhydrous Kiluaean olivine tholeiite at 1400°C, measured a drop in viscosity from 3.5 Pa s to 1.5 Pa s as the ambient pressure increased from 10^5 Pa (1 atmosphere) to 10^9 Pa. Contrary to the intuitively expected viscosity change, the observed trend has been attributed by Kushiro *et al.* (1976) to changes in the coordination-states of the cations in the liquid leading to melt depolymerization.

Considering vesicular lavas, on the other hand, among flows thicker than about 4 m, the increase in bubble distortion with depth as a result of compression may induce a noticeable contrast in the rheological characteristics of the flow near its base with respect to those of its upper layers. This hydrostatic influence, however, is of immediate significance only for examining the effective viscosity profile through a transverse section of a flow. As such, it cannot be used to judge the validity of the assumption of incompressible lava flow, since the latter is concerned with the consequences of dynamically initiated changes in pressure.

In order to treat a flow as incompressible, the velocity at which pressure signals travel through a fluid must be so large that the propagation of the resulting interactions in the fluid may be considered to be instantaneous under the conditions of observation. In other words, both the velocity v of the fluid and the speed at which changes in that velocity takes place must be small compared with the speed of sound c in the fluid, the latter being the propagation velocity of the pressure signals (Landau and Lifshitz, 1959).

The first condition may be expressed as:

$$v << c \qquad (5.33)$$

or, since $c = (1/\bar{\beta}\rho_l)^{1/2}$ (Mallock, 1910), as:

$$v << (1/\bar{\beta}\rho_l)^{1/2} \qquad (5.34)$$

The second requirement, which becomes superfluous if the flow is steady (that is, if the dimensions of the flow section of interest do not alter with time) may be written as:

$$L/t << c \qquad (5.35)$$

where L and t are the distance and time, respectively, over which the velocity of the fluid is observed to undergo a significant change.

Using values of 2500 kg m^{-3} and 10^{-6} Pa^{-1} for the mean lava density and compressibility (the second implying a typical vesicularity of 10% (v/v)), and assuming that velocities of $c/5$ or less are small enough to be considered negligible compared with c (a limit determined from practical engineering experience; Francis, 1975), Equation (5.34) indicates that for the first criterion to be satisfied, the velocity of the lava must be less than about 4 ms^{-1} (c = 20 ms^{-1}), which is commonly the case among Etnean flows. During the opening stages of an effusion, however, faster velocities and higher vesicle contents (the latter reducing the value of c) may be temporarily realized, suggesting that compressibility effects may then be of potential importance.

The time-scales over which appreciable changes in flow are seen to occur depend on the nature and the conditions of the observations being made. Thus it may take several minutes or hours (of the order of 10^2–10^4 s) for noticeable backflow-thickening behind a slowing flow-front to extend up to 100 m along the feeding channel, while only a minute or less (nominally 20 – 60 s) for thickening to occur over a similar distance behind a blockage (caused, for instance by a collapse of the inner margins of a levée) in a channel containing more fluid lava. Comparing the observed dynamic responses (in longitudinal section) of the lavas to the deceleration along only the 100-m-stretches (L = 100 m), it appears that in the first case, when t is at least 100 s, the characteristic velocity (L/t) is about 1 ms^{-1} or less, so satisfying, for the purposes of analysis, the second incompressibility condition as expressed by Equation (5.35). In the second case, however, with t being possibly 20 s, the characteristic velocity may reach 5 ms^{-1}, for which the effects of compressibility may no longer be insignificant.

When examining local, unsteady flow processes, therefore – especially among vesicle-rich, fluid young lavas close to their sources – the potential influence of fluid compressibility on the rheological and dynamical behaviour of the flow should be considered. On a larger scale, though, given that for much of their lifetimes the gross development of lava flows appears to occur under virtually steady conditions, it would seem at least a reasonable first approximation to treat them as incompressible media.

5.3.7 *Time-dependent rheological behaviour of sub-liquidus basaltic melts*

Time-dependent rheological behaviour has not been confirmed for avesicular basaltic melts in crystal–liquid equilibrium. *Apparent* rheopexy, however, may be detected among non-equilibrium, isothermal melts, owing to the general increase in the absolute viscosity of the sample at any given shear rate because of continuing crystallization and polymerization of the melt (for example, Murase and McBirney, 1973; Williams and McBirney, 1979; McBirney and Noyes, 1979; McBirney and Murase, 1984).

On the other hand, Shaw *et al.* (1968) detected thixotropic tendencies in their field samples of vesicular Makaopuhi Lava Basalt, exposed to maximum shear-rates of about 1 s^{-1}. Since similar behaviour was not observed when Shaw (1969) investigated the same, but bubble-free, material in the laboratory over the same temperature and shear-rate conditions, he inferred that the earlier determined thixotropy had been due to the deformation – and possibly bursting(?) – of the contained vesicles. If bubble bursting did occur, then the thixotropic effect is artificial, since the physical constitution of the sample must have varied during the experiment, the results contained being those of effectively a range of different samples with different vesicularities and, as such, not an accurate reflection of the intrinsic properties of a single sample. If, though, the crystal–vesicle–liquid properties remained constant throughout the experiment, then the thixotropic behaviour must be construed as a real phenomenon. Although Shaw *et al.* (1968) considered the time-dependent effect to be too small to be important for geological processes, it may cause potentially significant differences between direct rheological measurements made in the field – the absolute viscosities varying by a factor of 2 between the stirred and unstirred samples of Shaw *et al.* (1968, Fig. 9).

5.3.8 *Some applications of rheological studies to the interpretation of lava flow morphology*

When examining the rheological characteristics of lava flows, there are two distinct, but complementary, methods of investigation available. The first is to analyse in detail the rheological changes of a small batch (or element) of lava, with respect to its thermal history and to the stresses to which it has been subjected. Once attained, the gross behaviour of a flow may be estimated from the expected collective response of its individual elements, thermal gradients and dynamic conditions having been previously defined. Though theoretically attractive, there remain numerous practical difficulties with this approach. On the one hand, as shown above, there is as yet no straightforward means of predicting quantitatively the rheological characteristics of comparatively simple, constant-property suspensions, quite apart from crystallizing and vesiculating systems, whose suspending medium is simultaneously changing in composition. On the other, there is the evident problem of acquiring the necessary information about the internal conditions of a flow. Do local shear zones develop, for example, along which the bulk of the motion is concentrated? What are the nature of the cross-currents in a flow, which will affect the rate of spreading, as well as lava movement down a channel?

The second means of study is to consider a flow (or part of a flow) as a natural rheometer and to interpret its development in terms of its bulk rheological properties (that is, the properties of a hypothetical, homogeneous fluid, whose behaviour mimics that of the lava). Though a more empirical approach, being unable to pinpoint unequivocally what process or combination of processes is triggering the observed bulk rheological response, it is substantially more practicable than the alternative and is the one which has been most commonly adopted when investigating real lavas.

In applying bulk rheological calculations, it is essential to establish to what feature and its length-scale the measurements are being referred. Thus the bulk properties of an aa cauliflower (Kilburn, 1984) or other small surface prominence, such as a 'wave ridge' (as considered, for example, by Gauthier (1973)), are representative only of local surficial material, while the analyses of Wadge (1978) and Fitton *et al.* (1983) refer respectively to the properties of flow fronts and to the backflow region of a small lava tongue. Other morphological features which have been considered as rheological indicators include the pahoehoe – aa (Peterson and Tilling, 1980; Kilburn, 1981) and the aa–block (Cigolini *et al.*, 1984) lava transitions, the formation of salient lava tree moulds (Kilburn, 1984), and the shapes and dimensions of lava margins, whether flow fronts (Johnson, 1970) or lateral levées (Hulme, 1974; Moore *et al.*, 1978), the latter further influencing the dimensions of active lava channels.

Of these, it is the levée model of Hulme (1974) which has been most frequently applied (for example, Sparks *et al.*, 1976; Moore *et al.*, 1978). For the edge of a lava flow to continue advancing, the shear stresses to which it is being subjected must, at one point at least, exceed the local effective yield strength of the material. To illustrate the principle, Hulme (1974) considered the free gravitational flow of a stream of rheologically homogeneous lava with Bingham body characteristics. He demonstrated that the depth of the lava needs to exceed a critical value to enable the basal shear stresses (the maximum imposed shear stresses when only hydrostatic driving pressures are involved) acting on the flow margins to overcome their effective yield strength. Consequently, the thinning transverse profile of a lava stream results in the formation of stationary regions along both sides of the flow, where neither the maximum lateral nor longitudinal basal shear stresses can exceed the effective yield strength. Hence *initial* levées are produced which restrict the lateral spreading of the flow, but which allow its thicker central portion to move downslope within a channel.

Qualitatively, it appears that the basal width w_b of the *initial levées* are a measure of the ratio of the stresses retarding flow motion to those that encourage the lava's advance. The predicted relation between w_b and the effective yield strength of the lava is determined by the calculated equilibrium profile in cross-section of the flow margin, which itself depends upon assumptions concerning the details of the stress field. Consequently, quite apart from uncertainties introduced into the model by the processes which can modify the initial shape of a levée (such as accretion and channel overflows; see Chapter 4), the required assumptions also place restrictions upon the quantitative application of levée dimensions as rheological indicators. As they illustrate the types of problems which arise from the model dependency of bulk rheological analysis, it is instructive to briefly discuss some of these limitations.

5.3.9 *Equations describing the cross-sectional profile (lateral and longitudinal) of a lava flow*

The equilibrium shape of a flow margin is determined by the balance of the gravitational, frictional and rheological forces acting upon it. Hence, if a functional relation could be derived between these forces and the profile of a flow edge, it should in principle be possible to use field observations of the latter to estimate the bulk rheological state of that part of the lava *when it first came to rest.*

To derive any such relation, it is necessary to assume a rheological model for the lava and to impose boundary conditions upon the components of the stress field. In order to render the problem tractable, the simplifying assumptions have been made that: (1) the lava may be treated as a rheologically homogeneous body with a constant yield strength; (2) frictional effects are small enough to be neglected (although empirical correction factors may be later introduced into the idealized solution); and (3) the presence of material on either side of the section of interest will not significantly affect the stress system within the plane of that section.

Consider, therefore, the flow edge shown in Fig. 5.16. Notice that it may represent either a lateral

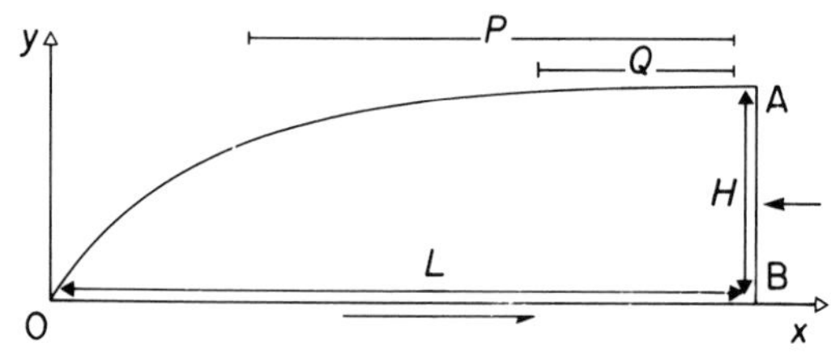

Fig. 5.16 The profile of a free-standing plastic body on a horizontal surface: a sketch defining the notation used to describe the shape of its surface. The filled, indented arrows represent force directions: $\frac{1}{2}\rho g H^2$ against the face AB in the direction of O, and τL parallel with the ground along OB away from O. The distances labelled P and Q show schematically the lengths over which, respectively, Equations (5.37) and (5.36) are valid.

margin or a flow snout. The origin is taken at O, with the Ox and Oy axes being horizontal and vertical respectively. Far away from the margin, the surface of the slope is small enough for the pressure distribution down AB to be approximated to a linear hydrostatic pressure variation. Thus the average force acting upon AB in the direction of O is given by $\frac{1}{2}\rho g H^2$. Assuming a plane, ground parallel stress system within the body of the lava, the hydrostatic force must be opposed by the shear force τL) acting away from O along the base of the flow. For static equilibrium, the basal shear stress τ is equal to the effective yield strength τ_y of the lava. Hence the force balance becomes:

$$\tfrac{1}{2}\rho g H^2 = \tau_y L$$

giving
$$H^2 = 2\tau_y L/\rho g \qquad (5.36)$$

Describing a parabolic profile, this equation has been previously derived by Orowan (1949), with respect to the shape of an ice sheet, and by Hulme (1974), who considered the outlines of the lateral margins of lava flows. It is valid, however, only when the basal slope is horizontal and along that part of the profile where the surface gradient is very small. Accordingly, it cannot be used to describe the shape of the markedly curved distal portion of a snout.

To overcome the surface-curvature limitation upon Equation (5.36), Nye (1967) and Johnson (1970) have re-analysed the problem, starting from a closer inspection of the stress directions established within the section. From fundamental plasticity theory (for example, Nadai (1963)), it can be shown that, for a free-standing plastic, the principal shear stresses are not simply aligned parallel with the slope of the supporting base (in this case, the horizontal ground). Indeed, they may be resolved along pairs of mutually perpendicular directions, each consisting of parts of cycloids (a useful introductory treatment is presented by Nye (1952)).

Incorporating such a stress field, Nye (1967) derived a modified profile equation of the form:

$$\tfrac{1}{2}\rho g H^2 + \tfrac{1}{2}\rho \tau_y H - \tau_y L = 0 \qquad (5.37)$$

Generated by a method of successive approximations to an ideal stress field, Equation (5.37) is theoretically valid only for distances from the origin (profile tip) greater than 0.3 $\tau_y/\rho g$ (Nye, 1967), which, in the case of a lava flow of density 2500 kg m^{-3} and a bulk effective yield strength of between 1–5 × 10^5 Pa, corresponds to upflow distances greater than 1–6 m.

An alternative derivation of the principal shear stress directions by Johnson (the results are presented in Johnson (1970), which cites Johnson (1965) for details of the derivation) yields the equation:

$$L = -(2\,\tau_y/\,\rho\,g)\ \ln\,[\cos\,(\rho\,g\,H/2\,\tau_y)] \quad (5.38)$$

In obtaining Equation (5.38), Johnson constrained the edge of the flow to meet the ground at 90°. This, however, appears to contradict his implicit requirements that the material remains plastic right up to its tip and does not form, for example, a partially rigid layer. Thus, as Nye (1967, p. 701) states, on approaching the origin the surface slope angle tends to 45° 'because assuming the material is plastic right up to the end this is the only value that is compatible with a free top surface and a bed which is a surface of maximum shear stress' (equivalent to the effective yield strength of the plastic). In addition, though not explicitly stated, Johnson's equation seems to have been derived on the assumption of a horizontal bed. As a result, the extension of Equation (5.38) to describe the snout profile of an inclined flow (Johnson, 1970, pp. 454 – 457) is not acceptable, since it does not take into account the adjusted gravitational stress component acting upon the material (relative to the horizontal case). Indeed, it is possible that Equation (5.38) may not be strictly applicable even to the case of a flat-lying material.

Similarly, Equations (5.36) and (5.37) are not applicable to plastic materials resting upon an incline. Nor can they be used to analyse curved margins with only short, nearly ground-parallel backflows. Hence the adoption of Equation (5.36) by Hulme (1974) to describe the form of the outer edges of lava lateral levées is not quantitatively valid, since the requirement of a small surface slope has not been observed. Accordingly, the apparent agreement obtained by Sparks *et al.* (1976) between the directly measured effective yield strengths of two small 1975 Etnean lava flows and the values calculated from the initial levée width–effective yield strength relation of Hulme (1974) may be fortuitous. Moreover, the uncertainties in the model also question the significance of the results of others who have used it to quantitatively compare levée structures, and their implied rheological properties, among, for example, lavas on the terrestrial planets (Moore *et al.*, 1978). These limitations, however, do not invalidate the qualitative usefulness of Hulme's treatment, which serves to illustrate the general nature of the relations between the factors involved in determining the equilibrium profile of an ideal levée.

In summary, therefore, attempts to describe the profile of an idealized free-standing plastic snout have met with only limited success. As a general rule (inferred from Nye (1967) Fig. 5), Equations (5.36) and (5.37), in addition to their surface-slope, horizontal-base and stress-field constraints, can be applied only to the bulk properties of snouts which extend for distances of the order of 10 $\tau_y/\rho\,g$ or more from their tips. Their quantitative application to lava flow margins thus appears to be restricted, particularly in the light of the extra complications of possibly non-horizontal bases and their different modes of rheological inhomogeneity.

5.4 Concluding comments

The recognition of crystallizing lavas as non-Newtonian fluids has led to a complete revision in the general approach to investigating the evolution of flows and flow-fields. Historically, Etna has played a key part in this change of ideas and continues, because of its accessibility and frequent eruptions, to be one of the few ideally situated natural laboratories for conducting the further studies that are necessary for better understanding lava rheology. For it is only with the accumulation of more rheological data from real lava flows, together with the testing of more refined measuring techniques, that the objectives listed at the beginning of the chapter – the prediction of a flow's development, the artificial manipulation of a lava, and the calculation of the energy requirements of effusive processes – are likely to be realized to the full.

6 Petrology and magmatic processes

'Oft liquid lakes of
burning sulphur flow, Fed from the fiery
springs that boil below.'

(Virgil, 70–90 BC, *The Aeneid*)

It is obviously impossible to observe magmatic processes within the subvolcanic environment. It is necessary, therefore, to gain most of the information indirectly, through such means as the experimental modelling of crystallization and melting processes in the laboratory often using compositionally simple analogues (Bowen, 1928; Morse, 1980), or by the examination of igneous intrusions which may be considered to be exposed portions of consolidated crustal magma reservoirs. Also, as discussed in Chapter 7, regions of magma storage and periods of magma movement may be identified by geophysical techniques. It is the erupted magma, however, that provides the direct link with the internal processes, for this material represents the end-product of all the mechanisms that have operated from generation in the source region to degassing on eruption. Consequently, the chemistry and mineralogy of the lavas and pyroclastics convey valuable information on the history of the magma.

When interpreting petrological data in terms of internal processes, it is necessary to proceed with caution. The processes which may have operated in the production of a suite of lavas are many and complex, including mantle heterogeneiity, variable depths of melting, variable degrees of partial melting, subsequent fractionation in either open or closed systems, crustal contamination and vapour phase fractionation. Some, or all, of these mechanisms may have operated to varying extents, and attempting to identify the effects of specific processes, without making invalid assumptions, may be difficult or impossible. Indeed, O'Hara (1977) and O'Hara and Mathews (1981) have demonstrated from a theoretical standpoint the likely complexity of the geochemical evolution of an open-system, periodically replenished magma reservoir.

In this chapter the petrology of Etnean volcanics is described and some models which may account for the observed variation are considered. The main rock types of Etna and their nomenclature have already been introduced in Chapter 3.

6.1 Isotope geochemistry

The following discussion on the isotope geochemistry of Etnean volcanics is based largely on the work of S. R. Carter and L. Civetta which is reported in Carter (1976), Carter and Civetta (1977) and Carter *et al.* (1978). Carter and Civetta (1977) analysed twenty-five lava samples for strontium- and lead-isotopes whilst Carter *et al.* (1978) analysed a further six of these samples for neodymium-isotopes. The samples included volcanics from the Iblean volcanic region to enable a broader understanding of the nature of the mantle source material involved in magma-generation in eastern Sicily. Although the analysed rocks from Etna are representative of the main petrological types found on the volcano, unfortunately they do not include all the main alkalic centres. There is thus a need for a detailed isotopic and trace element study of samples from Etna with good stratigraphic control similar to the recent investigation of Haleakala Volcano, East Maui, by Chen and Frey (1983).

Carter and Civetta (1977) consider that the low strontium-isotope ratios and the high Pb values of the Etnean lavas indicate that sialic crustal contamination has not been a significant process. On the basis of the $^{87}Sr/^{86}Sr$ ratios determined for the *basal tholeiitic volcanics* (0.70314 ± 4, 2σ to 0.70332 ± 5, 2σ), the *Paterno alkali olivine basalt* (0.70301 ± 4, 2σ) and the *alkalic series* (mean value 0.70352) Carter and Civetta propose that these three volcanic groups were derived from separate primary magmas generated from different source regions within a heterogeneous upper mantle. In addition, within the alkalic series, Carter and Civetta identified a further group with distinctive strontium-isotope characteristics which they called the *high-nickel series* (mean 0.70338). These values are lower than the estimated value of 0.705 for undifferentiated mantle assuming an initial ratio $^{87}Sr/^{86}Sr$ of 0.69899 and (Rb/Sr) Earth = 0.33 (Papanastassiou and Wasserburg, 1969) and this indicates that these source regions have been depleted in rubidium. The Etnean lavas have high lead isotope ratios, with values similar to those of typical volcanic oceanic islands plotting well to the right of the Geochron (Fig. 6.1). The highly radiogenic lead-compositions suggest that the mantle source region beneath Etna has undergone a multi-

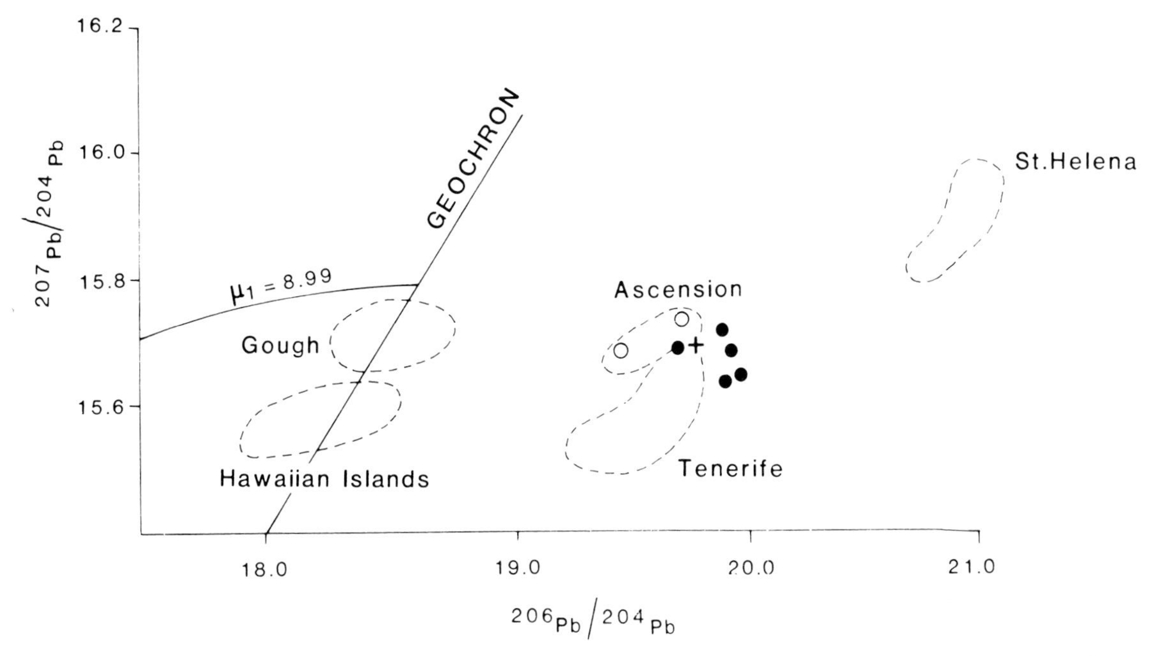

Fig. 6.1 Lead isotope ratios of Etnean lavas compared with those of young volcanic rocks from oceanic islands. Open circles: basal tholeiitic volcanics; filled circles: alkalic series; cross: Paterno Alkali Olivine Basalt. Etna data from Carter and Civetta (1977), other data from Faure (1977).

stage history involving depletion of lead relative to uranium and thorium (Carter and Civetta, 1977). Thus it would appear that the upper mantle beneath eastern Sicily is isotopically heterogeneous and has undergone a complex evolution. Carter and Civetta stress that no constraints can be placed on the relative depths and positions of the different source regions, but they describe a single eruptive unit, the Monte La Nave flow (0.1 km^3), in the north-west sector of the volcano which consists of some lava with the isotopic character of the alkalic series and other lava with the isotopic character of the high-nickel series. This isotopic variation within a single flow is significant in the consideration of the scale of the mantle heterogeneiity.

The basal tholeiitic volcanics show a positive correlation between $^{87}Sr/^{86}Sr$ and Ce/Nd (Carter and Civetta, 1977); see Fig. 6.2. It is possible to account for such a variation in Ce/Nd by differing degrees of partial melting of a source material where the concentration of neodymium in the melt is buffered by retention of neodymium in preference to cerium in a residual mineral phase. This process could explain the variation of Ce/Yb plotted against La indicating enrichment of light-rare-earth elements (LREE) relative to heavy-rare-earth elements (HREE) in the liquid during partial melting (for fuller discussion, see Fig. 6.3). Carter and Civetta, however, consider it most unlikely that the degree of partial melting in the source region should be inversely proportional to the $^{87}Sr/^{86}Sr$ ratio of the source material and suggest that more probably this correlation illustrates the coherent behaviour of rubidium and the LREE in the upper mantle.

In the partial melting of an ultrabasic assemblage, neodymium behaves in a more incompatible manner than samarium and, therefore, fractionation events tend to increase the Sm/Nd ratio in the mantle. Mantle material which has been subjected to depletion in LREE in its history will tend to have higher $^{143}Nd/^{144}Nd$ ratios than the predicted bulk earth value, 0.51264, for undifferentiated mantle. The Etnean volcanics (five samples of the basal tholeiitic volcanics and one hawaiite from the alkalic series) have

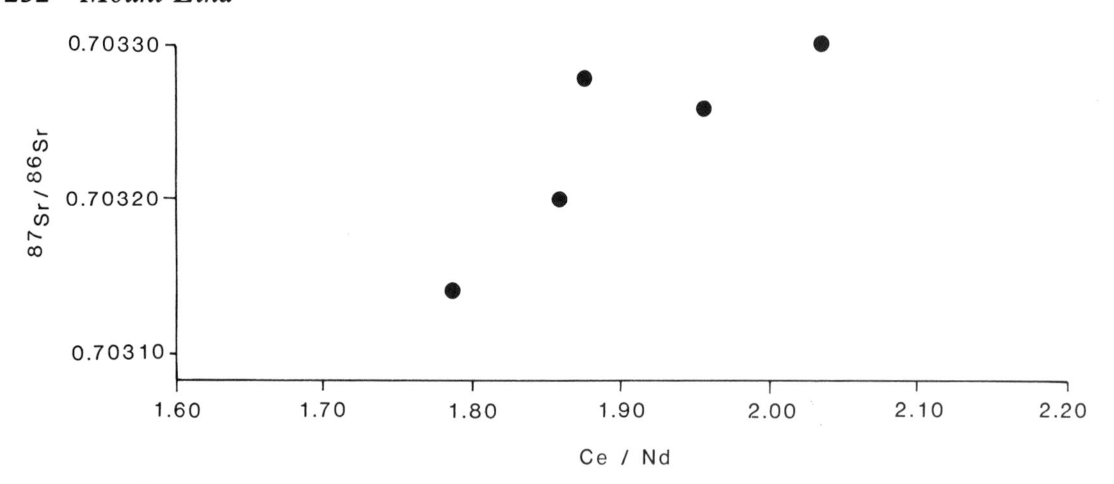

Figure 6.2 $^{87}Sr/^{86}Sr$ plotted against Ce/Nd for the basal tholeiitic volcanics. (After Carter and Civetta, 1977.)

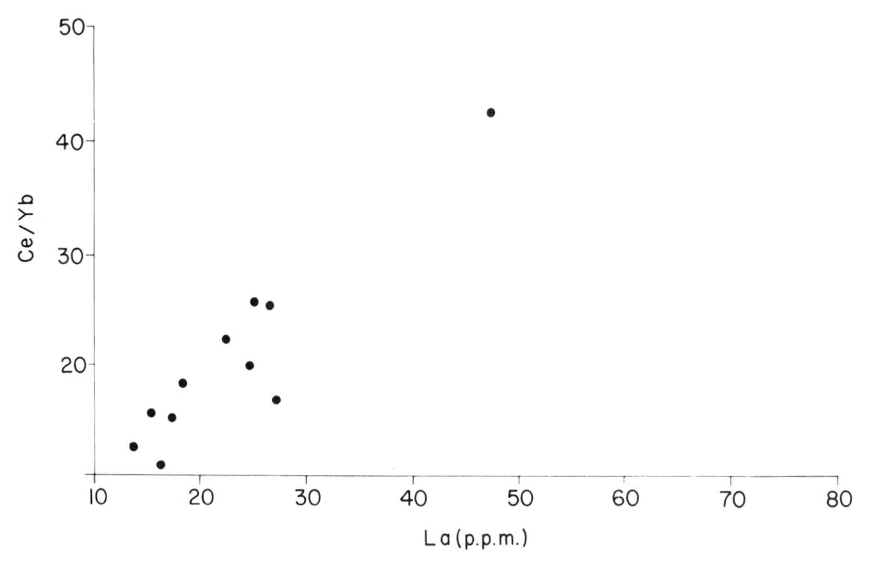

Fig. 6.3 Assuming that all the basal tholeiitic volcanics were derived from the same source material and taking the lanthanum concentration in primary liquids to be inversely related to the degree of partial melting, the varied values of Ce/Yb against La indicate that cerium and ytterbium ar not behaving similarly. Ytterbium shows little variation with differing degrees of partial melting suggesting that it is being retained in a residual mantle phase such as garnet. This could explain the enrichment of LREE (e.g. La and Ce) relative to HREE (e.g. Yb). Analytical data from Cristofolini *et al.* (1981).

$^{143}Nd/^{144}Nd$ values of 0.51292±3, 2σ to 0.51298±2, 2σ, (Carter *et al.* 1978). The Etnean volcanics, therefore, have higher neodymium isotope ratios than that predicted for undifferentiated mantle, supporting the interpretation from the strontium isotope data that the source region has been depleted in LREE at some stage in its history. The basal tholeiitic volcanics and the alkalic series, however, have Ce_N/Yb_N ratios of 5–10 and >10 respectively, which are much higher than the values of basalts from Iceland and the Reykjanes Ridge which have similar strontium isotope ratios (Carter and Civetta, 1977). To account for this apparent contradiction in which strontium and

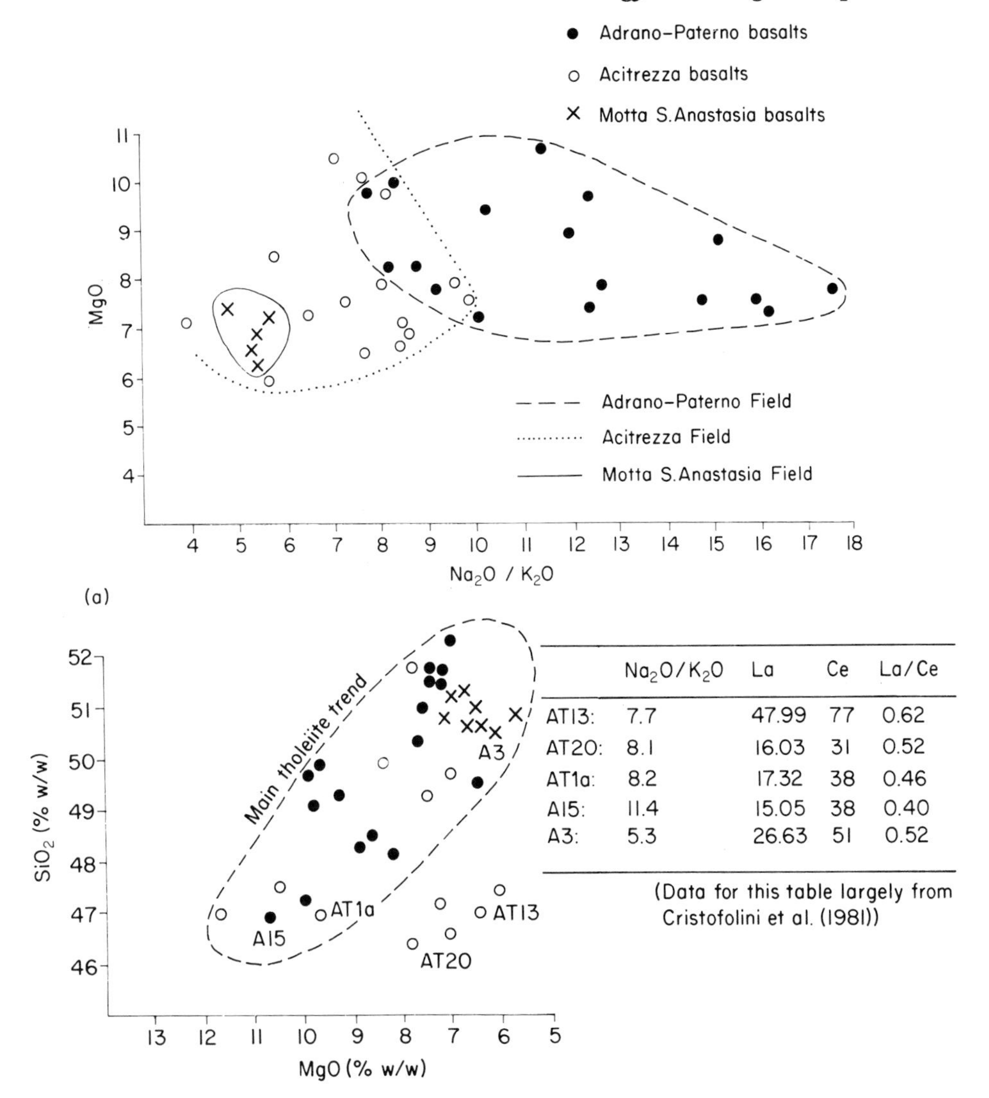

	Na_2O/K_2O	La	Ce	La/Ce
AT13:	7.7	47.99	77	0.62
AT20:	8.1	16.03	31	0.52
AT1a:	8.2	17.32	38	0.46
A15:	11.4	15.05	38	0.40
A3:	5.3	26.63	51	0.52

Fig. 6.4 (a) MgO plotted against Na_2O/K_2O for the basal tholeiitic volcanos showing differences in composition between the Adrano–Paterno, Acitrezza and Motta S. Anastasia basalts.

(b) SiO_2 plotted against MgO for the basal tholeiitic basalts showing the *main tholeiite trend*, the suggested compositional trend for the unaltered basalts. The Acitrezza basalts that lie outside this trend are considered to have undergone metasomatic alteration and show enrichment in the La/Ce *ratio*.

Analytical data taken from: Cristofolini (1972, 1974), Cristofolini and Puglisi (1974), Cristofolini *et al.* (1981), Duncan (1976b) and Tanguy (1978).

neodymium isotope data indicate a LREE-depleted source but the lavas themselves are relatively enriched in LREE, Carter *et al.* (1978) suggest that the source region was enriched in LREE at a late stage, sufficiently recently such that this event is not reflected in the strontium and neodymium isotope geochemistry. Such an event could have been mantle metasomatism, as discussed in Chapter 3. Holm and Munksgaard (1982) and Cortini and Hermes (1981) consider that mantle metasomatism was an important process in the genesis of the potassic volcanics of the Roman and Campanian volcanic provinces. The alternative possibility, that the high Ce_N/Yb_N ratios are due to small degrees of partial melting of a LREE depleted mantle with some residual phase such as garnet buffering the composition of Yb in the melt is considered unlikely by Carter and Civetta in view of the very small degrees of melting which would be required.

6.2 Basal tholeiitic volcanics

The basal tholeiitic volcanics have been subdivided, on the basis of their field relations, into three groups: the flood basalts between Adrano and Paterno, the volcanic plug at Motta S. Anastasia, and the submarine volcanics and high-level intrusives between Acitrezza and Acicastello. In addition, ancient lavas of tholeiitic affinity have been described in the Piedimonte area on the lower north-east flank of the volcano (Cristofolini and Romano, 1982). Atzori (1966) and Tanguy (1967), working independently, first recognized the subalkaline nature of these early lavas and their distinctiveness, both petrographically and chemically, from the mildly alkaline volcanics which make up the bulk of Etna. Subsequently, further investigation on these basal tholeiitic volcanics has been carried out by Cristofolini (1972, 1974), Cristofolini and Puglisi (1974), Duncan (1976b) and Tanguy (1978).

The submarine volcanics and intrusives at Acitrezza show some differences in their chemistry from that of the subaerial basalts between Adrano and Paterno (Fig. 6.4(a)). Tanguy (1978) considers these differences to reflect variations in the original magma chemistry. Cristofolini (1974) and Wells and Cristofolini (1977), in contrast, suggest that the differences are the result of metasomatic alteration of the Acitrezza basalts by hydrothermal activity of late-stage magmatic fluids interacting with solutions derived from sea-water or wet sediments (Cristofolini *et al.*, 1981). In the plot of MgO against Na_2O/K_2O (Fig. 6.4(a)), it can be seen that the Acitrezza basalts have broadly similar MgO-values to the Adrano–Paterno basalts but generally have lower Na_2O/K_2O values (< 10). The tholeiitic basalts from these groups, taken together, show a general correlation between MgO and SiO_2 (Fig. 6.4(b)), termed here the *main tholeiitic trend*. However, some of the Acitrezza basalts lie outside this field showing depletion in silicon dioxide and possibly also in magnesium oxide. REE (rare-earth element) data are available (Cristofolini *et al.*, 1981) for two of the Acitrezza basalts (AT20 and AT13) which lie off the main tholeiite trend and a selection of these data are presented in Fig. 6.4(b). These two samples show some enrichment in La/Ce relative to AT1a, an Acitrezza basalt which lies within the main tholeiite trend and has a REE chemistry similar to that of one of the Adrano subaerial basalts, A15. It is suggested that the Acitrezza basalts have undergone variable enrichment in certain incompatible elements including potassium, and depletion in some major elements through late-stage metasomatism.

The basalts from the volcanic plug at Motta S. Anastasia fall within, but towards the more-evolved end of, the main tholeiite trend (Fig. 6.4(b)). Like the Acitrezza basalts, however, they have low Na_2O/K_2O ratios and are relatively enriched in the LREE (Cristofolini and Puglisi, 1974; Cristofolini *et al.*, 1981). This enrichment in potassium and in the LREE may have resulted from concentration of volatile elements at high levels in the plug at a late stage when the magma was static prior to final consolidation.

It is suggested, therefore, that the tholeiitic basalts from the three groups of the basal tholeiitic volcanics belong to the same phase of magmatism, and that the main variation in magma chemistry is illustrated by the main tholeiitic trend in Fig. 6.4(b). In addition some of the basalts from Acitrezza have been subjected to late-stage alteration and as a result caution must be exercised in the interpretation of the original magma chemistry.

6.2.1 Petrography

It is necessary to have a good knowledge of the petrography of a suite of volcanic rocks before embarking with any confidence on a petrogenetic interpretation based on geochemical studies. The phenocryst mineralogy may provide information on pressure – temperature equilibrium conditions prior to eruption. In addition, resorption, reaction relations, inclusions and zoning in phenocrysts, as well as the presence of xenocrysts, are significant features concerning the processes that operated during ascent and possible storage of magma. The Adrano – Paterno tholeiitic basalts are considered first as they have not been subjected to any appreciable post-eruption alteration.

The Adrano–Paterno basalts are coarser-grained than the alkalic series lavas and have a well-developed sub-ophitic texture, no doubt because they cooled relatively slowly as thick flow units. Cristofolini (1973) suggests that these basalts were erupted at near-liquidus temperatures as they contain only phenocrysts of olivine rarely accompanied by plagioclase. The olivine phenocrysts, which are up to 1 mm in size, are typically rounded and may show signs of resorption. They range in composition from Fo_{86} in the olivine-normative basalts near Adrano to Fo_{74} in the quartz-normative basalts which occur near Paterno (Tanguy, 1978). Some olivine phenocrysts show marked iron-enrichment in their rims, up to Fo_{60}, and iron-rich olivines up to Fo_{42} are found in the groundmass (Cristofolini *et al.*, 1975; A. M. Duncan and R. M. F. Preston, unpublished data). In the quartz-normative basalts the olivine phenocrysts typically show resorption effects with alteration to iddingsite along the rims of crystals and within cracks. The occasional plagioclase phenocrysts are labradorite, with groundmass plagioclases being more sodic, ranging up to andesine in composition (Cristofolini, 1973).

Pyroxene, although not present as a phenocryst phase, is abundant in the groundmass. Two pyroxenes may be present: a calcium-rich pyroxene – subcalcic augite – and a calcium-poor pyroxene – pigeonite (Fig. 6.5). The subcalcic augites are similar in chemistry to augites in tholeiitic basalts from Hawaii (Fodor *et al.*, 1975). Tanguy (1978) estimates the pigeonite/augite ratio to be between 0.25 and 0.50 in the more siliceous tholeiites, but that pigeonite is rare or non-existent in the olivine-normative tholeiites.

Regarding the opaque mineralogy of these basalts, chromite occurs as inclusions within olivine phenocrysts, and ilmenite and titano-magnetite co-exist in the groundmass, with titanomagnetite becoming progressively more abundant in the quartz-normative tholeiites (Tanguy, 1978). The groundmass also contains an acidic glassy residuum which ranges in composition from rhyodacite in the olivine-normative tholeiites

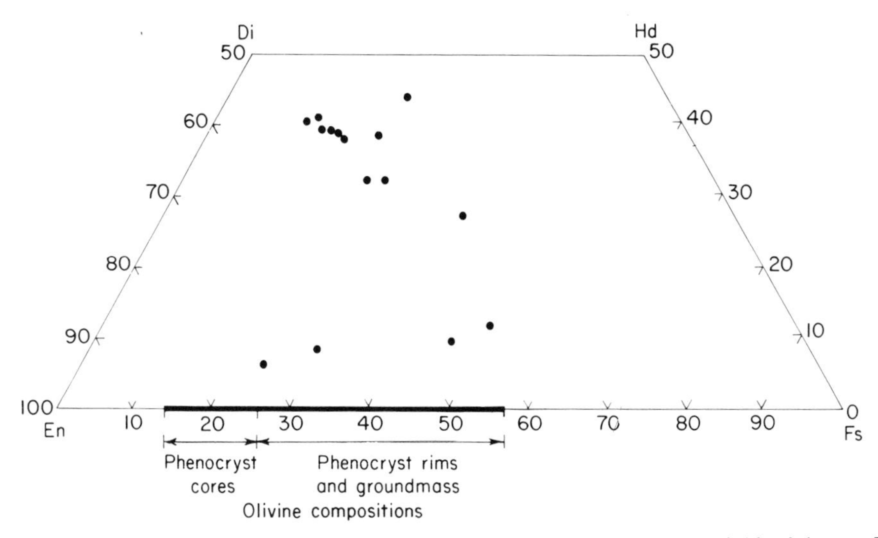

Fig. 6.5 Composition of groundmass pyroxenes and olivines and olivine phenocrysts in the Adrano – Paterno basalts of the basal tholeiitic volcanics. Olivine compositions, represented as Fe/(Fe + Mg) × 100, are plotted on the En – Fs tie line. Analytical data from Duncan (1976b) and Tanguy (1978).

Fig. 6.6 Pillow-like structures developed in the upper part of the Acitrezza intrusion. These are not pillows, however, because planes of early vesiculation (parallel to the hammer handle) pass from one block to another. Wells and Cristofolini (1977) suggest that these structures formed as the crystallizing magma stiffened and contracted while solutions derived from the sea or wet sediments penetrated along cracks and interacted with volatile components evolved from the magma. In the background can be seen one of the Cyclopean Islands with the intrusive basalt overlain by contact-metamorphosed Pleistocene marine clays. (Photograph: M. K. Wells.)

through to rhyolite in the quartz-normative tholeiites (Tanguy, 1978).

The Acitrezza basalts show considerable variability in their petrography (Cristofolini, 1974). The pillow lavas are hypersthene-normative basalts, similar in their petrography to the Adrano – Paterno tholeiites. The bulk of the Acitrezza intrusives are massive dolerites with olivine phenocrysts of comparable composition to those of the pillow lavas, but some of these olivines show evidence of disequilibrium being replaced by secondary clinopyroxene. In the uppermost parts of the intrusion there are thin veins of analcite dolerite which are related to joints and intimately associated with a rather dark dolerite (Fig. 6.6), referred to as the marginal facies by Wells and Cristofolini (1977). Near the margins of the intrusions, in close contact with the country rock of marine clays, larger bodies of analcite dolerite occur which are particularly well-developed in one of the Cyclopean Islands about 300 m offshore. These analcite dolerites are petrographically quite distinct from the Adrano – Paterno tholeiites and have an alkalic affinity with calcic augites, sometimes rimmed with aegirine, and no olivine. Wells and Cristofolini (1977) consider that these variable rocks of Acitrezza resulted from the single eruption of olivine-bearing tholeiite basalt magma, the likely nature of this initial magma being reflected in the rapidly congealed pillow lavas. They suggest, however, that the development of contraction joints in the more-slowly cooled associated intrusives provided access for solutions, from either sea-water or the wet sediments, to penetrate into the cooling igenous body. The complexity of this late-stage metasomatic activity has already been discussed.

6.2.2 *Geochemistry and petrogenesis*

Geochemically, the basal tholeiitic volcanics show limited but distinct chemical variation ranging from olivine-normative to quartz-normative tholeiite basalts. Cristofolini (1972, 1973) demonstrated that although olivine is generally the only liquidus phase on eruption of these lavas, the variation in their chemistry cannot be explained by olivine fractionation. In the MgO–SiO_2 and CaO–SiO_2 plots (Fig. 6.7) it can be readily seen that the basal tholeiitic volcanics do not lie on an olivine control line. Note the contrast of the basal tholeiitic volcanics trend with that of the tholeiite lavas from Kilauea, Hawaii (Wright, 1971). Cristofolini (1973) proposed that the variation reflects high-pressure processes and tentatively suggested

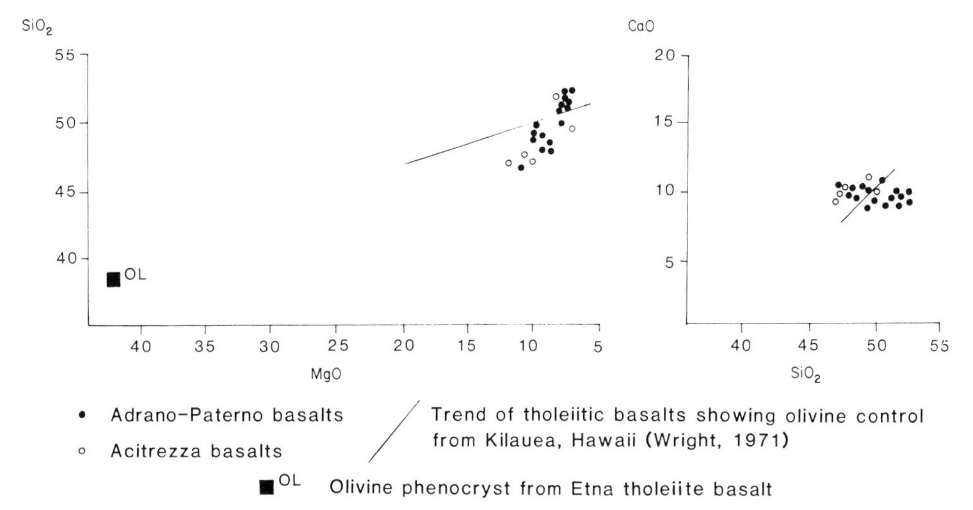

Fig. 6.7 SiO_2 plotted against MgO, and CaO plotted against SiO_2 for the basal tholeiitic volcanics showing the compositional variation in comparison to that of the tholeiitic basalts of Kilauea, Hawaii. Analytical data for Etna basalts from Cristofolini (1973) and Tanguy (1978), analysis of olivine phenocryst from Etna tholeiite basalt from Duncan (1976b) and Kilauea data from Wright (1971).

fractionation of garnet and clinopyroxene. Subsequent trace-element data, however, casts doubt on this model; scandium is enriched into garnet relative to silicate liquids (Irving, 1978) and the limited variation of Sc in the tholeiitic basalts (25 – 30 p.p.m.) does not support fractionation of garnet (Cristofolini *et al.*, 1981).

The Mg/Fe ratio of liquids in equilibrium with mantle material is controlled by the partition relations between the mafic minerals and the melt. The M' value ($M' = \mathrm{Mg}/\{\mathrm{Mg} + 0.85\,(\mathrm{Fe}'' + \mathrm{Fe}''')\}$) is a measure of the Mg/Fe″ ratio of the magma and based on the Mg/Fe partition relations for olivine – liquid determined by Roeder and Emslie (1970). Cox (1980) considers that liquids in equilibrium with 'typical' mantle material will have M' values greater than 60. What constitutes 'typical' mantle material is a matter of some debate, and Wilkinson and Binns (1977) and Wilkinson (1982) suggest that iron-enriched mantle may be significant in generating primary basalts with low M' values. The olivine normative basalts of the basal tholeiitic volcanics have M' values of around 0.65 indicating that they could represent magmas which have undergone only minimal modification during ascent. It is estimated (Basaltic Volcanism Study Project, 1981) that the nickel-content of terrestrial primary basaltic liquids ranges between 200–450 p.p.m. and therefore, the relatively high nickel content of these olivine-normative tholeiites (150–200 p.p.m.) also supports a primary, or near-primary origin (Duncan, 1976b).

Tanguy (1978) considers that the quartz-normative tholeiites were derived from the olivine-normative magma by moderate-to-low-pressure fractionation of 13% kaersutite, 6% olivine and 6% plagioclase. There is no direct evidence to support such a model as phenocrysts or xenocrysts of kaersutite have not been recorded in these tholeiitic basalts. Kaersutite is not a phase which would be expected to be in equilibrium with anhydrous tholeiitic basalt magma, though Tanguy does refer to some experimental work (Holloway and Burnham, 1972) which indicates that amphibole may be a possible liquidus phase at even relatively low f_{H_2O}. However, in the absence of further trace-element data and more specific experimental work, this mechanism must be regarded as rather speculative.

In addition, Tanguy suggests that the olivine-normative tholeiite basalt may represent the magma parental to the alkalic series and proposes a model involving remelting of the fractionating phases (kaersutite, olivine and plagioclase) from

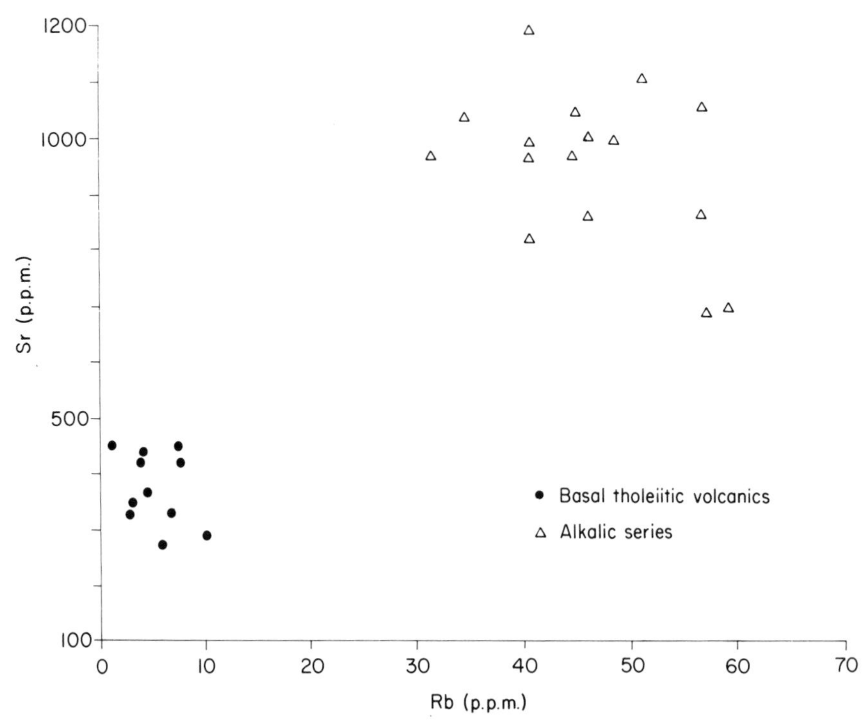

Fig. 6.8 Sr plotted against Rb for members of both the basal tholeiitic volcanics and the alkalic series. Analytical data from Cristofolini *et al.* (1981), Duncan (1976b) and Duncan and Preston (unpublished data).

the olivine-normative tholeiite magma at deeper levels generating a *femic* magma. This femic magma on subsequent differentiation gives rise to the alkalic series. Alternatively, Tanguy considers that high pressure fractionation (15–20 kbar) of orthopyroxene, clinopyroxene and minor plagioclase and titanomagnetite would generate a parental composition for the alkalic series. These proposals are considered unlikely for the following three reasons. Firstly, as already discussed, the strontium and neodymium isotope data indicate that the basal tholeiitic volcanics and the alkalic series are derived from different source regions and that they are not petrogenetically linked. Secondly, the basal tholeiitic volcanics and the alkalic series are stratigraphically distinct; and thirdly, in the Rb/Sr plot (Fig. 6.8) the basal tholeiitic volcanics and the alkalic series describe two distinct populations indicating that they are not related by any fractionation process. It should be noted, however, that Condomines *et al.* (1982) recognize some basalts with transitional Hf/Th ratios and suggest that they may have formed through mixing of magmas from both the alkalic series and the basal tholeiitic volcanics.

In conclusion, the basal tholeiitic volcanics may not be petrogenetically linked to the alkalic series and their chemical variation is a reflection of deep-seated processes. The range in strontium-isotope and Ce/Yb for these basalts indicates that they were derived from different sources in a heterogeneous mantle. The chemical variation in part may be caused by melting processes at varying depths where contraction of the (olivine+liquid) field with increasing pressure gives rise to progressively more magnesian primary liquids. Maaløe (1979) outlines such a mechanism to account for the chemical variation of the more magnesium-rich tholeiite basalts of Hawaii and active ocean ridges. An ascending diapir in the upper mantle would initiate partial melting at decreasing pressures generating progressively less magnesian primary liquids. The tholeiitic basalts, therefore, could represent discrete batches of magma generated at different levels in the mantle (Duncan and Guest, 1982).

6.3 Paterno alkali olivine basalt

The Paterno alkali olivine basalt, because of its insignificant volume in comparison to the rest of the volcanic products of Etna, hardly merits a section in its own right. Its importance, however, lies in the fact that it cannot be related to either the basal tholeiitic volcanics or the alkalic series. The low $^{87}Sr/^{86}Sr$ ratio of the Paterno alkali olivine basalt, 0.70301±4, 2σ, indicates that the magma was derived from a different (and distinctive) source region in the mantle than that which gave rise to the tholeiitic and alkalic magmas. In addition, the Paterno basalt dated at 210 000 BP (Condomines and Tanguy, 1976) was erupted after the onset of the basal tholeiitic volcanism but before the alkalic series activity (Chester and Duncan, 1982).

The Paterno basalt crops out as sheets and small plugs within the scoria of an ancient, eroded cone. This basalt is an attractive and distinctive rock-in-hand specimen being rich in olivine phenocrysts (typical mode: *phenocrysts* olivine 13%, plagioclase 3%, augite 1%; *groundmass* 83%). Small xenoliths of sandstone, generally only a few millimetres in size, also occur in the basalt; such xenoliths are relatively rare elsewhere on Etna. An analysis of the basalt is given in Table 6.1. The K_2O/Na_2O ratio of 0.17 is much lower than that of the alkalic series basalts and is rather low for alkali basalts generally which typically have values ranging from 0.16 to 0.78 (Wilkinson, 1974). The olivine phenocrysts, though fresh in appearance, are often rounded and show signs of resorption. These phenocrysts are magnesium-rich (Fo_{86}) and rich in nickel – 1773 p.p.m. (Duncan, 1976b) – compared with 849 p.p.m. for nickel in an olivine phenocryst from a hawaiite of the alkalic series. This forsteritic, nickel-rich olivine either crystallized from very mafic magma or represents a mantle-derived xenocryst. The clinopyroxene phenocrysts are calcic-augites and the plagioclases have an An-rich labradorite composition. The high M' (0.68), Ni (238 p.p.m.) and Cr (243 p.p.m.) values for the Paterno basalt (Duncan, 1976b) indicate that it may have represented a near-primary magma composition.

The ancient alkali olivine basalts recorded at the base of the volcanic succession in the Piedimonte area on the lower north-east flank of Etna (Spadea, 1972; Cristofolini *et al.*, 1977b) have a similar major-element chemistry, with $K_2O < 1\%$ (w/w) to the Paterno basalt. These basalts are more porphyritic than the Paterno basalt and, indeed, some are ankaramitic in character (e.g. mode of: *phenocrysts* olivine 6%, plagioclase 12%, augite 28%; *groundmass* 54%.) As well as phenocrysts of olivine (Fo_{86}), calcic-augite and plagioclase, rare relics of kaersutite occur (Spadea, 1972). Spadea suggests that these basalts represent the parental magma of the alkalic series. However, if the Piedimonte and Paterno basalts are related and represent an early phase of alkali olivine basalt magmatism, now largely obscured by younger lavas, the arguments above concerning the Paterno basalt would indicate that they are not genetically linked to the alkalic series.

6.4 The alkalic series

Lavas and pyroclastics of the alkalic series make up the main bulk of Etna representing over 98% by volume of the volcano. It is necessary for two reasons to consider the petrology of the alkalic series somewhat differently from both the basal tholeiitic volcanics and the Paterno alkali olivine basalt. Firstly, the volcanics of the alkalic series have been erupted over about the last 100 000 years and do not represent a single magmatic event. During this period of activity several different volcanic centres have been constructed, some with rather distinctive petrological characteristics. Indeed, the alkalic series is a collective term for a group of mildly alkaline volcanics within which several different trends have been recognized. Secondly, with virtually continuous discharge of basaltic magma throughout the last few hundred years, Etna is one of the few volcanoes in the world where it is possible to relate petrological investigations directly with geophysical and volcanological studies. Etna may be regarded as a large, natural,

Table 6.1 A selection of whole-rock major-element analyses and CIPW norms for Etnean lavas

	Sample numbers (see footnotes for explanation)									
	1	2	3	4	5	6	7	8	9	*10*
Analysis										
SiO_2	51.47	51.87	47.07	48.04	47.14	47.21	52.82	55.72	56.36	60.95
TiO_2	1.45	1.45	1.54	1.47	1.79	1.62	1.50	0.79	1.71	1.44
Al_2O_3	14.92	13.52	13.82	15.35	17.58	16.50	18.52	18.87	15.37	17.62
Fe_2O_3	0.94	3.20	3.45	3.32	3.25	4.43	6.82	4.85	4.72	3.07
FeO	9.07	8.75	7.76	6.28	7.10	6.45	1.00	1.52	5.00	1.93
MnO	0.18	0.19	0.13	0.18	0.17	0.21	0.17	0.11	0.16	0.14
MgO	9.60	7.68	11.68	9.74	5.54	6.23	3.22	2.66	3.07	1.19
CaO	9.10	9.24	9.30	9.52	11.47	11.06	7.57	6.27	6.36	3.92
Na_2O	3.10	3.16	2.58	3.80	3.96	3.20	5.06	5.39	4.18	5.66
K_2O	0.25	0.18	0.36	0.65	1.08	1.76	2.26	2.43	2.11	2.77
P_2O_5	0.20	0.19	0.28	0.37	0.74	0.51	0.73	0.36	0.69	0.41
CO_2	0.19	0.13	0.35	0.15	0.30	0.14	ng	ng	0.14	0.12
H_2O	0.37	0.62	2.20	0.38	0.61	0.31	ng	0.87	0.26	0.23
Total	100.84	100.18	100.52	99.25	100.73	99.63	99.67	99.84	100.13	99.45
CIPW norm										
Qz	–	1.77	–	–	–	–	–	0.55	8.67	7.85
Or	1.48	1.06	2.13	3.84	6.38	10.40	13.13	14.36	12.47	16.37
Ab	26.22	26.73	21.83	27.12	21.11	19.32	44.05	45.61	35.35	14.87
An	26.06	22.18	25.07	22.91	27.01	25.47	20.79	20.12	16.95	14.50
Ne	–	–	–	2.72	6.71	4.20	0.14	–	–	–
Di	14.44	18.24	13.63	17.52	20.35	20.94	10.67	6.72	8.10	1.77
Hy	19.00	21.62	12.63	–	–	–	–	3.51	6.49	3.94
Ol	8.5	–	13.67	16.20	8.44	8.17	4.24	–	–	–
Mt	1.36	4.64	5.00	4.81	4.71	6.42	–	2.97	6.84	2.50
Il	2.75	2.75	2.92	2.79	3.40	3.08	2.19	1.50	3.27	2.74
Ap	0.47	0.45	0.65	0.88	1.76	1.21	1.51	0.83	1.64	0.97
Hm	–	–	–	–	–	–	2.87	ng	–	1.34

ng = 'not given'

(1) Olivine tholeiite basalt, basal tholeiitic volcanics, from near Adrano (AD 1/30: Duncan, 1976b).
(2) Quartz tholeiite basalt, basal tholeiitic volcanics, from near Paterno (AD 2/91: Duncan, 1976b).
(3) Olivine tholeiite basalt, basal tholeiitic volcanics, from near Acitrezza (413: Tanguy, 1978).
(4) Paterno alkali olivine basalt from Paterno (AD 2/90: Duncan, 1976b).
(5) Hawaiite, alkalic series, from pre-Trifoglietto unit lava capping Terrace 4 Simeto Valley (AD 1/118: Duncan, 1976b).
(6) Hawaiite, alkalic series, 1974 flank eruption (Duncan, 1976b).
(7) Basic mugearite, alkalic series, from the Belvedere lavas exposed on the west wall, Valle del Bove (MES 81: Lo Giudice *et al.*, 1974).
(8) Mugearite, alkalic series, from Trifoglietto II (1032: Tanguy, 1978).
(9) Mugearite, alkalic series, from near Adrano, possibly correlates with Vavalaci (AD 2/33: Duncan, 1976b).

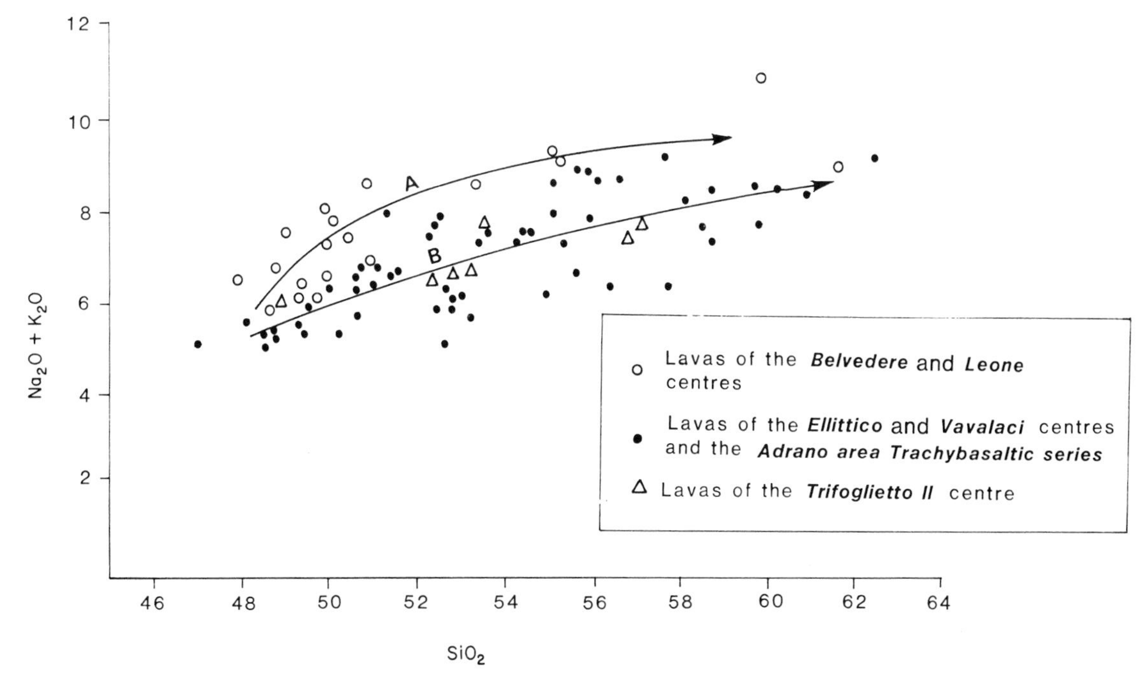

Fig. 6.9 $Na_2O + K_2O$ plotted against SiO_2 showing the variation of the different trends in the alkalic series. Analytical data from Cristofolini and Lo Giudice (1969), Duncan (1978), Lo Giudice (1971), Lo Giudice *et al.* (1974), McGuire (1980) and Romano and Guest (1979).

experimental petrological laboratory. Therefore the petrology of the alkalic series is relevant not only to Etnean studies but is of significance to basalt petrogenesis in general.

Three different trends are recognized in the alkalic series. These are (1) the normal trend, (2) the alkali-rich trend and (3) the low-titania trend. The normal trend does not show strong alkali enrichment (Fig. 6.9) and forms a rather transitional suite from nepheline-normative hawaiite through to quartz and hypersthene-normative mugearite and benmoreite. The volcanic units which crop-out on the flanks of Etna, the cone building lavas (e.g. *Ellittico, Vavalaci*, Adrano-area trachybasalts and the currently erupted products of *Mongibello*) generally belong to this normal trend. The alkali-rich trend shows more alkali enrichment than the normal trend as can be seen on the ($Na_2O + K_2O$) vs. SiO_2 plot (Fig. 6.9). Volcanics of this trend occur as units of horizontally bedded lavas (e.g. *Leone* and *Belvedere*) which crop out in the walls of the Valle del Leone and the Valle del Bove and have been interpreted as lava infilling ancient calderas (see Chapter 3). The lavas of the low-titania trend make up the *Trifoglietto II Centre* and are unusual in that they commonly contain kaersutite phenocrysts and show decreasing TiO_2 with increasing SiO_2 (see Fig. 6.18). The stratigraphic relationships of these three trends in the alkalic series are shown in Table 6.2. The presence of different trends within the alkalic series has been recognized by several workers. Klerkx (1968) describes the low-titania trend of the *Trifoglietto* lavas; Cristofolini (1971) uses titanium dioxide (TiO_2) concentrations to discriminate between different groups within the alkalic series, and Romano and Guest (1979) note the alkali-rich nature of the *Leone* and *Belvedere* lavas in relation to those of the *Ellittico* and *Vavalaci*. The trends identified in this account are not presented as definitive. Further study will no doubt reveal more complexity. Indeed, Carter (1976), as already discussed, describes a nickel-rich trend within the alkalic series but as yet there

Table 6.2 Stratigraphic relations of the different trends in the alkalic series

Centre	*Rock types*	*Trend*
Recent Mongibello	Mainly hawaiites	Normal
Leone	Hawaiites, basic mugearites	Alkali-rich
Ellittico	Hawaiites, basic mugearites, mugearites, benmoreites	Normal
Belvedere	Hawaiites, basic mugearites	Alkali-rich
Vavalaci	Hawaiites, basic mugearites, mugearites, benmoreites	Normal
Trifoglietto II	Basic mugearites, mugearites,	Low-titania
Pre-Trifoglietto II centres	Mainly hawaiites, but poorly exposed	Insufficient data

is not sufficient trace-element data for the volcano as a whole to assess the significance of such a trend.

The lavas of the alkalic series include hawaiites, basic mugearites, mugearites and benmoreites; the alkali basalts at one end of the series and the trachytes at the other are limited in their occurrence. Determining the relative volumetric abundance of the different lava types within volcanic centres and for the volcano as a whole is frustrated by the partial exposure. On Etna, a substantial portion of the surface area is covered by young lavas (< 2000 BP) and apart from outcrops in the walls of the Valle del Bove, older volcanics are poorly exposed.

6.4.1 *Petrography*

The lavas of the alkalic series are generally porphyritic with phenocrysts of plagioclase, augite, olivine and sometimes titanomagnetite and kaersutite. The more basic lavas often have a phenocryst content greater than 30% by volume, whereas the more silicic lavas tend to have fewer phenocrysts, some with less than 5%, with the more aphyric lavas showing a trachytic texture (Duncan, 1978). The modal analyses for a representative set of lavas of the alkalic series is given in Fig. 6.10 and this clearly shows the variation in phenocryst content and abundance. This variation is in agreement with the work of Marsh (1981), who from a theoretical viewpoint considers that the *eruption probability* of basaltic magma is likely to be greatest at 30 – 50 % crystallinity. Marsh argues that this is to be expected because, since *eruption probability* is the product of *thermal probability* and *rheological probability*, for lavas of similar crystallinity, viscosity will increase with silica content. The technique suggested by Marsh for using modal data of the phenocryst content of a suite of comagmatic lavas to determine the sequence of crystallization should be approached with some caution in the case of Etna, where there is evidence that polybaric crystallization may occur.

The phenocryst phases require close study as they contain valuable information regarding magmatic processes in operation prior to eruption. The chemistry, shape and zoning of the phenocryst phases place constraints on the models of fractional crystallization and magma-mixing that may be considered. The zoning in plagioclase phenocrysts records the physico-chemical history of the magma and the morphology of the crystals reflects the nature of the cooling of the melt from which they crystallized (Kuo and Kirkpatrick, 1982). The importance of this aspect of the petrography of the lavas of Etna was recognized by Cristofolini (1973) who noted that the complex zoning patterns in the plagioclase crystals provide significant information for the interpretation of a complex cooling history. Glomeroporphyritic aggregates are relatively common, these aggregates being generally composed of either predominantly plagioclase or of mainly augite with some olivine and titanomagnetite (Cristofolini, 1973; Cristofolini and Tranchina, 1980). Ultrabasic nodules, however, have not been recorded in the lavas of the alkalic series.

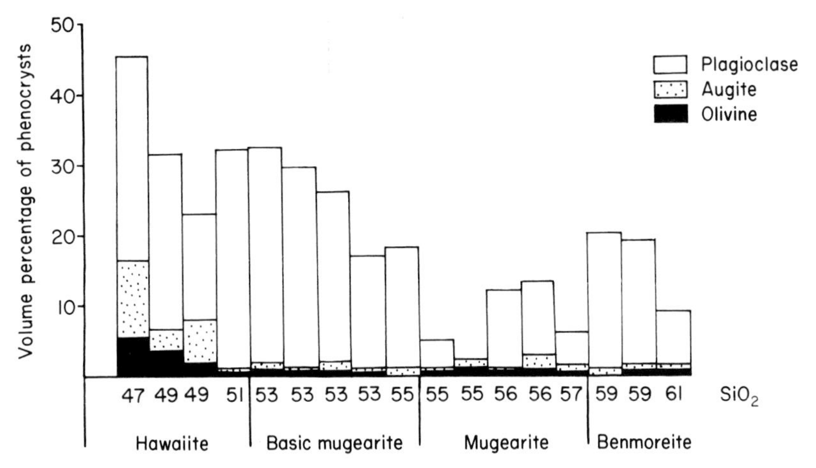

Fig. 6.10 Modal analyses of phenocryst content of lavas of the alkalic series from the Adrano area. (After Duncan, 1976b.)

Figure 6.11 shows the petrographic texture of some typical rocks of the alkalic series as represented in thin section. Glomeroporphyritic aggregates, one of plagioclase and one of augite, can be clearly seen in Fig. 6.11(b).

(a) Feldspars

In most of the lavas of the alkalic series, plagioclase is the dominant phenocryst phase. Indeed, some lavas contain up to 45% by volume of large plagioclase phenocrysts producing a distinctive rock type known locally as *cicirara* (Rittmann, 1973; Romano and Guest, 1979).

In many of the plagioclase phenocrysts there are zones of glassy inclusions, either occurring in the core of the crystal or forming distinctive growth bands parallel to the oscillatory zoning (Fig. 6.11(a)). Downes (1973), in a description of lavas of the 1971 flank eruption, suggests that the glassy inclusions in the plagioclase phenocrysts formed in the manner described by Bottinga *et al.* (1966) with the inclusions representing basaltic melt trapped during periods of rapid growth. Kuo and Kirkpatrick (1982) describe a similar skeletal texture in plagioclase megacrysts from mid-ocean ridge basalts and consider that this represents growth under conditions of considerable undercooling. A detailed electron microprobe analysis of plagioclase phenocrysts in a hawaiite lava (Duncan and Preston, in preparation) shows that in one particular crystal with a well-developed growth band of glassy inclusions there is no difference in the composition of the plagioclase between the zone of glassy inclusions and the relatively inclusion-free inner and outer zones of the phenocryst. In addition, not all the plagioclase phenocrysts (considering those of similar size) have zones of glassy inclusions indicating that they did not all experience the same growth history and this suggests that there is more than one crop of plagioclase phenocrysts in the hawaiite sample studied. A possible explanation of this would be magma-mixing. To account for the variation in morphology and zoning of plagioclase megacrysts in some mid-ocean ridge basalts, Kuo and Kirkpatrick (1982) suggest a model involving the mixing of two chemically distinctive magmas, both containing plagioclase phenocrysts, to form a hybrid magma of intermediate composition and temperature compared with the initial liquids. The more albite-rich plagioclase phenocrysts from the more evolved melt will be superheated in the hybrid, whereas the more anorthite-rich plagioclases from the more primitive melt will be undercooled. The superheated crystals will show some resorption and become mantled by more anorthite-rich material than the core. In contrast the undercooled crystals will show skeletal growth with a mantle more albite-rich than the core.

An investigation into the melt inclusions themselves has been carried out by Preston and Duncan

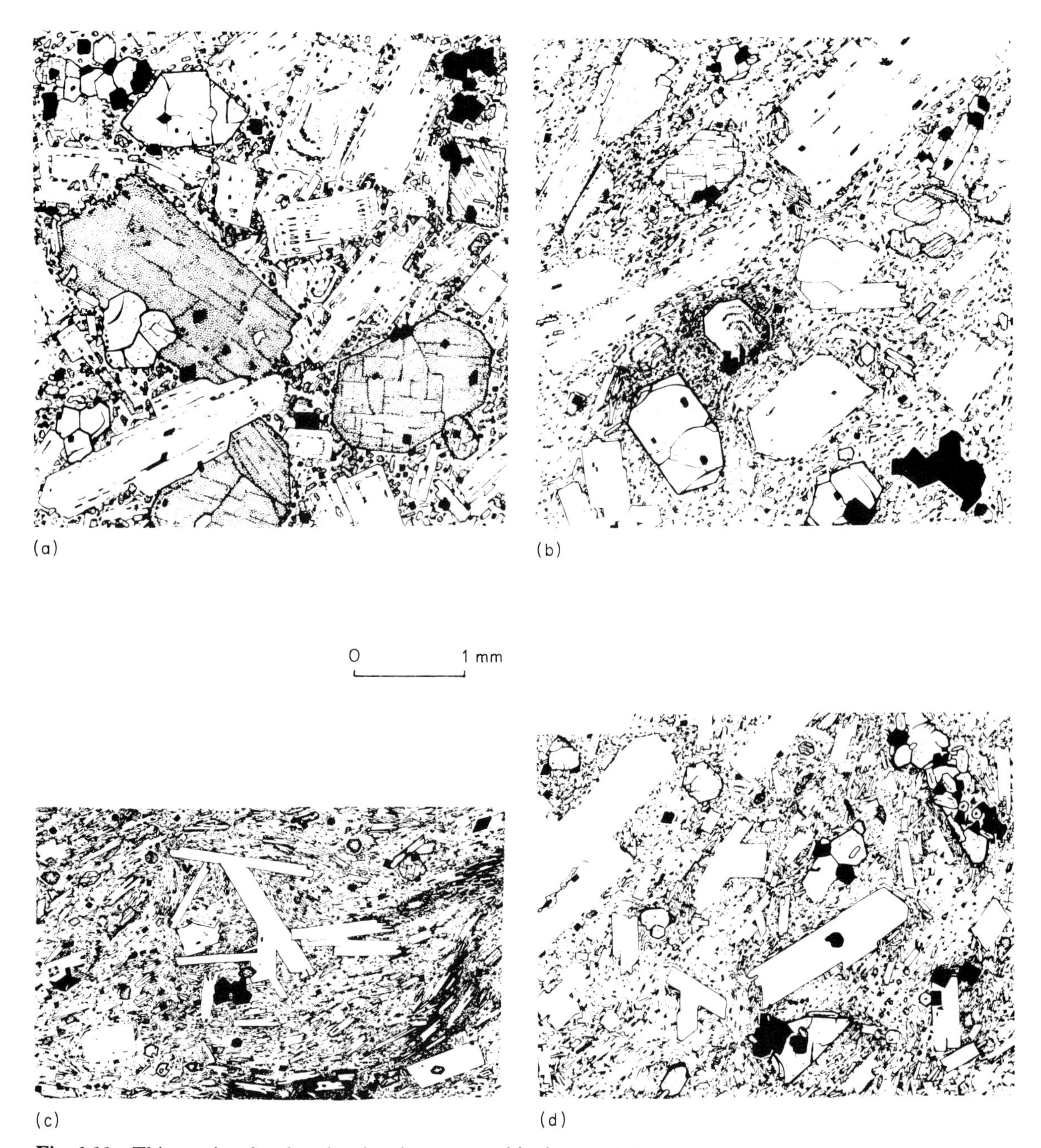

Fig. 6.11 Thin-section sketches showing the petrographic characteristics of rocks of the alkalic series. (a) Hawaiite, a highly porphyritic rock with euhedral phenocrysts of augite, plagioclase, olivine and minor titanomagnetite; note the zones of glassy inclusions in the plagioclase. (b) Basic Mugearite, not so strongly porphyritic with a lesser abundance of mafic minerals. (c) Mugearite only weakly porphyritic with a well-developed trachytic texture. (d) Benmoreite in which plagioclase is the main phenocryst phase with small olivines and augites; note the apatite phenocrysts with orientated opaque inclusions. (Thin-section drawings by the late Dr A. K. Wells and by Dr M. K. Wells.)

(1979). This work shows that the inclusions contain minute grains of chalcosine (Cu_2S) giving them an opaque nature in transmitted light. Many of the inclusions contain two parts: a spherical cavity lined with pyrite situated within, or at one end of, an area of glassy, but partly devitrified, silicon-rich material. Discrete grains of chalcosine occur within the silicon-rich part of the inclusions and also as isolated grains within the plagioclase. Preston and Duncan (1979) interpret the inclusions as trapped basaltic melt from which an immiscible, volatile-rich fluid separated during cooling. The inclusions in plagioclase phenocrysts in a quench sample of hawaiite collected during the 1983 eruption are completely clear, green glass. The pyrite coating of the spherical cavity precipitated from the volatile-rich fluid, this fluid being subsequently lost by leakage along cleavage planes or during the process of thin-section making.

Oscillatory zoning is commonly developed in the plagioclase phenocrysts of the alkalic series. Lofgren (1974) has demonstrated experimentally that compositional zoning in plagioclases may be generated by variations in pressure and temperature caused by eruption or movement of the magma. Vance (1962), however, considers such a mechanism unlikely because of the rapidity and regularity with which the variation must occur to produce the extremely fine-scale oscillatory zoning which is typical. In addition, Wiebe (1968) has shown, from a specific study of an intrusive body, that only major discontinuities in plagioclase zoning can be correlated between different crystals but there is no correlation in oscillatory zoning between crystals. According to Wiebe this indicates that repeated changes in the general environmental variables could account for the major, abrupt chemical discontinuities but they could not provide the mechanism for the oscillatory zoning. The origin of oscillatory zoning has been more generally attributed to kinetic growth models involving interaction between the rates of ionic diffusion and crystal growth (Bottinga *et al.*, 1966). A model for such a process of oscillatory zoning involving constitutional undercooling of the liquid adjacent to a growing, planar crystal face is described in some detail by Sibley *et al.* (1976). Lofgren (1980), however, considers that kinetic growth models do not provide a fully satisfactory mechanism capable of producing multiple oscillations and that with the lack of experimental data on oscillatory-zoned crystals some critical parameters are still to be identified. It is apparent, therefore, that caution must be exercised in the interpretation of zoning, but with a fuller understanding of the mechanisms involved, the study of such crystals should provide valuable information on the magmatic processes which operated during the growth of a phenocryst.

The plagioclase phenocrysts of the alkalic Etnean lavas range in composition from An_{80-55} in

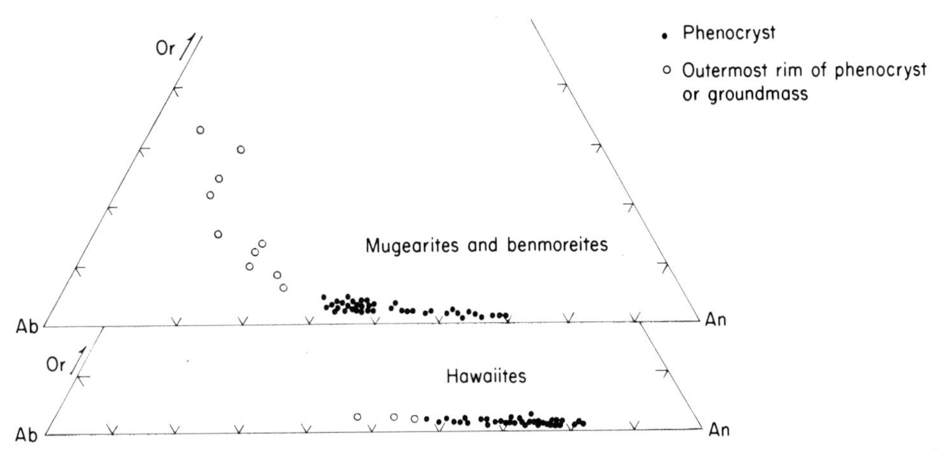

Fig. 6.12 Composition of phenocryst and groundmass plagioclases in lavas of the alkalic series. (Unpublished analytical data, Duncan and Preston.)

Fig. 6.13 Photomicrograph showing resorbed plagioclase phenocryst in a hawaiite lava (field of view is approximately 2.3 mm across.)

the hawaiites and basic mugearites to An $_{70-40}$ in the mugearites and benmoreites (Fig. 6.12). Groundmass feldspars are more alkalic with oligoclase, anorthoclase and sodic sanidine having been detected by XRD techniques (Lo Giudice, 1970; Tanguy 1973, 1978). Cristofolini (1973) notes that both the average and the core compositions of the plagioclases become more sodic with differentiation and that there is a relationship between the silica content of the rock and the An-content of the plagioclase cores. Even within one lava there is generally a considerable range in the composition of the plagioclase phenocrysts indicating the operation of fractional crystallization or magma-mixing. Morse (1980, p. 279 – 283) provides a useful discussion on the interpretation of the wide range in chemical variation of plagioclases from a basalt in terms of theoretical phase petrology using as an example a basalt from Picture Gorge, Oregon described by Lindsley and Smith (1971).

Plagioclase phenocrysts of the alkalic series are typically more calcic than plagioclase phenocrysts in hawaiites and mugearites from other mildly alkaline suites such as Hawaii (Macdonald and Katsura, 1964; Keil *et al.*, 1972), Terceira, Azores (Self and Gunn, 1976) and Mauritius (Baxter, 1975). Tanguy (1978) suggests that the abundance of calcic-plagioclase in Etnean lavas is due to the high CaO- and Al_2O_3-content of the magma. Another possible factor is provided by the work of Johannes (1978) who has shown that the An-content of a plagioclase in equilibrium with a given melt composition will be higher for hydrous than for anhydrous conditions.

The plagiocase phenocrysts in a sample of hawaiite lava from a prehistoric flow on the lower south-west flank of Etna have been investigated in some detail (Duncan and Preston, in preparation). This hawaiite, in common with many Etnean lavas, contains more than one group of plagioclase phenocrysts. Some of the plagioclase phenocrysts have a well-developed lath shape, whereas others have diffuse margins and profiles indicative of resorption (Fig. 6.13). As may be seen in the

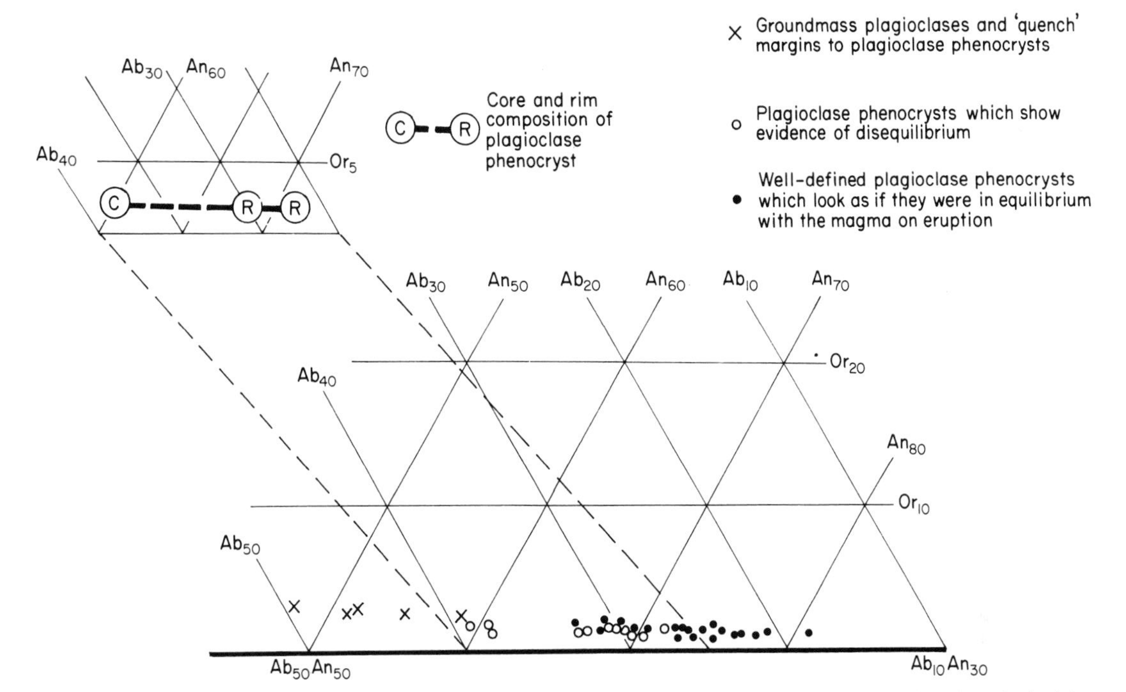

Fig. 6.14 Compositional variation of plagioclases in a single sample of hawaiite lava. (Unpublished analytical data, Duncan and Preston.)

Ab – An – Or plot (Fig. 6.14) these two groups – the euhedral lath-like phenocrysts (An $_{80-65}$) and the resorbed phenocrysts (An $_{70-60}$) are chemically distinct. Though the euhedral, lath-like phenocrysts show a range in composition no progressive variation from core to rim was observed. On some phenocrysts, however, there is a thin sodic-rim (An_{46}). Downes (1973) notes similar sodic-rims on plagioclase phenocrysts in 1971 lava quenched at the vent indicating that these rims grew at a pre-eruptive stage during the final ascent of the magma. Resorbed phenocrysts are more sodic than the euhedral, lath-like crystals and show some evidence of reverse zoning giving more calcic margins (Fig. 6.14). They must also have been in equilibrium with a more differentiated melt at a lower temperature and subsequently have been incorporated into a less-evolved melt at a higher temperature and have undergone partial melting and re-equilibrium with the liquid. This suggests a process of magma-mixing along the lines of that suggested by Kuo and Kirkpatrick (1982) for mid-ocean ridge basalts discussed above. Alternatively, the low-temperature crystals may have been derived from cumulate assemblages within the plumbing system.

(b) Pyroxenes

The clinopyroxene phenocrysts in the lavas of the alkalic series range from calcic-augite to augite in composition and show little evidence of iron-enrichment with differentiation (Cristofolini, 1973; Duncan and Preston, 1980). In the chemical variation of the phenocrysts from those in the hawaiites to those in the benmoreites there is an increase in silicon and a decrease in titanium and aluminium of the pyroxenes as the whole-rock chemistry becomes more silicic (Duncan and Preston, 1980). A similar relationship is recognized by Fodor *et al.* (1975) in the chemistry of clinopyroxenes from the alkalic lavas of Hawaii. In the Etnean clinopyroxenes there is a reasonable correlation between Al_z and Ti (Fig. 6.15), but there is excess Al_z which cannot be accounted for by the substitution mechanism of Le Bas (1962) with $Ti_y^{4+} + 2Al_z = M_y^{2+} + 2Si_z$. Duncan and

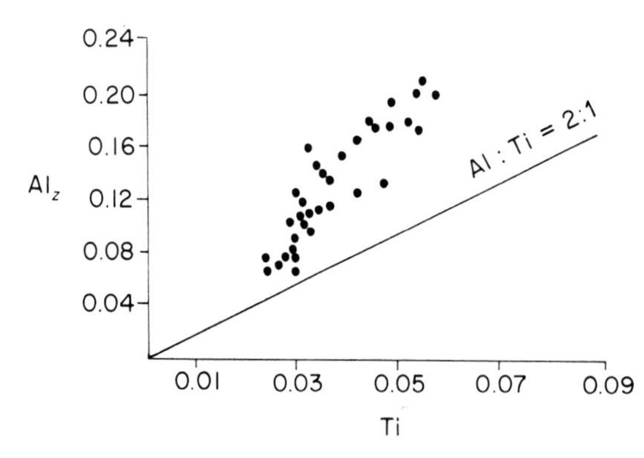

Fig. 6.15 Plot of Al_z against Ti (calculated on the basis of six oxygens) for clinopyroxenes from the alkalic series. (After Duncan and Preston, 1980.)

Preston (1980) suggest that the excess of Al_z may be partly balanced by Al entering into octahedral coordination with the effective substitution $2Al = M_y^{2+} + Si_z$. The increase in silicon and decrease in aluminium and titanium in the clinopyroxenes from the hawaiites to the benmoreites is no doubt due to the increase in silicon-activity of the melt with differentation.

The lack of iron-enrichment in the clinopyroxene phenocrysts with differentiation of the magma is clearly shown in Fig. 6.16. Duncan and Preston (1980) suggest that the higher Fe/Mg ratios in the clinopyroxene phenocrysts in the hawaiites may be due to prior crystallization of olivine which depleted the melt in magnesium. The importance of the order of crystallization of mineral phases in influencing the pyroxene chemistry is demonstrated by Barberi *et al.* (1971) who show that the rather subcalcic nature of augites in the Erta 'Ale basalts, Ethiopia, may be due to crystallization under low P_{H_2O} conditions; this would favour the crystallization of plagioclase feldspar and so deplete the residual melt in the 'Ca-Tschermack molecule'. A further point of note is that with fractionation the Fe^{3+}/Fe^{2+} ratio of the melt is likely to increase. According to Carmichael *et al.* (1974, p. 282), both enrichment in alkalis and decrease in temperature tend to increase the Fe^{3+}/Fe^{2+} ratio of the magma. The Fe_2O_3/FeO ratio of the lavas shows a general increase from the hawaiites to the benmoreites (Duncan, 1978). Such an increase in the Fe^{3+}/Fe^{2+} ratio of the melt, indicating relatively high f_{O_2}, will favour crystallization of magnetite and thereby deplete the amount of iron available for crystallizing pyroxenes (Duncan and Preston, 1980). It is apparent in Figure 6.17 that there is no sodium-enrichment

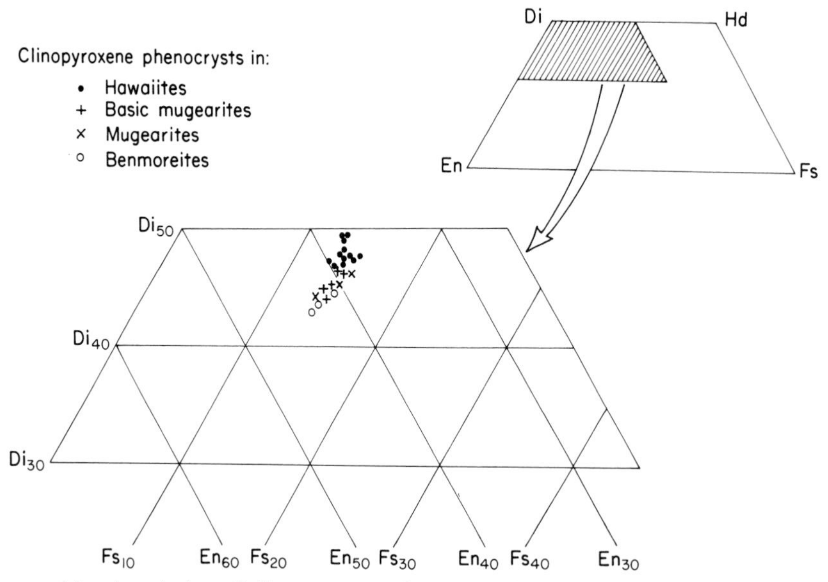

Fig. 6.16 Compositional variation of clinopyroxene phenocrysts of the alkalic series plotted on the pyroxene quadrilateral. (After Duncan and Preston, 1980.)

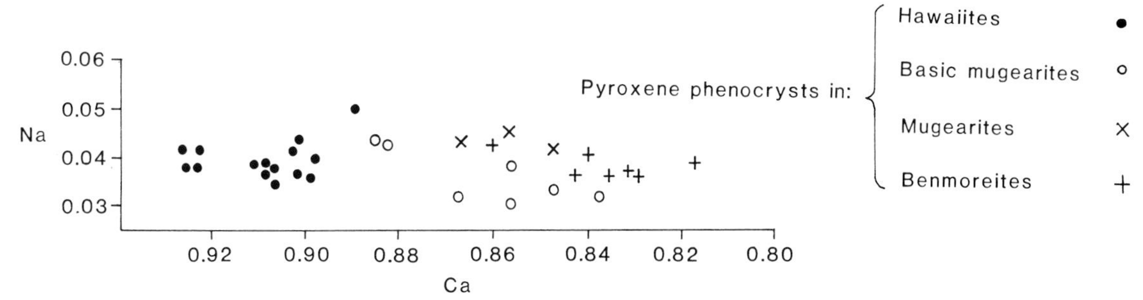

Fig. 6.17 Plot of atomic proportions of sodium against calcium for clinopyroxene phenocrysts from the alkalic series. (After Duncan and Preston, 1980.)

in the pyroxenes with differentiation, even though the whole-rock chemistry of the lavas shows alkali-enrichment with differentiation. Duncan and Preston (1980) suggest that the increase in Na in the melt leads to the crystallisation or more sodic plagioclase and that the magma is too alumina-rich for sodium to become an important constituent of any mineral other than feldspar or feldspathoid.

The calcic-augite phenocrysts in the hawaiites often show well-developed sector and oscillatory zoning (Downes, 1974; Duncan and Preston, 1980). Though this zoning in the pyroxenes implies considerable disequilibrium during growth there is no evidence of any chemical variation between core and rim within any one sector of a phenocryst. A similar lack of any core to rim variation, with the exception of chromium, is described by Shimizu (1981) for sector-zoned phenocrysts in an alkali olivine basalt from Bald Mountain, California. The oscillatory zoning is generally developed in the outer half of the phenocrysts from Etna and is represented chemically by silicon and magnesium varying antipathetically with aluminium and titanium (Duncan and Preston, 1980).

The sectors in these 'hour-glass' zoned phenocrysts can be visualized as pyramids with their apices at the centre of the crystal and their bases represented by the crystal faces (Deer, Howie and Zussmann, 1978). The $\{100\}$, $\{110\}$ and $\{010\}$ prism sectors show similar chemistry and are enriched in titanium, aluminium and iron but depleted in silicon and magnesium relative to the basal $\{11\bar{1}\}$ sectors (Duncan and Preston, 1980). This chemical variation between the basal and prism sectors is in accord with that observed in other examples of sector zoning in clinopyroxenes from alkali basalts (Hollister and Gancarz, 1971; Wass, 1973; Leung, 1974; Harkins and Hollister, 1977; and Shimizu, 1981). To account for the origin of sector-zoned augites, Duncan and Preston (1980) suggest a mechanism similar to that proposed by Leung (1974) and Downes (1974) involving the $\{11\bar{1}\}$ sectors growing too rapidly to maintain equilibrium with the melt. In addition Duncan and Preston suggest that the structure of the silicate melt may be important in influencing the distribution of elements between the liquid and the crystal. Alternatively, Nakamura (1973) and Dowty (1976) consider that it is the crystal structure presented by the growing face to the melt which controls the chemistry of the sectors in the clinopyroxene. Dowty (1976) suggests that during growth each crystal face has an adsorption layer that may be incorporated in part during growth; highly charged small cations being preferentially accepted into partially completed sites, termed proto-sites. For instance, the form $\{100\}$ has both M1 and M2 half-sites exposed, and Dowty predicts, therefore, that this sector should readily incorporate the highly charged and relatively small Al, Ti and Fe^{3+} ions.

The recent investigation into trace-element distribution in a sector-zoned augite carried out by ion probe analysis (Shimizu, 1981) supports the Dowty model for the origin of sector zoning. His investigation shows that the $\{100\}$ prism sector is enriched in incompatible elements relative to the basal sector. This does not support the model proposed by Duncan and Preston (1980) that the sector zoning is a result of the interaction between the rates of crystal growth and ionic diffusion in the melt which one would expect to lead to enrichment of incompatible elements in the rapidly growing basal sector. From the above discussion it is evident that many processes can operate to promote disequilibrium during crystal growth. Consequently, therefore, as discussed by Dowty (1976), it is important to be careful in using element-partitioning in minerals to indicate the physical conditions prevalent during crystal growth.

Dolfi and Trigila (1983) have carried out an interesting experimental investigation into the influence of water content in magma on the solid solution composition of crystallising clinopyroxenes. This experimental work was undertaken on a finely powdered sample of lava from the 1971 eruption of Etna at a pressure of 2 kbar, temperatures 970 – 1200° C and with water contents ranging between 0.1% and 2.8% $(H_2O)^{liq}$. This investigation showed a relation between the clinopyroxene composition and the water content of the melt. By coupling the correlation with the pressure-dependence of clinopyroxene composition, Dolfi and Trigila established a simple relation enabling the calculation of the amount of dissolved water in the melt of clinopyroxene- and plagioclase-bearing magma at known pressures in the crustal range. Bearing in mind the simplifications required by experimental investigations and assuming crystallization at 2 kbar, the relationship of Dolfi and Trigila, applied to the analytical data of Duncan and Preston (1980), suggests a dissolved water content of about 1% $(H_2O)^{liq}$ for the hawaiite magmas of Etna.

(c) Olivines

Olivine is present as phenocrysts or microphenocrysts in most of the lavas of the alkalic series. While the hawaiite lavas contain up to 5% by volume of olivine phenocrysts and have olivine in the groundmass, the more-evolved members of the series have less phenocrystic olivine and none in the groundmass. The composition of olivine crystallizing in basaltic melts is particularly sensitive to the Fe^{2+}/Mg ratio of the melt (Roeder and Emslie, 1970) and this is clearly reflected in the chemistry of the olivines of the alkalic series. The olivine phenocrysts in the hawaiites show normal zoning, ranging from Fo_{85} in the core to Fo_{70} in the rim, with groundmass compositions down to Fo_{60}. In the mugearites the olivine phenocrysts have compositions between Fo_{76-71} and in the benmoreities Fo_{70-60} (Duncan, 1976b). The olivine phenocrysts in the benmoreite lava sheets within the volcanic domes near Biancavilla show strong alteration with development of iddingsite, serpentine minerals and titanomagnetite; in some cases this alteration has gone to completion with titanomagnetic pseudomorphing after olivine. This alteration, however, is considered to be due to post-eruption fumarolic activity occurring within the domes, as lavas of similar composition which were erupted from the domes contain unaltered olivine.

(d) Kaersutite

Kaersutite amphibole occurs as phenocrysts in some of the lavas of the alkalic series, in particular the basic mugearites and mugearites of the pyroclastic sequence and the lower lava group of the Trifoglietto II centre (Klerkx, 1968; McGuire, 1982), in the lower tephra to the west of Giarre (Guest *et al.*, 1984), and occasionally in lavas of the other prehistoric centres (Cristofolini and Lo Giudice, 1969). Analytical data on these kaersutite phenocrysts are reported in Klerkx (1964), Cristofolini and Lo Giudice (1969) and Tanguy (1978). The kaersutite phenocrysts in these lavas typically show evidence of resorption with rounded outlines and also reaction relationships with the development of rims of titanomagnetite, and in some cases the kaersutite is totally pseudomorphed by titanomagnetite.

Information from experimental and field investigations (Holloway and Burnham, 1972; Cawthorn and O'Hara, 1976) suggests that kaersutite crystallizes from relatively hydrous basaltic magma. Kaersutite occurs in the pyroclastic sequence and the lower lava group of the Trifoglietto II centre, but is only rarely found in the more effusive middle and upper lava groups (McGuire, 1982) suggesting an association between kaersutite and the early volatile-rich explosive phase of activity of the Trifoglietto volcano. The resorbed and altered nature of the kaersutite phenocrysts indicates that they were not in equilibrium with the magma prior to eruption; indeed in one sample from the lower tephra a kaersutite crystal is mantled by euhedral augite. Kaersutite has generally been considered to be a high-pressure mineral (Green *et al.*, 1974) and its disequilibrium in the Etnean lavas may be due to instability at low pressures. Arculus and Wills (1980) consider that the low-pressure instability of amphibole in basaltic liquids is well illustrated in the mineralogy of lavas and associated plutonic nodules from the Lesser Antilles Arc, and that the preservation of amphibole in dacites and andesites is due to slower reaction rates or alternatively more rapid ascent from depth. Baxter (1978), however, demonstrates that kaersutite in alkali basalts and hawaiites from Mauritius is likely to have crystallized at the relatively low pressures of 1.5–3 kbar, equivalent to 5–10 km depth, with P_{H_2O} being (0.5–1.0) P_{total}. On the other hand, the disequilibrium in the Etnean kaersutites may be due to the reduction in P_{H_2O} of the magma at high levels in the conduit through progressive loss of volatiles by volcanic gaseous discharge. The kaersutite phenocrysts in the lavas are almost invariably rimmed with titanomagnetite, whereas the kaersutite crystals in the lower tephra, though showing signs of resorption, show no signs of alteration. This indicates that the alteration to titanomagnetite is likely to be a post-eruption process involving oxidation of the kaersutite in the more-slowly cooling lavas.

(e) Other minerals

Apatite is present in most of the lavas of the alkalic series (Klerkx, 1966; Downes, 1973), but is most abundant as microphenocrysts in the mugearites and benmoreites (Duncan, 1978). The crystallization of apatite in Etnean lavas has been studied in some detail by Klerkx (1966), with special reference to the lavas of the Trifoglietto II centre. Apatite microphenocrysts up to 0.2 mm long are relatively common in lavas with more than 54% (w/w) silica, i.e. the mugearites and benmoreites. The crystallization of apatite reflects a higher concentration of phosphorus pentoxide in the mugearites (0.8% (w/w)) relative to the hawaiites (0.6% (w/w)). These apatite phenocrysts show a distinctive brown pseudopleochroism caused by the inclusion of minute rods of titanomagnetite or hematite parallel to the *c*-axis (Klerkx, 1966). Where the apatite crystals are included in phenocrysts they do not contain the opaque inclusions. Indeed, in one sample where an apatite crystal is partly enclosed by an augite phenocryst, the part which is enclosed in the phenocryst is colourless whereas where it sticks out into the groundmass it shows the brown pseudopleochroism. This suggests that the inclusion of the iron oxide rods within the apatite occurs after crystal growth by late-stage reaction with the melt or groundmass involving diffusion of iron into the crystal (Duncan, 1976b). The occurrence of similar brown pseudopleochroic apatites has also been recorded in mugearites from Hawaii (Macdonald, 1968) and Gough Island (Le Maitre, 1962).

The opaque phase in the lavas of the alkalic series is titanomagnetite which occurs as microphenocrysts, inclusions in olivine and pyroxene phenocrysts and as granules in the groundmass. This suggests that the f_{O_2} must have been high enough to stabilize titanomagnetite at an early stage in the crystallization sequence of the magma. This may be the result of the relatively high P_{H_2O} of Etnean magma with dissociation of water, $2H_2O = 2H_2 + O_2$ (Hamilton and Anderson, 1967), giving rise to increased f_{O_2}. Microprobe analysis of titanomagnetites in Etnean hawaiites shows them to be relatively rich in components other than iron and titanium, with up to 5.5% (w/w) MgO and 6% (w/w) Al_2O_3. Ilmenite has not been detected in these lavas and it is not possible, therefore, to determine the f_{O_2} using the Buddington and Lindsley (1964) geothermometer.

Alkali feldspar and nepheline have been recorded in the groundmass of Etnean lavas (Cristofolini and Lo Giudice 1969; Tanguy, 1973; and Puglisi and Tranchina 1977) using XRD techniques. In addition Di Sabatino (1977) has detected groundmass leucite. Biotite has been recorded in some mugearites and benmoreites

(Kieffer, 1974b; Duncan, 1976b and McGuire, 1980) and is considered to be a late-stage magmatic or hydrothermal mineral. Bellia *et al.* (1980) have described the presence of orthopyroxene crystals in a lava erupted from the Monte Moio eccentric cone on the northern periphery of Etna, but the petrogenetic significance of the occurrence of this orthopyroxene has not yet been assessed.

6.4.2 *Geochemistry and petrogenesis*

The geochemistry of the lavas of the alkalic series shows continuous variation from hawaiite through mugearite to benmoreite (representative analyses are given in Table 6.1). It is considered that the series represents a broadly co-magmatic suite generated by differentiation from parental magmas of similar composition. The different trends recognized within the series reflects the operation of different physico-chemical processes during the ascent of the magma. It should be noted, however, that the differences in strontium isotope ratios determined by Carter and Civetta (1977) indicates that some of the magmas were derived from separate source areas in a heterogeneous mantle.

The chemical variation of the series is represented on Harker variation diagrams (Fig. 6.18). Though MgO would be a better index of differentiation for the more basic lavas, SiO_2 shows a greater range across the suite as a whole. Differentiation indices, such as the Thornton and Tuttle Index, the Larsen Factor and the Mafic Index, all combine data and this reduces their discrimination (Wright, 1974).

In many oceanic and continental alkali basalt volcanoes there is an apparent scarcity of products of intermediate composition (52 – 57% (w/w) SiO_2), commonly referred to as the Daly Gap. Chayes (1963, 1977) considers this gap to be of considerable petrological importance suggesting that there is not a continual evolution from basalt to trachyte by fractional crystallization. Other workers, in contrast, feel that the Daly Gap is more apparent than real and reflects either a sampling bias (Baker, 1968) or a discrimination in eruptive processes (Le Maitre, 1968; Gass and Mallick, 1968). A glance at Chayes (1977) will clearly demonstrate that this is an issue where feelings run high! On Etna there is no evidence of a Daly Gap (Fig. 6.18), though it must be admitted that it is very difficult to establish volumetric relationships between different rock types on an active volcano with a high rate of resurfacing. An areal sampling survey of Etna would merely reflect the composition of recently erupted lavas which are relatively uniform in composition and cover a large proportion of the surface area of the volcano. A survey of published analyses would show a clear bias reflecting interest in historic eruptive activity. The individual workers involved in producing the new geological map (Romano *et al.*, 1979) collected systematically and have come up with no evidence to support a scarcity of intermediate products relative to the benmoreites.

Though the chemical variation of the alkalic series is broadly similar to other mildly alkaline suites such as Gough Island (Le Maitre, 1962) and the Skye main lava series (Thompson *et al.*, 1972), there are some important differences. In comparison with Hawaii, the Etna series is lower in alkalis but richer in CaO and Al_2O_3, and shows a markedly different pattern of variation in TiO_2 (Cristofolini, 1973; Duncan, 1978). The alkalic series of Etna plots between the sodic trend of the Skye lavas and the potassic trend of the Gough volcanics. The alkalic series shows strong enrichment in LREE relative to the basal tholeiitic volcanics (Fig. 6.19), with values equivalent to those of Gough Island but on average showing greater concentrations than similar rocks from Hawaii and Reunion Island (Cristofolini *et al.*, 1981).

In terms of normative chemistry, the alkalic series, even after correction for oxidation of iron, shows a somewhat unusual trend ranging from nepheline-normative in the hawaiites through to hypersthene- and quartz-normative in the mugearites and benmoreites (Duncan, 1978). This trend appears to breach the low-pressure thermal divide of Yoder and Tilley (1962). Much experimental work has been undertaken over the last twenty years on the $CaO – MgO – Al_2O_3 – SiO_2$ system to provide information on basalt crystallization trends. Yoder and Tilley (1962) demonstrated that

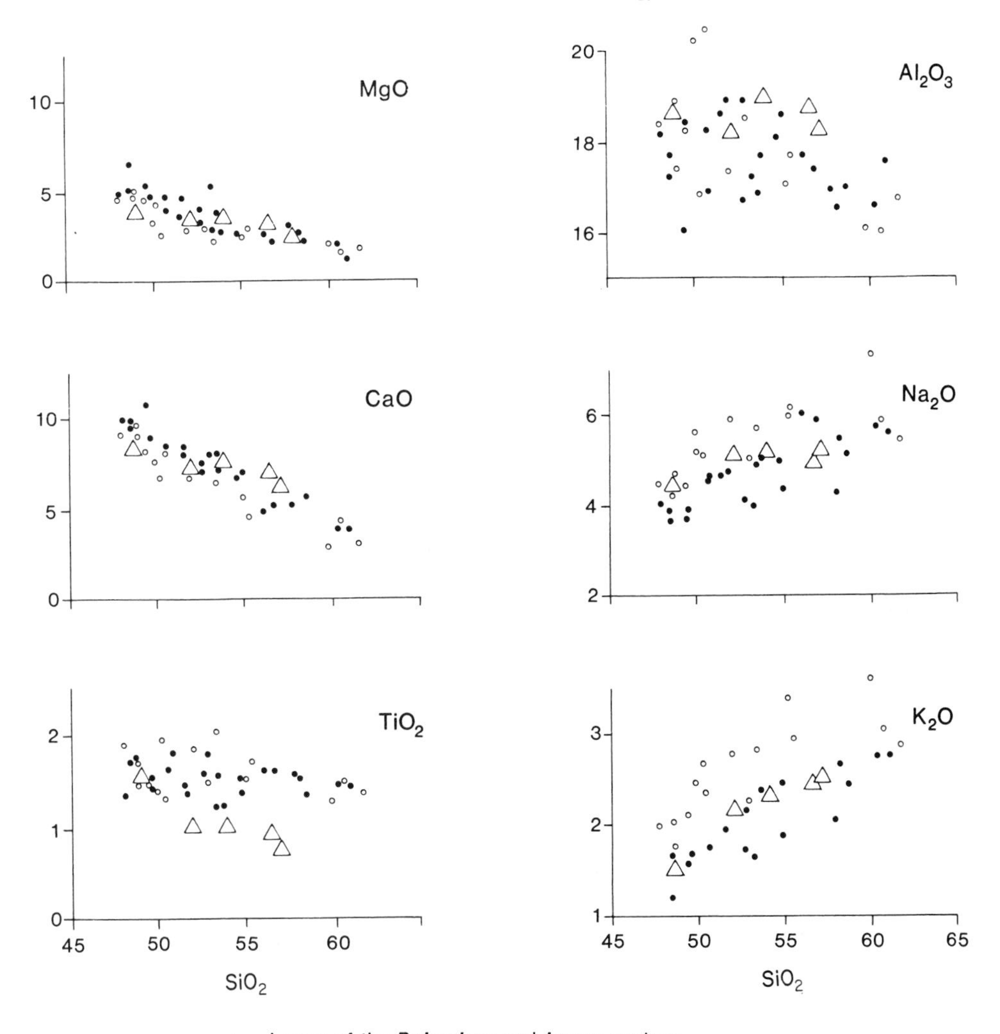

Fig. 6.18 Major-element variation diagrams for the different trends of the alkalic series (in % by weight). Analytical data from Cristofolini and Lo Giudice (1969), Duncan (1978), Lo Giudice (1971), Lo Giudice *et al.* (1974), McGuire (1980) and Romano and Guest (1979).

the Di – Fo – Ab plane is an equilibrium thermal divide at low pressures and considered that this is represented by the Cpx – Ol – Plag join in the generalized basalt tetrahedron. In point of fact the thermal divide may only approximate to the Di – Fo – An join as the effects of solid solution would cause the compositions of diopside, forsterite and anorthite to lie off the plane (Presnall *et al.*, 1978). O'Hara (1968) also recognized from experimental studies that at low pressures a thermal divide exists between tholeiitic and alkali basalts but his data suggest that this thermal divide is inoperative at pressures greater than 8 kbar. More recently, Presnall *et al.* (1978) have provided evidence based

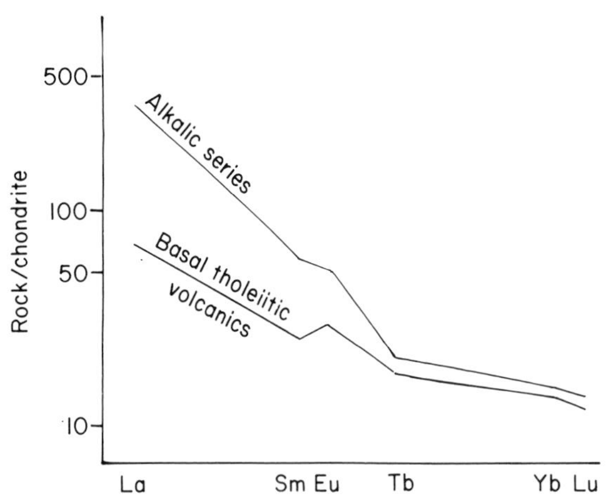

Fig. 6.19 Chondrite-normalized REE patterns of alkalic series (average of twelve analyses) and basal tholeiitic volcanics (average of ten analyses) based on one basaltic sample for each series. (After Cristofolini *et al.*, 1981.)

on a study of the liquidus phase relations on the Di–Fo–An join that the thermal divide may be inoperative above pressures as low as 4 kbar.

Miyashiro (1978), in a review of alkalic volcanic series, identifies three types of trend which contain 'alkalic' hypersthene-normative basalts.

Firstly, the *Coombs trend* covers hypersthene-normative basalts through to comendites and pantellerites (Coombs, 1963). The alkalic rocks of Bouvet, Ascension and Easter Islands and the continental volcanics of Nandewar, Australia, belong to this trend.

Secondly, alkalic volcanic series of the *straddle type* whose compositions lie across the position of the low-pressure thermal divide. The Skye main lava series (Thompson *et al.*, 1972) and the alkalic rocks of Terceira, Azores (Self and Gunn, 1976) display this type of association. In both cases the respective authors argue that high-pressure processes (at about 10 kbar), possibly involving variable degrees of partial melting, generated magmas with compositions astride the position of the low-pressure thermal divide. As the magmas ascended they underwent fractional crystallization at lower pressures where the low pressure thermal divide would be operative giving rise to contrasting undersaturated and oversaturated trends.

Thirdly, Miyashiro (1978) tentatively suggests a further type of straddle association, the *straddle-B type*, where the normative nepheline decreases with differentiation and the composition passes through the thermal divide becoming hypersthene- and quartz-normative. The alkalic series of Etna shows a straddle-B type association (Fig. 6.20). The differentiation of the magma of the alkalic series from hawaiite to benmoreite is considered to have taken place at moderate-to-low pressures, less than 5 kbar (Duncan, 1978; Cristofolini and Romano, 1982), where the thermal divide in the $CaO - MgO - Al_2O_3 - SiO_2$ system is likely to have been operative. One way to breach the thermal divide would be to fractionate an undersaturated phase not represented in the generalized basalt tetrahedron and thus drive the liquid through to oversaturated compositions. Cawthorn *et al.* (1973) explain the trend from nepheline-normative basanitoids and alkali basalts through to quartz-normative dacites in the calc-alkaline suite of Grenada in terms of fractional crystallization of undersaturated amphibole under hydrous conditions. On Etna, in the alkalic series there is petrographic evidence that titanomagnetite is a relatively early-crystallizing phase and fractionation of this, together with volatile loss of sodium in the open volcanic system, might account for the oversaturated nature of the trend. Romano (1970), Cristofolini (1973) and Rittmann (1974) have stressed the likely importance of vapour-phase fractionation of the alkalis in Etnean magmas.

The chemical variation of the alkalic series is largely controlled by moderate-to-low-pressure fractional crystallization of phases which are present as phenocrysts in the lavas (Lo Giudice, 1971; Cristofolini, 1973 and Duncan, 1978). Tanguy (1978) proposes a somewhat complex model involving differentiation from an olivine tholeiite basalt parental magma, but for the reasons already discussed this is considered unlikely. In the trace-element variation diagrams (Fig. 6.21) it can be seen that there is a kink in the trend for most elements around 52% (w/w) SiO_2. This change in the trend is considered to reflect a two-stage fractionation process. The first stage involves

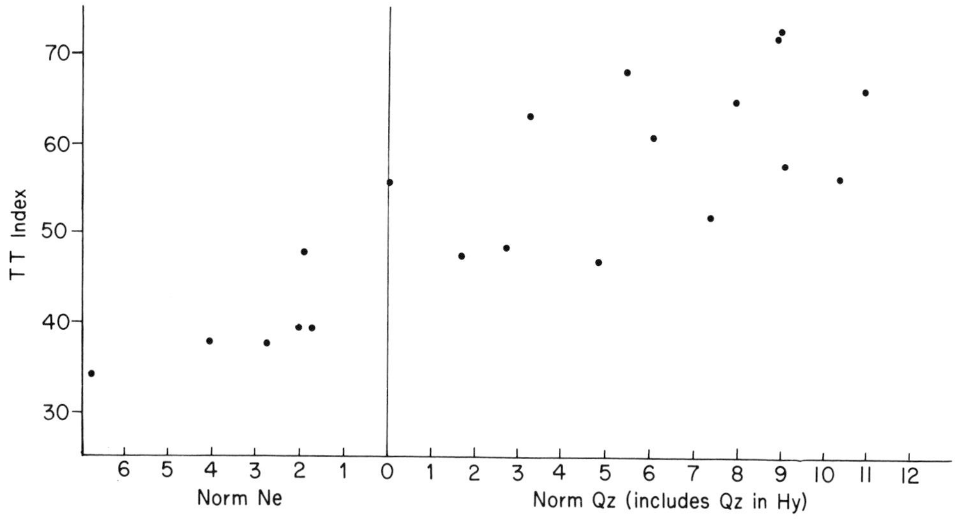

Fig. 6.20 Normative Ne or Qz plotted against the Thornton – Tuttle Differentiation Index (TT Index) for lavas of the alkalic series showing the straddle association across the position of the low-pressure thermal divide. (Analytical data from Duncan, (1976b).)

fractionation of predominantly mafic minerals which gives rise to the rapid depletion of magnesium oxide, nickel, chromium and cobalt from hawaiite to basic mugearite. The second stage requires fractionation of a plagioclase-rich extract to account for the decrease in strontium between basic mugearite and benmoreite. This is further supported by the MgO vs. Ni plot (Fig. 6.22) where it can be seen that the more basic lavas (MgO > 4% (w/w)) show good correlation with an olivine (+ clinopyroxene (?)) control line, while the more siliceous lavas show no such correlation. The CaO vs. MgO plot (Fig. 6.23) shows the chemical variation of the more siliceous lavas most effectively relative to the phenocryst compositions. These lavas (MgO < 4% (w/w)) show a trend projecting to intersect the augite – plagioclase tie line at approximately 60% plagioclase, 40% augite. This suggests that for the hawaiites the fractionation is largely controlled by olivine and augite whereas for the more siliceous lavas plagioclase and augite are the dominant phases (Duncan, 1978).

To test the feasibility of this fractionation model for the trachybasaltic volcanics (the alkalic series) of the Adrano area of Etna, Duncan (1978) determined whether it was possible to simulate the chemical variation of the lavas with a two-stage fractionation model involving removal of olivine, augite, plagioclase and titanomagnetite from a parental basic hawaiite melt. This was carried out using the graphical addition – subtraction technique after Bowen (1928). It was found that the chemical variation could be broadly accounted for by a first stage of fractionation of about 53% by weight of an extract of 53% augite, 26% plagioclase, 18% olivine and 3% titanomagnetite generating a residual liquid of basic mugearite composition. In the second-stage fractionation of 65% by weight of an extract of 70% plagioclase, 24% augite, 4% olivine and 2% titanomagnetite would give rise to a residual melt of benmoreite composition. Though relatively crude, this method of calculation nevertheless can demonstrate that the chemical variation of most of the major elements may be accounted for by fractionation of minerals present as phenocryst phases. The variation in the alkalis, on the other hand, cannot be solely explained by this simple model of crystal fractionation and, as suggested by Duncan (1978), vapour-phase fractionation may have allowed alkalis to escape from magma in the conduit as a volatile phase.

Lo Giudice (1971) in a study of the petrology of the lavas of the Vavalaci centre also demonstrates,

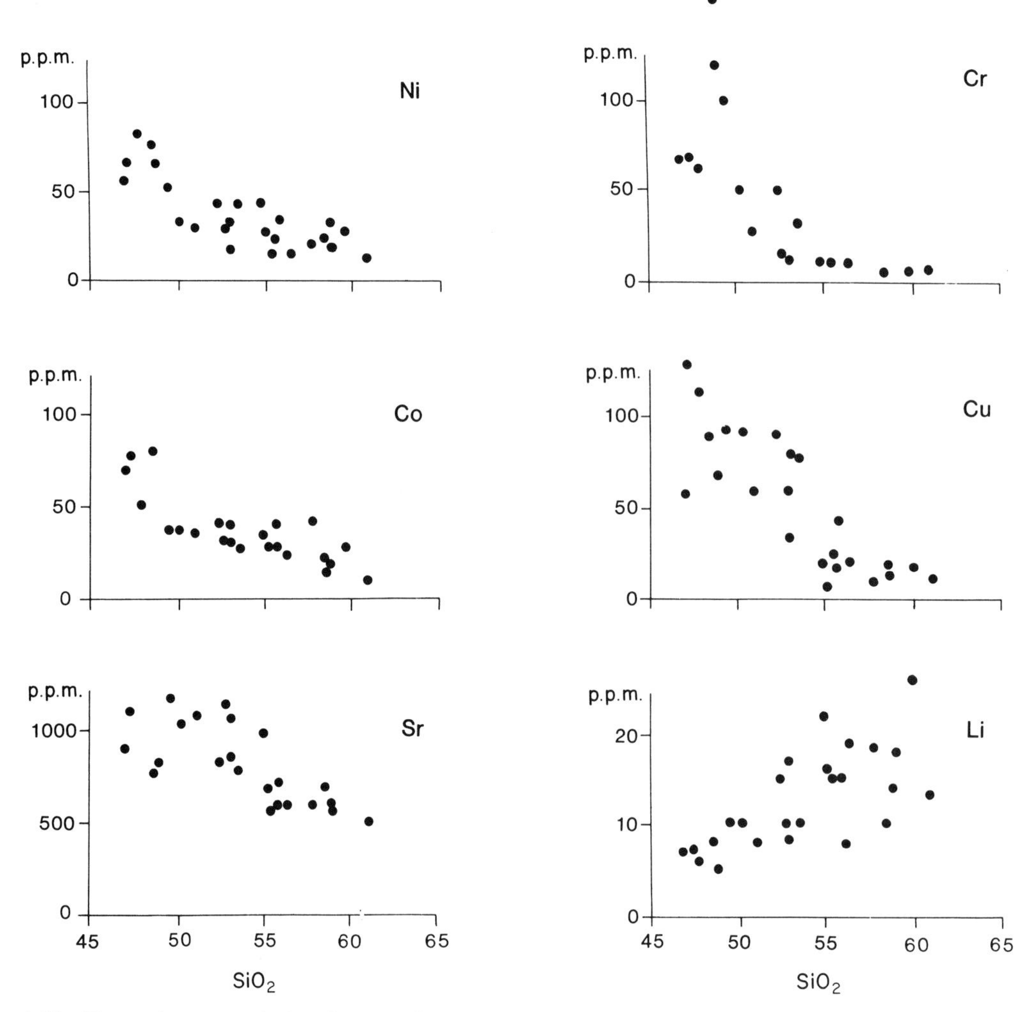

Fig. 6.21 Trace-element variation diagrams for lavas of the alkalic series. All samples are from the Adrano area and belong to the Normal alkalic trend. Trace-element concentrations expressed in p.p.m. (After Duncan, 1978.)

using the computation method of Bryan *et al.* (1969), that the chemical variation can be largely accounted for in terms of low-pressure fractionation of the minerals present as phenocryst phases. On the basis of the variation in nickel and thorium for the alkalic series, Condomines *et al.* (1982) propose that the chemical variation can be explained by initial crystallization dominated by olivine followed by fractionation of predominantly plagioclase and pyroxene.

The moderate-to-low-pressure fractionation model for the generation of the mugearites and benmoreities requires a rather different plumbing system from that which has operated in historic times. Guest and Duncan (1981) argue that over at least the last 200 years there has been little high-level storage of magma (see Chapter 7). Tanguy and Kieffer (1976 – 77) suggest that in historic times flank eruptions have been fed by magma that rises from depth and undergoes limited storage in a system of vertical dykes, which they envisage as active intrusions, located at the intersection of regional faults. It was proposed by Rittmann (1973) that extensive differentiation of magma

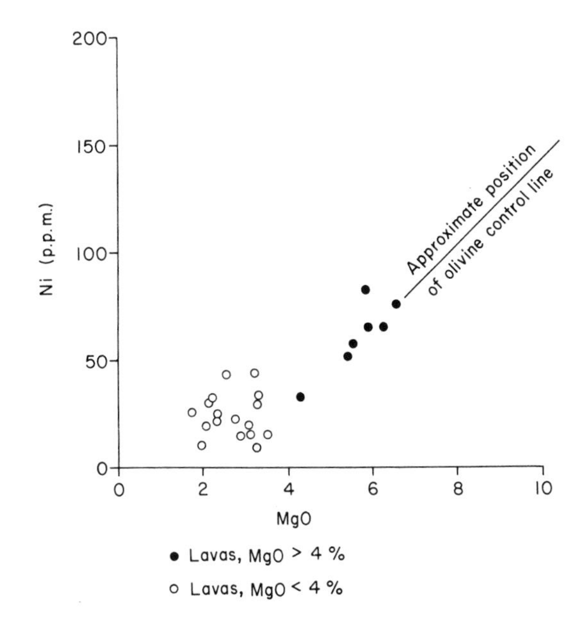

Fig. 6.22 Ni plotted against MgO for lavas of the alkalic series showing the approximate position of the olivine control line. (After Duncan, 1976b.)

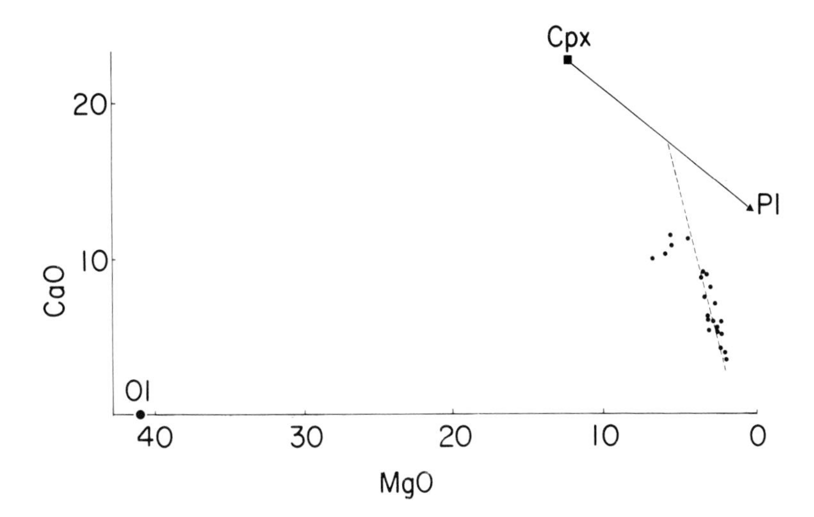

Fig. 6.23 CaO plotted against MgO for lavas of the alkalic series from the Adrano area (dots). The composition of olivine, clinopyroxene and plagioclase phenocrysts and the projection of the compositional trend for lavas with MgO<4%(w/w) are shown on the diagram. (After Duncan, 1978.)

could occur within the abyssal fissures when the upper part of the feeder dyke was closed. But Guest and Duncan (1981) consider that only a little differentiation occurs within these dyke systems and this is supported by the limited chemical variation during historic flank eruptions, as discussed towards the end of this chapter. It is likely that the moderate-to-low-pressure fractionation required to generate the more evolved magma compositions takes place in high-level magma reservoirs (Cristofolini, 1973; Condomines *et al.*, 1982; Duncan and Guest, 1982). The occurrence of high-level storage of magma in the past is supported by the presence of prehistoric calderas still recognizable on the upper slopes of Etna (Guest, 1980). For instance both the Vavalaci and Ellittico centres, some of whose lavas show evidence of being the products of extensive high-level fractionation, ended their activity with caldera collapse.

The petrogenesis of the alkali-rich and the low-titania trends has not yet been fully considered. The high alkali-content of the alkali-rich trend may be due to the fact that these lavas infilled calderas, presumably after a period of inactivity when magma would have been stored in the volcano under a closed system without loss of alkalis through vapour-phase fractionation. The low-titania trend is likely to be a result of fractionation of kaersutite, a titanium-rich amphibole, which is a common phenocryst phase in the lavas of this trend (Condomines *et al.*, 1982; McGuire, 1982).

In the preceding discussion on fractionation models a hawaiite composition, at the basic end of the alkalic series, has been taken as the parent magma. This parental hawaiite composition has an M'-value less than 0.58 and this makes it unlikely that it represents a primary composition (Duncan and Guest, 1982). Also, the Etnean hawaiites have nickel-contents less than 90 p.p.m. (Duncan, 1978) whereas Rhodes and Dungan (1977) suggest that magma resulting from a moderate degree of partial melting of mantle material should have nickel-contents of 200 – 300 p.p.m. The hawaiite parental magma of the alkalic series itself must be derived from a more primitive magma. Cristofolini and Romano (1982) and Duncan and Guest (1982) suggest that a lower crustal magma reservoir, possibly identified by the seismic survey of Sharp *et al.* (1980), acts as a site for the collection and differentiation of primary magma. On the basis of variation in the $^{230}Th/^{232}Th$ initial ratios of the alkalic series lavas and trace-element data, Condomines *et al.* (1982) consider that this deep-seated reservoir is the site of magma-mixing. They tentatively propose a relationship between changes in the $^{230}Th/^{232}Th$ initial ratios of the lavas and the formation of major calderas. However, the ages of these caldera events are not yet sufficiently well known for this correlation to be substantiated.

The differentiation of the primary magma or magmas in this deep reservoir is likely to involve crystallization of mafic minerals. The core compositions of some augite phenocrysts in hawaiite lavas from the Piedimonte area on the lower north-east flanks of Etna suggests that they equilibrated at pressures of nearly 5 kbar (Cristofolini *et al.*, 1982). Cristofolini *et al.* argue that these crystals have been derived from a cumulate mush which formed at depth within the crust and it may be that they represent accumulation from crystallization in a deep-seated reservoir. As more evolved hawaiite magma rises from the lower crustal reservoir, plagioclase becomes a progressively more important phenocryst phase. On the basis of the experimental studies of Knutson and Green (1975) on the crystallization of a hawaiitic liquid at different pressures and P_{H_2O} it is likely that crystallization of plagioclase in such liquids is suppressed to near-solidus temperatures at pressures approaching 5 kbar (Tanguy and Kieffer, 1976 – 77; Duncan and Guest, 1982). The hawaiite lava erupted in the 1974 flank eruption was atypical in that it contained no plagioclase phenocrysts, and Tanguy and Kieffer hold the view that this magma originated from 15–20 km depth, the position of the lower crustal reservoir. It may be, therefore, that this 1974 lava represents the nature of the parental magma generated by the deep crustal reservoir and does not show the effects of low-pressure crystallization shown by most of the historic lavas. For there to be extensive differentiation, however, significant high-level storage of magma must take place and this has not occurred in historic times. It is of interest that the lower crustal reservoir, which Sharp *et al.* (1980) interpreted as a framework of magma-filled fissures, coincides with the approximate depth of the brittle – ductile transition within the lithosphere beneath Etna suggested by Ghisetti and Vezzani (1982). The formation of a magma reservoir at this level, therefore, maybe a consequence of the ascending magma collecting at the base of the more rigid upper lithosphere.

6.5 Petrological variations in historic times

Petrological variations of Etnean lavas during the historic period can be considered on two scales. Firstly, petrological changes over the historic

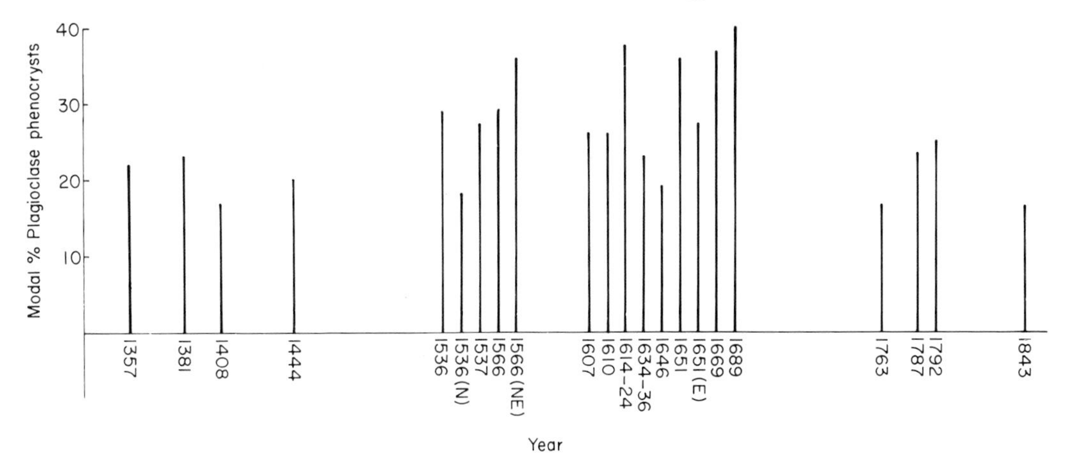

Fig. 6.24 Variation in the modal mineralogy of plagioclase phenocrysts in historic lavas between 1300 and 1850. Note that the sixteenth and seventeenth century lavas tend to have a high plagioclase phenocryst modal content. Indeed these lavas also tend to have fewer but larger plagioclase crystals than the other historic lavas.

period where there is a good knowledge of the eruptive record, and secondly, changes during actual eruptive episodes. The petrological information from both these lines of investigation integrated with volcanological and geophysical studies can provide a real contribution to the understanding of the magmatic processes operating in basaltic volcanoes.

As yet there is little information available on petrological variation in lavas over the historic period as a whole. Broadly speaking it appears that the magma has remained rather uniform in composition over this time, being hawaiitic in nature. Nevertheless some significant changes have been noted (Fig. 6.24). For instance, the lavas erupted in the seventeenth century, including the major eruption of 1669, are characterized by large plagioclase phenocrysts up to 4 mm in size giving rise to the distinctive *cicirara* texture. The presence of these large plagioclase phenocrysts indicates a rather different pre-eruption crystallization history for this magma than that of the subsequent magmas erupted after the seventeenth century which have lesser modal proportions of plagioclase phenocrysts with the larger plagioclase crystals being generally no greater than 2.5 mm. It may be that this *cicirara* texture results from storage of magma in a high-level crustal reservoir as has been suggested by Wadge (1977) to explain the volumetric relations of the 1669 eruption.

In the investigation of petrological changes during an eruptive event, to ensure good spatial and temporal control, it is necessary to collect the samples during the eruption. This was first undertaken during the 1971 eruption with somewhat contradictory results. Tanguy (1973) observed no significant variation in the petrology of the lavas of the 1971 eruption and was impressed by the uniformity of composition despite the duration and complexity of the eruption. On the other hand, Romano and Sturiale (1973) with a rather more extensive suite of samples did identify a slight change in magma composition during the eruption: the earliest lavas which were erupted at the highest altitude on the fissure were enriched in magnesia and pneumatolytic elements, such as sodium, titanium and iron, and depleted in silica relative to the later lavas erupted at lower altitudes. Romano and Sturiale explained this slight variation in terms of pre-eruption fractionation involving pneumatolytic differentiation in the upper parts of the conduit and fractional crystallization at deeper levels generating the more differentiated magma which fed the lower fissures. These preliminary studies, however, were hampered by lack of trace-element data and limitations in the sample suite. The investigation of small but significant changes in lava composition during an eruptive event as recognized by Romano and Sturiale in the 1971 eruption require a rigorous sampling programme and precise geochemical and petrographical analysis. Such an investigation of small changes in geochemistry and mineral composition of lavas was carried out by Scott (1983) for the March 1981 eruption.

The March 1981 eruption occurred on the northern slopes of the volcano with a radial fissure 7.5 km long opening on 17 March at 2600 m a.s.l. and migrating downslope to 1125 m a.s.l. where activity finished on 23 March (see Table 3.3). On the basis of geophysical evidence it is considered that the 1981 eruption drained a high-level radial dyke which was filled with magma in the late summer of 1980 (Sanderson, 1982a). The lavas are hawaiitic in composition and porphyritic in texture with phenocrysts of plagioclase, augite, olivine and minor titanomagnetite. The phenocryst content of the lavas increases steadily from around 25% to 32% with age and decreasing altitude of eruption (Scott, 1983). In their geochemistry, Scott shows that the early lavas are richer in alumina and strontium and poorer in ferric oxide (total), magnesia and calcium oxide compared to later and lower-altitude products. Since this was a short-lived, relatively high-effusion-rate eruption Scott argues that it preserves evidence of compositional variation within the magma storage body. He considers that the estimated seven-month residence time of the magma in the dyke was too short a period for the observed petrological variation to have developed through crystal-settling. Instead, Scott suggests that the variation can be best explained by different degrees of mixing of residual 1979 magma and fresh magma, of a similar composition to the early 1981 lava, during filling of the high-level dyke system in the late summer of 1980. Sanderson (1982b) measured significant decreases in gravity over the central and southern upper flanks of the volcano after the 1981 eruption and this is interpreted by Sanderson *et al.* (1983) as due to magma drainage from this region. Magma in such a storage area may have readily co-mingled with residual magma from the 1979 eruption stored beneath the South-east Crater and this lends support to Scott's model. However, some caution needs to be exercised as Sanderson (1982b), on the basis of inferred mass changes from direct gravimetric measurements, considers that the dykes which fed the August 1979 eruption were replenished from depth within three to nine months. A similar model involving magma mixing has been suggested by Fitton *et al.* (1983) to explain the chemical variation of the lavas of the 1982 eruption of Mount Cameroon, West Africa. Mount Cameroon is a basanite composite volcano which has erupted five times so far this century: 1909, 1922, 1954, 1959 and 1982. Fitton *et al.* have modelled the chemical variation of the 1982 lavas in terms of mixing a reservoir of magma close in composition to the 1959 lava with fresh magma slightly more basic than the last 1982 lava. This model of magma mixing is strongly supported by the strontium- and lead-isotopic variation of the lavas which cannot be explained in terms of a simple crystal fractionation process.

It is apparent from these preliminary studies that the integration of petrological data with geophysical and volcanological studies is obviously a crucial area of investigation which with careful interpretation can provide a valuable contribution to our understanding of magmatic processes.

6.6 Volcanic gases

The importance of volatiles in the petrogenesis of igneous rocks has been increasingly realised in recent years. Experimental studies have demonstrated the influence of volatiles in depressing liquidus and solidus temperatures in silicate systems, in controlling the crystallization sequence of silicate melts and more recently the role of carbon dioxide and water in affecting the composition of primary melts generated by partial melting of peridotite source materials. In a more direct way, even to the non-specialist, witnessing strombolian-type activity provides the observer with a spectacular introduction to magma-degassing with all senses: visual, aural and olfactory. Active volcanoes, such as Etna, provide an opportunity to sample magmatic gases directly.

There are three main ways to obtain information on volcanic gases (Anderson, 1975): (1) sampling

Fig. 6.25 French scientists collecting gases from the Bocca Nuova in 1969. (Photograph: J. E. Guest.)

of volcanic gases, (2) extraction of gases from lava rock and (3) the analysis of water from hot springs. Hot springs are probably dominated by heated groundwater and leached components and, therefore, provide little useful data on magmatic volatiles. Direct sampling of volcanic gases is the obvious approach but, unfortunately, it is generally a hazardous and technically difficult operation. This is clearly illustrated by the following statement of Tazieff (1970, p.5), regarding collection of gases from the North-east Crater: '. . . although the Bocca NE rim is sometimes accessible, our present-day protection suits do not allow us to stay there long enough, nor in a sufficiently relaxed state of mind to carry out accurate measurements.' (See Fig. 6.25.) In collecting the gas it is necessary to quench the gas sufficiently rapidly that the composition does not change fundamentally from that at magmatic temperatures. Otherwise, there is likely to be a change in the molecular gas composition with re-equilibration to different conditions. Contamination by atmospheric gases is another major problem, though this can be corrected for by subtracting nitrogen, argon and oxygen in atmospheric proportions (Nordlie, 1971). In addition, the composition of the gases are liable to change during the course of eruptions and are also very likely to vary depending on where they are collected relative to the active vent. Gases collected from fumaroles with temperatures substantially lower than that of the magma will have at least partly re-equilibrated and are likely to have reacted with the volcanic rocks through which they have passed. Extraction of gases by vacuum heating or crushing of lava samples can provide useful information, though the more insoluble volatile species may have been largely lost prior to solidification and care must be

Fig. 6.26 Tom Huntingdon collecting gases from a fissure in a crusted-over lava bocca at the base of the 1974 flank eruption cinder cone. (Photograph: A. M. Duncan.)

taken to avoid weathered or chemically altered specimens. A further line of investigation is the study of sublimates; the relationship between sublimates and associated lavas and volcanic gases is important in the understanding of near surface magmatic transport processes (Huntingdon, 1975). From this brief introduction it is clear that there are many problems in attempting to determine the volatile composition of a magma.

With its almost continual activity and accessible eruptions, Mount Etna would appear to be an excellent site for the investigation of the variation in the composition of volcanic gases during different styles of activity. Unfortunately, however, there has not been a sustained study of the volatile activity of Etna. The first real study of Etnean gases was carried out by a French team under the direction of Professor Tazieff, sampling gas emission from the Bocca Nuova in 1969 (Tazieff, 1970). This early work showed that when contamination was low it was evident that carbon dioxide was an important volcanic volatile constituent. Current knowledge on the composition of Etnean gases is largely based on the research carried out by Tom Huntingdon in the early 1970s (Huntingdon, 1973, 1975 and 1977). Huntingdon (1973) collected gases during the persistent activity near the North-east Crater in 1970 and, in the following year, at different vents at different phases during the 1971 eruption. The gases were collected at temperatures close to those of the active lava, around 1000°C, using the technique illustrated in Fig. 6.26. Adjusted analytical data of gases from Etna (in 1970), Kilauea (in 1918) and Erta' Ale are shown in Table 6.3. It can be seen that H_2O, SO_2 and CO_2 are the dominant species and that the gas

Table 6.3 Adjusted volcanic gas analyses from Kilauea, Erta'Ale and Etna. The analyses have been adjusted using numerical procedures based on thermodynamic calculations to restore the probable compositions of the erupted gases correcting for the effects of contamination and disequilibrium (Gerlach, 1979). This table is adapted from Table 1.3.5.1. of the *Basaltic volcanism of the terrestrial planets* (Basaltic Volcanism Study Project, 1981)

Volcano	*Volcanic gas compositions* (mole %)							
	H_2O	H_2	CO_2	CO	SO_2	S_2	H_2S	HCl
Kilauea								
1918 (1200°C)	52.30	0.79	30.87	1.00	14.95	0.12	1.03	0.14
Erta'Ale								
1971 (1075°C)	69.56	1.57	17.80	0.78	8.78	0.51	0.95	–
1974 (1125°C)	78.18	1.60	11.11	0.50	7.04	0.26	0.87	0.42
Etna								
1970	49.14	0.53	23.41	0.49	25.94	0.25	0.21	–

from Etna is richer in sulphur dioxide and poorer in carbon dioxide than the gas from Hawaii. The variation in the composition of the 1971 gases shows no obvious relation to time of collection, location of vent or altitude (Huntingdon, 1973); however, Huntingdon notes that the 1971 gases are lower in sulphur than the 1970 gases. Le Guern (1973) also recognized that the concentration of sulphur dioxide in gas collected during the 1971 eruption was much lower than that of gases collected in 1970. The compositions of the 1970 and 1971 gases, which Huntingdon (1973) recalculated to atomic proportions to eliminate the problems of disequilibrium, are illustrated in Fig. 6.27. Analysis of gases extracted from lava samples by Price (1980) confirms the lower concentration of sulphur in the 1971 gases relative to 1970, and Price suggests that this may be due to the more explosive nature of the 1971 eruption with, as has been proposed by Swanson and Fabbi (1973), increased violence of eruption being associated with volatile loss.

During the 1974 flank eruption (Guest *et al.*, 1974), Huntingdon was able to collect gas from a rather different eruptive environment. The sample was collected from a gas jet in a fracture in crusted lava at a small vent, situated at the base of the active cinder cone, which was feeding a small lava flow. The temperature of the gas was 1046°C and incandescent material could be seen in the crack just below the surface. Analysis of this gas by Hunting-

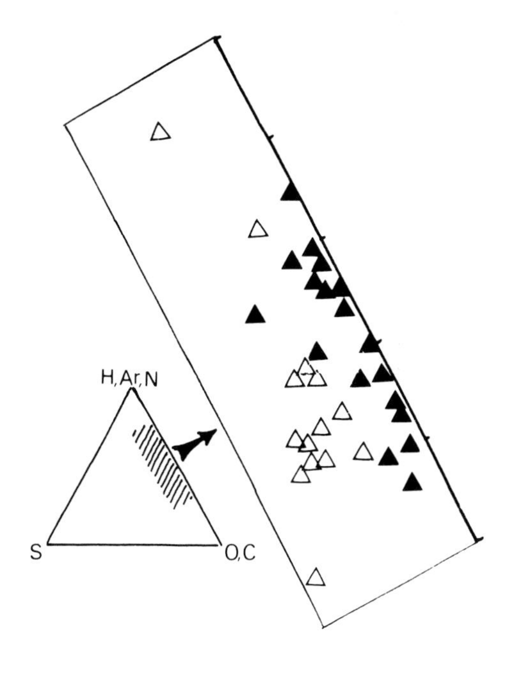

Fig. 6.27 Plot of analyses of 1970 and 1971 gases in terms of the percentage number of atoms. (After Huntingdon, 1973.)

don (1975) showed it to be very low in sulphur dioxide, about 0.01% (w/w), and Huntingdon suggests that this is due to the less soluble gases largely being discharged through the crater of the cinder cone with relatively degassed lava issuing from the foot of the cone. Huntingdon stresses that this has important implications regarding the collection of gases in that if separation of phases occurs at eruption this may give rise to misleading proportions for the molecular and atomic species in the magmatic volatiles.

Sato and Moore (1973) measured the oxygen and sulphur fugacities of magmatic gases from a series of hornitos close to the North-east Crater in 1970 using a solid-state electrolyte sensor probe. The gases ranged in temperature from 773 to 1057°C and a least squares fit of thirteen values yielded the relation:

$$\log f_{O_2} = 2.175 - 15110/\theta$$

where f_{O_2} is the oxygen fugacity in atmospheres and θ is the absolute temperature.

The Etnean values are about 0.9–2.2 log f_{O_2} units higher, within the temperature range measured, than values obtained in drill holes in the Makaopuhi lava lake (Sato and Wright, 1966). Gerlach (1979) restored the 1970 gas analysis for Etna at 1075°C and a f_{O_2} of $10^{-9.47}$ atmospheres and calculated an f_{O_2} range of $10^{+2.08}$ to $10^{+2.82}$ atmospheres at 860°C. Sato and Moore (1973) measured the f_{S_2} for 1970 Etna gases at $10^{-2.4}$ atmosphere for 860°C.

The study of sublimates and associated lavas can provide valuable information on the mobility of certain elements in a near surface magmatic environment. Between 1970 and 1976 Huntingdon (1977) collected and analysed ten pairs of sublimate and associated lava. Though the work was very preliminary in nature it demonstrated that sodium, potassium, zinc, rubidium, lead, copper and chlorine are relatively mobile and were enriched in the sublimates whereas silicon, calcium, iron, magnesium, aluminium and strontium were depleted relative to their concentration in the lavas. Le Guern and Bernard (1982) analysed sublimates collected in a silica tube from gas escaping from the surface of an active lava flow in 1976. They showed that at the high-temperature part of the tube (300 – 860°C) sulphates of sodium, potassium and iron were deposited; in the low-temperature region (below 200°C) sodium chloride, potassium chloride, calcium fluoride and chlorides of copper, nickel and zinc were deposited.

Price and Bailey (1980) analysed the gases extracted from plagioclase phenocrysts in lava erupted from the North-east crater in 1975. The plagioclase phenocrysts contained numerous inclusions of glass which often included vapour bubbles. The gases were extracted by vacuum heating and analysed by mass spectrometry. The gas extracted from the plagioclases is much richer in carbon dioxide than gas extracted from the whole-rock sample and Price and Bailey consider that this suggests that the magmatic gases at the time of crystallization of the plagioclase phenocrysts were much richer in carbon dioxide than at the time of quenching. This is to be expected as the lava melt will become strongly depleted in the more insoluble gases, such as carbon dioxide, relative to the more soluble gases, such as water vapour, on eruption, with the development of a separate vapour phase.

A recent development in the study of volcanic gases is the spectroscopic analysis of the plumes of active volcanoes. Remote sensing of the SO_2 concentration of the plume of Etna was carried out in 1975 by Haulet *et al* (1977) using a remote-sensing correlation spectrometer measuring absorption in the 3100 Å region. Measurements were made by driving along the Messina to Catania motorway at constant speed beneath the plume. The response of the spectrometer is directly proportional to the mean SO_2 concentration multiplied by the thickness of the plume. The volcano at that time was showing persistent activity with gentle effusion of degassed lava at a high altitude on the north flank of the volcano. The measurements of Haulet *et al.* (1977) provided a mean sulphur dioxide discharge rate of 3740 t d^{-1}. This measured output of sulphur dioxide from Etna is much greater than values determined by similar methods for volcanoes in Guatemala and Nicaragua, which discharge less than 400 t d^{-1} (Stoiber and Jepson, 1973). The solubility of sulphur in basaltic magma is strongly pressure-dependent; on the basis of experimental studies of the solubility of sulphur in $CaMgSi_2O_6$ and $NaAlSi_3O_8$ melts at high temperatures and pressures, Mysen and Popp (1980) consider that primary basaltic melts at 20 kbar may contain 1 – 1.5%(w/w) sulphur. On ascent, rapid decrease in pressure, and therefore solubility, may cause an immiscible sulphide melt to form and, because of its density relative to silicate melts, this is likely to undergo gravity settling. In the low-pressure eruptive environment, Anderson (1975) considers that basaltic magmas may contain up to 0.16%(w/w) sulphur. Degassing of the erupted lava could not account for the volume of sulphur dioxide discharged by Etna during the period of monitoring in 1975 (up to 3% (w/w) SO_2 of the mass of erupted magma; Wadge and Guest, 1981). Haulet *et al.* (1977) suggest that this discrepancy could be accounted for by degassing of a much greater mass of magma within the volcano plumbing system of which only a small proportion was erupted. From a study of Pacaya volcano in Guatemala, Stoiber and Jepson (1973) estimate that 80% of the discharge of sulphur dioxide was derived from 'intruded' magma that was not erupted. A similar relationship has been suggested for the discharge of carbon dioxide by Kilauea, the output of carbon dioxide is much greater than can be accounted for by degassing of the erupted volume of lava (Anderson, 1975). It seems apparent that volcanoes can act as a site for degassing of much larger volumes of mantle-derived material than are actually involved in the eruptive activity.

Carbonelle *et al.* (1982) quote a discharge rate for the volcanic plume of Etna of more than 11×10^6 t yr^{-1} carbon dioxide, measured in May 1977 using remote-sensing techniques. Their measurements, however, show that the CO_2-baseline in the ambient air on the slopes of the volcano was consistently more than the normal atmospheric background. They suggest that gaseous emanations from deep volcanic soil is significant and needs to be added to the measurements of discharge by the volcanic plume to give the total CO_2-flux of the volcanic pile.

In 1977 Malinconico (1979) monitored the variation in discharge from Etna using remote-sensing spectroscopy in July and August, during which time four short eruptions occurred. These eruptive episodes took place on 16 – 22 July, 5 – 6 August, 14 August and 24 August at the North-east Crater. During normal activity the discharge of sulphur dioxide was around 1000 t d^{-1} but output rose immediately prior to eruptions reaching a peak of around 5000 t d^{-1} at eruption. Malinconico suggests that fluctuations of SO_2-emission could provide a means for predicting eruptions on Etna. This is obviously an area worthy of further investigation and there is a need for monitoring the long-term variation in SO_2-discharge.

7 Internal plumbing

'Much of our knowledge of the mechanism of basaltic volcanoes has resulted from studies on Hawaii. Here for many years a team of scientists has kept a comprehensive record of various aspects of volcanic activity, like doctors attending some sleeping giant in an intensive care unit, continuously recording temperature, blood pressure and pulse rate.'

(M. K. Wells, 1971)

The analogy between a doctor and a volcanologist is a good one. To understand an active volcano it is not sufficient only to study the surface manifestations; we must delve deep into its bowels. Various techniques are available to probe the mysteries of the internal workings of a volcano: studies can be made of the composition, physical properties of the erupted material and the rates of activity; various geophysical techniques can be used to identify magma and track its movement below the surface; and the dissected corpses of long-dead volcanoes may provide valuable information on a volcano's anatomy. In addition theoretical modelling based on known physical properties of magma and the surrounding host rocks play an important part in developing new ideas (Wilson and Head, 1981).

Before the advent of geophysical techniques much of our understanding of the internal structure of volcanoes derived from the study of cores of ancient volcanoes laid bare by deep erosion. Classical studies of, for example, volcanic centres in the Scottish Tertiary volcanic province, as well as more ancient centres such as Glen Coe, provided considerable information about the nature of intrusive bodies within a volcanic pile and have led to speculation about their emplacement. From these studies and others it is clear that many different types of magma-emplacement occur within a volcano, ranging from simple dykes and sills to more complex forms such as ring dykes and cone sheets as well as massive gabbroic bodies of which Skaergaard in West Greenland has perhaps become the best-known. As well as these intrusive bodies large numbers of breccia pipes with different levels of dissection have been identified and many probably represent the downward extension of such surface features as the collapse pits of the Bocca Nuova and the Chasm in the summit region of Etna.

Despite an extensive literature on the internal structure of ancient volcanoes, it is often difficult to relate observations of currently active volcanoes with what is seen in the older dissected ones. Interpretations of the internal plumbing of active volcanoes often bear little resemblance to three-dimensional reconstructions made from field observations of dissected volcanoes. The one element that appears to be in common is the dyke; dense dyke swarms usually cut ancient volcanic structures and clearly play a major role in the transfer of magma to eruptive vents (Walker, 1974b). On a few volcanoes, such as some of those in the Galapagos, circumferential eruptive fissures have been considered as the upward extensions of ring dykes (McBirney and Williams, 1969). On Etna where the walls of the Valle del Bove expose some 1000 m vertical section into the side of the mountain, almost all of the intrusions are dykes (McGuire, 1982); any massive intrusive bodies if they exist must lie more than a kilometre below the present surface.

The lack of correspondence between the results of studies of high-level intrusions in old volcanoes and our understanding of the way magma is fed to the surface in modern active volcanoes probably results from a number of factors. Many of the intrusive bodies studied in the old volcanoes occurred at a late stage in the history of the volcano and may have played no part in the eruptive history. It is also probably wrong to imagine that every basaltic volcano has a similar internal structure and whereas, for example, ring dykes may be a dominant intrusive element of one kind of volcano, they may be absent under another where the tectonic regime is different. In addition, when studying an active volcano the concern is with identifying the magma pathways for individual events; in a dissected volcano only the cumulative results of many hundreds, of even thousands, of such events are seen. Many of these events may have lost their individual identity having been emplaced at different times in the cooling history of the surrounding rocks thus forming a complex intrusive body. Many such intrusions may have been 'failed eruptions' (Walker, 1974b) and the presence of such intrusions which never reach the surface confuse the story even more.

Despite the difficulties outlined above, it is still of critical importance that our studies lead to a complete understanding of the volcano's metabolism during life and the relation of these living processes to the dead carcass. Certainly many such links have been developed. The studies of Anderson (1951) on the emplacement of intrusions in

Scotland was the intellectual forerunner of more physically complex studies of fracture mechanisms of magma transport (Shaw, 1980); and the detailed examination of dykes near Shiprock in New Mexico has done much to develop our understanding of the flow of magma during the growth of dykes (Delaney and Pollard, 1981).

We have seen in the last chapter how petrological studies of erupted materials can place constraints on our understanding of the genesis and ascent of magma. The role of such studies in understanding the internal plumbing is two fold. Firstly, it can provide important information on the depth at which storage, crystallization and differentiation might have taken place; and secondly, major changes in the composition of erupted material with time may indicate wholesale changes in the internal plumbing of the volcano as it develops. Although petrological investigations of a volcano are valuable in their own right, Walker (1973b) has pointed out that such petrological studies can be greatly enhanced if volcanological considerations are taken into account. Thus the relative volumes of different compositions of rock erupted from an individual volcano must be considered in any petrogenetic scheme. Likewise because there may be a compositional (density) control on which magmas are erupted and which remain as intrusions below the surface a suite of lavas may not be compositionally representative of their intrusive counterparts and vice versa (Walker, 1974b). Where a volcano has emitted large quantities of pyroclastic material a simple suite of lavas may be totally unrepresentative of the general composition of magma entering the volcano.

The feedback from studies of the rheology of flowing lava to an understanding of the internal processes of volcanoes has also been important: thus the realization that magma may behave as a non-Newtonian liquid, as discussed in Chapter 5, may clearly influence interpretations of such processes as differentiation by crystal-settling and calculation of the rates of magma ascent based on entrainment of dense olivine nodules (Sparks *et al*, 1977).

Geophysical methods of volcano-monitoring provide a powerful tool in investigating the internal plumbing of a volcano. Such techniques have been used with considerable success in Hawaii and Japan. Seismological techniques provide information on the location of magma storage areas and can be used to trace pathways of magma ascent. Studies of ground deformation provide information on the emplacement of magma at shallow depth and can indicate when eruption is imminent. Changes in gravity can be interpreted in terms of magma movement as can magnetic and electrical surveys. On Hawaii a combination of these different types of geophysical survey has led to an understanding of the internal plumbing, particularly of Kilauea, probably unrivalled on any other volcano. In this chapter an attempt will be made to show how, by using techniques well established in volcanological research in Hawaii and elsewhere, a model of the internal plumbing of Etna may be developed.

7.1 Conduits and magma chambers

For most eruptions on Etna the feeding conduit, at least in the near surface regions, is a *dyke*. This is probably true for the majority of volcanoes, basaltic or otherwise, and on Etna, in common with most volcanoes with fissure vents, effusion tends to be localized on specific foci along the length of the dyke. Thus, although the dyke itself may be long, surface-tapping of magma only takes place from specific parts that, at most, represent one-third of the length of the fissure. Evidence that the dyke is more extensive is given by swarms of open fissures that open in association with the eruption and in which may be seen glowing lava that stops before it reaches the surface. The mechanism for focussing of upward flow in the fissure has been discussed by Delaney and Pollard (1981). Once an eruption has stopped it is common, especially with larger eruptions, to find tortuous open pipes descending vertically below the principal vents for distances of up to tens-of-metres; these presumably represent the path of ascending magma at least during the last stages of eruptions.

The feeding conduits to vents under the central conduit may not be simple dykes, although each of the individual vents that have given rise to repeated eruptions in the Central Crater may be related to fissure zones crossing the summit cones. However this repeated activity from single vents suggests that the conduits below these vents, at least in the near-surface region, consist of vertical, roughly cylindrical channelways. Nevertheless not all eruptions in the Summit Crater region occur from well-established vent areas such as the North-east Crater, the Chasm and the Bocca Nuova; but the high number of eruptions in this summit region suggests that there is what has been called a central conduit to the volcano. The nature of this conduit at depth is far from being understood. It must be considered a favoured pathway for magma rising into the volcano – a 'porous' column vertically below the Central Crater having a roughly cylindrical cross-section with a radius of perhaps 500 m. In the upper region (say the top few hundred metres to a kilometre) there are well-established 'open' passages that lead to the three craters that are almost continuously active.

Thus it may be considered that magma rises into the upper part of the volcano along pathways which may be of at least two types. There is the continuously open central conduit where magma tends to rise more frequently than elsewhere on the volcano and may either erupt from one of the permanent vents or it may escape laterally through fissures cutting the Summit Cone. Flank eruptions, on the other hand, erupt from fissures and the trends and locations of these fissures are controlled by the regional tectonics. The most extensive fissure-trends are the north-east rift and the weaker southern rift which are controlled by roughly parallel trending fissures. However, other regions where eruptions tend to concentrate, such as the high-density vent area on the western side of the volcano, may have a more complex tectonic control focussing activity in one specific region rather than on a linear trend.

Although simple plumbing diagrams for volcanoes often show dykes and central conduits extending uninterrupted to considerable depth, it would be naive to imagine that ascending magma follows such a straightfoward path. In a discussion of the fracture mechanisms of magma transport, Shaw (1980) considers magma ascent to occur in a plexus of conduits extending discontinuously from the melting source to the surface and involving incremental volumetric episodes of magma injection following fracture pathways governed by the stress states in the rock and the locally acting fluid pressure of magma. He considers dyke systems to be made up of lenticular segments of a variety of lengths. The size of each lenticular section of the dyke is considered to be short compared with the thickness of the lithosphere and to form a pattern consisting of a plexus of offset lenses. This concept of fracture propagation and dyke emplacement is based on field observations as well as theoretical studies (Pollard, 1976, 1977; and Hill, 1977). Equally the central conduit is unlikely to consist of a single column extending down to considerable depth; but instead probably consists of pods of magma rising through a relatively tortuous path within the central conduit. Below a few hundred metres the central conduit must consist of relatively hot rock of low tensile strength thus facilitating the rise of magma in this region. Once established it would become a favoured pathway for magma ascent unless there were an extremely long period of quiescence allowing the conduit to cool down and achieve a higher tensile strength.

The presence or absence of a high-level magma chamber within or just below the volcanic pile of Etna has long been a subject of debate. At a meeting of The Royal Society in London in 1972 devoted to the subject of Etna (Guest and Skelhorn, 1973) discussion focussed on this controversy. Rittmann (1973) held the view that there was no magma chamber at a high level under Etna but that magma is transported directly from its source to the surface in fissures. Differentiation occurs in individual dykes as discussed in the last chapter. On the other hand, Cristofolini (1973) considered that the petrochemistry of Etnean lavas could best be explained in terms of differentiation occurring in relatively large batches of magma so that the ratio between the amount of extruded lava and the total volume of magma is low. These conditions would require a much larger high-level storage area than available in individual dykes.

The term 'magma chamber' as used by Rittmann was in its classical sense of a body of liquid magma filling a major cavity below the volcano. However, magma storage areas need not necessarily have such simple geometry. Magma may be stored in a plexus of sills and dykes or in irregular veins within highly fractured rock. Because of the wide range of possibilities for the geometry of magma reservoirs the general term *magma storage area* will be used here; such storage areas may change in geometry with time. As well as considering the geometrical relations, the residence time of individual batches of magma within the volcano must be considered.

What then are the key questions that must be asked about the internal plumbing of Etna (or indeed any other volcano)? Firstly, is there a magma storage area and if so, where is it and what is its geometry? Secondly, what is the balance between magma supply rate into the volcano and the output rate of lava from it; and do these rates represent a steady state or not? Thirdly, what are the rates of magma ascent and residence times at different levels in the volcano? These questions will be discussed in the remaining parts of this chapter.

7.2 Ground deformation

It has long been known that ground deformation is a common phenomenon in volcanic districts, often resulting from shallow intrusion of magma. Particularly in more silicic volcanoes vertical and horizontal deformation is striking and large enough to be visible without the use of geodetic measurements. Massive movements have been observed in Japan where, for example, on Usu Volcano a tract of land nearly 3 m long and just over 0.5 km wide was elevated 150 m during a seven-month period in 1910, and then subsided by 36 m over the next five months (Imamura, 1930). During 1943 – 45 another dome on the same volcano caused a 1-km-diameter area of ground to rise 200 m. The existence of an intrusion was indicated by the extrusion of a dome rising 150 m above the uplifted area (Minakami *et al.*, 1951). Horizontal movements can be observed visually on most volcanoes where extensional fracturing takes place. The bulge that developed on the north flank of Mount St. Helens prior to the catastrophic eruption of 18 May 1980 was first recognized visually and later monitored by geodetic observations showing movements of as much as 1 m per day (Christiansen and Peterson, 1981).

Smaller movements that can be detected instrumentally have proved to be of considerable value in tracing the sub-surface migration of magma especially on basaltic volcanoes. Of particular importance have been the studies made at Kilauea in Hawaii where elevation changes were first noted by Wilson (1935) who measured vertical displacements of the ground surface of as much as 4 m of subsidence related to the sub-surface withdrawal of a lava column below Halemaumau in 1924. Since that time, measurement of ground deformation using a variety of techniques has become routine at the Hawaiian Volcano Observatory and as a result of these observations a pattern of deformation related to volcanism has emerged. The techniques used and the relation between deformation and volcanism has been summarized by Kinoshita *et al.* (1974) and only a brief summary is required here. It was T. A. Jaggar, a pioneer of Hawaiian volcanology, who first started measurements of ground tilt using a pendulum in 1916 (Jaggar and Finch, 1929). The general pattern of deformation on Hawaii starts with inflation of an area that may be about 12 km across near the top of the volcano with total uplift in the order of centimetres or tens of centimetres (Fig. 7.1), depending on the duration of the inflationary period. This swelling of the volcano both upwards and outwards is terminated at the start of a rift eruption during which the surface over the summit area subsides and contracts (Fig. 7.2). The rate at which the changes take place may be rapid especially during an eruption, and even normal pre-eruptive inflation can occur at a rate of several millimetres per day. Although measurements of vertical and horizontal deformation are made independently, the patterns of horizontal deformation are similar to those measured in the vertical plane. The centre of deformation need not be stationary and measurements by Fiske and Kinoshita (1969) show that

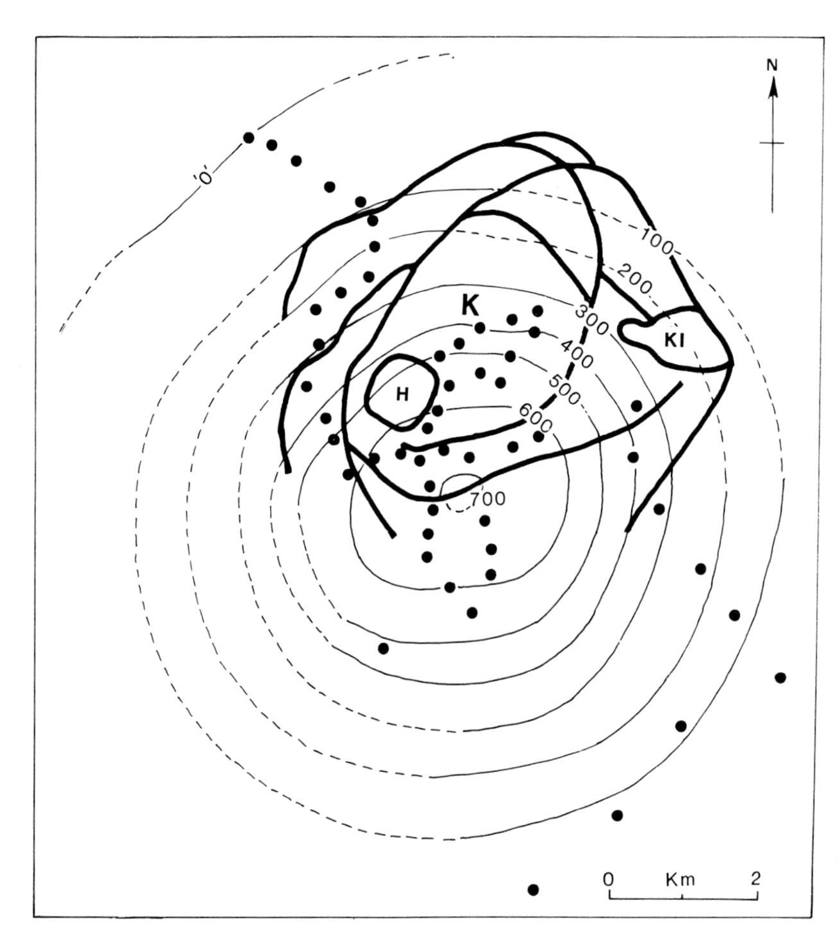

Fig. 7.1 Changes in elevation (in millimetres) at the summit of Kilauea volcano in Hawaii between January 1966 and October 1967. This period of inflation preceded the 1967–68 Halemaumau eruption. The thick lines are the borders of Kilauea Caldera (K), Halemaumau Crater (H) and Kilauea Iki Crater (KI). The dots represent principal levelling benchmarks. All the changes in elevation are referred to one benchmark, taken to be 'stable', lying between the Kilauea and Mauna Loa volcanoes. (After Fiske and Kinoshita, 1969, courtesy of *Science* (American Association for the Advancement of Science).)

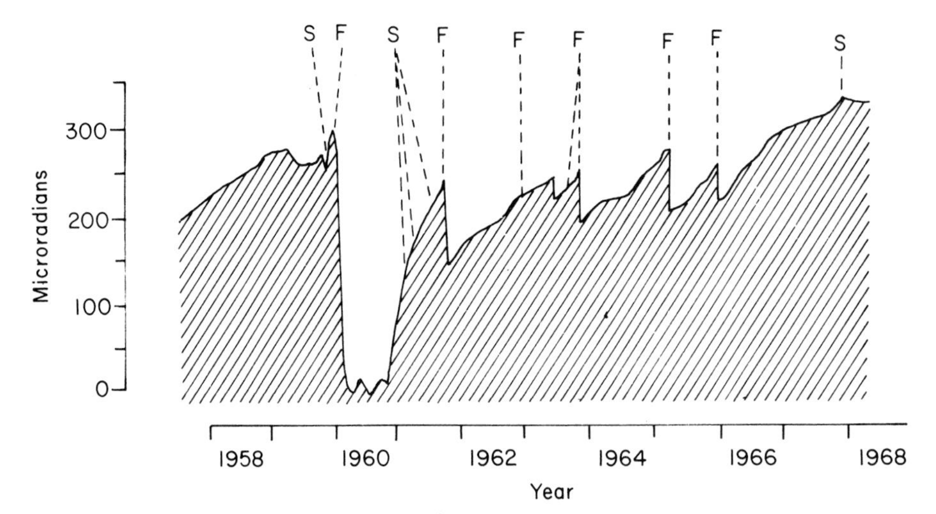

Fig. 7.2 Ground tilt measured daily at the Hawaiian Volcano Observatory on the rim of the Kilauea Caldera. It can be seen that summit eruptions (S) may occur during periods of increasing inflation but flank eruptions (F) result in a rapid deflation as magma moves away from the central conduit along a rift system. (After Fiske and Kinoshita, 1969, courtesy of *Science* (American Association for the Advancement of Science).)

prior to the 1967 – 68 eruption of Kilauea the inflation centre was displaced horizontally by more than 1 km in two weeks or less.

In order to interpret these deformation measurements in terms of a magma reservoir at depth below the Kilauea Caldera it is necessary to turn to theoretical models of the shape and amount of deformation that might be expected from intrusions of different depths and of different geometries. The first model of this type was provided by the Japanese geophysicist Mogi (1958). His model assumes that the earth's crust is a semi-infinite elastic body, and that deformation is caused by a small spherical source of hydrostatic pressure with a radius that is small compared with its depth.

Assuming the centre of uplift is known, together with the amount of deformation at different distances from the centre, it is possible to calculate the depth of the intrusion that is causing the observed deformation. In Fig. 7.3(a) representation of this model may be seen in which the ordinate is the percentage of maximum vertical uplift (Δh_0), while the abscissa is in units of depth (f) of the spherical source of pressure. As the depth changes the shape of the curve changes giving a steep curve for shallow sources and becoming flatter as the depth of the source increases. Because the indivi-

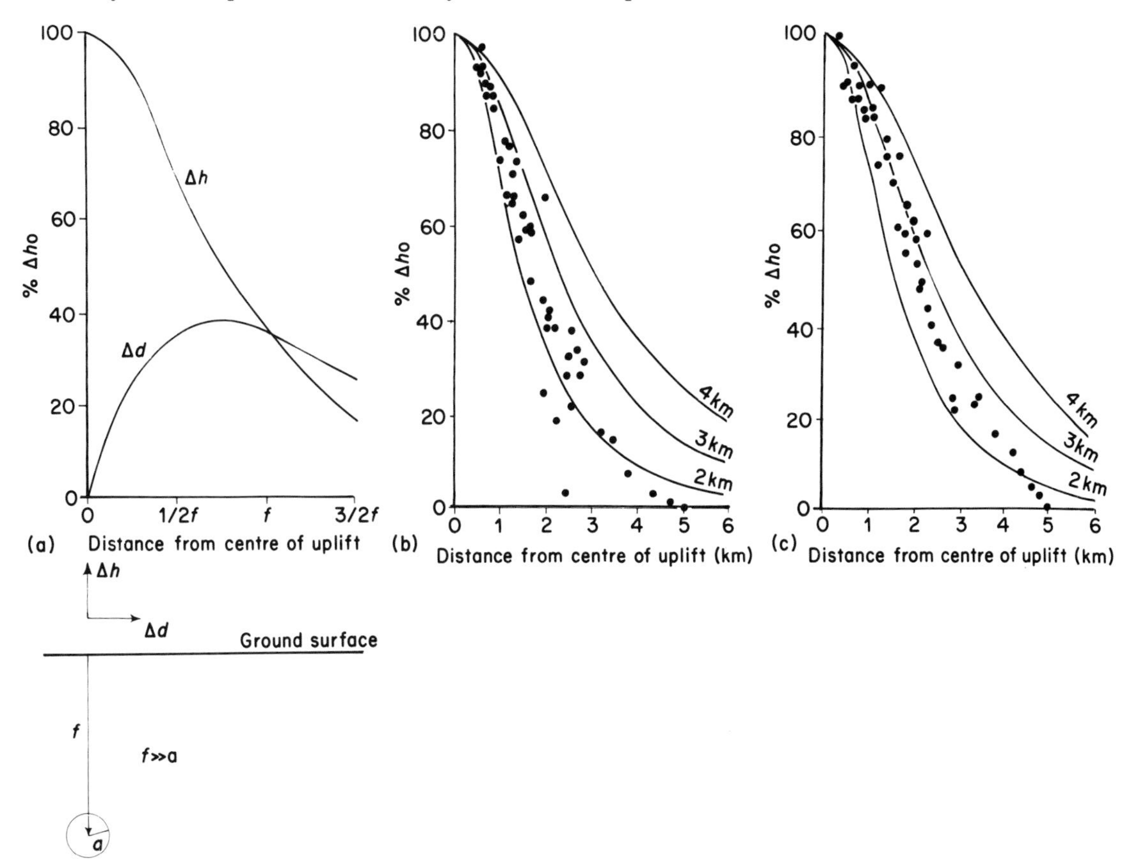

Fig. 7.3 (a) The theoretical vertical (Δh) and horizontal (Δd) displacement above a small spherical source (radius = a) of pressure at a depth (*f*) following the theory of Mogi (1958). (b) Vertical displacement of benchmarks around the summit of Kilauea (see Fig. 7.1) for the period January – July 1966 (maximum uplift is 107 mm). The distribution of data points suggests that the magma reservoir lies at a depth of between 2 – 3 km. (c) Vertical displacement of benchmarks on Kilauea for the period August – October 1967 (maximum uplift is 160 mm) indicating that the magma reservoir level is at about 3 km depth. All ordinate scales as percentage of Δh_0, the maximum uplift. (After Fiske and Kinoshita, 1969, courtesy of *Science* (American Association for the Advancement of Science).)

dual curves are sensitive to depth, it is possible to plot directly the deformation changes and ascertain the depth of source from a family of curves for different model depths (Figs 7.3(b) and 7.3(c)). As one might expect, the surface layers of a volcano do not behave as a perfect semi-infinite elastic body and some non-elastic deformation may be expected to take place especially immediately prior to eruption. Because of this the observations do not always fit the model precisely and Fiske and Kinoshita (1969) have observed that horizontal deformations prior to eruption were greater than would be predicted by the model. They interpret this in terms of rapid dilation as the magma reached the surface. Mogi's model has been of considerable importance in understanding deformation measurements on Hawaii and allowed the identification of a fairly shallow magma reservoir at about 2 – 4 km depth (Fig. 7.4) below the summit of Kilauea.

Although the Mogi model has had considerable apparent success, its use is limited to the inbuilt assumption that it relates to a point source and can only be used if the diameter of the magma reservoir is small by comparison with its depth below surface.

In an attempt to distinguish between magma storage areas of different shapes Dieterich and Decker (1975) used the techniques of finite-element modelling for a variety of shapes including spheres, horizontal lenses, vertical plugs, sills and dykes at various inclinations. These numerical models were then compared with actual measurements of vertical and horizontal ground deformation on Kilauea. They found that finite-element models appeared to provide better fits between the observed and computed data than those using the various existing elastic models which did not always explain observed differences between the vertical and horizontal deformations. The models of Dieterich and Decker illustrate that the shape of a shallow reservoir sensibly affects the pattern of surface displacement, but they point out that for

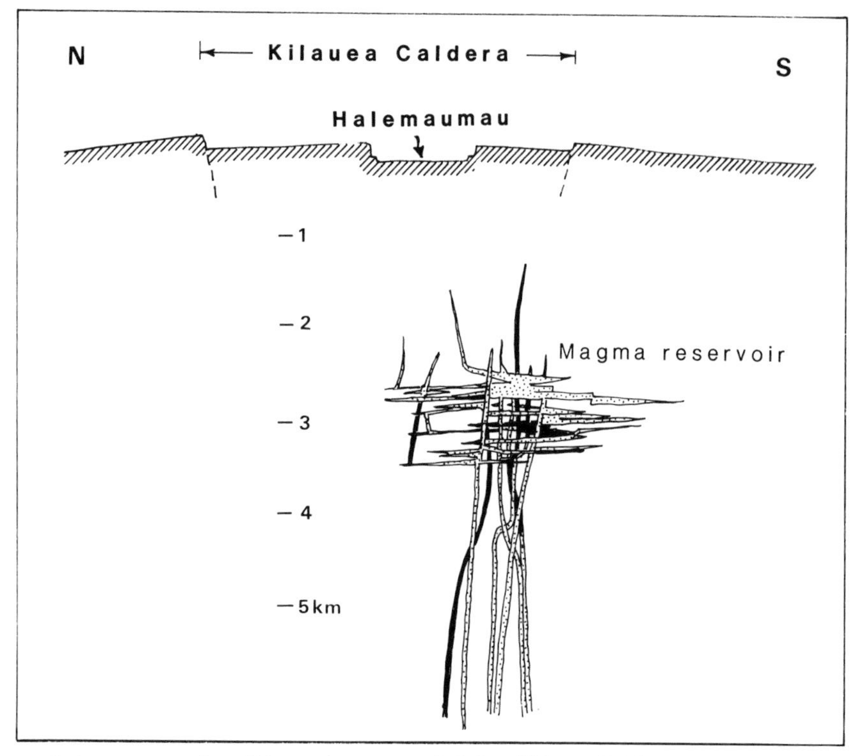

Fig. 7.4 A speculative cross-section of the magma reservoir below Kilauea Caldera based on ground-deformation studies. (From Fiske and Kinoshita, 1969, courtesy of *Science* (American Association for the Advancement of Science).)

some shapes of reservoir reliable estimates of the geometry and depth may be difficult to obtain if only vertical deformation data are available. By comparing their numerical models with data from Hawaii they demonstrate that summit deformation measurements fit best to a cylindrical chamber with a vertical axis and having a radius of 0.35 km. The depth of the top of the cylinder below the surface would be 0.7 km opposed to 2.5 km obtained using a point-source model. On the basis of these studies they suggest that the magma-storage region beneath the summit of Kilauea consists of several weakly interconnected, but generally stable, reservoir zones each of which approximates to a vertical cylinder with a height several times greater than its radius. Whether the cylinders are in reality simple cavities or closely interconnected plexus of dykes and sills is not known.

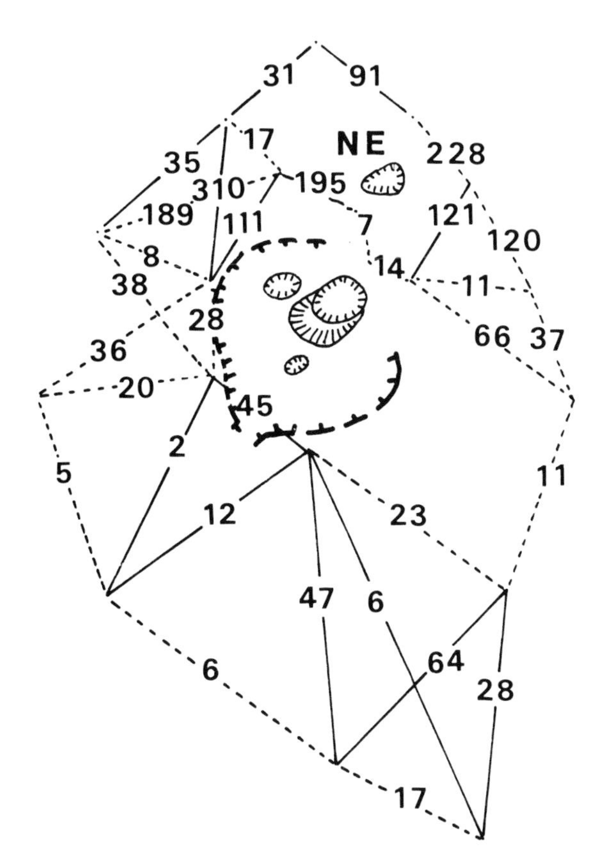

Fig. 7.5 An example of observed distance changes on the network of stations around the summit crater of Etna between June 1972 and July 1973. Solid lines between stations indicate a net increase in distance, dashed lines a net decrease. The differences in distances are given in millimetres. The heavy dashed line marks the rim of the Summit Crater which is about 500 m across. This pattern of deformation is interpreted in terms of expansion of a cylindrical column below the North-east Crater (NE). (After Wadge, 1976).

The evidence suggests that rift eruptions on Kilauea result from the outward growth of dykes from the central reservoir area along the rift zone until the dyke intersects the surface when lava erupts. The rift zones, which consist of parallel open cracks, eruptive fissures, faults and pit craters, have been interpreted in a number of ways. Moore and Krivoy (1964) conclude that the East Rift Zone of Hawaii consists of southward-dipping fractures related to gravity-sliding of the volcano's flank towards the sea. A northward-dipping fracture zone however, was proposed by Ryall and Bennett (1968). Nearly vertical fractures resulting from internal magma pressure were proposed by Fiske (1969) and Jackson and Swanson (1970). Based on the patterns of ground deformation Dieterich and Decker (1975) suggest that dykes feeding eruptions are inclined towards the south and open at least in part by dyke-injection pressures. Nevertheless gravity collapse by seaward sliding as occurs during major earthquakes may play a significant role.

These studies, and others, show that observations of ground deformation can be a powerful tool in predicting eruptions as well as in the identification of magma movement below the surface especially, as will be shown later in the chapter, if seismic data are also available.

Measurements of ground deformation on Hawaii have been of two types: (1) those that give a continuous record of movement and (2) those that give movements over intervals of time depending on the frequency of repetition of measurements. On Hawaii continuous measurements of tilt using various types of tilt meter have been of particular value, while non-continuous measurements have been made using water-tube tilt-metering, precise spirit-levelling and distance-measuring by electro-optical devices.

Only a few of these techniques have so far been used on Etna. The first measurements of ground deformation were made by Geoffrey Wadge (1976) and his colleagues from Imperial College London. Wadge set up a trilateration network with a diameter of about 2 km × 1.5 km around the summit of the volcano. The network consisted essentially of two concentric rings of benchmarks one at the foot and the other on the rim of the summit cone (Fig. 7.5). Electro-optical distance measurements were made between 1971 and 1974, the network being occupied six times during that period. In order to interpret these measurements, two assumptions were made. One was that distance changes could be considered to be a result of horizontal displacement of benchmarks and that any vertical component was neglible; and secondly, that the strain is homogeneous and elastic on the scale of the measurement distances. Wadge concluded that Mogi-type models did not explain the observed deformation. However the observed data provided a better fit with a model involving horizontal strain about an open cylindrical magma column where the strain is inversely proportional to the square of the distance from the centre of deformation. On the basis of these results, Wadge concluded that deformation in the summit region related to cylindrical columns of magma in the Chasm and under the North-east Crater. He suggested that substantial storage of magma occurred in the Chasm (Wadge, 1977) and that many flank eruptions resulted from radial fracturing, allowing magma to drain out of the Chasm reservoir to erupt on the flanks.

As we have seen, Etna is structurally complex and deformation studies restricted to the summit area can only be considered as part of the story. Unfortunately to monitor ground deformation over the whole volcano would be time-consuming and expensive. However, it is possible to make individual measurements in areas where movement is likely to occur. Wadge and his colleagues did this for a short period near the site of the 1974 eruption and a group from the International Institute of Volcanology in Catania, led by L. Villari (1983), have set up networks for measuring horizontal strain in a number of places on the volcano. One important region to study is the north-east rift, and repeated measurements across the rift in 1976 (Villari, 1977) showed expansion and con-

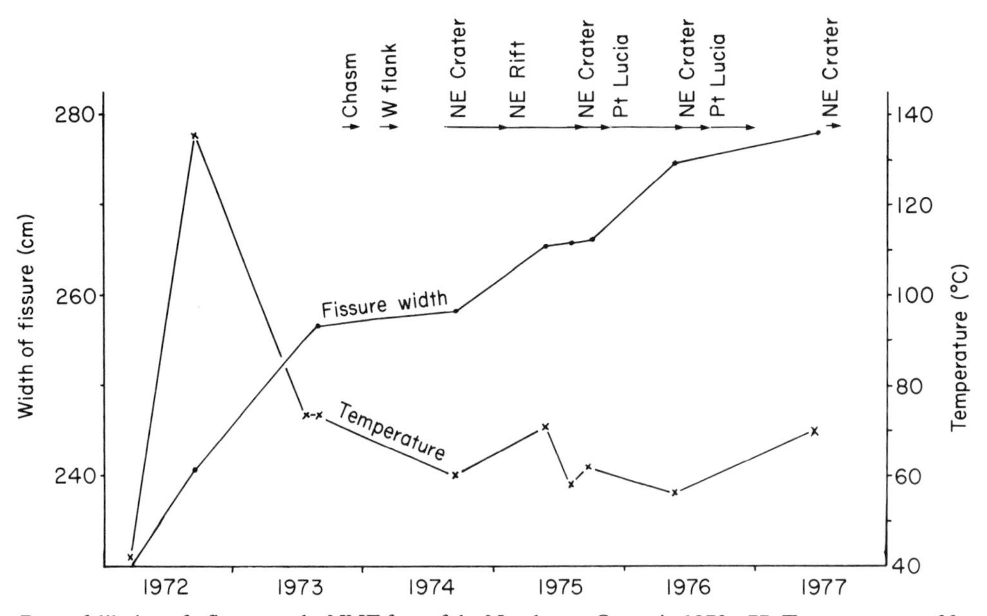

Fig. 7.6 Rate of dilation of a fissure at the NNE foot of the North-east Crater in 1972–77. Temperatures of fumaroles in the fissure are also shown. Eruptions during this period are indicated along the top of the diagram.

traction on the rift apparently related to volcanic activity: while quiet effusion of lava occurred on the rift, there was steady expansion; but when activity moved to the North-east Crater the rift closed.

Fissure dilation may also be measured directly with a tape. One NNE-trending fissure at the foot of the North-east Crater was monitored in this way for over four years until it was destroyed by volcanic activity in 1977. Measurements were made between two nails inserted on either side of the fissure. Temperatures of fumaroles in the fissure were monitored at the same time. The measurements showed a continuous widening of the fissure at varying rates of up to 1.5 cm per month. During periods of more rapid dilation, temperatures tended to rise but dropped when the rate of widening diminished (Fig. 7.6). When eruptions occurred elsewhere, the rate of opening decreased. One interpretation of these observations is that magma was intruding into the fissures running through the North-east Crater but that magma pressure was relieved when effusion took place from other parts of the plumbing system.

Although by the end of 1974 some measurements of vertical movement had been made by Wadge, there was no extensive network that could be repeatedly measured. In 1975 a team from the University of London Observatory established an 11-km-long levelling traverse across the summit of Mount Etna (Murray and Guest, 1982). The techniques used were similar to those employed in Hawaii except that measurements were made to a higher accuracy by the use of a micrometer attached to a Zeiss Ni2 level. This was done since it did not take significantly longer to make measurements this way and the amount of movement expected on Etna was not known. Relatively steep-sided volcanoes like Etna are not ideal for running precise levelling traverses mainly because many more stations must be occupied than on a relatively horizontal surface. The traverse established by this group followed the dirt track up the south of the mountain across the summit and down the northern track (Fig. 7.7). Although the technique employed and the radius of the traverse about the summit of the volcano were similar to those of Hawaii, the areal extent of the Hawaiian network around Kilaeua is considerably greater than that of Etna where the terrain imposes severe limitations on work of this kind. The traverse was precision-levelled nine times between July 1975 and July 1980. The technique of precise-levelling is fairly simple in principle, although tedious in practise (Fig. 7.8). An Invar 3 m rod is placed on a fixed station on the traverse. A sight is taken with the automatic level onto the rod from a distance that is controlled on a shallow slope by the amount of atmospheric refraction, and on a steep slope by the height of the pole, the instrument being less than 3 m below the top of the pole. The pole is then carried along the traverse to the other side of the level at an equivalent distance away as for the first reading. At this point the rod is usually held on a temporary stand firmly kicked into the ground. With the rod held in place, the level is then moved to a new station beyond the rod at a suitable distance and a new reading is taken. This procedure is repeated along the traverse with fixed stations at suitable intervals along it. The measurements allow the relative heights between fixed stations to be established and repeated occupations of the stations give the changes in elevation with time. Ideally all the turning points are marked by nails as in Hawaii where many of the traverses run along paved roads, but on Etna lack of suitable positions for driving in nails makes this impossible. Thus speed and efficiency of the work depends on the experience of the team. When the 11-km-long traverse was originally set up across Etna it took about six days to measure but with experience it could be completed in 2½ – 3 days depending on weather conditions. Speed in completing the traverse is important as ground movements may take place within the time period of measurement. All the measurements are relative and on Kilauea are related to a 'stable' station off the Kilauea edifice. However on Etna there is no location within range of the traverse that may be taken as stable. One way of obviating this problem would be to run a traverse down to a tide-gauge on the coast but this would involve a traverse of about 20 km long and the errors involved could negate the exercise. In Hawaii the 'stable' station is occasionally levelled to the coast.

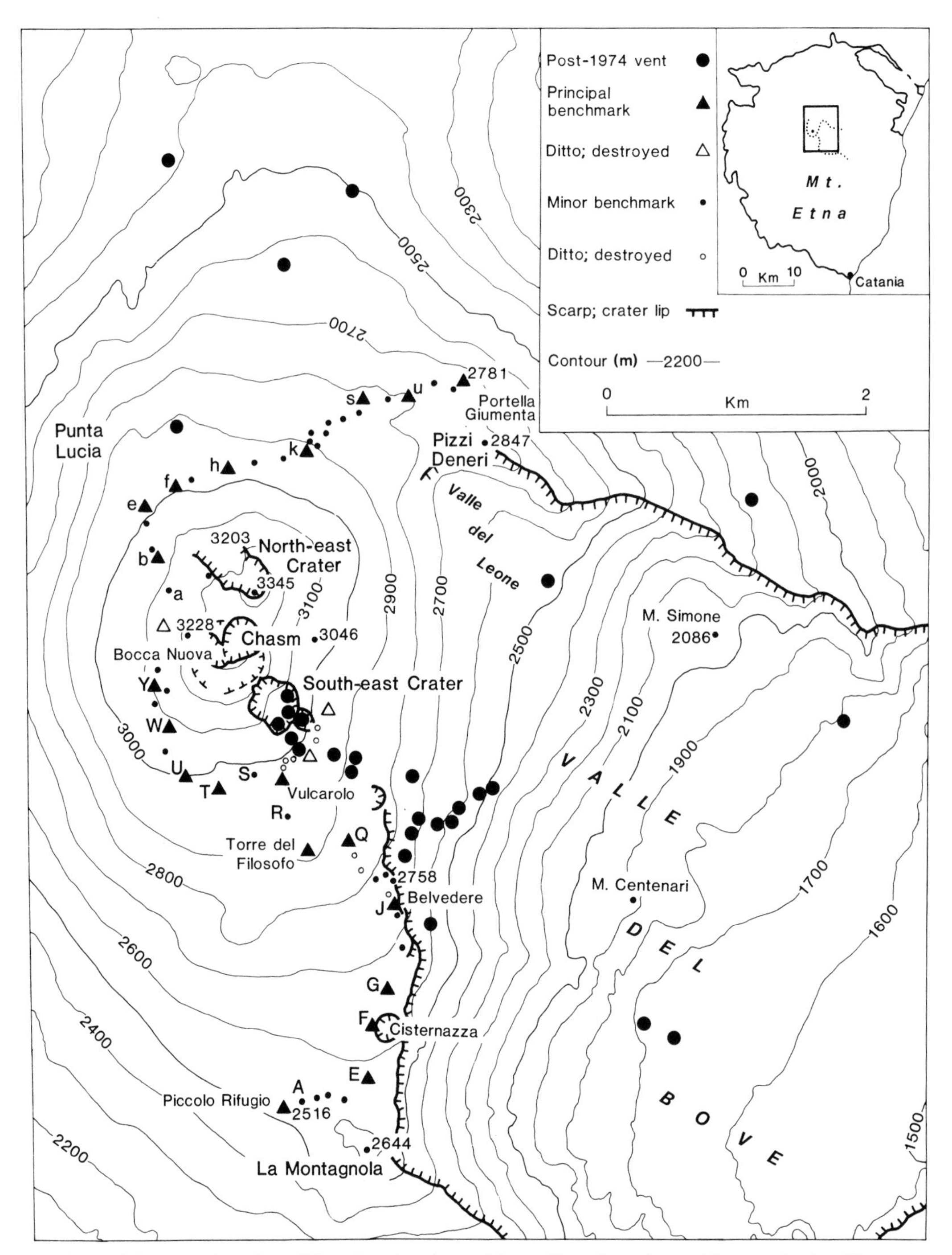

Fig. 7.7 Map of the summit region of Etna showing the positions of benchmarks used in a precise-levelling traverse across Etna between 1975 and 1980. South of the summit, stations are labelled in upper-case letters and on the northern side in lower-case letters. The sites of vents active during the period of levelling are indicated and it will be noted that these cluster in the region showing most deformation, around the South-east Crater and Belvedere. (From Murray and Guest, 1982.)

Fig. 7.8 The University of London Observatory levelling team on the south flank near the foot of the Summit Cone, seen in the background. (Photograph: J. E. Guest.)

Errors in levelling may be expressed as $\pm Z\sqrt{K}$ where K is the distance (in kilometres) and Z is a quantity which decreases with increasing precision of levelling. For the Etnean traverse, observed variations allow a value of 0.7 ± 0.6 to be derived for Z giving a mean expected error of 2.3 mm over the total length of the traverse (Murray and Guest, 1982).

When this five-year study was initiated it was expected that patterns of movement similar to those in Hawaii would be observed. However the changes in elevation showed a quite different pattern. The most dramatic changes were on the northern flank where drops of as much as 84 cm between stations 500 m apart were observed during a period of one year (Murray *et al.*, 1977). The whole of the area where this high rate of deflation was observed consists of a large fan of lavas erupted from the North-east Crater. All the stations that showed a substantial lowering of the ground surface were on fresh lavas erupted after 1974. It was also noted that elsewhere on the traverse where benchmarks were sited on relatively young lavas there was a tendency for these stations to drop relative to adjacent stations off the flow (Fig. 7.9). Murray and Guest (1982) therefore concluded that these large movements on the northern flank result from compaction and possible downward sliding of lava flows on a steep slope rather than being of a more deep seated origin.

On the southern flank of the volcano where most of the benchmarks were sited on old rocks there were small relative movements that were restricted to specific localities (Figs 7.10 and 7.11). Over the length of the traverse there was no overall pattern of movement that could be considered comparable

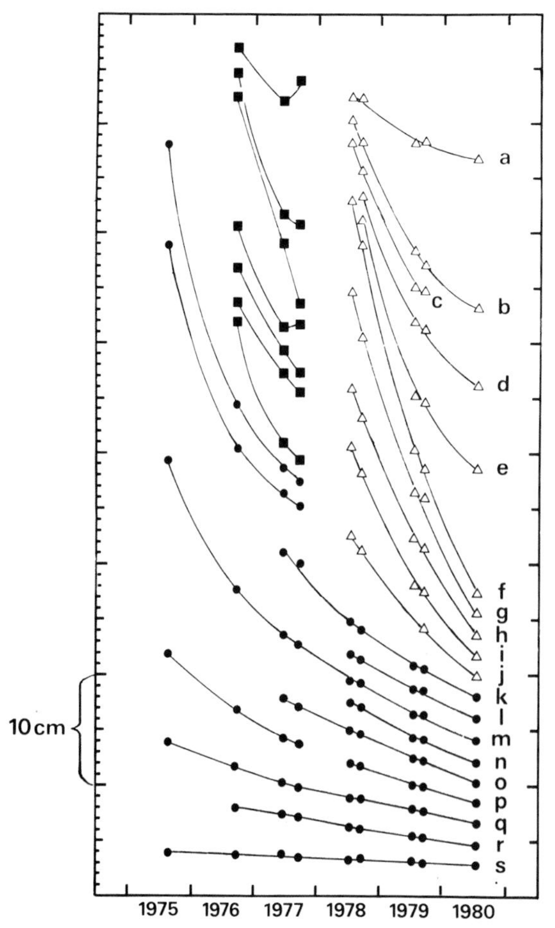

Fig. 7.9 Graph to show the relative vertical movement with time for benchmarks on the northern flank of Etna. Locations of benchmarks are shown in Fig. 7.7. All these stations are on fresh lava flows from the North-east Crater. Solid circles represent those installed on flows erupted between 1966 and 1971; solid squares those on lavas of September – November 1975; and open triangles those on flows produced during the winter of 1977/78. The vertical axis indicates the amount of vertical movement relative to station 'u' situated off the flow field. (From Murray and Guest, 1982.)

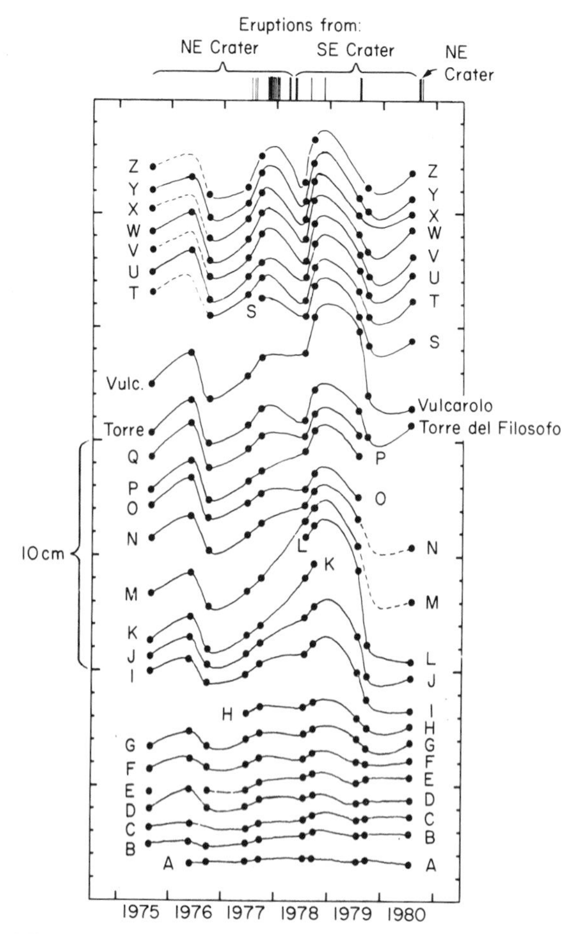

Fig. 7.10 Graph of the changes in altitude of individual benchmarks with time relative to the Piccolo Rifugio base station at the southern end of the traverse. Positions of benchmarks are shown in Fig. 7.7. From Murray and Guest, 1982.)

to that observed in Hawaii. Because all the movements referred to a base benchmark at the end of the traverse situated on the mountain and thus liable to movement also, it could be that the whole region of the traverse moved relative to the rest of the mountain. To test this possibility and whether there was an Hawaiian-type pattern of inflation and deflation but over a broader area, thirty-two dry-tilt stations were set up strategically around the mountain. These stations each consisted of three benchmarks about 30 – 60 m apart in a roughly equilateral triangle. They were installed between May 1976 and June 1977. These again were similar to those set up in Hawaii. Tilt of the surface is obtained by measuring changes in relative height between each of the three stations. This is done by placing the automatic level equidistant from each benchmark to within 20 cm and levelling to an Invar rod set up on each benchmark in turn. As far as possible, calm, cloudy days were chosen for measurements so as to reduce the effects of

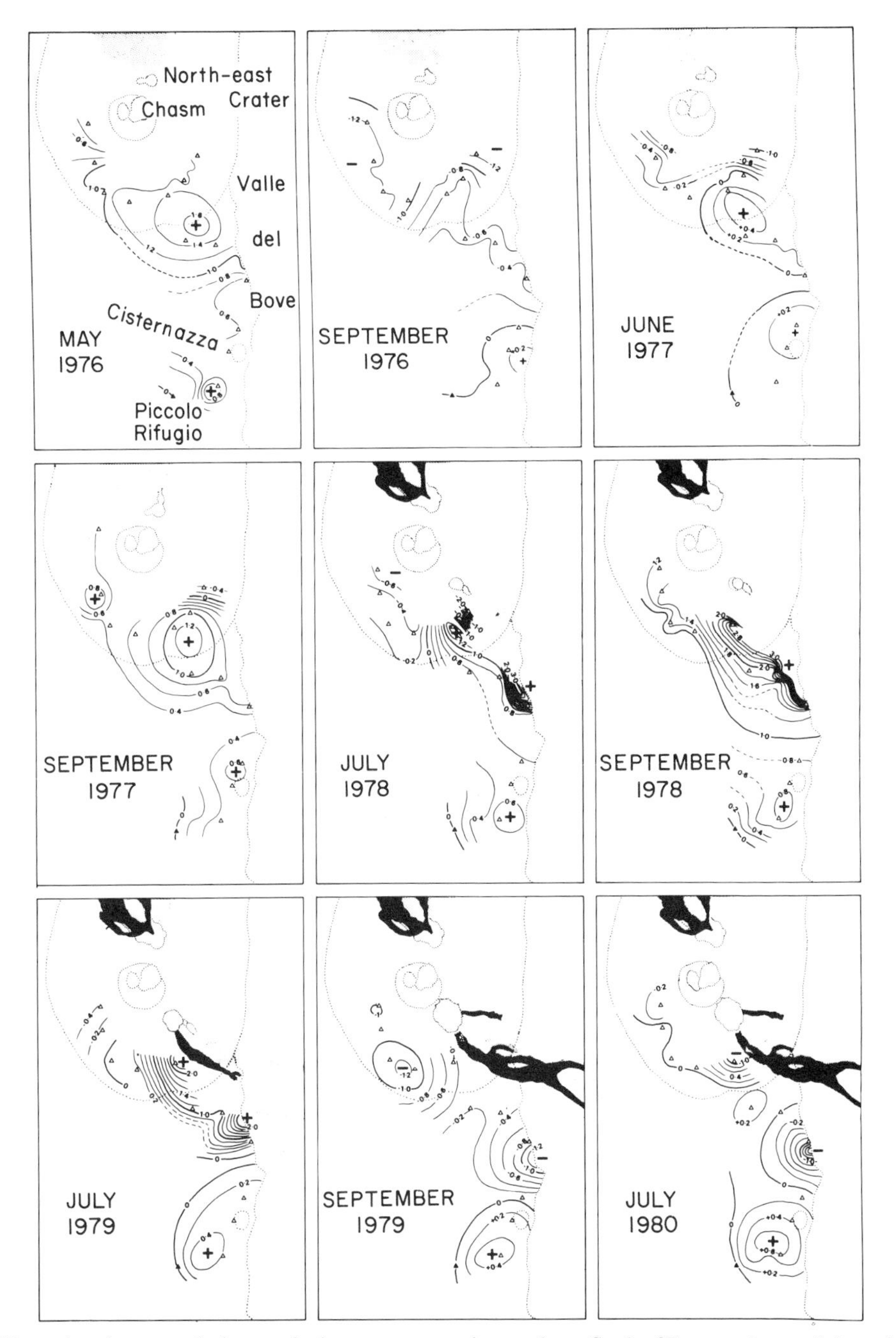

Fig. 7.11 Maps showing cumulative vertical movement on the southern flank of Etna as observed since the levelling traverse was first occupied in July – August 1975. The numbers indicate amount of vertical movement in centimetres. Positive and negative signs are approximate positions of centres of inflation or deflation; open triangles represent the principal benchmarks. The lavas erupted from vents in the map area are shaded. It should be noted that the main area of movement occurred in the Vulcarolo, Torre del Filosofo, Belvedere region which was close to the activity associated with the South-east Crater that started in early 1978. An area of inflation also developed near the southern end of the traverse and this region continued to inflate after July 1980 (Murray, 1982b). This centre of inflation may well have been related to the eruption in 1983 which occurred just downslope from this area. (From Murray and Guest, 1982.)

atmospheric tremor and atmospheric refraction. These tilt stations were measured within a few days of running the levelling traverse. Again, the measurements showed no pattern of changing tilt of the type seen in Hawaii. Movements were observed which could be related to local block movements or movements of the volcano related to the regional structural trends, although it was difficult to relate such movements to any specific trend.

On the basis of these observations, Murray and Guest (1982) came to the conclusion that at least over the five-year period of observations, when a variety of different types of volcanic activity occurred, there was no evidence of movements associated with a shallow magma-storage area and that any major magma-storage area under the volcano had to be at a depth considerably below the volcanic pile, at least in the region of 10 – 20 km below the surface.

As well as measuring their own dry-tilt stations, the University of London Observatory group continued occupying three Imperial College dry-tilt stations. Previously Wadge had observed relatively large movements at these stations although he was unable to relate the tilt vectors to volcanic activity. However the measurements made from 1975 onwards did not show such large changes, and it is difficult to interpret these differences in observations since they were made using different techniques and levelling crews.

Although the levelling traverse and dry-tilt stations showed no overall pattern of inflation and deflation related to filling and emptying of a shallow storage area, the traverse did show vertical movements of a few centimetres in specific areas apparently associated with volcanic activity. Because most of these movements were observed to take place over short distances of about 1 km (Fig. 7.10) it was assumed that they were real, relative to adjacent sections of the traverse. The most persistent area that showed movement was centred approximately 1 km to the south-east of the Central Crater (Fig. 7.11). In this small region there tended to be inflation before activity at the North-east Crater, followed by deflation. The largest amount of inflation occurred between August 1975 and May 1976 and was followed by three months of strombolian activity at the North-east Crater; after this there was a complex deflation. Reinflation occurred again until a new vent area opened on 29 April 1978 leading to a succession of eruptions. This new crater was later called the South-east Crater and lies 600 m north of the centre of the inflation area. As these eruptions continued from the South-east Crater and other fissure vents to the north-east, inflation areas paralleling these fissures developed.

If a Mogi model is assumed for these small deformation areas, there is a good correspondence of the data with a source near to 1.6 km below the surface for the deformation occurring between 1976 and 1977 (Fig. 7.12). A depth of about 1000 m was computed for deformations between June and September 1977. The form of the deformation (Murray and Guest, 1982) may be interpreted in terms of the emplacement of a dyke prior to and during the eruption that started from the South-east Crater in 1978. Clearly magmatic pressure in this dyke was influenced by effusive activity occurring on the northern side of the volcano. If this interpretation is correct then we have evidence that fissure-opening and dyke-emplacement can occur as much as two years before the actual outbreak of an eruption and this observation may have significance when residence times of magma in the volcano are considered. Measurements of fumarole temperatures (Guest, 1973a) had certainly suggested similar time periods between the beginning of dyke emplacement and the onset of eruption prior to the 1971 eruption. About a year before the onset of the 1971 eruption the Bocca Nuova collapsed and this was followed by a sharp increase in the temperature of fumaroles in the Central Crater between the Bocca Nuova and the area that was to become the new eruptive site. This phenomenon was interpreted by Guest (1973a) as resulting from magma intruding into the 1971 fissure system before the lava outbreak occurred.

From the observations of ground movement on Etna over nearly a decade, it is evident that Etna behaves in a strikingly different way from Hawaii and by implication suggests that its plumbing is quite different. Nevertheless it must be remem-

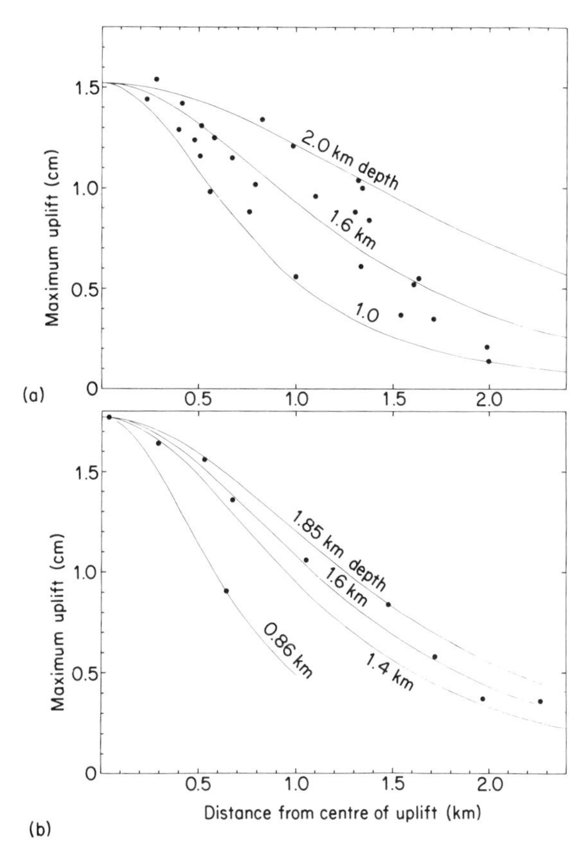

Fig. 7.12 The amount of uplift versus distance from centre of uplift for the periods (a) July/August 1975 to May 1976 and (b) September 1976 to September 1977. Solid circles show the actual measurements while the curves show the expected amount of uplift for various source depths calculated from Mogi's (1958) equations, assuming maximum uplifts of (a) 1.52 cm and (b) 1.80 cm.

bered that measurements have only been made for a relatively short period and that they may be unrepresentative or only a small part of a much longer term deformation pattern on the volcano. Certainly measurements made by Wadge appeared to show more ground movement than those made after 1975 and it could be that these larger movements represented readjustment of the volcano after the large 1971 eruption which involved at least 50×10^6 m^3 (Wadge *et al.*, 1975) and possibly as much as 70×10^6 m^3 of erupted lava (Rittmann *et al.*, 1971). During much of the decade after 1971 the volcano showed a steady-state output of magma at a rate of 0.3 m^3 s^{-1} with a maximum volume for an individual eruption of 25×10^6 m^3 of lava; under these conditions it could be that less deformation occurs. Ground deformation before the major 1983 flank eruption however showed a similar pattern to that before the much smaller 1978 eruption (Murray, 1982b).

The conclusions that can be drawn from the ground-deformation studies so far are as follows:

(1) That during the period of study there was no large-scale and persistent storage area for the magma within the volcanic pile;
(2) That small-scale storage of magma may have occurred in shallow dykes in different places for as much as two years before an eruption;
(3) The volume of this stored material is difficult to determine and depends on the conditions of emplacement;
(4) If the small-scale ground-deformation results mainly from magma pressure then the amount of storage is small; but if the dyke is emplaced passively as a result of tectonic dilation of fissures then much larger amounts of magma could be emplaced within the dyke without there being accompanying broad-scale vertical ground-deformation.

It is quite clear that a much more extensive ground-deformation network is required on Etna in which both vertical and horizontal measurements are made simultaneously. Assuming that the measurements made so far are representative of a longer period in the volcano's history then future networks must span areas where dyke emplacement is most likely such as in the rift zones and other nodes of activity so that the dilation of fractures and emplacement of dykes of magma can be monitored wherever they may occur.

7.3 Seismic studies

Because Mount Etna is thought to lie close to the boundary between two major plates, deep-seated earthquakes associated with plate movement occur. As with all other volcanoes, whether they lie at plate margins or not, there are also seismic manifestations that are more directly related to the volcanic process. Clearly, however, the distinction between tectonic and volcanic earthquakes become blurred in a tectonically active zone, as tectonism and volcanism must be intimately associated. According to Shimozuru (1971) volcanic earthquakes are defined as 'earthquakes which occur at and around volcanoes at relatively shallow depths'; they may occur up to about 10 km away from the active centres and their foci are usually less than 10 km below the surface. Magnitudes are usually small although some of fifth- and sixth- magnitude have been known to occur. Nevertheless although the intensity may be high, damage is usually localized.

Minakami has proposed a classification for volcanic earthquakes based on the nature of the seismograms. Type-A volcanic earthquakes have focal depths between about 1 km and 10 km beneath and around the volcano and show distinct P- and S-phases. The type-B earthquakes occur at less than 1 km depth, usually concentrated immediately below the eruptive centre, and because they are shallow in depth the seismograms obtained from more than about 1 km from the source show no clear P- and S-phases. Explosion quakes have foci just below the crater and when felt, usually when standing close to a crater that is active or is just awakening from a period of inactivity, are felt as a short, sharp shock sometimes associated with a heard-thump. Volcanic tremors are long-duration or continuous vibrations of the ground which can sometimes be strong enough to be felt close to an active centre; they are considered to be generated by magmatic processes and may often be a precursor to impending activity. However, like explosion quakes, tremor can occur without any eruptive activity and may be related to shallow intrusion.

The study of seismic activity at a volcano is of critical importance as it provides information about the movement of magma, fissure opening and associated tectonism, and on many volcanoes can assist greatly in prediction, especially where patterns of seismic activity can be recognized as characteristic of different kinds of volcanic activity. Ryan *et al.* (1981) have built an ingenious three-dimensional model of the internal structure of Kilauea's magmatic reservoir and transport system by plotting all the earthquake foci obtained between 1969 and 1974. This model shows a well-defined central magma-storage area below Kilauea at about 2 – 6 km depth, as determined from the ground-deformation studies discussed earlier in this chapter. They were also able to show the feeding pipes to different active areas during this time.

Although the earliest reports of earthquakes in the Etnean region go back to the Classical era, reliable records are probably only available from the mid-sixteenth century. This catalogue of earthquakes over such a lengthy period, together with the long record of volcanic activity, provides an excellent opportunity to examine statistically the relations between earthquakes and volcanic activity. Sharp *et al.* (1981) searched for such a relation using non-stationary Poisson statistics. Only earthquakes with a minimum intensity of 5 on the modified Mercalli scale were selected. From this study they were unable to find a correlation between earthquakes in structural zones adjacent to Etna, but found a significant relation between flank eruptions and earthquakes in the zone immediately surrounding the volcano. However, there was no such correlation with the onset of persistent summit activity, even when this preceded flank activity. Sharp *et al.* (1981) suggest that these represent plate movement that triggered activity or actively opened fissures allowing magma to ascend. They preferred the latter explanation in which the volcano acts passively to an externally generated fracture event giving rise to flank eruptions. Summit eruptions, on the other hand, are considered to result from magma rising up an already-open conduit.

Although Sharp *et al.* found no correlation between the onset of volcanic activity and earthquakes in the adjacent region, and although tectonic earthquakes in adjacent regions may not be directly related to the rise of magma or an eruption, they can be considered as possible triggers for an eruption that is pending or as giving a boost to a shallow intrusion that might otherwise not have led to an eruption. However, although such effects, together with tidal influences, and changes in atmospheric pressure and rainfall could contribute to the onset of an eruption, statistically they may only show weak correlation or indeed no significant relationship at all.

Instrumental observations of earthquakes in the Etnean region are available from about the beginning of this century. Recently a new seismometer-network was set up by the University of Catania with the specific intention of investigating earthquakes associated with Mount Etna. The first station was established in 1967 with a second one in 1970. By 1973 there was a total of six stations each with short-period vertical seismometers. The aim of the study was to examine earthquakes, explosions quakes and tremor; a detailed report on studies up until 1981 has been given by Cosentino *et al.* (1982). From these studies it appears that flank eruptions are usually heralded by seismic phenomena. Seismic activity starts between two and ten days before the event (usually about 3 – 5 days) and increases in frequency and energy as the eruption approaches. The quakes have a shallow depth of between 1 km and 5 km and the magnitude does not normally exceed 4.5. During the 1974 eruption on the west flank of the volcano, seismicity began ten days before the eruption with increasing intensity towards the start of the eruption and decreasing during the eruption. The second phase of activity at this site was an almost exact repetition of the seismic activity before the first phase, and the end of the eruption coincided with a short seismic crisis. The 1981 eruption on the north flank was announced by seismic activity that started three days before the eruption. Terminal eruptions on the other hand are not normally preceded by earthquake activity and even for those flank eruptions such as the one that opened in late-April 1978 from fissures near the summit of the volcano there were no earthquakes prior to the opening of the summit vent, although fissures that opened lower down the flanks were accompanied by quakes. Only one summit eruption from the North-east Crater in September 1980 was apparently preceded by a long-term increase in seismic activity.

The conclusions from these observations appear to be that magma may rise freely up the region of the central conduit and that, for most of the time, open pathways exist. Even when persistent activity moves downslope from the summit to the north-east rift, as it did in 1975, there was little change in seismic activity with only a few low-energy shocks. Flank eruptions do not have any long-standing channelways that are open and before these can occur fissure opening takes place either by tectonic movement or from pressure by the ascending magma.

Explosion shocks precede and accompany most eruptions. However, they need not necessarily be precursors of vent opening or eruptions and they commonly occur in the summit region, presumably as a result of magma activity a short distance below the surface.

Although eruptions associated with the central conduit at or near the summit are not heralded by an increased in the number of earthquakes, they are usually characterized by a sudden increase in tremor amplitude up to several days before an eruption. Again, however, the onset of tremor or an increase in the number of earthquakes, they indicate forthcoming eruptive activity and collapse deep in the Bocca Nuova can sometimes give felt-tremor as much as 300 m away from the Bocca in the Central Crater.

Volcanic tremor is usually considered to be the result of magma or gas movement below the surface. Several explanations have been put forward including continuous cracking as the magma advances through opening fissures, supersonic gas flows and turbulent motion of a vapour gas – magma mixture. Schick *et al.* (1982) and Cosentino (1982) considered this last explanation to be relevant on Etna. From their studies of tremor, Schick *et al.* consider that there are two sources of tremor on Etna, one being a flat disc of magma acting as a small magma-storage area of 2 km diameter about 2 km below the Central Crater. This is an interesting interpretation as the filling and emptying of such a chamber should produce ground movement which is not observed. However it would be in general agreement with the idea of Wadge (1976) that although most eruptions are fed from magma stored in a column under the Chasm there is a subsidiary chamber that feeds larger flank-eruptions. The other source of tremor is that which apparently corresponds with the movement of magma up the central conduit.

The outcome of seismic observations on Etna so far is extremely encouraging. Enlargement of and continued observation from the existing network could help to provide considerably more information about the internal plumbing of Etna. Of particular interest is the study of volcanic tremor; much more work is required to identify the origin of this phenomenon and thus learn more about the nature and rate of magma movement below the surface. Observation of tremor may remain the only predictive tool for persistent activity, but an increase in earthquake activity is most likely to provide the best prediction for flank eruptions. Even then because such activity may be related to tectonic movements and also the intrusion of magma without eruption, use of these data at least in the near future cannot be totally successful in predicting the onset of new eruptive activity.

Seismic studies have another important function in the examination of the internal structure of volcanoes. By observing the way that seismic waves generated from some distance away from the volcano pass below it, it is possible to look for possible magma chambers. This technique is known as shadowgraphing and has been used successfully in a number of volcanic regions. The first identification of a possible body of magma below Etna was made by Machado (1965) who compared the observed and theoretical seismic intensities of the Messina 1908 earthquake. From this study he observed a large region of negative anomaly which he attributed to the absorption of seismic energy by a magma chamber below Etna, estimated to be at 5 km depth and have an area of 40 km × by 100 km across.

In 1968 a large refraction profile was conducted along the northern part of Sicily running just to the north of Etna. Interpretation of the later arrivals showed that the Sicily coast has a typical continental crust but with a low-velocity zone in the range of 9 – 24 km, interpreted as a high-temperature zone caused by magma chambers below Etna (Cassinis *et al.*, 1970). To investigate the structure and physical properties of the anomaly further, a group from the University of Cambridge installed a seismic network of short-period seismometers over an area of about 60 km × 50 km around the perimeter of Mount Etna. The network was operated from the end of October 1977 until January 1978. In this experiment they used localized travel time delays of seismic waves from shots fired at sea and regional earthquakes and teleseisms as well as conducting wave-form analyses. Four shots were fired at sea to determine a crustal model for the area. Although the profile was not reversed it was in good agreement with the one previously obtained in 1968. The rest of the experiment relied on natural seismic activity, and travel time residuals were obtained by comparing theoretical travel times with observed ones using P-wave arrival times. The highest residuals were found on the opposite side of the network from the direction of the incident ray path indicating that there is a low-velocity zone under the volcano. Qualitatively, the region of delay corresponds roughly to an ellipsoidal body of tens-of-kilometres in lateral extent. It appears to have a long axis oriented NNE. To study this further a triaxial ellipsoidal body of different sizes and depth was tested for a best fit to the data. In all, 20 000 models were examined and the best fit was obtained for an anomaly at 20 km depth of the dimensions 22 km × 31 km × 4 km (Fig. 7.13). High-frequency attenuation across the anomaly indicated that it was not rigid. From the velocity reduction of about 16% it was suggested that the body is not completely molten and consists of 14% of melt perhaps trapped in a network of fissures and corresponding to about 1600 km^3 of magma. As a result of this experiment it seems possible that magma rises from below the Moho and is trapped in this storage area at 20 km before ascending to the surface. The validity of the experiment depends on the assumption that a low-velocity region below a volcano is a magma-storage area – a not-unreasonable assumption. The resolution of the experiment did not allow the identification of any secondary storage area that might occur above this.

7.4 Gravimetric measurements

The study of changes in the earth's gravitational

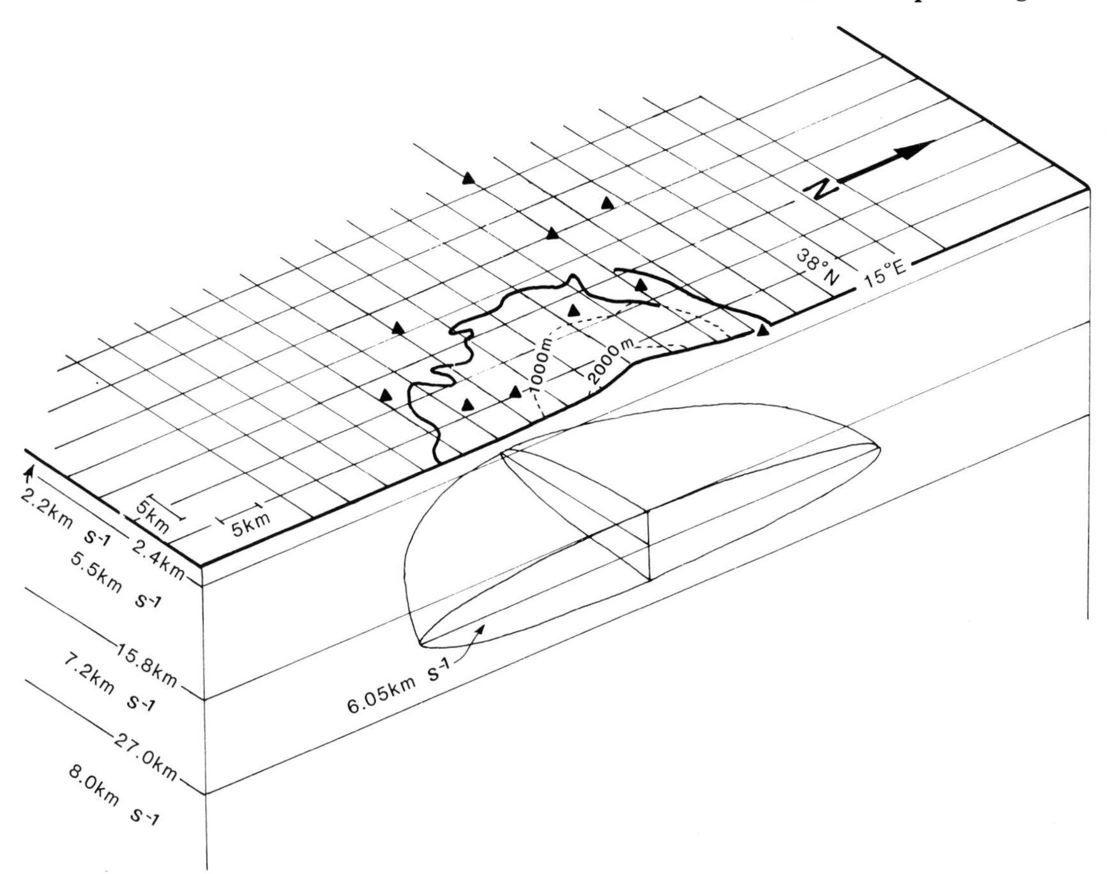

Fig. 7.13 Three-dimensional diagram of the crustal model and low-velocity anomaly beneath Etna. Crustal layer velocities and depths are indicated, and the ellipsoidal anomaly is shown centred beneath the volcano in the 7.2 km s^{-1} layer. For scale a 5-km grid is marked on the surface and the outline of Etna is indicated by a thick line. Solid triangles show locations of Seismometers (From Sharp *et al.*, 1980, courtesy of *Nature*.)

field both in space and time can be used successfully to investigate sub-surface structures. Gravity anomalies are common on volcanoes and are usually associated with caldera structures either as a positive or a negative anomaly depending on the volcano. Calderas on the Big Island of Hawaii have positive anomalies which tend to be offset from the summit caldera.

A detailed gravimetric study of Etna was made by Klerkx and Evrard (1970). The most striking feature of their study is the steep-sided 10-km-diameter 'high' centred on the southern wall of the Valle del Bove and covering much of the Valle itself and the flanks to the south. This anomaly probably relates to a high concentration of dense rocks under this region although whether it is related to the Valle del Bove is not clear. Its southern margin corresponds to the Tardaria Caldera rim and it may be related to this old volcanic centre which, although now largely obscured, may well have been the largest caldera on Mount Etna. Another striking anomaly is the negative one to the north of this which is slightly offset from the Valle del Leone and may relate to that caldera, but it is actually centred on one of the areas of high volcanic activity.

Small secular changes in the acceleration due to the force of gravity can indicate changes in mass below the volcano but can also occur as a result of vertical ground movement. Timothy Sanderson from Imperial College, London (Sanderson, 1982a,b) has used this technique to investigate where magam resides before eruption. In September 1979 he set up ninety-two gravity stations around the volcano. Each station was sited on a stable massive lava outcrop or a permanent building. All the measurements made at these stations were referred to a home station and the whole network was tied into stations of the Italian Geodetic Commission. Corrections were made for tidal variations and errors of 8 – 15 μgal were expected as a result of instrument error, datum inaccuracies and effects of the water table. Gravity changes in the range of −36 μgal to +48 μgal observed between September 1979 and August 1980 are unlikely to be due to chance. To test that such movements were not a result of elevation changes, some of the stations of the network were chosen to coincide with the University of London Observatory levelling line described earlier; it was found that changes in elevation were of an order-of-magnitude too small and in the wrong direction to explain the gravity changes. Sanderson therefore assumed that the measured changes in the gravitational acceleration resulted from a change in mass below the surface. During the time measurements were made eruptions took place from the North-east Crater in September 1980 and February 1981, and on the north flank in March 1981. It is assumed that the changes in gravity resulted from magma movements associated with these eruptions and that the magma was fed from one localized region in each case. To model these magma movements Sanderson proposed that the magma rises passively into vertical fissures in which gas pressure and magma level are variable. The magma is thus filling a void and the amount of strain is relatively small. Such a model is consistent with the ground-deformation studies. Using a vertical dyke model of a size necessary to contain the mass of the erupted material, and setting the vertical extent of the dyke as 1 km (this is not a sensitive parameter) it is possible to search for an optimum depth and azimuth of dyke to fit the gravity-change data. In the case of the 1981 eruption the optimum fit gives a dyke with an azimuth of 335 ± 5° and a length of 14±3 km. This trend corresponds well with the fissure systems developed during the north flank eruption. The 1981 eruption is therefore considered to result from draining of a radial dyke which was charged with magma near to sea level six-to-twelve months before the eruption occurred.

Applying the same technique to the North-east Crater eruptions in September 1980, it was found that there was no optimum model and the changes are interpreted as the filling of small radial dykes as the magma ascended fairly rapidly. This eruption therefore is considered to be the result of magma ascending uninterrupted from depth to the North-east Crater in an open conduit.

Continuation of these high-precision gravity measurements on the established stations could provide important information about the volcano's internal plumbing. Clearly, in the interpretation of such measurements certain assumptions have to be made about the internal state of the volcano because gravity changes can result from a variety of different processes including de-gassing of magma, opening of fissures, forcible injection of magma, filling of fissure voids by magma. Different interpretations can be made depending on what is considered to be the cause of the gravity change. However, as is becoming clear in this chapter, each of the geophysical techniques employed depends to some extent on the results of other types of examination of the volcano, slowly refining the assumptions that must be made in the construction of models.

7.5 Magma budget and ascent rate

As well as knowing the geometry of the plumbing system of a volcano, it is also important for a complete knowledge of the system to know the velocity and volumetric ascent rates of magma in space and time. In some parts of the system, ascent rates may be high while in others magma may have residence times up to several years or even decades. Some of the magma will never reach the surface either because it remains in a conduit after an eruption or because it may intrude into the volcanic pile but never erupt; thus the output of lava represents only a part of the magma budget.

As discussed in an earlier chapter, the output of magma from *flank eruptions* is apparently in a steady state. Estimates of *total* erupted volumes for both persistent and flank activity between 1971 and 1981 (Wadge and Guest, 1981) indicate that magma may be released at the surface either as virtually continuous effusion close to the overall output rate or as a series of short, higher-effusion-rate eruptions with repose periods keeping the average output at the steady-state rate (Fig. 7.14). For much of the decade the limiting size of an eruption was about 25×10^6 m^3 of erupted lava as indicated by the envelope bounding the cumulative output plot shown in Figure 7.14. Thus the longer the repose time following an eruption the larger is the potential size of the next eruption up to the limit of 25×10^6 m^3. However, this simple pattern was broken twice between 1971 and 1983. The first was in 1971 when a flank eruption gave rise to a total volume of more than 50×10^6 m^3 of lava, and the second in 1983 when about 100×10^6 m^3 of lava were erupted on the south flank. Following the 1971 eruption only small amounts of lava were erupted until sufficient time had elapsed to bring the volcano back into the steady-state condition. Thus the evidence suggests that the total plumbing system of Etna gives an overall steady-state output. The amount of material forming intrusions into the volcanic pile is unknown but if this averages to a constant ratio with the output, then magma is supplied from the deep reservoir at a steady rate. Furthermore the constant output indicated by flank eruptions since the mid-eighteenth century (Fig. 4.38) would suggest that the same style of plumbing system has operated for some 200 years. The much higher output noted during the early-seventeenth century would indicate that at that time the plumbing system was different, giving individual eruptions that generally emitted larger volumes of lava than those in the following centuries. Because the volume of lava erupted at the summit before about 1965 is unknown it is not possible to tell if the ratio between output from flank eruptions and that from persistent activity has always remained the same, or if the periods of high output from the flanks result from less persistent activity. The long 1614

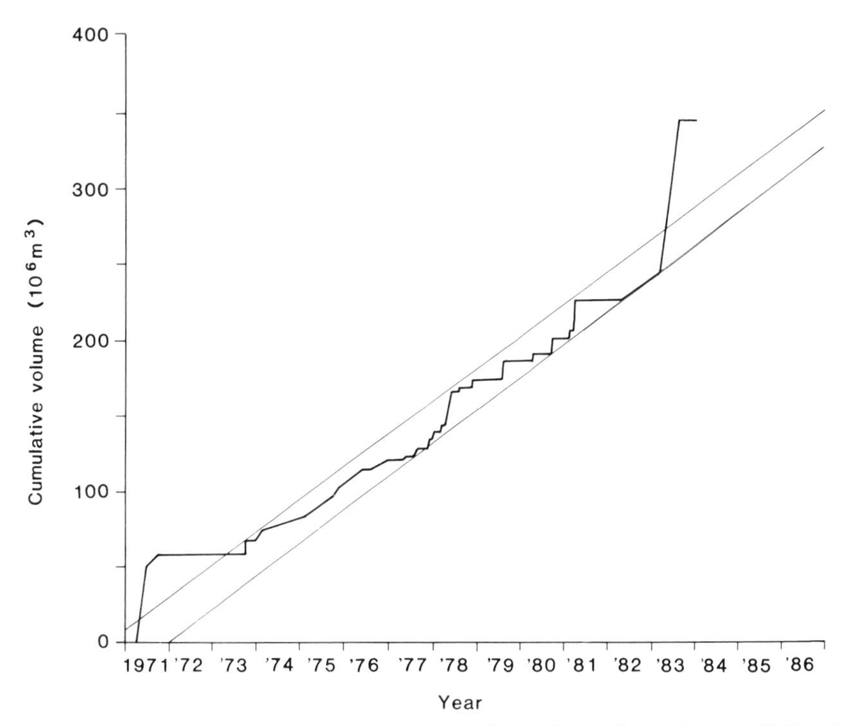

Fig. 7.14 The cumulative volume of magma erupted at Etna from 1971 to the beginning of 1984. (Modified from Wadge and Guest, 1981.)

– 24 eruption could well represent a transfer of persistent activity from the summit to the north-east rift as a result of blockage in the central conduit.

Magma ascent velocities are difficult to determine but the theoretical models of Wilson and Head (1981) suggest that, for strombolian activity to occur, ascent velocities must be less than 0.5 ms^{-1}; with higher velocities fire-fountains occur. On Etna true fountaining has rarely been observed suggesting that the maximum ascent velocity at least in the upper part of the Etna plumbing system is about 0.5 ms^{-1}. If this velocity is then accepted for long-lived eruptions, like the North-east Crater persistent activity during 1966 – 71, the feeding conduit near the surface need only have had a diameter of about 1.5 m to give the observed effusion rate of just under 1 m^3 s^{-1}, assuming that the density of the magma in the near-surface part of the vent is similar to that of the lava erupted. However where the effusion rates are much larger in flank eruptions, vents of greater cross-sectional areas (usually fissures) are required.

Assessment of the way that magma rises into the volcano from depth cannot be determined simply from activity at the surface. Several models could be proposed to explain the observed activity. One extreme model could be that magma leaves the deep-seated magma chamber continuously at a rate equalling the observed output plus an unknown amount forming intrusive bodies below the volcano. The magma's passage to the surface would probably be discontinuous owing to changes in shape of the conduit geometry and variations in velocity especially near the surface. Thus, although during long periods of steady-state effusion at the summit conditions below the surface remain fairly constant, changes in conduit geometry could result in a series of short, higher-effusive-rate eruptions. The opening of fissures on the flank could divert magma from the central conduit system delivering lava to the surface at a higher rate than is possible through the smaller cross-sectional area of the central conduit. In some cases a proportion of the magma entering the volcano may slowly fill a fissure even when activity is occurring elsewhere until a critical volume is reached and the dyke disgorges itself through fissures at the surface.

The other extreme model is that magma is released in pulses from the deep-seated reservoir in response to the local stress field. These pulses may travel quickly to the surface or may in part have residence times of up to a year or so in high-level fissures before eruption.

In reality, magma uprise is probably a combination of both the models outlined above and the process will only be further understood by more continuous geophysical monitoring than has been carried out so far. However, an important component in monitoring the movement of magma within the plumbing system is careful measurement of the output of lava from both persistent and flank activity over a longer period of time than has been done so far.

7.6 Summary and discussion

It would appear that if there is a major storage area for magma under Etna it may be a large reservoir at about 20 km below sea level. This is fed from a deeper source below the Moho. Most of the observations argue that there is no permanent high-level storage area, although there is some suggestion from work on volcanic tremor that storage occurs about 2 km below the summit, a conclusion that is not supported by other observations. Several techniques suggest that magma is stored in dykes within or just below the volcanic pile for many months (or even as much as two years) before a flank eruption. However it is not clear how much of the magma later erupted is stored at a high level before eruption, and it is quite possible that only a small part of the total magma is wedged into fissures opened sometime before the eruption takes place. Gravity models however can be produced which would be consistent with all the magma being emplaced ready for eruption many months before.

For persistent activity at the summit there appears to be an almost continuously open conduit to depth and most persistent activity is seismically quiet. Gravity data also suggest that magma involved in summit activity rises quickly from depth without storage, certainly in the top few kilometres of the conduit.

One of the problems of determining a model for the plumbing is to know how representative of historical times are the last few years for which there is geophysical data and also how representative is historical time for the whole of the volcano's history. It has been noted that the historical output rate has changed with time and that there was a period in the late-sixteenth and the seventeenth centuries when the output rate was considerably higher than in the period afterwards. During this time of high output, the texture of the erupted lava was different with the size of the plagioclase phenocrysts being much larger (Chapter 6). This clearly suggests that conditions within the uprising magma were different, and that probably the magma ascent rate and volcano plumbing were also different (Guest and Duncan, 1981; Duncan and Guest, 1982). Further back in the history of the volcano, as discussed in the last chapter, the range of compositions of material erupted suggests that there were high-level magma storage areas. Thus the present geophysical information may well be indicative of the state of the volcano at the present time but almost certainly the internal plumbing has changed throughout the volcano's history (Fig. 7.15). This does not necessarily mean that in prehistoric times when there is evidence for high-level magma storage that such reservoirs were in existence continuously and it is quite possible that for most of the history of the volcano it has been similar to the present but that for limited periods the plumbing was different.

It has also been argued that throughout the history of the volcano the position of the central conduit has shifted with time. Sartorious vön Waltershausen (1880), recognizing that the Trifoglietto cone had been partly buried by products of a more recent centre near the present one, postulated that the central conduit had moved northwards with time. This view was commonly accepted until the 1970s (Rittmann, 1973). Lyell (1858) on the other hand took a different view considering that Etna had a twin axis that operated simultaneously, one being Trifoglietto and the other Mongibello, near the present summit. This idea was supported by the observations of Mario Gemmellaro (quoted by C. Gemmellaro, 1860) that the ancient Trifoglietto dykes radiated from an area close to the present summit. Thus Lyell considered that Trifoglietto was a subsidiary cone to the larger Mongibello edifice.

Stratigraphic studies made over the last ten years have tended to support the views of Lyell but have also shown that the construction of Etna was more complex than envisaged by workers during the mid-nineteenth century. The Trifoglietto cone was buried by the Vavalaci lavas which built up a large structure, the top of which eventually collapsed to give the Vavalaci Caldera. The dykes in the Valle del Bove (Fig. 7.16) consist of two sets of dykes trending north-east and north-west, intersecting near the middle of the projected Vavalaci Caldera. This suggests that there was a long-standing centre of activity here that was at least contemporaneous with Trifoglietto. The next cone to be built up was that of Ellittico on the northern rim of the Vavalaci Caldera and this was followed by the Piano Cone which again suffered caldera collapse situated near the rim of the old Vavalaci Caldera close to where it is intersected by the Ellittico Caldera.

Based on the present evidence therefore, there has been no simple northward movement of the centre of activity and the present summit cone lies less than 2 km to the north-west of the middle of the Vavalaci Caldera. It is in this region, offset from the summit, that the two ancient dyke swarms in the Valle del Bove intersect and from which the majority of historical fissures radiate (Wadge, 1977). This observation may suggest that this is the main centre of the Mongibello Cone which has suffered repeated collapses (Guest, 1980). Clearly, however, the principal near-surface conduit since Trifoglietto times has occupied slightly different positions on the construct. Whether these shifts in position are shallow deviations of the conduit or of more deep-seated origin is unknown; but McGuire (1983) has suggested that magma rising from depth enters a 'clearing house' below the area marked by the intersection of dykes and fissures, and it is from here that magma is distributed to other parts of the volcano including

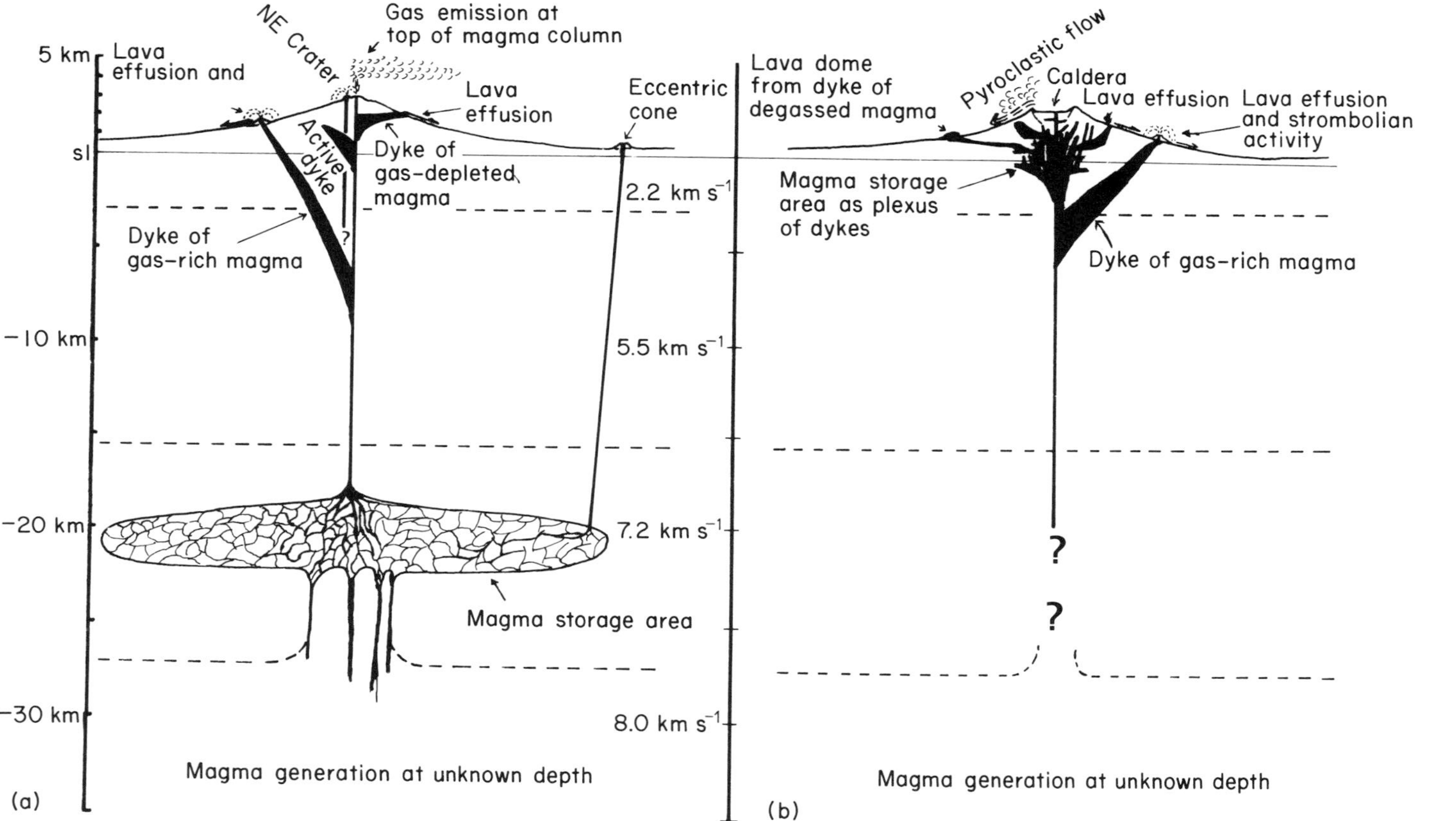

Fig. 7.15 (a) Interpretation of the internal structure of Mount Etna as it has been during the last 300 years. Magma rises up a central conduit from the deep magma storage area and a column of magma is probably always present to levels of less than one km below the volcano's summit even when effusion is not taking place. Persistent activity takes place from the top of the column when it is at or near ground level, and de-gassing from the column in the Summit Crater takes place continuously. Fissure-opening allows magma to leave the central conduit at different depths to produce flank eruptions that normally have higher effusion rates than the persistent activity. Dykes leaving the central conduit at depths below a few kilometres are still gas-rich giving rise to flank eruptions that have associated strombolian activity; whereas dykes radiating from high in the column contain gas-depleted magma (the gas having escaped up the central conduit to the summit region) and lava effusions are not accompanied by strombolian activity. Activity occurring close to the summit associated with the central conduit system is gas-rich and normally give rise to strombolian activity. The depth at which the North-east Crater magma column joins the central conduit is not known.

Eccentric eruptions such as that at Moio on the northern perimeter of the volcano may be associated with independent conduits directly from the magma storage area although there is a possibility that they are caused by long dykes from the central conduit. In this diagram the magma storage area and the seismic velocities are taken from Sharp *et al.* 1980.

(b) Similar to (a) but representing the volcano in pre-Valle del Bove times. In this interpretation a magma storage area possibly consisting of a plexus of dykes existed within the volcanic pile, at least at times when lavas of more-evolved compositions were erupted. Possibly during this time normal activity was similar to that in (a), but associated with the high-level storage complex were caldera collapses, pyroclastic flows and the emplacement of lava domes. (From Guest and Duncan, 1981, courtesy of *Nature*.)

the summit region. Such an hypothesis remains to be tested by future geophysical monitoring.

It must be concluded that the plumbing of Etna is complex and far from easy to understand. Unlike many other basaltic volcanoes it does not fit the model originally developed for Kilauea, perhaps not surprisingly given the relatively simple structural environment of Hawaii in the middle of a plate compared with the complex and not yet understood structural environment of Etna.

The relation between the regional tectonics and volcanism is difficult to determine. This results in part from a lack of understanding of the tectonics of this part of the Mediterranean and it is thus only possible to relate active fissure trends to known structural patterns in the region. The matter is further complicated by the fact that there is a stress field in the volcano imposed by the vast bulk of the mountain itself. The large active faults on the volcano's seaward flank in part at least result from seaward sliding of the eastern flank of the mountain: a process that led to extreme failure resulting in the Valle del Bove. Such seaward creep of the unbuttressed flank of the volcano must clearly play a part in opening of fissures that allow magma to reach the surface. Major changes in topography such as the opening of the Valle del Bove must also modify the stress system and it is notable that the styles of volcanism indicative of high-level magma-storage ceased after the Valle del Bove had been formed. For a better understanding of this complex volcano, extensive geophysical and volcanological surveillance over a long time period is required.

Fig. 7.16 Dykes in the wall of the Valle del Bove. (Photograph: J. E. Guest.)

8 Volcanic hazard on Etna

'A large area which
has been flooded with lava
is perhaps the most hideous and appalling
scene of desolation anywhere
to be found on the surface
of the globe.'

(Sir Archibald Geikie, 1885)

Assessing the threat from a volcano demands as complete a knowledge as possible of its long- and short-term behaviour. As this becomes better understood, more effective land-management policies, emergency procedures and mitigation techniques can be drawn up and implemented to reduce the vulnerability of exposed communities.

In this respect, it is helpful to make a distinction between a 'risk' and a 'hazard', terms which, in general use, are often treated as if interchangeable. Thus, while a *hazard* may be considered as the likelihood of being affected by a particular (volcanic) phenomenon, the *risk* provides a measure of the loss (for example, death, destruction of property, or economic decline) that is expected to follow as a result of that phenomenon. In a more concise form, the relation between the two may be presented as (modified after Fournier d'Albe, 1979): *risk equals the product of hazard and expected loss.*

Consequently, the potential risk facing a village in a highly hazardous region may be less than that for a city – with a larger population and of greater economic importance – in a relatively less hazardous district. At the same time, although a town at risk from a nearby eruption must be in a hazardous area, the converse association need not hold true.

The definition also clearly demonstrates that the reduction of volcanic risk may be achieved by lowering the value of an area, through evacuation or restricted development, or by manipulating the source of the hazard so as to decrease its potential threat. The first approach may be considered as a broadly passive response, that is reacting to volcanic events without attempting to control them. This is the most reliable policy from the point of view of saving life, but it is also inevitably expensive and, if permanent relocation should be necessary, can be psychologically traumatic. When lives are not in immediate danger, therefore, such as when an encroaching lava is still several days flowage away from a given settlement, there is at least a good economic argument for considering an active response, whereby some effort is made to alter the course of the flow.

There are accordingly three steps to a complete hazard analysis: (1) identifying the nature of the hazard; (2) determining when and where it will occur; and (3) preparing remedial measures to mitigate its effect. The first of these has to be determined from the behaviour of the volcano as established from the historical and geological records. The same information can be used to assess the long-term vulnerability of different areas on the volcano and so allow appropriate land-management policies to be initiated. This is essentially the objective of *general* prediction (following the terminology of Walker (1974a)). *Specific* prediction, on the other hand, is concerned with the routine monitoring of the volcano (using geophysical, geochemical and phenomenological techniques) in order to identify the timing, location, style and magnitude of an impending eruption. Once the outbreak has started, elements of both methods can be used to evaluate its probable mode of development, from which a first appraisal can be made as to the feasibility of mitigation.

8.1 The sources of hazard on Mount Etna

Flank effusions have posed the greatest hazard to Etnean settlements in historical times. Unless actually erupted in a populated area, the lavas rarely present an immediate threat to human life, their fronts commonly slowing to less than walking pace within distances of 1 – 2 km from the vent. Only occasionally, and upon the unwary, have they had a terminal effect. During the 1928 eruption, three men (this figure is open to question) apparently elected to stay an extra night in their threatened homes outside Mascali. By the following morning, on 9 November, the houses, and their contents, had been consumed by the flows (Jaggar, 1928b, quoting press reports). Yet more dramatically, at least thirty-six spectators from Bronte were reportedly killed in 1843 when the front of the lava suddenly exploded upon encountering marshy ground (Rodwell, 1878). Similarly, two officials narrowly escaped serious injury during the opening stages of the 1983 eruption, when an explosion at a nearby lava front moving over snow caused them to lose control of their vehicle. These apparently phreatic events are especially pernicious owing to their suddenness and unpredictability. Despite the 1983 incident, it is not uncommon, for example, for a whole flow field to develop in a snow-covered district without such an occurrence, suggesting that its basal crust develops quickly to provide an efficient thermal insulator. When this is ruptured, however, so allowing a comparatively large amount of trapped groundwater to come into contact with incandescent material, the conditions are appropriate for an unexpected explosion.

In general, though, it is immovable property which is most endangered by lava flows. In the case of fields and houses, destruction is absolute, and while it is possible to rebuild and relocate entire towns and villages (for instance, Belpasso and a major part of Catania in 1669, and Mascali in 1928), buried farmland can only be reclaimed after several generations of weathering. Assuming, therefore, that Etna's historical behaviour will be representative of its activity for at least the next few hundred years, the principal goal of hazard assessment becomes to determine the vulnerability of different areas to invasion by lavas. Before developing this aspect in more detail (in the section on general prediction and hazard analysis), it is prudent to consider the other major sources of hazard on the volcano, from the rare paroxysms which affect whole regions to the more frequent, less violent phenomena with more restricted spheres of influence.

At the more catastrophic end of the spectrum are the ignimbrite- and caldera-forming eruptions and large-scale phreatomagmatic events (Chapter 4). Because these styles of activity can obliterate large areas very rapidly, their resumption would constitute a much greater hazard to all parts of the mountain than has been experienced in recorded history. They are unlikely to recur, however, unless there is a major change either in the magma storage system or in the surface conditions of the volcano. Thus, on the one hand, Etna's prehistoric ignimbrites are associated with mugearitic and benmoreitic lavas, considerably more evolved than the hawaiites typical of the last 2 – 3 millenia or more, while, on the other, the large phreatomagmatic cones, such as Trifoglietto II, appear to have formed during periods of harsher and wetter climate (Chapter 4). Consequently, any return to such activity is expected to be preceded by a gradual change (probably requiring at least several hundreds-to-thousands of years) in either eruptive patterns, involving long periods of dormancy for differentiation to produce a suitably evolved magma, or general climatic conditions, neither of which appears to be happening at present.

Less vehement explosions, in contrast, are common occurrences on Etna, ranging from sporadic ultravulcanian outbursts to continuous strombolian activity (Chapter 4). Their impact, however, is usually confined to the immediate vicinity of a vent and the expelled lithic blocks or juvenile bombs rarely have a lethal range of more than 300 – 500 m, while the accompanying blast-waves set-up in the atmosphere have a yet more limited effect. Indeed, it is the fine ashes, particularly from strombolian activity, which may ultimately cause the most disruption – even thin tephra blankets having the potential to reduce crop yields and clog machinery.

By mixing with rain or melt water, thicker tephra blankets on the volcano's upper slopes may also endanger developed areas through the generation of lahars. Several prehistoric examples have been recognized both below the Valle del Bove and near Biancavilla (Chapter 4). Few, though, have been described in the historical record. The best documented is the mudflow of March 1755, triggered after an eruption at the summit when it was blanketed with ice and snow. According to Lyell (1858), the reputedly-hot lahar swept down through the Valle del Bove and on towards the sea, leaving a deposit over 2 km wide and up to 10 m thick. In view of the frequency of summit activity and the ubiquitous preservation there of snow and ice below layers of ash and lava (Fig. 8.1), it is notable that comparable lahars do not appear to have been more common. A possible explanation is that because of a general cooling in the European climate during the eighteenth century, Etna may have been able to maintain a comparatively thicker cover of snow and ice at high altitude (Duncan *et al.*, 1981). In consequence, it is uncertain whether or not the current conditions at the summit are suitable for producing large lahars. If they should

Fig. 8.1 Intercalated layers of ice and tephra in the summit region of Etna. Protected by the insulating properties of the pyroclastic material, ice accumulations such as these may survive for several months or possibly years.

occur, however, one of the more vulnerable parts of the volcano would seem to be between the Valle del Bove and the coast (Duncan *et al.*, 1981).

Based on instrumental records extending back to the turn of the century, Etna's eastern slopes also appear to be especially prone to seismic activity (Fig. 8.2). With focal depths of generally less than 6 km, most of these earthquakes have been attributed to tectonic movements rather than magmatic activity (Lombardo and Patane, 1982), although the first is often associated with the onset of the second (Sharp *et al.*, 1981). During this short period of instrumental observation, few of the earthquakes have exceeded magnitude 6 on the Modified Mercalli (MM) scale, two exceptions being the events of 1911 and 1914 (magnitudes 6 – 6.5 on the MM scale, or 9 – 10 on the MSK(-64) scale, as used in Fig. 8.2), which caused considerable damage in the built-up areas around Santa Venerina and Linera (Cosentino, 1982). From the historical record, however, there is also evidence that more violent earthquakes may occur at intervals of several centuries, such as the devastating events of 1169 and 1693, which together caused the loss of up to 115 000 lives (see Table 3.3).

A more localized menace from ground movement is surface collapse. As described in Chapter 4, the formation of pits and the collapse of vent walls are typically related to the loss of support from subterranean magma. Although dramatic foundering has been observed in the summit region – from the widening of the Bocca Nuova to the subsidence of the summit cone – this appears to be a less common process among flank vents, presumably because the latter are not additionally subjected to the destabilizing action of persistent

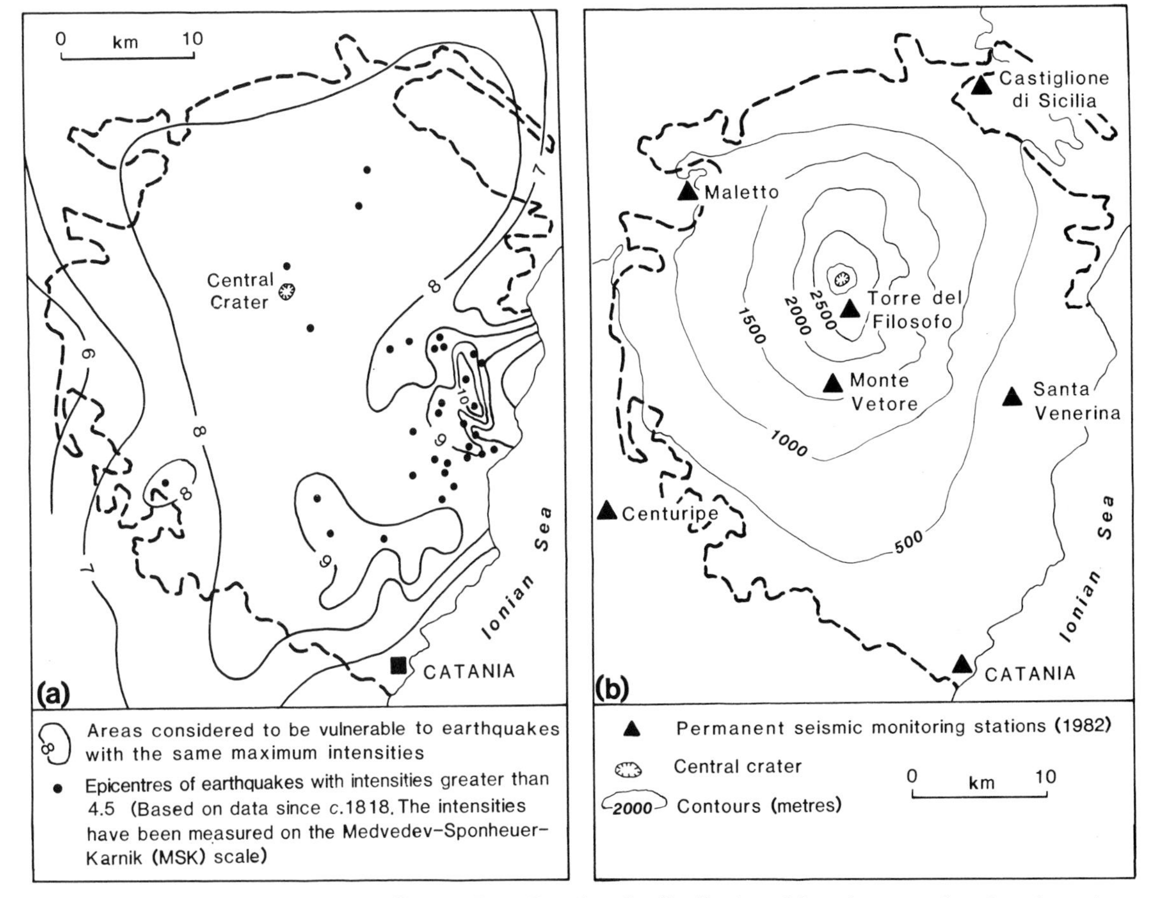

Fig. 8.2 (a) A seismic intensity map of Mount Etna. Based on the distribution of the epicentres of earthquakes, of known intensity, recorded between 1818 and 1973, the lines of equal seismic intensity have been calibrated on the MSK (−64) scale (after Barbano *et al.*, 1980). Note the concentration of epicentres towards the lower ESE flanks of the volcano. (b) The locations of the seven short-period, vertical-component seismometers, which compose the basic seismic monitoring net on Mount Etna. (From Cosentino, 1982.)

activity, either in the form of mechanical disturbance, due to oscillations in magma level, or of chemical degradation by gases.

Volcanic gases and aerosols are also a source of hazard in their own right. In addition to water, Etnean gases contain a high proportion of carbon dioxide and sulphur dioxide (Gerlach, 1979, 1983; also see Chapter 6, Section 6.6). Most of the exhalation tends to occur from the open vents at the summit, the prevailing northwesterlies keeping the plume at high altitude above the surrounding region. Nevertheless, during phases of strong degassing, the meteorological conditions may be suitable for the precipitation of unusually acidic rain over Etna's fertile south-eastern flanks. However, the degree to which crops and water supplies may be adversely affected has yet to be established. Near a more sheltered vent, on the other hand, calmer winds may be more favourable to the temporary collection in hollows of dense and asphyxiating carbon dioxide; such pockets of gas may prove fatal if their CO_2 concentrations should increase above the order of 8% by volume (Faivre-Pierret and Le Guern, 1983).

8.2 Specific prediction and hazard assessment

Two common handicaps to alleviating the impact of an eruption are a lack of preparedness before the event and uncertainty, after the initial outbreak, as to whether or not the eruption will enter a menacing phase. Etna's 1979 flank activity, for example, started with the reawakening of the South-east Crater on 16 July. At 3000 m, the strombolian activity was not in itself especially hazardous; rather, it provided an extra novelty for visiting tourists. Two-and-a-half weeks later, however, lava emerged from several new vents on the Eastern and North-eastern slopes, the largest destroying some orchards and endangering the town of Fornazzo. But despite the eighteen-day interval, emergency services were only directed to Fornazzo once the effusion was under way. If, however, it had been possible to specify sooner that the town was at risk, an earlier official presence could have been made felt, if only to reassure the anxious population.

It is the improvement of this situation which is the main objective of specific prediction and hazard assessment, that is, the detailed monitoring of the volcano to identify the likely time, place and style of an imminent eruption. To this end, Etna has become a valuable testing ground for a variety of techniques. However, as with other volcanoes, basaltic or otherwise, no single method has emerged which, by itself, can offer a definitive forecast of activity. Thus, while flank eruptions are often preceded by shallow seismic crises, shallow seismic crises do not always herald an eruption. Similarly an increase in ground temperature does not automatically indicate the approach of an outburst, being only a pointer to the possible injection of magma at shallow levels, without being able to signal whether or not it will break through the surface. To reduce the ambiguity of interpretation, therefore, several monitoring methods need to be operating simultaneously, the purpose being to define a common trend among the independently derived data.

This approach has been used to advantage in other basaltic volcanic regions, such as Hawaii and Iceland. Unfortunately the individual behaviour of a volcano is often too idiosyncratic to be of predictive value elsewhere (compare, for instance, the results of the ground-deformation studies in Hawaii and on Etna, as outlined in Chapter 7). Accordingly each volcano must be monitored for a length of time much greater than the typical interval between eruptions, in order to establish a base level of normal non-eruptive behaviour and thereby to recognize what constitutes a significant increase in activity.

Such a programme has been developing on Etna since the mid-1970s, using geophysical and geochemical techniques, especially seismic and ground-deformation studies (a brief summary has been given by Villari (1983)). In addition to the information that these methods have provided about the plumbing system of the volcano (Chapter 7), they are now beginning to resolve short-term behavioural patterns that have a forecasting potential.

8.2.1 Seismic studies

Whether stimulated by, for example, the opening and closing of fissures, or the vibrations induced by rapid fluid motion or vesiculation, the migration of magma is typically associated with some form of seismic phenomenon (Chapter 7). By tracing the passage of earthquake focal depths, it is possible, in principle, to follow the progress of an inferred magma body from depths of several kilometres up to the surface. Thus, despite the complications arising from non-magmatic behaviour (such as the localized settling of the volcanic interior), seismic monitoring remains a powerful tool for detecting the first indications of magma ascent and for identifying the possible areas of an imminent eruption.

The core of the Italian seismic network of automatic, continuously recording instruments is shown in Fig. 8.2(b). Although the geometry of the net has left virtually the whole of the northern flank uncovered, so prohibiting a complete volcano-wide study of seismic activity and introducing large error margins into epicentre and focus determinations (Villari, 1983), a review of the data acquired between 1973 and 1981 has allowed Cosentino (1982) to specify three trends in the association between seismicity and eruptive activity:

(1) The flank eruptions on the western and northern sides of the Valle del Bove, and also the 1981 north flank activity, have been preceded by a significant increase in the frequency and energy released by shallow seismic phenomena (at depths of 1 – 5 km) some 2 – 10 days before an eruption (Figure 8.3), no single earthquake exceeding a magnitude (MM scale) of 4.5 (data from the 1974 west flank eruption are less comprehensive since only one seismic station was then in commission);

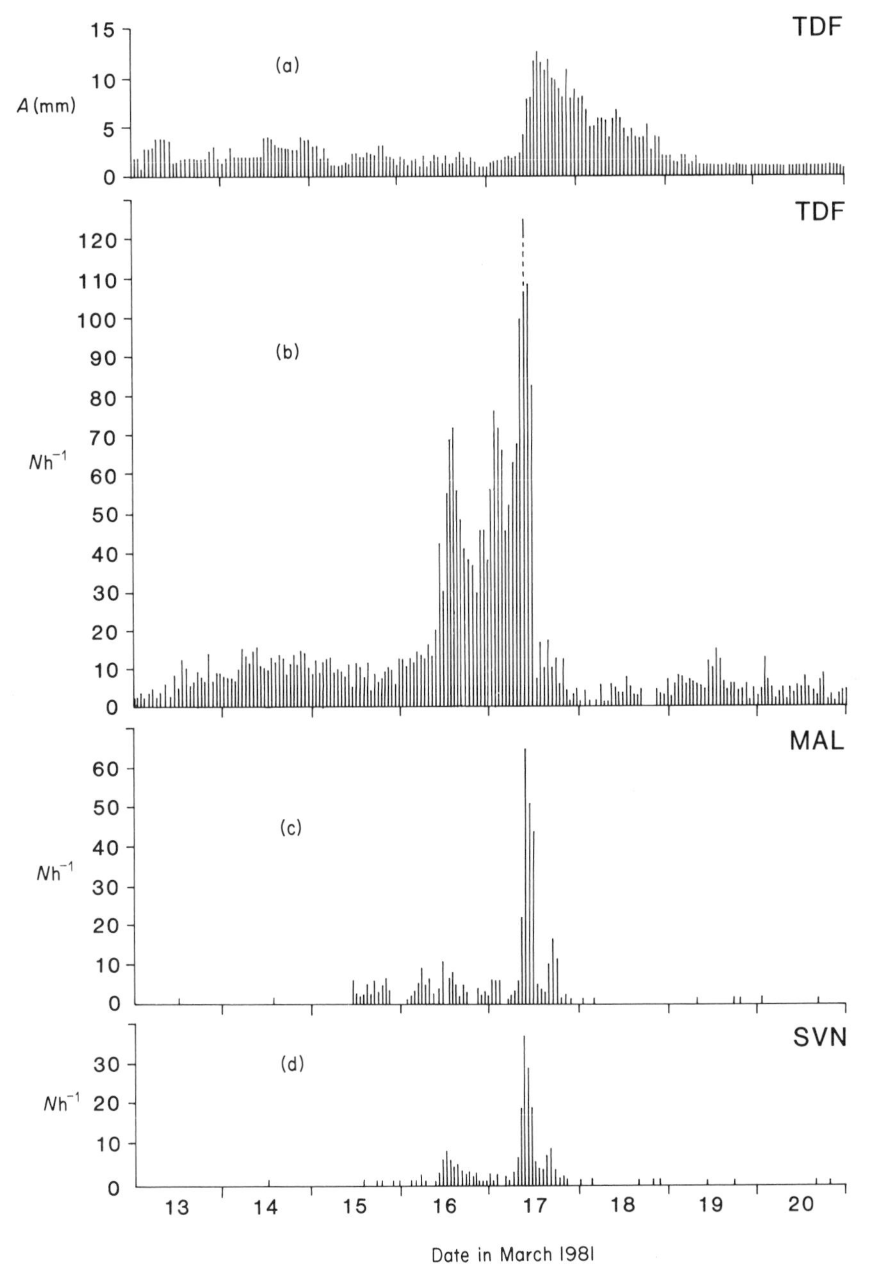

Fig. 8.3 Seismic signals recorded before and during the opening phases of Etna's 17–23 March 1981 north flank eruption.

(a) Changes in the half-amplitude A of the tremors detected at the Torre del Filosofo station. The period of high half-amplitude values (17–20 March) corresponds to that in which most of the lava was effused; the peak value on 17 March is associated with the phase of the fastest discharge and most vigorous degassing of the lava.

(b,c,d) Changes in the frequency (Nh^{-1} numbers per hour) of the tremors detected at (b) the Torre del Filosofo, (c) Maletto and (d) Santa Venerina stations. The increase in the tremor frequency immediately before the eruption appears to have been related to the opening of shallow fissures ahead of the migrating magma.

The station locations are shown in Fig. 8.2(b). (After Cosentino *et al.*, 1981; Cosentino, 1982.)

(2) Most eruptions on or near the Summit Cone have not been preceded by significant changes in seismic activity in the days leading up to an eruption. On occasion, however, the beginning of an eruption has been characterized by a sudden increase in harmonic tremor, possibly the result of the rapid and turbulent degassing of the magma; and

(3) A marked increase in explosive activity (detected seismically as 'explosion 'quakes'), particularly at vents in the summit area, does not necessarily indicate the imminence of lava effusion.

Even with a small seismic net, therefore, eight years of monitoring has allowed the identification of potentially significant seismic crises, which, when indeed associated with eruptions, have been observed several days before the volcanic outburst itself. One of the most promising developments was the warning issued by the Istituto di Scienze della Terra of Catania University the day before the 17 March (1981) north flank eruption (Cosentino *et al.*, 1981). It was in response to the announcement that Romolo Romano, of the Istituto Internazionale di Vulcanologica in Catania, was reconnoitering the area in a helicopter when the first of the fissures opened.

8.2.2 *Ground-deformation studies*

The introduction of new material from depth generally results in some distortion of the volcanic pile. The degree to which this deformation becomes manifest at the surface depends upon the shape and mass of the new material, the depth and mode (permissive or forcible) of intrusion, and the bulk compressibility of the fluid magma and the solid host rocks. However, as indicated by the description in Chapter 7 of the techniques available, the interpretation of ground-deformation data is necessarily model-dependent because of the flexibility allowed in estimating the influencing parameters. The immediate predictive value of such studies is further inhibited by the current inability to distinguish between phases of simple intrusion and potential extrusion. Their major importance, therefore, is for locating the likely sites for an eruption, which on Etna may be recognized months or possibly years in advance (Murray and Guest, 1982; Murray, 1982b; see also Chapter 7).

8.2.3 *Other geophysical techniques*

In combination, seismic and ground-deformation methods currently provide the most promise for being able to follow the migration of a magma and to indicate where and when it is likely to erupt. Several other geophysical studies, however, have also been conducted on Etna and though none is yet sufficiently advanced to permit specific predictions to be made, they have been able to indicate areas of potentially higher-than-average vulnerability and also to offer the possibility of placing tighter constraints on the interpretations of seismic and deformation data. The techniques may be grouped into three general classes according to the type of physical effect of the magma on the volcano which they are trying to detect: thermal, electromagnetic and gravimetric.

Thermal surveys rely on identifying areas of greater-than-average surface temperatures, brought about through the conductive or convective transfer of heat from an underlying magma. Basaltic melts typically rise fast enough to bring the magma to the surface more quickly than their heat can be conducted through the low-conductivity host rocks. Consequently, any thermal variations preceding an eruption are most likely to be produced by convective heat transfer through heated groundwater or juvenile gases (Francis, 1979; Bourlet and Bourlet, undated).

Zones of high thermal anomaly have been identified around Etna's upper slopes from both infrared images taken from space (De Carolis *et al.*, 1975; Archambault *et al.*, 1979b) and direct ground-temperature measurements (e.g. Archambault *et al.*, 1979a; Archambault *et al.*, undated; Bourlet and Bourlet, undated). A major difficulty in interpretation lies in distinguishing anomalies due to underlying magmas from the superficial effects of recent lava flows, changes in vegetation and soil conditions, and seasonal variations in surface water content. Nevertheless, Archambault *et al.* (1979b) recognized on satellite images an important and apparently long-lived (that is, since it was first distinguished in 1978) thermal 'high' extending over some 50 km^2 and running from the Citelli region (east of the Valle del Leone), along the western wall of the Valle del Bove, to the vicinity of the Monti Silvestri cones (at about 1800 – 1900 m a.s.l. on the southern rift). This they have interpreted as a zone covering a preferred magma-feeding or-storage system, which is thus subject to frequent heating and delineates an area of potentially high vulnerability to an eruption.

Short-term temperature changes apparently related to eruptive activity have also been recorded by a pilot ground-temperature monitoring system in the Monti Silvestri – Calcarazzi region (Archambault *et al.*, undated.) The location of the network and the results obtained during 1980 and part of 1981 are shown in Fig. 8.4. While there appears to have been a significant temperature increase coinciding with the resumption of South-east Crater activity (from April to August 1980), the possible precursory signals (in early April) are rather less striking. In addition, there seems to have been no systematic relation between the observed temperature changes and the North-east Crater eruptions, although these may to some extent have been masked by the effects of the south flank activity. However, in view of the fact that the monitoring stations are situated some 5 – 6 km from the summit area, the results have proved sufficiently encouraging for the French operators to install a second network between the Torre del Filosofo and the South-east Crater (on the south flank between 2920 and 3050 m). After a few preliminary difficulties, including strikes by lightning, these sensors, inserted to depths of up to 120 cm, have since been linked to the Argos satellite communications system, thereby allowing the data to be relayed directly to France (Archambault, 1982). With the two networks operating in tandem, it is hoped that it will be possible to better outline the size and shape of local thermal anomalies while they develop, as well as to quantify which ranges of temperature-rise and rate of increase indicate a strong probability of an eruption.

The high temperature (about 1100°C) of a magma also provides it with electrical and magnetic properties markedly different from those of the solidified host rocks. Thus both electrical resistivity and magnetisation decrease with rising temperature, the latter finally disappearing once the Curie temperature of 600°C has been surpassed. Consequently, the ascent of fresh magma should be detectable through local distortions in either the natural magnetic and electric fields at the surface of the volcano or fields externally induced by artificial means. In both cases, the observed reduction in field strength will depend upon the size, shape and depth of the new material, while the migration of juvenile volatiles may also lower the resistivity of the enclosing medium.

Reviews of the volcanological applications of magnetic and electromagnetic (with electrical) surveying methods have been presented by Robach (1983) and Halbwachs (1983) respectively. On Etna, special attention has been paid to electromagnetic induction and self-potential techniques – the first analysing the form of the secondary magnetic fields induced in the substrata by an artificial electromagnetic field, the second investigating the potential differences naturally created by electrochemical processes in the ground. Though neither method has been utilized for specific prediction, preliminary studies indicate that they are sufficiently sensitive to be of value in detecting the arrival of new magma. Hence electromagnetic profiling has been able to identify shallow (less than 1500 m deep) structural weaknesses (Van Ngoc *et al.*, 1979), heat sources (Van Ngoc *et al.*, 1980), and water-saturated layers that may increase the local hazard from sudden phreatic explosions (Van Ngoc *et al.*, 1982), while a week-long self-potential survey was apparently able to record the motion of the magma feeding the 1983 flank eruption (Van Ngoc *et al.*, 1983).

The shifting of magma will additionally influence the local gravitational field, not only because of the displacement of a large mass of material, but also through attendant changes in ground elevation and, if close enough to the surface, variations in magmatic density caused by vesiculation and different degrees of magma compression (Sanderson

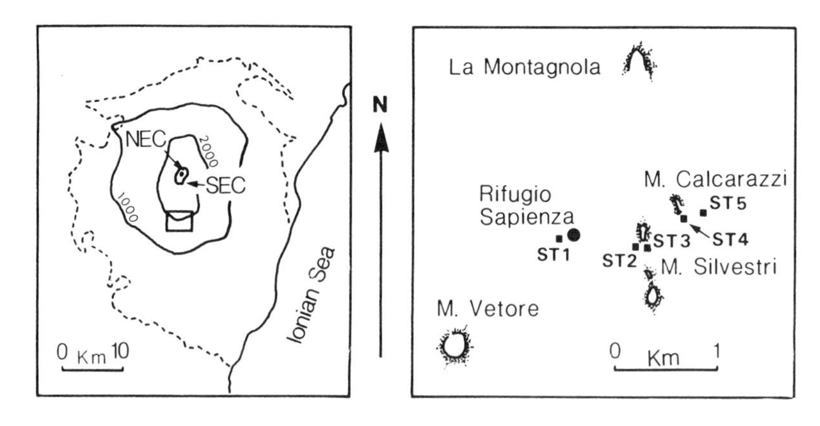

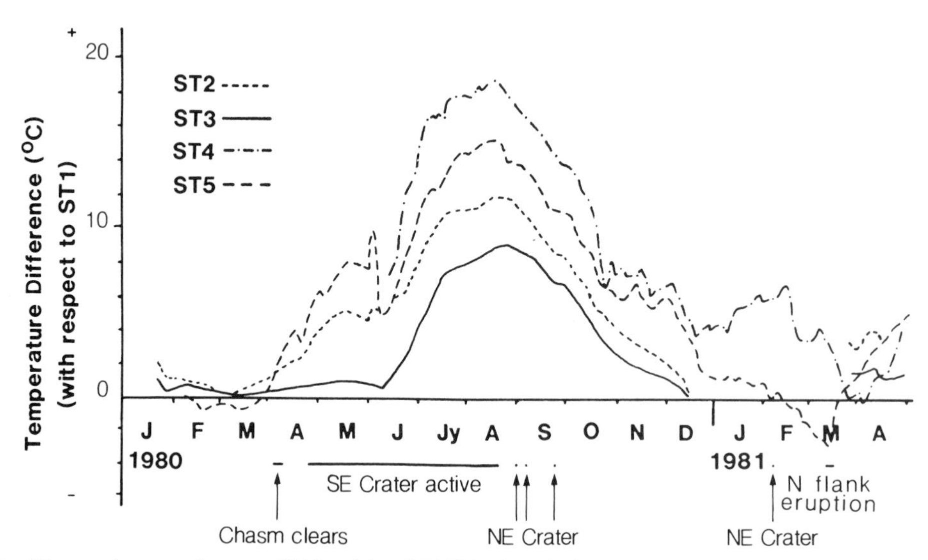

Fig. 8.4 Changes between January 1980 and April 1981 in the relative ground-temperatures (120 cm depth) measured on Etna's south flank at about 1900 m a.s.l. Some of the variations seem to have been related to eruptive activity, heat being transferred from new magma to the monitoring area by the convection of groundwater and possibly escaping juvenile gases.
In order to remove seasonal thermal variations, the temperatures are quoted as the differences from those measured at the Sapienza Reference Station (ST1), which appears to lie outside the zone of groundwater convection. (Data from Archambault *et al.*, undated.)

et al., 1983). The interpretation of gravity data is further complicated by the dependence of the nature of the observed anomaly on the depth and shape of the disturbing mass. For gravimetric data to be of value for hazard assessment, therefore, the number of unknown quantitites must be reduced using independently obtained estimates, such as of the geometry of the feeding system from geological and seismic data, or of changes in surface elevation from ground-deformation studies. Thus Sanderson (1982a) and Sanderson *et al.* (1983) have been able to combine ground-deformation and gravimetric data to constrain models of the feeding systems active during Etna's September 1980 (North-east Crater) and March 1981 (north flank) eruptions, and to identify an area of potentially high vulnerability on the mountain's western slopes. They also demonstrated the possibility of detecting permissive near-surface magma movement, which may not necessarily be accompanied by either surface-elevation changes or seismic phenomena.

8.2.4 *Geochemical studies*

Geophysical surveillance methods rely on detecting a magma directly through its effects on its surroundings. Geochemical techniques, in contrast, are concerned with monitoring volcanic constituents themselves, notably the early-released gases which are the first phases to arrive at the surface.

The initial chemical compositions of these gases are sensitive to the composition, temperature and depth (ambient pressure) of the parent magma at the time of their escape. In theory, the presence and ascent of a degassing intrusion should be observable from the exhalation of high-temperature gases at the surface and from differences in their compositions. As mentioned in Chapter 6, however, there are logistical and technical difficulties in adequately sampling such materials, in addition to the complications introduced by compositional changes due to rapid equilibration of the gases to the new environmental conditions and the effects of contaminating reactions with the atmosphere, groundwater, and the ashes and lavas of the volcanic pile. As a consequence, no unambiguous chemical parameter (such as the proportion of a particular gas species, or the ratio of one species to another) has been identified as a precursor to eruptions on Etna, although there are some indications that increases in the rates of discharge of sulphur dioxide (Zettwoog and Haulet, 1978; Malinconico, 1979; Jaeschke *et al*, 1982) and of hydrogen sulphide (Jaeschke *et al.*, 1982) may become useful for predictive purposes.

8.2.5 *The limitations of geophysical and geochemical methods for specific prediction*

The collection of physical and chemical data provides quantitative estimates of the values of selected parameters, changes in which may be related to magmatic activity. Though still in the early stages of development, seismic and ground-deformation studies have already proved of value in identifying potential eruption centres, notably before the 1981 (Cosentino *et al.*, 1981) and 1983 (Murray, 1982b) flank effusions, and the preliminary results from other techniques are also encouraging. However, even when different methods yield evidence consistent with the ascent of a magma, it is not yet possible to assert whether or not it will break through the surface.

A limiting factor is the empirical nature of the data interpretation. For example, as shown respectively by Murray and Guest (1982) and Sanderson (1982a), many of the observed ground-elevation and gravity changes may be explained in terms of a number of assumed magma bodies of different geometries at different positions, the preferred model being generally chosen on the basis of geological studies of dissected parts of the cone (such as the Valle del Bove). With continued monitoring, however, and the introduction of additional techniques, new geophysical and geochemical data may be used to test the consistency of earlier models and to propose more realistic alternatives.

By thus developing a better understanding of the plumbing system of the volcano and of the processes operating beneath the surface, more reliable announcements are likely to be forthcoming about the time and place of an approaching eruption, and possibly also about the manner in which that eruption will develop. At the moment, this third aspect of specific prediction relies wholly on empirical studies, observers using their experience of previous eruptions to evaluate the possible behaviour of the one in progress. A key example of this approach, particularly relevant to Etna, is the assessment of the growth of a lava flow-field.

8.3 The empirical determination of the relative vulnerabilities of Etnean districts

8.3.1 *Studies of lava flow development*

Owing to the complex interaction of the factors

controlling lava flow development (Chapters 4 and 5), it is not yet possible to specify exactly, during the height of an eruption, what will be the final dimensions of a flow-field. However, thanks to the large number of Etna's recorded eruptions, empirical studies (notably those of Walker (1973a, 1974a), Wadge (1978), Lopes and Guest (1982) and Romano and Sturiale (1982)), comparing the relative variation of selected effusion characteristics (such as the final lengths and widths of flow-fields versus their rates of effusion and the altitudes of the source vents), have enabled some general trends to be recognized, from which a lava's probable *maximum* areal extent can be estimated.

Walker (1974a) was the first to emphasize the association among Etnean (aa) lavas that, although flows effused at the same altitude show a scattering of final lengths (Fig. 8.5), the maximum flow length tends to increase with decreasing altitude – a trend which he attributed to a corresponding increase in hydrostatic magma driving pressures at lower elevations. From the improved data of Lopes and Guest (1982; see Fig. 8.5, this book), the variation may be approximately described by the relation:

$$L_{max} = 19.94 - 1.26\, h^2_v \qquad (\text{for } 0.3 \leq h_v \leq 3.2) \qquad (8.1)$$

where the maximum potential flow length (L_{max}) and source vent altitude (h_v) are both measured in kilometres.

If the average ground slope angle below the vent can be assigned a constant value $\alpha°$, then, applying simple trigonometry, the greatest distance likely to be covered by a flow may also be expressed in terms of the altitude range Δh_{max} that it has passed through, where:

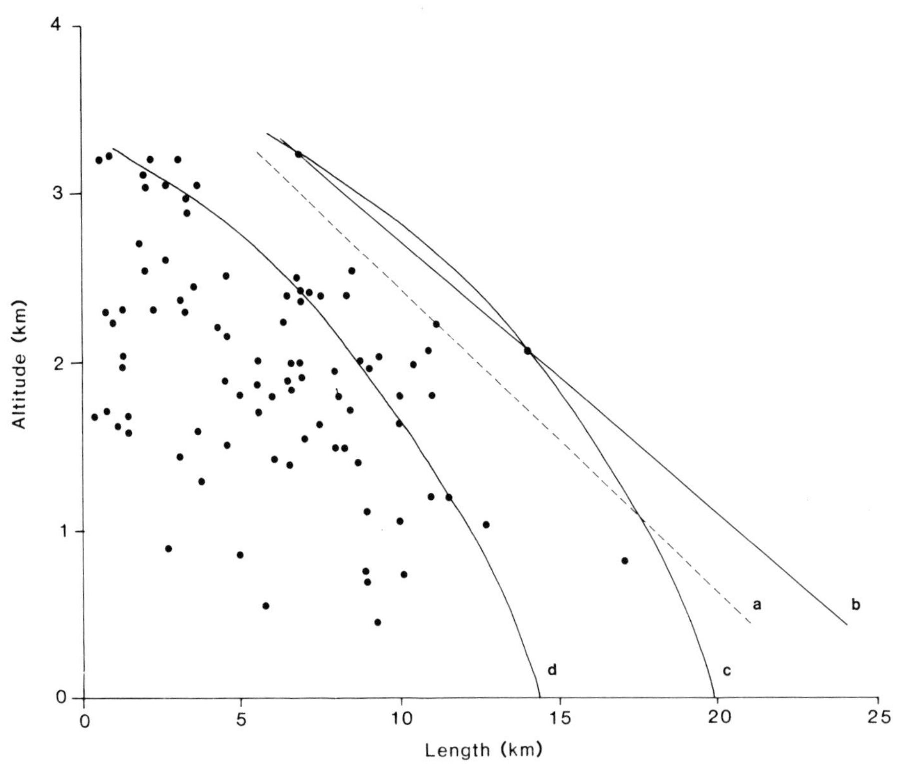

Fig. 8.5 The variation with the altitudes of their source vents of the lengths of eighty-six Etnean flow fields. The four curves describe: (a) the limiting envelope of Walker (1974a); (b) the limiting envelope of Lopes and Guest (1982); (c) the limiting envelope described by Equation (8.1); and (d) the 80% envelope described by Equation (8.5). (Data from Lopes and Guest, 1982.)

$$[\Delta h_{max} = h_v - h_b = L_{max} \sin \alpha] \quad (8.2)$$
$$(\text{for } 0.3 \leq h_v \leq 3.2;\ 0 \leq h_b)$$

and h_b is the (basal) altitude of the tip of the flow, in kilometres.

The maximum potential width of a flow-field at any given position also increases with decreasing altitude (Lopes and Guest, 1982; see Fig. 8.6, this book). This appears to be a response to the general shallowing of Etna's regional slopes towards sea level, the largest relative changes in maximum width, between 1400 m and 2200 m a.s.l., coinciding with Etna's most rapid change in regional gradient.

From Fig. 8.6, the relation between maximum potential flow width (W_{max}; km) and altitude (h; km) is approximately described by:

$$W_{max} = 4.05\, e^{-0.26 h^2} \quad (\text{for } 0 \leq h \leq 3) \quad (8.3)$$

The maximum potential area (A_{max}) of a flow may then be estimated by integrating Equation (8.3) over the range of altitudes covered by the lava and dividing by the average gradient (tan α) of the surface. Thus:

$$A_{max} = \frac{4.05}{\tan \alpha} \int_{h_b}^{h_v} e^{-0.26 h^2}\, dh \quad (8.4a)$$

which may be rewritten as:

$$A_{max} = \frac{14.1}{\tan \alpha} \int_{h^*_b}^{h^*_v} (2\pi)^{-1/2} e^{-0.5 h^{*2}}\, dh^* \quad (8.4b)$$

where $h^* = 0.72\, h$.

The function to be integrated in Equation (8.4b) is the same as that describing the shape of the statistical normal distribution curve and, as such, can be readily evaluated between the desired limits with the use of standard normal probability tables.

As an illustration, consider the effusion of a lava from a vent at 2350 m a.s.l., below which the average ground slope angle is 10°. From Equations (8.1) and (8.2), respectively, the maximum flow length and lowest altitude to which it will descend are calculated to be about 13.0 km and 100 m a.s.l. Setting $h = 0.1$ in Equation (8.3) indicates that the width of the flow is unlikely to

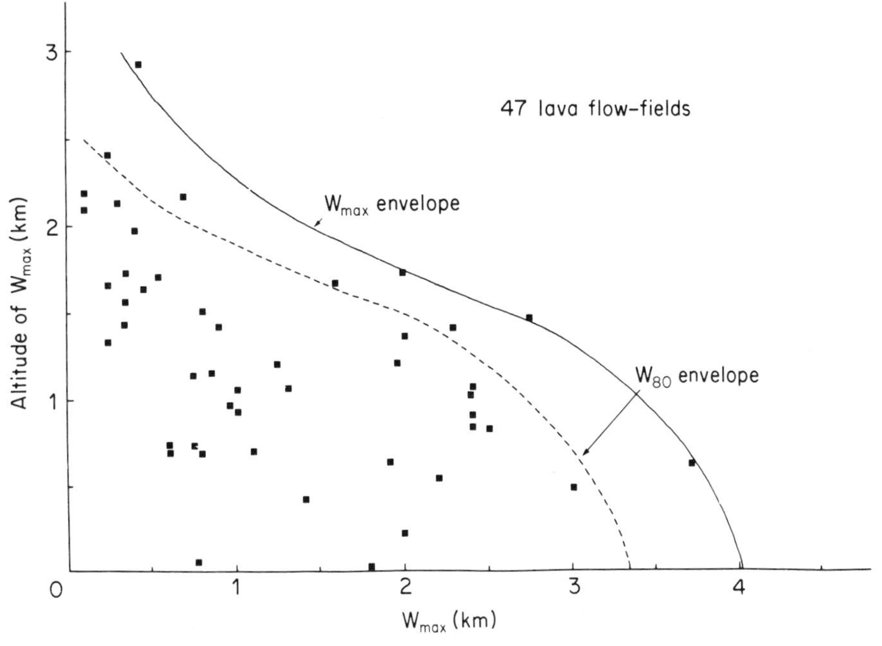

Fig. 8.6 The variation in the maximum widths of 47 Etnean flow fields with the altitudes at which they are widest. The two curves describe: (a) the limiting envelope described by Equation (8.3); and (b) the 80% envelope described by Equation (8.7). (Data from Lopes and Guest, 1982.)

exceed 4.0 km, while evaluation of Equation (8.4b) between the limitsd 0.07 km (= $0.72h_b$) and 1.69 km (= $0.72h_v$) yields a maximum potential flow-field area of 34.6 km^2.

These figures represent extreme limiting values, especially A_{max}, which has been calculated on the perhaps-unrealistic assumption that a flow-field not only attains its maximum potential length, but also its maximum potential width *at all altitudes*. As an attempt to reduce unreasonable overestimation, the equations of the maximum envelopes presented above have been translated along the length- and width-axes of Figs 8.5 and 8.6, respectively, so that they enclose 80% of the recorded data. The modified equations corresponding to Equations (8.1.), (8.2), (8.3) and (8.4b) are:

$$L_{80} = 14.48 - 1.26\,h_v^2 \qquad (\text{for } 0.3 \leqslant h_v \leqslant 3.2) \qquad (8.5)$$

$$\Delta h_{80} = h_v - h_{b,80} = L_{80} \sin\alpha \quad (\text{for } 0.3 \leqslant h_v \leqslant 3.2;\ 0 \leqslant h_{b,80}) \qquad (8.6)$$

$$W_{80} = 4.05\,e^{-0.26\,h^2} - 0.63 \qquad (\text{for } 0 \leqslant h \leqslant 2.5) \qquad (8.7)$$

$$A_{80} = \frac{14.1}{\tan\alpha}\int_{h^\star_{b,80}}^{h^\star_v} (2\pi)^{-1/2}\,e^{-0.5\,h^{\star 2}}\,dh^\star - \frac{0.63}{\tan\alpha}(h_v - h_{b,80}) \qquad (\text{for } 0.3 \leqslant h_v \leqslant 2.5;\ 0 \leqslant h_{b,80}) \qquad (8.8)$$

where the subscript '80' designates the 'eight-percent envelope'.

Repeating the previous example with the modified equations yields the results: $L_{80} = 7.6$ km, $h_{b,80}$ = 1050 m, W_{80} (at the toe of the flow, $h = h_{b,80}$) = 2.4 km, and A_{80} = 9.9 km^2, the linear flow dimensions showing approximately 40% reductions, the area decreasing by just over 70%. In principle, this form of analysis may be extended to cover any given fraction of the recorded data. However, when the desired data fraction falls below about 70%, the shapes of the limiting envelopes may begin to deviate significantly from those in the worked examples. Consequently, the method of fixing the approximate position of an envelope by translating the maximum envelope parallel with one of the axes of the graphs will become increasingly less acceptable; instead, the shape and position of each new envelope will have to be determined independently.

Nevertheless, in spite of its not accounting either for the vagaries introduced by local topography, this approach does provide the opportunity to rapidly prepare provisional, graded hazard maps at the outset of an eruption, given only the altitude of the source vent and the average downslope gradient. Thus, for example, the area enclosed by the 40%-limits may be considered to be that under immediate threat from an effusion, while districts beyond the 80%-limits are tentatively classified as 'safe'. With such guidelines, preliminary emergency procedures may be initiated within a matter of hours after the start of an eruption, to be later amended as necessary in the light of on-the-spot field observations.

For more general hazard assessment, Equations (8.1) and (8.2) may be applied in reverse, to estimate the highest point from which a lava can issue and still reach a specified altitude (the latter equivalent to h_b). Once this has been established, topographic constraints may be used to outline the boundaries of the catchment area for a particular town or district (Fig. 8.7), the catchment area being defined as that region in which an eruption must occur in order to present a potential hazard (Guest and Murray, 1979).

In addition, the data from Fig. 8.5 may be used to evaluate empirically the probability P_b that a lava will bury a vulnerable district. This will vary with the distance d that the lava has to cover and with the value of its maximum potential length. As a first approximation, Kilburn (1983c) assumed that the frequencies of lava lengths, expressed as fractions of L_{max}, were uniformly distributed, the probability of a lava travelling a distance greater than or equal to d then being given by:

$$P_b = 1 - (d/L_{max}) \qquad (\text{for } 0 \leqslant d \leqslant L_{max})$$
$$P_b = 0 \qquad (\text{for } d > L_{max}) \qquad (8.9)$$

The observed frequency-distribution of relative lava lengths, however, as determined from the points plotted in Fig. 8.5 and using Equation (8.1) for L_{max} is presented in Fig. 8.8. Though there is an overall tendency for fewer flows to reach the

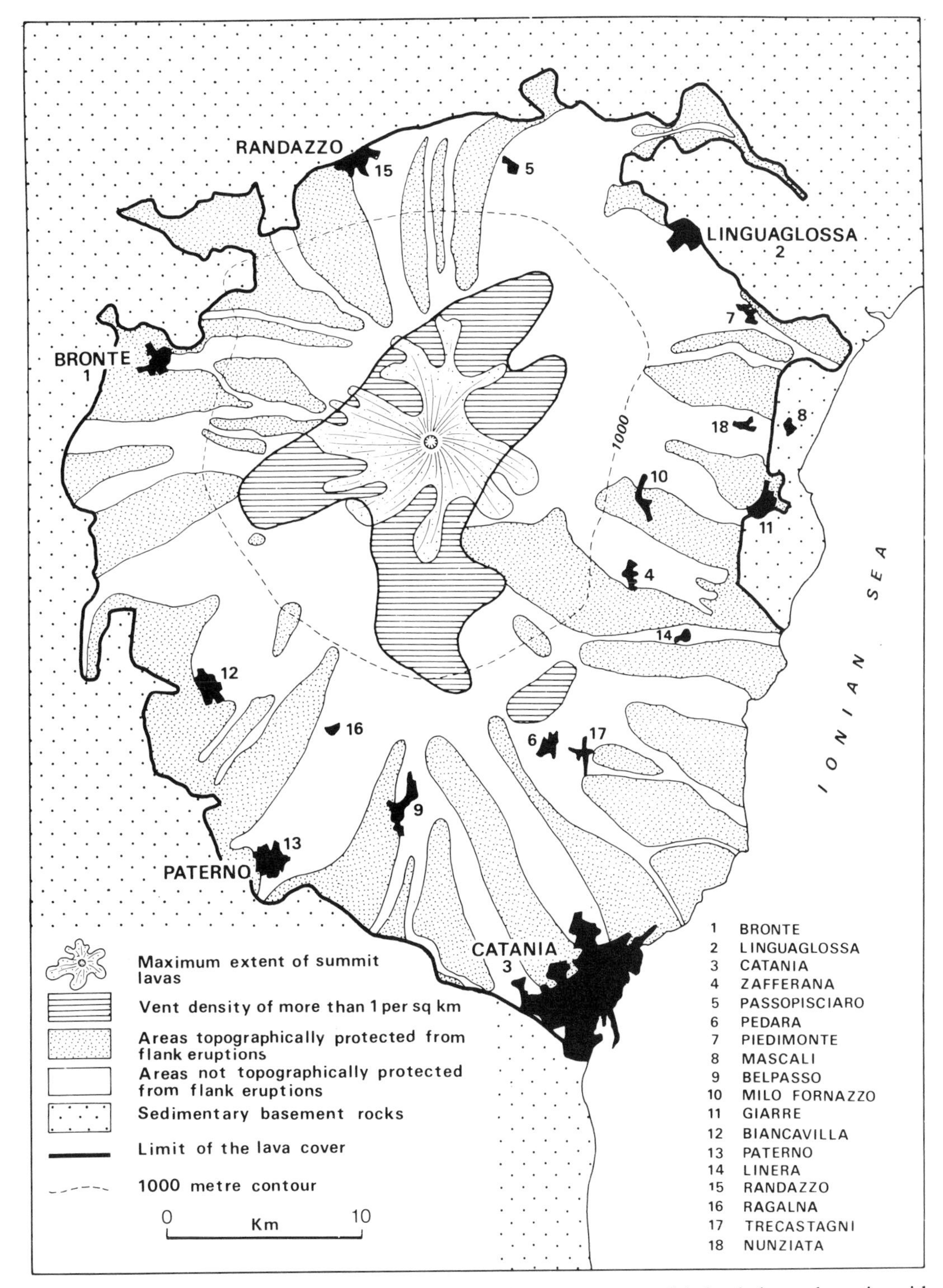

Fig. 8.7 The locations of eruption catchment areas of selected Etnean towns, and their relation to the region with vent number-densities greater than one vent per square kilometre. (Data from Guest and Murray, 1979, courtesy of the *Geographical Journal* (The Royal Geographical Society).)

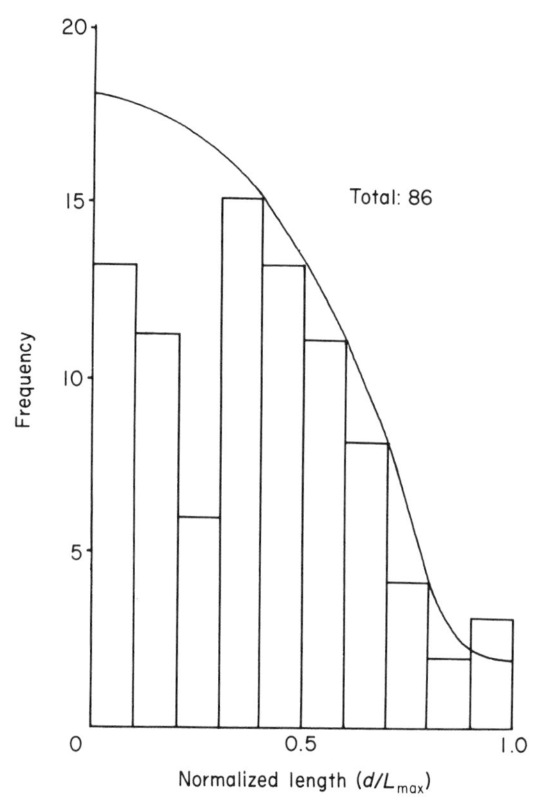

Fig. 8.8 The frequency distribution of the normalized lengths of eighty-six Etnean flow fields. The enclosing curve has been fitted empirically.

longer relative length range, the apparently regular variation between 0.4 L_{max} and L_{max} is not continued at shorter relative lengths. Since the original data (from Lopes and Guest, 1982) were mostly gathered from Etna's principal effusions, a bias towards underestimating the number of shorter flow-fields at any given altitude is to be expected. A hypothetical curve has therefore been fitted to the frequency histogram in Fig. 8.8, which closely follows the longer relative flow length data, but overestimates the numbers of relatively shorter flows compared with the recorded frequencies. By normalizing the area under the curve such that it equals unity, an approximate probability chart showing the variation of P_b with the minimum relative flow length which must be achieved (here equal to d/L_{max}) may be constructed and is found (Fig. 8.9) to give values consistently lower than those obtained from Equation (8.9). Thus, for example, a lava has a 50% chance of reaching or exceeding half its maximum potential flow length, assuming a uniform frequency-distribution, but only a 30% chance according to the empirically derived curve (Fig. 8.9).

The delineation of catchment areas (Fig. 8.7) and the estimation of P_b represents the first two stages in quantifying the vulnerabilities of particular districts to lava flows. The third factor to be considered is the chance that an eruption will in fact occur inside a given catchment area.

8.3.2 *The temporal and spatial distributions of Etnean flank eruptions*

The probablility P_t of an eruption occuring inside a catchment area within a specific interval of time may be expressed as the product of: (1) the probability P_e that an eruption will occur anywhere on the volcano, and (2) the probabilities (P_{Az} and P_{Alt} that, when it does so, it will be within the azimuthal (sectoral) and the altitudinal ranges occupied by the catchment area of interest respec-

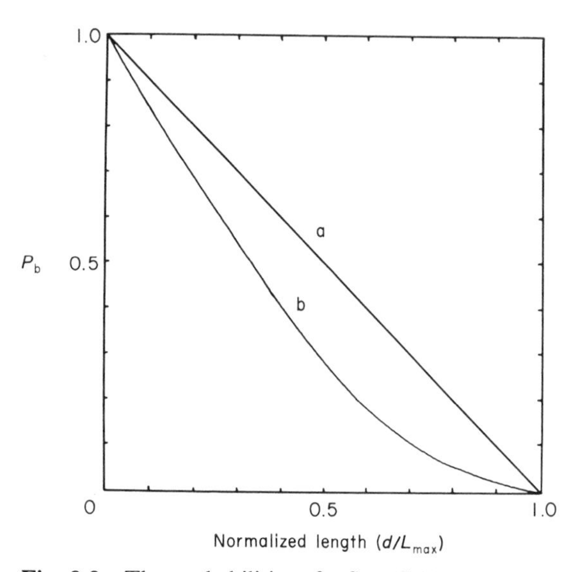

Fig. 8.9 The probabilities of a flow field achieving a given fraction (d/L_{max}) of its maximum potential length. Curve (a), described by Equation (8.9), has been derived assuming that the flow field lengths are uniformly distributed. Curve (b) has been derived assuming that the flow field lengths are distributed according to the empirically determined curve in Fig. 8.8.

tively. This leads to a measure of the vulnerability (V) of an area being written as:

$$V = P_t P_b$$
$$= P_e P_{Az} P_{Alt} P_b \quad (8.10)$$

A relative vulnerability (RV) scale may then be established by normalizing each value of V from Equation (8.10) with respect to an arbitrary standard, which, for convenience, has been chosen as the vulnerability of Catania (V_{Cat}). Hence:

$$\mathrm{RV} = V/V_{Cat}$$
$$= (P_e P_{Az} P_{Alt} P_b)/(P_e P_{Az} P_{Alt} P_b)_{Cat} \quad (8.11)$$

Since the probability of an eruption occurring anywhere on the volcano remains the same regardless of the position of the area of interest, Equation (8.11) may be simplified to:

$$\mathrm{RV} = (P_{Az} P_{Alt} P_b)/(P_{Az} P_{Alt} P_b)_{Cat} \quad (8.12)$$

In the absence of a physical model of Etna's plumbing system, the required probabilities have to be empirically determined from analyses of the past behaviour of the volcano. Any estimates are, in consequence, time-averaged approximations and, as such, cannot be used to realistically describe fluctuations in eruptive patterns over time-scales much longer or shorter than that used to derive the average values. It is pertinent, therefore, to investigate the temporal and spatial distributions of Etnean eruptions and the nature of any variations which may be related to the time-scales being considered. Once these have been established, it will be possible to better evaluate the limitations to the approach outlined above for quantifying the vulnerabilities of Etnean settlements to lava flows.

8.3.3 *Patterns in the frequencies of Etna's historic eruptions*

Several attempts have been made to find a systematic pattern in Etna's frequency of eruptions. Yet, although each refinement of the historical record allows the reassessment of earlier models (for example, Imbò (1928) revising the model of Riccò (1907)), an element of subjectivity invariably influences the recognition of a particular cycle or sequence. This is to be expected because of the empirical nature of the studies involved and contention as to what constitutes a significant event in terms of the volcano's dynamic behaviour. In particular, while flank eruptions may be easily distinguished as discrete episodes, summit activity is much harder to catalogue because there is often no clear dividing-line between active and passive phases.

Caution must therefore be applied when interpreting the results of statistical analyses of Etna's total eruptive frequency. Considering the period from 1500 to 1880, for example, Wickman (1966), recognizing the uncertainties in his data, has suggested that the lengths of the repose intervals between 'major eruptions' (Wickman, 1966, p. 388) on Etna show evidence of a random behaviour, described in this case by an exponential frequency-distribution. The implication of this conclusion is that the probability of an eruption occurring within a fixed interval of time remains the same, irrespective of when the previous eruption took place. Some of the results of Wickman's model are listed in Table 8.1, which gives the probability of no eruption occurring within a speci-

Table 8.1 The probability, $P_t(0)$, of no eruption occurring within t years of the last eruption, using the Wickman model

Length of interval t (yr)	*Probability of no eruption,* $P_t(0)$ *(– see footnote)*
1	0.86
2	0.73
3	0.63
4	0.53
5	0.46
6	0.39
7	0.34
8	0.29
9	0.24
10	0.21
20	0.04
30	0.01

Following from the exponential distribution determined by Wickman (1966) for the repose intervals between Etna's eruptions, the probability $P_t(0)$ may be shown to be (Wickman, 1966): $P_t(0) = e^{-\lambda t}$ where t is the length of the interval in years and λ is an eruption frequency characteristic, which, for Etna, is 0.156 yr^{-1}.

fied number of years after the last outburst; for instance, there is a probability of 0.86 that a repose interval will last for 1 yr, 0.21 that it will last for 10 yr, and 0.04 that it will last for 20 yr.

Although this model allows at least a first estimate to be made of the likelihood of a repose interval achieving a certain length, it cannot be used to make a specific statement as to either the date of the next eruption, or whether it will occur at the summit or on the flanks. Moreover, it provides a representation only of eruptive behaviour averaged over nearly 400 years, and so cannot resolve any shorter-term ordering which may exist in the arrangement with time of the different length repose intervals.

Apparently more relevant to hazard studies is the pattern empirically derived by Imbò (1928) of the recurrence of Etna's flank eruptions, since it is these which constitute the principal menace of the volcano. Presenting a plot similar to that in Fig. 8.10, which shows the variation with time of the lengths of the repose intervals between 1755 and 1983 (Imbò's analysis examines the period from 1755 to 1908), he pointed out that, over time-spans of a few decades, the different length intervals exhibit, in a qualitative fashion, a tendency to gather into alternating groups of longer and shorter duration.

Using this apparent clustering, Imbò (1928) divided the sequence of eruptions from 1755 to 1908 into three groups: 1755 – 1809, 1809 – 1865, and 1865 – 1908, consisting of, respectively, nine, six and seven eruptions. These he related to an episodic flushing out of magma from the volcano and its subsequent filling-up, the former opening a phase with three or four eruptions in quick succession (up to 4 – 5 yr apart), the latter bringing it to a close with eruptions after longer intervals (of the order of 10 – 15 yr). Imbò also noted that a number of the effusions in each period occurred along the same general direction, suggesting some structural control upon the grouping characteristics. Using Imbò's eruption frequency criterion, it may be postulated that two further phases have been completed since 1908, namely 1908 – 1942 and 1942 – 1971 (see Fig. 8.10). On this basis, it appears that, after an increase between the first two clusters, the successive periods of those since 1809 have been decreasing in the order of 56, 43, 34 and 29 yr. Should the trend continue, therefore, the present phase, which started with the 1971 eruption, may be expected to finish before the year 2000. Moreover, given that the previous four phases have ended with repose intervals of between 12 and 16 yr, it may transpire that the 1983 effusion marks the final, or penultimate, flank eruption of the

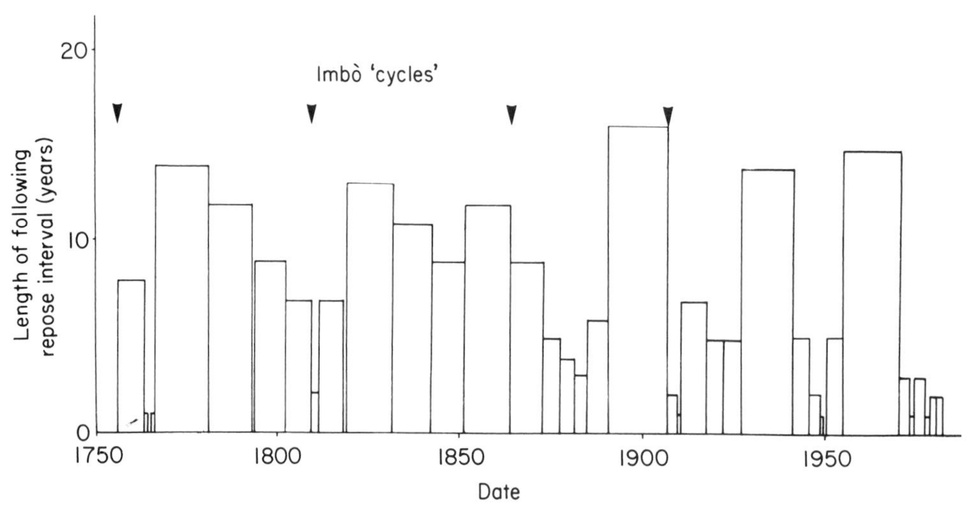

Fig. 8.10 The distribution with time of flank eruptions on Etna between 1755 and 1983. The ordinate shows the length of the interval until the next flank eruption, and the arrows indicate the limits of the cycles originally postulated by Imbò (1928).

current sequence, Etna's activity in the interim being concentrated near to the summit.

This inference, however, is purely qualitative and poorly constrained. Hence, if the current Imbò phase should continue for longer than anticipated, a case could be made that the change in periodicity itself follows a possibly cyclical pattern. On the other hand, it may be that, if not a spurious feature, the repose period clustering is a subsidiary effect of shifts in the dominant vent directions every few decades or so. This assumption appears to be implicit in the alternative extension of the Imbò model by Bullard (1976), who lengthened the third phase to 1928, so also giving the initial Imbò trio a more regular periodicity than when first postulated (52, 56 and 63 yr, as opposed to 52, 56 and 43 yr). The subject of such a structural control will be returned to in the next section.

A rather different approach to identifying some underlying trend in the timing of Etna's flank eruptions has been attempted by Casetti *et al.* (1981). Analysing the distribution of the dates of the onset of flank activity between 1323 and 1980 (sixty-five events altogether), they found that some 17% occurred in November, with secondary peaks in March (about 14%) and May (about 15.5%). Unable to attribute this clustering to seasonal climatic changes (for example, greater rainfall, whose percolation through the ground towards any shallow magma body could increase the chances of an opening phreatic or phreatomagmatic event), they have suggested that it could be an effect of fluctuations in the Earth's change in rotational velocity, it passing through two periods, March – April and November, when it switches from deceleration to acceleration, thereby increasing the centrifugal pull on the crust and encouraging the widening of fissures.

In common with the Imbò model, however, the study of Casetti *et al.* does not enable any definitive statement to be made as to when the next flank eruption will occur, but only indicates those times when, other factors being equal, the odds appear to be more favourable. Indeed, what the search for rhythmic behaviour has so far demonstrated is that when it comes to predicting the date of the next flank eruption, all times are possible, but some are more possible than others, the choice depending upon the time-scales being considered (decades with the Imbò model, months with the treament of Casetti *et al.*), as well as upon the factor which is identified as having the main controlling influence on the eruptive pattern (hence the different extensions of the original Imbò model).

At the present stage of analysis, therefore, there is some evidence that the probability of an eruption occurring on Etna within a given interval may show one or more periodic variations with time. Of particular importance from the point of view of general hazard assessment are the postulated Imbò clusters, since they involve fluctuations over periods of several decades, which compare with the common time-scales of land-management policies. As yet, the existence of the groupings is supported solely by qualitative evidence, and more rigorous analysis may show them to be statistically not significant. Although this uncertainty restricts the value of absolute vulnerability (V) determinations, it will not, as shown by Equation (8.12), affect the evaluation of relative vulnerability, which is more dependent upon the spatial distribution of the eruption centres.

8.3.4 *The location of Etna's flank eruptions*

Every area on Mount Etna has a chance of becoming a future site of an eruption. However, although there are vents to be found scattered all over the mountain, the majority are confined to within a few specific zones, arranged in a roughly radial pattern about the summit.

This concentration is well demonstrated by maps depicting the change in the number-density of vents per unit area, two examples being given in Fig. 8.11 (after Guest and Murray, 1979) and 8.12(a) (after Cristofolini and Romano (1980), developing the analysis of Frazzetta and Romano (1978)). In spite of the differences in detail, the independently determined maps do show the same overall clustering of vents along, in order of decreasing average number-density, the north-east and southern rift zones and to the east-northeast and west of the summit.

These zones appear to have been important

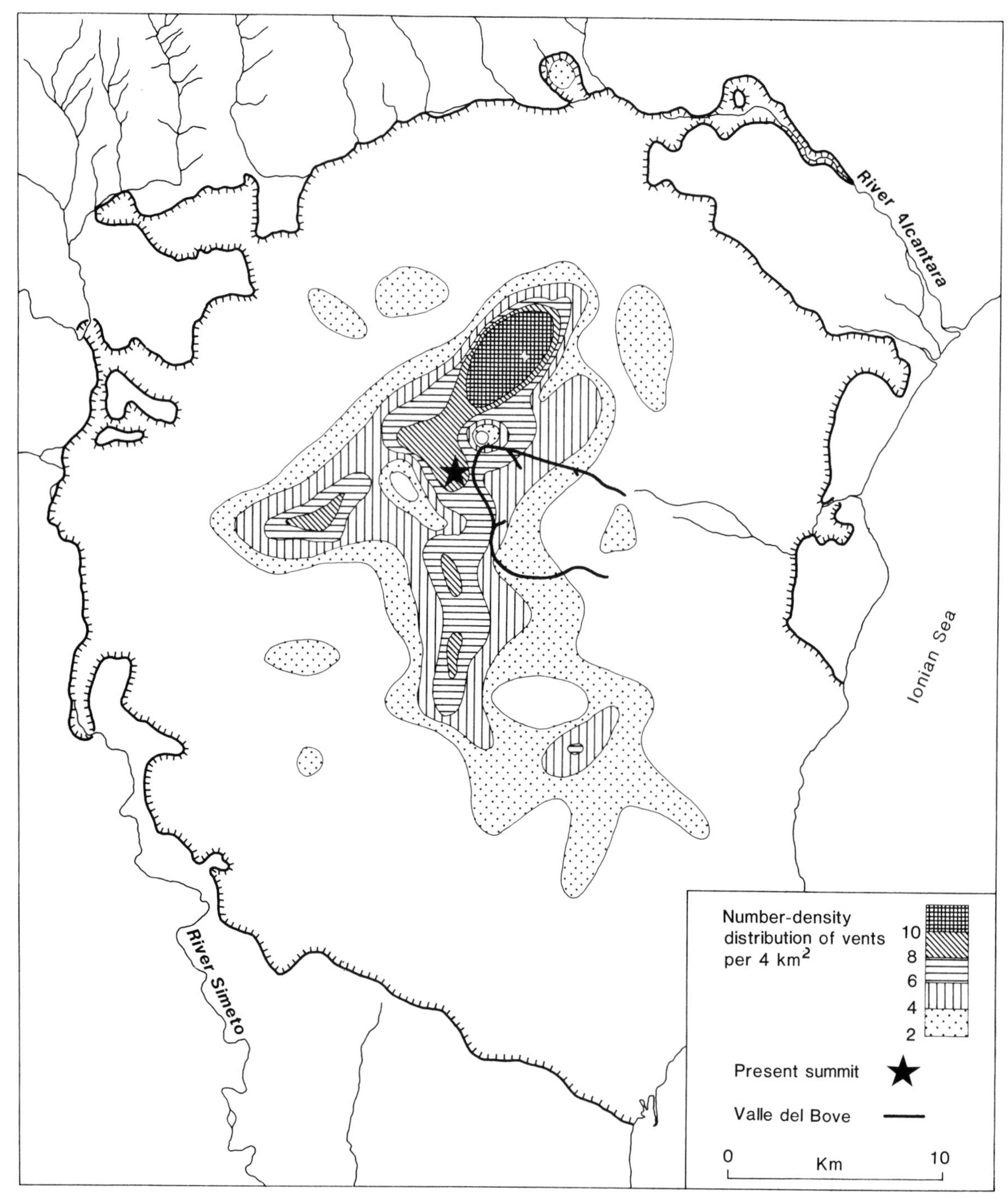

Fig. 8.11 The number-density distribution of Etnean vents. (From Guest and Murray, 1979; compare with Figure 8.12(a).)

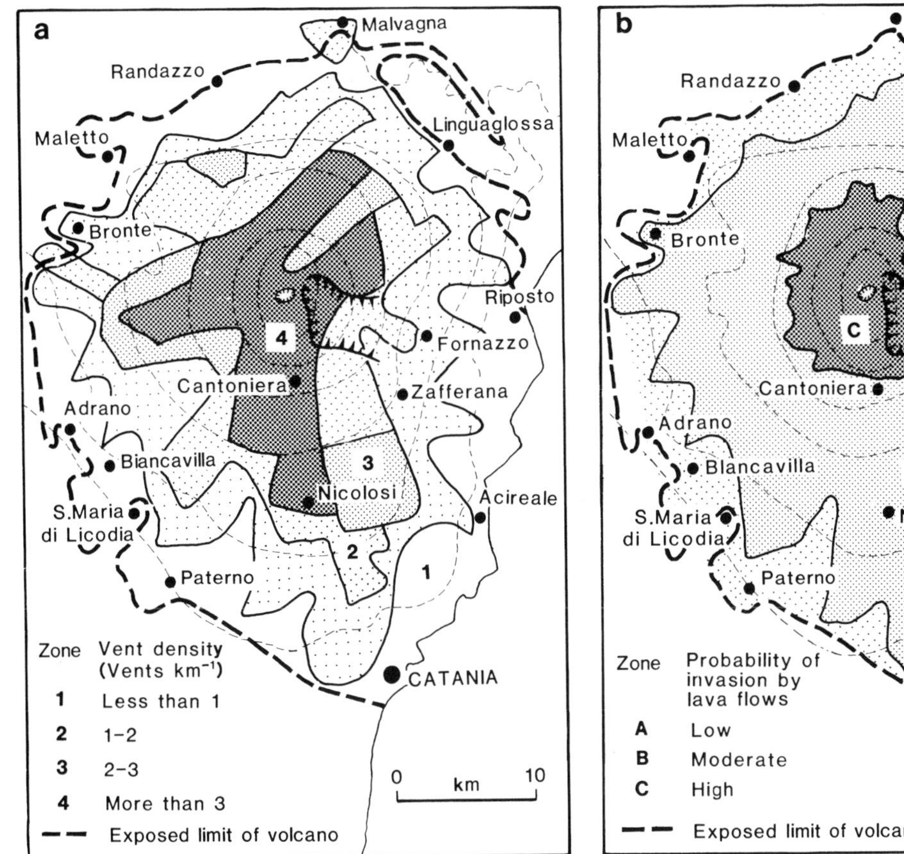

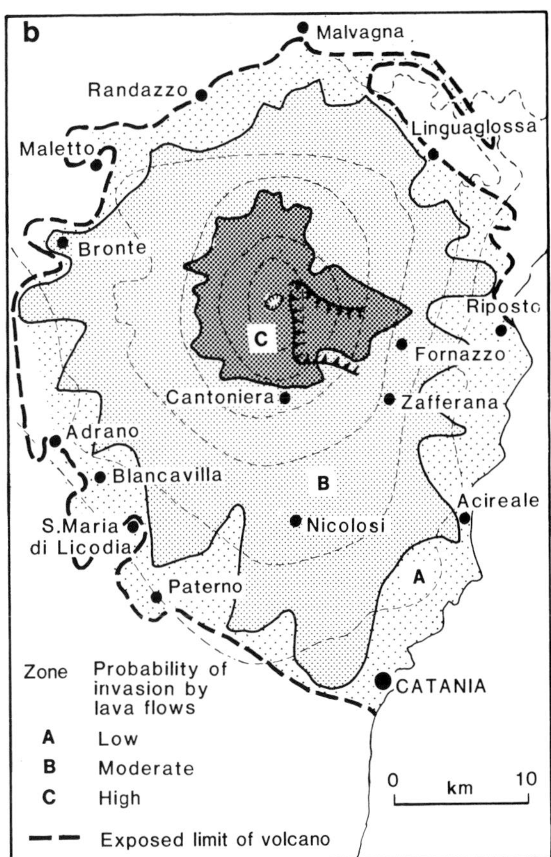

Fig. 8.12 Hazard maps of Mount Etna showing (a) the number-density distribution of vents on the volcano, and (b) areas of different relative vulnerability to invasion by lava flows. By combining the lettered and numbered regions delineated on the two maps, it is possible to divide the volcano into ten categories of area, based on the relative, long-term (on a millenial time-scale) hazard that they face from effusive and localised explosive activity. A ten-point hazard-scale, corresponding to the area categories, may thus be established as, in order from the least to the greatest hazard A1, A2, B1, B2, B3, B4, C1, C2, C3, and C4. (After Cristofolini and Romano, 1980; compare Fig. 8.12(a) with Fig. 8.11.)

eruptive regions for at least the last few thousand years, suggesting a major structural influence upon vent distribution. Figure 8.13(a(i)) shows the location by sector (centred upon the Central Crater) of 130 undated cones and cone clusters (identified on the 1:50 000 geological map of Mount Etna (Romano *et al.*, 1979), which provides the best available, if incomplete, guide to the distribution of prehistoric flank vents). Because, with the exception of the southern rift zone, which falls almost entirely within the south sector, the high-vent-density areas occupy large portions of more than one sector, the data in Figure 8.13(a) may be rearranged to discriminate between vents with higher- and lower-vent-density associations, the latter being grouped together by sector (Figure 8.13(a(ii)). The corresponding histograms for the flank vents and vent clusters which have been active between 1536 and 1983 are shown in Fig. 8.13(b).

The similarity between Fig 8.13(a(ii)) and 8.13(b(ii)) indicates the consistent importance of the high-vent-density zones (whose boundaries have been visually determined) in both the prehistoric and historic samples. The agreement between the sectoral distributions (Figs 8.13(a(i))

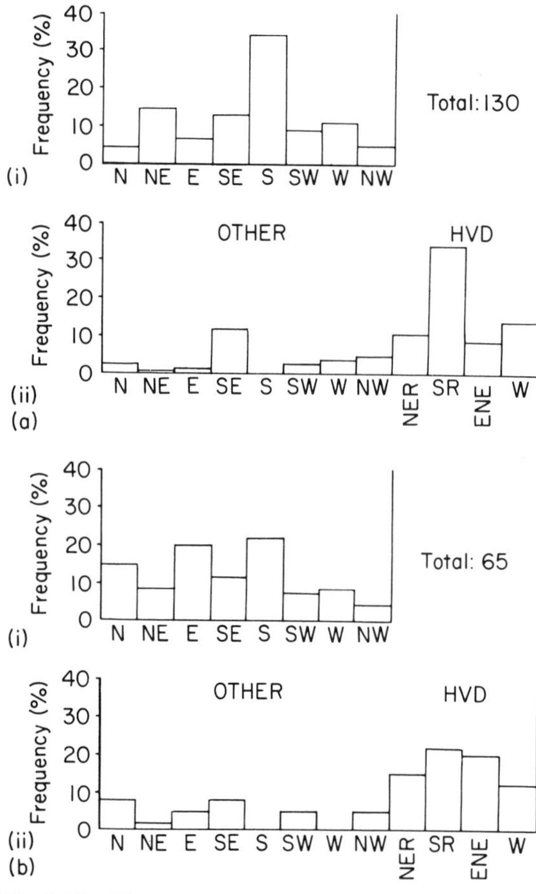

Fig. 8.13 The locations of Etna's flank vents. Frequency distributions of (a) prehistoric adventive cones (130 vents); and (b) vents active between 1536 and 1983 (65 vents), by (i) sector, centered upon the Central Crater; and (ii) rift zone and non-rift areas, the latter being divided into sectors as in (i).

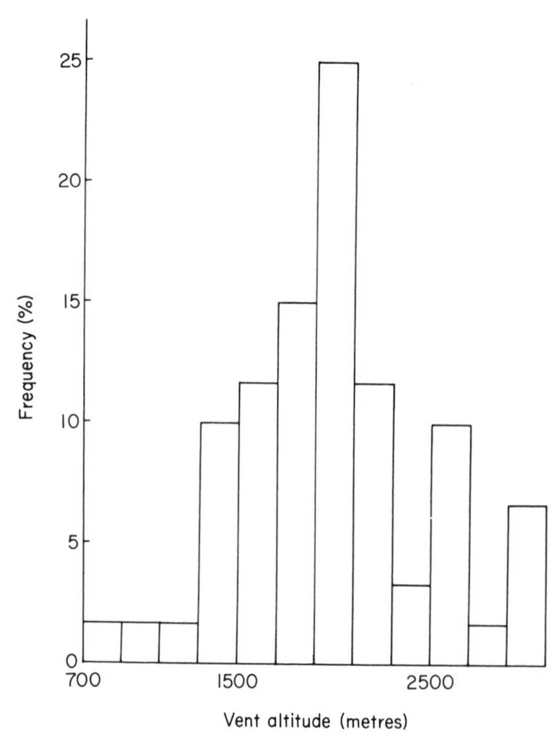

Fig. 8.14 The frequency distribution of the altitudes of historic and prehistoric Etnean flank vents (195 vents).

and 8.13(b(i)), on the other hand, is less well-defined, most notably between the north and east sectors, both of which appear to have been comparatively more active during the 1536 – 1983 period. It is not known whether the difference is the effect of some bias introduced by the method of sampling, in particular the choice of sector to which a vent on a sector boundary should be allocated (compare, for example, the data presented by Duncan *et al.* (1981)), or whether it reflects a genuine long-term shift, oscillatory or otherwise, in the favoured districts of activity. Whatever the cause of the variation, however, until its nature has been identified, sectoral estimates of P_{Az}, at least for periods of the order of 400–500 yrs and possibly longer, can be determined only from time-averaged values, using the observed normalized frequency distributions (such as in Fig. 8.13) of vents whose age-range coincides with the selected time-scale; thus Fig. 8.13(b(i)) may be used where the average distribution over about 500 years is required, while Figs 8.13(a(i)) and 8.13(b(i)), combined and renormalized, may be used for intervals of some 3000 – 4000 years.

This form of approximation becomes increasingly unacceptable as the time-scale is reduced, owing to the corresponding decrease in the size of the sample to be analysed. Nevertheless, there is reasonable evidence (Table 8.2), that, over a 50 – 60 yr time-span, sequences of flank eruption tend to concentrate alternately along either the ENE – W high-vent-density regions or the NE – S rift zones. Hence, since 1755, four broad groupings may be recognized according to the dominant pair of areas: 1755 – 1802/09 (NE – S), 1802/09 – 1869

(ENE – W), 1874 – 1928/47 (NE – S) and 1928/47 – (?)1979/81 (ENE – W), the first three being similar to the Imbò eruption cycles, as modified by Bullard (1976; see also the previous section). It is therefore possible that the major 1983 eruption has ushered in the beginning of predominantly north-east – southern rift flank activity for the next half century. In this respect, it is also noteworthy that, on a number of occasions, two or more successive flank eruptions have occurred within the same immediate vicinity, the later vents typically opening at higher altitudes (Imbò, 1928: Wadge, 1977). Examples which may be cited are the 1883, 1886 and 1892 sequence on the southern rift, the eruptions of 1911 and 1923 on the northern rift, and the 1950 – 51, 1956 and 1971 (main phase) effusions along the east-north-east trend. There is consequently little foundation for the notion that an area recently affected by a lava flow will be substantially safer in the near future.

Also evident from Figs 8.11 and 8.12(b) is a general increase in vent density with increasing altitude. A response not only to the decrease in surface area of the volcano at higher altitudes (the area of land below 1000 m is 1141 km^2, between 1000 and 2000 m, 499 km^2, and above 2000 m, 100 km^2 (Duncan *et al.*, 1981)), the variation is also partly due to a peak at intermediate altitudes in the absolute numbers of preserved vents. Figure 8.14 shows the height distribution of the flank eruptive centres (including prehistoric cones). More than half are clustered within the range 1700 – 2300 m, the mean altitude being approximately 1940 m.

However, owing to the variation with position and vent morphology in the rate of vent preservation, it is not feasible to unambiguously identify any changes that may have occurred in the mean vent altitude since prehistoric times. Guest and Murray (1979) have calculated that the rate at which new ground is covered by lavas increases with altitude, averaging from about 0.1 km^2 per year below 1000 m to something of the order of 0.3 km^2 per year above 2000 m. Accordingly, combined with the upward decrease in the surface area of the volcano, the vents at higher altitudes are expected to be buried more rapidly than those on the lower slopes. Furthermore, below about 2000 m, there appears to be an increase in the proportion of vents which build large cinder-cones around themselves, possibly reflecting a tendency for lower-flank features to tap deeper magmas before they have lost some of their volatiles (Guest and Duncan, 1981). Being high relief features resistant to erosion, cones are likely to be identifiable for longer than simple fissures, which are much more vulnerable to burial by later effusions. In general, therefore, it is the lower cones which have the greater life-expectancies, as well as the larger areas in which to accumulate their numbers. Thus, by virtue of preservational bias, most of the surviving prehistoric cones are those that were built up at lower levels and so their observed altitude distribution cannot be accepted as representative of the total contemporary vent distribution, nor be used as a standard to compare with the altitude-distribution of historic flank-vents. Moreover, with the possible exception of the prehistoric cone population of the south sector (which contains forty-five cones and cone clusters), there are too few vents per sector in either the historic or prehistoric samples (Figs 8.13(a(i)) and 8.13(b(i)) to allow a satisfactory statistical analysis of any variations in their altitudinal distributions within individual sectors.

The inadequacy of the available data for assessing the significance of any changes in mean vent altitude with either time or radial position effectively prohibits the rigorous evaluation of P_{Alt} for different time-scales. In view also of the limitations to the P_{Az} calculations, it is evident that the detailed determination of relative vulnerabilities using Equation (8.12) is not practical given the current state of understanding of Etnean behaviour. If, however, it is assumed that the vent distributions established over periods of several centuries or more will be representative of their average distribution over similar lengths of time into the future, then vent density maps, such as Figs 8.11 and 8.12a, can be prepared for the desired time-scale and, when combined with maps of the appropriate catchment areas (for instance, Figure 8.7), may be used to develop a provisional quantitative analysis of the likelihood of an eruption occurring within a particular catchment area.

Table 8.2 The locations, with respect to the principal high-vent-density regions, of flank vents active between 1755 an 1983

Date of eruption	*High-vent-density region*				*Other*
	NE rift zone	*S rift zone*	*ENE zone*	*W zone*	*(By sector)*
1755					E
1759		√			
1763		√		√	
1764/5	√				
1766		√			
1780		√			
1792/3		√			
1802			√		
C					
1809	√				
1811/12			√		
1819			√		
1832				√	
1843				√	
1852/3			√(?)		E(?)
1865			√		
1869			√		
C					
1874	√				
1879	√	√			
1883		√			
1886		√			
1892		√			
1908		√(?)			E(?)
1910		√			
1911	√				
1918					NW
1923	√				
1928			√		
C					
1942		√			
C					
1947	√				
1949					NW
1950/51			√(?)		E(?)
1956			√		
1971		√(?)	√		
1974				√	
1975	√				
1978			√		
1979			√		E(?)
1981	√				NW
C(?)					
1983		√			

C designates changeover period from one pair of preferred high-vent-density regions to another.
(?) indicates element of ambiguity in allocating vent to a particular region.

8.3.5 A preliminary assessment of the relative vulnerabilities of selected settlements on Etna and the construction of general hazard maps

The proposed relative vulnerability analysis relies on the assumptions that:

(1) Etna's future flank behaviour and average vent-density-distribution over the time-scale of interest will be similar to those already recorded;
(2) Areas of equal average vent-density share the same chance of containing a future eruptive centre;
(3) Eruptions are expected to occur only within the areas enclosed by a specified vent density contour, determined from the observed vent-density-distribution established over the appropriate time-interval; this region is designated as the 'total eruption area' (tea); and
(4) The changes in topography caused by an eruption will not seriously alter the relative likelihood of an eruption occurring in any catchment area.

Consider, for example, the evaluation of very long-term (over thousands of years) relative vulnerabilities. The vent distribution in Figure 8.11 may be taken as representative of the average conditions over this length of time, with the total eruption area being defined as the region within the '2 vents per 4 km²' contour, since few cones occur outside this limit. To simplify the calculation, the volcano has been divided into four types of area whose average vent densities have been assigned the values 0, 1, 2, and 3 vents km^{-2}. These correspond to the regions in Fig. 8.11 with:

(1) less than 2 vents per 4 km^2;
(2) from 2 to 6 vents per 4 km^2;
(3) from 6 to 10 vents per 4 km^2; and
(4) more than 10 vents per 4 km^2.

By superimposing the catchment areas from Fig. 8.7, it is possible to determine the area ($A_{ø,c}$; km^2) of each catchment area with an average vent density of ø vents km^{-2}. The theoretically expected number of vents (E_c) in the catchment area thus becomes:

$$E_c = \sum_{\phi=1}^{\phi=3} \phi A_{\phi,c} \qquad (8.13)$$

which, when divided by the expected number of vents in the total eruption area (E_{tea}) gives a first approximation to the probability of an eruption occurring within that catchment area (P_t). Hence:

$$P_t = \frac{E_c}{E_{tea}} = \frac{\sum_{\phi=1}^{\phi=3} \phi A_{\phi,c}}{\sum_{\phi=1}^{\phi=3} \phi A_{\phi,tea}} \qquad (8.14)$$

To obtain a measure of the probability that a lava will subsequently reach the district of interest, an average vent altitude ($\bar{h}_v$) for a catchment area may in principle be estimated from:

$$\bar{h}_v = \frac{\sum_{\phi=1}^{\phi=3} \bar{h}(\phi A_{\phi,c})}{\sum_{\phi=1}^{\phi=3} (\phi A_{\phi,c})} \qquad (8.15)$$

where $\bar{h}$ is the mean altitude of the area with a vent density of ø.

Owing to the irregular outlines of the catchment areas and of the vent density and altitude contours, however, it is more convenient in the first instance to estimate $\bar{h}_v$ visually, taking due account of the 'weighting' effect of the different vent density areas. From this value of $\bar{h}_v$ an average distance $\bar{d}$ to the settlement may be measured directly from a map (allowing for any necessary deviations to bypass local topographic obstacles), and an estimate of the average maximum potential flow length $\bar{L}_{max}$ calculated from Equation (8.1). Hence a figure for an average P_b may be determined from Fig. 8.9 and so the relative vulnerability of the settlement (as defined by Equation (8.11)) estimated from:

$$RV = (P_t\, P_b)/(P_t\, P_b)_{Cat} \qquad (8.16)$$

This method of analysis has been applied to thirteen of Etna's principal settlements, the data and results for which are presented in Table 8.3. For each district, two RV-values have been calculated using the different P_b estimates from the curves shown in Fig. 8.9. Both sets of results arrange the settlements in virtually the same order of relative vulnerability (the exceptions being Paternò and Biancavilla). Because of the simplifications used in the study, however, the absolute RV-values should only be used as rough comparative guides and not be considered as indicating exactly how much more or less vulnerable is one town with respect to another. Indeed, it is more realistic to use the calculated values to collect the settlements together into larger classes of comparable vulnerabilities. Thus, based upon the observed dispersion of their vulnerabilities (Table 8.3) the thirteen selected towns may be gathered into six classes and arranged in order from the most (I) to least (VI) vulnerable over an approximately 3000 – 4000-year time-span;

(I) Zafferana.
(II) Bronte, Catania, Linguaglossa, Milo-Fornazzo.
(III) Giarre, Nicolosi.
(IV) Belpasso.
(V) Baincavilla, Nunziata, Paternò.
(VI) Mascali, Randazzo.

The relative vulnerabilities of the same settlements over shorter time-scales of a few hundred years may be similarly analysed using the vent-density distribution established between 1536 and 1983. This distribution is virtually identical with that shown in Fig. 8.11 for average vent-densities greater than 1 vent km^{-2} (4 vents per 4 km^2). Indeed, since all but three (1669, 1928 and 1981) of the flank eruptions during this period have taken place in the zone enclosed by the '4 vents per 4 km^2' contour, this has been selected as the outer limit of the relevant total eruption area. Following the method outlined above, the volcano may again be divided into four types of zone, this time with assigned average vent-density values of 0, 1.25, 2 and 3 vents km^{-2}, which correspond in Fig. 8.11 to the regions of:

(1) Less than 4 vents per 4 km^2;
(2) From 4 to 6 vents per 4 km^2;
(3) From 6 to 10 vents per 4 km^2; and
(4) More than 10 vents per 4 km^2.

The data used and the relative vulnerabilities obtained are presented in Table 8.4. As before, the settlements may be gathered into broader classes of comparable relative vulnerabilities, yielding the following arrangement, in order of decreasing vulnerability:

(I) Linguaglossa.
(II) Bronte.
(III) Belpasso, Nunziata, Zafferana.
(IV) Catania, Giarre, Milo-Fornazzo, Paternò.
(V) Biancavilla, Mascali.
(VI) Randazzo.
(VII) Nicolosi.

These class divisions have been determined from the apparent clustering of the calculated RV-values for the 500-year period only, and their boundary limits are not the same as those used for the longer-term classification. Comparison between the two lists, however, does demonstrate how the relative vulnerabilities of areas may vary over different lengths of time, the change in this case being due (as inferred from an examination of the corresponding approximate measures of vulnerability V in Tables 8.3 and 8.4) to the significant decreases in the shorter-term vulnerabilities of Biancavilla, Catania, Milo-Fornazzo, Nicolosi, Randazzo, and Zafferana.

Though currently restricted by the available data to time-spans lasting for several centuries or longer, the form of the analyses presented above may be applied to any locality on Etna once the associated catchment area has been determined from a topographic map and the limits to lava lengths inferred from Equation (8.1). By dividing the volcano into a grid pattern, therefore, the potential exists for constructing long-term vulnerability maps at scales of resolution finer than those which have been previously employed (such as by Guest and Murray (1979); Cristofolini and Romano (1980); Duncan *et al.* (1981)).

By juxtaposing Figs 8.12(a) and 8.12(b), for example, Cristofolini and Romano (1980) have qualitatively identified ten classes of vulnerability zone covering the Etnean region (listed in the caption to Figure 8.12), from which the very-long-term (over millenia) comparative vulnerabilities of the populated and agriculturally productive sectors (here taken to lie below 1000 m a.s.l.),

Table 8.3 The relative vulnerabilities of selected Etnean settlements on time-scales of the order of 1000 yr (E_{tea} = 380 vents)

Settlement	$\bar{h}_v$ (km)	$\bar{d}$ (km)	$\bar{L}_{max}$ (km)	P_t	$(P_b)_{UN}$	$(P_t P_b)_{UN}$ ($=V'_{UN}$)	RV_{UN}	$(P_b)_{EMP}$	$(P_t P_b)_{EMP}$ ($= V'_{EMP}$)	RV_{EMP}
Catania	0.9	15.7	18.9	0.073	0.17	0.012	1.00	0.10	0.007	1.00
Belpasso	1.5	10.0	17.1	0.014	0.41	0.006	0.46	0.26	0.004	0.49
Paternò	1.1	13.2	18.4	0.013	0.28	0.004	0.29	0.17	0.002	0.30
Biancavilla	1.8 1.0	12.1 5.0	15.8 18.7	0.009 0.002	0.23 0.73	0.004	0.28	0.14 0.50	0.002	0.31
Bronte	1.8	10.5	15.8	0.034	0.33	0.011	0.90	0.21	0.007	0.97
Randazzo	2.2 1.4	10.0 6.5	13.8 17.5	0.007 0.001	0.27 0.63	0.003	0.20	0.16 0.42	0.002	0.20
Linguaglossa	1.8 1.2	12.1 7.2	15.8 18.1	0.025 0.015	0.23 0.60	0.015	1.19	0.14 0.40	0.010	1.30
Mascali	1.7 1.2	14.1 10.0	16.3 18.1	0.007 0.002	0.13 0.45	0.002	0.14	0.07 0.29	0.001	0.16
Nunziata	1.7	10.7	16.3	0.012	0.34	0.004	0.33	0.22	0.003	0.36
Giarre	1.8 1.2	12.5 8.2	15.8 18.1	0.017 0.006	0.21 0.55	0.007	0.55	0.23 0.36	0.006	0.84
Milo-Fornazzo	2.0 1.2	7.9 3.8	14.9 18.1	0.015 0.004	0.47 0.79	0.010	0.82	0.30 0.56	0.007	0.92
Zafferana	2.0 1.2	10.0 5.0	14.9 18.1	0.035 0.014	0.33 0.72	0.020	1.61	0.20 0.49	0.014	1.90
Nicolosi	0.8	1.1	19.1	0.007	0.94	0.007	0.53	0.76	0.005	0.73

Subscripts $_{UN}$ and $_{EMP}$ correspond to uniform and empirical distributions of flow-field length. See Fig. 8.9.

Table 8.4 The relative vulnerabilities of selected Etnean settlements on time-scales of the order of 100 yr (E_{tea} = 230 vents)

Settlement	$\bar{h}_v$ (km)	$\bar{d}$ (km)	$\bar{L}_{max}$ (km)	P_t	$(P_b)_{UN}$	$(P_t P_b)_{UN}$ $(=V'_{UN})$	RV_{UN}	$(P_b)_{EMP}$	$(P_t P_b)_{EMP}$ $(=V'_{EMP})$	RV_{EMP}
Catania	1.2	18.0	18.1	0.034	≃0.01	0.000(3)	1.00	≃0.01	0.000(3)	1.00
Belpasso	1.7	12.6	16.1	0.029	0.22	0.006	1.88	0.16	0.005	1.36
Paternò	1.3	14.0	17.8	0.022	0.21	0.005	1.36	0.15	0.003	0.97
Biancavilla	1.9	12.6	15.4	0.004	0.18	0.000(7)	0.20	0.10	0.000(4)	0.12
Bronte	2.0	10.8	14.9	0.045	0.27	0.012	3.57	0.17	0.008	2.25
Randazzo	2.3	10.4	13.0	0.002	0.20	0.000(4)	0.12	0.12	0.000(2)	0.07
Linguaglossa	2.0	11.5	14.9	0.077	0.23	0.018	5.21	0.15	0.011	3.40
Mascali	1.7	14.1	16.3	0.007	0.13	0.001	0.26	0.07	0.000(5)	0.14
Nunziata	1.7	11.2	16.1	0.020	0.30	0.006	1.76	0.19	0.004	1.12
Giarre	1.8	13.0	16.1	0.020	0.19	0.004	1.12	0.11	0.002	0.65
Milo-Fornazzo	2.2	8.3	13.0	0.013	0.36	0.005	1.38	0.24	0.003	0.92
Zafferana	2.2	10.8	13.0	0.040	0.17	0.007	2.00	0.09	0.004	1.06
Nicolosi	U	U	U	U	U	U	U	U	U	U

U = undefined by model.
Subscripts $_{UN}$ and $_{EMP}$ correspond to uniform and empirical distributions of flow-field length. See Fig. 8.9.

considered as a proportion of the total area in each sector below 1000 m, appears to be, from most to least vulnerable: S and SE, NE, E, W, SW, N, and NW.

Considering shorter-term vulnerabilities, Guest and Murray (1979) have estimated the likely maximum extent of lava coverage over periods of about 500 yr, using the constraints provided by:

(1) The present-day topography of the volcano;
(2) The maximum potential length of a flow (from the data of Walker (1974b)); the use of Equation (8.1) instead does not materially influence the result); and
(3) The assumption that eruptions are unlikely to occur in areas with vent densities less than or equal to 1 vent km^{-2}.

The resulting map (Fig. 8.15) highlights those areas which are topographically protected from lavas, given the restrictions above. From this, Duncan *et al.* (1981) have determined the proportion of land, by sector and by altitude, which lies in the lava shadow zones. Their figures (Table 8.5) indicate that the areas in sectors below 1000 m may be arranged in the following order of decreasing long-term vulnerability: NE, S, N and E, SW, W, SE, and NW. Comparing this list with that for the millenial time scale, it appears that the south, south-east, east and north-east sectors of the volcano may be considered as being generally the most vulnerable, with the north-west emerging as the least-threatened sector.

Though it does not allow for the occasional low-flank eruptions occurring outside the 1 vent km^{-2} vent-density (which, by virtue of their locations, are those most likely to affect developed areas), the shadow-zone map in Fig. 8.15, if suitably modified from time to time to account for topographic changes caused by new activity, does offer some guidance when land-use decisions have to be made that involve choosing the best districts for future long-term investment. It does not, however, diminish the need for the detailed, quantitative relative-vulnerability zoning of the volcano, which remains a major objective for future studies.

8.4 The manipulation of lava flows

Techniques for controlling the growth of a flow-field divide naturally into two categories: those which seek to change its environmental setting, and those which aim to alter the lava's structure itself. The first include the construction of dams or diversion barriers, and the excavation of the area in the path of a flow. The second, in contrast, rely on redirecting a flow by piercing its margins, or attempting to slow its progress by hastening solidification. Both general approaches have been attempted on Etna, but, as on other volcanoes, neither can claim to have yet scored an unqualified success. The chief handicap is a lack of experience – a reflection certainly not of a shortage of effusions but of deterring economic, political and social considerations (Chapter 9).

Indeed, Etna offers a classic example of the issues involved. During the calamitous 1669 eruption, Diego Pappalardo and some fifty others from the neighbourhood of Catania endeavoured to divert a major lava stream away from their homes by breaching its chilled margins with makeshift picks and axes, water-soaked hides being used as protection from the heat. In this enterprise – the earliest of its kind anywhere on record – the ambitious group were successful, but at the cost of sending the new flow that resulted in the general direction of Paternò. Unimpressed, about 500 armed Paternesi encouraged the first group to desist. The breach healed, the flow resumed its original course and joined the several others which eventually overwhelmed a large part of Catania.

More significantly, the civil unrest aroused by this episode led to the declaration that those interfering with a lava flow could be held liable for any damage that may subsequently occur, a decree formally ratified by the Bourbon monarchy in the nineteenth century and only suspended, apparently for the first time, during the 1983 eruption. Partly through legal restraint, therefore, detailed feasibility studies of the mitigation techniques which could be used on Etna are still at a preliminary stage (Maugeri and Romano, 1980 – 81) and, in spite of the experience gained in 1983, a reliable assessment of their relative merits can only be

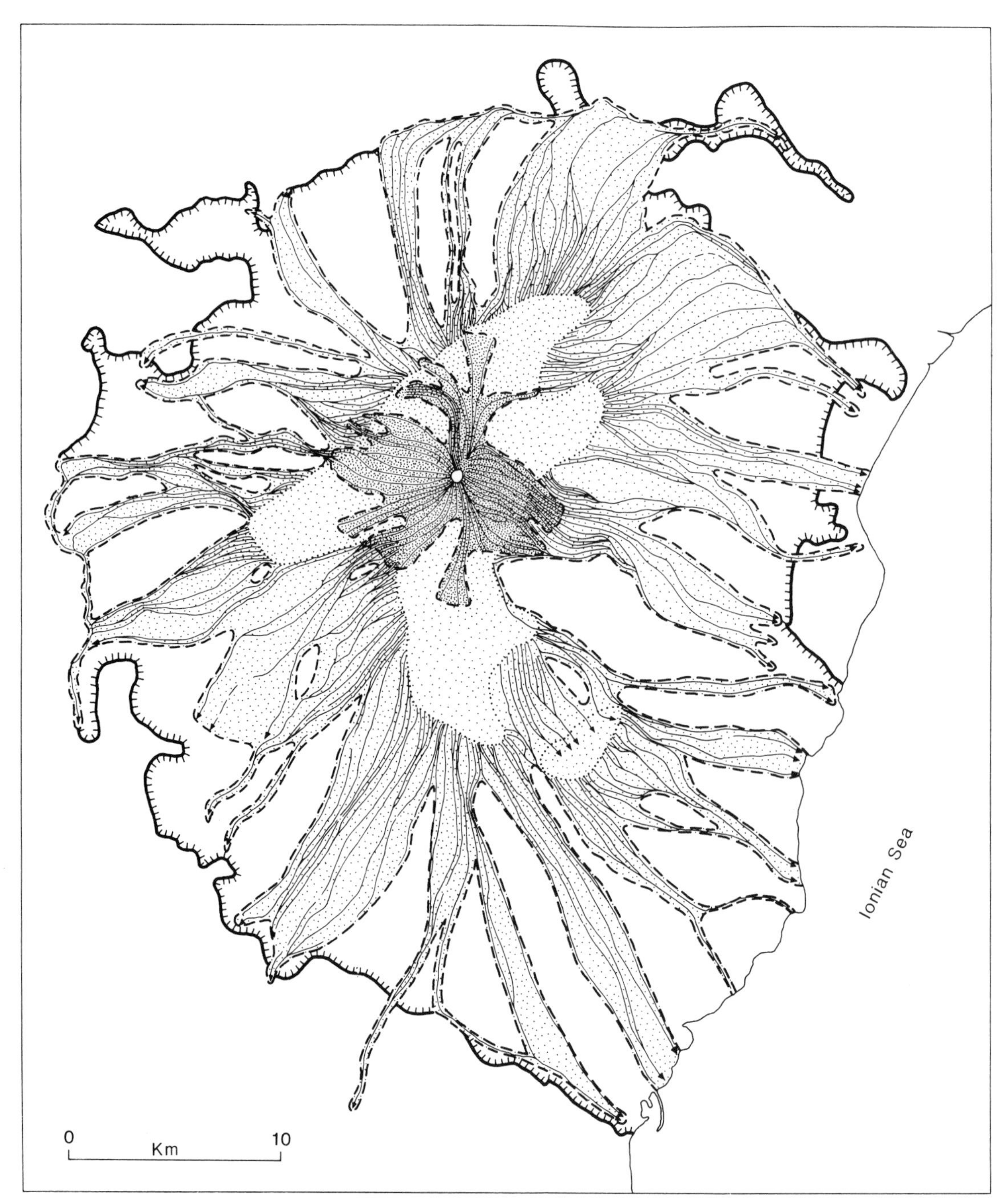

Fig. 8.15 The delineation of shadow zones, topographically protected from lava flows of flank eruptions. The map shows the maximum extent of lava flows erupted from the perimeter of the area having vent-number-densities greater than 1 vent km^{-2}. The directions of the flows have been estimated using the present-day topography from maps with a 25-m contour interval. The maximum flow field lengths were computed from the data of Walker (1973a). The closely stippled area represents the maximum coverage of lavas effused from the summit. Since eruptions rarely occur outside the 1 vent km^{-2} region, the unshaded parts of the volcano provide a guide to those areas topographically protected from lava flows. With future topographic changes, however, the shadow zone boundaries will alter. (After Guest and Murray, 1979.)

conducted in light of the attempts which have been made on volcanoes elsewhere.

8.4.1 *Dams and diversion barriers*

The popular analogy relating the mode of advance of a lava to the motion of a 'caterpillar'-tractor tread carries with it the notion that a flow overcomes obstructions by shouldering them aside. In general, however, because of the growth of a chilled crust, the snout velocity of even a thick lava (up to 10 m or more high) tends to have slowed sufficiently within only a few days of its eruption to exert a surprisingly small thrust against any obstacle it encounters. It is thus not uncommon for a flow to be held up for a matter of hours as it piles up behind and then overflows the flimsiest of dry-stone walls, rather than cause the wall to collapse. Even hastily constructed ramparts of soil or volcanic cinders, though prone to puncturing by the denser lava, can hinder a flow long enough to gain valuable time for more thorough emergency measures to be carried out downslope. During the second week of the 1983 eruption, for example, several cinder ramparts were thrown up at about 10 – 20 m intervals along the western side of the main channel (Fig. 8.16), in a bid to prevent a newly budded satellite stream from completely destroying the already partially engulfed Ristorante Corsaro (Fig. 8.17). Each rampart was about 3 m high, 10 – 15 m long before bending upslope, to contain the spreading of the flow, and had a basal width of some 4 – 5 m. With regard to the primary objective the barriers proved ineffectual, the originally 2-m-thick lava stream surmounting the obstacles before burying the restaurant and adjacent outhouses in the space of a few hours.

They did, however, arguably buy time for the completion of a further defence barrier alongside a new house less than 100 m downflow. Of similar dimensions to the earlier cinder-banks, but composed chiefly of aa rubble, the wall was intended to

Table 8.5 Areas on Mount Etna currently shaded by topography from flank eruptions(1) plotted by altitude zone and sector

	Sector								
	N	*NW*	*W*	*SW*	*S*	*SE*	*E*	*NE*	*Total*
Below 1000 m									
Overall area (km^2)	94	42	89	154	314	218	132	98	1141
Shaded area (km^2)	40	30	45	68	97	105	57	19	461
Shaded area (%)	43	71	51	44	31	48	43	19	40
Between 1000–2000 m									
Overall area (km^2)	47	71	77	76	69	48	48	63	499
Shaded area (km^2)	22	33	24	4	3	25	2	3	116
Shaded area (%)	47	46	31	5	4	52	4	5	23
Total below 2000 m									
Overall area (km^2)	141	113	166	230	383	266	180	161	1640
Shaded area (km^2)	62	63	69	72	100	130	59	22	577
Shaded area (%)	44	56	42	31	26	49	33	14	35

The area of land lying above 2000 m is 110 km^2 and the total area of the volcano is 1750 km^2

(1) Assuming that flank vents open only within those areas of the volcano with vent number-densities greater than 1 vent per square kilometre; for further discussion, see Figure 8.15 and the main text.

(Data from Duncan *et al.*, 1981.)

Fig. 8.16 Cinder ramparts constructed in the path of a new lava stream, April 1983. Scooping material directly from the mountainside, several cinder ramparts were hastily erected during the early stages of Etna's south flank eruption, in a bid to inhibit the progress of a satellite lava stream (front left), recently budded from the main flow (middle distance, running across the photograph). The new stream, advancing from left to right, has just surmounted one rampart. A second embankment is nearing completion some 10 – 20 m downslope. Note that the ramparts have been given an arcuate form in plan view, in an attempt to contain both the advance and spreading of the tongue. (Photograph C. R. J. Kilburn.)

act as a divertor and was thus orientated just off parallel from the principal direction of flow. The operation appears to have been successful. Though much taller than the barrier the edge of the lava, which, because of a local shallowing in slope had thickened to nearly 9 m, did not spread over to the other side but simply ran along the apex of the wall. It is always possible that the barrier had been fortuitously positioned close to what would have been the natural periphery of the stream had it been allowed to develop unhindered. Nevertheless, as the threatened house lay less than 30 m away, even a marginal effect on behalf of the wall may well have made the difference between its destruction and escape. Unfortunately the building was eventually consumed during a later phase of the eruption.

The principal elements in barrier design have been discussed by Macdonald (1962, 1972), based on the behaviour of the protective walls built during the 1960 eruption of Kilauea. These were all constructed with locally available materials, for the most part aa clinkers and broken-up fragments of massive lava, supplemented, where necessary, by clinkers and soil. The general conclusions arrived at were that:

(1) The walls should be made of the densest material available, to reduce the possibility of their being buoyed away by the lava;

Fig. 8.17 The Ristorante Corsaro, at about 1900 m a.s.l. on Etna's southern flanks, partially engulfed by aa lava during the first week of the 1983 eruption. By the following morning, 3 April, the building had been completely overwhelmed. (Photograph: C. R. J. Kilburn.)

(2) The components should be preferably angular and irregular, to increase the amount of mechanical locking between them;
(3) The walls should have trapezoidal cross-sections, widening downwards. The broad base is necessary to increase the frictional resistance of the wall along the ground and to reduce the chances of a flow pushing it over. In the case of rubble barriers, the ratio of basal width to wall height should be of the order of 3:1 (similar to that initially used for the major 1983 Etnean barriers (Lockwood, 1983)).

A gently sloping face on the eruption side allows the encroaching lava to overlap the base of the wall and push downwards upon it, improving the stability of the structure, rather than pushing the wall only laterally and making it more likely to topple. A shallow-sloping lee side is also an advantage because, if the wall should be surmounted, the lava will pass over more slowly and less readily erode the top surface;
(4) Large outward projections on the eruption side of a wall should be avoided, as these provide some support for the lava and reduce the effective height of the barrier. Where such salients are not removable, the wall should there be built higher than the sections on either side; and
(5) The walls should have sufficient freeboard to minimize the chance of any overflows. Although on occasion a small overflow may effectively raise the height of the barrier (Lockwood, 1983), this process cannot be relied upon, since even a small amount of lava may be sufficiently erosive to lead eventually to a breach being cut through the wall.

Local topography also plays an important role in determining the design, use and location of a barrier. Dams, for example, whose purpose is to contain a flow-field, should be aligned roughly at right angles to the main direction of motion and are consequently subjected to the maximum thrust that the lava can provide. They are accordingly best-suited to shallow terrain at distances far from a vent, where low flow-front velocities, and hence thrusts, will more commonly prevail. Moreover, they must also be built to a height substantially greater than the flow thickness in order to accommodate the effect of ponding.

Diversion barriers, in contrast, by cutting diagonally across the path of the flow, are more appropriate in steeper areas, where the gradient of the diverted path, shallower than the original, is large enough to keep the flow moving at a reasonable velocity and reduce its expected degree of thickening alongside the barrier; for the same reason, the new route for the lava should be as even as possible, with even small shrubs and boulders being cleared out of the way (Macdonald, 1962). Also in contrast to dams is the apparently reduced necessity for diversion barriers, at least in some cases, to be even as high as the encroaching lava, a feature important to bear in mind when assessing the cost of construction. An instance of a low barrier diverting a thick lava, in addition to that cited above, occurred during the 1955 eruption of Kilauea (Bolt *et al.*, 1975), when an 8-m-thick aa-flow, approaching the village of Kapoho, had its course changed by an old railway embankment about one-third its height. It appears that the shear stresses on the upper portion of the lava were insufficient to cause its deformation, with only the guiding lower layers, below the level of the embankment, showing appreciable flowage.

Such suitably low stress conditions, however, will not always be met, particularly when dealing with fluid lavas on comparatively steep slopes. Furthermore, it is not unusual during long eruptions for streams from later phases to take the same path as, and flow over, earlier, stagnating tongues. By raising the local topography, therefore, the older lavas will diminish the working height of any previously installed barriers, so reducing their efficiency compared with when they confronted the younger flows. As mentioned below, this proved to be a common problem during the major diversion attempts on Etna in 1983.

8.4.2 *Altering the gross structure of a flow*

As the Catanesi demonstrated in 1669, the open-channel structure common to aa lavas offers the possibility of diverting the main stream, or of reducing its discharge, by breaking down the marginal levées of the flow. Although this may still in part involve digging away at a flow either by hand or by machine (as on Etna in 1983), it is generally acknowledged that the use of explosives currently provides a more efficient, quicker, and probably safer approach to the problem. Regardless of differences in method, however, the essential principles remain unchanged from those laid down by Finch and Macdonald (1949). Developed from the lessons learned after the 1935 and 1942 bombing operations on the lavas from Mauna Loa, these guidelines bear being repeated in full.

> 'Where the lava river is still open and confined between levées, breaking down of the levée therefore will allow the liquid lava to escape to one side and form a new flow, robbing the old flow of part or all of its supply of liquid lava. If topographic conditions are favourable, the new flow may move off at a high angle to the direction of the older flow, and reach some entirely different destination. More commonly, however, because the older flow was guided by the direction of steepest slope or pre-existing topographic depressions, the new flow follows the same direction and moves downslope along the edge of the older one. However, the advance of the lava as a whole is greatly delayed because the diverted flow may take days, or even weeks, to reach the point attained previously by the older flow. When the second flow has reached the danger point, it also can be [breached], thus still further delaying the advance of the lava front.
>
> A long stretch of the flow, or several separate points on the flow, may be suitable for [breaching]. If so, in general it appears advisable to select the lowest suitable site for [breaching] first. If it then becomes necessary to [breach] the flow again at a later date the higher sites are still available. On the other hand, if the higher sites are [breached] first the new lava streams advanc-

ing along the edges of the older one may so alter conditions that the lower sites are no longer suitable. In general, it appears desirable to wait as long as is safely possible before [breaching] the flow. Every day which [breaching] is delayed brings the eruption that much closer to an end, and, in general, sees the rate of extravasation diminished. Premature [breaching] may result in the process having to be repeated, whereas a single bombing might have sufficed had it been delayed a little longer. Care must be taken, however, to allow a sufficient margin of time to cover the possibility of periods of bad weather with low visibility (when bombing is impossible) and rapid forward spurts of the flow' (Finch and Macdonald, 1949, pp. 1–2; '[breach]' here replaces 'bomb' in the original).

If, however, the lava should develop as a tube-fed pahoehoe flow (for example, the Etnean lavas of 1614–24, 1651, 1764–65 and 1792), the additional possibility arises of puncturing the tube roof with the intention of blocking the established conduit with the disrupted material, generating an overflow and the birth of a new stream. This was attempted during bombing of the 1935 lavas from Mauna Loa, but the success of the manoeuvre remains equivocal (compare, for instance, the discussions of Macdonald (1972) and Lockwood and Torgerson (1980)).

Although restricted by resources and topographic conditions, the manner in which the charges are introduced into the lava will also be determined by the precision with which the breaching must be undertaken. Several methods were considered before the 1983 experiment on Etna, including aerial bombing, the use of artillery and manually emplaced devices. At the time of the decision, a principal concern was that the break should be sited on the western side of the main feeding channel, away from the endangered tourist facilities. Thus one of the reasons that the method finally chosen was the manual emplacement of dynamite was that it avoided the possibility of a stray bomb or shell breaching the wrong levée and sending a new flow to the east.

Allied to lava breaching is the as-yet-untested idea of reshaping the vent area and encouraging the main stream to develop towards a less valuable district. This technique would seem particularly well suited to cases when cinder cones grow up around a vent, allowing the feeding lava to collect on the inside with a surface at a higher level than the surrounding terrain. Simple fissure eruptions, on the other hand, since they rarely involve the raising of the source much above ground level, would seem less amenable to such a method. Under these conditions, the necessary change in vent morphology could be achieved only by excavating the pre-flow surface – an undesirable proposition in that it carries the possibility of opening an entirely new vent and considerably worsening the situation.

On broadly similar lines, the useful breaching of a flow can only be attempted when a lava has developed a well-defined channel or tube system. Among aa channels, in particular, it would seem that little benefit can be expected from piercing a lateral levée unless it has built itself up sufficiently to permit the level of the active channel to stand above the neighbouring surface. During its early stages of development, therefore, when a flow appears to be a more-or-less homogeneous stream, the method of flow-breaching would seem to afford little chance of protection.

8.4.3 *Altering the fabric of a lava flow*

The most direct way of stopping a flow is to accelerate those processes which naturally provide its resistance to motion – in other words, to increase its rate of solidification (particularly in the outer, restraining margins) either by quenching the melt to a glass or by raising its rates of crystal nucleation and growth. In the case of an undercooled lava, at least four mechanisms may be considered:

(1) Lowering the temperature of the melt;
(2) Increasing the rate of exsolution of water and related volatiles and encouraging the continued expansion of the consequent vesicles;
(3) Stirring the melt; and
(4) Seeding the melt with foreign nuclei.

Water is an obvious choice for cooling large volumes of lava. Under ideal conditions, 1 m^3 of water should be able to reduce the temperature of about 0.75 m^3 of basalt from 1100°C to 100°C. This ratio, however, yields a somewhat optimistic minimum value of the amount of water likely to be needed to chill a given volume of lava, not least because the outer layers, despite being intensely fractured by their rapid chilling (Bjornsson *et al.*, 1982), provide an increasing impedance to water percolation. As the crust thickens, therefore, for every cubic metre of water arriving at the edge of the hot interior, a larger volume of water will have to have been pumped onto the flow surface. There is, nevertheless, some evidence that water spraying can be usefully employed to slow down a lava.

The first recorded attempt appears to have been made in 1960 by Fire Chief Eddie Bento and colleagues from the Hawaii Fire Department (Macdonald, 1962; Bolt *et al.*, 1975). Turning their hoses on the lava that was steadily engulfing Kapoho, they found that they could locally check its advance for up to several hours (Bolt *et al.*, 1975), while the dowsing of stationary margins cooled the crust sufficiently to prevent the radiant heat from igniting wooden structures only a few metres away (Macdonald, 1962).

Similarly, towards the close of the October 1983 eruption of Miyakejima, (one of the Izu Islands in Japan) the 5-m-high flow fronts passing through Ako were sprayed with sea water for periods of 1 – 2 d. Although the lavas were by then covering only a few metres a day, having inundated some 80% of the village, 38 of the 40 sites selected for spraying finally ceased to advance about a day earlier than those that had been left untouched (Japan Meteorological Agency, 1983).

By far the most concerted efforts at lava chilling, however, were those undertaken in 1973 to save the town and harbour of Vestmannaeyjar, the principal fishing centre in Iceland. Water spraying was continued for several weeks during the main phase of the effusion and successfully inhibited the lavas' progress, apparently by producing internal ramparts which the flows had to negotiate (Williams and Moore, 1973). more conjectural is whether or not the operation had any significant influence upon the final length of the flows, which Thorarinsson (1979) has suggested may not have been much different from their undisturbed natural reach. With regard to stopping the flows, Tazieff (1977) has further argued that the dowsing could only have been expected to be of limited value, on the grounds that similar lavas were at the same time flowing into the sea and proceeding underwater for several days before halting. This behaviour, though, may in part be attributable to the different gravitational shear stresses acting upon the flows. Thus, while the water-sprayed tongues were advancing over surfaces with about a 5° inclination, those entering the sea were encountering angles of up to 30° (estimated from the maps in Einarsson (1974)). Among flows of comparable thicknesses, therefore, the ambient shear stresses imposed on the offshore lavas would have been up to five times greater than those generated on land, and so the coastal flows would have had to acquire correspondingly larger bulk effective viscosities before coming to rest.

As a cautionary digression, it is worth recording here that arrangements were also prepared to tackle the offshore lavas threatening to close the entrance to the harbour. The plan was to use high explosives to hasten the cooling of the flows by breaking their insulating crusts. The day before the experiment, however, it was calculated that the detonation of even small charges of about ten kilogrammes could potentially initiate a runaway mixing process, in which all the lava would exchange its heat with the water above it, thereby rapidly releasing some 2 – 4 Mt of energy (Colgate and Sigurgeirsson, 1973). The technique, therefore, has still be be tested.

Involving less dramatic repercussions is the possibility of explosively agitating a lava on land. In addition to the circumstantial experimental evidence that stirring may enhance the rate of crystal nucleation in an undercooled magma (Emerson, 1926; Gibb, 1974; Corrigan, 1982), there is tentative support for the notion that such an effect can indeed be induced artifically in an actively flowing lava. During the 1935 Mauna Loa eruption, the US Air Corps attacked a tube-fed pahoehoe flow which was approaching Hilo, on the Hawaiian coast (summaries have been given by Bolt *et al.* (1975), Bullard (1976) and Lockwood and Torgerson (1980)). As well as rupturing the main feeding tube, the explosions also apparently accelerated the transformation of the lava (its surface layers, at least) from the pahoehoe- to aa-state, thus helping the collapsed roof material to clog the enclosed passageway (Jaggar, 1939; Finch and Macdonald, 1949). Lockwood and Torgerson (1980), however, could find no evidence of significant blockages during field studies of the bombed area in the late 1970s – possibly due to an obscuring effect by post-bombing effusion or because the plugs were dislodged downstream soon after their growth. Yet, despite remaining an unresolved issue, there are sufficient favourable indications to warrant further investigations.

8.4.4 *Mitigating lava flow hazard on Etna*

Though each may prove of value under specific conditions, not all of the techniques outlined above can be regarded as being generally applicable to an eruption on Mount Etna. Most evidently restricted is the use of water cooling. As an idea of the rate of pumping which might be necessary, for several days during the height of the Vestmannaeyjar operation some 1.0 m^3 s^{-1} were required to have an effect on the lava (Jónsson and Matthíasson, 1974). Such is the low level of Etna's water table, comparable volumes are not readily available apart from near the base of the volcanic pile, the region statistically expected to be least often disrupted by an effusion. Indeed, in some of the upper inhabited levels of the volcano, water supplies are still delivered twice daily by lorry.

Topographic conditions and land usage are also inhibiting factors. With the exception of the Valle del Bove, few areas on Etna above 700 m – the region most prone to historic activity – have surface inclinations of less than 5° (Walker, 1977). As a general rule-of-thumb, therefore, artificial embankments are likely to be more efficient as diversion barriers than dams for all but the longer, low-altitude lavas. At the same time, the steeper slopes also reduce the possibility of diverting a flow – whether by barrier or levée breaching – into a completely different area of the volcano. Thus, when dealing with flows threatening the major developed regions below 1000 m (1500 m in some southern and south-eastern districts), the intensity of land usage for urban and agricultural purposes is such that there are not many areas of comparatively low value into which the flows may be directed. Furthermore, owing to insufficient precision, the use of artillery or bombers to attack a flow in a prosperous area can only be considered as a last resort when other methods have failed.

The restraints on diversion become less rigid, however, if the flow can be interfered with on Etna's higher slopes. This has been well illustrated by the events during the 1983 south flank eruption, of which a brief account is given below, based largely upon the reports of Lockwood (1983), Romano (1983), Taubes (1983) and Volpe (1984).

Following a series of strong earthquakes first felt during the night of 26–27 March, Etna's 1983 south flank eruption started on the morning of the 28th with the opening of a 750 m-long fissure between the altitudes of 2350 and 2450 m. Disrupting the tourist cable-car system and burying several restaurants, chalets and other small buildings, the main aa stream had extended 3.5 km by 3 April. Twenty days later it had advanced a further 3 km, reinforcing local fears that the three towns of Ragalna, Nicolosi and Belpasso (10 km, 12 km and 14 km downslope respectively) were under serious threat from inundation. However, from Equations (8.1) and (8.5), setting h at 2.25, it is apparent that, although the maximum potential length of the flow (L_{max}) was 13 km, there was an empirical chance of only 1-in-5 of it reaching more than 7.5 km (L_{80}), even neglecting the topographic protection to Nicolosi and Ragalna (indeed, as it was to turn out, the flow field did not extend more than approximately 7 km). Nevertheless, at the time, lava was still being discharged at a steady rate of about 10 m^3 s^{-1}, similar to that of the earlier phases. Accordingly, it was agreed to make an attempt to breach the margin of the feeding channel at a high level and to force a new stream to grow parallel with the course of the existing flow, on the assumption that it would take about the same time as had already elapsed to reach the tip of the flow-field, while robbing the earlier stream of its supply. Thus it was hoped to gain time to arrange further defence measures should the eruption not have stopped in the interval.

The site chosen for the experiment, at about 2200 m, is shown in Fig. 8.18. The western margin was selected to avoid a further threat to the Rifugio Sapienza and the remaining tourist facilities on the east, and because about one kilometre downslope, next to Monte Vetore, there existed a natural ponding area, in which some of the lava could be collected if a barrier was thrown across the route to the Astrophysical Observatory (Fig. 8.18). Preparations for the operation, involving some 200 men, were started during the first week in May. By Monte Vetore work began on the construction of a huge rubble blockade, about 10 m high, 30 m wide at its base, and approximately 400 m long.

At the proposed blasting site, bulldozers were used to excavate the upper reaches of a diversion channel (about 50 000 m^3 volume), as well as to gouge out a roughly-15 m section from the western levée of the flow (up to 6 m tall with a base about 10 m wide (Fig. 8.19)), leaving a 3 m-thick wall to be punctured by explosives.

Because of the narrow margin of error allowed in locating the breach, it was necessary for the charges to be put into place by hand. The plan devised by the blast engineers, Lennart Abersten and Giovanni Ripamonti, was to inject some fifty-to-sixty charges into three rows of holes drilled through the thinned margins. However, the temperature of the newly exposed wall was considerably higher than the 200°C maximum safe-handling temperature of the Gel-A dynamite to be used. Cooling of the holes was thus attempted by dowsing with water and packing with dry-ice. To this end, neither method proved satisfactory, but, in combination, they were able to chill the levée sufficiently for it to thicken into the flow. With the effusion rate remaining steady, the narrowing of the active channel promoted local overflows which, though comparatively thin, managed to bury a number of the lowermost drill holes.

As a result of these problems, the deadline for the attempt, originally scheduled for May 7, was delayed by a week. The difficulty of placing the dynamite was eventually overcome with the use of pneumatic hoses, designed to inject the charges simultaneously through steel pipes standing out from the lava margin (Fig. 8.19) and to provide the engineers with a minimum of 30 s to get clear. Announced by a bugle call, the detonation finally took place at 04.09 local time on 14 May. Whether

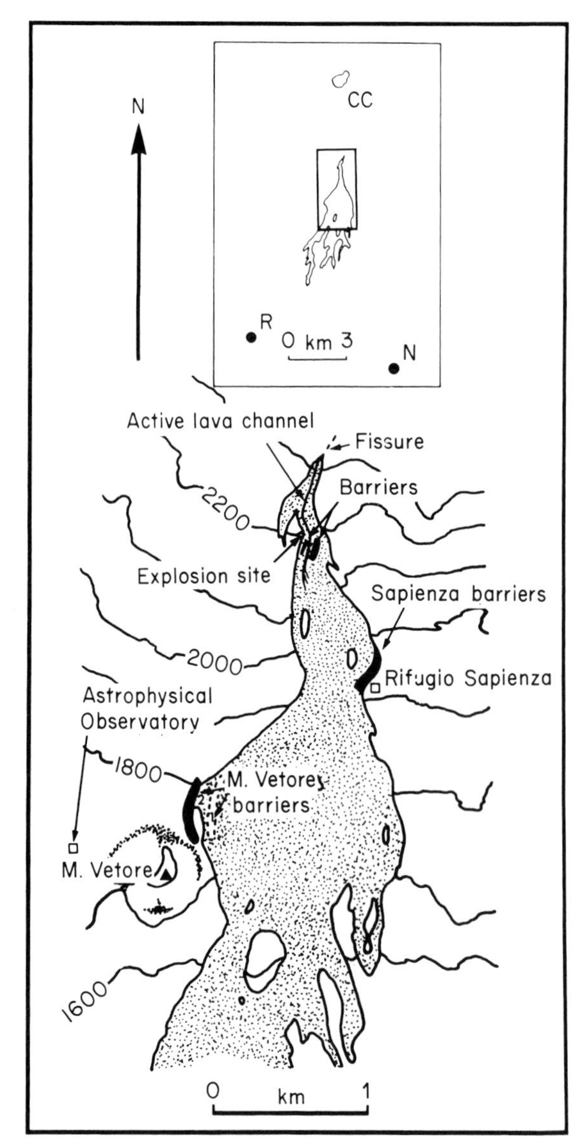

Fig. 8.18 The upper reaches of the 1983 lava flow field, just before the explosive breaching attempt on 14 May, showing the locations of the diversion barriers and the explosion site. The inset shows the position of the flow field with respect to the Central Crater (CC) and the towns of Ragalna (R) and Nicolosi (N). (After Romano, 1983).

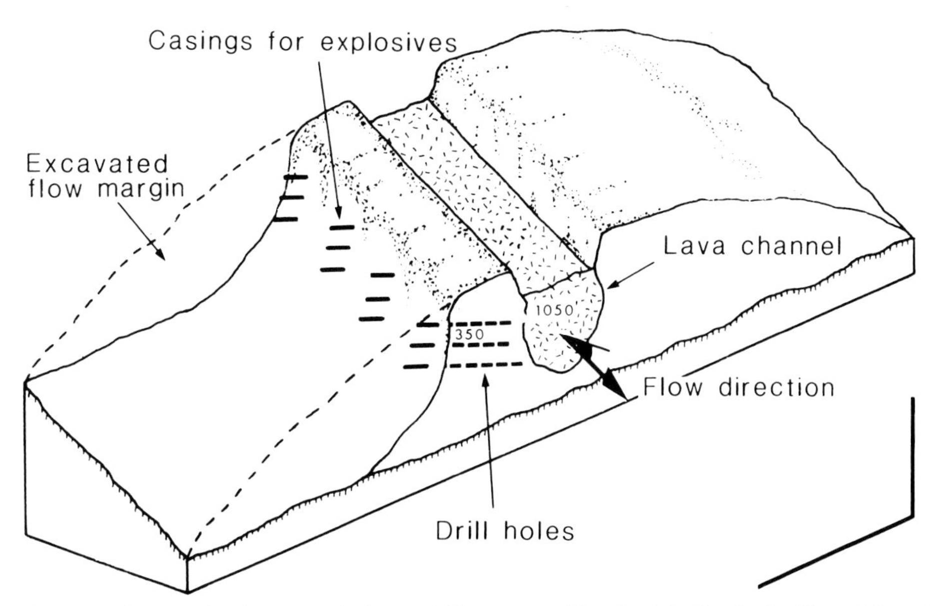

Fig. 8.19 A schematic cross-section through the partially excavated lava levée before its final breaching with explosives on 14 May 1983. The figures on the front face indicate the estimated temperatures (°C) within the levée. The scale bars (bottom right) represent approximately 5 m and refer only to the overall dimensions of the front face. The longitudinal section of the flow has not been drawn to scale. (After Lockwood, 1983; Volpe, 1984.)

or not the decision to go ahead was influenced by political or media pressure or was simply a scientific compromise to pre-empt further hindrance from the frequent overflows remains a point of discussion. In the event, though, the blasting did not occur under the anticipated conditions: artificial cooling had caused the levée to increase by up to 3.5 m in height and 2 – 3 m in thickness, and the loss of the lowest drill holes meant that only 80% of the intended 500 kg of dynamite could be used, with none of it in the key basal region of the levée. Consequently, the breach which resulted was smaller than had been calculated and allowed only some 20% of the lava to find its way from the mainstream into the artificial channel. Together with the reduced size of the gap and the comparative coolness of the treated levée, this low flow rate allowed the rapid healing of the breach and in less than two days it had closed up completely.

At the same time, however, a major blockage developed in the feeding channel about 500 m downstream, apparently initiated by some of the debris that had been blown into the flow (any contribution from melt stirring is not known). Quite unexpectedly, the obstruction succeeded in achieving what the earlier breach could not, by diverting the lava into the lower reaches of the man-made channel and thence towards the south-west. Within a few days, some 65% of the flow was being re-routed in the direction of Monte Vetore and of the new embankment, one of the largest structures of its kind ever to have been built. As each new tongue banked up against the barrier, so more rubble was added to increase its height. The race was continued for several days and it was not until the evening of 27 May, by which time the barrier had almost doubled in volume to 150 000 m^3, that the lava finally managed to well over the top. The following morning a new barrier was started about 100 m further west and, in part sheltered by its predecessor, was successful in containing the western advance of the flow-field.

The south-westward siphoning of the lava also relieved some of the pressure on the Sapienza complex, which had previously been threatened with total burial by local offshoots from the main channel. During the temporary respite after the explosion, work was started on another barrier adjacent to the Rifugio Sapienza, which had narrowly escaped destruction in mid-April. Situated within a shallow depression, the barrier, from almost the beginning of its construction, was frequently encroached upon by new tongues of lava. Indeed, when only nine days old, on 29 May, its top was covered by the upper layers of a passing flow margin, which, rather than constituting a threat to the barrier's stability, actually improved the structure by adding a further 2 m to its height. Thereafter the continued shoring-up of the embankment preserved its integrity until the end of the eruption, on 6 August, so ensuring that the remaining tourist facilities below emerged largely unscathed (Fig. 8.20).

At a cost of more than £3 million, the attempt at manipulating the lava stands as a landmark in volcanology and as a tribute to the workers involved. The diversion barriers were particularly successful in stemming the spread of the flow in key areas. Indeed, during the later stages of its development, the flow-field naturally entered a phase of spreading in the Monte Vetore vicinity with the formation of a large secondary bocca field. Even without the breaching attempt, therefore, the Vetore embankments may well have been needed to protect at least the approaches to the Astrophysical Observatory and the adjacent hotel and tourist chalets.

The explosion experiment, however, has been a source of some controversy (see, for example, the discussion in *Volcano News*, **15** (1983)). As already mentioned, it seems unlikely, on empirical grounds, that the flow field would have extended much further downslope whether or not the breaching had been attempted, and that, having reached its maximum natural length, it would have then proceeded to thicken and spread laterally. It is questionable, therefore, that the blasting attempt and its consequences had any significant influence upon the distal growth of the flow-field, although it may have reduced the degree of spreading along its middle reaches. In addition, it is possible that the temporary siphoning-off of some of the lava may have been important in gaining time for work to begin on the principal Sapienza diversion barrier (Lockwood, 1983). It has also provided valuable experience, by highlighting problems in the details of excavating and blasting a flow margin – a typical example being the difficulties arising from the channel overflows unintentionally induced by the chilling of the target levée. Thus, if for no other reason, the explosion attempt can be justified by having increased the awareness of the problems involved and allowing a more mature assessment to be made for tackling future effusions, for it is almost certain that an eruption will occur in which flow-breaching offers the only real hope of saving valuable property.

In essence, the 1983 operation has demonstrated the utility of an integrated approach to lava flow control, rather than completely relying on one method alone. The effusion, however, was perhaps better suited than most to some attempt at manipulation, being readily accessible along its whole length, having a well-established feeding system that maintained a reasonably steady discharge, and being of a long-enough duration for even delayed experiments to be carried out. Moreover, because of its south flank location, the flow-field continued to present a threat for most of its 18.5-week lifetime. On several other occasions, lavas have caused most of their damage within only a few days of eruption, regardless of their ultimate durations. In such cases, a response swifter than that in 1983 becomes of paramount importance.

Anticipating this need, Maugeri and Romano (1980 – 81) have suggested that permanent foundations for diversion barriers be constructed at key locations around the volcano, to be rapidly reinforced by a special civil-defence force once the imminence of an eruption is known. Though commendable in principle, there are some discouraging practical aspects that need to be faced. The first is the sheer size of Etna. Even considering only the densly populated and cultivated zones below 1000 m, the area to be protected covers some 1141 km^2 and at least twelve major settlements, each with 10 000 (or more) inhabitants (1971 census). Using a conservative estimate of £500 000 for a combined foundation and diversion channel, and assuming an average of three per major settlement, the cost of just a basic protection scheme would be of the order of £18 million (1983 prices). Although a

(a)

(b)

Fig. 8.20 Views, taken after the end of the eruption, of the series of barriers which protected part of Etna's main south flank tourist complex from the 1983 lava flows.

(a) A series of artificial embankments, seen running diagonally to the left of the Rifugio Sapienza (large building, lower centre), and from left to right above the Sapienza and the base station of the cable-car system (lower right), were successful in diverting the later lava streams (filling the top and left of the photograph, the general downslope direction being towards the bottom) away from the tourist facilities. Some earlier tongues of lava, which did impinge on the area, have been cleared from around the Sapienza and the cable-car base station.

(b) Looking upslope towards the Rifugio Sapienza from the top of one of the artificial embankments (the middle barrier of the three running diagonally in Fig. 8.20(a)). The black diverted lavas can be seen to the left and apparently above the upper embankment. The visible height of the Sapienza is about 17 m.

(Photographs: J. E. Guest.)

fraction of the value of the property to be protected, this is nevertheless a substantial capital outlay for a project which can neither guarantee an area's safety nor assert that no adverse environmental consequences will result. Thus, (1) a barrier might either be surmounted by a lava before it can be reinforced, or its presence may simply be rendered irrelevant by the opening of a vent on its downslope side; (2) the new barriers and diversion channels may upset local drainage patterns sufficiently to affect agricultural productivity in the area.

It is here that the 1983 operation acquires a further significance. Its very undertaking has eased the legal and psychological (namely, that Acts-of-God should not be tampered with by mortals) restraints against interfering with lavas and, in so doing, may have helped pave the way towards establishing as a routine procedure the tackling of any flow, even if in a remote area, in order to refine manipulative techniques and to improve the speed of their implementation.

There are also strong practical and economic incentives for initiating such a programme. Firstly, the testing of techniques on flows in uninhabited areas runs a lesser risk of unfortunate consequences than if tried out in a valuable zone. Secondly, because of the increasing prosperity of the Etnean region, the expense of several trial runs could be offset by the salvation of one town, thanks to the accumulated experience.

Together, therefore, Etna's frequent effusions and economic importance provide the necessary availability of lavas and the motivation to test lava control techniques. Such practice will not invariably make the methods perfect, but it could help them to become standard weapons against the action of lava flows, whether on Etna or elsewhere.

9 Volcanic hazards: human response and adjustment

'Any study of environmental hazards will necessarily involve an examination of the complex interactions between physical and human systems, since no hazard can exist unless it is perceived and in turn provokes a human response.'

(Whittow, 1980)

The development of the Etna region (Chapter 2) to its present position of economic pre-eminence within Sicily came about through the profitable exploitation of the resources of the volcano by man and, indeed, the definition of resources is bound up with the notion of interaction between man and environment, because 'neither the environment nor parts of the environment are resources until they are . . . capable of satisfying mankind's needs' (Mitchell, 1979, p. 1). Hazards also involve the interplay of man and environment, because unless man is present, even the most extreme natural events cannot be said to be harmful; the continued occupation of a region like Etna involves a trade-off between the risks and benefits of a particular location. In the last chapter (Chapter 8) the nature and characteristics of the physical threat posed by volcanological phenomena – particularly lava flows – to various sectors and zones on the volcano were discussed; the present chapter seeks to examine this threat in relation to the inhabitants of the region.

9.1 The conceptual framework

Research into natural hazards has been reviewed on several occasions (White, 1973; Burton, *et al.*, 1978; Mitchell, 1979; Warrick, 1979) and from these works it is possible to devise a framework into which the hazards experienced by the inhabitants of Etna may be placed. Every hazard provokes a response and this response may modify and adjust both the threat from the hazard itself and the human use of the particular area (Fig. 9.1). No matter whether the response involves an individual, a single cultural group or a society, the number of adjustments is not infinite and depends on two factors. The first of these is the theoretical range of adjustments available and the second the particular process of decision-making adopted by the in-

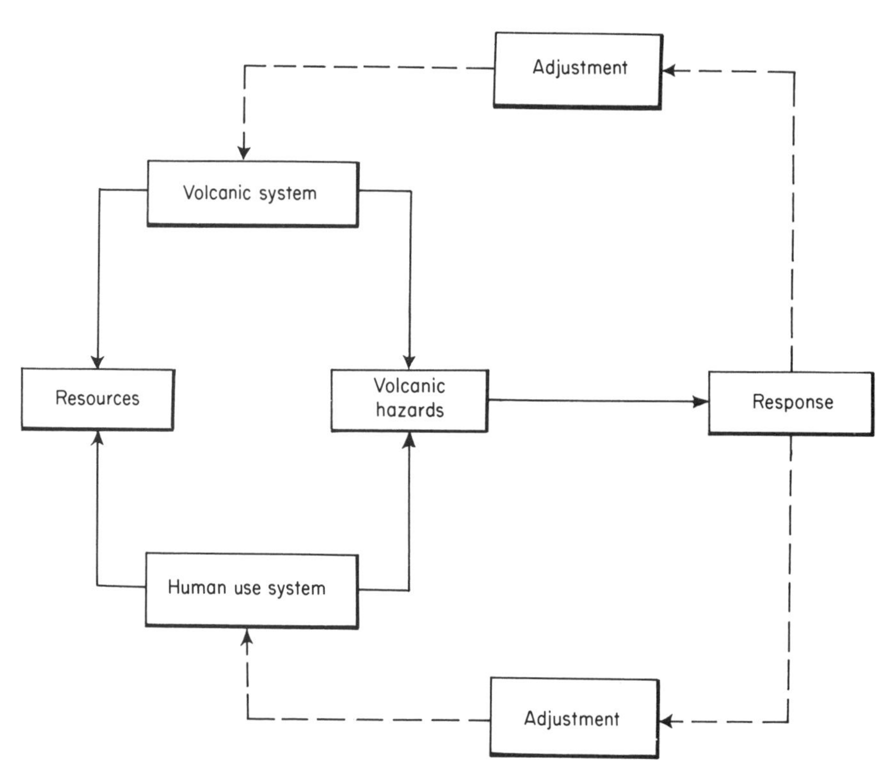

Fig. 9.1 The nature of the human response and adjustment to volcanic hazards. (Modified from Burton *et al.*, 1978 and Warrick, 1979.)

habitants of the given region.

At every stage of technological development there exists a theoretical range of adjustments which may be chosen by an individual or a community. Thus the range which is available today is greater than it was, say, 100 years ago and is probably smaller than in the future. For most common types of geophysical hazard, tables have been constructed showing the theoretical adjustments available at the present time (Burton *et al.*, 1968), but this task has not been carried out for either volcanic hazards in general or for lava flows in particular, despite the fact that this field has been reviewed on a number of occasions (Macdonald, 1972; Warrick, 1979; Williams and McBirney, 1979). Since lava flows are the main type of volcanic hazard currently experienced by the inhabitants of Etna, Table 9.1 has been constructed to consolidate existing information on this topic and, although fairly self-explanatory, certain points require elaboration. All adjustments involving technology (i.e. modifying the hazard and the loss potential) or requiring highly developed social and administrative systems (i.e. spreading losses and planning for losses), may be viewed as simply alternatives to loss-bearing. Even in technically advanced countries such as the USA and Japan these alternatives have only been available for a relatively short time and for most of recorded history the inhabitants of volcanic regions throughout the world have had little option but to bear losses. A further point is that well-formulated hazard mapping, based on the application of *general predictive* modelling (Chapter 8), is probably the ideal basis for future land-use planning on active volcanoes, as the flanks may be divided into zones of relative risk so that new developments may be concentrated into areas which are comparatively safe. It is important to note that the reason why many hazardous areas on active volcanoes are occupied is because the inhabitants make the judgement that the advantages of a potentially dangerous location more than outweigh the risks, and this aspect of human decision-making implies that all zoning policies must take into account the ratio of benefits-to-costs, if they are to be effective in gaining public support. A final point relates to insurance and public relief. Within the hazard literature it has often been noted that these forms of adjustment, though fully justified on economic, social and ethical grounds, often have the serious drawback of encouraging sub-optimal locational decisions (Burton *et al.*, 1978), since the inhabitants of disaster-prone regions are shielded to some extent from the consequences of their own folly, while continuing to reap often-subtantial economic benefits. In New Zealand, for example, insurance has encourged new buildings on shifting foundations (O'Riordan, 1974) and has increased potential losses. To be truly effective both insurance and external relief should be linked to effective zoning policies, so that existing property and livelihoods are indemnified, but new development discouraged in particularly hazard-prone areas.

The mechanisms by which individuals and wider cultural groups make decisions about how to respond to natural disasters is still much debated in the literature and, although much psychological and economic theory is now available, there is nothing approaching a consensus view (Burton *et al.*, 1978; Warrick, 1979). The particular perception of individuals and the corporate perceptions of wider cultural groups, however, are believed to be of crucial importance in decision making (Simon, 1959; White, 1973). These perceptions depend upon a complex amalgam of environmental, social and psychological factors; research in a number of countries on a variety of hazards allows certain generalizations to be made about the ways in which decisions are made. These generalizations are based mainly on research carried out on a variety of hazards of which few are related to volcanic activity, but it is interesting that the few studies of decision-making that have been carried out in volcanic regions have produced very similar findings.

Material wealth has been shown to be a crucial variable in conditioning responses. Not only does wealth correlate with other socio-economic variables like education levels, but also influences the ability of individuals and social groups to recover from the effects of a natural disaster. In other words, though the effects of a natural disaster may

Table 9.1 The theoretical range of adjustments to hazards from lava flows

Affect the cause	*Modify the hazard*	*Modify the loss potential*	*Adjust to losses*		
			Spread the losses	*Plan for losses*	*Bear the losses*
Types of adjustment					
No known way of altering the eruptive mechanism	(1) Protect high-value installations (2) Alter lava flow direction (3) Arrest forward motion	(1) Introduce warning systems (2) Prepare for a disaster through civil-defence measures (3) Introduce land-planning measures to control future development in particularly hazard-prone areas	(1) Public relief from national and local government (2) Government-sponsored and supported insurance schemes (3) International relief from agencies such as the United Nations Disaster Relief Office	Individual family or company insurance	Individual family, company or community loss-sharing
Examples and notes					
	(a)	(b)	(c)	(d)	
	Use of explosives and bombing to divert flows; has been tried in Hawaii Emergency barriers tried in Hawaii and Japan Barriers to divert future flows from inhabited areas; have been suggested for the town of Hilo (Hawaii) Control forward advance by watering the flow margin; limited success in Hawaii and Heimaey (Iceland)	Warning systems only available on certain well-monitored volcanoes, in technologically advanced countries, e.g. USA (Hawaii and volcanoes showing signs of activity in the continental USA), Japan and Iceland Emergency evacuation plans have been formulated in several countries, e.g. USA, Japan and Soufriere de Guadeloupe	Public relief available in most countries; the most comprehensive schemes are in the technologically most developed countries, e.g. Canada, USA, Japan and New Zealand Government-sponsored insurance schemes available in several countries, e.g. USSR and New Zealand UN Disaster Relief Office established only	Possible to a certain extent in more-developed countries, but even in the USA it is limited by the discretion of individual companies	This is the traditional form of adjustment and is still widely practised in many volcanic areas

Table 9.1 (contd.)

Affect the cause	*Modify the hazard*	*Modify the loss potential*	*Adjust to losses*		
			Spread the losses	*Plan for losses*	*Bear the losses*
Examples and notes (contd.)					
		Land-planning policies are in operation in some areas where 'general prediction' and hazard-mapping have been carried out (see Chapter 8). See references for details	in 1972. May be of great benefit to developing countries in the face of major losses in the future; international relief given by many developed countries in the past, e.g. Paricutin eruption, Mexico		

Format: based on Burton *et al.* (1968).

Information from:

(a) Mason and Foster, 1953; Macdonald, 1962, 1972; US Corps of Engineers, 1966; Macdonald and Abbott, 1970; Grove, 1973; Williams and McBirney, 1979.

(b) Hawaiian Civil Defense, Department of Defense, 1971; Macdonald, 1972; UNESCO, 1972, 1974; Nakano *et al.*, 1974; United Nations, 1976; Booth, 1977, 1979; Fournier d'Albe, 1979; Warrick, 1979; Sorenson and Gersmehl, 1980; Westercamp, 1980/81.

(c) Gerasimov and Zvonkova, 1974; O'Riordan, 1974; Burton *et al.*, 1978; Warrick, 1979.

(d) White, 1974; Warrick, 1979.

be roughly egalitarian, wealth is associated with the ability to take locational risks and survive (Haas *et al.*, 1977; Grayson and Sheets, 1979). Hence following the eruptions of Paricutin Volcano (Mexico) in the 1940s, Nolan (1979) found that the richer, better-educated families could liquidate their assets and choose whether to leave the region or not, while many in the poorer Indian communities had no choice at all and were forced to remain. Wealth and education also make it more likely that risks will be accurately perceived and appropriate adjustments chosen. This is significant when the responses of nation states at different levels of development are being compared, because national wealth is strongly related to the range of adjustments which may be adopted (Table 9.1).

A complicating factor, however, is the provision of external aid either in the form of help for a devastated region from the national government, or in the case of a Third World country, from abroad. Here the perceptions of aid donors may differ markedly from those expressed in the region or nation involved. This factor was important in 1961 when the response of well-intentioned decision-makers in London to an eruption which took place on the small Atlantic island of Tristan da Cunha was immediate evacuation, first to a small uninhabited island and then, by way of Capetown, to Britain. In Britain the islanders generally found the man-made environment – of unaccustomed diseases, motor traffic and all the pressures associated with high-technology living – far less to their liking than the island they had left. All but fourteen returned in 1963, the general reaction being that if another eruption occurred they would prefer to remain and cope (Blair, 1964). Unfortunately, so unsettling was evacuation that some time later

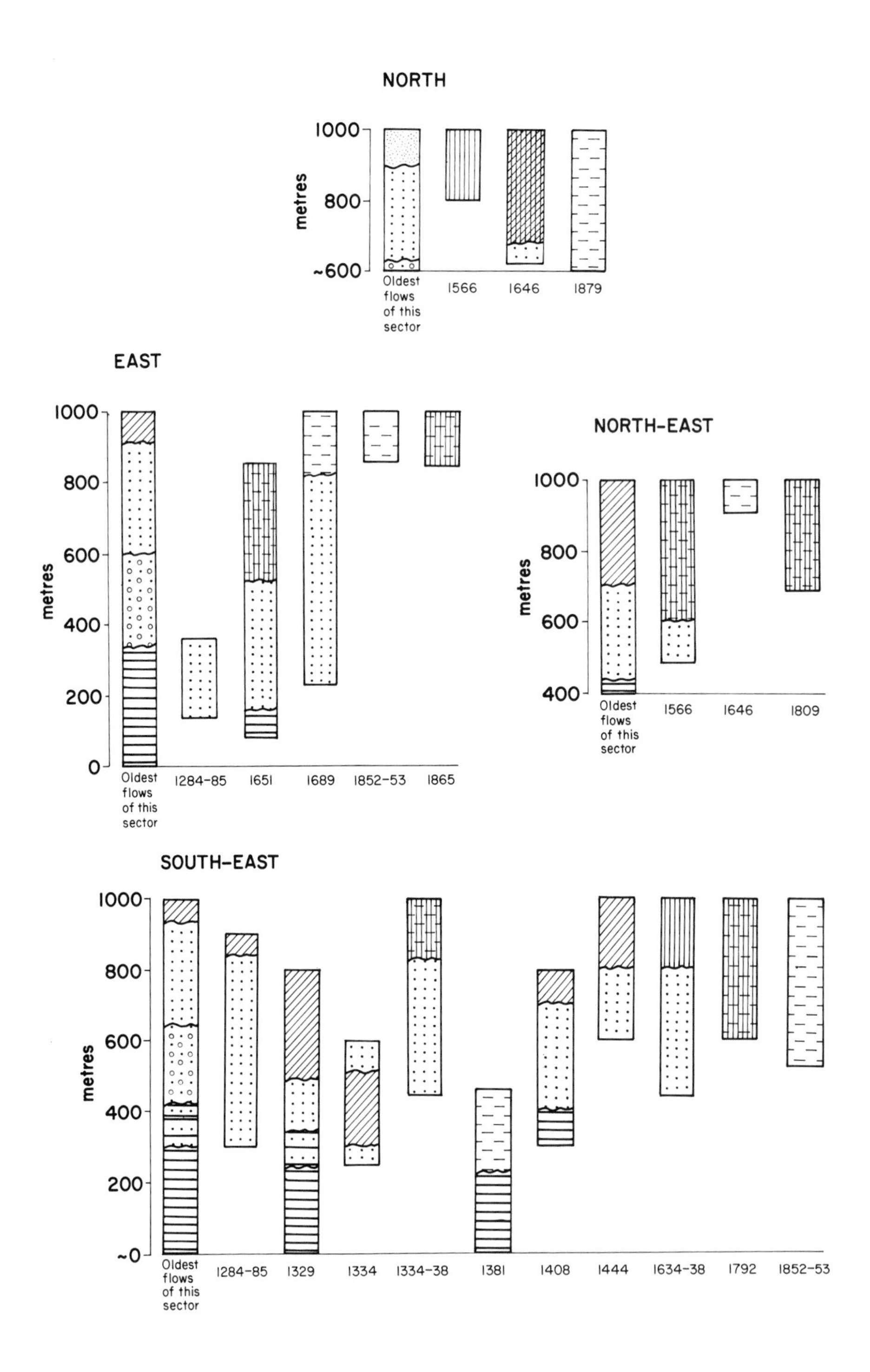

Fig. 9.2 Vegetation succession on lava flows of different ages on the flanks of Etna. (Compiled from Speranza, 1960; Rochefort, 1961; Romano *et al.*, 1979; Durbin, 1981. Extra information from the analysis of vertical air photographs.)

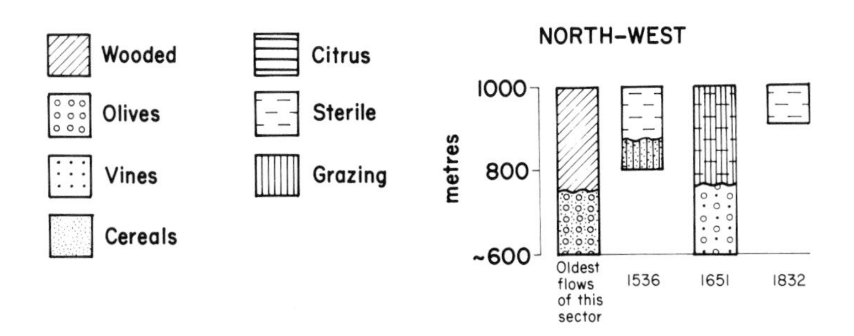

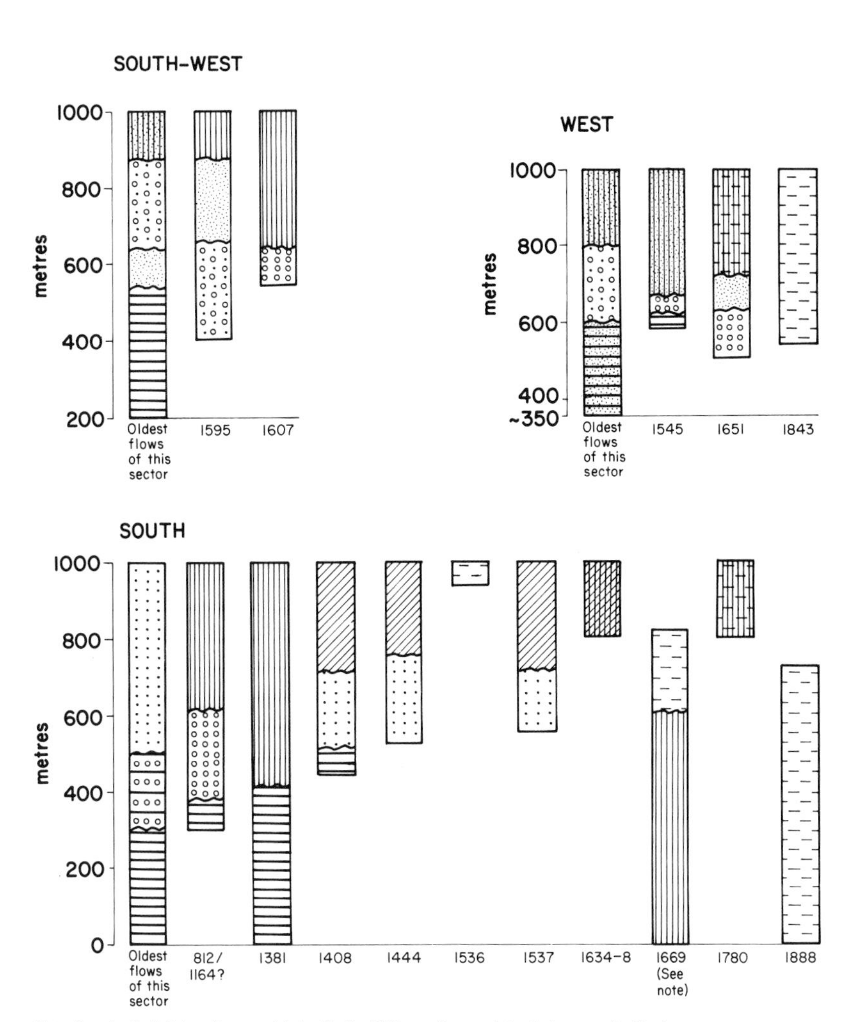

Note: Pyroclastic fall deposits associated with the 1669 eruption are intensively cropped with vines

35 out of the total population of 250 returned to Britain (Burton *et al.*, 1978).

Experience is also an important control over individual and group responses to hazards. Broadly the longer the experience and the more frequent the exposure to a particular hazard, the more likely it is that future threats will be accurately assessed; Caucasian and Japanese residents who have lived in potentially dangerous areas of Hawaii for over fifteen years generally perceive the probability of future losses in a manner which coincides with scientific forecasts. In contrast comparative newcomers have only a sketchy impression of the true risks they run (Hodge *et al.*, 1979). The hazards faced by the people of Hawaii may be classified as high-probability but low-risk, but when hazards are of low-probability but high-risk, experience may have the opposite effect, and long occupation of an area may instill a false sense of security. In 1975, for instance, certain areas on the slopes of Mount Baker (Washington, USA) were closed because of minor hydrothermal activity which, it was believed, was a precursor to more violent volcanism. Mount Baker, like Mount St. Helens, is a classic example of a low-probability but high-risk volcano with the last significant eruption occurring in 1870 (Simkin *et al.*, 1981). The reaction of holiday-makers showed significant polarization, with those who had visited the volcano many times without incident resenting the closure far more than those who were visiting for the first time and had no previous experience on which to call (Hodge *et al.*, 1979).

Urban and rural dwellers often show differences in response with the former, because of their greater mobility and the fact that they live in largely man-made environments, being less aware than the latter of the true risks they run. Thus in the Puna District of Hawaii farmers are prepared to risk utilizing potentially dangerous land for agriculture, but play safe by not actually living in these areas (Murton and Shimabukuro, 1974). In contrast Hawaiian town- and city-residents consistently either underestimate or overestimate the threat they face, in spite of being made aware of the true state of affairs through the dissemination of considered scientific information (Hodge *et al.*, 1979). Also in many urban areas natural hazards are viewed as events which will happen at some indefinite time in the future, whereas man-made 'hazards' like traffic, crime and pollution may be far more pressing and immediate (Gollant and Burton, 1969; Burton *et al.*, 1978).

The system of beliefs held by the population of hazard-prone areas may be of critical importance in determining a particular course of action when faced by a potential or actual disaster. A good example of this is reported by Warrick (1979) who, by using information collected by Murton and Shimabukuro (1974) amongst the inhabitants of the Puna District (Hawaii), was able to show how the more elderly members of the native Hawaiian cultural group are often prepared to do nothing when faced by losses from lava flows, even though they are fully aware of the consequences of their inaction. Indeed during an eruption in 1955, one elderly man even refused to save his personal belongings and thereby suffered a total loss. This response to a natural hazard, so difficult for outsiders to comprehend, is perfectly consistent with the system of beliefs held by this particular culture. These Hawaiians believe that the native goddess Pele controls their fate and, hence, no preventative action is either necessary or advisable.

There are additional features of the response of individuals and societies to natural hazards which have not yet been confirmed by empirical studies carried out in volcanic regions. Two of these are significant to the present study. The first is the frequent observation that individual traits of personality are frequently of critical importance in determining a person's reaction to a hazard (Baumann and Sims, 1972). These traits include varying senses of inner control, differing perceived roles within a society, and the ability to cope and survive by improvization. A second feature is the accuracy with which people are able to estimate the true probability of a dangerous natural event occurring at some time in the future. In this regard it has been found that the so-called *gambler's fallacy* often applies, in which the occurrence of an event at a specific place in a particular year makes it appear less likely to happen again in the near future, regardless of the true probabilities involved.

For societies it is common to classify responses to natural hazards into three categories: *folk or pre-industrial*; *modern technological or industrial*; and *comprehensive or post-industrial* (White 1973). The principal characteristics of these are listed in Table 9.2. It should be emphasized, however, that these are merely generalized categories derived from research on a large number of different types of hazard and are merely yardsticks against which the specific response in a given area may be measured (Natural Hazards Research Working Paper, 1970; Mitchell, 1979). The comprehensive/post-industrial response is very much the ideal from a planning point of view, since it incorporates the best elements of the other categories. Its implementation requires an approach to land planning which, while recognizing the true character of the physical threat, at the same time attempts to harmonize technology to both the natural environment and the perceptions of the individuals faced by the danger. It is doubtful whether any society has yet fully reached this stage in its response to volcanic hazards, although the hazard warning system currently in use in Hawaii probably comes closest to the ideal (Sorensen and Gersmehl, 1980). The stages from pre-industrial to post-industrial should not be seen as necessarily sequential, because the characteristics of more than one form of response may be found in a given volcanic region at the same time (White, 1973). This is often the case in developing countries where some sections of society may act in a manner little changed over centuries, while others adopt an industrial or even a post-industrial form of reaction.

9.2 Mount Etna: hazard response and adjustment

To some extent an examination of the responses and adjustments made by the inhabitants of Etna to the threat posed by volcanic hazards is hampered by the lack of detailed social surveys of the processes of decision-making. Such surveys would enable a comparison to be drawn between the responses of the residents of Etna and those of people in other hazardous regions. Fortunately, study in the Etna region is assisted by both the quality and continuity of historical records, which in many cases contain information on the reactions of the population to eruptions from the Classical Era onwards, and by the high standard of contemporary source materials in the form of academic publications and newspapers. It is upon these that the following account is based.

Responses of people in the region to the hazard posed by Etna are at the present time in transition from typical pre-industrial orientations to ones more characteristic of post-industrial societies (Table 9.2). In common with many areas that have been integrated into the western industrial economy at a late stage, there is little evidence to suggest that the region has ever passed through a typical intermediate industrial stage. It is, therefore, both appropriate and convenient to adopt an historical subdivision and examine pre-industrial before post-industrial responses.

9.2.1 *Pre-industrial responses*

On Etna charactersitic pre-industrial responses may be recognized in the reaction of the population to eruptions from the Classical Era until the early years of the twentieth century. In essence, responses changed little over time and were dominated by most of the features listed in Table 9.2, as being typical of societies at this stage in their development. It is clear that most actions taken following a disaster were both indigenous in character and dominated by either individual action or action by small groups. External aid played only a small part in the response, although from time to time exceptions did occur. The Roman authorities, following the eruption of 122 BC when large quantities of ash caused many roofs in Catania to fail, granted the city relief from taxes for a period of ten years (Rodwell, 1878). Later, after the catastrophic eruption of 1669, aid was sent to Catania by the Spanish Viceroy. In the latter case this aid was seen as something of a mixed blessing and was somewhat resented by the city, for whilst troops restored order by executing looters, there was a fear that this was merely a cover to allow the Palermo authorities to steal the revered veil of St. Agatha, which was believed to be a

Table 9.2 The varying response to natural hazards in three different types of society

Folk or pre-industrial society	*Modern technological or industrial society*	*Comprehensive or post-industrial society*
(1) Wide range of adjustments	(1) Relatively narrow range of adjustments	Combines features of the two types of response and, therefore, incorporates a greater range of adjustments than is found in the technological response and is tailored to the needs of the particular society and hazard; this response involves a number of capital and organizational requirements
(2) Action by individuals or small groups	(2) Requires co-ordinated action by societies	
(3) Emphasis on harmonization with nature, rather than using technology to control nature	(3)Emphasis on technological control over nature, rather than harmonization	
(4) Low capital requirements	(4) High in capital requirements	
(5) Responses vary over short distances	(5) Responses tend to be uniform	
(6) Flexible responses and easily abandoned if unsuccessful	(6) Responses inflexible and difficult to change	

Adapted from White, 1973; and Mitchell, 1979.

defence against lava flows (Mack-Smith, 1968).

Although in detail the range of adjustments was large, throughout the pre-industrial era, loss-bearing was the dominant form of involuntary response. Inundation of agricultural land by lava flows represented a semi-permanent reduction in the land available for agriculture, since land was effectively sterilized for many generations. On the outskirts of Catania the 1669 lava flow still remains virtually uncropped, being used in the main for housing, industry and the grazing of animals, while older contiguous flows carry some of the most intensively worked land on the whole volcano (see Chapter 2). The enhanced rainfall of the south-eastern flank and the low altitude of this particular flow make it more susceptible than most of the volcano to the effects of weathering processes, yet after three centuries it has not regained anything like its former fertility. On the other hand, throughout history many older flows have slowly been brought back into productive use, so that while land has been lost new land has been slowly re-colonized.

Detailed land-use histories of the communes on the slopes of Etna have not been published, but land-use mapping (Fig. 9.2) makes it possible to estimate the rate at which areas sterilized by lava flows have been brought back into production. Even low-altitude flows on the well-watered south, south-east and east flanks of the volcano remain sterile for at least 150 years and are only capable of supporting rough grazing after 200 years and require in excess of 300 years before cash crops like vines may be grown. On Etna certain flows exceeding 700 years in age are accurately dated (Romano *et al.*, 1979) and it is significant that even these are neither so well-weathered, nor so intensively cultivated, as the oldest flows of the volcano. Within other sectors of the volcano the area of land lying below the 1000 m contour is smaller (Table 9.3) and in general rainfall is lower, so reducing the effectiveness of chemical weathering. This effect probably accounts for the fact that lava flows of similar ages on opposite sides of the volcano show very dissimilar rates of re-colonization (Fig. 9.2), though clearly there could be other reasons for these contrasts apart from weathering and such factors as varying land-use histories, other environmental limitations and the economic feasibility of particular types of agriculture (Chapter 2) immediately spring to mind and cannot be ruled out. It is not only the intensity of cropping that is strongly dependent upon the rate of weathering and thus the age of the flow, but also the range of crops which may be grown within a given altitudinal range. This phenomenon may be seen in all sectors, but is perhaps best demonstrated by data from the south. Here the oldest flows can support the cultivation of vines up to 1000 m and citrus and olives up to 500 m, yet even dated historical flows in excess of 500 years old cannot support the cultivation of vines above 750 m and normally land above this height is used for low-intensity rough grazing (Fig. 9.3) or for woodland. Because weathering processes operate more quickly and colonization pressures are greater at lower altitudes there is far less difference between the land-uses on flows of different ages at low levels. Hence, once flows are more than 500 years old the highest limit of citrus cultivation is relatively unaffected by age (Fig. 9.2).

Before the twentieth century, the actual processes of recolonization involved several of the characteristics listed in Table 9.2 as being typical of the pre-industrial response. The emphasis was upon harmonization with nature, with the succession of new land-uses closely mirroring the stages of re-colonization that would have occurred naturally on these lava surfaces. Indeed the early stages were wholly natural and involved initial colonization by lichens and mosses and somewhat later by higher-order plants, including grasses. Following this, hardy trees – mostly almonds, figs and pistacchios – were planted until the lavas were sufficiently well-weathered and covered by the depth of soil required for the cultivation of cash crops (King, 1973a). These were usually citrus fruits at low levels, and vines and olives above.

Although all sectors were broadly uniform as far as the methods of re-colonization were concerned, with the initiative being taken by individual or small groups of farmers using the traditional techniques of peasant agriculture, including large amounts of labour and relatively little capital, there were detailed variations over both time and space. Thus the introduction of the prickly pear cactus (*Opuntia ficus-indica*) into the region from South America some 300 years ago, increased the options open to farmers, since its powerful roots were found to be most effective in assisting the break-up of lava flows (King, 1973a). Also present-day land-use maps and aerial photographs give some indication that, in the past, farmers had a fairly accurate idea of the true potential of different areas of land for re-colonization. Near to the town of Nicolosi on the south flank of Etna, for instance, air-fall ash and other pyroclastic materials associated with the 1669 eruption appear to have been intensively cultivated with vines for a considerable period of time, whereas lavas of a similar age remain either sterile or are used for rough grazing.

Throughout the recorded history of Etna losses from lava flows have not been equally spread amongst the different sectors of the volcano. In the seventeenth century the south sector lost over 13% of its principal area of cultivation below 1000 m, with over 96% of this occurring in the single eruption of 1669. For the later part of the pre-industrial era between 1500 and 1900, a period for which reliable records of eruptions are available for the

Table 9.3 Land below 1000 m, which has been covered by lava flows between AD 1500 and 1900

	Sector								
	N	*NW*	*W*	*SW*	*S*	*SE*	*E*	*NE*	*Total*
Area (km²)	94	42	89	154	314	218	132	98	1141
Area (% of total)	8	4	8	13	28	19	12	9	
Land covered by lava flows AD 1500–1900 (km²)	6	9	12	5	49	4	9	4	98
Land covered by lava flows AD 1500–1900 (% area of each sector)	6	21	13	3	15	2	7	4	

Note: The area of land lying above 1000 m is 609 km², and the total area of the volcano is 1750 km².

Fig. 9.3 A 'late-prehistoric' lava flow at around 1600 m on the south flank of the volcano. Even flows of this age at high levels have not yet achieved their full productivity. (Photograph: D. K. Chester.)

whole volcano (Wadge, 1977), it is possible to calculate the area of each sector below 1000 m which was lost to cultivation. As Table 9.3 shows, in this period certain sectors suffered losses over wide areas, whilst others escaped virtually unscathed.

It is significant that, although any losses were a catastrophe for those affected, in certain sectors a given area of land-loss had far more serious consequences than in others. For example between 1500 and 1900 the north-west and east sectors both lost 9 km² of land, but the effect on the north-west sector was far more serious for the local economy, since this represented some 21% of the main cultivated area in comparison with only 7% in the east (Table 9.3). Given this background of very severe losses in particular sub-regions of the volcano at specific times in history, it is not surprising that rural distress was an aspect of pre-industrial loss-bearing which attracted the attention of contemporary writers.

In the first century BC the historian Diodorus suggested that the *Sican* people were driven from their homes to western Sicily as a result of a much earlier and very violent eruption (King, 1973a), while it is reported that following the eruption of 126 BC disease was widespread (Rodwell, 1878), though it is possible that this account refers to the Island of Lipari rather than to Etna. In the Middle Ages the eruption of 1169 caused the writer Ludovico Aurelio to comment on the large-scale destruction of wheat, vines and timber. This disaster was exacerbated by a large tectonic earthquake which probably preceded the eruption and reduced Catania to ruins causing the deaths of an estimated 15 000 people (Hyde, 1916). Accounts of agricultural losses and rural distress have survived for several eruptions of the fourteenth, fifteenth and sixteenth centuries (vön Waltershausen, 1880), but far more information is available for eruptions which occurred in the seventeenth century. This is because this century saw more flank eruptions than those which either preceded or succeeded it, with many of these causing losses on the southern flanks of the volcano where the main centres of population and learning were located (Duncan *et al.*, 1981). The largest and most widely reported eruption occurred in 1669 and contemporary accounts survive in English and French as well as in Italian. Also this eruption was the first to be witnessed by a scientific observer – Alfonso Borelli, an amateur naturalist and Professor of Mathematics at the University of Catania. His account makes clear the total devastation wrought to the agricultural economies of the fourteen villages which were destroyed (Rodwell, 1878). According to the Earl of Winchilsea this caused 27 000 peasants to be made homeless (Winchilsea, 1669) which was in addition to losses suffered by the city of Catania, where the population was reduced from 20 000 to 3 000. Although eighteenth and nineteenth century agricultural losses were less than those of the seventeenth century, contemporary commentators still wrote vivid accounts of localized rural distress. In the eighteenth century the eruption of 1792 caused distress in the vicinity of Zafferana (Ferrara, 1818), while later the 1843 eruption which affected Bronte not only sterilized over 1.5 km^2 of land below 1000 m, but was also responsible for the deaths of several tens of people – an unusual occurrence on Etna and caused by an explosion at the flow front. This eruption also brought about temporary agricultural losses to a wide area due to both the deposition of large quantities of air-fall ash and the occurrence of 'acid rain', which was apparently produced by flushing of the eruptive plume (Rodwell, 1878). The Zafferana area again suffered distress during the eruption of 1852 – 53 when large stands of timber were destroyed (vön Waltershausen 1880); while later much agricultural land was sterilized by lava flows in 1865 (east sector); in 1879, when lava almost reached the River Alcantara and cut communications on the northern flanks; and in 1886, when over 400 ha of fertile land were desolated (Hyde, 1916).

Semi-permanent sterilization of land and temporary yet severe rural distress were not the only forms of loss-bearing characteristic of the Etna region in pre-industrial times and throughout the recorded history of the volcano towns and villages have also suffered the direct effects of lava flows and other forms of volcanic activity. Figure 9.4 and Table 9.4 summarize the details of urban losses for the period up to the close of pre-industrial era (around 1900), but it must be borne in mind that, for the earlier part, losses were probably much greater than is apparent in the more remote regions of the volcano due to a lack of literate observers. There is also good evidence to suggest that certain early flank eruptions were ignored by historians (Wadge, 1977) but, these qualifications apart, it is of interest that urban losses have not been equally spread amongst the settlements of the region. At one extreme, Catania has been threatened, partially or wholly destroyed by volcanic activity on seven occasions, whereas Acireale – the second city of Etna – has throughout its long history never been invaded by lava flows and has only once been seriously damaged by earthquakes (in 1693). The five largest towns in the region in the nineteenth century – Paterno, Giarre, Adrano, Bronte and Biancavilla – have also never been invaded by lava flows, though several have been threatened from time to time (see Table 9.4). The main effect has been the destruction of small towns and villages on the southern and south-eastern flanks; only occasionally have settlements outside these two sectors been damaged. There are two reasons for this pattern of losses. First, the southern and south-eastern sectors contain 70% of the total population of the region, but only some 40% of the land area and, thus, they have a greater population at risk. Furthermore, as discussed in Chapter 2, the vast majority of the population of these sectors is urban. A second reason is that most flank

Table 9.4 The effects of eruptions and earthquakes (*in italics*) on the settlements of the region during the pre-industrial era

Date	*Settlements affected*	*Nature of the actual and potential loss*	*Response and adjustment*
693 BC	Catania	City destroyed by lava	Rebuilt on the same site
425 *or* 424 BC	Catania	North side of the city destroyed by lava near to Ognina	Rebuilt on the same site
396 *or* 394 BC	Acireale	City threatened by lava and narrowly escaped disaster. Lava entered the Ionian Sea just north of the city	Several small villages are now located on this flow
122 BC	Catania	Pyroclast fall deposits caused roofs to fail	Repairs effected and the city continued to grow
AD 40(?)	Catania	Pyroclast fall deposits covered the city	City rehabilitated
AD 252 *or* 253	Catania	City threatened and lava stopped just short of the Roman settlement	Much of the central business district of the city was subsequently built on this flow
1169	*Catania*	*City destroyed by an earthquake; 15 000 people killed*	*Rebuilt on the same site*
1371 *or* 1381	Catania	City threatened and lava entered the Ionian Sea to the north of the main built-up area in the vicinity of Ognina	Eventually the city expanded over this lava
1408	(a) Trecastagni (b) Pedara	Town destroyed by lava Town destroyed by lava	Both towns were relocated a short distance from this flow
1444	*Towns affected are uncertain*	*Earthquakes on the volcano and collapse at the summit*	
1444	Catania	City threatened by lava	Several villages were subsequently built on this flow
1536	Randazzo	Lava came to within 1.5 km of the town	A small hamlet was later built on this flow
1537		*Earthquakes felt all over Sicily and collapse at the summit. Probably caused damage to several towns and villages*	
1537	Nicolosi	Town destroyed by lava	Rebuilt and a thriving community by the time of the 1633 earthquake
1566	Linguaglossa	Town threatened and narrowly escaped disaster	Eventually the town expanded over this flow
1595 (possibly 1062)	Adrano	Town threatened by lava	Little subsequent settlement on this flow
1607 *or* 1610	Adrano	Town threatened and lava came to within 1.5 km of the town centre	Little subsequent settlement on this flow
1633	*Nicolosi*	*Earthquakes on the volcano and the town was partially destroyed*	*Probably rebuilt in part by 1669*
1646	North flank settlements	A long flow which is reported to have destroyed several villages	The village of Passopisciaro was later built on this flow

Table 9.4 (contd.)

Date	*Settlements affected*	*Nature of the actual and potential loss*	*Response and adjustment*
1651 (ended 1653)	Bronte	Town threatened and narrowly escaped disaster	Eventually the town expanded over this flow
1669	*Nicolosi (11 March)*	*Town partially destroyed by an earthquake before the eruption*	*Rebuilt on the same site*
1669	Belpasso (12 March)	Town destroyed, causing 8 000 people to be made homeless	The town was subsequently rebuilt on a new site (Mezzocampo). The 'air' there was found to be unhealthy and the town was relocated on its present site in 1695, about 1 km away from the 1669 flow. In 1900 the town had only just recovered its 1669 population
1669	S. Pietro Clarenza (13 March)	Town destroyed	The town was later relocated a short distance away from the flow
1669	Mascalucia (13 March)	Town destroyed	The town was later relocated a short distance away from the flow
1669	Camporotondo (13 March)	Town destroyed	The town was later relocated a short distance away from the flow
1669	S. Giovanni di Gelermo (15 March)	Lava reached the town, but it is uncertain whether it was totally destroyed	The town was later relocated a short distance away from the flow
1669	Misterbianco (25 March)	Town destroyed	The town was later relocated more than 2 km away from the flow
1669	Catania (12–23 April)	City destroyed, 17 000 out of the 20 000 inhabitants were made homeless. The keep of the castle was the only substantial building to remain	The city was subsequently rebuilt on the same site. By the time of the 1693 earthquake the city had a population 24 000
1669	Fourteen small villages on southern flank	Villages destroyed	Some of these villages were later relocated near to the flow; the fate of others is uncertain
1689	Macchia	Several small villages were destroyed and lava threatened the outskirts of the town	This lava flow is now intensively settled and the town has expanded over its lower portions
1693	*Catania*	*The city was destroyed by a major earthquake, causing the deaths of 18 000 people*	*The city was subsequently rebuilt and by 1800 had a population of 45 000*
1693	*Acireale*	*Probably most of the city was destroyed*	*Rebuilt on the same site*
1792	Zafferana	Lava approached the town and caused widespread losses on the outskirts	Little subsequent settlement on this flow
1811	Milo	Lava approached and threatened the town	Little subsequent settlement on this flow
1832	Bronte	Lava approached to within 2 km of the town centre	Little subsequent settlement on this flow

Table 9.4 (contd.)

Date	*Settlements affected*	*Nature of actual and potential loss*	*Response and adjustment*
1843	Bronte	Lava breached the main road 2.8 km to the south of the town	Little subsequent settlement on this flow
1852/3	Zafferana	Lava threatened the town and came to within 0.5 km of the town centre	The town rapidly expanded over this flow
1865	*Macchia*	*Certain villages in the vicinity of the of the town were damaged and in Macchia fifty-two people were killed*	*The town and villages were rehabilitated*
1879	Various small settlements on the north flank, especially Passopisciaro	Lava approached close to village of Passopisciaro (between Randazzo and Linguaglossa)	The village subsequently expanded over this flow
1886	Nicolosi	Lava threatened the town	Little subsequent settlement on this flow
1892	Nicolosi	Lava approached and threatened the town	Virtually no subsequent settlement on this flow; except for isolated buildings

Based on information in Rodwell (1878); vön Waltershausen (1880); Hyde (1916); Baedeker (1930); King (1973a) and Stothers and Rampino (1983).
Note: (?) Indicates a doubtful eruption.

eruptions of the pre-industrial era occurred on the southern and south-eastern flanks (Duncan *et al.*, 1981), this being particularly true of several of the very destructive flows which were erupted between the start of the fifteenth century and the close of the seventeenth century.

Although loss-bearing was the principal form of adjustment involuntarily practised by the urban inhabitants of the Etna region, several exceptions are recorded in the historical record and most of these were attempts to mitigate the truly massive losses caused by the 1669 eruption. As discussed in Chapter 8, this eruption was notable for it was one of the first attempts anywhere in the world to actually modify the hazard (see Table 9.1), by deliberately trying to alter the direction of a lava flow (Macdonald, 1972). Diego Pappalardo of Catania and his colleagues, although successful in reducing the forward movement of the flow, nevertheless vividly illustrated the problems of diversion, since this action incensed the inhabitants of Paterno whose town was now threatened (see Fig. 9.4). As a result of the ensuing social protest, diversion was declared illegal and was not repeated for another 300 years. During the 1669 eruption futile attempts were also made to arrest the forward movement of lava threatening Catania by the rapid construction of walls (Rodwell, 1878), while the ancient city walls caused the flows to be diverted into the Ionian Sea for several days. Eventually the walls were breached and lava invaded the city (vön Waltershausen, 1880).

Perhaps the most remarkable feature of urban loss-bearing in the Etna region is that even though settlements may have been destroyed on several occasions they were invariably either rebuilt on, or as near as possible to, their original sites (Table 9.4); as far as may be determined from the historical record, abandonment was not a feature of the pre-industrial response. Catania, even though it was destroyed on several occasions by volcanic activity and twice by earthquakes is, somewhat paradoxically, the easiest case to understand, since even in its ruined state it would have possessed more advantages for regrowth than any alternative location. As discussed in Chapter 2 these advant-

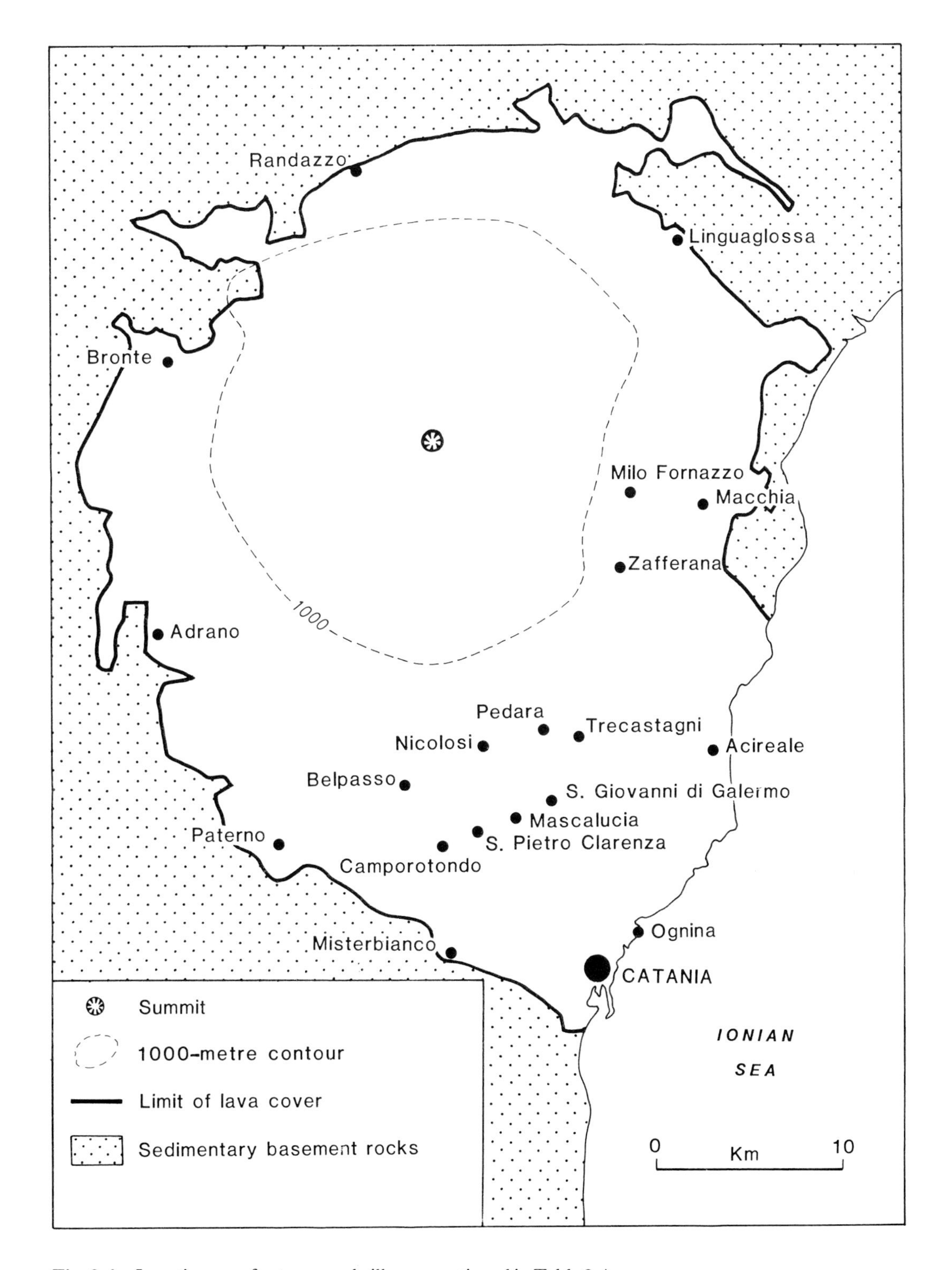

Fig. 9.4 Location map for towns and villages mentioned in Table 9.4.

ages would have included its established role as the commercial and transport focus of the agriculturally most prosperous part of the highly productive Etna region, its functions as a port, and (not least) the traditions of its inhabitants in the professions, trade and industry. Furthermore, research from other parts of the world strongly suggests that relocation of established cities following natural disasters is rarely given serious consideration, because of a range of positive factors similar to those mentioned above. It is also pointed out in these studies that even if these locational advantages do not exist then other, more intangible, influences may well play a part in stimulating rebuilding. In writing of the 1972 Nicaraguan earthquake which devastated the city of Managua, Burton *et al.* (1978) noted that the city's infrastructure, its everyday activity and its inhabitants' attachment to it combined to create an inertia that made rebuilding inevitable. Whether inertia acted as an influence upon the residents of Catania is an open question since the published historical accounts do not provide an answer, and discussion must of necessity remain purely speculative.

The rebuilding of smaller towns and villages following devastation by lava flows presents a much more complex picture and often relocation as near as possible to their original sites is normal (Table 9.4). This is in marked contrast to the case of both Catania and the numerous towns and villages that were destroyed by earthquakes and which were invariably rebuilt in their original positions. The reasons for this contrast are difficult to find, but it seems likely that the nature of losses is important, as is also the relative difficulties of rebuilding settlements destroyed by earthquakes on the one hand and lava flows on the other. Writing of the 1669 eruption, both Rodwell (1878) and King (1973a) note that the lava took some eight years to cool and that for many months following the end of the eruption peasants could still boil water on the flow, suggesting that it would have been an unsuitable surface for rapid rebuilding especially given the fairly rudimentary civil engineering techniques then available. It should also not be forgotten that, whereas even after the 1669 eruption not all of Catania was destroyed so that rebuilding could take place gradually over a long period (Admiralty, 1945; King 1973a), in the case of smaller towns and villages losses were often total and a new site was clearly essential. Earthquake losses although catastrophic at the time caused no sterilization of building land and so reconstruction could take place on the same site regardless of the size of the settlement affected.

Many centuries before they were sufficiently well-weathered to allow agricultural colonization, many lava flows were used for the siting of new villages and also provided cheap land over which existing towns and villages could expand (Table 9.4). This practice has continued to the present day and much of the post-1945 expansion of Catania and many smaller towns may be observed to have taken place on otherwise barren lava surfaces.

No account of the pre-industrial era is complete without some reference being made to the system of beliefs held by the inhabitants of Etna, since these go some way to explaining many aspects of the response. As early as the eighth century BC the Greek poet Hesiod was speculating on the mechanisms responsible for volcanic activity; and throughout the Classical Age a succession of writers sought some rationale for both eruptions of the volcano and for the losses suffered by the people who lived on its flanks. Within this tradition (Table 9.5) several important common elements are evident: the most important was the belief that, regardless of whether activity was explained using mythological, religious or scientific frames of reference, eruptions were unpredictable and inevitable. All mankind could do was to propitiate the forces which controlled the volcano and its eruptions; Lucilius Junior records that in the first century AD it was common for people to climb the mountain and offer incense to appease the gods (Hyde, 1916).

This belief, that loss-bearing was unavoidable and is an expression to an individual of supernatural punishment or vengeance, may be traced into the Christian Age and may be said to be a characteristic of the whole pre-industrial era. Thus it is recorded by the Earl of Winchilsea that as the 1669 lava flows approached Catania, religious processions were 'followed by great multitudes of

Table 9.5 Views of classical authors on the volcanic activity of Etna

Writer	*Work*	*Views on Etna*
Greek poets		
Hesiod (eighth century BC) Aeschylus (*c*.525–*c*.456 BC) Pindar (*c*.522–*c*.442 BC)	*Theogony* *Prometheus Bound* *First of the Phythian Odes for Hieron*	Volcanic activity was explained as struggles of the rebellious giants Typhoëus (Typhon) or Enceladus who were imprisoned beneath Etna. An alternative tradition holds that the crater represented the forge of Hephaestus (Vulcan), where the bolts of the gods were manufactured
Roman poets		
Cicero (106–43 BC) Vergil (70–19 BC) Ovid (*c*.43 BC–AD 17)	*De Divinatione* *Aeneid* *Metamorphoses*	
Homer (the poet probably lived in the ninth century BC, but the events probably represent an amalgam of historical events, legends and folk tales going back to the time of the Trojan War, i.e. twelfth century BC)	*Odyssey*	Homer made eastern Sicily the scene of many of the adventures of Odysseus, but made no direct mention of an eruption of Etna. This possibility implies that the volcano was quiet at this time. However, he pictures the blinded Cyclops throwing rocks after the hero's ship and some commentators have suggested this may refer to an eruption. Since the time of Pliny the Elder (AD 23–79), a series of small islands near to Acitrezza – 7 km north of Catania, and named the *Scoglie dei Ciclopi* – have been related to this adventure
'Scientific' theories of Roman writers		
Lucretius (*c*.98–*c*.55 BC) Justinus	*De Rerum Natura* (Book 6) *Historiae Phillippicae*	Eruptions caused by winds, which gather inside the mountain and drive out flames that reside in the bowels of the earth. Alternatively the winds rush through hollows at the base of the mountain when the sea ebbs, while other winds were generated within the mountain itself
Lucilius Junior (it is generally accepted that Lucilius was encouraged to write this didactic poem by Seneca (4 BC–AD 65))	*Aetna* (probably written between AD 65 and 79)	Provided the first comprehensive model of Etnean activity in a poem of 644 hexameters (see text). He dismissed the idea of any connection between Etna and Vulcan or the Cyclops. At the time it would appear that people ascended the mountain and offered incense to placate the gods. Lucilius says he has no belief in this practice
Heroic deeds		
Lucilius Junior Seneca (and other writers)	*Aetna* *Senecae Naturalium Quaestionum*	During an eruption (possibly 693 BC) two heroic youths, named Anapias and Amphinomus, placed their parents on their shoulders and bore them through the flaming streets of Catania. It was claimed, in the legend, that the lava parted for them; statues were constructed in honour of the *Pii Fratres*
Relationship between Etna and historical events		
Livy (59 BC–AD 17) Virgil (70–19 BC)	 *Georgics*	Eruption of 44 BC thought to portend the death of Caeser

Compiled from information in Rodwell (1878); Hyde (1916); Johnston-Lavis (1918); Romano (1982) and Stothers and Rampino (1983).

people, some of them mortifying themselves with whips, and other signs of penance, with great complaints and cries, expressing their dreadful expectation of the events of those prodigious fiery inundations' (Winchilsea, 1669, p. 17). Another well-known example of the appeasement of God's wrath concerns the frequent use of the veil of St. Agatha to arrest the progress of lava flows. During the eruption of AD 252 lava approached Catania and its inhabitants rushed to the tomb of St. Agatha, who had been martyred the year before, and carried her veil to the flow front. It was claimed at the time that the lava was immediately halted (vön Waltershausen 1880). Following this success the efficacy of the veil was tested on several occasions, perhaps the most famous being during the eruption of 1669 when it was suggested that the veil prevented the complete destruction of Catania. After part of the city had been destroyed the citizens brought out the veil, whereupon the flow changed course to the south-east and flowed into the sea, forming a huge promontory which afterwards acted as a breakwater (Hyde, 1916). Even at the close of the nineteenth century the veil was still in regular use and in 1886 when Nicolosi was threatened (Table 9.4) the people of the town carried pictures of their three patron saints from the church to the *Altarelli*, an open-air chapel above the town. This had no effect on the lava, but later the Bishop of Catania arrived with the revered veil and soon after the flow reached the Altarelli it first divided and then stopped (Hyde, 1916). These successes apart, throughout the history of Etna far more towns have been destroyed by lava than have been saved from a similar fate through Divine intervention (see Table 9.4). In the absence of any real alternatives to loss bearing this particular feature of the pre-industrial response is perfectly understandable.

A second common element within the system of beliefs held by the inhabitants was that the disasters, though terrible at the time, had a positive role in stimulating personal acts of heroism and self-sacrifice. An early incident, for instance, (recorded by Seneca, Lucilius Junior and others) concerned the bravery of Anapias and Amphinomus (Table 9.5) – this quickly became part of both recorded and oral history; while later the already-quoted story of Diego Pappalardo and his fellow citizens was accorded a similar status. It is of interest that this tradition of lauding heroic deeds has continued into the twentieth century and the story is related by King (1973a) of Monsignor Nicotra, parish priest of the village of S. Alfio, which was threatened during the 1928 eruption. He announced that he would offer his life to save the village and his request was granted; the village was saved and he died four months later. Today this story is already gaining the status of a folk legend.

Although mythology and religious belief were the usual means by which losses were explained, from the time of the ancients onwards there existed a minority 'scientific' tradition that sought a more rational understanding. Amongst Classical authors the most complete model was that proposed by Lucilius Junior in the poem *Aetna*, written between AD 65 and 79 (Table 9.5). In this poem an eruption is first described in detail and then natural processes are invoked in order to explain its principal characteristics. Lucilius argues that the agents responsible for eruptions are wind and air (*spiritus*), for without them no 'fire' (sic) is possible. These agents 'jostle one another inside the mountain and, in the struggle to escape crowding, drag with them everything that stands in the way' (Hyde, 1916, p. 411). Periods of quiescence, according to Lucilius Junior, indicate that the winds causing eruptions come from within rather than from outside the volcano, and closure of the channels through which the material moves not only delays eruptions, but also increases the violence of subsequent outbursts. Unfortunately this early scientific tradition did not continue and, though careful descriptions of individual eruptions are a feature of the literature of the region from the twelfth century AD onwards (Rodwell, 1878), few, if any, new models were proposed until the late-eighteenth and early-nineteenth centuries. The gradual growth in scientific understanding during the nineteenth century, however, was one of the factors which eventually led to the close of pre-industrial era around 1900 and a pronounced yet gradual change in the nature of the perception, response and adjustment to the threat posed by periodic flank eruptions.

9.2.2 *Post-industrial responses*

When describing an historical sequence it is rarely justifiable to divide it into discrete periods, and the choice of 1900 as marking a break between a distinct pre-industrial and an equally clear-cut post-industrial form of response is adopted here for convenience alone. Indeed, not only did change begin in, and accelerate during the course of, the nineteenth century but, as Table 9.2 implies, some elements of the traditional response continue unchanged in all post-industrial societies. On Etna, for example, the willingness of many to appeal to the Deity as a means of averting personal disaster remains a constant response and was a feature of both the 1971 and 1983 eruptions. What makes responses and adjustments to major flank eruptions that have occurred in the present century so different is that a consensus emerged which held that even if losses could not be prevented, something should be done to mitigate their worst effects both to individuals and to the region as a whole.

One of the most important influences on this evolving consensus was political and involved the gradual integration of the region into Italian national life. This meant that for the first time natural disasters were viewed in national rather than purely local terms with the result that public relief became a real alternative to involuntary loss-bearing (see Table 9.1). Although unification of Sicily with the mainland occurred in 1860, it was not until the early years of the present century that the national government became a real factor in the process of adjustment. One reason for this delay was that between 1860 and the Messina earthquake of 1908, Sicily suffered no major natural disaster and on Etna the eruptions of 1879, 1886 and 1892 (Table 9.4) only caused limited damage (Admiralty, 1944). A further reason was, as King (1973a, p. 13–14) notes, that 'the immediate post-Unification period was remarkable for the ignorance that prevailed about the real conditions of life in Sicily and southern Italy in general, for few politicians ventured south of Rome.' So great was the disaster at Messina, however, with some 98% of all the houses destroyed and a death toll of around 80 000 in the city alone, that the civil powers were virtually forced to act, with troops being used to maintain law-and-order and to construct temporary dwellings (Baedeker, 1930). Considering the scale of the disaster this aid was modest in the extreme and, in the immediate aftermath of the catastrophe, probably less useful than the relief aid provided from America and the salvage work undertaken by the mercantile marines of Russia, Germany and Great Britain, but it did at least establish the precedent of state-intervention in assisting the victims of natural disasters.

In all major flank eruptions since 1900 (Table 9.6) the State has become progressively more involved in providing public relief. Hyde (1916), for instance, writing of the 1910 eruption which threatened the town of Nicolosi and the village of Borello, notes how the army was quickly pressed into service and provided hundreds of wagons to allow the evacuation of people and property. The eruptions which occurred during the inter-war years (1923 and 1928) enabled the fascist authorities to demonstrate their efficiency in coping with emergencies. Apart from a partially successful fight against organized crime, the twenty-one years of fascist rule (1922 – 43) has less political impact on Sicily than many other regions of Italy (Mack-Smith 1968). The Mussolini government, however, was keen to 'manufacture' prestige and a favourable impression of itself both nationally and in the international press; such initiatives as improvements in communications, water supply, tentative land reform together with public disaster relief admirably served these goals of policy while fundamentally changing little in this rather backward island (King, 1973a). In the eruptions of 1923 and 1928 the army was used to maintain order and to organize evacuation where necessary, but in 1928 it was also responsible for emergency housing, the distribution of relief funds (provided by the Mussolini Cabinet) and in helping to dismantle and remove factory equipment which was threatened by the lava (Jaggar, 1928a, 1928b, 1929). These eruptions also saw the first personal involve-

Table 9.6 The effects of twentieth-century flank eruptions on the inhabitants of the region

Date	*Location of eruption*	*Effects on the inhabitants*
1908	High-level eruption, south-east sector (3000–2200 m)	Minor eruption; little (if any) effect on the main populated parts of this sector
1910	High-level eruption, south sector (3000–1950 m)	A serious eruption, with lava threatening Nicolosi and the adjacent village of Borello (a suburb of Belpasso). Large areas of agricultural land and woodland were destroyed
1911	Eruption associated with the north-east rift (2500–1650 m)	Lavas associated with this eruption caused the road between Linguaglossa and Randazzo to be cut. Virtually no damage to housing, but some agricultural losses
1918	High-level eruption, north-west sector (3100–1900 m)	Minor eruption; little (if any) effect on the main populated parts of this sector
1923	Boccas opened successively down the north-east rift (2400–1800 m)	Lavas from this eruption caused the road between Linguaglossa and Randazzo to be cut, together with the narrow-gauge railway line. Significant agricultural losses were caused and some houses were destroyed on the outskirts of Linguaglossa
1928	Main lava flows from a fissure (1200 m), east sector	Probably the most serious eruption since 1669. Lava totally destroyed the town of Mascali and cut all major road and rail links on the east side of the volcano. It was estimated that 700 houses were destroyed, 5000 people made homeless and 16 km^2 laid waste. Total losses estimated at $18 million ($US at 1928 prices). At least two people reported killed
1942	High-level eruption, south-west sector (3000–2240 m)	Minor eruption; little (if any) effect on the main populated parts of this sector
1947	Eruption associated with north-east rift (3050–2200 m) and flowed down north sector	Virtually no effects on settlements, but destroyed 0.4 km^2 of woodland and 0.5 km^2 of cultivated land
1949	Fractures near summit and lava flowed down north, north-west and south sectors	Little (if any) effect on the main populated parts of these sectors
1950–51	Fissures opened in Valle del Bove (2800–2250 m), east sector	Lava threatened the town of Fornazzo and cut the road to the town in several places
1971 (April)	Two fissures opened near to the summit, south sector	Lava destroyed the Etna Observatory and the upper part of the cable-car route
1971 (May)	Fissures opened (about 1800 m), east sector	The towns of Fornazzo and S. Alfio were threatened by lava, which also caused significant losses to agricultural land and woodland
1974	Eruption associated with two vents, west sector (about 1675 m)	Relatively minor eruption; little (if any) effect on the main populated parts of this sector
1978	Several fissures active, Valle del Bove (2800–2500 m), east sector	Largely confined to the Valle del Bove, relatively little damage, except to rough grazing land

Table 9.6 (contd.)

Date	*Location of eruption*	*Effects on the inhabitants*
1979	Eruption associated with two main events in the Valle del Bove, east sector (1800–1700 m)	Large flows cut a minor road and threatened the main road communications to the town of Fornazzo. Limited agricultural and woodland losses
1981	North-west sector (2500–1800 m)	A serious eruption; lava threatened the town of Randazzo and the village of Montelaguardia (3.5 km east of Randazzo). All road and rail communications to the east were severed and 250 farm buildings were destroyed, in addition to many animals. 4 km^2 of land were inundated, about 2.5 km^2 of this being agriculturally productive and the rest used for woodland and rough grazing. Total losses of the order of $10 million ($US at 1981 prices)
1983	South sector (about 2400 m)	A major eruption which destroyed much of the tourist complex at around 1900 m together with large areas of woodland and agriculturally productive land. According to some authorities the towns of Ragalna, Nicolosi and many small villages were threatened, but in the event were saved from destruction. Total losses estimated at greater than $30 million ($US at 1983 prices)

Compiled from information in Hyde (1916); Ponte (1923); Jaggar (1928b, 1929); Booth and Francis (1972); Clapperton (1972); King (1973a); Guest and Murray (1980); VEST (1981); Kilburn (1983a, 1983b); Lockwood (1983) and numerous other sources.

ment of national leaders with the affairs of the region at times of natural disaster. In 1923 the King of Italy and the Prime Minister – Benito Mussolini – visited the scene of the disaster, and the latter placed a seaplane at the disposal of Professor Ponte of the Etna Vulcanological Institute so that he could report on the progress of the eruption. In honour of the visit and the interest shown in the area by these national leaders (as well as, no doubt, for more obvious political reasons) the *Accademia Gioenia di Catania* named the new craters formed by the 1923 eruption after these two visitors (Ponte, 1923). For equally obvious political reasons these names are not in common use today.

Since 1945 no eruption has wrought destruction on the scale of 1928 (Table 9.6) and the reaction of the authorities to the eruptions of 1971, 1981 and 1983 is generally accepted by commentators to have been reasonably successful (King, 1973a; VEST, 1981), with orderly evacuation where necessary, the brisk mobilization of aid and the rapid restoration of communications. In addition most of the ultimate cost of these eruptions has been borne by national and local government. From the middle of the 1970s it became apparent both to national government and on Etna that the existing state provision was probably not adequate to cope with either a large volcanic eruption, or a large earthquake, of the scale that has been all too common in the past.

Several natural disasters have been widely reported in the national and international press and have been the subject of careful research. From these works it is clear that, whilst financial provision and political will are adequate, effective relief is severely hampered by poor administration, logistical difficulties in ensuring that aid actually reaches victims, and the lengthy period it takes for regions to recover following a catastrophe. Some of these problems are not new and as early as 1924 it is reported that Mussolini, on a visit to Messina, was appalled when he discovered that victims of the 1908 earthquake were still housed in makeshift accommodation (Admiralty, 1945). What is extremely worrying to policy-makers is that similar problems are still occurring more than fifty years later, even though in material terms Italy has become one of the more prosperous countries in the world. Hence in 1982 the Pope made a visit to certain villages in western Sicily which were still suffering from the effects of an earthquake in 1968. Logistical problems in making sure aid reaches victims were also highlighted by experience following this earthquake since, even though the government and other agencies provided money, clothing and blankets, these took too long in reaching those in need and the 50 000 people made homeless were forced to live in tents and other unsatisfactory accommodation for months on end (Haas and Ayre, 1969; King, 1973a). Furthermore, criminal organizations were allowed to exploit the situation, racketeers buying up livestock and land at cheap prices hoping eventually to make a profit out of the distress of this poor region.

A detailed study of the 1963 Vaiont Dam overflow in northern Italy, which claimed the lives of nearly 2 000 people (Quarantelli, 1979), suggests that maladministration is the major problem confronting the Italian authorities in their attempts to provide effective disaster relief. In particular, Quarantelli lists the difficulties involved in evolving means whereby Italian politicians can actually work together in emergencies when they are often drawn from opposite ends of a very wide and mutually antipathetic political spectrum, when all disasters can become 'political footballs' in which blame is easily attached by opponents to any decisive action and where the main aid-providing agency – the army – is unsure of its powers and lacks specialized training and effective civilian direction.

On Etna, although the stimulus for a reconsideration of the organization of disaster relief stems in part from the lessons learnt from natural disasters elsewhere in Sicily and on the mainland, local circumstances have also been important. In September 1979 nine tourists were killed and about twenty injured during an explosion at the summit of Etna (Guest *et al.*, 1980a) – the first fatalities on the volcano since the eruption of 1928 (Jaggar, 1928b, 1929). This event was widely reported by the media and had the effect of further concentrating the minds of politicians on the issue of disaster planning. In October 1979 a scientific and technical consultative committee (Comitato di consulenza Techico-Scientifico per il vulcano Etna) was set up, with experts being drawn from the University of Catania and the International Institute of Volcanology, also in Catania, to advise the civil authorities on volcanic and earthquake hazards in the region (Cristofolini and Romano, 1980). Experience from the mainland, especially from the Avellino earthquake of 1980, and the 1983 eruption of Etna, implies that public administration is much improved from the position described by Quarantelli (1979) as having been common in the early 1960s (Fig. 9.5). In a letter to the editor of the journal *Disasters*, a member of International Disaster Institute in London, suggests that much press disquiet over the handling of the 1980 earthquake was unfair to the Italian authorities in view of the scale of the disaster, the fact that it occurred at night and in an area consisting of numerous scattered hilltop villages. This correspondent points out that within one week essential services had been restored and that the majority of survivors were housed in temporary accommodation (Stephenson, 1981). Furthermore, as a result of the previous somewhat unsatisfactory administrative arrangements, the Italian authorities in both the Friuli earthquake of 1976 and the Avellino disaster were quick to appoint an Extraordinary Commissioner to co-ordinate the relief effort (Anon., 1981, 1982). A similar initiative was adopted during the 1983 eruption of Etna, when the Minister of Civil Protection acted to integrate the actions of civil, military and scientific personnel (Page, 1983). Whether a relief effort of the scale needed to deal with a major eruption of Etna could be mounted in the near future is an open question, but it is encouraging to see that the authorities are at least taking the threat seriously.

A second factor which has made responses and adjustments so different in the twentieth century

Fig. 9.5 The 1981 lava which nearly destroyed the town of Randazzo. Within a few weeks landowners had marked out property lines and the authorities had constructed a temporary road. (Photograph: D. K. Chester.)

than in preceding centuries, is the growth in material wealth. The process of development (Chapter 2) has been responsible in part for the ability of the authorities to draw up plans for comprehensive public relief and to provide adequate funding to make these plans possible. Some idea of the amount of money needed to deal with major disasters is evident from consideration of the 1980 Avellino earthquake when the State had to make around $US 1.3 billion available in immediate disaster aid, while the total economic loss is estimated at over $US 12 billion (Anon., 1981, 1982). This latter figure, moreover, ignores the cost of the inevitable slowing of economic activity (possibly of the order of $US 2 billion). Although far less, the costs of the 1983 eruption of Etna are still significant to national and regional economies and after one month property losses alone were estimated at over $US 30 million (Kilburn, 1983a). At a more personal level, however, this increased wealth means that today alternatives to simple loss-bearing are possible. Small agricultural holdings are still common in the Etna region, with individual plots as small as 2 ha being a feature of the southern and south-eastern flanks (D. S. Walker, 1967), but today many farmers own parcels of land in different areas, with the result that they are much less likely to suffer a total loss and be rendered destitute should an eruption destroy significant quantities of their land. This ability of farmers to survive as a result of the system of land-holding that has evolved was of importance during the 1971 eruption (Table 9.6). Seven farmers in the commune of S. Alfio lost land, four losing eight vineyards, one lost ten, one twenty and the worst-affected seventy, yet most of these farmers possessed land elsewhere and could therefore spread their losses (Clapperton, 1972).

Fig. 9.6 A house destroyed by lava during the 1979 eruption. At the present time few householders are insured against losses and have to rely on the State or their own resources. (Photograph: D. K. Chester.)

Perhaps of greater significance, especially for the future, is the fact that increased wealth now allows both commercial organizations and individuals to 'plan for losses' by means of insurance (Table 9.1). Insurance against natural disasters is available in Italy, even though it is not backed by government guarantees and reserve funds, as is the case in Spain, Switzerland, New Zealand and several other countries. Earthquakes are covered by extensions to standard fire policies and these are individually negotiated by Italian insurance companies (Bolt, 1978) but, surprisingly, risks arising from volcanic activity are rarely covered (Associazione Nazionale Fra Le Imprese Assicuratrici, 1982, personal communication). Cover, however, is available through the international insurance market and the actions of London underwriters are typical; London-based companies and syndicates generally write insurance against natural disasters by means of extensions to standard fire policies. These special endorsements indemnify policyholders against losses resulting from volcanic eruptions, earthquakes and fires resulting from seismic activity. The world is divided into categories of risk and, for each, minimum premiums are recommended by national associations of companies. Using these for guidance, underwriters calculate premiums by means of their knowledge of geological history, the type of building involved and the nature of the business being performed (Fire Offices' Committee, London, 1982, personal communication). The uptake of policies within the region is probably small and the general impression seems to be that people are generally not 'insurance-minded', believing that the government will come to their aid in time of disaster (Fig. 9.6). In addition the premiums demanded are probably beyond the resources of many individuals, farmers and small businessmen. Given the rapid industrial development of the region in recent years (Chapter 2) and the influx of investment and companies from the mainland and abroad, it seems likely that in the future the position will change, and that insurance will become a more important factor in the post-industrial response.

A third element in the evolving consensus that something should be done to mitigate the worst effects of eruptions is related to the progressive application of scientific knowledge to the twin goals of hazard-modification and loss-reduction (Table 9.1). Until the mid-1970s most investigations were of a pure research character, although from the 1920s onwards there were occasional initiatives on the part of scientists to arrest the forward motion of lava flows and alter their directions. During the 1923 eruption, for instance, it is recorded that, under the direction of Professor Ponte, scientists from the (then) Etna Volcanological Institute introduced carbon dioxide into some of the eruption craters to prevent, or at least reduce, explosive activity by preventing combustible gases combining with oxygen. According to reports at the time this action was considered to have been fairly successful (Ponte, 1923). Later, in 1928, an attempt was made to construct artificial channels to divert the main lava front from its relentless advance on the town of Giarre by means of a safe route to the coast, but fortunately the lava stopped before the efficacy of this measure could be put to the test (Jaggar, 1929). Since the 1920s no flank eruption has caused as much damage as that of 1928 (Table 9.6). During both the 1971 and 1983 eruptions scientific knowledge was applied to modifying the threat and reducing potential losses. In 1971 Haroun Tazieff made a plea for the Italian air force to be allowed to bomb certain eruption fissures to halt, or change the course of the flows (King, 1973a), but this suggestion was overruled by the authorities who were worried about the unpredictable consequences of such action. In particular they were concerned about causing losses in areas which would not otherwise have been affected.

Action taken during the 1983 eruption is interesting because for the first time in recent years an attempt was made to divert a lava flow from its natural course. This eruption started on 28 March at around 2400 m on the southern flank of the volcano. In less than one month it had caused damage estimated at over $US 30 million to the valuable tourist complex, which had developed during the preceding twenty-five years (Table 9.6; also see Chapter 2). In response to lobbying by the inhabitants of towns and villages at lower levels on the volcano, who feared the further erosion of their livelihoods and the eventual destruction of their homes, two actions were taken by the authorities. First, an ancient law was suspended which made individuals liable for losses caused by the diversion of lava flows. This statute had been enacted following the attempt in 1669 by men from Catania to divert lava from their city and the trouble this caused with the inhabitants of Paterno, who would have suffered considerable losses if this action had been successful (Kilburn, 1983a, 1983b; and Chapter 8). Secondly, on the invitation of the Minister for Civil Protection, a committee of scientific advisers was set up under Professor Barberi of the University of Pisa to advise on the best solutions that could be adopted in the circumstances.

The committee sugggested that earthen lava-diversion barriers should be rapidly constructed at two sites to protect high-value installations and that, as a secondary measure, a breach should be made in the main lava channel in order to deflect some of the lava to a new course and so 'buy' time until the barriers were in place. The diversion attempt involved the use of explosives to break the lava channel at around 2200 m and, because of its spectacular nature, attracted the attention of press and television reporters from many countries of the world. Unfortunately the media largely missed the point of this exercise and saw the diversion as the principal, and in some cases the sole, response of the authorities. Many critical reports appeared which implied that this action was based on political considerations, elections being due in June, so that the authorities could demonstrate in a visible way that they were doing something positive to prevent further losses. Criticism also focussed on the cost of the diversion and the fact that villages further down the mountain were not in any immediate danger. Most scientific observers were, in contrast, of the opinion that the operation was reasonably successful (Lockwood, 1983). The barriers successfully saved the high-value installations they were designed to protect and the cost of the whole operation was probably less than the value of the property that would have been lost if no action had been taken (see Chapter 8 for a detailed discussion).

The iniatives taken in 1983 and in earlier eruptions represented attempts by scientists to assist the civil powers while eruptions were actually in progress and were, as a result, planned at short notice and on an *ad hoc* basis. In line with the new spirit of preparedness which entered Italian disaster-planning in the 1970s it is now realized that if measures designed to either modify the hazard or its loss potential (Table 9.1) are to be fully effective in future eruptions, especially if these are of a large scale and located in densely populated areas, then measures have to be both scientifically justified and planned in advance. In addition it is considered essential that these initiatives should be fully supported and understood by the authorities; at the present time three regional centres are proposed to co-ordinate state efforts in the event of future natural catastrophes. Recent research, therefore, has focused upon the appropriateness (for Etna) of several forms of adjustment. This research has included investigations of planning policies to restrict development in particularly hazard-prone areas, evaluations of possible techniques to protect high-value installations, and the assessment of a number of measures designed to alter the directions of future lava flows or to halt their progress. In Chapter 8 recent attempts to construct *general predictive* models (Walker, 1974a) of Etnean activity were discussed and the refinement of these into hazard maps provides a means of zoning the volcano into areas of differing volcanic risk (Booth, 1979). Although all the general predictive models proposed for Etna come to broadly similar conclusions, leaving only a few discrepancies to resolve (see Chapter 8), further research is required before these may be used as a practical basis for land-use planning. All models present their conclusions in map form usually supplemented by a written statement, and it might be thought a simple task to use these maps to steer new economic development into relatively safe areas, through a system of physical planning controls (Duncan *et al.*, 1981). Unfortunately these maps cover the whole volcano at a broad scale and, although they are suitable documents for planning the location of large-scale developments which could be sited virtually anywhere on the lower slopes of Etna, for the majority of projects this is not the case since all the alternative locations may be restricted to one commune or even a single town. To remedy this unsatisfactory situation scientists from both the University of Catania and the International Institute of Volcanology (Catania) have recently begun a detailed hazard-study of the area around the towns of Milo and Zafferana. This area has been affected by flank eruptions on many occasions (Tables 9.4 and 9.6) and is probably one of the most potentially hazardous tracts on the whole volcano, but in the future other areas will be treated to a similarly detailed investigation.

Statistical modelling is a further field in which research is required before hazard maps may be fully employed for land-use planning. So far, published general predictive models have been largely qualitative in character, and it has not been possible to specify the statistical probability of losses occurring in specific areas of the volcano (Maugeri and Romano, 1980 – 81). In the view of Barberi and Gasparini (1976, p. 227) 'in order to take a decision on the basis of a cost–benefit analysis, urbanists and civil engineers need . . . more complete information than is provided in such qualitative maps.' For Vesuvius, maps based upon the probability of losses resulting from either lava flows or the opening of eruptive fissures have been available for some time (see Scandone and Cortini, 1982), based in part on statistical procedures first developed by Wickman (1966, 1976). Probabilistic hazard maps may be only readily compiled for volcanoes which have been reasonably active and possess well-documented eruption chronologies, since long repose periods or limited historical records make it impossible to determine whether documented eruptions are typical of the activity over the whole life of the volcano. Both these criteria are met by Etna and it seems only a question of time before probabilistic hazard maps are constructed.

In view of the success of various preventive and defensive measures taken in several parts of the world to modify the hazard posed by lava flows (Table 9.1), it is not surprising that in recent years applied volcanological research has been concerned with choosing the most appropriate adjustments of this type for Etna. This work has only just started but already some preliminary findings have been published (Maugeri and Romano, 1980 – 81) and these are summarized in Table 9.7. Although this table is fairly self-explanatory, two points need clarification. First, the evaluations are largely based on scientific criteria and, with the exception of the limited experience gained during the 1983 eruption, there has not been sufficient research carried out on the ratio of costs-to-likely-benefits. In other words the question of whether investment would be better directed to alternative measures including insurance, civil defence and state compensation, has not yet been answered satisfactorily. Secondly, to be effective the measures proposed by Maugeri and Romano require the formation of an 'intervention unit' to complete the defensive structures once an eruption has started. They envisage that this could be a specially trained military corps, which could also be used for assisting the civil powers in the event of other natural disasters. This is a very useful suggestion, especially considering many of the logistical problems which have reduced the effectiveness of the official response in the past and, in view of the new spirit of concern and involvement with disaster planning, may become an accepted part of pre-disaster preparedness in the near future.

Table 9.7 Recent evaluation of different techniques designed to modify the hazard from lava flows

Technique	*Evaluation*
Diversion of lava at eruption sites or through the rupturing of flow levées on the flanks of the volcano	Considered to be only practicable at high levels on the volcano and in the Valle del Bove. At lower levels any diversion would still cause damage and diversion is not therefore thought to be a viable option
Control the forward advance of lava flows by cooling the flow fronts with water	Not considered to be a viable option, since in Iceland such an operation required 0.9 $m^3 s^{-1}$ of water and this volume is not available on Etna, except near to the sea
Defensive works to protect high-value installations	Defence works could be of limited success and might include dams, barriers and cleared flow-ways. However, probably only justified for the protection of high-value installations in areas of high hazard-potential. On Etna defence works could be partly constructed before the event and finished during the event; provided the civil powers could effectively mobilize the labour required

Based on Maugeri and Romano (1980–81).

9.3 Conclusion: prospects for the future

From the foregoing discussion it is clear that during recent years significant progress has been made in formulating effective means of adjustment and response to volcanic and other geophysical hazards, which are commensurate with Italy's status as a relatively wealthy, developed country. It is also evident that many of these initiatives are at the planning stage and it can only be hoped that the region is not afflicted by any major natural disaster before all the measures are implemented.

There remain certain areas in which further efforts are necessary before the response of the Etna region may be truly described as comprehensive. Perhaps the greatest need is for a programme of mass scientific education, so that the inhabitants of the region, including political leaders, may be made fully aware of the true nature of geophysical risk. Maugeri and Romano (1981) suggest that this could take the form of scientists giving lectures to local groups, but an even greater need is for an informed press adequately briefed by expert personnel before, during and after a future eruption. In Italy there have been several instances of the press publishing misleading information about natural disasters, of which the attempt during the 1983 eruption to divert lava flows is but the latest example. This is due in part to official indifference over the need for properly organized press briefings and, in the absence of reliable, scientifically sound information, what has been published has often been of an alarmist or sensational character and has, indeed, sometimes hindered relief efforts (Quarantelli, 1979). On Etna, an example of the way in which unchallenged press reports can easily cause mass panic occurred a few years ago when newspapers carried a story that an astrologer had predicted an imminent earthquake in Catania. Many people fled from the city and in so doing caused a major traffic jam. If an earthquake had, through coincidence, struck at this time, then the relief effort would have been severely impeded. Civil authorities, at both the national level and in the Etna region, therefore need to ensure that the press is supplied with accurate information from reputable scientific sources.

A further requirement is for the integration of local and regional economic plans on the one hand and disaster contingency plans on the other. At the moment many areas of Etna are being developed and many new buildings are located in potentially hazardous locations. As Maugeri and Romano (1980 – 81, p. 183) note 'in some cases the solution considered the best is hindered not so much by the need to protect already . . . built areas as by the provisions of local and regional building plans with which it is now difficult to interfere.' As a solution they suggest that new legislation is called for and it is to be hoped that this aspect of land-use planning will receive detailed attention from policy makers in the near future.

Finally, better surveillance of the volcano is needed. As discussed in Chapter 8 specific prediction of eruptions on Etna as elsewhere is still in its infancy, but surveillance would enable plans to be drawn up at the first sign of possible activity and ensure an effective response to any emergency. All disaster plans have been made on the assumption that future activity will mirror that of the historic past, involving persistent, mildly strombolian activity at the summit and the periodic eruption of lava on the flanks. It has been known for some time, however, that in the prehistoric past the volcano gave rise to more explosive activity (Duncan *et al.*, 1981), including pyroclastic flows (Duncan, 1976a). These flows were associated with more-evolved magmas and different styles of eruption from those which have characterized historical activity. Although in the short and medium terms it is probably safe to assume that Etna will continue to act as it has done throughout the period for which records are available, it would be prudent to focus part of any surveillance programme on monitoring any changes in either eruptive style or lava petrology. Similar comments apply to the possible risks from lahars (volcanic mudflows) and slope failure induced by oversteepening of slopes by successive lava flows covering the same area. Both these processes have probably occurred at earlier stages in the volcano's evolution (see Chapters 3 and 4) but, again, comprehensive surveillance should ensure that appropriate action can be taken if the warning signs are recognized. In short, when assessing potential hazards, it is probably unsafe to assume that the past is always an infallible guide to the future.

References

Ackermann, N. L. and Shen, H. T. (1979) Rheological characteristics of solid – liquid mixtures. *A.I.Ch.E. Journal*, **25**, 327 – 332.

Admiralty (1944) *Italy*, (BR 517, vol. 1) Naval Intelligence Division, London.

Admiralty (1945) *Italy*, (BR 517c, vol. IV) Naval Intelligence Division, London.

Affronti, F. (1967) Straordinario gradiente pluviometrico del Monte Etna. *Schweiz Met. Zentralanstalt Veröffentlichungen*, **4**, 115 – 123.

Affronti, F. (1969a) Inversioni Termiche estive sul Monte Etna. *La Meteorologie*, **10 – 11**, 109 – 117.

Affronti, F. (1969b) Polveri da esplosioni dell 'Etna e nucleazioni. *Riv. di. Meteorol.*, **21**, 41 – 55.

Aitken, M. J., Fleming, S. J., Doell, R. R. and Tanguy, J. C. (1968) Thermoluminescent study of lavas from Mt. Etna and other historic flows: preliminary results, in *Thermoluminescence of Geological Materials* (ed. J. D. McDougall). Academic Press, London, pp. 359 – 366.

Alexandrovichi, H.M., Pavlnichenko, M. M. and Mateiko, F. F. (1962) *Doklady Akad. Nauk. SSSR*, **6**, 168. (Quoted by Jinescu, 1974.)

Alvarez, W. (1972) The rotation of the Corsica–Sardinia microplate. *Nature*, **235**, 103–105.

Ambrosetti, P., Azzaroli:, A, Bonadonna, F. P, and Follieri, M. (1972) A scheme of Pleistocene chronology for the Tyrrhenian side of central Italy. *Boll. Soc. Geol. Ital.*, **88**, 3 – 10.

Anderson, A. T. (1975) Some basaltic and andesitic gases. *Rev. Geophys. Space Phys.*, **13**, 37 – 55.

Anderson, E. M. (1951) *The Dynamics of Faulting and Dyke Formation, with Application to Britain*, Oliver and Boyd, Edinburgh.

Anon. (1669a) An answer to some inquiries concerning the eruptions of Mount Aetna, 1669, communicated by some inquisitive merchants now residing in Sicily. *Phil. Trans. R. Soc., Lond.*, **4**, 1028 – 1034.

Anon. (1669b) A chronological account of several Incendiums or fires of Mt. Aetna. *Phil. Trans. R. Soc., Lond.*, **4**, 967 – 969.

Anon. (1977) *Popolazione Residente e Presente dei Communi: Censimenti dal 1861 — 1971*, Tome II, Istituto Centrale di Statistica, Rome.

Anon. (1979) *Commendio Statico Italiano*, Istituto Centrale di Statistica, Rome.

Anon. (1981) The earthquake in southern Italy on 23 November 1980 (Part one). *Italy: Documents and Notes*, New Series (No. **16**), 31 – 59.

Anon. (1982) The earthquake in Southern Italy on 23 November, 1980 (Part two). *Italy: Documents and Notes*, Third Series (No. **1**), 9 – 41.

Archambault, C. (1982) Remote monitoring of Etna. *Argos Newsletter*, No. **15** (October), 1 – 5.

Archambault, C. and Tanguy, J. C. (1976) Comparative temperature measurements on Mount Etna lavas, problems and techniques. *J. Volcanol. Geotherm. Res.*, **1**, 113 – 125.

Archambault, C., Stoschek, J. and Tanguy, J. C. (1979a) Mise en évidence d'anomalies thermiques dans la basse zone du secteur sud de l'Etna. *Centre*

National d'Etudes des Telecommunications (CNET) de Lannion, Note Technique NT/CPM/FMI/110.

Archambault, C., Stoschek, J. and Tanguy, J. C. (1979b) Etablissement d'une carte thermique du massif de l'Etna à patir des données transmises par le satellite météorologique NOAA V. Interprétation structurale et corrélations avec les phases éruptives de Avril-Mai 1978. *Centre National d'Etudes des Telecommunications (CNET) de Lannion, Note Technique NT/CPM/FMI/111.*

Archambault, C., Scarpinati, G., Stoschek, J. and Tanguy, J. C. (undated). Analyse et surveillance thermiques de volcans actifs. *Bulletin PIRPSEV*, No. **66**, CNRS-INAG, Paris.

Arculus, R. J. and Wills, K. J. A. (1980) The petrology of plutonic blocks and inclusions from the Lesser Antilles Island Arc. *J. Petrol.*, **21,** 743 – 799.

Argyriadis, I., de Graciansky, P., Marcoux, J. and Ricou, L. E. (1980) The opening of the Mesozoic Tethys between Eurasia and Arabia – Africa, in *Geology of the Alpine chains born of the Tethys* (eds J. Aubouin, J. Debelmas and M. Latreille), *Memoire Bureau de Récherches Géologiques et Miniéres*, **115,** 199 – 214.

Arrhenius, S. (1887) Uhr die innere Reibung verdunnter wasseviger Losungen. *Z. Physik. Chemie.*, **1,** 285 – 298.

Arzi, A. A. (1978) Critical phenomena in the rheology of partially melted rocks. *Tectonophysics*, **44,** 173 – 184.

Atzori, P. (1966) La parete lavica fra Adrano e Biancavilla. *Atti Accad. Gioenia Sci Nat. (Catania)*, **18,** 50 – 70.

Baedeker, K. (1930) *Southern Italy and Sicily with Excursions to Sardinia, Malta, Tripoli and Corfu*, Karl Baedeker, Leipzig (George Allen and Unwin, London).

Bagnold, R. A. (1954) Experiments on a gravity-free dispersion of large solid spheres in a Newtonian fluid under Shear. *Proc. R. Soc., Lond.*, **225A,** 49 – 63.

Bagnold, R. A. (1966) The shearing and dilation of dry sand and the 'singing' mechanism. *Proc. R. Soc., Lond.*, **295A,** 219 – 232.

Baker, I. (1968) Intermediate oceanic volcanic rocks and the Daly Gap. *Earth Planet. Sci. Lett.*, **4,** 103 – 106.

Barbano, M. S., Cosentino, M., Lombardo, G., and Patanè, G. (1980) Isoseismal maps of Calabria and Sicily earthquakes (Southern Italy). C. N. R., Progetto Finalizzato Geodinamica, Publ. No. 341.

Barberi, F. and Gasparini, P. (1976) Volcanic hazards. *Bull. Int. Ass. Eng. Geol.*, **14,** 217 – 232.

Barberi, F., Bizouard, H. and Varet, J. (1971) Nature of the clinopyroxene and iron enrichment in alkalic and transitional basaltic magmas. *Contrib. Mineral. Petrol.*, **33,** 93 – 107.

Barberi, F., Civetta, L., Gasparini, P., Innocenti, P., Scandone, R. and Villan, L. (1974) Evolution of a section of the Africa-Europe plate boundary: palaeomagnetic and volcanological evidences from Sicily. *Earth Planet. Sci. Lett.*, **22,** 123 – 132.

Barberi, F., Bizouard, H., Capaldi, G., Ferrara, G., Gasparani, P., Innocenti, F., Joron, J. L., Lambret, B., Treuil, M. and Allegre, C. (1978) Age & nature of basalts from the Tyrrhenian abyssal plain. *Init. Rep. DSDP*, **Leg 42, XLII,** *509—514.*

Barry, R. G. and Chorley, R. J. (1971) *Atmosphere, Weather and Climate*, Methuen, London.

Barth, T. F. W. (1962) *Theoretical Petrology*, John Wiley, New York.

Basaltic Volcanism Study Project (1981) *Basaltic Volcanism on the Terrestrial Planets*, Pergamon, New York.

Baumann, D. D. and Sims, J. H. (1972) The tornado threat: coping styles of the north and south. *Science*, **176,** 1386 – 1392.

Baxter, A. N. (1975) Petrology of the older series lavas, Mauritius, Indian Ocean. *Bull. Geol. Soc. Am.*, **86,** 1449 – 1458.

Baxter, A. N. (1978) Ultramafic and mafic nodule suites in shield-forming lavas from Mauritius. *J. Geol. Soc. Lond.*, **135,** 565 – 583.

Beccaluva, L., Deriu, M., Macciotta, G., Savelli, C. and Venturelli, G. (1977) Geochronology & magmatic character of the Pliocene – Pleistocene volcanism in Sardinia (Italy). *Bull. Volcanol.*, **40,** 153 – 168.

Beccaluva, L., Colantoni, P., Di Girolamo, P. and Savezzi, C. (1981) Upper-Miocene submarine volcanism in the Strait of Sicily (Banco senza Nome). *Bull. Volcanol.*, **44 – 3,** 537 – 581.

Beckinsale, M. and Beckinsale, R. (1975) *Southern Europe : The Mediterranean and Alpine Lands*, Hodder and Stoughton, London.

Bellia, S., Carapezza, M., Lucido, G., Nuccio, P. M. and Valenza, M. (1980) Aspetti magmatologici e ruolo dell·'H_2O rella eroluzione del Vulcano di Moio (Sicilia) *Mineral. Petr. Acta*, **24,** 107 – 122.

Bernoulli, D. and Lemoine, M. (1980) Birth and evolution of the Tethys: the overall situation, in *Geology of the Alpine chains born of the Tethys* (eds J. Aubouin, J. Debelmas and M. Latreille), *Memoires Bureau de Récherches Géologiques et Miniéres,* **115,** 168 – 179.

Bigazzi, G., Bonadonna, F. P., Ghezzo, C., Giuliani, O., Radicati Di Brozolo, F. and Rita, F. (1981) Geochronological study of the Monte Amiata lavas (Central Italy). *Bull. Volcanol.*, **44 – 3,** 455 – 465.

Biju-Duval, B., Dercourt, J. and Le Pichon, X. (1977) From Tethys Ocean to the Mediterranean Seas: a plate tectonics model of the evolution of the Western Alpine System, in *Structural History of the Mediterranean Basins* (eds B. Biju-Duval and L. Montadent) Editions Technip. Paris, pp. 143 – 164.

Birch, F. and Dane, E. B., Jr. (1942) Viscosity, in *Handbook of Physical Constants* (eds F. Birch, J. F. Schairer and H. C. Spicer). *Geol. Soc. Am. Spec. Pap.*, **36,** 131 – 137.

Bird, R. B., Stewart, W. E. and Lightfoot, E. N. (1960) *Transport Phenomena*, John Wiley and Sons, New York.

Björnsson, H., Björnsson, S. and Sigurgeirsson, Th. (1982) Penetration of water into hot rock boundaries of magma at Grímsvötn. *Nature*, **295,** 580 – 581.

Blackburn, E. A., Wilson, L. and Sparks, R. S. J. (1976) Mechanisms and dynamics of strombolian activity. *J. Geol. Soc., Lond.*, **132,** 429 – 440.

Blair, J. P. (1964) Home to Tristan da Cunha. *National Geographic*, **125** (Jan.), 60 – 81.

Blok, A. (1969) Southern Italian agro-towns. *Comparative Studies in Society and History* **11,** 121 – 135.

Boccaletti, M., Nicolich, R. and Torturici, L. (1984) The Calabrian Arc and the Ionian Sea in the dynamic evolution of the Central Mediterranean. *Marine Geol.*, **55,** 219 – 245.

Bolt, B. A. (1978) *Earthquakes: A Primer*, W. H. Freeman, San Francisco.

Bolt, B. A., Horn, W. L., Macdonald, G. A. and Scott, R. F. (1975) *Geological Hazards*, Springer-Verlag, Berlin.

Bonney, T. G. (1899) *Volcanoes*, John Murray, London.

Booth, B. (1977) Mapping volcanic risk. *New Scientist*, **22nd September,** 743 – 745.

Booth, B. (1979) Assessing volcanic risk. *J. Geol. Soc., Lond.*, **136,** 331 – 340.

Booth, B. and Francis, P. (1972) Etna erupts and will erupt again. *Geographical Magazine*, **44** (7), 472 – 481.

Borelli, G. A. (1670) *Historia et Meteorologia Incendii Aetnaei Anno 1669 ac Responsio ad Censuras Honoratti Fabri contra Librum de Vi Percussionis*, Regio Julio.

Bottinga, Y. and Weill, D. F. (1972) The viscosity of magmatic silicate liquids: a model for calculation. *Am. J. Sci.*, **272,** 438 – 475.

Bottinga, Y., Kudo, A. and Weill, D. (1966) Some observations on oscillatory zoning and crystallisation of magmatic plagioclase. *Am. Mineral.*, **51,** 792 – 806.

Bourlet, F. and Bourlet, Y. (undated) Etude des anomalies thermiques et hydriques sur le versant N.E a Citelli et sur le versant sud a la Montagnola. *Bulletin PIRPSEV*, **No. 73,** CNRS-INAG, Paris.

Bowen, N. L. (1928) *The Evolution of the Igneous Rocks*, Princeton University Press, Princeton.

Brea, L. B. (1957) *Sicily Before the Greeks*, Thames and Hudson, London.

British Society of Rheology (1966) *Bulletin*, **3,** 7.

Brodkey, R. S. (1967) *The Phenomena of Fluid Motions*, Addison-Wesley Publ. Corp., Mass.

Bruggeman, D. A. G. (1935) Berechnung verscheidener physikalischer konstanten von heterogenen Substanzen I. *Ann. der Physik*, **5,** 636 – 679.

Brunelli, F. and Scammacca, B. (1978) Le grotte dell' Etna : stato attuale delle conoscenze. *Process: Setimana Speleologica Catanese e Seminario Sulle Grotte Laviche*, Club Alpino Italiano, Gruppo Grotte, Catania, pp. 201 – 204.

Bryan, W. B., Finger, L. W. and Chayes, F. (1969) Estimating proportions in petrographic mixing equations by least-squares approximation. *Science (New York)*, **163,** 926 – 927.

Brydone, P. (1776) *A Tour Through Sicily and Malta; In a Series of Letters to William Beckford Esq.*, A. Strachan and T. Cadell (two vols.), London.

Buddington, A. F. and Lindsley, D. H. (1964) Iron – titanium oxide minerals and synthetic equivalents. *J. Petrol.*, **5,** 310 – 357.

Bullard, F. M. (1976) *Volcanoes of the Earth*, University of Texas Press, Austin.

Burton, I., Kates, R. W. and White, G. F. (1968) *The Human Ecology of Extreme Geophysical Events*, Working paper 1, Dept. of Geography, University of Toronto.

Burton, I., Kates, R. W. and White, G. F. (1978) *The Environment as Hazard.* Oxford University Press, New York.

Buscalioni, L. (1909) L'Etna e la sua vegetazione con Particolare Riguardo alla Genesi della Valle del Bove. *Boll. Soc. Geog. Ital.*, **46,** 221 – 50, 369 – 400.

Caire, A. (1970) Sicily in its Mediterranean Setting, in *Geology and History of Sicily* (eds W. Alvarez and K. H. A. Gohrbandt) R.E.S.L., Tripoli, pp. 145 – 170.

Campagnoli, C. C. (1979) The organisation of tourism in Sicily. *Wiener Geog. Schriften*, **53/54**, 132 – 142.

Caputo, M., Panza, G. F. and Postpischl, D. (1970) Deep structure of the Mediterranean basin. *J. Geophys. Res.*, **75**, 4919 – 4923.

Carapezza, M. (1962) Un esempio di eruzione laterale da faglia nell' apparato erruttivo etneo. *Acta miner. Alpina*, **8**, 249 – 276.

Carbonelle, J., Dajlevic, D., Zettwoog, P. and Sabroux, J. C. (1982) Gas output measurements from an active volcano. *Bull. Volcanol.*, **45 – 3**, 267 – 268.

Carmichael, I. S. E., Turner, F. J. and Verhoogen, J. (1974) *Igneous Petrology*, McGraw-Hill, New York.

Carter, S. R. (1976) *Petrology and Geochemistry of the Lavas of Mt. Etna, Sicily*. D. Phil. thesis, University of Oxford.

Carter, S. R. and Civetta, L. (1977) Isotope and trace element variations in the eastern Sicilian volcanics: genetic implications of the heterogeneous nature and development of the source regions. *Earth Planet. Sci. Lett.*, **36**, 168 – 180.

Carter, S. R., Evensen, N. M., Hamilton, P. J. and O'Nions, R. K. (1978) Continental volcanics derived from enriched and depleted source regions: Nd- and Sr- isotope evidence. *Earth Planet. Sci. Lett.*, **37**, 401 – 408.

Casetti, G., Frazzetta, G. and Romano, R. (1981) A statistical analysis in time of the eruptive events on Mount Etna (Italy) from 1323 to 1980. *Bull. Volcanol.*, **44**, 283 – 294.

Cassinis, R., Cosentino, P., Ponzini, G. S. and Rinscetti, M. (1970) Contributo all'esplorazione geofisica lungo la costa etnea. *Convegno Internazionale sulle Acque Sotterranee*, December 11, Palermo.

Castiglione, M. (1958) Sulla natura delle vulcaniti della zona etnea. *Boll. Sed. Accad. Gioenia Sci. Nat.*, (ser 4) **4**, 325 – 42.

Cawthorn, R. G and O'Hara, M. J. (1976) Amphibole fractionation in calcalkaline magma genesis. *Am. J. Sci.*, **276**, 309 – 329.

Cawthorn, R. G., Curran, E. B. and Arculus, R. J. (1973) A petrogenetic model for the origin of the calc-alkaline suite of Grenada, Lesser Antilles. *J. Petrol.*, **14**, 327 – 337.

Channell, J. E. T., D'Argenio, B. and Horvath, F. (1979) Adria, the African promontory in Mesozoic Mediterranean palaeogeography. *Earth Sci. Rev.*, **15**, 213 – 292.

Chayes, F. (1963) Relative abundance of intermediate members of the oceanic basalt-trachyte association. *J. Geophys. Res.*, **68**, 1519 – 1534.

Chayes, F. (1977) The oceanic basalt-trachyte relation in general and in the Canary Islands. *Am. Mineral.*, **62**, 666 – 671.

Chen, C.-Y. and Frey, F. A. (1983) Origin of Hawaiian tholeiite and alkalic basalt. *Nature*, **302**, 785 – 789.

Chester, D. K. and Duncan, A. M. (1979) Interrelationships between volcanic and alluvial sequences in the evolution of the Simeto River Valley, Mount Etna, Sicily. *Catena*, **6**, 293 – 315.

Chester, D. K. and Duncan, A. M. (1982) The interaction of volcanic activity in Quaternary times upon the evolution of the Alcantara and Simeto Rivers, Mount Etna, Sicily. *Catena*, **9**, 319 – 342.

Chong, J. S., Christiansen, E. B. and Baer, A. D. (1971) Rheology of concentration suspensions. *J. Appl. Polymer Sci.*, **15**, 2007 – 2021.

Christiansen, R. C. and Paterson, D. W. (1981) Chronology of the 1980 eruptive activity, in *The 1980 Eruption of Mount St. Helens, Washington* (eds P. W. Lipman and D. R. Mullineaux. *US Geol. Surv. Prof. Pap.*, **1250**, 17 – 30.

Cigolini, C., Borgia, A. and Casertano, L. (1984) Intra-crater activity, aa - block lava, viscosity and flow dynamics : Arenal volcano, Costa Rica. *J. Volcanol. Geotherm. Res.*, **20**, 155 – 176.

Civetta, L., Orsi, G., Scandone, P. and Pece, R. (1978) Eastwards migration of the Tuscan anatectic magmatism due to anticlockwise rotation of the Apennines. *Nature*, **276**, 604 – 606.

Clapperton, C. M. (1972) Patterns of physical and human activity on Mount Etna. *Scott. Geogr. Mag.*, **88**, 160 – 167.

Clarke, B. (1967) Rheology of coarse settling suspensions. *Trans. Inst. Chem. Eng.*, **45**, 251 – 256.

Colantoni, P., Lucchini, F., Rossi, P. L., Sartori, R. and Savelli, C. (1981) The Palinuri Volcano and magmatism of the south-eastern Tyrrhenian Sea (Mediterranean). *Marine Geol.*, **39**, M1 – M12.

Colgate, S. A. and Sigurgeirsson, Th. (1973) Dynamic mixing of water and lava. *Nature*, **244**, 552 – 555.

Collins, D. J. and Wayland, H. (1963) Hydrodynamic interactions of sub-microscopic particles. 1: Viscometric studies. *Trans. Soc. Rheol.*, **7**, 275 – 293.

Comitato per La Carta dei Suoli (1966) *Carta dei Suoli D' Italia*, A. and R. Senatori, Firenze.

Condomines, M. and Tanguy, J. C. (1976) Age de l'Etna determine par la methode du desequilibre radioactif $^{230}Th/^{238}U$. *C. R. Acad. Sci., Paris*, **282D**, 1661 – 1664.

Condomines, M., Tanguy, J. C., Kieffer, G. and Allegre, C. J. (1982) Magmatic evolution of a volcano studied by $^{230}Th - ^{238}U$ disequilibrium and trace elements systematics: the Etna case. *Geochem. Cosmochim. Acta*, **46**, 1397 – 1416.

Coombs, D. S. (1963) Trends and affinities of basaltic magmas and pyroxenes as illustrated on the diopside – olivine – silica diagram. *Mineral. Soc. Am. Spec. Paper*, **1**, 227 – 250.

Corrigan, G. M. (1982) Supercooling and the crystallisation of plagioclase, olivine and clinopyroxene from basaltic magmas. *Mineral. Mag.*, **46**, 31 – 42.

Cortini, M. and Hermes, O. D. (1981) Sr isotopic evidence for a multi-source origin of the potassic magmas in the Neapolitan area (S. Italy). *Contrib. Mineral. Petrol*, **77**, 47 – 55.

Cosentino, M. (1982) Relationship between seismicity and eruptive activity of Mt. Etna, in *Mount Etna Volcano, a Review of the Recent Earth Sciences Studies*. (ed. R. Romano), *Mem. Soc. Geol. Ital.*, **23**, 174 – 181.

Cosentino, M., Cristofolini, R., Ferri, M., Lombardo, G., Patanè G., Romano, R., Viglianisi, A. and Villari, P. (1981) L'eruzione dell'Etna del 17 – 23 Marzo 1981. Rapporto preliminare. *Rend. Soc. Geol. Ital.*, **4**, 249 – 252.

Cosentino, M., Lombardo, G., Patane, G., Schick, R. and Sharp, A. D. L. (1982) Seismological researches on Mount Etna: state of the art and recent trends, in *Mount Etna Volcano, a Review of the Recent Earth Sciences Studies* (ed R. Romano), *Mem. Soc. Geol. Ital.*, **23**, 159 – 202.

Cox, K. G. (1980) A model for flood basalt vulcanism. *J. Petrol.*, **21**, 629 – 650.

Cox, K. G., Bell, J. D. and Pankhurst, R. J. (1979) *The Interpretation of Igneous Rocks*, Allen and Unwin, London.

Cristofolini, R. (1967) La successions dell' attivita vulcanica sull pendici sud-occidentali dell'Etna. *Atti dell Accad. Gioenia Sci. Nat. (Catania)*, **VI, 18**, 283 – 294.

Cristofolini, R. (1971) La distribuzione del titanio nelle vulcaniti etnee. *Period. Mineral. Roma*, **40**, 41 – 66.

Cristofolini, R. (1972) I basalti a tendenza tholeiitica dell'Etna. *Period. Mineral. Roma*, **41**, 167 – 200.

Cristofolini, R. (1973) Recent trends in the study of Etna. *Phil. Trans. R. Soc., London*, **274A**, 17 – 35.

Cristofolini, R. (1974) La massa subvolcanica di Acitrezza (Etna). *Rend. Soc. Ital. Mineral. Petrol.*, **30**, 741 – 770.

Cristofolini, R. (1979) An outline of the volcanism at Mt. Etna in the light of its morphostructural features. *Proc. 15th Meeting Geomorphological Survey and Mapping*, Modena, Italy.

Cristofolini, R. and Lo Giudice, A. (1969) Le latitandesiti di un complesso intermedio tra Trifoglietto e Mongibello affiorante tra la Valle del Bove ed Adrano-Biancavilla (Etna). *Rend. Soc. Ital. Mineral. Petrol.*, **25**, 227 – 261.

Cristofolini, R. and Puglisi, D. (1974) Caratteri petrografici dell' Affioramento basaltico di Motta S. Anastasia (Etna). *Rend. Soc. Mineral. Petrol.*, **30**, 771 – 800.

Cristofolini, R. and Romano, R. (1980) *Pericoli da Attività Vulcanica Nell' Area Etnea*, Comitato di consulenza Tecnico-Scientifico per il vulcano Etna, Catania.

Cristofolini, R. and Romano, R. (1982) Petrologic features of the Etnean volcanic rocks, in *Mount Etna Volcano, a Review of the Recent Earth Sciences Studies* (ed. R. Romano), *Mem. Soc. Geol. Ital.*, **23**, 99 – 116.

Cristofolini, R. and Tranchina, A. (1980) Aspetti, petrologici delle vulcaniti Etnee: caratteri dei fenocristalli isolati ed in aggregati. *Rend. Soc. Ital. Mineral. Petrol.*, **36**, 751 – 773.

Cristofolini, R., Preston, R. M. F. and Wells, M. K. (1975) Microprobe analysis of minerals from basal lavas of the Adrano area, Etna. *UK Research on Mount Etna, 1974*, The Royal Society, p. 11.

Cristofolini, R., Ghisetti, F., Rinscetti, M. and Vezzani, L. (1977a) Neotectonics, seismicity and volcanic activity in North-eastern Sicily. *VI Colloq. Geol. Aegean Reg., Proc. 2*, 757 – 766.

Cristofolini, R., Patanè, G., Puglisi, D., Rasa, R. and Tranchina, A. (1977b) Il basso versante nord-orientale dell'Etna nei dintorni di Piedimonte Etneo: studio geologico e morfo-strutturale. *Boll. Soc. Geol. Ital.*, **96**, 695 – 712.

Cristofolini, R., Albini, A., Di Girolamo, P. and Stanzione, D. (1981) Geochemistry of some volcanic rocks from south-eastern Sicily: rare earth and other trace element distribution. *Bull. Volcanol.*, **44 – 1**, 95 – 107.

Cristofoloni, R., Patanè, G. and Recupero, S. (1982) Morphologic evidence for ancient volcanic centres and indications of magma reservoirs underneath Mt. Etna, Sicily. *Geogr. Fis. Dinam. Quat.*, **5**, 3 – 9.

Cucuzza-Silvestri, C. (1949) L' eruzione dell'Etna del 1947. Parte I : Fenomeni erruttivi. *Bull. Volcanol.*, **9**, 81 – 111.

Cuccuzza-Silvestri, C. (1957) L'Etna del 1956. *Atti Accad. Gioenia Sci. Nat.*, **11**, 29 – 98.

Cumin, G. (1938) La pastorizia Etnea. *Riv. Geog. Ital.*, **45,** 9 – 21.

Cumin, G. (1954) L'eruzione laterale etnea del novembre 1950 – dicembre 1951. *Bull. Volcanol.*, **15,** 70pp.

Debazac, E. F. (1965) Les Pineraies de Calabre et de Sicile. *Revue Forestière Francaise*, **10,** 662 – 673.

De Beaumont, E. J. B. A. L. (1834) *Recherches sur le Mont Etna*. (Quoted by Lyell, 1858.)

De Beaumont, E. J. B. A. L. (1836) Recherches sur la structure et sur l'origine du Mont Etna. *An. Mines Carbur. Paris*. (ser.3), **9,** 175 – 216, 575 – 630.

De Bruijn, H. (1951) General discussion on 'The size and shape factor in colloidal systems.' *Discuss. Faraday Soc.*, **11,** 86.

De Carolis, C., Lo Giudice, E. and Tonelli, A. M. (1975) The 1974 Etna eruption: multispectral analysis of Skylab images reveals the vegetation canopy as a likely transducer of pre-eruptive volcanic emission. *Bull. Volcanol.*, **39,** 371 – 384.

Deer, W. A., Howie, R. A. and Zussmann, J. (1978) *Rock-forming Minerals, Vol. 2a, Single Chain Silicates*, Longmans, London.

Delaney, P. T. and Pollard, D. D. (1981) Deformation of host rocks and flow of magma during growth of minette dykes and breccia-bearing intrusions near Shiprock, New Mexico. *US Geol. Surv. Prof. Pap.*, **1202,** (61pp).

Delano-Smith, C. (1979) *Western Mediterranean Europe: A Historical Geography of Italy, Spain and Southern France since the Neolithic*, Academic Press, London.

De Saussure, H. (1879) Mount Etna. *Nature*, **20,** 544 – 545.

Dewey, J. F., Pitman, W. C., Ryan, W. B. F. and Bonnin, J. (1973) Plate tectonics and the evolution of the Alpine System. *Bull. Geol. Soc. Am.*, **84,** 3137 – 3180.

Dieterich, J. H. and Decker, R. W. (1975) Finite element modelling of surface deformation associated with volcanism. *J. Geophys. Res.*, **80,** 4094 – 4102.

Di Girolamo, P. (1978) Geotectonic settings of Miocene-Quaternary volcanism in and around the eastern Tyrrhenian Sea border (Italy) as deduced from major element geochemistry. *Bull. Volcanol.*, **41,** 229 – 250.

Di Paola, G. M. (1973) The Island of Linosa (Sicily Channel). *Bull. Volcanol.*, **37 – 2,** 149 – 174.

Di Re, M. (1963) Hyaloclastites and pillow lavas of Acicastello (Mt. Etna). *Bull. Volcanol.*, **25,** 281 – 284.

Di Sabatino, B. (1977) Significato petrologico della presenza di leucite in lave di stirpe atlantica: eruzione dell'Etna della primavera 1971. *Period. Mineral.*, **46,** 45 – 57.

Dolfi, D. and Trigila, R. (1983) Clinopyroxene solid solutions and water in magmas: results in the system phonolitic tephrite- H_2O. *Mineral. Mag.*, **47,** 347 – 352.

D'Orville, Count J. P. (1764) *Sicula, quibus Siciliae veteris rudera illustrantur*, Amstelodami.

Downes, M. J. (1973) Some experimental studies on the 1971 lavas from Etna. *Phil. Trans. R. Soc., Lond.*, **274A,** 55 – 62.

Downes, M. J. (1974) Sector and oscillatory zoning in calcic augites from Mount Etna, Sicily. *Contrib. Mineral Petrol.*, **47,** 187 – 196.

Dowty, E. (1976) Crystal structure and crystal growth. II. Sector zoning in minerals. *Am. Mineral*, **61,** 460 – 469.

Duffield, W. A., Stieltjes, L. and Varet, J. (1982) Huge landslide blocks in the growth of Piton de la Fournaise, La Reunion, and Kilauea Volcano, Hawaii. *J. Volcanol. Geotherm. Res.*, **12,** 147 – 160.

Duncan, A. M. (1976a) Pyroclastic flow deposits in the Adrano area of Mount Etna, Sicily. *Geol. Mag.*, **113,** 357 – 363.

Duncan, A. M. (1976b) *Petrology and Geology of the Volcanic Rocks of the Adrano Area, Mount Etna, Sicily*, Ph.D. Thesis, University of London.

Duncan, A. M. (1978) The trachybasaltic volcanics of the Adrano area, Mount Etna, Sicily. *Geol. Mag.*, **115,** 273 – 285.

Duncan, A. M. and Guest, J. E. (1982) Mount Etna: variations in its internal plumbing. *Geophys. Surveys*, **5,** 213 – 227.

Duncan, A. M. and Preston, R. M. F. (1980) Chemical variation of clinopyroxene phenocrysts from the trachybasaltic lavas of Mount Etna, Sicily. *Mineral. Mag.*, **43,** 765 – 770.

Duncan, A. M., Chester, D. K. and Guest, J. E. (1981) Mount Etna Volcano: Environmental impact and problems of volcanic prediction. *Geog. J.*, **147,** 164 – 179.

Durbin, C. S. (1981) *The Climatology of a Volcano: Mount Etna, Sicily*, unpublished BSc thesis, University of Liverpool.

Durbin, C. S. and Henderson-Sellers, A. (1981) Meteorological importance of the volcanic activity of Mount Etna. *Weather*, **36,** 284 – 291.

Einarsson, T. (1949) *The Eruption of Hekla 1947 — 1948 IV, pt 3* (eds T. Einarsson, G. Kjartansson and S.

Thorarinsson), Visindafelg Islendinga and Museum of Natural History, Reykjavík, Iceland.

Einarsson, T. (1974) *The Heimaey Eruption: In Words and Pictures, Heimskringla, Reykjavík.*

Einstein, A. (1906) Eine neue Bestimmung der Molekuldimensionen. *Ann. Physik (Lz), (4)*, **19**, 289 – 306.

Einstein, A. (1911) Berichtigung zu meiner Arbeit: Eine neue Bestimmung der Molekuldimensionen. *Ann. Physik (Lpz), (4)*, **34**, 591 – 592.

Emerson, N. B. (1978) *Pele and Hiiaka*, Charles E. Tuttle Co., Rutland, Vermont.

Emerson, O. H. (1926) The formation of aa and pahoehoe. *Am. J. Sci.*, **12**, 109 – 114.

Eveson, G. F. (1959) The viscosity of stable suspensions of spheres at low rates of shear, in *Rheology of Disperse Systems* (ed. C. C. Mill), Pergamon Press, London, pp. 61 – 83.

Eveson, G. F., Ward, S. G. and Whitmore, R. L. (1951) Anomalous viscosity in model suspensions. *Discuss. Faraday Soc.*, **11**, 11 – 14.

Faivre-Pierret, R. and Le Guern, F. (1983) Health risks linked with inhalation of volcanic gases and aerosols, in *Forecasting Volcanic Events* (eds. H. Tazieff and J. C. Sabroux, Elsevier, Amsterdam, Chapter 7.

Faure, G. (1977) *Principles of Isotope Geology*, John Wiley & Son, New York.

Fazzelus, T. (1558) *De Rebus Siculis decades duae, nunc primum in lucem editae; his accessit totius operis index locupletissimus*, folio, Panormi.

Ferrara, F. (1773) *Storia generale dell' Etna, che comprende la descrizione di questa montagna: la storia delle sue eruzioni e dei suoi fenomeni*, F. Pastore, Catania.

Ferrara, F. (1818) *Descrizione dell'Etna con la Storia delle eruzione e il Catalogo dei prodotti*, Palermo.

Filoteo, A. (also known as Antonio Filoteo Degli Omadei) (1590) *Aetnae Topographia*, folio, Perugia.

Finch, R. H. and Macdonald, G. A. (1949) Bombing to divert lava flows. *The Volcano Letter*, No. **506**, 1 – 3.

Finetti, I. (1981) The structure of the Calabro-Sicilian Arc: krikogenesis rather than subduction in *Sedimentary Basins of Mediterranean Margins* (ed. F. C. Wezel), Tecnoprint, Bologna, pp. 465 – 485.

Finley, M. I. (1968) *A History of Sicily: Ancient Sicily to the Arab Conquest*, Chatto and Windus, London.

Fiske, R. S. (1969) Anatomy of an active volcano – Kilauea 1965 – 1968. (abstract) *EOS Trans. AGU*, **50**, 113.

Fiske, R. S. and Kinoshita, W. T. (1969) Inflation of Kilauea volcano prior to its 1967 – 1968 eruption. *Science*, **165**, 341 – 349.

Fitton, J. G., Kilburn, C. R. J., Thirlwall, M. F. and Hughes, D. J. (1983) 1982 eruption of Mount Cameroon, West Africa. *Nature*, **306**, 327 – 332.

Fodor, R. V., Keil, K. and Bunch, T. E. (1975) Contribution to the mineral chemistry of Hawaiian rocks: IV. Pyroxenes in rocks from Haleakala and West Maui Volcanoes. Maui, Hawaii. *Contrib. Mineral. Petrol.*, **50**, 173 – 195.

Formica, C. (1968) L'Esportazione dalla Sicilia dei Prodotti Ortofrutticoli. *Boll. Soc. Geog. Ital.*, **105**, 561 – 586.

Foshag, W. F. and Gonzalez R. J. (1956) Birth and development of Paricutin Volcano, Mexico. *US Geol. Surv. Bull.*, **965 – D**, 489pp.

Fournier d'Albe, E. M. (1979) Objectives of volcanic monitoring and prediction. *J. Geol. Soc., London.*, **136**, 321 – 326

Francaviglia, A. (1959) L' imbasamento sedimentario dell' Etna ed il golfo pre-etneo. *Boll. Serv. Geol. Ital.*, **81**, 593 – 684.

Francis, J. R. D. (1975) *Fluid Mechanics for Engineering Students*, 4th edn, Edward Arnold, London.

Francis, P. W. (1979) Infrared techniques for volcano monitoring and prediction – a review. *J. Geol. Soc., Lond.*, **136**, 355 – 359.

Frank, T. (1933) *An Economic Survey of Ancient Rome. Vol. 1: Rome and Italy of the Republic*, John Hopkins Press, Baltimore.

Frankel, N. A. and Acrivos, A. (1967) On the viscosity of a concentrated suspension of solid spheres. *Chem. Eng. Sci.*, **22**, 847 – 853.

Frazzetta, G. and Romano, R. (1978) Approcio di studio per la stesura di una carta del rischio vulcano (Etna-Sicilia). *Mem. Geol. Soc. Ital.*, **19**, 691 – 697.

Frazzetta, G. and Villari, L. (1981) The feeding of the eruptive activity of Etna volcano. The regional stress field as a constraint to magma uprising and eruption. *Bull. Volcanol.*, **44 – 3**, 269 – 282.

Freeman, E. A. (1892) *Sicily. Phoenician, Greek, and Roman. (The story of the Nations, vol. 31)*, Fisher Unwin, London.

Frisch, H. L. and Simla, R. (1956) The viscosity of colloidal suspensions and macromolecular solutions, in *Rheology, Vol. 1* (ed. F. R. Eirich) Academic Press, New York, pp. 523 – 613.

Fujii, N. and Uyeda, S. (1974) Thermal instabilities during flow of magma in volcanic conduits. *J. Geophys. Res.*, **79**, 3367 – 3369.

Fuster, J. M., Arana, V., Brandle, J. L., Navarro, M., Azonso, U. and Aparicio, A. (1968) *Geology and Volcanology of the Canary Islands: Tenerife*. Instituto

'Lucas Mallada' consejo superior de investigaciones cieutificas, Madrid.

Garrec, J. P., Lounowski, A. and Plebin, R. (1977) Study of the influence of volcanic fluoride emissions on the surrounding vegetation. *Flouride*, **10,** 152 – 156.

Gasparini, C., Iannaccone, G., Scandone, P. and Scarpa, R. (1982) Seismotectonics of the Calabrian Arc. *Tectonophysics*, **84,** 267 – 286.

Gass, I. G. and Mallick, D. I. J. (1968) Jebel Khariz: an upper Miocene stratovolcano of comendite affinity on the South Arabian coast. *Bull. Volcanol.*, **32,** 33 – 88.

Gauthier, F. (1973) Field and laboratory studies of the rheology of Mount Etna lava. *Phil. Trans. R. Soc., Lond.*, **274A**, 83 – 98.

Gay, E. C., Nelson, P. A. and Armstrong, W. P. (1969) Flow properties of suspensions with high concentrations. *A. I. Ch. E. Journal*, **15,** 815 – 822.

Gemmellaro, C. (1852) *Breve ragguaglio dell' eruzione dell' Etna del 21 Agosto 1852*, Catania.

Gemmellaro, C. (1860) La vulcanologia dell' Etna. *Atti Accad. Gioenia Sci. Nat.* (ser. 2) **15,** 27 – 140.

Gemmellaro, G. (1828) *Quadro istorico topografico delle eruzioni dell' Etna*, (Catania, 1824); London edition, 1828, Vol. 1).

Gerasimov, I. P. and Zvonkova, T. V. (1974) Natural hazards in the territory of the U.S.S.R.: study, control and warning, in *Natural Hazards: Local, National, Global* (ed. G. F. White, Oxford University Press, London, pp. 243 – 255.

Gerlach, T. M. (1979) Evaluation and restoration of the 1970 volcanic gas analyses from Mount Etna, Sicily. *J. Volcanol. Geotherm. Res.*, **6,** 165 – 178.

Gerlach, T. M. (1982) Interpretation of volcanic gas data from tholeiitic and alkalic mafic lavas. *Bull. Volcanol*, **45,** 235 – 244.

Gerlach, T. M. (1983) Intrinsic chemical variations in high-temperature volcanic gases from basic lavas, in *Forecasting Volcanic Events*. (eds H. Tazieff and J. C. Sabroux), Elsevier, Amsterdam, Chapter 24.

Ghisetti, F. and Vezzani, L. (1981) Contribution of structural analysis to understanding the geodynamic evolution of the Calabrian Arc (S. Italy). *J. Struct. Geol.*, **3**, 371 – 381.

Ghisetti, F. and Vezzani, L. (1982) Different style of deformation in the Calabrian arc (southern Italy): implications for a seismotectonic zoning *Tectonophysics*, **85,** 149 – 165.

Gibb, F. G. F. (1974) Supercooling and the crystallization of plagioclase from a basaltic magma. *Mineral Mag.*, **36,** 641 – 653.

Giese, P., Gorler, K., Jacobshagen, V. and Reutter, K. J. (1980) Geodynamic evolution of the Apennines and Hellenides, in *Mobile Earth* (eds H. Gloss *et al.*), I. G. P. Research Report F. R. G., Boppard, Boldt, pp. 71 – 87.

Golant, S. and Burton, I. (1969) *The Meaning of a Hazard: Application of the Semantic Differential.* Natural Hazards Research Working Paper 7, University of Colorado Institute of Behavioural Science, Boulder.

Goldsmith, H. L., and Mason, S. G. (1967) The microrheology of dispersions, in *Rheology, Theory and Applications, Vol. IV* (ed. F. R. Eirich), Academic Press, New York, Chapter 2.

Gorshkov, G. S. (1959) Gigantic eruption of the volcano Bezymianny. *Bull Volcanol.*, **20,** 77 – 112.

Graves, R. (1955) *The Greek Myths*, Penguin, Harmondsworth.

Grayson, D. K. and Sheets, P. D. (1979) Volcanic disasters and the archaeological record, in *Volcanic Activity and Human Ecology* (eds P. D. Sheets and D. K. Grayson), Academic Press, New York, pp. 623 – 633.

Greeley, R. (1971) Observations of activity forming lava tubes and associated structures, Hawaii. *Modern Geology*, **2,** 207 – 223.

Green, D. H., Edgar, A. D., Beasley, P., Kiss, E. and Ware, N. G. (1974) Upper mantle source for some hawaiites, mugearites and benmoreites. *Contrib. Mineral. Petrol.*, **48,** 33 – 43.

Grindley, G. W. (1973) Structural control of volcanism at Mount Etna. *Phil. Trans. R. Soc., Lond.*, **274A,** 165 – 175.

Grove, N. (1973) Volcano overwhelms an Icelandic village. *National Geographic*, **144** (July), 40 – 67.

Gruntfest, I. J. (1963). Thermal feedback in liquid flow; plane shear at constant stress. *Trans. Soc. Rheol.*, **7,** 195 – 207.

Guest J. E. (1973a) The summit of Mount Etna prior to the 1971 eruptions. *Phil. Trans. R. Soc., Lond.*, **274,** 63 – 78.

Guest, J. E. (1973b) Fumarole temperature increases on the summit cone of Mount Etna, Sicily, 1972. *J. Geol. Soc., Lond.*, **129,** 311 – 315.

Guest, J. E. (1980) Calderas and stratigraphy of the upper part of Mount Etna. *UK Research on Mount Enta, 1977 – 79*, The Royal Society, pp. 7 – 9.

Guest, J. E. (1982) Styles of eruption and flow morphology on Mt. Etna, in *Mount Etna Volcano, a Review of the Recent Earth Sciences Studies* (ed. R. Romano), *Mem. Soc. Geol. Ital.*, **23**, 49 – 73.

Guest, J. E. and Duncan, A. M. (1981) Internal plumbing of Mount Etna. *Nature*, **290**, 584 – 586.

Guest, J. E. and Murray, J. B. (1979) An analysis of hazard from Mount Etna Volcano. *J. Geol. Soc., Lond.*, **136**, 347 – 354.

Guest, J. E. and Murray, J. B. (1980) Summary of volcanic activity on Etna 1977 – 1979, in *UK Research on Mount Etna, 1977 – 1979*, The Royal Society, 50 – 53.

Guest, J. E. and Skelhorn, R. R. (eds) (1973) Mount Etna and the 1971 eruption. *Phil. Trans. R. Soc., Lond.*, **274A,** 179pp.

Guest, J. E., Huntingdon, A. T., Wadge, G., Brander, J. L., Booth, B., Carter, S. and Duncan, A. (1974) Recent eruption of Mount Etna. *Nature*, **250,** 385 – 387.

Guest, J. E., Murray, J. B., Kilburn, C. R. J., Lopes, R. M. C. and Fidczuk, P. (1980a) An eyewitness account of the Bocca Nuova explosion on 12 September 1979, in *UK Research on Mount Etna, 1977 – 1979*, The Royal Society, pp. 46 – 50.

Guest, J. E., Underwood, J. R. and Greeley, R. (1980b) Role of lava tubes in flows from the Observatory Vent, 1971 eruption on Mount Etna. *Geol. Mag.*, **117,** 601 – 606.

Guest, J. E., Chester, D. K. and Duncan, A. M. (1984) The Valle del Bove, Mount Etna: its origin and relation to the stratigraphy and structure of the volcano. *J. Volcanol. Geotherm. Res.*, **21,** 1 – 23.

Guest, J. E., Greeley, R. and Wood, C. (in press) The 1614 – 24 lava flow of Mount Etna.

Guirand, F. (1968) Greek Mythology, in *New Larousse Encyclopedia of Mythology*, Hamlyn, pp. 85 – 167.

Haas, J. E. and Ayre, R. S. (1969) *The Western Sicily Earthquake of 1968*, National Academy of Sciences, Washington.

Haas, J. E., Kates, R. W. and Bowden, M. J. (1977) *Reconstruction Following Disaster*, MIT Press, Cambridge, Mass.

Halbwachs, M. (1983) Electrical and electromagnetic methods, in *Forecasting Volcanic Events* (eds H. Tazieff and J. C. Sabroux), Elsevier, Amsterdam, Chapter 34.

Hamelin, B., Lambret, B., Joron, J. L., Treuil, M. & Allègre, C. J. (1979) Geochemistry of basalts from the Tyrrhenian Sea. *Nature*, **278,** 832 – 834.

Hamilton, D. L. and Anderson, G. M. (1967) Effects of water and oxygen pressures on the crystallisation of basaltic magma, in *Basalts, Vol. 1* (eds H. H. Hess and A. Poldervaart). John Wiley and Son, New York, pp. 445 – 482.

Hamilton, Sir. W. (1768 – 72) Observations on Mount Vesuvius, Mount Etna, and other Volcanoes: In a series of letters, addressed to the Royal Society to which are added Explanatory Notes by the author, hitherto unpublished. *Phil. Trans. R. Soc., Lond.*, **57 – 61**.

Hamilton, Sir W. (1771) Account of a journey to Mount Etna in a letter to Mathew Maty. *Phil. Trans. R. Soc., Lond.*, **60,** 1 – 20.

Hamilton, Sir W. (1772) *Observations on Mount Vesuvius, Mount Etna and Other Volcanoes of the Two Sicilies*, London.

Hamilton, Sir W. (1776) *Campi Phlegraei. Observations on the Volcanoes of the Two Sicilies*, Naples.

Hammill, M. (1979) Contrasting cinder cones on the flanks of Mount Etna, Sicily. *Geol. Mag.*, **116,** 135 – 138.

Hardee, H. C., and Larson, D. W. (1977) The extraction of heat from magmas based on heat transfer mechanisms. *J. Volcanol. Geotherm. Res.*, **2,** 113 – 144.

Harkins, E. and Hollister, L. S. (1977) Sector zoning of clinopyroxene from a weakly metamorphosed diabase. *Am. Mineral.*, **62,** 390 – 394.

Hatch, F. H., Wells, A. K. and Wells, M. K. (1972) *Petrology of the Igneous Rocks*, 13th edn, Thomas, Murby, London.

Hatschek, E. (1911) *Kolloid. Zh.*, **8,** 34. (Quoted by Sibree, 1934.)

Haulet, R., Zettwoog, P. and Sabroux, P. C. (1977) Sulphur dioxide discharge from Mount Etna. *Nature*, **268,** 715 – 717.

Hawaiian Civil Defense, Department of Defense (1971) *The State of Hawaii Plan for Emergency Preparedness: Disaster Assistance*, Vol. 3, Honolulu.

Hawkesworth, C. J. and Vollmer, R. (1979) Crustal contamination versus enriched mantle: ^{143}Nd/^{144}Nd and ^{87}Sr/^{86}Sr evidence from the Italian volcanics. *Contrib. Mineral. Petrol.*, **69,** 151 – 165.

Heezen, B. C., Gray, C., Segre, A. G. & Zarudski, E. F. K. (1971) Evidence of foundered continental crust beneath the central Tyrrhenian Sea. *Nature*, **229,** 327 – 329.

Hill, D. P. (1977) A model for earthquake swarms. *J. Geophys. Res.*, **82,** 1347 – 1352.

Hill, W. B. (1981) *An Investigation into Possible Lichenometric Dating of Lava Flows, Mout Etna, Sicily*, unpublished BA thesis, University of Liverpool.

Hodge, D., Sharp, V. and Marts, M. (1979)

Contemporary responses to volcanism: case studies from the Cascades and Hawaii, in *Volcanic Activity and Human Ecology*. (eds P. D. Sheets and D. K. Grayson) Academic Press, New York, pp. 221 – 247.

Hoffmann, F. (1839) Geonostische Beobachtungen. Gesammelt auf einer Reise durch Italien und Sicilien, in den Jahren 1830 bis 1832. *Archiv. f. Min.*, **13**, 3 – 726.

Hollister, L. S. and Gancarz, A. J. (1971) Compositional sector zoning in clinopyroxenes from the Narce area, Italy. *Am. Mineral.*, **56**, 959 – 979.

Holloway, J. R. and Burnham, C. W. (1972) Melting relations of basalt with equilibrium water pressures less than total pressure. *J. Petrol.*, **13**, 1 – 29.

Holm, P. M. and Munksgaard, N. C. (1982) Evidence for mantle metasomatism: an oxygen and strontium isotope study of the Vulsinian district, central Italy. *Earth Planet. Sci. Lett.*, **60**, 376 – 388.

Houston, J. M. (1964) *The Western Mediterranean World. An Introduction to its Regional Landscapes*, Longmans, London.

Houwink, R. (1971) Rheological behaviour of matter, in *Elasticity, Plasticity and Structure of Matter* (eds. R. Houwink and H. K. de-Decker), Cambridge University Press, Cambridge, Chapter 1.

Hulme, G. (1974) The interpretation of lava flow morphology. *Geophys. J. R. Astr. Soc.*, **39**, 361 – 383.

Huntingdon, A. T. (1972) The eruption of Mount Etna, 1971. *Sci. prog. Lond.*, **60**, 107 – 119.

Huntingdon, A. T. (1973) The collection and analysis of volcanic gases from Mount Etna. *Phil. Trans. R. Soc., Lond.*, **274A**, 119 – 128.

Huntingdon, A. T. (1975) Observation and studies of Mount Etna 1974 with particular reference to the volatile phase. *UK Research on Mount Etna, 1974*, The Royal Society, pp. 27 – 30.

Huntingdon, A. T. (1977) Mount Etna sublimates *UK Research on Mount Etna, 1975 – 1976*, The Royal Society, pp. 51 – 52.

Hutton, J. (1788) Theory of the earth; or an investigation of the laws observable in the composition, dissolution and restoration of land upon the globe. *Trans. R. Soc. (Ed.)*, **1**(2), 209 – 304.

Hyde, W. W. (1916) The volcanic history of Etna. *Geog. Rev.*, **1**, 401 – 418.

Imamura, A. (1930) Topographical changes accompanying earthquakes on volcanic eruptions. *Publs. Earthquake Investigations in Foreign Languages (Tokyo)*, No. **25**, (143pp).

Imbò, G. (1928) Sistemi eruttivi Etnei. *Bull. Volcanol.*, **15**, 89 – 119.

Imbò, G. (1965) *Catalogue of the Active Volcanoes of the World including Solfatara Fields (Vol. 18), Italy*, International Association of Volcanology, Rome.

International Geographical Union (1977) *Working Group on Environmental Perception: Circular No. 1*, Institute for Environmental, Studies, University of Toronto.

Irving, A. J. (1978) A review of experimental studies of crystal/liquid trace element partitioning. *Geochim. Cosmochim. Acta*, **42**, 743 – 770.

Jackson, D. B. and Swanson, D. A. (1970) Kilauea deformation: East Rift. (abstract) *EOS Trans. AGU*, **51**, 441.

Jaeschke, W., Berresheim, H. and Georgii, H. W. (1982) Sulphur emissions from Mt. Etna. *J. Geophys. Res.*, **87**, 7253 – 7461.

Jaggar, T. A. (1928a) Eruption of Etna. *The Volcano Letter*, **No. 202,** (Nov. 8th).

Jaggar, T. A. (1928b) The eruptions of Etna. *The Volcano Letter*, **No. 204,** (Nov. 22nd).

Jaggar, T. A. (1929) More about Etna. *The Volcano Letter*, **No. 211,** (Jan. 10th).

Jaggar, T. A. (1939) Expedition to the lava-bombing site. *The Volcano Letter*, **No. 465,** 1 – 3.

Jaggar, T. A. and Finch, R. M. (1929) Tilt records for thirteen years at the Hawaiian Volcano Observatory. *Bull. Seismol. Soc. Am.*, **19**, 38 – 51.

Japan Meterological Agency, Office of Volcanic Observation (1983) Report of 1983 Miyakejima eruption to the Smithsonian Institution. *SEAN Bull.*, **8**(10), 2 – 5.

Jashemski, W. F. (1979) Pompeii and Mount Vesuvius, AD 79, in *Volcanic Activity and Human Ecology* (eds P. D. Sheets and D. K. Grayson), Academic Press, New York, pp. 587 – 623.

Jeffrey, D. J. and Acrivos, A. (1976) The rheological properties of suspensions of rigid particles. *A.I.Ch.E. Journal*, **22**, 417 – 432.

Jinescu, V. V. (1974) The rheology of suspensions. *Intern. Chem. Eng.*, **14**(3), 394 – 420.

Johannes, W. (1978) Melting of plagioclase in the system Ab – An – H_2O and Qz – Ab – An – H_2O at PH_2O = 5 kbar, an equilibrium problem. *Contrib. Mineral. Petrol.*, **66**, 295 – 303.

Johnson, A. M. (1965) *A Model for Debris Flow*, unpublished PhD dissertation, The Pennsylvania State University, Univ. Park, Penn., USA.

Johnson, A. M. (1970) *Physical Processes in Geology*, Freeman, Cooper and Co., San Francisco.

Johnston-Lavis, H. J. (1918) *Bibliography of the Geology and Eruptive Phenomena of the More Important Volcanoes of Southern Italy*, University of London Press, London.

Jónsson, V. Kr. and Matthíasson, M. (1974) Hraunkoeling á Heimaey (Chilling of lava on Heimaey). *Tímarit Verkfroedingafélags Islands*, **59**, 70 – 83.

Karam, H. J. and Bellinger, J. C. (1968) Deformation and breakup of liquid droplets in a simple shear field. *Ind. Eng. Chem. Fundam.*, **7**, 576 – 581.

Keil, K., Fodor, R. V. and Bunch, T. E. (1972) Contributions to the mineral chemistry of Hawaiian rocks II. Feldspars and interstitial material in rocks from Haleakala and West Maui Volcanoes, Maui, Hawaii. *Contrib. Mineral. Petrol.*, **37**, 253 – 276.

Keller, J. (1980) The island of Salina, in *The Aeolian Islands – an Active volcanic Arc in the Mediterranean Sea* (ed. L. Villari), *Rend. Soc. Ital. Mineral. Petrol.*, **36**, 489 – 524.

Keller, J. (1981) Alkali basalts from the Tyrrhenian Sea Basin: magmatic & geodynamic significance. *Bull. Volcanol.*, **44**, 327 – 337.

Keller, J., Ryan, W. B. F., Ninkovitch, D. and Altherr, R. (1978) Explosive volcanic activity in the Mediterranean over the past 200,000 years, as recorded in deep-sea sediments. *Bull. Geol. Soc. Am.*, **89**, 591 – 604.

Kieffer, G. (1970a) Une ultime phase d'activite explosive de la Valle del Bove (Etna) vieille de 5000±130 ans et ses ensiegnements sur l'histoire recente du grand volcan Sicilien. *C.r. Acad. Sci., Paris*, **270D**, 3198 – 3201.

Kieffer, G. (1970b) Les dépôts détritique et pyroclastiques du versant oriental de l'Etna. *Atti. Accad. Gioenia Sci. Nat.* (Catania) (ser.7), **2**, 3 – 32.

Kieffer, G. (1971) Dêpots et niveaux marins et fluviatiles de la région de Catane (Sicile). *Mediterranée*, **5 – 6**, 591 – 627.

Kieffer, G. (1973) Une éruption à caractères Katmaiens, à l'origine de coulées ponceuses et de coulées responsable de la formation de la caldeira du Cratère Elliptique de L'Etna (Sicile). *C.r. Acad. Sci., Paris*, **277D**, 2321 – 2324.

Kieffer, G. (1974a) Existence probable d'une caldeira d'une quinzaire de kilomètres de diamètre dans la structure de l'Etna (Sicile). *Geol. Mediterr.*, **1**, 133 – 138.

Kieffer, G. (1974b) Un aspect particulier du volcanisme ancien de L'Etna (Sicile). C. r. Acad. Sci., Paris, **278D**, 1549 – 1552.

Kieffer, G. (1975) Pillows and hyaloclastites associated to subaerial lavas at the South-West of the base of Mount Etna (Sicily, Italy). *Geol. Mediterr.*, **2**, 179 – 184.

Kieffer, G. (1979) L'activité de L'Etna pendant les derniers 20 000 ans. *C. r. Acad. Sci., Paris*, **288D**, 1023 – 1026.

Kieffer, G. (1982) Les explosions phreatiques et phreatomagmatiques terminales a L'Etna. *Bull. Volcanol.*, **44**, 655 – 660.

Kilburn, C. R. J. (1981) Pahoehoe and aa lavas: a discussion and continuation of the model of Peterson and Tilling. *J. Volcanol. Geotherm. Res.*, **11**, 373 – 389.

Kilburn, C. R. J. (1983a) The Etna diversion. *Geographical Magazine*, **55**, 338 – 339.

Kilburn, C. R. J. (1983b) Playing with fire. *Guardian*, London, (19th May).

Kilburn, C. R. J. (1983c) Studies of lava flow development, in *Forecasting Volcanic Events* (eds. H. Tazieff and J. C. Sabroux), Elsevier, Amsterdam, Chapter 8.

Kilburn, C. R. J. (1984) *A Study of the Morphological and Rheological Development of the Basaltic aa Lavas on Mt. Etna, Sicily*, PhD Thesis, University of London.

King, R. (1971) Mediterranean island in torment. *Geographical Magazine*, **44**, 178 – 85.

King, R. (1973a) *Sicily*, David and Charles, Newton Abbot.

King, R. (1973b) *Land reform: The Italian Experience*, Butterworth, London.

King, R. (1975) Geographical perspectives on the evolution of the Sicilian mafia. *Tijd. Econ. Soc. Geog.*, **66**, 21 – 34.

King, R. and Strachan, A. (1978) Sicilian agro-towns, *Erdkunde*, **32**, 110 – 123.

Kinoshita, W. T., Swanson, D. A. and Jackson, D. B. (1974) The measurement of crustal deformation related to volcanic activity at Kilauea Volcano, Hawaii, in *Physical Volcanology* (eds L. Civetta, P. Gasparini, G. Luongo and A. Rapolla), Elsevier, Amsterdam, Chapter 4.

Klerkx, J. (1964) Sur la presence de syntagmatite a l'Etna. *Ann. Soc. Geol. Belg.*, **87B**, 147 – 157.

Klerkx, J. (1966) La crystallisation de l'apatite dans les lavas de l'Etna. *Ann. Soc. Geol. Belg.*, **89B**, 450 – 458.

Klerkx, J. (1968) *Etude Géologique et Pétrologique de la Valle del Bove (Etna)*, Thèse présentée pour l'obtention du grade de docteur en sciences géologiques et minéralogiques, Université de Liége.

Klerkx, J. (1970) La caldera de la Valle del Bove: sa signification dans l'evolution de l'Etna (Sicile). *Bull. Volcanol.*, **34,** 726 – 737.

Klerkx, J. and Evrard, P. (1970) Les anomalies gravimetriques de Etna (Sicile) et l'evolution du Trifoglietto. *Ann. Soc. Geol. Belg.*, **93,** 145 – 147.

Knutson, J. and Green, T. H. (1975) Experimental duplication of high-pressure megacrysts/cumulate assemblage in a near saturated hawaiite. *Contrib. Mineral. Petrol.*, **52,** 121 – 132.

Kubiena, W. L. (1953) *The Soils of Europe*, Thomas Murby, London.

Kuo, L-C and Kirkpatrick, R. J. (1982) Pre-eruption history of phyric basalts from DSDP Legs 45 and 46: Evidence from morphology and zoning patterns in plagioclase. *Contrib. Mineral Petrol.*, **79,** 13 – 27.

Kushiro, I. (1980) Viscosity, density and structure of silicate melts at high pressures, and their petrological applications, in *Physics of Magmatic Processes* (ed. R. B. Hargraves), Princeton University Press, New Jersey, Chapter 3.

Kushiro, I. Yoder, H. S., Jr and Mysen, B. O. (1976) Viscosities of basalt and andesite melts at high pressures. *J. Geophys. Res.*, **81,** 6351 – 6356.

Landau, L. D. and Lifshitz, E. M. (1959) *Fluid Mechanics*, Pergamon, Oxford.

Le Bas, M. J. (1962) The role of aluminium in igneous clinopyroxenes with relation to their parentage. *Am. J. Sci.*, **260,** 267 – 288.

Le Guern, F. (1972) *Etudes dynamiques sur la phase gazense eruptive*. CEA-R14383, Commissariat a l'Energie Atomique.

Le Guern, F. (1973) The collection and analysis of volcanic gases. *Phil. Trans. R. Soc., Lond.*, **274A,** 129 – 135.

Le Guern, F. and Bernard A. (1982) Etudes des mechanismes de condensation des gaz magmatique – exemple de l'Etna (Italie). *Bull. Volcanol.*, **45,** 161 – 166.

Le Guern, F., Tazieff, H., Vavasseur, C. and Zettwoog, P. (1982) Resonance in the discharge of the Bocca Nuova, Etna (Italy), 1968 – 1969. *J. Volcanol. Geotherm, Res.*, **12,** 161 – 166.

Le Maitre, R. W. (1962) Petrology of volcanic rocks, Gough Island, South Atlantic. *Bull. Geol. Soc. Am.*, **73,** 1309 – 1340.

Le Maitre, R. W. (1968) Chemical variation within and between various rock series – a statistical approach. *J. Petrol.*, **9,** 250 – 252.

Lenk, R. S. (1967) A generalized flow theory. *J. Appl. Polymer Sci.*, **11,** 1033 – 1042.

Lenk, R. S. (1978) *Polymer Rheology*, Applied Science Publishers Ltd, London.

Leung, I. S. (1974) Sector-zoned titanaugites: morphology, crystal chemistry and growth. *Am. Mineral*, **59,** 127 – 138.

Leviton, A. and Leighton, A. (1936) Viscosity relationships in emulsions containing milk fat. *J. Phys. Chem.*, **40,** 71 – 80.

Lindsley, D. H. and Smith, D. (1971) Chemical variations in the feldspars. *Carnegie Inst. Washington Yearb.*, **69,** 274 – 278.

Lipman, P. W. and Mullineaux, D. R. (eds) (1981) The 1980 eruption of Mount St. Helens. *US Geol. Surv. Prof. Pap.*, **1250,** (844pp.).

Locardi, E., Lombardi, G., Funiciello, R. and Parotto, M. (1977) The main volcanic groups of Latium (Italy): relations between structural evolution and petrogenesis. *Geol. Romana*, **15,** 279 – 300.

Lockwood, J. G. (1983) Diversion of lava flows at Mount Etna. *Volcano News*, **15,** 4 – 6.

Lockwood, J. P. and Torgerson, F. A. (1980) Diversion of lava flows by aerial bombing – lessons from Mauna Loa volcano, Hawaii. *Bull. Volcanol.*, **43,** 727 – 741.

Lofgren, G. (1974) Temperature-induced zoning in synthetic plagioclase feldspar, in *The Feldspars* (eds W. S. Mackenzie and J. Zussman), Manchester University Press, pp. 362 – 375.

Lofgren, G. (1980) Experimental studies on the dynamic crystallisation of silicate melts, in *Physics of Magmatic Processes* (ed. R. B. Hargraves), Princeton, New Jersey, pp. 487 – 551.

Lo Giudice, A. (1970) Caratteri petrografici e petrochimici delle lave del Complesso di Vavalaci (Etna). *Rend. Soc. Ital. Mineral. Petrol.*, **26,** 687 – 731.

Lo Giudice, A. (1971) La differenziazione magmatica nelle lave del complesso di Vavalaci (Etna). *Period. Mineral. Roma*, **40,** 241 – 259.

Lo Giudice, A., Romano, R. and Sturiale, C. (1974) Geologia e petrologia delle vulcaniti della parete occidentale della Valle del Bove (Etna). *Rend. Soc. Ital. Mineral. Petrol.*, **30,** 801 – 838.

Lo Giudice, E., Patane, G., Rasa, R. and Romano, R. (1982) The structural framework of Mt. Etna, in *Mount Etna Volcano: a Review of Recent Earth Science Studies* (ed. R. Romano), Mem. Soc. Geol. Ital., **23,** 125 – 158.

Lombardo, G. and Patanè, G. (1982) Etnean seismicity from macroseismic data and its relations with main tectonic features. in *Mount Etna Volcano: a Review of Recent Earth Science Studies* (ed. R. Romano),

Mem. Geol. Soc. Ital., **23,** 166 – 173.

Lopes, R. and Guest, J. E. (1982) Lava flows on Etna, a morphometric study, in *The Comparative Study of the Planets* (eds A. Coradini and M. Fulchignoni, D. Reidel, Dordrecht.

Lucchini, F., Rossi, P. L., Simboli, G. and Cristofolini, R. (1982) Confronto geochimico fra i prodotti magmatici, basici del Trias-Giura nell'area Tetidea, in *Guida alla geologia del Sudalpino centro-orientale* (eds A. Castellarin and G. B. Vai), *guida geol. reg. S.G.I.*, 133 – 141, Bologna.

Lucretius (100 BC) *The Nature of the Universe*, Penguin Classic, 1951 (translated by R. E. Latham).

Lyell, Sir C. (1830) *Principles of Geology*, 1st edn. John Murray, London.

Lyell, Sir C. (1847) *Principles of Geology*, 7th edn, John Murray, London.

Lyell, Sir C. (1849) On craters of denudation, with observations on the structure and growth of volcanic cones. *Q. J. Geol. Soc., Lond.*, **6,** 209 – 234.

Lyell, Sir C. (1858) On the structure of lavas which have consolidated on steep slopes; with remarks on the mode of origin of Mount Etna, and on the theory of 'Craters-of-Elevation'. *Phil. Trans. R. Soc., Lond.*, **148,** 703 – 86.

Maaløe, S. (1979) The compositional range of primary tholeiitic magma evaluated from major element trends. *Lithos*, **12,** 58 – 72.

Macciotta, G., Venturelli, G. and Beccaluva, L. (1978) Geochemistry of mafic Cainozoic volcanics from Sardinia (Western Mediterranean). *Bull Volcanol.*, **41,** 56 – 78.

McBirney, A. R. and Murase, T. (1984) Rheological properties of magmas. *Ann. rev. Earth Planet. Sci.*, **12,** 337 – 357.

McBirney, A. R. and Williams, H. (1969) Geology and petrology of the Galapagos Islands. *Geol. Soc. Am. Mem.*, **118.**

McBirney, A. R. and Noyes, R. M. (1979) Crystallisation and the layering of the Skaergaard Intrusion. *J. Petrol*, **20,** 487 – 554.

Macdonald, G. A. (1962) The 1959 and 1960 eruptions of Kilauea volcano, Hawaii and the construction of walls to restrict the spread of the lava flows. *Bull. Volcanol.*, **24,** 249 – 294.

Macdonald, G. A. (1968) Composition and origin of Hawaiian lavas, in *Studies in Volcanology* (eds R. R. Coats, R. L. Hay and C. A. Anderson), *Geol. Soc. Am. Mem.*, **116,** 477 – 522.

Macdonald, G. A. (1972) *Volcanoes*, Prentice-Hall, New Jersey.

Macdonald, G. A. and Katsura, T. (1964) Chemical composition of Hawaiian lavas. *J. Petrol.*, **5,** 82 – 133.

Macdonald, G. A. and Abbott, A. T. (1970) *Volcanoes in the Sea: the Geology of Hawaii*, University of Hawaii Press, Honolulu.

McGetchin, T. R., Settle, M. and Chouet, B. A. (1974) Cinder cone growth modeled after North-east Crater, Mount Etna, Sicily. *J. Geophys. Res.*, **79,** 3257 – 3271.

McGuire, W. J. (1980) *The Volcanic Geology of the Southern Wall of the Valle del Bove, Mount Etna, Sicily*, PhD Thesis, CNAA, Luton College of Higher Education.

McGuire, W. J. (1982) Evolution of the Etna volcano: Information from the Southern Wall of the Valle del Bove Caldera. *J. Volcanol. Geotherm. Res.*, **13,** 241 – 271.

McGuire, W. J. (1983) Prehistoric dyke trends on Mount Etna; implications for magma transport and storage. *Bull. Volcanol.*, **46,** 9 – 22.

Machado, F. (1965) The Messina earthquake of 1908 and the magma chamber of Etna. *Bull. Volcanol.*, **28,** 375 – 380.

McKenzie, D. P. (1977) Can plate tectonics describe continental deformation? in *Structural History of the Mediterranean Basins* (eds B. Biju-Duval and L. Montadent), Editions Technip, Paris, pp. 189 – 197.

Mackenzie, J. K. (1950) The elastic constants of a solid containing spherical holes. *Proc. Phys. Soc.*, **63B,** 2 – 11.

Mack-Smith, D. (1968) *A History of Sicily : Vol. 1 Medieval Sicily 800 – 1713; Vol.2 Modern Sicily after 1713*, Chatto and Windus, London.

Mahood, G. and Hildreth, W. (1983) Nested calderas and trapdoor uplift at Pantelleria, Straits of Sicily. *Geology*, **11,** 722 – 726.

Malin, M. C. (1980) Lengths of Hawaiian lava flows *Geology*, **8,** 306 – 308.

Malinconico, L. L. (1979) Fluctuations in SO_2 emission during recent eruptions of Etna. *Nature*, **278,** 43 – 45.

Mallock, A. (1910) The damping of sound by frothy liquids. *Proc. R. Soc. Lond.*, **84A,** 391 – 395.

Mancini, F. (1966) *Breve commento alla Carta sei Suoli D' Italia*, R. Coppini, Firenze.

Mancini, F. and Ronchetti, G. (1968) *Potenzialità dei Suoli Italiani*, Pubblicazione dell' Accademia Italiana de Scienze Forestali, R. Coppini, Firenze.

Marinelli, G. (1975) Magma evolution in Italy, in *Geology of Italy* (ed. C. H. Squyres), Earth Sciences Society, Tripoli, pp. 165 – 219.

Marsh, B. D. (1981) On the crystallinity, probability of occurrence, and rheology of lava and magma. *Contrib. Mineral. Petrol.*, **78,** 85 – 98.

Mason, A. C. and Foster, H. L. (1953) Diversion of lava flows at O Shima, Japan. *Am. J. Sci.*, **251,** 249 – 258.

Massa, G. A. (1708) *Della Sicilia grand' Isola del Mediterraneo in prospettiva e il Monte Etna o il Mongibello esposto in veduta da un religioso della Compagnia di Gesu*, folio, Palermo.

Maugeri, M. and Romano, R. (1977) Volcanic mudflows on Mount Etna (Sicily). *Proc. Int. Symp. on the Geotechnics of Structurally Complex Formations, A.G.I.*, **II,** 185 – 188.

Maugeri, M. and Romano, R. (1980 – 81) *Suggestions for the Preventive and/or Defensive Works against Lava Flows in the Etnean Area*, Publ. **149,** Istituto Internazionale di Vulcanologia, Catania.

Mercalli, G. (1907) *I vulcani attivi della Terra*. Ulrico Hoepli, Milan.

Meteorological Office (1962) *Weather in the Mediterranean. Vol. 1*, HMSO, London.

Metzner, A. B. and Whitlock, M. (1958) Flow behaviour of concentrated (dilatant) suspensions. *Trans. Soc. Rheol.*, **2,** 239 – 254.

Miller, A. A. (1963) *J. Polymer Sci*, **A1,** 1857. (Quoted by Lenc, 1978.)

Milone, F. (1960) *Sicilia La natura e l'uomo*, Paulo Boringhieri, Torino.

Minakami, T., Ishiskawa, T. and Yagi, K. (1951) The 1944 eruption of Volcano Usu in Hokkaido, Japan. *Bull. Volcanol.*, **11,** 45 – 157.

Mitchell, B. (1979) *Geography and Resource Analysis*, Longman, London.

Miyashiro, A. (1978) Nature of alkalic volcanic rock series. *Contrib. Mineral. Petrol.*, **66,** 91 – 104.

Mogi, K. (1958) Relations between eruptions of various volcanoes and the deformations of the ground surface around them. *Bull. Earthquake Res. Inst.*, **36,** 94 – 134.

Monheim, R. (1971) Die Agrostadt Siziliens: ein städtischer Typ agrarischer Grossiedlungen. *Geog. Z.*, **59,** 204 – 225.

Mooney, M. (1958) in *Rheology*, vol. 2, (ed. F. R. Eirich), Academic Press, New York.

Moore, J. G. (1975) Mechanism of formation of pillow lava. *Am Scientist*, **63,** 269 – 277.

Moore, J. G. and Krivoy, H. L. (1964) The 1962 flank eruption of Kilauea Volcano and the structure of the east rift zone. *J. Geophys. Res.*, **69,** 2033 – 2045.

Moore, J. G. and Fiske, R. L. (1969) Volcanic substructure inferred from dredge samples and ocean-bottom photographs, Hawaii. *Bull. Geol. Soc. Am.*, **80,** 1192 – 1202.

Moore, H. J., Arthur, D. W. G. and Schaber, G. G. (1978) Yield strengths of flows on the Earth, Mars and Moon. *Proc. Lunar Planet. Sci. Conf. 9th*, 3351 – 3378.

Morrison, S. R. and Harper, J. C. (1965) Wall effect in couette flow of non-Newtonian suspensions. *Ind. Eng. Chem., Fundam.*, **4,** 176 – 181.

Morse, S. A. (1980) *Basalts and Phase Diagrams*, Springer-Verlag, New York.

Mountjoy, A. B. (1970) Planning and industrial developments in eastern Sicily. *Geography*, **55,** 441 – 444.

Muir, I. D. and Tilley, C. E. (1961) Mugearites and their place in alkali igneous rock series. *J. Geol.*, **69,** 186 – 203.

Murase, T. (1981) Thermophysical properties of some magmatic silicate liquids. *Bull. Volcanol. Soc. Japan*, **26(3),** 161 – 185. (In Japanese.)

Murase, T. and McBirney, A. R. (1973) Properties of some common igneous rocks and their melts at high temperatures. *Bull. Geol. Soc. Am.*, **84,** 3563 – 3592.

Murray, J. B. (1975) Map of the summit area of Mount Etna in 1973. *UK Research on Mount Etna, 1975 – 1976*, The Royal Society, p.46.

Murray, J. B. (1980a) Map of the summit area of Mount Etna in September 1978. *UK Research on Mount Etna, 1977 – 1979*, The Royal Society, p. 33 – 36.

Murray, J. B. (1980b) Changes in the North-East Crater region in 1976 – 78, *UK Research on Mount Etna, 1977 – 1979*, The Royal Society, p. 37 – 42.

Murray, J. B. (1980c) The Bocca Nuova : its history and possible causes of the September 1979 eruption. *UK Research on Mount Etna, 1977 – 1979*, The Royal Society, p. 49 – 50.

Murray, J. B. (1982a) *Summita del Mt. Etna Settembre 1981* Ordnance Survey, Southampton.

Murray, J. B. (1982b) Les deformations de l'Etna a la suite de l'eruption 1981. *Bull. PIRPSEV*, **No. 57,** (30 pp).

Murray, J. B. and Guest, J. E. (1982) Vertical ground deformation on Mt. Etna, 1975 – 1982. *Bull. Geol. Soc. Am.*, **93,** 1166 – 1175.

Murray, J. B., Guest, J. E. and Butterworth, P. S. (1977) Large ground deformation on Mount Etna

Volcano. *Nature*, **266,** 338 – 340.

Murton, B. J. and Shimabakuro, S. (1974) Human adjustment and volcanic hazard in Puna District, Hawaii, in *Natural Hazards: Local, National, Global.* (ed. G. F. White), Oxford University Press, New York, 151 – 161.

Mysen, B. O. and Popp, R. K. (1980) Solubility of sulphur in Ca Mg Si_2 0_6 and Na Al Si_3 O_8 melts at high pressure and temperature with controlled f_{O_2} and f_{S_2}. *Am. J. Sci.*, **280,** 78 –92.

Nabelek, P. I., Taylor, L. A. and Lofgreu, G. E. (1978) Nucleation and growth of plagioclase and the development of textures in high-alumina basaltic melt. *Proc. Lunar Planet, Sci. Conf. 9th*, 725 – 741.

Nadai, A. (1963) *Theory of flow and fracture of solids*, Vol. II McGraw-Hill Book Co., New York.

Nakamura, Y. (1973) Origin of sector-zoning in igneous clinopyroxenes. *Am. Mineral.*, **58,** 986 – 990.

Nakano, T., Kadomura, H., Mizutani, T., Okuda, M. and Sekiguchi, T. (1974) Natural hazards: report from Japan, in *Natural Hazards : Local, National, Global.* (ed. G. F. White, Oxford University Press, New York, 231 – 243.

Natural Hazards Working Paper (1970) *Suggestions for Comparative Field Observations on Natural Hazards*, Working paper, **16,** Department of Geography, University of Toronto.

Nelson, S. A. (1981) The possible role of thermal feedback in the eruption of siliceous magmas. *J. Volcanol. Geotherm. Res.*, **11,** 127 – 137.

Newton, I. S. (1687) *Philosophiae naturalis principia mathematica*, book 2, 1st edn.

Ninkovich, D. and Hays, J. D. (1972) Mediterranean island arcs and origin of high potash volcanoes. *Earth Planet. Sci. Lett.*, **16,** 331 – 345.

Nolan, M. L. (1979) Impact of Paricutin on five communities, in *Volcanic Activity and Human Ecology* (eds P. D. Sheets and D. K. Grayson), Academic Press, New York, pp. 293 – 335.

Nordlie, B. E. (1971) The composition of the magmatic gas of Kilauea and its behaviour in the near surface environment. *Am. J. Sci.*, **271,** 417 – 463.

Nye, J. F. (1952) The mechanics of glacier flow *J. Glaciol.*, **2,** 82 – 93.

Nye, J. F. (1967). Plasticity solution for a glacier snout. *J. Glaciol.*, **6,** 695 – 715.

Ogniben, L. (1960) Nota illustriva della schema geologico del Sicilia nord-orientale. *Riv. Miner. Siciliana*, **64/65,** 183 – 212.

Ogniben, L. (1966) Lineamenti idrogeologici dell' Etna. *Riv. Miner. Siciliana*, **100/102,** 151 – 173.

Ogniben, L. (1970) Paleotectonic history of Sicily, in *Geology and History Sicily* (eds. W. Alvarez and K. H. A. Gohrbandt) P.E.S.L., Tripoli, pp. 133 – 143.

O'Hara, M. J. (1968) The bearing of phase equilibria studies in synthetic and natural systems on the origin and evolution of basic and ultrabasic rocks. *Earth Sci. Rev.*, **4,** 69 – 133.

O'Hara, M. J. (1977) Geochemical evolution during fractional crystallization of a periodically refilled magma chamber. *Nature*, **266,** 503 – 507.

O'Hara, M. J. and Mathews, R. E. (1981) Geochemical evolution in an advancing, periodically replenished, periodically tapped, continuously fractionated magma chamber. *J. Geol. Soc. Lond.*, **138,** 237 – 277.

Olsson, W. A. (1974) Grain size dependence of yield stress in marble. *J. Geophys. Res.*, **79,** 4859 – 4862.

O'Riordan, T. (1974) The New Zealand natural hazard insurance scheme: application to North America, in *Natural Hazards: Local, National, Global.* (ed. G. F. White), Oxford University Press, New York, 217 – 219.

Orowan, E. (1949) (Remarks during meeting on the flow of ice and other solids), in Joint meeting of the British Glaciological Society, The British Rheologist's Club and the Institute of Metals. *J. Glaciol.*, **1,** 231 – 240.

Ovid [Publins Ovidius Naso] (43BC – AD17) *Metamorphoses* Penguin Classic 1955 (translated by M. M. Innes).

Page, C. (1983) Race against time on Mount Etna. *Guardian*, London (14 May).

Papanastassiou, D. A. and Wasserburg, G. J. (1969) Initial strontium isotopic abundances and the resolution of small time differences in the formation of planetary objects. *Earth. Planet. Sci. Lett.*, **5,** 361 – 376.

Pecora, A. (1968) *Sicilia: Le regione D' Italia*, Vol. 17, Unione Tipografico Editice Torinese.

Peterson, D. W. and Tilling, R. I. (1980) Transition of basaltic lava from pahoehoe to aa, Kilauea volcano, Hawaii: field observations and key factors. *J. Volcanol. Geotherm Res.*, **7,** 271 – 293.

Pichler, H. (1970) Volcanism in eastern Sicily and the Aeolian Islands, in *The Geology and History of Sicily* (eds W. Alvarez and K. H. A. Gohrbandt), P.E.S.L., Tripoli, pp. 261 – 281.

Pichler, H. (1980) The Island of Lipari, in *The Aeolian Islands – an active Volcanic Arc in the Mediterranean Sea* (ed. L. Villari), *Rend. Soc. Ital. Mineral.*, **36,** 75 – 100.

Pieri, M. (1975) An outline of Italian Geology, in *Geology of Italy* (ed. C. H. Squyres) Earth Sciences Society, Tripoli, pp. 75 – 143.

Pinkerton, H. (1978) *Methods of Measuring the Rheological Properties of Lava*, Ph.D. Thesis, University of Lancaster.

Pinkerton, H. and Sparks, R. S. J. (1976) The 1975 sub-terminal lavas, Mount Etna: a case history of the formation of a compound lava field. *J. Volcanol. Geotherm Res.*, **1,** 167 – 182.

Pinkerton, H. and Sparks, R. S. J. (1978) Field measurements of the rheology of lava. *Nature*, **276,** 383 – 384.

Platania, G. (1902 – 1903) Acicastello – Ricerche geologiche e vulcanologiche. *Atti e Rend. Acc. Sc. e Lett. e Anti Zelanti.* ser. 3, **2,** (56 pp), Acireale.

Pollard, D. D. (1976) On the form and stability of open fractures at the earth's crust. *Geophys. Res. Letters*, **3,** 513 – 516.

Pollard, D. D. (1977) On the mechanical interaction between a fluid-filled fracture and the earth's surface. *J. Geophys. Res.*, **53,** 27 – 57.

Polunin, O. (1969) *Flowers of Europe : A Field Guide.* Oxford University Press, London.

Ponte, G. (1911) Sulla cenere vulcanica dell' eruzione Etnea del 1911. *Atti. R. Accad. Lincei.* (ser. 5), **21,** 209 – 16.

Ponte, G. (1923) The recent eruption of Etna. *Nature*, **112,** 546 – 548.

Ponte, G. (1953) Sull ' eruzione etnea del 1950 – 51. *Bull. Volcanol.* (ser. 2) 13.

Presnall, D. C., Dixon, S. A., Dixon, J. R., O'Donnell, T. H., Brenner, N. L., Schrock, R. L. and Dycus, D. W. (1978) Liquidus phase relations on the join Diopside – Forsterite – Anorthite from 1 atm to 20 kbar: their bearing on the generation and crystallisation of basaltic magma. *Contrib. Mineral Petrol.*, **66,** 203 – 220.

Preston, R. M. F. and Duncan, A. M. (1979) Electron-microprobe investigation of melt inclusions in plagioclase phenocrysts from Mount Etna. *Mineral. Mag.*, **43,** 181 – 183.

Price, W. F. (1980) Comparison of gases trapped in rapidly cooled lavas from eruptions of Etna. *UK Research on Mount Etna 1977 – 1979*, The Royal Society, pp. 25 – 27.

Price, W. F. and Bailey, D. K. (1980) A carbon dioxide-rich volatile phase in Mount Etna volcanism. *Mineral Mag.*, **43,** 675 – 677.

Puglisi, D. and Tranchina, A. (1977) Variazioni petrografiche e petrochimiche entro due successioni laviche affioranti sul versante nord-orientale dell' Etna (zona di Piedimente Etneo). *Mineral. Petr. Acta*, **21,** 65 – 91.

Quarantelli, E. L. (1979) The Vaiont Dam overflow: A case study of extra-community responses in massive disasters. *Disasters*, **3,** 199 – 212.

Ram, A. (1967) High shear viscometry, in *Rheology, Theory and Applications*, Vol. IV (ed. F. R. Eirich), Acadmic Press, New York, Chapter 3.

Rammelsberg, C. F. A. (1849) Ueber die mineralogischen Gemengtheile der Laven (Aetnalava). *Z. dt. geol. Ges. (Berlin)*, **1,** 232 – 244.

Recupero, G. (1815) *Storia naturale e generale dell' Etna. Opera postuma con annotazioni del suo nipote Agatino Recupero*, Stampa R. Catania, Universita, pp. 1 – 2.

Reiner, M. (1934) The theory of non-Newtonian liquids. *Physics*, **5,** 321 – 341.

Reiner, M. (1960) *Deformation, strain and flow*, H. K. Lewis, London.

Reiner, M. (1964) The Deborah Number. *Physics Today*, **17(1),** 62.

Reynolds, O. (1885) On the dilatancy of media composed of rigid particles in contact. With experimental illustrations. *Phil. Mag.*, **20,** 469 – 481.

Rhodes, J. M. and Dungan, M. A. (1977) The nature of primary ocean floor basalts. *Basaltic Volcanism Study Project 1*, (**Contrib.** 7), 50 – 52.

Riccardi, M. (1958) Carta delle variazioni della popolazione in Sicilia dal 1901 al 1951. *Boll. Soc. Geog. Ital.*, **95,** 339 – 352.

Riccò, A. (1892) L'Eruzione dell' Etna. *Nuova. Antol.*, **41,** (18pp).

Riccò, A. (1894) Breve relazione sui terremoti del 7 e 8 Agosto 1894 avvenuti nelle contrade Etnee. *Boll. Oss. Moncalieri (Torino)* (ser. 2), **14,** (10) . . .

Riccò, A. (1897) Stato del cratere centrale dell' Etna dal 2° semestre 1895 al 1° semestre 1897. *Boll. Soc. Sismol. Ital.*, **3,** 61 – 63.

Riccò, A. (1898) Determinazioni della Gravità relativa fatte nelle regioni Etnee e nella Sicilia orientale. *Atti. R. Acad. Lincei* (ser. 5), **7** (2), 3 – 14.

Riccò, A. (1907) Periodi di riposo dell' Etna. *Boll. dell' Acc Gioenia di Scienze Naturali (Catania)*, **94,** 2 – 6.

Riccò, A. (1909) Eruzione Etnea del 28 Aprile 1908. *Boll. Sed. Accad, gioenia (Catania)*, **2 (5/6),** 11 – 12.

Riccò, A. (1910) Sur l'eruption de l'Etna du 28 mars 1910. *C. R. hebd. Seanc. Acad. Sci. Paris*, **150,** 1078 – 1081.

Riedesel, J. H. vön (1767) *Reise durch Sicilien und Gross-Griechenland*, Zürich.

Rikli, M. (1943) *Das Pflanzenkleid der Mittelmeerlander, Vols 1 – 3*, H. Huber, Berne.

Rittmann, A. (1962) *Volcanoes and their Activity*, John Wiley/Interscience, New York.

Rittmann, A. (1963) Vulkanismus and Tektonik des Äetna. *Geol. Rdsch.*, **53,** 788 – 800.

Rittmann, A. (1973) Structure and evolution of Mount Etna. *Phil. Trans. R. Soc. London* **274A,** 5 – 16.

Rittmann, A. (1974) The geochemical importance of pyromagma. *Bull. Volcanol.*, **38,** 1 – 17.

Rittmann, A., Romano, R. and Sturiale, C. (1971) L'eruzione etnea dell' aprile – giugno 1971 *Atti del Accad. gioenia Sci. Nat. (Catania)*, **VII 3,** 1 – 29.

Robach, F. (1983) Geomagnetism and volcanology, in *Forecasting Volcanic Events* (eds H. Tazieff and J. C. Sabroux, Elsevier, Amsterdam, Chapter 33.

Robson, G. R. (1967) Thickness of Etnean lavas. *Nature*, **216,** 251 – 252.

Rochefort, R. (1961) *Le travail en Sicile Etude de Geographie Sociale*. Presses Universitaires de France, Paris.

Rochefort, R. (1972) La population Italien en 1971. *Revue geog. du Lyon*, **47,** 385 – 393.

Rodwell, G. F. (1878) *Etna: A History of the Mountain and its Eruptions*, C. K. Paul and Co, London.

Roeder, P. L. and Emslie, R. F. (1970) Olivine – liquid equilibrium. *Contrib. Mineral Petrol.*, **29,** 275 – 289.

Rogers, A. (1970) Migration and industrial development: The southern Italian experience. *Econ. Geog.*, **46,** 111 – 135.

Romano, R. (1970) Tectonic control of magmatic differentiation: an example. *Bull. Volcanol.*, **34,** 823 – 832.

Romano, R. (1982) Succession of volcanic activity in the Etnean area, in *Mount Etna Volcano, a Review of the Recent Earth Sciences Studies*. (ed. R. Romano), *Mem. Soc. Geol. Ital.* **23,** 27 – 49.

Romano, R. (1983) Report of 1983 Etna eruption to the Smithsonian Institution. *Sean Bull.*, **8(7),** 10 – 11.

Romano, R. and Sturiale, C. (1971) L'Isola di Ustica – Studio geovulcanologico e Magmatologico. *Riv. Miner. Siciliana*, **22,** 3 – 61.

Romano, R. and Sturiale, C. (1973) Some considerations on the magma of the 1971 eruption. *Phil. Trans. R. Soc. Lond.*, **274A** 37 – 43.

Romano, R. and Villari, L. (1973) Carateri petrologici e magmatologici del vulcanismo ibleo. *Rend. Soc. Ital. Mineral. Petrol.*, **29,** 453 – 483.

Romano, R. and Sturiale, C. (1975) Geologia della Tavoletta 'Monte Etna Sud' (F. 262 – IIISO). *Boll. Soc. Geol. Ital.*, **94,** 1109 – 1148.

Romano, R. and Guest, J. E. (1979) Volcanic geology of the summit and northern flank of Mount Etna, Sicily. *Boll. Soc. Geol. Ital.*, **98,** 189 – 215.

Romano, R. and Sturiale, C. (1981) Geologia del versante Sud-orientale Etneo, F° 270 IV (NO, NE, SO, SE). *Boll. Soc. Geol. Ital.*, **100,** 15 – 40.

Romano, R. and Sturiale, C. (1982) The historical eruptions of Mt. Etna (volcanological data) in *Mount Etna Volcano, a Review of the Recent Earth Sciences Studies*. (ed. R. Romano), *Mem Soc. Geol. Ital.* **23,** 75 – 97.

Romano, R., Sturiale, C., Lentini, F. *et al.* (1979) *Carta Geologica del Monte Etna*, C. N. R. Prog. Fin. Geodinamica, 1:50 000.

Roscoe, R. (1952) The viscosity of suspensions of rigid spheres. *Brit. J. Appl. Phys.*, **3,** 267 – 269.

Rutgers, R. (1962) Relative viscosity of suspensions of rigid spheres in Newtonian liquids. *Rheol. Acta.*, **2,** 202 – 210.

Rutley, F. (1878) The mineral constitution and microscopic character of some of the lavas of Etna, in *Etna: A History of the Mountain and its Eruptions* (ed. G. F Rodwell), C. and K. Paul, London, pp. 135 – 142.

Ryall, A. and Bennett, D. L. (1968) Crustal structure of southern Hawaii related to volcanic processes in the upper mantle. *J. Geophys. Res.*, **73,** 4561 – 4582.

Ryan, M. P., Koyanagi, R. Y. and Fiske, R. S. (1981) Modelling the three-dimensional structure of macroscopic magma transport systems: application to Kilauea Volcano, Hawaii. *J. Geophys. Res.*, **86,** 7111 – 7129.

Sadron, C. (1953) in *Flow Properties of Disperse Systems* (ed. J. J. Hermans), North-Holland Publishing Co., Amsterdam, p.131 (Quoted by Goldsmith and Mason, 1967.)

Sanderson, T. J. O (1982a) Direct gravimetric detection of magma movements at Mount Etna. *Nature*, **297,** 487 – 490.

Sanderson, T. J. O. (1982b) *Mount Etna: Direct Gravimetric Detection of Magma Movements*, PhD Thesis University of London.

Sanderson, T. J. O., Berrino, G., Corrado, G. and Grimaldi, M. (1983) Ground deformation and gravity changes accompanying the March 1981 eruption of Mount Etna. *J. Volcanol. Geotherm. Res.*, **16,** 299 – 315.

Sato, M. and Wright, T. L. (1966) Oxygen fugacities directly measured in magmatic gases. *Science*, **153,** 1103 – 1105.

Sato, M. and Moore, J. G. (1973) Oxygen and sulphur

fugacities of magmatic gases directly measured in active vents of Mount Etna. *Phil. Trans. R. Soc. Lond.*, **274A,** 137 – 146.

Scandone, P. (1979) Origin of the Tyrrhenian Sea and Calabrian Arc. *Boll. Soc. Geol. Ital.*, **98,** 27 – 34.

Scandone, R. and Cortini, M. (1982) Il Vesuvio: un vulcano ad alto rischio. *Le Scienze (edizione Italiana di Scientific American)*, **28,** 92 – 106.

Scarfe, C. M. (1973) Viscosity of basic magmas at varying pressure. *Nature Physical Science*, **241,** 101 – 102.

Schick, R., Cosentino, M., Lombardo, G. and Patane, G. (1982) Volcanic tremor at Mount Etna. A brief description, in *Mount Etna Volcano, a Review of the Recent Earth Sciences Studies* (ed. R. Romano), *Mem. Soc. Geol. Ital.*, **23,** 191 – 196.

Scott, S. C. (1983) Variations in lava composition during the March 1981 eruption of Mount Etna and the implications of a compositional comparison with earlier historic eruptions. *Bull. Volcanol.*, **46,** 393–412.

Scott Blair, G. W. (1968) *Rheol. Acta.*, **4,** 53. (Quoted by Lenk, 1978.)

Scott Blair, G. W. (1969) *Elementary Rheology*, Academic Press, London.

Scrope, G. J. P. (1825) *Considerations on Volcanoes, the Probable Causes of their Phenomena and their Connection with the Present State and Past History of the Globe; Leading to the Establishment of a New Theory of the Earth.* W. Phillips and G. Yard, London.

Sekiya, S. and Kikuchi, Y. (1980) The eruption of Bandai-San. *J.C.S.I. U.T.*, **3,** 91 – 172.

Self, S. and Gunn, B. M. (1976) Petrology, volume and age relations of alkaline and saturated peralkaline volcanics from Terceira, Azores. *Contrib. Mineral, Petrol.*, **54,** 293 – 313.

Settle, M. (1979) The structure and emplacement of cinder cone fields. *Am. J. Sci.*, **279,** 1089 – 1107.

Sharp, A. D. L., Davis, P. M. and Gray, F. (1980) A low-velocity zone beneath Mout Etna and magma storage. *Nature*, **287,** 587 – 591.

Sharp, A. D. L., Lombardo, G. and Davis, P. M. (1981) Correlation between eruptions of Mount Etna, Sicily, and regional earthquakes as seen in historical records from AD 1582. *Geophys. J. R. Astr. Soc.*, **65,** 507 – 523.

Shaw, H. R. (1969) Rheology of basalt in the melting range. *J. Petrol.*, **10,** 510 – 535.

Shaw, H. R. (1972) Viscosities of magmatic silicate liquids: an empirical method of prediction. *Am. J. Sci.*, **272,** 870 – 893.

Shaw, H. R. (1980) The fracture mechanisms of magma transport from the mantle to the surface; Chapter 6 in *Physics of Magmatic Processes* (ed. R. B. Hargraves), Princeton University Press, Princeton, New Jersey.

Shaw, H. R., Wright, T. L., Peck, D. L. and Okamura, R. (1968) The viscosity of basaltic magma: an analysis of field measurements in Makaopuhi lava lake, Hawaii. *Am. J. Sci.*, **261,** 255 – 264.

Shimizu, N. (1981) Trace element incorporation into growing augite phenocryst. *Nature*, **289,** 575 – 578.

Shimozuru, D. (1971) A seismological approach to the prediction of volcanic eruptions, in *The Surveillance and Prediction of Volcanic Activity*, UNESCO, Paris, pp. 19 – 45.

Sibley, D. F., Vogel, T. A., Walker, B. M. and Byerly, G. (1976) The origin of oscillatory zoning in plagioclase: a diffusion and growth controlled model. *Am. J. Sci.*, **276,** 275 – 284.

Sibree, J. O. (1934) The viscosity of froth. *Trans. Faraday Soc.*, **30,** 325 – 331.

Sigvaldason, G. E. (1974) Chemical composition of volcanic gases. In: *Physical Volcanology* (eds L. Civetta, P. Gasparini, G. Luongo and A. Rapolla), Elsevier, Amsterdam, Chapter 9.

Silvestri, O. (1866) Sulla Eruzione dell' Etna nel 1865, studi geologici e chemici. *Atti. Soc. Ital. Sci. Nat. (Milano)*, **9,** 50 – 67.

Silvestri, O (1867) I Fenomeni vulcanici presentati dell' Etna nel 1863 – 1866, considerati in rapporto alla grande eruzione del 1865. Studii di geologia – Chimica. *Atti. Accad. Gieonia. Sci. Nat.* (ser. 3), **1,** 53 – 319.

Silvestri, O. (1881) Petrografia e mineralogia micrografica delle roccie eruttive dell' Etna e degli altri centri vulcanici (ora spenti) della Sicilia. *Boll. R. Com. Geol. Ital.*, **12,** 583 – 585.

Silvestri, O. 1886 La recente eruzione dell' Etna. *Nuova Antol.* (ser. 3), **4,** 22 – 36.

Simkin, T., Siebert, L., McClelland, L., Bridge, D., Newhall, C. and Latter, J. H. (1981) *Volcanoes of the World.* Hutchinson-Ross, Stroudsburg.

Simon, H. A. (1959) Theories of decision-making in economic and behavioral science. *Am. Econ. Rev.*, **49;** 253 – 283.

Skelland, A. H. P. (1967) *Non-Newtonian Flow and Heat Transfer*, John Wiley & Sons, New York.

Smit, P. P. A. (1965) Calculation of some physical constants of dispersions and real mixtures. *Kolloid. Zh.*, **205,** 122 – 128.

Sorensen, J. H. and Gersmehl, P. J. (1980) Volcanic

hazard warning system: Persistence and transferability. *Environmental Management*, **4,** 125 – 136.

Spadea, P. (1972) Alcalibasalt tra le lave antiche del l'Etna nell' area di Piedimonte Etneo (Etna NE). *Rend. Soc. Ital. Mineral. Petrol.*, **28,** 297 – 338.

Sparks, R. S. J. (1978) The dynamics of bubble formation and growth in magmas: a review and analysis. *J. Volcanol. Geotherm. Res.*, **3,** 309 – 324.

Sparks, R. S. J. and Pinkerton, H. (1978) Effect of degassing on rheology of basaltic lava. *Nature*, **276,** 385 – 386.

Sparks, R. S. J., Pinkerton, H. and Hulme, G. (1976) Classification and formation of lava levées on Mount Etna, Sicily. *Geology*, **4,** 269 – 271.

Sparks, R. S. J., Pinkerton, H. and Macdonald, R. (1977) The transport of xenoliths in magmas. *Earth Planet. Sci. Lett*, **35,** 234 – 238.

Speranza, F. (1960) *Dei limiti altrimetrici dell vegetazione sull' Etna*, Catania.

Stein, N. (1971) Die Industrialisierung an der Südostküste Sizilliens. *Erde*, **102,** 180 – 207.

Stella-Starabba, F. (1928) Sulle lave dell' eruzione dell' Etna del 1928. La variazioni della composizione chimica durante il periodo effusivo. *Bull. Volcanol.*, **15/18,** 56 – 69.

Stephenson, R. S. (1981) The Italian earthquake: Relief operations. *Disasters*, **5,** 71 – 72.

Stoiber, R. E. and Jepson, A. (1973) Sulphur dioxide contributions to the atmosphere by volcanoes. *Science*, **182,** 577 – 578.

Stothers, R. B. and Rampino, M. R. (1983) Volcanic eruptions in the Mediterranean before AD 630 from written and archaeological sources. *J. Geophys. Res.*, **88,** 6357 – 6371.

Streckeisen, A. L. (1967) Classification and nomenclature of igneous rocks – Final report of an enquiry. *Neues Jahrb. Mineral. Abh.*, **107,** 144 – 214.

Sturiale, C. (1967) Su alcune piroclastiti del basso versante meridonale dell' Etna. *Rend. Soc. Ital. Mineral. Petrol.*, **23,** 427 – 452.

Sturiale, C. (1968) Le formazione eruttive submarine a Nord di Catania. *Rend. Soc. Ital. Mineral. Petrol.*, **24,** 313 – 346.

Sugden, D. E. and John, B. S. (1976) *Glaciers and landscape*, Edward Arnold, London.

Sulerzhitzky, L. D. (1969) Radiocarbon dating of volcanoes; in *Volcanoes and their Roots, IAVCEI Symposium, Oxford*, pp. 85 – 94.

Swanson, D. A. (1972) Magma supply rate at Kilauea Volcano, 1952 – 1971. *Science*, **175,** 169 – 170.

Swanson, D. A. and Christiansen, R. L. (1973) Tragic base surge in 1790 at Kilauea Volcano. *Geology*, (Oct.), 83 – 86.

Swanson, D. A. and Fabbi, B. P. (1973) Loss of volatiles during fountaining and flowage of basaltic lava at Kilauea Volcano, Hawaii. *J. Res. U.S. Geol. Survey*, **1,** 649 – 658.

Sylos-Labini, P. (1964) Precarious employment in Sicily. *Int. Labour Rev.*, **89,** 268 – 285.

Symonds, J. A. (1874) *Sketches in Italy and Greece*, Smith and Elder, London.

Tanguy, J. C. (1967) Presence de basaltes à caractère tholeiitique dans la zone de l'Etna (Sicile). *C. r. Acad. Sci., Paris*, **264D,** 21 – 24.

Tanguy, J. C. (1973) The 1971 eruption: petrography of the lavas. *Phil. Trans. R. Soc. Lond.*, **274A,** 45 – 53.

Tanguy, J. C. (1978) Tholeiitic basalt magmatism of Mount Etna and its relations with the Alkaline Series. *Contrib. Mineral. Petrol.*, **66,** 51 – 67.

Tanguy, J. C. (1979) The storage and release of magma on Mount Etna: a discussion. *J. Volcanol. Geotherm. Res.*, **6,** 179 – 188.

Tanguy, J. C. (1981) Les éruptions historiques de l'Etna: Chronologie et localisation. *Bull. Volcanol.* **44,** 586–640.

Tanguy, J. C. and Kieffer, G. (1976 – 77) The 1974 eruption of Mount Etna. *Bull. Volcanol.*, **40,** 1 – 14.

Taubes, G. (1983) The battle of Etna. *Discover*, **4(7),** 12 – 19.

Taylor, G. I. (1932) The viscosity of a fluid containing small drops of another fluid. *Proc. R. Soc. Lond.*, **138A,** 41 – 48.

Taylor, H. P. and Turi, B. (1976) High ^{18}O igneous rocks from the Tuscan magmatic province, Italy. *Contrib. Mineral. Petrol.*, **55,** 33 – 54.

Tazieff, H. (1970) New investigation on eruptive gases. *Bull. Volcanol.*, **34,** 1 – 18.

Tazieff, H. (1977) La Soufrière, volcanology, and forecasting. *Nature*, **269,** 96 – 97.

Tazieff, H. (1983) Estimating eruptive peril: some case histories; in *Forecasting Volcanic Events* (eds H. Tazieff and J. C. Sabroux), Elsevier, Amsterdam, pp. 547 – 559.

Thomas, D. G. (1961) Transport characteristics of suspensions: II. Minimum transport velocity for flocculated suspensions in horizontal pipes; III Laminar-flow properties of flocculated suspensions. *A.I.Ch.E. Journal*, **7,** 423 – 437.

Thomas, D. G. (1963) Non-Newtonian suspensions, part 1. Physical properties and laminar transport characteristics. *Ind. Eng. Chem.*, **55,** 18–29.

Thomas, D. G. (1965) Transport characteristics of

suspensions: VIII. A note on the viscosity of Newtonian suspensions of uniform spherical particles. *J. Colloid. Sci.*, **20,** 267–277.

Thompson, R. N., Esson, J. and Dunham, A. C. (1972) Major element chemical variation in the Eocene lavas of Skye, Scotland. *J. Petrol.*, **13,** 219–253.

Thorarinsson, S. (1979) On the damage caused by volcanic eruptions with special reference to tephra and gases, in *Volcanic Activity and Human Ecology* (eds P. D. Sheets and D. K. Grayson), Academic Press, New York, pp. 125–159.

Tozer, D. C. (1965) Heat transfer and convection currents. *Phil. Trans. R. Soc. Lond.*, **258A,** 252–271.

Turi, B. and Taylor, H. P. (1976) Oxygen isotope studies of potassic volcanic rocks of the Roman province, Central Italy. *Contrib. Mineral. Petrol.*, **55,** 1–32.

Ugolini, F. C. and Zasoski, R. J. (1979) Soils derived from tephra; in *Volcanic Activity and Human Ecology* (eds P. D. Sheets and D. K. Grayson) Academic Press, New York, pp. 83–114.

UNESCO (1972) *The Surveillance and Prediction of Volcanic Activity*, UNESCO, New York.

UNESCO (1974) *Report on Proceedings of the Regional Seminar on the Surveillance and Prediction of Volcanic Activity, Guadeloupe, 28 June – 2 July 1974.* Document SC74/W38, UNESCO, New York.

United Nations (1976) *Disaster Prevention and Mitigation: Vol. 1: Volcanological Aspects*, United Nations, New York.

US Corps of Engineers (1966) *Review Report on Survey for Lava Flow Control, Island of Hawaii.* State of Hawaii. US Department of the Army. Honolulu, Hawaii: Corps of Engineers, Ford Armstrong.

Vagliasindi, C. (1950) A review of three papers in Italian by C. Emiliani. *J. Geol.*, **58,** 284–285.

Van Bueren, H. G. (1961) *Imperfections in Crystals*, North-Holland Publishing Co., Amsterdam.

Vance, J. A. (1962) Zoning in igneous plagioclase: normal and oscillatory zoning. *Am. J. Sci.*, **260,** 746–760.

Vand, V. (1948) Viscosity of solutions and suspensions; I, II, III. *J Phys Chem.*, **52,** 277–321.

Van Ngoc, P., Boyer, D. and Kieffer, G. (1979) Localisation précise d'une fissure profonde sous les Monts Silvestri (Etna, Sicile) par les méthodes électromagnétiques et sa relation avec la 'rift zone' du volcan. *C. r. Acad. Sc. Paris* (Série D), **289,** 69–72.

Van Ngoc, P., Boyer, D. and Kieffer, G. (1980) Sur l'existence d'une zone de forte conductivité électrique, en relation avec les éruptions sur le versant nord-est de l'Etna (Sicile). *C.r. Acad. Sc. Paris* (Série D), **290,** 443–446.

Van Ngoc, P., Boyer, D. and Kieffer, G. (1982) Sur la structure interne profonde d'un secteur du flanc sud de l'Etna et sa relation avec l'évolution structurale du volcan Sicilien. *C.r. Acad. Sc. Paris* (Série II), **295,** 891–894.

Van Ngoc, P., Boyer, D. and Tanguy, J. C. (1983) Sur le mécanisme de l'eruption de mars 1983 à l'Etna d'après les résultats de Polarisation Spontanée. *C.r. Acad. Sc. Paris* (Série II), **297,** 177 – 180.

Van Wazer, J. R., Lyons, J. W., Kim, K. Y. and Colwell, R. E. (1963) *Viscosity and Flow Measurement*, Interscience, New York.

Varekamp, J. C. (1981) Relations between tectonics and volcanism in the Roman Province, Italy; in *Tephra Studies* (eds S. Self and R. S. J. Sparks), Reidel, Dordrecht, pp. 219 – 225.

Varnes, D. J. (1978) Slope movement: types and processes, in *Landslide Analysis and Control*, Transportation Res. Board, N.A.S., Spec. Rep. **11 – 33.**

VEST – Volcanic Eruption Surveillance Team (1981) Etna erupts again: A VEST report on the March 1981 eruption of Mount Etna, Sicily. *Earthquake Information Bulletin*, **13,** 134 – 140.

Villari, L. (1970) Studio petrologico di alcuni campioni dei pozzi Bagno dell'Acqua e Gadir (Isola di Pantelleria). *Rend. Soc. Ital. Mineral Petrol.*, **26,** 353 – 376.

Villari, L. (1977) *How do the Summit of Etna Deform During Alternating Phases of its Persistent Activity*, open file report **1/77,** International Institute of Volcanology, Catania.

Villari, L. (ed) (1980) The Aeolian Islands – An active volcanic arc in the Mediterranean Sea. *Rend. Soc. Ital. Mineral. Petrol.*, **36,** 1 – 193.

Villari, L. (1983) Volcano Surveillance and volcanic hazard assessment in the Etnean area; in *Forecasting Volcanic Events* (eds H. Tazieff and J. C. Sabroux, Elsevier, Amsterdam, pp. 131 – 147.

Virgil [Publius Vergilius Maro] (70 – 19 BC) *The Aenied.*

Vita-Finzi, C. (1969) *The Mediterranean Valleys: Geological Changes in Historical Time.* Cambridge University Press, Cambridge.

Vita-Finzi, C. (1975) Late Quaternary alluvial deposits in Italy, in *Geology of Italy* (ed. C. H. Squyres, Earth Sciences Society, Tripoli, pp. 329 – 341.

Volpe, A. (1984) Deviazione della colata lavica dell' Etna del 14/5/1983 *5° Congresso Nazionale dei Geologi: Geologia e Protezione Civile* (Pre-prints).

vön Abich, O. W. H. (1836) *Vues illustratives de quelques*

phénomènes géologiques prises sur le Vesuve et l'Etna, pendant les années 1833 et 1834. I. Kuhr, Paris.

vön Buch, L. (1818 – 19) Uber die Zasammensetzung der basaltischen Inseln und über Erhebungskrater. *Abhandl. Preuss, Akad. Wiss. (Berlin)*, 51 – 68.

vön Waltershausen, Sartorius W. (1848 – 61) *Atlas des Aetna . . . mit Beihülfe von S. Cavallari, C. F. Peters and C. Roos*, S. Schmidt (Part 1), Berlin; Geographisches Institut (Parts 2 – 8); Weimar.

vön Waltershausen, Sartorius W. (1880) *Der Ätna*, Vols I and II. Engelman, Leipzig.

Wadge, G. (1976) Deformation of Mount Etna, 1971 – 1974. *J. Volcanol. Geotherm. Res.*, **1**, 237 – 263.

Wadge, G. (1977) The storage and release of magma on Mount Etna. *J. Volcanol. Geotherm. Res.*, **2**, 361 – 384.

Wadge, G. (1978) Effusion rate and the shape of aa lava flow-fields on Mount Etna. *Geology*, **6**, 503 – 506.

Wadge, G. (1982) Steady-state volcanism: evidence from eruption histories of polygenetic volcanoes. *J. Geophys. Res.*, **87**, 4035 – 4049.

Wadge, G. and Guest, J. E. (1981) Steady-state magma discharge at Etna 1971 – 1981. *Nature*, **294**, 548 – 550.

Wadge, G., Walker, G. P. L. and Guest, J. E. (1975) The output of Etna volcano. *Nature*, **255**, 385 – 387.

Walker, D. S. (1967) *A Geography of Italy*, Methuen, London.

Walker, G. P. L. (1967) Thickness and viscosity of Etnean lavas. *Nature*, **213**, 484 – 485.

Walker, G. P. L. (1973a) Lengths of lava flows. *Phil. Trans. R. Soc. Lond.*, **274A**, 107 – 118.

Walker, G. P. L. (1973b) The imbalance between volcanology and geochemistry. *Q. J. Geol. Soc. Lond.*, **129**, 684.

Walker, G. P. L. (1974a) Volcanic hazards and the prediction of volcanic eruptions; in *The Prediction of Geological Hazards*. Misc. Paper 3, Geological Society, London, pp. 23 – 41.

Walker, G. P. L. (1974b) Eruptive mechanisms in Iceland; in: *Geodynamics of Iceland and the North Atlantic Area*. (Ed. Kristjansson), D. Reidel, Dordrecht-Holland, pp. 189 – 201.

Walker, G. P. L. (1975) The strombolian scoria fall deposits of 1669 and 1974. *UK Research on Mount Etna 1974*, The Royal Society, pp. 24 – 26.

Walker, G. P. L. (1977) Slope angles of the Etna volcano. *UK Research on Mount Etna, 1975 – 1976*, The Royal Society, pp. 7 – 8.

Walker, G. P. L. (1981a) Characteristics of two phreatoplinian ashes, and their water flushed origin. *J. Volcanol. Geotherm. Res.*, **9**, 395 – 407.

Walker, G. P. L. (1981b) Generation and dispersal of fine ash and dust by volcanic eruptions. *J. Volcanol. Geotherm. Res.*, **11**, 81 – 92.

Walker, G. P. L. and Croasdale, R. (1972) Characteristics of some basaltic pyroclastics. *Bull. Volcanol.*, **35**, 303 – 317.

Ward, S. G. and Whitmore, R. L. (1950a) Studies of the viscosity and sedimentation of suspensions. Part 1 – The viscosity of suspensions of spherical particles. *Brit. J. Appl. Phys.*, **1**, 286 – 290.

Ward, S. G. and Whitmore, R. L. (1950b) Studies of the viscosity and sedimentation of suspensions. Part 2 – The viscosity and sedimentation of suspensions of rough powders. *Brit. J. Appl. Phys.*, **1**, 326 – 328.

Warrick, R. A. (1979) Volcanoes as hazard: an overview; in *Volcanic Activity and Human Ecology*. (eds P.D. Sheets and D. K. Grayson). Academic Press, New York, 161 – 189.

Washington, H. S., Aurousseau, M. and Keyes, M. G. (1926) The lavas of Etna. *Am. J. Sci.*, **12**, 371 – 408.

Wass, S. Y. (1973) The origin and petrogenetic significance of hour-glass zoning in titaniferous clinopyroxenes. *Mineral. Mag.*, **39**, 133 – 144.

Wells, M. K. and Cristofolini, R. (1977) Post-consolidation growth of pyroxene in submarine basalt, Acitrezza, Sicily; in *UK Research on Mount Etna, 1975 – 1976*, The Royal Society, pp. 43 – 47.

Weltmann, R. N. and Green, H. (1943) Rheological properties of colloidal solutions, pigment suspensions, and oil mixtures. *J. Appl. Phys.* **14**, 569 – 576.

Westercamp, D. (1980/81) Assessment of volcanic hazards at Soufrière de Guadeloupe, F. W. I. *Bulletin Bureau De Recherches Geologiques et Minieres*, **Sect. 4 (2)**, 187 – 192.

Westervelt, W. D. (1963) *Hawaiian Legends of Volcanoes* C. E. Tuttle Co., Rutland, Vermont.

Wezel, F. C. (1967) I terreni quaternari del substrato dell' Etna. *Atti Acc. Gioen. Sc. Nat. (Catania)*, **VI 18**, 271 – 282.

Wezel, F. C. (1975) Flysch successions and tectonic evolution of Sicily during the Oligocene and early Miocene; in *Geology of Italy* (ed. C. H. Squyres), Earth Sciences Society, Tripoli, pp. 105 – 129.

White, G. F. (1973) Natural hazards research, in *Directions in Geography* (ed. R. J. Chorley, Methuen, London, pp. 193 – 212.

White, G. F. (1974) Natural hazards research: concepts, methods and policy implications; in *Natural Hazards: Local, National, Global*. (ed. G. F.

White), Oxford University Press, New York, pp. 3 – 16.

Whitford-Stark, J. and Wilson, L. (1976) Atmospheric motions produced by hot lava. *Weather*, **31,** 25 – 27.

Whittow, J. (1980) *Disasters*, Penguin, Harmondsworth.

Wickmann, F. E. (1966) Repose period of volcanoes. *Ark. Minerol. Geol.*, **4,** 291 – 367.

Wickmann, F. E. (1976) Markov models of repose – period patterns of volcanoes; in *Random Processes in Geology* Springer-Verlag, Berlin, pp. 135 – 161.

Wiebe, R. A. (1968) Plagioclase stratigraphy: a record of magmatic conditions and events in a granite stock. *Am. J. Sci.*, **266,** 690 – 703.

Wilkinson, J. F. G. (1974) The mineralogy and petrography of alkali basaltic rocks; in *The Alkaline Rocks*, (ed. H. Sørenson), John Wiley and Sons, New York.

Wilkinson, J. F. G. (1982) The genesis of mid-ocean ridge basalt. *Earth Sci. Rev.*, **18,** 1 – 57.

Wilkinson, J. F. G. and Binns, R. A. (1977) Relatively iron-rich lherzolite xenoliths of the Cr-diopside suite; A guide to the primary nature of anorogenic tholeiitic andesite magma. *Contrib. Mineral. Petrol.*, **65,** 199 – 212.

Williams, H. (1941) Calderas and their origin. *Univ. of Calif. Publs. Bull. Dept. Geol. Sci.*, **25,** 239 – 346.

Williams, H. and McBirney, A. R. (1979) *Volcanology*, Freeman Cooper, San Francisco.

Williams, P. S. (1951) Some effects of (sic) concentrated suspensions of variations in particle size and shape *Discuss. Faraday Soc.*, **11,** 47 – 55.

Williams, R. S. and Moore, J. G. (1973) Iceland chills a lava flow. *Geotimes*, **18,** 14 – 17.

Wilson, L. (1980a) Relationships between pressure, volatile content and ejecta velocity in three types of volcanic explosion. *J. Volcanol. Geotherm Res.*, **8,** 297 – 313.

Wilson, L. (1980b) Volcanic explosion clouds: density, temperature and particle content estimates from cloud motion. *J. Geophys. Res.*, **85,** 2567 – 2572.

Wilson, L. and Head, J. W. (1981) Ascent and eruption of basaltic magma on the Earth and Moon. *J. Geophys. Res.*, **86,** 2971 – 3001.

Wilson, R. M. (1935) Ground surface movement at Kilauea Volcano, Hawaii. *Univ. of Hawaii Res. Publ.*, **No. 10,** 56.

Winchilsea, Earl of (1669) *A True and Exact Relation of the Late Prodigious Earthquake and Eruption of Mount Etna or Montegibello as it Came in a Letter Written to His Majesty from Naples. Together with a More Particular Narrative of the Same, as it is Collected out of Several Relations sent from Catania*, Newcomb, London.

Wood, C. (1976) Caves in rocks of volcanic origin; in *The Science of Speleology*, Academic Press, Chapter 4.

Wright, T. L. (1971) Chemistry of Kilauea and Mauna Loa lava in space and time. *US Geol. Survey Prof. Paper*, **735** (40 pp).

Wright, T. L. (1974) Presentation of chemical data for igneous rocks. *Contrib. Mineral. Petrol.*, **48,** 233 – 248.

Yoder, H. S. and Tilley, C. E. (1962) Origin of basaltic magmas: an experimental study of natural and synthetic rock systems. *J. Petrol.*, **3,** 342 – 532.

Zettwoog, P., and Haulet, R. (1978) Experimental results on the SO_2 transfer in the Mediterranean obtained with remote sensing devices. *Atmos. Env.*, **12,** 795 – 796.

Index

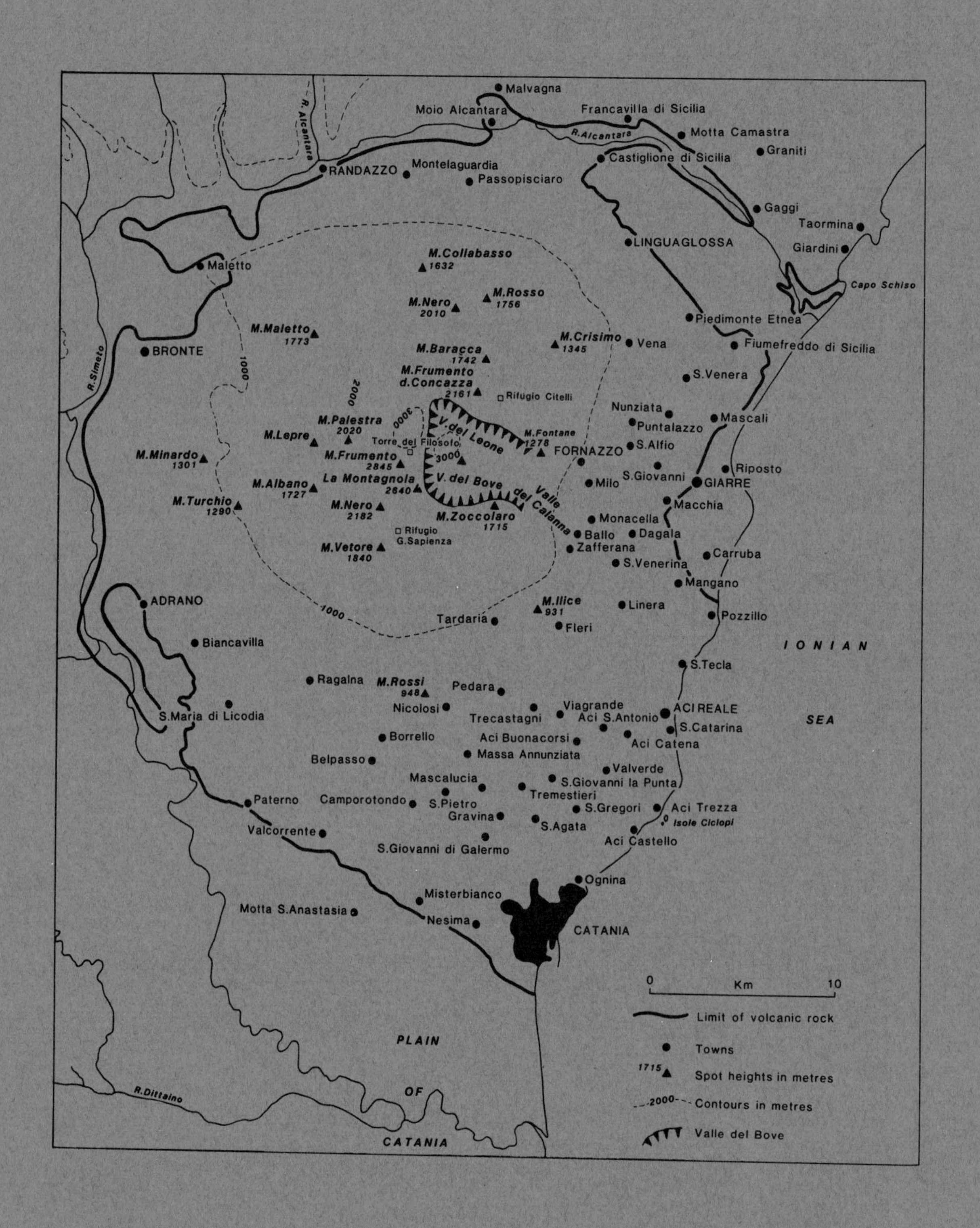

Malvagna
Moio Alcantara
Francavilla di Sicilia
R. Alcantara
Motta Camastra
Graniti
Castiglione di Sicilia
RANDAZZO
Montelaguardia
Passopisciaro
Gaggi
Taormina
Giardini
Capo Schiso
LINGUAGLOSSA
Maletto
M.Collabasso 1632
M.Rosso 1756
M.Nero 2010
M.Maletto 1773
BRONTE
R.Simeto
1000
2000
3000
M.Baracca 1742
M.Crisimo 1345
Vena
Piedimonte Etnea
Fiumefreddo di Sicilia
S.Venera
M.Frumento d.Concazza 2161
Rifugio Citelli
Nunziata
Mascali
Puntalazzo
M.Palestra 2020
M.Lepre
V. del Leone
M.Fontane 1278
FORNAZZO
S.Alfio
Torre del Filosofo
M.Frumento 2845
M.Minardo 1301
S.Giovanni
Riposto
GIARRE
Milo
M.Albano 1727
La Montagnola 2640
V. del Bove
Valle del Calanna
M.Turchio 1290
M.Nero 2182
M.Zoccolaro 1715
Macchia
Monacella
Rifugio G.Sapienza
Ballo
Dagala
Zafferana
M.Vetore 1840
Carruba
S.Venerina
Mangano
ADRANO
M.Ilice 931
Linera
Tardaria
Pozzillo
Fleri
Biancavilla
IONIAN
S.Tecla
Ragalna
M.Rossi 948
Pedara
S.Maria di Licodia
Nicolosi
Trecastagni
Viagrande
ACI REALE
Aci S.Antonio
S.Catarina
SEA
Borrello
Aci Buonacorsi
Aci Catena
Belpasso
Massa Annunziata
Valverde
Mascalucia
S.Giovanni la Punta
Tremestieri
Paterno
Camporotondo
S.Pietro
S.Gregori
Aci Trezza
Gravina
S.Agata
Isole Ciclopi
Valcorrente
Aci Castello
S.Giovanni di Galermo
Ognina
Misterbianco
Motta S.Anastasia
Nesima
CATANIA
0 Km 10
Limit of volcanic rock
Towns
1715 Spot heights in metres
2000 Contours in metres
Valle del Bove
PLAIN
OF
CATANIA
R.Dittaino